# Scotland

## THE ROUGH GUIDE

## Rough Guide credits

| | |
|---|---|
| Series editor: | Mark Ellingham |
| Text editors: | Kate Berens, Samantha Cook |
| Editorial: | Martin Dunford, John Fisher, Jonathan Buckley, Greg Ward Jules Brown, Graham Parker, Jo Mead |
| Production: | Susanne Hillen, Andy Hilliard, Gail Jammy, Vivien Antwi, Alan Spicer |
| Cartography: | Melissa Flack |
| Finance: | Celia Crowley, Simon Carloss |
| Publicity: | Richard Trillo |
| Administration: | Tania Hummel |

Thanks to the following for their help in the preparation of this guide:

Sue Beattie and Simon Oakley; Tracy Bonham; Anthony Briant; Val and Gordon Humphreys; Kate and Nat Middleton; Cathy and Emma Rees; Roger Spalding; Tom Strang; Caledonian MacBrayne ferries; Historic Scotland; Loganair; National Trust for Scotland; the Scottish Tourist Board; everyone at the regional tourist boards, especially Aberdeen, Caithness, Dundee, Fort William & Lochaber, Ross & Cromarty, Sutherland; individual thanks should also go to Gordon Adam, Rachel Gosling, Gillian Harrower, Angus McMillan, Helen Cheyne at Forth Valley, David Summers at the Highland Regional Council, Margaret Anderson at Kirkcaldy, Donald Pow at Loch Lomond, Stirling & the Trossachs, Jackie Selway at Perthshire, and Kyle MacKay at St Andrews & Northeast Fife. Thanks also to Andrew Tibber for proofreading; to Gail Jammy for typesetting the book (twice!); to Melissa Flack and Sam Kirby for the maps; and finally to Kate Berens for providing a sound base, and Sam Cook for taking over the reins with such aplomb.

This first edition published 1994 by Rough Guides Ltd, 1 Mercer Street, London WC2H 9QJ.

Distributed by the Penguin Group:

Penguin Books Ltd, 27 Wrights Lane, London W8 5TZ
Penguin Books USA Inc., 375 Hudson Street, New York 10014, USA
Penguin Books Australia Ltd, 487 Maroondah Highway, PO Box 257, Ringwood, Victoria 3134, Australia
Penguin Books Canada Ltd, 10 Alcorn Avenue, Toronto, Ontario M4V 1E4, Canada
Penguin Books (NZ) Ltd, 182–190 Wairau Road, Auckland 10, New Zealand

Rough Guides were formerly published as Real Guides in the United States and Canada.

Typeset in Linotron Univers and Century Old Style to an original design by Andrew Oliver.
Printed in the UK by Cox & Wyman Ltd, Reading, Berks.

**Illustrations** in Part One and Part Three by Ed Briant.
Basics and Contexts illustrations by Henry Iles..

Mapping is based upon the Ordnance Survey maps with the permission of the Controller of Her Majesty's Stationery Office, © Crown copyright.

# Scotland

## THE ROUGH GUIDE

Written and researched by
**Donald Greig, Rob Humphreys, Phil Lee,
Gordon McLachlan, Mike Parker, Sally Roy,
Tania Smith and Mark Whatmore**

Additional account by
Geoffrey Young

THE ROUGH GUIDES

# LIST OF MAPS

## MAP SYMBOLS

**REGIONAL MAPS**

- ▬▬ Railway
- ▬▬ Motorway
- ▬▬ Road
- ▬ ▬ Ferry route
- ······ Waterway
- ▬ ▬ ▬ Chapter division boundary
- ▬▬ ▬▬ Scottish borders
- ▬▬▬ County boundary
- ▥ Stately home
- ♛ Castle
- ▲ Mountain peak

- ⌂ Abbey
- ∴ Ruins
- ♟ Museum
- ▦ National Park

**TOWN MAPS**

- ▬ Wall
- ⓘ Tourist Office
- ✉ Post Office
- ▮ Building
- ⊞ Church
- ⊞ Cemetery
- ▦ Park

# CONTENTS

Introduction  vii

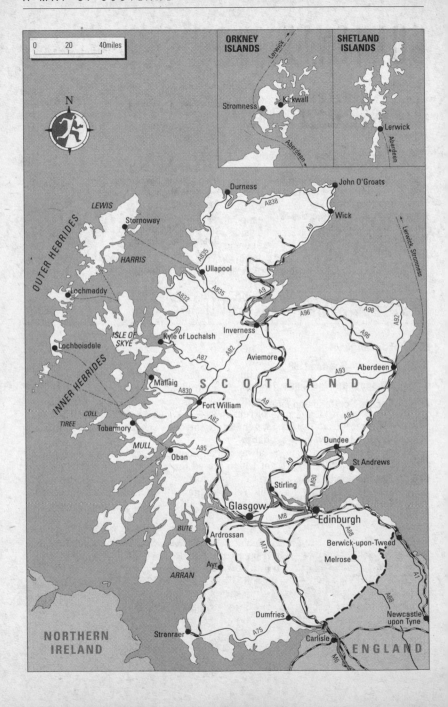

# INTRODUCTION

Reaching north from the English border, **Scotland** is a nation of stock images. Its landscapes are constantly reproduced on postcards and in glossy picture books; and the "bonnie Scotland" idyll of kilts, sporrans and bagpipes is about as familiar a set of cultural symbols as it's possible to get. Whatever your view of this, the reality can't help but be an improvement, and while the authorities milk the very "Scottishness" of Scotland for all it's worth, the real pleasures of the country need no tourist-board hype. It is, quite simply, despite an abysmal climate, a wonderfully rewarding and diverse place to travel. The main urban centres of Edinburgh and Glasgow are two of Britain's most complex and intriguing cities, perfectly complementing each other and only thirty miles apart; and the countryside more than lives up to all the praise that has been heaped upon it – whether you're visiting the wooded dales that weave across the south of the country, touring the at times supremely remote lochs, glens and mountains of the Highlands, or hopping the sea-battered islands that arc around its west and north coasts.

Of all Scotland's geographical features, it is the Great Glen, the geological fault slicing across the Highlands from Fort William to Inverness, which has had the most historical significance. For centuries it marked the "Highland line", with the Gaelic-speaking, cattle-raising clans concentrated to the north and west, and the English-speaking Scots, distinguished by their Norman-style feudal loyalties and allegiances, dominant to the south and east. These two linguistically distinct Scotlands developed on separate lines, their mutually antagonistic populations creating the first of several overlapping sources of national tension. After the Reformation, religion became another flashpoint, not just between Catholic and Protestant, but amongst a host of reformist sects, and later still industrialization divided the rural from the urban, generating the class-conscious, socialist-minded cities of central and eastern Scotland.

In the background there has always been Scotland's problematic relationship with England. In 1707, the Act of Union united the English and Scottish crowns, ending centuries of dynastic warfare, and shortly afterwards, in 1745, the failure of Bonnie Prince Charlie's Jacobite rebellion gave the English and their Scottish allies the opportunity to bring the Gaels to heel. However, the union only partly integrated the two nations, and Scotland's relationship with its more powerful neighbour remains an anomalous one. Although they retain a separate legal and educational system, the Scots have no regional assembly, few autonomous powers, and are effectively governed from London. Since 1979, English voters have kept the Conservative Party in power, while the huge majority of Scots have consistently favoured the opposition – the Liberal Democrats in the Highlands and islands and the Labour Party in the cities. This has fuelled renewed ill-will towards the union, with many Scots feeling resentful and disenfranchized. The attitude in England, meanwhile, is one that is ready to recognize – indeed patronize – the harmless symbols of Scottish nationhood (the tartan, pipes, kilts and so forth), while being very reluctant to hand over any real power or independence to the Scottish people.

## Where to go

If you're short of time, you can still sample a little of everything, beginning with either – or both – of the country's great cities, Glasgow and Edinburgh, before moving on up the west coast, where stunning land and seascapes are studded with reminders of Scotland's long and fractious history.

Travelling around mainland Scotland is comparatively easy: the road network reaches almost every corner of the country, the trains serve the major towns and an extensive bus system links all but the most remote of villages. Hikers are better served: all of the country's parks and most of the wilderness areas are criss-crossed by well-used walking trails. Without your own transport, it's more difficult to move around the islands, where, especially on the Western Isles, bus services deteriorate and are often impossible to coordinate with ferry sailing times. Almost all of the ferries are operated by *Caledonian MacBrayne*, who provide a splendidly punctual and efficient service, along with various island-hopping discount tickets to reduce the substantial costs of ferry travel. Reasonably priced accommodation is available almost everywhere, at its least expensive (and sometimes grimmest) in the youth hostels, and more popularly in hundreds of family-run B&Bs.

The majority of visitors begin their tour of Scotland in the capital, **Edinburgh**, a handsome and ancient town famous for its magnificent castle and the Palace of Holyroodhouse, as well as for the excellence of its museums – not to mention the **Edinburgh International Festival**, a world-acclaimed arts shindig held for three weeks, from the middle of August. From here it's just a short journey west to the capital's rival, lively **Glasgow**, a sprawling industrial metropolis that was once the second city of the British Empire. In recent years, though its industrial base remains in decline, Glasgow has done much to improve its image, but it's still a rough-and-ready city, blessed in particular by an impressive set of architectural reminders of its late eighteenth- and nineteenth-century heyday.

Heading south is underrated **Southern Scotland**, which features some of the country's finest scenery, especially among the elevated river valleys surrounding **Moffat** and in the forests and flat-peaked hills of the **Galloway Forest Park**, close to the **Solway coast**. Away to the east lie the better-known ruins of the four medieval Border abbeys of Melrose, Dryburgh, Jedburgh and Kelso. **Jedburgh** is the pick of the bunch, but the trim town of **Melrose**, tucked into the one of the prettiest parts of the valley of the River Tweed, is the best peg on which to hang your visit, especially as it's close to **Abbotsford**, the intriguing, treasure-crammed mansion of Sir Walter Scott.

To the north of Edinburgh, across the Firth of Forth, **Central Scotland and Fife**'s varied landscape embraces deep and shadowy glens, jagged-edged mountains and the well-walked hills of the **Trossachs**. It's here you'll also find the impressive remains of **Stirling** castle and, on the coast, well-heeled **St Andrews**, home of golf. **Northeast Scotland**, further north still, has less to offer, though you could consider following the **Speyside** malt whisky trail, or making a fleeting visit to oil-rich **Aberdeen**, the nation's third largest city, or **Deeside**, home to Queen Victoria's "dear paradise", Balmoral.

Most visitors move on from the central belt to **Argyll**, a sparsely populated territory of sea lochs and mountains. Mainland Argyll points out towards the southernmost reaches of the **Hebrides**, the long chain of rocky islands necklacing Scotland's Atlantic shoreline. **Bute** and **Arran**, with its striking granite peaks, are reached by ferry from Ardrossan in Ayrshire; from Oban you can reach the gorgeous scenery of **Mull**, and the quieter islands of **Islay** and **Jura**, wonderful places for a walking holiday.

Up along the coast, reached by boat from Mallaig or Kyleakin, is **Skye**, the most visited of the Hebrides, made famous by the exploits of Flora MacDonald, who smuggled Bonnie Prince Charlie "over the sea to Skye" after his defeat at the Battle of Culloden. The harsh rocky promontories that make up the bulk of the island are serrated by scores of deep sea lochs, together creating some of the western coast's fiercest scenery. The island also boasts the snow-tipped **Cuillins**, whose clustered summits offer perhaps the most challenging climbing in the country, and the bizarre rock formations of the Quiraing ridge on the **Trotternish peninsula**. The only settlement of any size is **Portree**, draped around the cliffs of a narrow bay, but many visitors prefer to explore the isolated hotels, B&Bs and youth hostels scattered across the island.

From Uig, on the west coast of Skye, and from Oban and Ullapool, there are frequent boats out across to the **Western Isles**, an elongated archipelago extending south from the single island of **Lewis and Harris**, to the uninhabited islets below **Barra**. The Isles are some of the last bastions of the Gaelic language, and you'll find many road signs in Gaelic only. Of the islands, Lewis is distinguished by the prehistoric standing stones of **Callanish**, one of the best preserved monuments of its type in Europe, while North Harris possesses a remarkably hostile landscape of forbiddingly bare mountains giving way to the wide sandy beaches and lunar-like hills of South Harris.

Back on the mainland, the **Highlands**, whose multitude of mountains, sea cliffs, glens and lochs cover the northern two-thirds of the country, are probably the region most commonly associated with Scotland. Their great popularity belies their stark remoteness, despite a number of internationally known sights, not least **Loch Ness**, midway along the Great Glen and home to the eponymous monster. **Inverness**, near the site of the **Battle of Culloden**, is an obvious base for exploring the region, although **Fort William**, at the opposite end of the Great Glen, close by **Ben Nevis**, Scotland's highest peak, is a possible alternative, especially if you're heading off west. In the far north, boats leave for the cluster of islands that make up the agricultural **Orkneys**, where **Kirkwall**, the largest settlement, is justifiably proud of its mighty medieval cathedral. Some sixty miles further north lies the most far-flung part of Scotland, the hundred-odd islands – of which only twenty are inhabited – that constitute the **Shetlands**. You've got to be fairly determined to make it this far north, but the sea- and wind-buffeted islands, whose only town is unremarkable **Lerwick**, offer some of the country's wildest scenery and finest bird-watching.

## When to go

The pressure systems rolling in off the Atlantic pretty much control Scotland's volatile **climate**, especially on the west coast, where a bright, sunny morning can soon turn into a wet and windy afternoon. The west coast is appreciably wetter than the rest of the country, but milder in winter, due to the moderating influence of the Gulf Stream. There's no way of predicting when the fine weather will arrive – though spring and early autumn have proved good bets in recent years; you just have to trust your luck and be well prepared, even in high summer. Always pack warm and waterproof clothing – and an umbrella.

## SCOTLAND'S CLIMATE

Average daily maximum temperatures in °C and monthly rainfall in mm

|  | Jan | Feb | March | April | May | June | July | Aug | Sept | Oct | Nov | Dec |
|---|---|---|---|---|---|---|---|---|---|---|---|---|
| **Dumfries** | | | | | | | | | | | | |
| °C | 5.6 | 6.0 | 8.2 | 11.2 | 14.4 | 17.3 | 18.3 | 18.1 | 15.9 | 12.9 | 8.6 | 6.8 |
| mm | 103 | 72 | 66 | 55 | 71 | 63 | 77 | 93 | 104 | 106 | 109 | 104 |
| **Edinburgh** | | | | | | | | | | | | |
| °C | 6.2 | 6.4 | 8.5 | 11.2 | 14.2 | 17.1 | 18.4 | 18.2 | 16.3 | 13.3 | 9 | 7.1 |
| mm | 47 | 39 | 39 | 38 | 49 | 45 | 69 | 73 | 57 | 56 | 58 | 56 |
| **Fort William** | | | | | | | | | | | | |
| °C | 6.3 | 6.7 | 8.6 | 11.2 | 14.5 | 16.6 | 17.2 | 17.3 | 15.4 | 12.8 | 8.8 | 7.3 |
| mm | 200 | 132 | 152 | 111 | 103 | 124 | 137 | 150 | 199 | 215 | 220 | 238 |
| **Lerwick** | | | | | | | | | | | | |
| °C | 5.1 | 4.9 | 6 | 7.8 | 10 | 12.5 | 13.7 | 14 | 12.5 | 10.3 | 7.4 | 6 |
| mm | 127 | 93 | 93 | 72 | 64 | 64 | 67 | 78 | 113 | 119 | 140 | 147 |
| **Perth** | | | | | | | | | | | | |
| °C | 5.7 | 6 | 8.4 | 11.8 | 14.9 | 18 | 19.1 | 18.6 | 16.2 | 12.9 | 8.5 | 6.6 |
| mm | 70 | 52 | 47 | 43 | 57 | 51 | 67 | 72 | 63 | 65 | 69 | 82 |
| **Tiree** | | | | | | | | | | | | |
| °C | 7.2 | 7 | 8.3 | 10.3 | 12.7 | 14.8 | 15.8 | 16.1 | 14.7 | 12.6 | 9.6 | 8.2 |
| mm | 120 | 71 | 77 | 60 | 56 | 66 | 79 | 83 | 123 | 125 | 123 | 123 |
| **Wick** | | | | | | | | | | | | |
| °C | 5.6 | 5.7 | 7.3 | 9.3 | 11.3 | 14.2 | 15.4 | 15.4 | 14.1 | 11.8 | 8.2 | 6.5 |
| mm | 81 | 58 | 55 | 45 | 47 | 49 | 61 | 74 | 68 | 73 | 90 | 82 |

## HELP US UPDATE

We've endeavoured to make this guide as up-to-date as possible, but it's inevitable that some of the information will become inaccurate between now and the preparation of the next edition. Readers' updates and suggestions are very welcome – please mark letters "Scotland Update" and send them to:

Rough Guides, 1 Mercer Street, London WC2H 9QJ,
or Rough Guides, 375 Hudson Street, 4th Floor, New York, NY 10014.

## TRAVELLING FROM ENGLAND, IRELAND AND EUROPE

**Crossing the border from England into Scotland is straightforward, with train and bus services forming part of the British national network. Flights are another option, though fares tend to be high. If you're driving from the south the two main routes run up the east side of England via the A1 and up the west side of the country using the M6 and the A74. Though roads have been improved considerably over recent years, neither of these approaches offers motorway driving the whole way.**

By the early summer of 1994 the Channel Tunnel should be open, and running a frequent train service – *Le Shuttle* – that crosses from Calais to Folkestone in 35 minutes. From Folkestone to London it's a couple of hours on the train, and then a further 4hr 30min to Edinburgh or Glasgow. For foot passengers, frequent through trains will run between London and various major European cities, operated by British Rail and the French and Belgian train companies. For information on journey times and fares, call ☎0303/271 100.

See p.4 for the full picture on airlines and routes.

### FLIGHTS

You can fly to Scotland's **main airports** – Edinburgh, Glasgow and Aberdeen – in an hour or so from all three London airports as well as from various English provincial airports and Ireland. There's usually a confusingly wide array of fares. The best deals are special-offer tickets sold within seven days of departure – it's pot luck as to whether any flight has these bargain fares, but

certainly worth a phone call. No refund is payable in the event of cancellation, and your stay must cover at least one Saturday. The next cheapest seats are *Apex* tickets, available on all flights, at about half the price of a full-price economy class scheduled ticket. The full amount for *Apex* must be paid at least two weeks before departure, and only 50 percent of the price will be returned if the booking is cancelled.

There are flights almost hourly to Edinburgh and Glasgow from London, and about six or so a day to Aberdeen. As a broad guide to what you're likely to pay, reckon on around £90 for the cheapest fare from London to Edinburgh or Glasgow on *British Airways*, *British Midland* or *Air UK*, around £110 for an *Apex* on this same route and up to £200 or more for the full fare. See p.4 for the full picture on airlines and routes.

Flights from other parts of Britain are less frequent but similarly pricy. About one flight a day leaves Birmingham Airport for Edinburgh, Glasgow and Aberdeen – the cheapest return fares to all three with *British Airways* hover around £80. From the south of England, *Loganair*'s cheapest flight to Edinburgh from Southampton is around £129 return. Coming from **Ireland** by air from Dublin, there are three flights a day to Edinburgh and Glasgow – *Aer Lingus*' *Apex* fare to both is around £100, while an ordinary return might be as much as three times that amount. From Belfast things work out much cheaper. *British Airways* has one flight a day to Glasgow; the *Apex* fare is around £60. Again, see p.4 for full details of airlines and their routes. It's also worth checking fares through a specialist agency such as Campus Travel or STA Travel, as they may be able to offer special deals – again, we've listed addresses on p.4.

### TRAINS

Glasgow and Edinburgh are both served by frequent direct **British Rail** InterCity services from London, and easily reached from other main English towns and cities, though you may have to change trains en route. Ordinary second-class **fares** are high, and first class costs an extra 33 percent, but in many cases you can take advantage of five types of reduced-fare ticket (see p.4), all of which come with their own restrictions and

## AIRLINE ADDRESSES AND ROUTES FROM ENGLAND, IRELAND AND EUROPE

**Aer Lingus**
Dublin Airport, Dublin, Eire ☎01/3444777
*Dublin to Edinburgh and Glasgow.*

**Air France**
Blvd Blanqui 74, Paris ☎44.80.22.22
*Paris to Edinburgh and Glasgow.*

**Air UK**
Stansted House, Stansted Airport,
Stansted, Essex ☎0345/666777
*London to Edinburgh, Glasgow and Aberdeen.*
*Leeds to Edinburgh.*
*Humberside to Edinburgh and Aberdeen.*
*Jersey to Edinburgh.*
*Amsterdam to Edinburgh, Glasgow and Aberdeen.*
*Stavanger to Aberdeen.*

**British Airways**
156 Regent St, London ☎0345/222111
*London to Edinburgh, Glasgow and Aberdeen.*
*Manchester to Aberdeen.*
*Birmingham to Edinburgh, Glasgow and Aberdeen.*
*Bristol to Edinburgh, Glasgow and Aberdeen.*

**British Midland**
Donington Hall, Castle Donington,
Derby ☎0345/554554
*London to Edinburgh and Glasgow.*
*East Midlands to Glasgow.*
*Belfast to Glasgow.*
*Paris to Edinburgh via London.*

**Business Air**
Kirkhill Business House, Howmoss Drive,
Dyce, Aberdeen ☎0382/66345
*East Midlands to Edinburgh and Aberdeen.*
*Esbjerg to Aberdeen.*

**Icelandair**
Reykjavik Airport, 101 Reykjavik ☎91/690100
*Reykjavik to Glasgow.*

**Loganair**
Trident House, Renfrew Rd,
Paisley ☎031/ 333 3338
*Leeds to Aberdeen.*
*Southampton to Edinburgh.*

**Lufthansa**
Hauptbahnhof 2,
60329 Frankfurt-am-Main ☎069/255255
*Frankfurt to Edinburgh.*

**Sabena**
Kardinaal, Mercierstraat 35,
Brussels 1000 ☎0509/2030
*Brussels to Edinburgh and Glasgow.*

**SAS**
Froesundaviks Alle 1, Soina, 9–16187,
Stockholm ☎08/7970000
*Stavanger to Aberdeen.*

## FLIGHT AGENTS IN BRITAIN

**Campus Travel**
52 Grosvenor Gdns, London SW1 ☎071/730 2101
*Also many branches around the country.*

**Council Travel**
28A Poland St, London W1 ☎071/437 7767

**STA Travel**
86 Brompton Rd, London SW7 ☎071/937 9971
Offices nationwide.

**Travel Cuts**
295 Regent St, London W1 ☎071/637 3161

conditions. On Sundays, on many long-distance services, you can convert your second-class ticket to a first-class one by paying a £5 supplement – well worth it if you're facing a six-hour journey on a popular route.

In decreasing order of cost, **Savers** are return tickets that can be used on all trains on Saturdays, Sundays and public holidays, on most weekday trains outside rush hour for the outward journey and all trains for the return leg. If you buy a return ticket at any station outside the rush hour, you'll routinely be issued with a *Saver*. **SuperSavers**, cheaper still, cannot be used on Fridays nor on

half a dozen other specified days of the year, and are not valid for any peak-hour service to or from London. *Saver* and *SuperSaver* tickets are valid for one month (outward travel has to be within two days of the date on the ticket), and are valid on London Underground if your journey involves crossing from one London station to another. **Apex** tickets are issued in limited numbers on certain InterCity journeys of 150 miles or more, and have to be booked at least seven days before travelling; a seat reservation is included with the ticket. The rock-bottom **SuperApex** tickets have to be booked fourteen days in advance, and are available in limited numbers on InterCity services from London to Edinburgh, Glasgow and Motherwell. **Children** aged 5–15 inclusive pay half the adult fare on most journeys – but there are no discounts on *Apex* and *SuperApex* tickets. Under-5s travel free.

To take the London–Edinburgh service as an example, an ordinary single fare costs £61, which is more than the majority of the reduced return fares: a *Saver* return costs £69; *SuperSaver* £59; an *Apex* costs £44; a *SuperApex* just £29. For all these tickets you should book as far in advance as you possibly can – many *Apex* and *SuperApex* are sold out weeks before the travel date.

**Journey times** from London can be as little as 4hr 30min to Edinburgh and 5hr to Glasgow; from Manchester reckon on around 2hr 30min to Edinburgh and 3hr to Glasgow. From either of these two points allow another 2hr 30min to Aberdeen and 3hr 30min to Inverness. These cities are all served by overnight **sleeper trains,** reservations for which cost an additional £25 and can be made at any mainline train station. An expensive but easy, way of bypassing the long drive north is to put your car on the train, using the **Motorail** service, details of which are available from the InterCity Motorail Office, PO Box 44, Edinburgh EH1 1BA (☎0345/090700). Reckon on paying at least £100 to take a car up to Edinburgh from London and back.

### BUSES

Inter-town **bus** services (known as **coaches** in Scotland and the rest of Britain) duplicate many train routes, often at half the price of the train or less. The frequency of service is often comparable to the train, and in some instances the difference in journey time isn't great enough to be a deciding factor; buses are also reasonably comfortable, and on longer routes often have drinks and sandwiches available on board. Two of the main operators between England and Scotland are *Scottish Citylink Coaches* (☎031/557 5717) and *Caledonian Express* (☎0738/33481), both of which offer reduced rates to children, students, people under 25 and senior citizens. Direct buses run from **London**, **Birmingham**, **Manchester** and **Newcastle** to **Edinburgh**, **Glasgow**, **Aberdeen and Inverness**. Tickets are widely available from bus stations and hundreds of agents throughout England. Typical fares from London to Glasgow and Edinburgh –

journeys of around 7hr 30min – cost £38 return, while to Aberdeen or Inverness the journey takes around twelve hours and the ticket costs about £47 return. There's a 25 percent **discount** on bookings made seven days in advance.

### FERRIES

The only way to get to Scotland direct by ferry **from Europe** is on the three-times weekly *P&O Scottish Ferries* service from **Bergen** in Norway to **Aberdeen** via **Lerwick** on Shetland. The journey to Lerwick takes twelve hours, with a single fare of £55. From there it's another fourteen hours and £50 on to Aberdeen. If you want to take your car on either journey, add another £50 or so.

There's a greater choice of ferry services from Europe to ports in England, the most convenient of which are those to Newcastle or Hull in northeast England, from where it's an easy two-hour drive across the border into Scotland. *North Sea Ferries* sail daily to Hull from **Rotterdam** and **Zeebrugge**; both crossings take about fourteen hours and, for two people with a small car, cost from around £150 single from Rotterdam and twice as much from Zeebrugge. From **Scandinavia**, *Color Line* also sail to Newcastle from Bergen via Stavanger, as do *Scandinavian Seaways* who run two services a week from June to the beginning of August from Esbjerg in Denmark and one a week from Gothenburg in Sweden. Both crossings take about 24 hours, and fares run from about £300 single from Denmark and £370 single from Sweden – again for two people and a car. A further alternative is to take one of the very frequent ferries to England from the **French ports**; there's more choice of sailings this way, though the drive up to Scotland from the south coast can easily take a full day. There are regular crossings with *Hoverspeed, Stena Sealink* and *P&O* from Calais to Dover, the shortest route, for which the lowest fare for a small car and two adults is £70. For full details of ferry routes and prices call the ferry companies direct.

From **Ireland** ferries run from **Larne** and **Belfast** in Northern Ireland to **Stranraer**. *Stena Sealink* and *P&O European Ferries* both have several crossings daily, taking 2hr 15min – reckon on £180 return for a small car and two people with *Stena* and £233 return with *P&O* to Stranraer.

# TRAVELLING FROM NORTH AMERICA

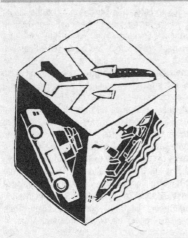

Of Scottish cities, only one – **Glasgow** – is reachable direct by air. Flights into Edinburgh tend to route through London (*British Airways*) or Dublin (*Aer Lingus*); to get to Aberdeen or Inverness you'll have to hop on a shuttle from London on *British Airways*. *Loganair* fly to the Scottish islands via Glasgow or Edinburgh. See p.4 for the full picture on flying to Scotland from other parts of Britain.

## SHOPPING FOR TICKETS

Barring special offers, the cheapest fare is usually an **Apex** ticket, although this will carry certain restrictions: you have to book – and pay – at least 21 days before departure, spend at least seven days abroad (maximum stay three months), and you tend to get penalized if you change your schedule. There are also winter **Super Apex** tickets, sometimes known as "Eurosavers" – slightly cheaper than an ordinary Apex, but limiting your stay to between 7 and 21 days. Some airlines also issue **Special Apex** tickets to people younger than 24, often extending the maximum stay to a year. Many airlines offer youth or student fares to **under 25s**; a passport or driving licence are sufficient proof of age, though these tickets are subject to availability and can have eccentric booking conditions. It's worth remembering that most cheap return fares involve spending at least one Saturday night away and that many will only give a percentage refund if you need to cancel or alter your journey, so make sure you check the restrictions carefully before buying a ticket.

**Travelling to Scotland from North America, your choice of arrival point will depend largely on whether your itinerary also includes England. If it does, you'll almost certainly stand to save on the airfare by flying into London and making your way up to Scotland from there.**

Figure on 6hrs 30mins **flying time** from New York to any of the British airports, 11hrs 30mins from the West Coast (it's an hour extra coming back, due to headwinds). Most eastbound flights cross the Atlantic overnight, reaching Britain the next morning, although a few flights from the East Coast leave early in the morning, landing late the same evening, just as everything is shutting down.

You can normally cut costs further by going through a **specialist flight agent** – either a **consolidator**, who buys up blocks of tickets from the airlines and sells them at a discount, or a **discount agent**, who wheels and deals in blocks of tickets offloaded by the airlines, and often offers special student and youth fares and a range of other travel-related services such as travel insurance, rail passes, car rentals, tours and the like. Bear in mind, though, that penalties for changing your plans can be stiff. Remember too that these companies make their money by dealing in bulk – don't expect them to answer lots of questions. Some agents specialize in **charter flights**, which may be cheaper than anything available on a scheduled flight, but again departure dates are fixed and withdrawal penalties are high (check the refund policy). If you travel a lot, **discount travel clubs** are another option – the annual membership fee may be worth it for benefits such as cut-price air tickets and car rental.

Regardless of where you buy your ticket, the **fare** will depend on the season. Fares to Britain are highest from around early June to mid-September, when the weather is best; they drop during the "shoulder" seasons – mid-September to early November and mid-April to early June – and you'll get the best prices during the low season, November through April (excluding Christmas and New Year when prices are hiked up and seats are at a premium). Note also that flying on weekends ordinarily adds $20–60 to the round-trip fare; the prices qouted below assume midweek travel.

## FLIGHTS FROM THE USA

Transatlantic fares are very reasonable, thanks to intense competition. Any local travel agent should be able to access airlines' up-to-the-minute fares, although in practice they may not have time to research all the possibilities and you might want to call the airlines direct.

Several airlines fly direct from **Eastern US** "gateway" cities **to Glasgow** – not nearly as many as to London, but enough to ensure a decent choice and competitive fares. Low-season, midweek Apex fares from New York (*Aer Lingus, British Airways*), Boston (*Aer Lingus, Northwest*) and Washington, DC (*United*) hover around the $500 mark, from Chicago (*American*) reckon on around $575; peak-season prices are likely to run $150–200 higher.

Flying to **London**, low-season fares are rather cheaper, hovering around the $400–450 mark from New York City, Boston or Washington, DC, $500 or so from Atlanta, Chicago, St Louis or Miami, and around £600 from Denver, Dallas-Fort Worth. Flying to **Manchester** in the north of England is another possibility though this doesn't work out much cheaper than the direct fare to Glasgow.

Flying from **West Coast USA to Scotland** is two hops at best. From LA you can fly nonstop to London and change there for a shuttle flight; from other cities, your best bet is to make for an Eastern gateway city and then on to Glasgow. Midweek fares from LA or San Francisco to Glasgow start at $600 in the low season. Again, the fares **to London** will invariably be cheaper, starting as low as $500 from LA or San Francisco.

## FLIGHTS FROM CANADA

*Air Canada* and *British Airways* fly nonstop **to Glasgow** from their gateway cities of Toronto, Montréal and Vancouver (*Air Canada* also fly from Toronto to Edinburgh via London). Low-season midweek Apex fares start at Can$550 from Toronto or Montréal, Can$750 from Vancouver. High-season travel will add a premium of Can$300–400.

You won't necessarily save any money by flying **to London**, although you will have a greater choice of carriers, and it's certainly a good idea if you're coming from any other Canadian city. In addition to Toronto, Montréal and Vancouver you can fly nonstop to London from Ottawa, Halifax, Edmonton and Calgary with either *Air Canada* or *Canadian Airlines*.

## PACKAGES AND INCLUSIVE TOURS

Although you may want to see Scotland at your own speed, you shouldn't dismiss out of hand the idea of a **package deal**. Many agents and airlines put together very flexible deals, sometimes amounting to no more than a flight plus car or train pass and accommodation, and these can actually work out better value than the same arrangements made on arrival – especially fly-drive deals, as car rental is expensive in Britain. A package can also be great for your peace of mind, if only to ensure a worry-free first week.

Many **tour** operators specialize in travel to Scotland. Most can do packages of the standard highlights, and many organize walking or cycling

## NORTH AMERICAN AIRLINES AND ROUTES

**Aer Lingus**  ☎1-800/223-6537
*Boston and New York
via Dublin or Shannon to London.*

**Air Canada**  ☎1-800/776-3000
*Montréal, Toronto and Vancouver
to Glasgow and London.*

**Air India**  ☎1-800/223-7776
*New York and Toronto to London.*

**American Airlines**  ☎1-800/433-7300
*Boston, Chicago, Dallas-Fort Worth,
Los Angeles, Miami, Nashville,
New York, Raleigh/Durham to London.
Chicago to Glasgow.*

**British Airways**  ☎1-800/247-9297
*New York to Glasgow.
Atlanta, Baltimore, Boston, Charlotte, Chicago,
Dallas-Fort Worth, Houston, Los Angeles, Miami,
New York, Orlando, Philadelphia, San Francisco,
Seattle, Washington, DC to London, with connec-
tions to Glasgow, Edinburgh, Aberdeen and
Inverness.*

**Canadian Airlines**  ☎1-800/426-7000
*Calgary, Edmonton, Toronto
and Vancouver to London.
Toronto to Manchester.*

**Continental Airlines**  ☎1-800/231-0856
*Denver, Houston and Newark
to London.*

**Delta Airlines**  ☎1-800/241-4141
*Atlanta, Cincinnati, Miami and
Orlando to London
Atlanta to Manchester.*

**Kuwait Airways**  ☎1-800/458-9248
*New York to London.*

**Northwest Airlines**  ☎1-800/225-2525
*Minneapolis to London.
Boston to Glasgow.*

**TWA**  ☎1-800/221-2000
*St Louis to London.*

**United Airlines**  ☎1-800/538-2929
*Los Angeles, New York,
San Francisco, Seattle and
Washington, DC to London .
Washington, DC to Glasgow.*

**US Air**  ☎1-800/622-1015
*New York to London.*

**Virgin Atlantic Airways**  ☎1-800/862-8621
*Boston, JFK, Miami, Newark
and Orlando to London.*

## DISCOUNT TRAVEL AGENTS, CONSOLIDATORS AND TRAVEL CLUBS IN NORTH AMERICA

**Air Brokers International**, 323 Geary St, Suite 411, San Francisco, CA 94102 (☎1-800/883-3273). Consolidator.

**Council Charter**, 205 E 42nd St, New York, NY 10017 (☎1-800/223-7402). Youth-oriented charter broker.

**Council Travel**, 205 E 42nd St, New York, NY 10017 (☎1-800/743-1823 or 212/661-1450); 312 Sutter St, San Francisco, CA 94108 (☎415/421-3473); and many other regional outlets. The country's largest student and youth-oriented discount agent.

**Discount Travel International**, Ives Building, 114 Forrest Ave, Suite 205, Narberth, PA 19072 (☎215/668-7184). Discount travel club, membership $45.

**Moment's Notice**, 425 Madison Ave, New York, NY (☎212/486-0503). Travel club.

**Nouvelles Frontières**, 12 E 33rd St, New York, NY 10016 (☎212/779-0600); 1001 Sherbrook E, Suite 720, Montréal H2L IL3 (☎514/526-8444); and other US and Canadian locations. Discount travel agent.

**STA Travel**, 48 E 11th St, New York, NY 10003 (☎1-800/777-0112 or 212/477-7166); 106 Geary St, San Francisco, CA 94108 (☎415/391-8407); and several other offices on the East and West coasts. Major discount agent specializing in student and youth deals.

**Stand Buys**, 311 W Superior St, Chicago, IL 60610 (☎1-800/548-1116). Travel club.

**Travel Cuts**, 187 College St, Toronto, Ont. M5T 1P7 (☎416/979-2406); and outlets on most Canadian university campuses.The principal student/youth discount agency in Canada.

**UniTravel**, 1177 N Warson Rd, St Louis, MO 63132 (☎1-800/325-2222). Consolidator.

## NORTH AMERICAN TOUR OPERATORS TO SCOTLAND

**British Coastal Trails**, 1001 B Ave, Suite 302, Coronado, CA 92118 (☎619/437-1211). Walking trips in the Highlands and Borders.

**British Travel International**, PO Box 299, Elkton, VA 22827 (☎1-800/327-6097). Agent for all independent arrangements: air tickets, rail and bus passes, hotels, and a comprehensive B&B reservation service.

**Especially Britain**, PO Box 121398, Fort Worth, TX 76121-1398 (☎1-800/869-0538). Fly-drives and independent tours built around the *Scottish Explorer* and *National Trust for Scotland* passes (see p.30).

**Hostelling International USA**, PO Box 37613, Washington, DC 20013 (☎202/783-6161). Affiliated with the Scottish Youth Hostels Association, organizes walking, cycling and general youth tours.

**Journeys Through Scotland**, 35 S Encino Rd, South Laguna, CA 92677 (☎1-800/521-1429).

**Lynott Tours**, Empire State Bldg, 350 5th Ave, #6219, New York, NY 10118 (☎1-800/221-2474). Special-interest tours, hotel and castle stays, self-drives.

**Mountain Travel/Sobek**, 6420 Fairmount Ave, El Cerrito, CA 94530 (☎1-800/227-2384). Hiking and cycling tours.

**Renaissance Travel**, 5720 Buford Way, Norcross, GA 30071 (☎1-800/43-SCOTS). Scottish specialist.

**Scottie Line Travel**, PO Box 506, Chagrin Falls, OH 44022 (☎1-800/875-SCOT). "Easy walking tours".

**Scottish Connections**, 304 Victory Rd, Marina Bay, North Quincy, MA 02171 (☎617/770-4172). Scotland tours.

**Sterling Tours**, 2707 Congress St, Suite 2-G, San Diego, CA 92110 (☎1-800/727-4359). Scottish specialist offering a variety of independent itineraries, some packages.

trips through the countryside, with any number of theme tours based around Scotland's literary heritage, history, pubs, gardens, theatre, golf – you name it. A few possibilities are listed in the box above, and a travel agent will be able to point out others; bear in mind that bookings made through travel agents cost no more than going through the tour operator. For a full listing, contact the *Scottish Tourist Board* (see p.15). Be sure to examine the fine print of any deal, and make sure the operator is a member of the *United States Tour Operator Association* (*USTOA*) or approved by the *American Society of Travel Agents* (*ASTA*).

# TRAVELLING FROM AUSTRALIA AND NEW ZEALAND

**There are no direct flights to Scotland from anywhere in Australia or New Zealand, so you will have to route through London and then travel north.**

Daily flights connect London with Melbourne, Sydney, Brisbane and Perth, with no great difference in the fares. With *Garuda*, the least expensive airline, a return ticket from Sydney to London should cost you around Aus$1600 in the low season – mid-November to mid-December. With *British Airways*, *Thai* or *Malaysian* airlines add at least another Aus$100. From Auckland expect to pay around NZ$1170 single or NZ$2050 return in the low season – October to November – with *Qantas*.

## AIRLINES IN AUSTRALASIA

**Air New Zealand**, Air New Zealand House, Queen St, Auckland (☎09/357 3000).

**British Airways**, 64 Castlereagh St, Sydney (☎02/258 3300); Dilworth Building, Queen St Auckland (☎09/367 7500).

**Garuda Airlines**, 175 Clarence St, Sydney (☎02/262 2011); WestPac Tower Bldg, 10th Floor, 120 Albert St, Auckland (☎09/366 1855).

**Malaysian Airways**, 11th Floor, Amex Tower 388, George St, Sydney (☎0/364 3590); 12th Floor, Swanson Centre, 12–26 Swanson St, Auckland (☎09/373 2741).

**Qantas**, Qantas International Centre, International Square, Sydney (☎02/ 236 3636).

**Thai International Airways**, Kensington Swan Bldg, 22 Fanshawe St , Auckland (☎09/377 0268).

## DISCOUNT AGENTS IN AUSTRALASIA

**Anywhere Travel**, 345 Anzac Parade, Kingsford, Sydney (☎02/663 0411).

**Brisbane Discount Travel**, 360 Queen St, Brisbane (☎07/229 9211).

**Budget Travel**, PO Box 505, Auckland (☎09/309 4313).

**Discount Travel Specialists**, Shop 53, Forrest Chase, Perth (☎09/221 1400).

**Flight Centres**, Circular Quay, Sydney (☎02/241 2422); Bourke St, Melbourne (☎03/ 650 2899); plus branches nationwide except in the Northern Territory. National Bank Towers, 205–225 Queen St, Auckland (☎09/309 6171); Shop 1M, National Mutual Arcade, 152 Hereford St, Christchurch

(☎09/379 7145); 50–52 Willis St, Wellington (☎04/472 8101); plus branches nationwide.

**Passport Travel**, 320b Glenfarrie Rd, Malvern, Melbourne (☎03/824 7183).

**Topdeck Travel**, 45 Grenfell St, Adelaide (☎08/410 1110).

**STA**, 732 Harris St, Sydney (☎02/212 1255); CAE Shop, 256 Flinders St, Melbourne (☎03/347 4711); 100 James St, Northbridge, Perth (☎09/227 7299).

**STS Travel**, 10 High St, Auckland (☎09/309 9995); 233 Cuba St, Wellington (☎04/385 0561); 223 High St, Christchurch (☎03/379 9098).

**Tymtro Travel**, Suite G12, Wallaceway Shopping Centre, Chatswood, Sydney (☎02/411 1222).

The add-on cost to either Glasgow or Edinburgh will be anything between Aus$200 and Aus$300 (NZ$250–350) depending on the season, from Auckland, between NZ$250 and NZ$350, so you might want to consider travelling on by bus or train from London.

Numerous discount agents can supply these and other low-price tickets. One of the most reliable operators is *STA* (*STS* in New Zealand), who can also advise on **visa regulations** for Australian and New Zealand citizens – and for a fee will do all the paperwork for you.

# VISAS, CUSTOMS REGULATIONS AND TAX

**Citizens of all the countries of Europe – except Albania, Bulgaria, Poland and the states of the former Soviet Union – and citizens of Canada, Australia and New Zealand can enter Britain with just a passport, generally for up to three months. Citizens of all other nationalities require a visa, obtainable from the British Consular office in the country of application. US citizens can travel in Britain for up to six months without a visa, but for longer stays, should apply to the British Embassy in Washington, DC (see below). All overseas consulates in Scotland are detailed in the listings sections for Edinburgh and Glasgow.**

Travellers coming into Britain directly from another **EC** country do not have to make a declaration to **customs** at their place of entry and can effectively bring almost as much wine or beer across the Channel as they like. However, there are still strict restrictions – details of which are prominently displayed in all duty free outlets – on **tax- or duty-free** goods, so you can't invest in a stockpile of cheap cigarettes, wherever you're coming from.

There are **import restrictions** on a variety of articles and substances, from firearms to furs derived from endangered species, none of which should bother the normal tourist. However, if you need any clarification on British import regulations, contact HM Customs and Excise, New Kings Beam House, 22 Upper Ground, London SE1 9PJ (☎071/620 1313). You cannot bring pets into Britain on holiday, as strict quarantine restrictions apply to animals brought from overseas (except Northern and Southern Ireland).

Many goods in Britain, with the chief exceptions of books and food, are subject to **Value Added Tax** (VAT), which currently increases the cost of an item by 17.5 percent. Visitors from non-EC countries can save a lot of money through the Retail Export Scheme, which allows a refund of VAT on goods to be taken out of the country – though savings will usually be minimal, if anything, for EC nationals, because of their own VAT rates. Note that not all shops participate in this scheme – those doing so display a sign to this effect – and that you cannot reclaim VAT charged on hotel bills or other services.

## BRITISH EMBASSIES ABROAD

**Australia** Commonwealth Ave, Yarralumla, Canberra, ACT 2600 (☎062/270-6666).

**Canada** 80 Elgin St, Ottawa, ON K1P 5K7 (☎613/237-1530).

**Ireland** 31–33 Merrion Rd, Dublin 4 (☎01/695211).

**Netherlands** General Koningslaan 44, Amsterdam (☎676 43 43).

**New Zealand** Reserve Bank Bldg, 2 The Terrace, PO Box 1812, Wellington (☎04/726-049).

**USA** 3100 Massachusetts Ave NW, Washington, DC 20008 (☎202/462-1340).

## MONEY, BANKS AND COSTS

The basic unit of currency in Britain is the **pound sterling (£)**, divided into 100 pence (p). Coins come in denominations of 1p, 2p, 5p, 10p, 20p, 50p and £1 – there's a rare £2 coin in circulation as well. *Bank of England* and **Northern Ireland banknotes are legal tender in Scotland; in addition the** *Bank of Scotland,* **the** *Royal Bank of Scotland* **and the** *Clydesdale Bank* **issue their own banknotes in denominations of £1, £5, £10, £20, £50 and £100 – legal tender in the rest of Britain, no matter what shopkeepers south of the border might say. Shopkeepers will carefully scrutinize any £20 or £50 notes, as forgeries are widespread, and you'd be well advised to do the same. The quickest test is to hold the note up to the light to make sure there's a thin wire filament running from top to bottom; this is by no means foolproof, but it will catch most fakes.**

### CARRYING MONEY

There are no exchange controls in Britain, so you can bring in as much money as you like. The easiest and safest way to carry your money is in travellers' cheques, available for a small commission (usually one percent) from any major bank. The most commonly accepted travellers' cheques are *American Express*, followed by *Visa* and *Thomas Cook* – most cheques issued by banks will be one of these three brands. You'll usually pay commission again when you cash each cheque, normally another one percent or so, or a flat rate – though

no commission is payable on Amex cheques exchanged at Amex branches. Make sure to keep a record of the cheques as you cash them, so you'll be able to get the value of all uncashed cheques refunded immediately if you lose them.

Most hotels, shops and restaurants in Scotland accept the major **credit cards** – *Access/MasterCard, Visa, American Express* and *Diners Club* – although they're less useful in the rural areas, and smaller establishments all over the country, such as B&Bs, will often accept cash only. You can get cash advances from selected banks and bureaux de change on credit cards, though there will invariably be a minimum amount you can draw.

If you have a PIN, *Visa* and *Access/ Mastercard* can also be used at Bank of Scotland and *Royal Bank of Scotland* cashpoint machines. *Bank of Scotland* and *Royal Bank of Scotland* cashpoints also take *Lloyds* and *Barclays* cashcards, while *Clydesdale* takes *Midland* and *National Westminster*.

### BANKING HOURS

In every sizeable town in Scotland, and some surprisingly small villages, you'll find a branch of at least one of the big four high-street banks: *Bank of Scotland, Royal Bank of Scotland, Clydesdale* and *TSB Scotland*. Basic **opening hours** are Monday to Friday 9.15am till 4 or 4.45pm, though all are open until 5.45pm on Thursdays. Almost everywhere banks are the best places to **change money and cheques**; outside banking hours you'll have to use a **bureau de change**, widely found in most city centres, often at train stations or airports. Avoid changing money or cheques in hotels, where the rates are normally very poor.

### EMERGENCIES

If, as a foreign visitor, you run out of money or there is some kind of emergency, the quickest way to get **money sent out** is to contact your bank at home and have them wire the cash to the nearest bank. You can do the same thing through *Thomas Cook* or *American Express* if there is a branch nearby. Americans and Canadians can also have cash sent out through *Western Union* (information in UK ☎0800/833833) to a nearby bank or post office. Make sure you know when it's likely to arrive, since you won't be notified by the receiving office. Remember, too, that you'll need some form of identification when you pick up the money.

## COSTS

Scotland has become an expensive place to visit, although in general it is marginally less pricy than England. The minimum expenditure, if you're camping, hitching a lot of the time and preparing most of your own food, would be in the region of £20 a day, rising to around £25 a day using the hostelling network, some public transport and grabbing the odd meal. Couples staying at budget B&Bs, eating at unpretentious restaurants and visiting a fair number of tourist attractions are looking at around £40 each per day – if you're renting a car, staying in comfortable B&Bs or hotels and eating well, you should reckon on at least £60 a day per person. Single travellers should budget on spending around sixty percent of what a couple would spend (single rooms cost more than half a double). If you're visiting **Edinburgh**, which can get pricy, allow at least an extra £5 or so a day to get full pleasure out of the place, though, unlike London, accommodation prices are no higher in Scotland's capital than in the rest of the country. For more detailed information on the cost of accommodation, transport and eating, see the relevant sections below.

## INSURANCE, HEALTH AND EMERGENCIES

**Wherever you're travelling from, it's a good idea to have some kind of travel insurance, which covers you for loss of possessions and money too, as well as the cost of all medical and dental treatment. If you're travelling to Scotland from elsewhere in Britain, you may well be covered by your domestic insurance policies, but if you do need extra cover, _Endsleigh_ are about the cheapest British insurers, offering a month's travel cover for around £20. Their policies are available from most youth/student travel specialists or direct from their main Scottish offices at 7–9 Shandwick Place, Edinburgh (☎031/228 4878) and 178 Hope St, Glasgow (☎041/332 5252). In London they're based at 97–107 Southampton Row (☎071/ 580 4311). Whatever your policy, if you have anything stolen, get a copy of the police report of the incident, as this is essential to substantiate your claim.**

In the **US and Canada** you should also check the insurance policies you already have carefully before taking out a new one. You may discover that you're covered already for medical and other losses while abroad. Canadians especially are usually covered by their provincial health plans, and holders of ISIC cards are entitled (outside the USA) to be reimbursed for $3000-worth of accident coverage and sixty days of in-patient benefits up to $100 a day for the period the card is valid. Students may also find their health coverage extends during vacations, and many bank and charge accounts include some form of travel cover; insurance is also sometimes included if you pay for your trip with a credit card.

If you do want a specific travel insurance policy, there are numerous to choose from: short-term combination policies covering everything from baggage loss to broken legs are the best bet and cost around $50 for fifteen days, $80 for a month, $150 for two months, $190 for three months. One thing to bear in mind is that none of the currently available policies covers theft; they only cover loss while in the custody of an identifiable person – though even then you must make a report to the police and get their written statement. Two companies you might try are _Travel Guard_, 110 Centrepoint Drive, Steven Point, WI

54480 (☎1-800/826-1300 or 715/345-0505), or *Access America International*, 600 3rd Ave, New York, NY 10163 (☎1-800/284-8300 or 212/949-5960).

## HEALTH

No vaccinations are required for entry into Britain. Citizens of all **EC** countries are entitled to free medical treatment at National Health Service hospitals; citizens of other countries will be charged for all medical services except those administered by accident and emergency units at National Health Service hospitals. Thus a **US** citizen who has been hit by a car would not be charged if the injuries simply required stitching and setting in the emergency unit, but would if admission to a hospital ward were necessary. Health insurance is therefore extremely advisable for all non-EC nationals.

In additon to all the usual accidents and calamities that might arise, you should be prepared to encounter the **midge** (*Culicoides impunctatus*), a tiny biting fly found all over Scotland, particularly in the Highlands and islands, during the summer. Midges love still, damp conditions and can make outdoor life a misery. You'll soon notice if they're around; cover up arms and legs and try and avoid wearing dark colours, which attract them. Various repellents are worth a try, among them *Autan* and *Jungle Juice,* widely available from pharmacists.

**Pharmacists** can dispense only a limited range of drugs without a doctor's prescription. Most are open standard shop hours, though in large towns some may close as late as 10pm – local newspapers carry lists of late-opening pharmacies. **Doctors' surgeries** tend to be open from about 9am to noon and then for a couple of hours in the evening; outside surgery hours, you can turn up at the casualty department of the local hospital for complaints that require immediate attention – unless it's an emergency, in which case ring for an ambulance, ☎999.

### EMERGENCIES

For Police, Fire Brigade, Ambulance and, in certain areas, Mountain Rescue or Coastguard, dial ☎999.

## THE POLICE

For the most part the Scottish **police** continue to be approachable and helpful to visitors. If you're lost in a major town, asking a police officer is generally the quickest way to get help – alternatively, you could ask a **traffic warden**, a much maligned species of law-enforcer responsible for parking restrictions and other vehicle-related matters. They're distinguishable by their flat caps with a yellow band, and by the fact that they are generally armed with a book of parking-fine tickets; police officers on street duty wear a peaked flat hat with a black and white chequered band, and are generally armed with a truncheon (baton) – rarely a gun.

As with any country, Scotland's major towns have their dangerous spots, but these tend to be inner-city housing estates where no tourist has any reason to be. The chief risk on the streets is pickpocketing, so carry only as much money as you need, and keep all bags and pockets fastened. Should you have anything stolen or be involved in some incident that requires reporting, go to the local police station (addresses in the major cities are listed in the guide); the ☎999 number should only be used in emergencies.

# INFORMATION AND MAPS

**If you want to do a bit of research before arriving in Scotland, you should contact the British Tourist Authority (BTA) in your country or write direct to the main office of the Scottish Tourist Board (STB), marking your letter Information Department – the addresses are given below. The BTA and the STB will send you a wealth of free literature, some of it just rosy-tinted advertising copy, but much of it extremely useful – especially the maps, city guides and event calendars. If you want more hard facts on a particular area, you should approach the area tourist boards, which are listed overleaf. Some are extremely helpful, others give the impression of being harassed to breaking point by years of understaffing, but all of them will have a few leaflets worth scanning before you set out.**

**Tourist offices** (sometimes called Tourist Information Centres) exist in virtually every

Scottish town – you'll find their phone numbers and opening hours in the relevant sections of the *guide*. The average opening hours are much the same as standard shop hours, with the difference that in summer they'll often be open on a Sunday and for a couple of hours after the shops have closed on weekdays; opening hours are generally shorter in winter, and in more remote areas the office may well be closed for the season. All centres offer information on accommodation (and can usually book rooms – see "Accommodation"), local public transport, attractions and restaurants as well as town and regional maps. In many cases their services are free, but a growing number of offices make a small charge for an accommodation list or a town guide with an accompanying street plan.

## MAPS

Most bookstores will have a good selection of maps of Scotland and Britain in general, but see the box on p.17 for a list of travel specialists. Of the many North American outlets, the *British Travel Bookshop* in New York, in particular, stocks a phenomenal array. *Rand McNally Map and Travel* is also a good bet; they have 24 stores nationwide. For details of your local branch, and direct-mail maps call ☎1-800/333-0136 ext 2111.

Virtually every service station in Scotland stocks one or more of the big **road atlases**. The

### SCOTTISH TOURIST BOARD OFFICES

**Scotland**: 23 Ravelston Terrace, Edinburgh EH4 3EU (☎031/ 332 2433).

**England**: 19 Cockspur St, London SW1 5BL (☎071/930 8661 or 8662 or 8663).

### BRITISH TOURIST AUTHORITY OFFICES

**Australia**: 210 Clarence St, 4th Floor, Sydney, NSW 2000 (☎02/267 4555).

**Canada**: 111 Avenue Rd, Suite 450, Toronto, Ontario M5R 3J8 (☎416/925-2175).

**Ireland**: 123 Lower Bagot St, Dublin 2 (☎ 01/661 4188).

**New Zealand**: Suite 305, 3rd Floor, Dilworth Building, corner of Customs and Queen streets, Auckland (☎649/303 1446).

**USA**: 2580 Cumberland Pkwy, Suite 470, Atlanta, GA (☎404/432-9641).

625 N Michigan Ave, Suite 1510, Chicago, IL (☎312/787-0490).

World Trade Center, Suite 450, 350 S Figueroa St, Los Angeles, CA (☎213/628-3525).

551 5th Ave, Suite 701, New York, NY 10176 (☎212/986-2200).

## AREA TOURIST BOARDS IN SCOTLAND

**Angus Tourist Board**, Administration Offices, Market Place, Arbroath, Angus DD11 1HR (☎0241/72609).

**Aviemore and Spey Valley Tourist Board**, Grampian Road, Aviemore, Invernessshire PH22 1PP (☎0479/810363).

**Ayrshire Tourist Board**, Suite 1005, Prestwick Airport, Prestwick, Ayrshire KA9 2PL (☎0292/284196).

**Banff and Buchan Tourist Board**, Collie Lodge,Banff AB45 1AU (☎0261/812319).

**Caithness Tourist Board**, Whitechapel Rd, Wick, Caithness KW1 4EA (☎0955/2596).

**City of Aberdeen Tourist Board** , St Nicholas House, Broad St, Aberdeen AB9 1DE (☎0224/632727).

**City of Dundee Tourist Board**, 4 City Square, Dundee DD1 3BA (☎0382/27723).

**Clyde Valley Tourist Board**, Horsemarket, Ladyacre Rd, Lanark ML11 7LQ (☎0555/2544).

**Dumfries and Galloway Tourist Board**, Campbell House, Bankend Rd, Dumfries DG1 4TH (☎0387/53862).

**Dunoon and Cowal Tourist Board**, Tourist Information Centre, 7 Alexander Parade, Dunoon, Argyll PA23 8AB (☎0369/3785).

**East Lothian Tourist Board**, Brunton Hall, Musselburgh, East Lothian EH21 6AE (☎0368/63353).

**Edinburgh Marketing**, Waverley Market, 3 Princes St, Edinburgh EH2 2QP (☎031/557 1700).

**Forth Valley Tourist Board**, Annet House, High St, Linlithgow, West Lothian EH49 7EJ (☎0506/844600).

**Fort William and Lochaber Tourist Board**, Cameron Centre, Cameron Square, Fort William, Invernessshire PH33 6AJ (☎0397/703781).

**Gordon District Tourist Board**, St Nicholas House, Broad St, Aberdeen AB9 1DE (☎0224/276276).

**Greater Glasgow Tourist Board**, 39 St Vincent Place, Glasgow G1 2ER (☎041/204 4400).

**Inverness, Loch Ness and Nairn Tourist Board**, Castle Wynd, Inverness IV2 3BJ (☎0463/234353).

**Isle of Arran Tourist Board**, Information Centre, The Pier, Brodick, Isle of Arran KA27 8AU (☎0770/2140).

**Isle of Bute Tourist Board**, 15 Victoria St, Rothesay, Isle of Bute PA20 0AJ (☎0700/502151).

**Isle of Skye and South West Ross Tourist Board**, Tourist Information Centre, Portree, Isle of Skye IV51 9BZ (☎0478/2137).

**Kincardine and District Tourist Board**, 45 Station Rd, Banchory, Kincardineshire AB31 3XX (☎03302/2066).

**Kirkcaldy District Council**, Information Centre, South St, Leven, Fife KY8 4PF (☎0333/429464).

**Loch Lomond, Stirling and Trossachs Tourist Board**, 41 Dumbarton Rd, Stirling FK8 2QQ (☎0786/475019).

**Midlothian Tourism**, 7 Station Rd, Roslin, Midlothian EH25 9PF (☎031/440 2210).

**Moray Tourist Board**, 17 High St, Elgin, Moray IV30 1EG (☎0343/543388).

**Orkney Tourist Board**, Information Centre, 6 Broad St, Kirkwall, Orkney KW15 1DH (☎0856/872856).

**Perthshire Tourist Board**, 45 High St, Perth PH1 5TJ (☎0738/38353).

**Ross and Cromarty Tourist Board**, Information Centre, North Kessock, Inverness IV1 1XB (☎046373/505).

**Scottish Borders Tourist Board**, 70 High St, Selkirk TD7 4DD (☎0385/63435).

**Shetland Island Tourism**, Market Cross, Lerwick, Shetland ZE1 0LU (☎0595/3434).

**St Andrews and North East Fife Tourist Board**, Tourist Information Centre, 2 Queens Gardens, St Andrews, Fife KY16 9TE (☎0334/72021).

**Sutherland Tourist Board**, The Square, Dornoch, Sutherland IV25 3SD (☎0862/810400).

**Western Isles Tourist Board**, 4 Beach St, Stornaway, Isle of Lewis PA87 2XY (☎0851/703088).

**West Highlands and Islands of Argyll Tourist Board**, Albany St, Oban PA34 4AR (☎0631/63122).

best of these are the large-format ones produced by the *AA*, *RAC*, *Collins* and *Ordnance Survey*, which cover all of Britain at around 3miles:1in and include larger-scale plans of major towns.

You could also invest in the excellent **fold-out maps** published by *Michelin* and *Bartholomew*, the latter includes clear town plans of the major cities.

## MAP OUTLETS IN THE UK

**Edinburgh**

*HMSO Books*, 71 Lothian Rd, EH3 9AZ (☎031/228 4181).

*Thomas Nelson and Sons Ltd*, 51 York Place, EH1 3JD (☎031/557 3011).

**Glasgow**

*John Smith and Sons*, 57–61 St Vincent St (☎041/221 7472).

**London**

*Daunt Books*, 83 Marylebone High St, W1 (☎071/224 2295).

*National Map Centre*, 22–24 Caxton St, SW1 (☎071/222 4945).

*Stanfords*, 12–14 Long Acre, WC2 (☎071/836 1321).

*The Travellers Bookshop*, 25 Cecil Court, WC2 (☎071/836 9132).

## MAP OUTLETS IN NORTH AMERICA

**Chicago**

*Rand McNally*, 444 North Michigan Ave, IL 60611 (☎312/321-1751).

**Montréal**

*Ulysses Travel Bookshop*, 4176 St-Denis (☎514/289-0993).

**New York**

*British Travel Bookshop*, 551 5th Ave, NY 10176 (☎1-800/448-3039 or 212/490-6688).

*The Complete Traveler Bookstore*, 199 Madison Ave, NY 10016 (☎212/685-9007).

*Rand McNally*, 150 E 52nd St, NY 10022 (☎212/758-7488).

*Traveler's Bookstore*, 22 W 52nd St, NY 10019 (☎212/664- 0995).

**San Francisco**

*The Complete Traveler Bookstore*, 3207 Filmore St, CA 92123 (☎415/923-1511).

*Rand McNally*, 595 Market St, CA 94105 (☎415/777-3131).

**Seattle**

*Elliot Bay Book Company*, 101 South Main St, WA 98104 (☎206/624-6600).

**Toronto**

*Open Air Books and Maps*, 25 Toronto St, M5R 2C1 (☎416/363-0719).

**Vancouver**

*World Wide Books and Maps*, 1247 Granville St.

**Washington, DC**

*Rand McNally*, 1201 Connecticut Ave NW, Washington, DC 20036 (☎202/223-6751).

## MAP OUTLETS IN AUSTRALASIA

**Adelaide**

*The Map Shop*, 16a Peel St, Adelaide, SA 5000 (☎08/231 2033).

**Brisbane**

*Hema*, 239 George St, Brisbane, QLD 4000 (☎07/221 4330).

**Melbourne**

*Bowyangs*, 372 Little Bourke St, Melbourne, VIC 3000 (☎03/670 4383).

**Perth**

*Perth Map Centre*, 891 Hay St, Perth, WA 6000 (☎09/322 5733).

**Sydney**

*Travel Bookshop*, 20 Bridge St, Sydney, NSW 2000 (☎02/241 3554).

If you're after more detail, the most comprehensive **maps** of Scotland are produced by the **Ordnance Survey** series – renowned for its accuracy and clarity. The 204 maps in their 1:50,000 (a little over 1mile:1in) *Landranger* series cover the whole of Britain and show enough detail to be useful for most walkers. Their more detailed 1:25,000 *Pathfinder* series is invaluable for serious hiking but only covers the more popular outdoor recreational areas and National Parks. The full *Ordnance Survey* range is only available at a few big-city stores, although in any walking district of Scotland you'll find the relevant maps in local shops or tourist offices.

# GETTING AROUND

**As you'd expect, the efficiency of Scotland's train and bus services is largely dictated by geography and population density. The majority of Scots live in the central belt, which spreads from Glasgow in the west to Edinburgh, virtually on the east coast. Public transport here is efficient and most places are easily accessible by train and bus. To the south and north it can be a different story; off the main routes public transport services are few and far between, particularly in more remote regions such as the northern Highlands, although with careful planning practically everywhere is reachable and you'll have no trouble getting to the main tourist destinations. In most parts of Scotland, especially if you take the scenic back roads, the low level of traffic makes driving a wonderfully unstressful experience.**

## TRAINS

Always something of a national joke, recent government policies have led to a severe decline in **rail services** all over Britain, and Scotland is no exception. For the time being, under-subsidized Scotrail, British Rail's Scottish operator, runs the majority of train services, reaching all the major towns, sometimes on lines rated as among the great scenic routes of the world. For a **run-down of the different fares available**, see "Travelling from England, Ireland and Europe".

You can buy tickets for Scotrail trains at stations or from major travel agents. For busy long-distance InterCity routes, it's advisable to **reserve** a seat. Seat reservations to Edinburgh, Glasgow, Aberdeen or Inverness are included in the price of the ticket if you book in advance. The ticket offices at many rural and commuter stations are closed at weekends; in these instances

there's sometimes a vending machine on the platform. If the machines aren't working, you can buy your ticket on board, but if you've embarked at a station that does have a machine and you haven't bought a ticket, there's a spot fine of £10.

ScotRail offer a number of **travel cards** and **special tickets** that are available to British nationals and foreign visitors alike. The *Freedom of Scotland Travelpass* gives unlimited train travel and is valid on all *CalMac* west coast ferry links (see ferry information on p.21) as well as offering 33 percent reductions on many buses and on some *P&O* Orkney and Shetland ferries. It costs £95 for 8 consecutive or £130 for 15 consecutive days and comes complete with timetables and a card allowing discounts at tourist attractions, shops and restaurants throughout Scotland. The *ScotRail Rover* is perhaps the most flexible option, allowing unlimited travel on ScotRail for varying periods; prices range from £59 for 4 days out of 8 consecutive days travel to £110 for 12 out of 15 days. ScotRail also do three other regional *Rover* passes: the *West Highland* (covering the area from Glasgow to Fort William) which costs £35 for four days travel out of eight; the *North Highland*, which for the same price is valid on all lines from Thurso to Aberdeen; and the *Festival Cities*, which includes routes from Glasgow to Edinburgh and Stirling, and costs £19.50 for three days travel out of seven.

For **North American visitors**, the standard *BritRail Pass,* available from British Rail agents outside Britain (see below) which allows unlimited travel in England, Scotland and Wales for 8

---

**TRAIN OFFICES AND AGENCIES IN NORTH AMERICA**

**British Rail International**, 1500 Broadway, New York, NY 10036 (☎1-800/677-8585 or 212/575-2667); 94 Cumberland St, Toronto, ON M5R 1A3 (☎416/929-3333).

**CIE Tours International**, 108 Ridgedale Ave, Morristown, NJ 07690 (☎1-800/522-5258 or 201/292-3438).

**Rail Europe**, 226–230 Westchester Ave, White Plains, NY 10604 (☎1-800/848-7245 or 914/682-2999); and branches in Santa Monica, San Francisco, Fort Lauderdale, Chicago, Dallas, Vancouver and Montréal.

days ($219), 15 days ($339), or a month
($495).The *BritRail Flexipass* gives free travel in
the same areas on 4 days out of 8 ($189), 8 days
out of 15 ($269) or 15 days out of a month ($395).
The *Freedom of Scotland Travelpass* costs $145
for 8 days, $205 for 15 days and $259 for 22 days.

Two passes are available only in Britain itself,
both valid for one year. The **Young Person's
Railcard** costs £16 and gives 33 percent reductions on all standard, *Saver* and *SuperSaver* fares
to full-time students and those between 16–24
years of age. A **Senior Citizens' Rail Card**, also
£16 and offering thirty percent reductions is available to those who have reached retirement age.
For both passes you'll need to show proof of age
and have two passport-size photographs.

## BUSES

Travelling around Scotland by bus may take a
little longer than using the train, but works out
considerably cheaper. There's a plethora of
regional companies, but by far the biggest
national operators are *Scottish Citylink* coaches
and *Caledonian Express*. With the price of train
travel becoming exorbitant, their services are so
popular that for busy routes and on any route at
weekends and during holidays it's a very good
idea to buy a "reserved-journey ticket", which
guarantees you a seat.

UK residents under 25, in full-time education
or of retirement age, can buy a *Caledonian
Express* **Discount Coach Card**, which costs £7,
is valid for one year and entitles the holder to a
30 percent discount on fares. Two special deals
are available to foreign travellers: the
**Britexpress** card, which costs £12 and provides
thirty percent reductions on fares over a 30-day
period, and a **Tourist Trail Pass**, which offers

unlimited travel on the *Caledonian Express*
network; an 8-day pass costs £65 for students
and under-23s, £90 for others; a 15-day pass £95
and £135 respectively; a 30-day pass £133 and
£190. In England you can obtain both from major
travel agents, at Gatwick and Heathrow airports
and at the British Travel centre in London. In
Scotland outlets include St Andrew Square Bus
Station, Edinburgh, and Buchanan Bus Station,
Glasgow, as well as other local bus stations. In
**North America** these passes are available at
travel agents or direct from *British Travel
International*, PO Box 299, Elkton, VA 22827 (☎1-
800/327-6097).

**Local bus services** are run by a bewildering
array of companies, and it's increasingly the case
that private companies duplicate the busiest
routes in an attempt to undercut the commercial
opposition, leaving the remoter spots neglected.
As a general rule, the further away from urban
areas you get, the less frequent and more expensive bus services become.

Those rural areas not covered by other forms
of public transport are served by the **postbus**
network, which operates 140 mini-buses carrying
mail and about eight fare-paying passengers.
They set off in the morning – in remote northern
areas this may be as late as 11am, when the mail
arrives at the post office – and deliver mail to
every cottage, farm and shop in the area. It's an
extremely cheap way to travel, costing about £2
or so for every twenty miles, and can be a
convenient way of getting to hidden-away B&Bs.
You can get a booklet of routes and timetables
from the *Royal Mail Public Relations Unit*, West
Port House, 102 West Port, Edinburgh EH3 9HS
(☎031/228 7407).

If you're **backpacking**, it's worth investigat-
ing a small outfit called *Go Blue Banana*, whose
minibus calls at Edinburgh, Perth, Aviemore,
Inverness, Skye, Fort William, Glencoe, Oban and
Loch Lomond every two days except Monday,
stopping at independent hostels en route. You can
hop on and off wherever you like, and a ticket, for
one circuit but with no time limit, costs £45.
Further details are available from their office at 12
Rutland Square, Edinburgh (☎031/228 2281).

## DRIVING AND HITCHING

If you want to cover a lot of the country in a short
time, or just want more flexibility, you'll need
your own transport. In order to **drive** in Scotland

you must have a current driving licence; foreign nationals will need to supplement this with an international driving permit available from national motoring organizations for a small fee. If you're bringing your own car into the country you should also carry your vehicle registration or ownership document at all times. Furthermore, you must be adequately insured, so be sure to check your existing policy.

Scotland remains one of the few countries in the world where you drive on the left, a situation that can lead to a few tense days of acclimatization for overseas drivers. **Speed limits** are 30–40mph (50–65kmph) in built-up areas, 70mph (110kmph) on motorways and dual carriageways and 50mph (80kmph) on most other roads. As a rule, assume that in any area with street lighting the speed limit is 30mph (50kmph) unless stated otherwise.

The three major motoring organizations, the *Automobile Association (AA)*, the *Royal Automobile Club (RAC)* and *National Breakdown*, all operate 24-hour emergency **breakdown**

services. The *AA* and *RAC* also provide many other motoring services, including a reciprocal arrangement for free assistance through many overseas motoring organizations – check the situation with yours before setting out. On motorways the *AA* and *RAC* can be called from roadside booths; elsewhere ring ☎0800/887 766 for the *AA*, ☎0800/828 282 for the *RAC* and ☎0800/400 600 for *National Breakdown* – though in remote areas, particularly in the Highlands, you may have a long wait for assistance. You can ring these emergency numbers even if you are not a member of the respective organization, although a substantial fee will be charged.

Like the rest of Britain, it's inadvisable for anyone travelling alone to **hitch** in Scotland, even in the central region where there's a good motorway network and a lot of traffic. Things are less problematic in remote areas, especially in the Highlands, where there's a long tradition of giving lifts, but locals clearly have priority, and you may have to wait a long time before you're picked up.

## MOTORING ORGANIZATIONS

**American Automobile Association**, 1000 AAA Drive, Heathrow, FL 32746 (☎1-800/566-1166 or 407/444-7000).

**Australian Automobile Association**, 212 Northbourne Ave, Canberra ACT 2601 (☎61/6247-7311).

**Automobile Association**, Fanum House, Basingstoke, Hants RG21 2EA (☎0256/20123).

**Canadian Automobile Association**, 2 Carlton St, Toronto, ON M4B 1K4 (☎416/964-3002).

**New Zealand Automobile Association**, PO Box 1794, Wellington (☎64/473-8738).

**Royal Automobile Club**, PO Box 100, RAC House, 7 Brighton Rd, S Croydon CR2 6XW (☎081/686 0088).

## CAR RENTAL FIRMS IN BRITAIN

**Avis**, 100 Dalry Rd, Edinburgh EH11 2DW (☎031/337 6363).

**Budget**, Royal Scot Hotel, Edinburgh Airport, 111 Glasgow Rd, Edinburgh EH12 (☎031/334 7740).

**Eurodollar**, Shrubhill Service Station, Leith Walk, Edinburgh EH7 (☎031/556 5515).

**Europcar**, 24 E London St, Edinburgh EH7 (☎031/661 252).

**Hertz**, 10 Picardy Place, Edinburgh EH1 3JT (☎031/556 8311).

**Holiday Autos**, 25 Savile Row, Mayfair, London W1X 1AA (☎071/491 1111).

**Mitchell Self Drive**, 32 Torphichen St, Edinburgh EH3 (☎031/229 5384).

## CAR RENTAL FIRMS IN THE US

**Alamo** ☎1-800/327-9633.

**Avis** ☎1-800/722-1333.

**Budget** ☎1-800/527-0700.

**Europe By Car** ☎1-800/223-1516.

**Hertz** ☎1-800/654-3131.

**Holiday Autos** ☎1-800/422-7737.

**National Car Rental** ☎1-800/CAR-RENT.

## CAR AND MOTORBIKE RENTAL

**Car rental** in Scotland is expensive, and, especially if you're travelling from North America, you'll probably find it cheaper to arrange things in advance through one of the multinational chains. If you do rent a car, the least you can expect to pay is around £140 a week – the rate for a small hatchback from *Holiday Autos*, the most competitive rental agency; reckon on paying £40 per day direct from one of the multinationals, £5 or so less at a local firm. Most companies prefer you to pay with a credit card, otherwise you may have to leave a deposit of at least £100. There are very few automatics at the lower end of the price scale – if you want one, you should book well ahead. To rent a car you need to show your driving licence; few companies will rent to drivers with less than one year's experience and most will only rent to people between 21 and 70 years of age.

**Motorbike rental** is ludicrously expensive, at around £45 a day/£200 a week for a 500cc machine, and around £80/£300 for a one-litre tourer, including everything from insurance, helmets and luggage.

## FERRIES

Scotland has 130 inhabited islands, and ferries play an important part in travelling around the country. Most ferries carry cars and vans, for which advance reservations can be made – highly advisable, particularly during the busy summer season from April to October. Of the major operators, *Caledonian MacBrayne* (abbreviated by most people and throughout this book to *CalMac*) covers the majority of routes.

*CalMac* have a virtual monopoly on services on the River Clyde and those to the Inner and Outer Hebrides, sailing to 23 islands altogether. They aren't cheap, but they do have two types of **reduced fare pass**, the *Island Hopscotch* and the *Island Rover*. The *Hopscotch* covers a range of economy fares for cars and passengers on 23 preplanned routes which are valid for three months from the date of the first journey. There are two types of *Island Rover*, for 8 and 15 consecutive days, which offer unlimited travel on *CalMac* ferries, though you must inform them of your exact itinerary in advance and fares will vary accordingly. Schedules vary and are highly complicated, but you can get details from the address below.

*P&O Scottish Ferries* sail to Orkney and Shetland from Aberdeen and Scrabster (Thurso). To Shetland from Aberdeen takes 14hr and costs

---

### FERRY OFFICES AND INFORMATION IN SCOTLAND

**Caledonian MacBrayne Ltd**, The Ferry Terminal, Gourock, Renfrewshire PA19 1QP (☎0475/650100).

**Orkney Islands Shipping Co Ltd**, Head Office, 4 Ayre Rd, Kirkwall KW15 1QX (☎0856/872044).

**P&O Scottish Ferries**, PO Box 5, Jamieson's Quay, Aberdeen AB9 8DL (☎0224/572615).

**Western Ferries (Clyde) Ltd**, 16 Woodside Crescent, Glasgow G3 7UT (☎041/332 9766).

---

about £50 for a foot passenger, plus £120 or so for a car. Aberdeen to Orkney takes 8hr, Scrabster to Orkney 1hr 50min, which costs £15 or so, plus a further £40 for a car. For both routes you should book if you are taking a vehicle. *P&O* offer no passes.

In addition, *Western Ferries* operate between Gourock and Dunoon on the mainland to the islands of Islay and Jura; fares start at about £1 for foot passengers to about £5 for a car. The various Orkney islands are linked by the services run by the *Orkney Islands Shipping Co Ltd.* – fares hover around £6 return for foot passengers plus £15 for a car. Numerous small operators round the Scottish coast run day-excursion trips; their phone numbers are listed in the relevant guide chapters.

It is possible to book ferry tickets in advance from **North America**, if you know exactly when you'll be making the crossing. For ferries around the Scottish islands, contact *Scots American* (☎201/768-1187). For sailings to/from Northern Ireland, try *Scots American* or *British Rail International* (☎1-800/677-8585). These companies can also take reservations for travel on ferries between England and France, Belgium or the Netherlands. *Bergen Line* (☎1-800/323-7436) and *Scandinavian Seaways* (☎1-800/533-3755) operate ferries between England and Scandinavia.

## INTERNAL FLIGHTS

Scotland has seventeen internal airports, many of them on the islands and useful if you are short on time. Flights between the islands are mainly operated by *Loganair* (☎041/889 3181), with *British Airways* (☎0345/222111) flying between Edinburgh, Glasgow, Aberdeen and Inverness and to some of the main islands. Airports are listed over the page; call them direct for further details.

## AIRPORTS IN SCOTLAND

**Aberdeen Airport** ☎0224/722331.

**Barra Northbay Airport** ☎08715/283.

**Benbecula Airport** ☎0870/2051.

**Campbeltown Airport** ☎0586/552571.

**Dundee Airport** ☎0382/643242.

**Edinburgh Airport** ☎031/333 1000.

**Fair Isle Airstrip** ☎03512/224.

**Glasgow Airport** ☎041/887 1111.

**Inverness Airport** ☎0463/232471.

**Islay Airport** ☎0496/2361.

**Kirkwall Airport** ☎0856/872421.

**Stornaway Airport** ☎0851/702256.

**Sumburgh Airport** ☎0950/60654.

**Tingwall Airstrip** ☎0595/843306.

**Tiree Airport** ☎08792/456.

**Unst Airport** ☎095781/404.

**Wick Airport** ☎0955/2215.

# ACCOMMODATION

The prevalence of bed and breakfast (B&B) and youth hostels in Scotland ensures that budget accommodation is easy to come by. There are also scores of upmarket hotels, ranging from bland business-oriented places in the centres of the big towns and plush converted country mansions and ancient castles. Most tourist offices will book all kinds of accommodation for you when you arrive, though the fee for this service varies considerably. In some areas you will pay a deposit that's deducted from your first night's bill (usually ten percent), in others the office will take a percentage or flat-rate commission – on average around £2 – and occasionally it's free. Another useful service operated by the majority of tourist offices is the *Book-a-bed-ahead* service, which locates accommodation in your next port of call. This will cost at least £2.20.

## HOTELS AND B&Bs

The STB operates a nationwide system for grading **hotels, guest houses and B&Bs**, which is updated annually – although by no means everyone participates, and you shouldn't assume that a B&B, in particular, is no good if it's ungraded. There are so many of these establishments in Scotland that the grading inspectors can't possibly keep track of them all, and in the rural backwaters some of the most enjoyable

## ACCOMMODATION PRICE CODES

Throughout this book, accommodation **prices** have been graded with the numbers below, according to the cost of the least expensive double room in high season. The bulk of the recommendations will fall in categories ② to ⑤; recommendations in the highest categories are limited to places that are especially attractive. Bear in mind that many of the swanky hotels often slash their tariffs at the weekend when the business types have gone home, and that many of the cheaper places will also have more expensive rooms. Note that in our accommodation listings price codes are not given for youth hostels – they all come into the lower end of the ① category.

| | | |
|---|---|---|
| ① under £20 | ④ £40–50 | ⑦ £70–80 |
| ② £20–30 | ⑤ £50–60 | ⑧ £80–100 |
| ③ £30–40 | ⑥ £60–70 | ⑨ over £100 |

accommodation is to be found in welcoming and beautifully set houses whose facilities may technically fall short of official standards. Everything in this scheme is graded into four categories: Approved, Commended, Highly Commended and Deluxe. Within these, one to five Crowns are awarded for "facilities" which theoretically cover the condition of buildings and grounds, the quality of the food and general comfort as well as the warmth of welcome and the efficiency and friendliness shown by the staff. It's probably also worth using the the grades supplied by the *AA* and the *RAC* as they independently combine evaluation of facilites with a degree of subjective judgement. Though there's not a hard and fast correlation between standards and price, you'll probably be paying in the region of £30–35 per night for a double room at a one-star hotel (breakfast included), rising to around £70 in a three-star, and from around £120 for a five-star. In some larger towns and cities you'll find that the big hotels often offer cut-price deals at the weekend to fill the rooms vacated by the week's business trade, but these places tend to be soulless multinational chain operations. If you can afford it, stay in a refurbished old building – many towns have atmospheric coaching inns and such like, while out in the countryside you'll find converted mansions and castles, often with brilliant restaurants attached.

At the lower end of the scale, hotels merge almost imperceptibly into B&Bs – often known as **guest houses** in resorts and other tourist towns. These range from ordinary private houses with a couple of bedrooms set aside for paying guests and a dining room for the consumption of a rudimentary breakfast, to rooms as well furnished as those in hotels costing twice as much, with delicious home-prepared breakfasts, and an informal hospitality that a larger place couldn't match. B&Bs are also graded by the STB, the *AA* and the *RAC*. As a guideline to costs, it's easy to find a grade one STB place for under £25 per night a double; grade four places go for around £70. As many B&Bs, even the pricier ones, have a very small number of rooms, you should certainly book a place as far in advance as possible.

Another important point to remember in rural Scotland is that many B&Bs, as well as hotels, are only open for the summer season, roughly from Easter to October. You'll always find somewhere to stay outside this period, but the choice may be pretty limited.

## YOUTH HOSTELS

The network of the **Scottish Youth Hostels Association** (**SYHA**) consists of some eighty properties, usually offering bunk-bed accommodation in single-sex dormitories or smaller rooms. A few of these places are spartan establishments of the sort traditionally associated with the wholesome, fresh-air ethic of the early hostels, but most have moved well away from this and are beginning to offer private facilities with no curfew.

All the youth hostels referred to in the *Guide* are official SYHA properties unless stated otherwise. For Scottish residents, membership – which includes membership of the hostelling associations in the sixty countries affiliated to the **International Youth Hostels Association** (**IYHF**) – costs £2.50 per year for under-18s, £6 for others, and can be obtained either by writing to or visiting the SYHA offices listed overleaf, or in person at most SYHA hostels. Visitors from elsewhere in Britain and foreign nationals who wish to join the IYHF can do so at the SYHA offices or most Scottish youth hostels for a £9 fee. Youth hostel members are allowed half-price entry to National Trust for Scotland properties (see p.30).

At any time of the year, particularly in the Grade 1 youth hostels, it's best to **book your place** well in advance, and it's essential at Easter, Christmas and between May and August. You can book by post or telephone; in both cases your bed will be held until 6pm on the day of arrival. Some hostels, particularly in the Highlands, are closed for the whole of the winter except for the Christmas and New Year period. Even if you

---

**SYHA GRADES AND COSTS**

All SYHA hostels are **graded** to indicate their level of facilities. **Grade 1** hostels, which cost £6.15, are the top of the range, including free hot showers, and, occasionally, extended opening hours. At **Grade 2** hostels – the most common – the rate is £4.80 per night, and hot showers are usually available for a small fee; **Grade 3** (£3.65) places are the simplest, with limited facilities. We've given the grades for each hostel in the guide.

Over most of Scotland students aged 18–25 can get a £1 reduction on admission prices on production of a valid student card. The cost of hostel **meals**, where available, is low: breakfast is around £2.50, and evening meals start at just £3.70. Nearly all hostels have kitchen facilities, for those who prefer self-catering.

## SYHA OFFICES

**Aberdeen**: 11 Ashvale Place, AB1 6QD (☎0224/588156).

**Ayr**: Craigweil House, Craigweil Rd, KA7 2XJ (no phone).

**Dundee**: 86 Bell St, DD1 1JG (☎0382/22150).

**Edinburgh**: 161 Warrender Park Rd, EH9 1EQ (☎031/229 8660).

**Glasgow**: 12 Renfield St, G2 5AL (☎041/226 3976).

**Stirling**: 7 Glebe Crescent, FK8 2JA (☎0786/451181).

haven't booked, always phone ahead – we've given phone numbers in the *Guide*. Most hostels are closed from 10am to 5pm with an 11pm curfew, but some are open all day. Length of stay is normally unlimited. It's worth getting a copy of the *SYHA Handbook*, which clarifies the intricacies of the system, and lists every hostel in the association; it's available from the address below.

Allied to the SYHA, the **Gatliff Hebridean Hostels Trust** is a charitable organization that rents out very simple croft accommodation in the Hebridean Islands. Accommodation is very basic, almost primitive, but the settings are spectacular. These places are ungraded, and many have no phones. There's also the **Independent Backpackers Hostels Association**, an association of 37 independent hostels, mainly situated in the Highlands and islands, though including three in Edinburgh. These are mostly family-run places with no membership and no curfew, and most are open all year. Housed in buildings ranging from crofthouses to converted churches, they all have dormitories, hot showers, common rooms and self-catering kitchens, while many organize a

range of outdoor activities. Prices range from £2–8 per person per night. A brochure listing all the properties is available from *The Independent Backpackers Hostels Scotland*, c/o The Loch Ness Backpackers Lodge, Leiston, Drumnadrochit, Invernessshire IV3 6UT (☎04562/807).

## CAMPING, CARAVANNING AND SELF-CATERING

There are hundreds of **campsites** in Scotland, most of which are open from April to October. The most expensive sites, which charge about £8 to pitch a tent, are usually well equipped with shops, a restaurant, a bar and occasionally sports facilities. At the other end of the scale, farmers sometimes offer pitches on their land for as little as £2 per night. The *AA* list and grade campsites in their publication *Camping and Caravanning in Britain and Ireland*, and the area tourist boards can all supply lists of their recommended sites.

In the most popular parts of rural Scotland – especially in the Highlands and the islands – tents have to share space with **caravans**. The great majority are permanently moored at their sites, where they are rented out for **self-catering** holidays, and the ranks of nose-to-tail trailers in the vicinity of some of Scotland's finest scenery might make you think that half the population of Britain shacks up in a caravan for the midsummer break. You may prefer more robust self-catering accommodation, and there are thousands of STB-approved properties for rent by the week, ranging from city penthouses to secluded cottages. The least you can expect to pay for four-berth self-catering accommodation in summer would be around £150 per week, but for something special – such as a well-sited coastal

## YOUTH HOSTEL ASSOCIATIONS

**Australia**: *Australian Youth Hostels Association*, PO Box 61, Strawberry Hills, Sydney, 2012, New South Wales (☎02/212-1266).

**Canada**: *Canadian Hostelling Association*, 1600 James Naismith Drive, Suite 608, Gloucester, ON K1B 5N4 (☎613/748-5638).

**England**: *Youth Hostel Association* (*YHA*), Trevelyan House, 8 St Stephen's Hill, St Albans, Herts AL1 2DY (☎0727/855 215). London shop and information office: 14 Southampton St, London WC2E 7HY (☎071/836 8541). There are fifteen other YHA city locations throughout England.

**Ireland**: *An Óige*, 39 Mountjoy Square, Dublin 1 (☎01/363111).

**New Zealand**: *Youth Hostels Association of New Zealand*, PO Box 436, Christchurch 1 (☎03/799-970).

**Northern Ireland**: *Youth Hostel Association of Northern Ireland*, 56 Bradbury Place, Belfast, BT7 1RU (☎0232/324733).

**USA**: *American Youth Hostels*, PO Box 37613, Washington, DC 200013 (☎202/783-6161).

cottage – you should budget for twice that amount. Several agencies let self-catering accommodation, including *Dundas Property Agency*, 61–63 Broughton St, Edinburgh EH1 3RJ and *Finlayson Hughes*, 45 Church St, Inverness IV1 1DR and the *NTS*, 5 Charlotte St, Edinburgh. If money is no object try *Blandings*, 225 Ebury St, London SW1W 8UT, who rent upmarket properties all over Britain. Failing that, scan the pages of the *Sunday Times* or *Observer*, both of which carry numerous adverts for holiday cottages.

Another cheap self-catering option, especially if you're staying a week or more, is **campus accommodation.** Many Scottish universities open their halls of residence to overseas visitors during the summer break, and rooms vary from tiny single rooms in long, lonely corridors, to relatively comfortable places in small shared apartments. The *British Universities Accommodation Consortium* (*BUAC*) have full details: contact them at PO Box 581, University Park, Nottingham NG7 2RG (☎0602/504 571).

# FOOD AND DRINK

**Though the Scots still tend to regard eating as a necessity rather than the focal point of the day, the quality of Scottish food has improved by leaps and bounds in recent years. Scots produce – superb meat, fish and game, a wide range of dairy products, the best soft fruit in Europe and a bewildering variety of traditional baked goodies – is of outstanding quality and has to some extent been rediscovered of late; bear in mind, too, that in the larger cities, the presence of various immigrant communities has led to a fine array of ethnic restaurants.**

### FOOD AND DRINK

In many hotels and B&Bs you'll be offered a **Scottish breakfast;** similar to its English counterpart of sausage, bacon and egg but with the addition of porridge – properly made with genuine oatmeal and traditionally eaten with salt rather than sugar, though the latter is always on offer. You may also be served kippers or Arbroath smokies (delicately smoked haddock with butter), or a large piece of haddock eaten with a poached egg on top. Oatcakes (plain, slightly salty biscuits) and a "buttery" – a butter-enriched bread related to the French croissant – will often feature. Scotland's staple drink, like England's, is **tea**, drunk strong and with milk, though **coffee** is just as readily served everywhere.

The quintessential Scots dish is **haggis**, a sheep's stomach bag stuffed with spiced liver, offal, oatmeal and onion and traditionally eaten with bashed neeps (mashed turnips) and chappit tatties (mashed potatoes). The humble haggis has become rather trendy in recent years, and you can even, in the big cities, get an occasional vegetarian version. Other staples include steak and kidney pie and shepherd's pie (minced beef covered with mashed potato and baked), as well as **stovies**, a tasty mash of onion and fried potato heated up with minced beef. In this cold climate home-made soup is generally welcome; try **Scots broth**, made with combinations of lentil, split pea, mutton stock or vegetables and barley.

Scots **beef** is delicious, especially the Aberdeen Angus breed; menus will specify if your steak falls into that fine category. **Venison**, the meat of the red deer, also features large – low in cholesterol and very tasty, it's served roasted or in casseroles, often flavoured with juniper or with a whisky sauce. If you like **game** and can afford it, splash out on grouse, the most highly prized of all game birds, strong, dark and succulent, best eaten with bread sauce. Pheasant is also worth a try; less rich than other game, more like a particularly tasty chicken – you can eat it stuffed with oatmeal or with a mealie pudding, a kind of vegetarian black pudding made from onion, oatmeal and spices.

Scotland has a huge variety of fresh **fish** to choose from. In the coastal towns, prawns, oysters, crab and scallops are always available, while inland salmon is a must, especially the more delicately flavoured wild salmon – though this will always cost more than the farmed variety. Both are served either hot with melted butter, small new potatoes and a creamy Hollandaise sauce, or cold in a salad. Trout is also farmed in Scotland, often fried in oatmeal and eaten with bacon. Look out especially for the wild brown trout, whose firm pink flesh is nearly as good as salmon.

**Puddings**, often smothered in butterscotch sauce or syrup, are taken very seriously in Scotland. One traditional favourite is Cranachan, made with toasted oatmeal steeped in whisky and folded into whipped cream flavoured with fresh raspberries; on the same lines, Atholl Brose, related to the English syllabub, is made with oatmeal, whisky and cream. For the ultimate dessert decadence try the clootie dumpling, a sweet, stodgy fruit pudding soaked in a cloth for hours. If it all sounds a bit rich you might prefer the black bun, a peppery fruit cake encased in a thin pastry and traditionally eaten at New Year, or the many homemade shortbreads – far superior to the commercial varieties. One Scottish institution that satisfies the Scots sweet tooth is the **high tea**, consisting of a cooked main course and a plethora of cakes, washed down with tea or coffee and eaten between about 5 and 6.30pm.

As for **fast food**, fish and chips is as popular in Scotland as in England and "**chippies**" abound, serving battered fish – invariably known as a "fish supper" even if eaten at lunchtime – haggis, and oatmeal-based numbers such as black and mealie puddings. For alternative fast food in the major towns there are all the usual **pizza** and **burger** outlets, and the more recent **baked potato** shops.

## WHERE TO EAT

For **budget food** in Scotland you'll find hordes of **cafés** – which range from the most basic "greasy spoons" to vaguely French-style **brasseries**, where you can have anything from a glass of wine to a cup of coffee, as well as a simple meal. Many provincial towns have **tearooms** of sorts,

where you can sample Scottish baking. Some of the cheapest places to eat in Scotland are the **pubs,** many of which serve food all day – indeed, in the smallest villages these might be your only options.

The ranks of Scottish **gastronomic restaurants** grow with each passing year, with cordon bleu chefs producing high-class dishes with a Scottish slant that certainly rival their English and European counterparts. Outside Edinburgh and Glasgow many of these are found in hotels but are happy to serve non-residents, though you could easily land up paying from £25–50 a head. Travelling around Scotland, you can track down the best food by looking for pubs, restaurants and cafés belonging to the **Taste of Scotland** scheme. This is sponsored by the STB and aims to promote good regional cooking using fresh local ingredients. The scheme has around four hundred members, who are regularly inspected, and publishes an annual guide to its restaurants, which is available from the STB and leading bookshops, or direct from *Taste of Scotland*, 33 Melville St, Edinburgh EH3 7JF.

In central Scotland, particularly in Edinburgh and Glasgow, the **Indian** and **Chinese** communities ensure there is a good choice of restaurants, offering quality meals at fair prices. Some of the **French** restaurants in Edinburgh are excellent, and Scotland's large **Italian** community means there are numerous good trattorias. On the whole, though, you won't find the range of choice that exists south of the border, and outside the big cities **vegetarians** are still looked on somewhat askance, though the *Taste of Scotland* members do their best to remedy this.

The restaurant listings in the *Guide* include a mix of high-quality and budget establishments. As a general rule on **costs**, if we call a place inexpensive, you can expect to pay under £10 a head, without drinks; moderate means it will cost between £10 and £20; expensive from £20 to £30; and very expensive over £30.

## DRINK

Like the rest of Britain, Scottish **pubs**, which originated as travellers' hostelries and coaching inns, are *the* great social institution, and the pub crawl, a drunken trawl through as many pubs as possible in one night, is a national pastime. The focal points of any community, the local British pub can vary from oak-beamed and ingle-nooked inns with heaps of atmosphere, open fires and polished brass fittings, to blaring, noisy theme pubs, lined wall-to-wall with juke boxes and pinball machines. Most pubs are owned by large breweries who favour their own cask-conditioned real ales served from the distinctive Scottish tall font (for more on types of beer, see below). Many of them, especially outside the big cities, are no-nonsense spit and sawdust public bars with an almost exclusively male clientele, making some visitors, especially women, feel highly uncomfortable. However, there are plenty of places that can be as welcoming as the full name, "public house", suggests, along with – in Edinburgh and Glasgow at least – a rash of upbeat, trendy café-bars favoured by a young, pre-clubbing set.

Scotland was ahead of England in changing to all-day **opening hours** and pubs are generally open from Monday to Saturday 11am–11pm, with "last orders" called by the barstaff about fifteen minutes before closing time. On Sunday the hours are reduced; many pubs are closed in the afternoon and last orders are called at 10.30pm. In general, you have to be 16 to enter a pub unaccompanied, though some places have special family rooms for people with children, and beer gardens where younger kids can run free. The legal drinking age is 18.

## BEER

**Beer** is the staple drink in Scotland's pubs, the indigenous variety a thick, dark **ale** with a full head served in pints or half-pints at room temperature, much like the English bitter (in Scotland known as **heavy**). Scottish beers are graded by the shilling: a system used since the 1870s and indicating the level of potency – the higher the shilling mark, the stronger, or "heavier" the beer. A pint costs anything from £1.20 to £2, depending on the brew and the locale of the pub.

Scotland's biggest name breweries are *McEwan's* and *Younger's*, part of the mighty *Scottish and Newcastle* group, and *Tennents*, owned by the English firm *Bass*. The beers produced by these companies tend to be heavier, smoother and stronger than their English equivalents, especially *McEwan's Export*, a mass-produced, highly potent brew, and *Tennents' Fowler's Wee Heavy*, a famously tasty smooth ale. *Younger's Tartan*, though less flavoursome, is Scotland's biggest seller.

However, if you really want to discover how good Scottish beer, once renowned throughout

the world for its strength, can be, look out for the products of the small **local breweries** scattered throughout Scotland. Edinburgh's *Caledonian Brewery* makes nine good cask beers, operating from Victorian premises that preserve much of their original equipment, including the only direct-fired coppers left in Britain. Others to look out for are *Bellhaven*, a brewery near Edinburgh whose 80 shilling *Export* is a typical Scottish ale; *Maclays*, a hoppy, lightish ale brewed in Alloa; and *Traquair*, in the Borders, who do a wonderfully smooth *House Ale*. The dry, fruity *Alice Ale*, brewed in Inverness, and the *Orkney Brewery's Raven Ale* could be life-savers in the north, where good beer is hard to come by.

Blond pilsner beers, or **lagers**, are served all over Scotland, along with European and American bottled varieties, but the major Scottish brews have little to fear from these pale and often tasteless competitors. **Wines** sold in pubs are generally appalling – strange in view of the excellent selection sold in off-licences and supermarkets.

## WHISKY

Scotland's national drink is **whisky** – *uisge beatha*, the "water of life" in Gaelic – traditionally drunk in pubs with a half-pint of beer on the side, a combination known as a "nip and a hauf".]

Whisky has been produced in Scotland since the fifteenth century, and really took off in popularity after the 1780 tax on claret made wine too expensive for most people. The taxman soon caught up with illicit whisky distilling and drove the stills underground, and today many malt distilleries operate on the site of simple cottages that once distilled the stuff illegally. In 1823 Parliament revised its Excise Laws, in the process legalizing whisky production, and today the drink is Scotland's chief export. There are two types of whisky: **single malt**, made from malted barley, and **grain whisky**, which, relatively cheap to produce, is made from maize and a small amount of malted barley in a continuous still. **Blended**, which accounts for more than ninety percent of all sales, is as the name suggests, a blend of the two types.

Grain whisky forms about seventy percent of the average bottle of blended whisky, but the distinctive flavour of the different blends comes from the malt whisky which is added to the grain in different quantities. The more expensive the blend, the higher proportion of skilfully chosen and aged malts that have gone into it. Among many brand names, *Johnnie Walker, Bells, Teachers* and *The Famous Grouse* are some of the most widely available. All have a similar flavour, and are often drunk with mixers such as lemonade or mineral water.

Despite the dominance of the blended whiskies, **single malt whiskies** are infinitely superior, and best drunk neat to appreciate their distinctive flavours. Malt whisky is made by soaking barley in water for two or three days until it swells, after which it is left to germinate for up to twelve days, allowing the starch in the barley seed to become soluble. The malted barley is dried and peated, mashed with hot water and fermented with yeast to convert the sugar into crude alcohol, which is then twice distilled and the vapours condensed as a spirit, aged for a minimum of three years in oak casks. Single

malts vary enormously depending on the peat used for drying, the water used for mashing, and the type of oak cask used in the maturing process, but they fall into four distinct groups – Highland, Lowland, Campbeltown and Islay, with the majority falling into the Highland category and being produced largely on Speyside. You can get the best-known blends – among them *Glenlivet, Glenmorangie, MacAllan, Talisker, Laphroaig, Highland Park* and *Glenfiddich*, the top seller – in most of the pubs.

Most distilleries have a highly developed nose for PR and offer free tours that range from slick and streamlined to small and friendly. All of them offer visitors a "wee dram" as a finale, and you can buy bottles of the stuff – though prices are no lower at source than in the shops. See *Argyll* and *Northeast Scotland* for more on whisky.

## POST AND PHONES

Virtually all post offices are open Mon–Fri 9am–5.30pm, Sat 9am–12.30 or 1pm; in small communities you'll find sub-post offices operating out of a shop, open the same hours, even if the shop itself is open for longer. Stamps can be bought at post office counters, from vending machines outside, or from an increasing number of newsagents, usually in books of four or ten. A first-class letter to anywhere in the British Isles currently costs 25p and should – in theory – arrive the next day; second-class letters

cost 19p, and take from two to four days. Airmail letters of less than 20g (0.7oz) to EC countries also cost 25p, to non-EC European countries 28p and elsewhere overseas from 41p. Pre-stamped aerogrammes conforming to overseas airmail weight limits of under 10g can be bought for 39p from post offices only.

Public **payphones** are operated by *British Telecom* (*BT*) and, less commonly, by its rival *Mercury*, and in towns, at least, are widespread. Many *BT* payphones take all coins from 10p upwards, although an increasing proportion of *BT* and all of *Mercury's* payphones only accept **phonecards**, available from post offices and newsagents which display *BT's* green or *Mercury's* blue logo. These cards come in denominations of £1, £2, £4, £5 and £10; remember, though, that *Telecom* and *Mercury* cards are not interchangeable. All *Mercury* phones and some *BT* phones accept credit cards too.

### OPERATOR SERVICES AND PHONE CODES
Operator ☎100
Directory assistance ☎192
Overseas directory assistance ☎153
International operator ☎155

## INTERNATIONAL CALLS

To call **overseas from Scotland** dial ☎010, then the appropriate country code and finally the number, including the local code minus any initial zero. Country codes include:

USA and Canada ☎ 1

Ireland ☎353

Australia ☎61

New Zealand ☎64

To **telephone Scotland** from overseas it's ☎011 from the US and Canada, ☎0011 from Australia and ☎00 from New Zealand, followed in all cases by 44, then the area code minus its initial zero, and finally the number.

Inland calls are cheapest between 6pm and 8am, and the *Mercury* rate is cheaper than *BT's* over long distances. **Reduced rate periods** for most **international calls** are 8pm–8am from Monday to Friday and all day on Saturday and Sunday, though for Australia and New Zealand it's midnight–7am and 2.30–7.30pm daily. Any number that begins ☎0800 is free.

Throughout the *Guide*, telephone numbers are prefixed by the area code, except in the case of the big cities, when the area code is indicated once only, in a shaded box. **From April 16, 1995 all telephone codes in Britain will be changed**. The digit 1 will be inserted after the initial 0 in all area codes, and the code for dialling abroad will become 00 instead of 010.

## OPENING HOURS AND HOLIDAYS

**General shop hours are Mon–Sat 9am–5.30 or 6pm, although shops are increasingly opening on Sunday and late-night in the larger towns, with Thursday or Friday the favoured evenings. No Scottish shops sell alcohol on Sundays, however. The big supermarkets also tend to stay open until 8pm or 9pm from Monday to Saturday, as do many of the stores in the shopping complexes that are springing up on the outskirts of many major towns. Many provincial towns still retain an "early closing day" when shops close at 1pm – Wednesday is the favourite.**

Unlike in England, Scotland's "**bank holidays**" mean just that: they are literally days when the banks are closed rather than general public holidays, and they vary from year to year. They include 2 January, the Friday before Easter, the first and last Monday in May, the first Monday in August, St Andrew's Day (30 November), Christmas Day (25 December) and Boxing Day (26 December).

New Year's Day, January 1, is the only fixed **public holiday**, but all Scottish towns and cities have a one-day holiday in both spring and autumn – dates vary from place to place but normally fall on a Monday. If you want to know the exact dates, you can get a booklet detailing them from *Glasgow Chamber of Commerce*, 30 George Square, Glasgow G2 1EQ.

## SIGHTS, MUSEUMS AND MONUMENTS

**Apart from the really big museums, and a number of attractions high on the tourist trail, Scotland's tourist season runs from Easter to October and outside this period many indoor attractions are shut – though ruins, parks and gardens are normally accessible year-round. We've given full details of opening hours and admission charges in the *Guide*.**

Many of Scotland's most treasured sights – from castles and country houses to islands, gardens and tracts of protected landscape – come under the control of the privately run **National Trust for Scotland**, 5 Charlotte Square, Edinburgh EH2 4DU (☎031/226 5922) or the state-run **Historic Scotland**, 20 Brandon St, Edinburgh EH3 5RA (☎031/244 3101), shown respectively as the "NTS" or "HS" in the *Guide*. Both organizations charge an entry fee for most places, and these can be quite high, especially for the more grandiose NTS estates. If you think you'll be visiting more than half a dozen owned by the NTS, or more than a dozen owned by Historic Scotland, it's worth taking **annual membership** (NTS £23, family £38; HS £14, family £28), which allows free entry to their properties.

In addition, both the NTS and HS offer short-term passes that give discounts on admission prices. The **National Trust Touring ticket**, which costs £9 for an adult and £15 for a family, is valid for seven days and gives free admission to all their properties. The HS **Scottish Explorer** seven-day ticket allows free entry to seventy monuments, castles and other properties and costs £8 or £17 for a family; a two-week equivalent is a little less than twice the price. **Members of the IYHF** (see p.23) are automatically eligible for half-price entry into all NTS properties.

A lot of Scottish **stately homes** remain in the hands of the landed gentry, who tend to charge in the region of £5 for admission to edited highlights of their domain. Many other old buildings, albeit rarely the most momentous structures, are owned by local authorities, and admission is often cheaper, sometimes free. Municipal art galleries and museums are usually free, as are most of the **state-owned museums**, although "voluntary" donations are normally solicited.

The majority of fee-charging attractions in Scotland have 25–50 percent **reductions** for senior citizens, the unemployed, full-time students and children under 16, with under-5s being admitted free almost everywhere. Proof of age will be required in most cases. The entry charges given in the *Guide* are the full adult charges.

**North Americans** can buy the Scottish Explorer and National Trust Touring passes at a travel agent or directly from *Especially Britain* (see under "Travelling from North America"). A further option, only open to overseas visitors, is the **Great British Heritage Pass**, which gives free admission to some six hundred sites throughout Britain, many of which are not run by the National Trust for Scotland or Historic Scotland. Costing $50 (Can$60) for 15 days, or $75 (Can$90) for a month, it can be purchased through most travel agents, *British Airways* offices or the British Travel Centre in London.

## THE MEDIA

### NEWSPAPERS AND MAGAZINES

The principal **British daily newspapers** are all available in Scotland, often in a specific Scottish edition. The tabloids are as popular as in England – among them Rupert Murdoch's sex-and-scandal *Sun*, the self-consciously ridiculous *Daily Sport*, and the vaguely left-wing *Mirror*, the only tabloid that manages anything approximating an antidote to the Sun's reactionary politics. The "quality" end of the market is cornered by the Murdoch-owned *Times*, the staunchly Conservative *Daily Telegraph*, the *Independent*, which strives worthily to live up to its name, and the *Guardian*, which inhabits a niche marginally left of centre.

The **Scottish press**, in the main rather staid and parochial, produces two major serious daily newspapers, the fiercely right-wing *Scotsman* and the slightly less-so *Herald*, published in Edinburgh and Glasgow respectively. Scotland's biggest selling daily paper, though, is the down-market *Daily Record*, from the same group as the *Daily Mirror*. The provincial daily press is probably more widely read than its English counterpart, with Aberdeen's *Press and Journal*, Dundee's fiercely parochial *Courier and Advertiser* and the *Inverness Courier* enjoying the largest regional circulations.

Many national **Sunday newspapers** have a Scottish section north of the border, but Scotland's own Sunday "heavy" is the wholly serious and somewhat dull *Scotland on Sunday*. Far more fun is the anachronistic *Sunday Post*, published by Dundee's mighty Thomson and Legg publishing group and read by over half of the population. It's a wholesome paper, uniquely Scottish, and has changed little since the 1950s, since when its two long-running cartoon strips,

*Oor Wullie* and *The Broons*, have acquired something of a cult status.

When it comes to **specialist periodicals**, the best-selling weekly news magazine is the dry, scholarly *Economist*. The earnest socialist alternative, the *New Statesman and New Society*, has so few readers that it's stuck with the nickname "The Staggers", while the satirical bi-weekly *Private Eye* is a much-loved institution that prides itself on printing the stories the rest of the press won't touch, and on surviving the consequent stream of libel suits. Scottish **monthlies** include the *Scottish Field*, a low-brow version of England's *Tatler*, covering the interests and pursuits of the landed gentry, and the widely read *Scots Magazine*, an old-fashioned middle-of-the-road publication which promotes family values, a stiff upper lip and lots of good fresh air. *USA Today* is the most widely available **North American paper**, though only the larger newsagents will stock it; you can also find *Time* and *Newsweek* in quality bookstores and newsagents. For visitors to Glasgow and Edinburgh, the fortnightly **listings magazine** *The List* is a must, covering all events in both cities.

## TELEVISION AND RADIO

In Scotland there are four main **television channels**, the state-owned BBC1 and 2, and the independent commercial channels, ITV and Channel Four. Though assailed by government critics of late, the **BBC** is just about maintaining its worldwide reputation for in-house quality productions, ranging from expensive costume dramas to intelligent documentaries – split between the avowedly mainstream BBC1 and the more rarefied fare of BBC2. The populist STV, Grampian and Border companies together form the **ITV** network in Scotland, complemented by the more eclectic and less mainstream broadcasting of the partly subsidized **Channel Four**. Rupert Murdoch's multi-channel BSkyB has a monopoly of the satellite business, presenting a blend of movies, news, sport, re-runs and overseas soaps, and **cable** TV companies are beginning to appear in Scotland. But for the time being the old terrestrial stations still attract the majority of viewers.

Market forces are eating away too at the BBC's **radio** network, which has five stations catering for a range of tastes: Radio One, almost exclusively mainstream pop music; Radio Two, MOR music; Radio Three, predominantly classical music; Radio Four, a blend of current affairs, arts and drama; and Radio Five, the newest station, a mix of sport and news. Radio One has rivals in the form of commercial radio all over Scotland – most stations are far less raucous and teen-targeted than their English equivalents – while Classic FM has lured people away from Radio Three, by offering a less earnest approach to its subject. The BBC also operates several regional Scottish stations, presenting a worthy mix of local news and Top Twenty hits.

## ANNUAL EVENTS

Scotland offers a huge range of annual events, reflecting contemporary culture and heritage as well as its world-renowned tartan image. Many tourists will want to home straight in on bagpipes, ceilidhs and Highland Games, but it's worth bearing in mind that there's more to Scotland than this: numerous regional celebrations perpetuate ancient customs and accentuate the differences between Scotland and England, while the Edinburgh Festival and Glasgow's Mayfest are arts festivals on an international scale. Scotland's sporting events range from Highland Games, International Rugby and golf championships to homegrown pastimes such as curling – an activity that can be

## EVENTS CALENDAR

**December 31 and January 1**: Hogmanay and Ne'er Day. More important to the Scots than Christmas. Festivities revolve around the "first-footing", when at midnight crowds of revellers troop into neighbours' houses bearing gifts. Traditionally the first foot should be a dark-haired stranger carrying coal and salt (so the house won't lack for warmth or food), and a bottle of whisky (for obvious reasons).

**December 31**: Flambeaux procession at Comrie. Locals parade through the streets carrying flaming torches to welcome New Year.

**January 1**: Stonehaven fireball ceremony. Locals swing fireballs on long sticks to welcome New Year and ward off evil spirits.

**January 1**: Kirkwall Boy's and Men's Ba' Games, Orkney. Mass, drunken football game through the streets of the town, with the castle and the harbour the respective goals – as a grand finale the players jump into the harbour.

**January 11**: Burning of the Clavie, Burghead, Moray. Burning tar barrel is carried through the town and then rolled down Doorie Hill. Charred fragments of the Clavie offer protection against the evil eye.

**Last Tuesday in January**: Up-Helly-Aa, Lerwick, Shetland. Norse fire festival culminating in the burning of a specially built Viking longship. Visitors will need an invite from one of the locals.

**End of January**: Burns Night. Burns suppers all over Scotland. Dinners held to commemorate Scotland's greatest poet; haggis, whisky and lots of poetry recital.

**February**: Scottish Curling Championship held in a different (indoor) venue each year.

**February**: Aberdeen Angus Bull Sales at Perth.

**February**: Scotland v. England Rugby Union

**March 1**: Whuppity Scourie at Lanark. Local children race round the church beating each other with home-made paper weapons as they go; a representation (it's thought) of the chasing away of winter or the warding off of evil spirits.

**March**: Scotland v. France Rugby Union.

**March**: Edinburgh Folk Festival.

**April**: Scottish Grand National at Ayr; not quite as testing as the English equivalent steeplechase but an important event on the Scottish racing calendar.

**April**: Rugby 7s (seven-a-side rugby tournament) in full swing all over the Borders.

**April**: Kate Kennedy procession at St Andrews. An exclusively male university tradition in honour of distinguished figures in the town and university's history. The role of Kate, niece of the founder of the university, and mythologized as a great beauty, is always played by a first-year student.

**April**: Shetland Folk Festival.

**May 1**: Beltane Fire festival on Calton Hill in Edinburgh.

**May**: Mayfest; Glasgow's recent and very successful answer to the Edinburgh Festival.

**May**: Scottish FA Cup Final in Glasgow.

**Late May**: Atholl Highlanders Parade at Blair Castle, Perthshire; the annual parade and inspection of Britain's last private army by their colonel-in-chief, the Duke of Atholl.

**Late May**: Scottish Hebridean Islands Peak Race; the biggest combined sailing and fell running competition in the world.

**June–August**: Riding of the Marches in the border towns of Hawick, Selkirk, Annan, Dumfries, Duns, Peebles, Jedburgh, Langholm and Lauder. The Rides originated to check the boundaries of common land owned by the town and also to commemorate warfare between the Scots and the English. Nowadays individual Ridings have their own special ceremonies, though they all start with a parade of pipes and brass bands.

**June**: Shinty Camanachd Cup Final, usually in Inverness. Finals of the intensely competitive games between the northern towns who play Scotland's own stick-and-ball game.

**June**: Royal Highland Agricultural Show, Ingliston, near Edinburgh. Scotland's biggest and best.

**June**: Highland Games at Campbeltown, Aberdeen and Grantown-on-Spey.

**July**: Scottish Open Golf Championship held at a different venue annually.

**July**: Glasgow International Folk Festival.

**July**: Highland Games at Caithness, Elgin, Glengarry, North Uist, Inverness, Inveraray, Mull, Lewis, Durness, Lochaber, Dufftown, Halkirk.

**August**: Edinburgh International Festival and Fringe. One of the world's great arts jamborees, detailed in full on p.84.

**August**: Edinburgh Military Tattoo held on the Castle esplanade; massed pipe bands and drums by floodlight.

**August**: World Pipe Band Championship at Glasgow.

**August**: International Horse Trials at Blair Atholl.

**August**: Horse festival on South Ronaldsay in Orkney. Small children dress as horses and drag decorative wooden ploughs along the beach in a competition to turn the straightest furrows.

**August**: Northern Meeting Piping Championships at Inverness.

**August**: Highland Games at Mallaig, Skye, Dornoch, Aboyne, Strathpeffer, Assynt, Bute, Glenfinnan, Argyllshire, Glenurquhart and Invergordon.

**September**: Highland Games at Braemar.

**September**: Ben Nevis Race for amateurs to the top of the highest mountain in Scotland and back again.

**October**: The National Mod. Competitive festival of all aspects of Gaelic performing arts, held in varying venues.

**October**: Glenfiddich Piping Championships at Blair Atholl for the world's top ten solo pipers.

**November**: St Andrew's Day celebrations at St Andrews.

**loosely described as bowls on ice, which originated in Scotland nearly five hundred years ago and is now played all over the world – and shinty, a simple form of hockey. Soccer is the national game, and weekly league matches are held from August to May.**

It's important to bear in mind that a few of the smaller, more obscure events, particularly those with a pagan bent, are in no way created for tourists, and indeed, do not always welcome the casual visitor. If in doubt, check at the local tourist office. The STB publishes a weighty and complete list of Scottish events annually in December: it's free and you can get it from area tourist offices or direct from their headquarters.

## HIGHLAND GAMES

Despite their name, **Highland Games** are held all over Scotland, from May until mid-September: they vary in size and differ in the range of events they offer, and although the most famous are at Oban, Cowal and especially Braemar, often the smaller ones are more fun. They probably originated in the fourteenth century as a means of recruiting the best fighting men for the clan chiefs, and were popularized by Queen Victoria to encourage the traditional dress, music, games and dance of the Highlands; various royals still attend the Games at Braemar. The most distinctive events are known as the **"heavies"** – tossing the caber, putting the stone, and tossing the weight over the bar – all of which require prodigious strength and skill. Tossing the caber is the most spectacular, when the athlete must run carrying an entire tree trunk and attempt to heave it end over end in a perfect, elegant throw. Just as important as the sporting events are the **piping competitions** – for individuals and bands – and **dancing competitions,** where you'll see girls as young as three years old tripping the quick, intricate steps of such traditional dances as the Highland Fling.

The list above includes some of the better-known Games; for the smaller, local games, check at individual tourst offices.

# SPORT AND OUTDOOR PURSUITS

Many visitors bypass Scotland's main cities and come purely for the beautiful scenery. There are vast tracts of land where you'll never see a soul, ideal walking for even the toughest hiker, and spectacular mountains on which some of the world's great mountaineers have cut their teeth and which in winter provide great skiing. For more sedate walkers, numerous marked trails range from hour-long ambles to coast-to-coast treks. The coast, lochs and rivers give opportunities for fishing as well as sailing and numerous water-sports, and there are plenty of fine beaches for less structured fresh-air activities or just slobbing around. Scotland is also known as the "home of golf": it's cheaper here and there are proportionally more courses than anywhere else in the world. For specific details on where to go to watch or participate in any of the following activities, contact the Scottish Sports Council, 1–3 Colme St, Edinburgh (☎ 031/225 8411).

## CLIMBING AND WALKING

The whole of Scotland offers good opportunities for gentle hillwalking, from the smooth, grassy hills and moors of the **Southern Uplands** to the wild and rugged country of the northwest. Scotland has three **Long Distance Footpaths** (LDPs) which will take days to walk, though you can, of course, just do part of them. The **Southern Upland Way** crosses Scotland from coast-to-coast in the south, and is the longest at 212 miles. The best-known is the **West**

---

### SAFETY IN THE SCOTTISH HILLS

Scottish mountains are not high, but, due to rapid weather changes, they are potentially extremely dangerous and should be treated with respect. Every year, in every season, climbers and hill walkers die on Scottish mountains. If the weather looks as if it's closing in, *get down fast*. It is essential that you are properly equipped – even for what appears to be an easy climb in apparently settled weather – with proper warm and waterproof layered clothing, supportive footwear and adequate maps, a compass (which you should know how to use) and food. Always leave word of your route and what time you expect to return.

The STB publishes a helpful leaflet, *Enjoy the Scottish Hills in Safety*, available from tourist offices.

---

**Highland Way**, a 95-mile hike from Glasgow to Fort William via Loch Lomond and Glen Coe. The gentler **Speyside Way**, in Aberdeenshire, is a mere thirty miles.

Scotland's main climbing areas are in the **Highlands**, which boast many challenging peaks as well as great hill walks. There are 279 mountains over 3000ft (914m) in Scotland, known as **Munros** after the man who first classified them: many walkers "collect" them, and it's possible to chalk up several in a day. Serious climbers will probably head for **Glen Coe** or **Torridon** which offer difficult routes in spectacular surroundings.

Major walks are covered in the *Guide*, along with numerous short walks from accessible towns and villages, but if you want more details the tourist offices are generally helpful. As for serious walking and climbing guidebooks, the *Scottish Mountaineering Club District Guides*, available in large bookshops, are the best to go for: blow-by-blow accounts of climbs written by professional mountaineers.

## CYCLING

Despite the recent boom in the sale of mountain bikes, **cyclists** are treated with notorious neglect by many motorized road users and by the people who plan the country's traffic systems. Very few of Scotland's towns have proper cycle routes, but if you're hell-bent on tackling the congestion, pollution and aggression of city traffic, get a **helmet** and a secure **lock** – cycle theft in Scotland is an organized and highly effective racket. The rural backroads are infinitely more enjoyable, particularly in the gentle landscape of the south of the country, whose generally amiable gradients and decent density of pubs and B&Bs make it a perfect area for cycle touring. Your main problem out in the countryside will be finding any spare parts – only inner tubes and tyres are easy to find.

Cycling is popular in the highland walking areas, but cyclists should remember to keep to rights of way and to pass walkers at considerate speeds. Footpaths, unless otherwise marked, are for pedestrian use only.

Transporting your **bike** by train is a good way of getting to the interesting parts of Scotland without a lot of stressful pedalling. Bikes are not allowed on InterCity express trains, but on other inter-town routes are carried at £3 per journey. **Bike rental** is available at shops in most large towns and many tourist centres, but the specimens on offer are often pretty derelict – alright for a brief spin, but not for any serious touring. Expect to pay in the region of £8–10 per day, £40–60 per week.

Britain's biggest **cycling organization** is the *Cycle Touring Club* or *CTC* (Cotterell House, 69 Meadrow, Godalming, Surrey, GU7 3HS; ☎0483/417217), which supplies members with touring and technical advice as well as insurance. A recommended country-wide guide is their *Route Guide to Cycling in Britain and Ireland*, a third of which covers Scotland .

## GOLF

There are over four hundred **golf courses** in Scotland, where the game is less elitist, cheaper and more accessible than anywhere else in the world. The game as it's known today took shape in the sixteenth century on the dunes of Scotland's east coast, and today you'll find some of the oldest courses in the world on these early coastal sites, known as "links". If you want a round of golf, it's often possible just to turn up and play, though it's sensible to phone ahead and book, and essential for the championship courses (see below).

**Public** courses are owned by the local council, while **private** courses belong to a club. You can play on both – occasionally the private courses require that you be a member of another club, and the odd one asks for introductions from a member, but these rules are often waived for overseas visitors and all you need to do is pay a one-off fee. The cost of one round will set you back between around £5 for small, nine-hole courses, up to more than £20 for eighteen holes. Simply pay as you enter and play. In remote areas the courses are sometimes unmanned – just put the admission fee into the honour box. Most courses have **resident professionals** who give lessons, and some rent equipment at reasonable rates. Renting a caddy car will add an extra few pounds depending on the swankiness of the course.

Scotland's **championship** courses, which often host the British Open tournament, are renowned for their immaculately kept greens and challenging holes, and though they're favoured by serious players, anybody with a valid handicap certificate can enjoy them. **St Andrews** (☎0334/75757) is *the* destination for golfers: it's the home of the *Royal and Ancient Golf Club*, the worldwide controlling body that regulates the rules of the game. Of its five courses, the best known is the Old Course, a particularly intriguing ground with eleven enormous greens and the world-famous "Road Hole". If you want to play, there's no introduction needed, but you'll need to book months in advance and have a handicap certificate – handicap limits are 24 for men and 36 for women. You could also enter your name for the daily right-to-play lottery – contact the club before 2pm on the day you'd like to play. One of the easiest championship courses to get into is *Carnoustie*, in Angus (☎0241/53249), though you should still try and book as far ahead as possible. No handicap certificate is required for play here before 1.30pm on Saturday and 11am on Sunday. Other championship courses include *Gleneagles* in Perthshire (☎076/463543); *Royal Dornoch* in Sutherland (☎0862/810219); and *Turnberry* in Ayrshire (☎0655/31000). A round of golf at any of these will set you back at least £20, double that if you rent a human caddy – and you'll be expected to tip over and above that. Near Edinburgh, *Muirfield*, considered by professional players to be one of the most testing grounds in the world, is also one of the most elitist – women can only play if accompanied by a man and aren't allowed into the clubhouse.

## DISABLED TRAVELLERS

Scotland has numerous specialist tour operators catering for physically handicapped travellers, and the number of non-specialist operators who welcome clients with disabilities is increasing. For more information on these operators, you should get in touch with *Disability Scotland*, Princes House, 5 Shandwick Place, Edinburgh EH2 4RG (☎031/229 8632). They have a comprehensive computer database covering all aspects of disabled holidays in Scotland publish a full directory, and are happy to deal with queries. There's also the *Royal Association for Disability and Rehabilitation (RADAR)*, 25 Mortimer St, London W1N 8AB (☎071/637 5400), who publish their own guide to holidays and travel abroad (see below), as well as being a good source of all kinds of information and advice, and *Mobility International*, 228 Borough High St, London SE1 1JX (☎071/403 5688), who put out a quarterly newsletter that keeps up-to-date with developments in disabled travel; their North American office is at PO Box 3551, Eugene, OR 97403 (☎503/343-1284).

Should you go it alone, you'll find that Scottish attitudes towards travellers with disabilities are often begrudging, and years behind advances towards independence made in North America and Australia. Access to theatres, cinemas and other public places has improved recently, but **public transport** companies rarely make any effort to help disabled people, though some *British Rail InterCity* services now accommodate wheelchair users in comfort. Wheelchair users and blind or partially sighted people are automatically given 30–50 percent reductions on train fares, and people with other disabilities are eligible for the **Disabled Persons Railcard** (£14 per year), which gives a third off most tickets. There are no bus discounts for the disabled, and of the major **car rental** firms only *Hertz* offer models with hand controls at the same rate as conventional vehicles, and even these are in the more expensive categories. **Accommodation** is the same story, with modified suites for people with disabilities available only at higher-priced establishments and perhaps the odd B&B.

Useful **publications** include *RADAR*'s annually updated *Holidays in the British Isles; A Guide For Disabled People*. Two other publications to look out for are *The World Wheelchair Traveller* by Susan Abbott and Mary Ann Tyrrell (AA Publications), which includes basic hints and advice, and our own *Nothing Ventured/Able to Travel: Disabled People Travel the World* by Alison Walsh (Rough Guides), which has practical advice and inspiring accounts of disabled travel worldwide.

## DIRECTORY

**Beaches** Scotland is ringed by fine beaches and bays, most of them clean and many of them deserted even in high summer – perhaps hardly surprising given the bracing winds and icy water. Few people come to Scotland for a beach holiday, but it's worth sampling one or two, even if you never shed as much as a sweater. A rash of slightly melancholy seaside towns lies within easy reach of Glasgow, while on the east coast, the relatively low cliffs and miles of sandy beaches are ideal for walking. Bizarrely enough, given the low temperature of the water, the beaches in the northeast are beginning to figure on surfers' itineraries, attracting enthusiasts from all over Europe. Perhaps the most beautiful beaches of all are to be found on Scotland's islands: endless, isolated stretches that on a sunny day can be the epitome of the Scottish Hebridean dream.

**Drugs** Likely-looking visitors coming to Britain from Holland or Spain can expect scrutiny from Customs officers on the lookout for hashish (marijuana resin). Being caught with possession of a small amount of hashish or grass will lead to a fine, but possession of larger quantities or harder narcotics could mean imprisonment or deportation.

**Gaelic** In some areas of Scotland, particularly in the Hebridean islands, road signs are almost exclusively in Gaelic. In the *Guide*, the Gaelic translation is given – in italics and parentheses – the first time any village or island is mentioned, after that the English name is used.

**Electricity** In Britain the current is 240V AC. North American appliances need a transformer and adaptor; Australasian appliances only need an adaptor.

**Laundry** Coin-operated laundries are found in nearly all Scottish cities and some towns, and are open about twelve hours a day from Monday to Friday, less on weekends. A wash followed by a spin or tumble dry costs about £2 – "service washes" (your laundry done for you in a few hours) cost about £1 extra.

**Public toilets** Found at all train and bus stations and signposted on town high streets: a fee of 10p or 20p is usually charged.

**Smoking** Although many Scots still smoke, the last decade has seen a dramatic change in attitudes towards smoking and a significant reduction in the consumption of cigarettes. Smoking is now outlawed from just about all public buildings and on public transport, and many restaurants and hotels have become totally non-smoking. Smokers are advised, when booking a table or a room, to check their vice is tolerated there.

**Time** Greenwich Mean Time (GMT) is in force from late October to late March, after which the clocks go forward an hour for British Summer Time (BST). GMT is five hours ahead of the US Eastern Standard Time and ten hours behind Australian Eastern Standard Time.

**Tipping and service charges** In restaurants a service charge is usually included in the bill; if it isn't, you should leave a tip of 10–15 percent or so. Some restaurants are in the habit of leaving the total box blank on credit-card counterfoils, to encourage customers to add another few percent on top of the service charge. There's no need to, and if you're paying by credit card, check that the total box is filled in before you sign. Taxi drivers expect a tip in the region of ten percent. You do not have to tip bar staff.

**Videos** Visitors from North America planning to use their video cameras in Britain should note that Betamax video cassettes are less easy to obtain in Scotland, where VHS is the commonly used format, so bring a supply with you.

# PART TWO

## THE

# GUIDE

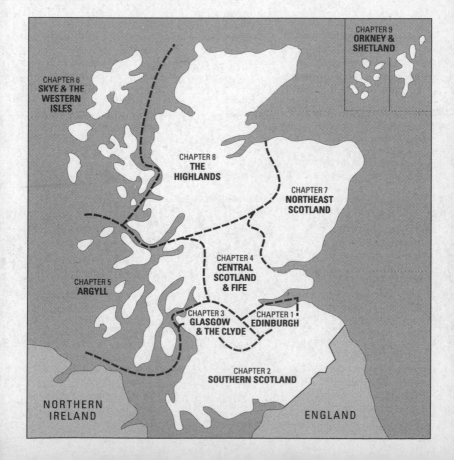

CHAPTER 9
**ORKNEY &
SHETLAND**

CHAPTER 6
**SKYE & THE
WESTERN
ISLES**

CHAPTER 8
**THE
HIGHLANDS**

CHAPTER 7
**NORTHEAST
SCOTLAND**

CHAPTER 4
**CENTRAL
SCOTLAND
& FIFE**

CHAPTER 5
**ARGYLL**

CHAPTER 3
**GLASGOW
& THE CLYDE**

CHAPTER 1
**EDINBURGH**

CHAPTER 2
**SOUTHERN SCOTLAND**

NORTHERN
IRELAND

ENGLAND

# CHAPTER ONE

# EDINBURGH

**W**ell-heeled **EDINBURGH**, the showcase capital of Scotland, is a cosmopolitan and cultured city. Its setting is undeniably striking; perched on a series of extinct volcanoes and rocky crags which intrude on the generally flat landscape of the Lothians, with the sheltered shoreline of the Firth of Forth to the north. "My own Romantic town", Sir

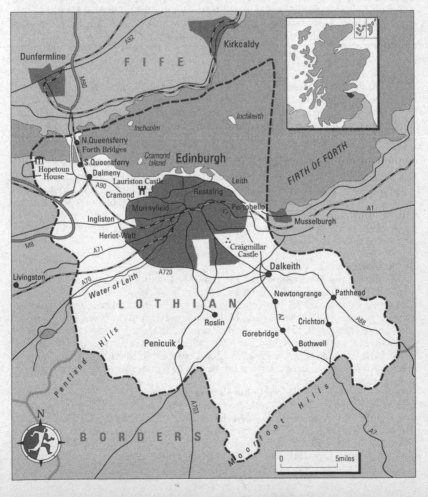

Walter Scott called it, although it was another native author, Robert Louis Stevenson, who perhaps best captured the feel of his "precipitous city", declaring that "No situation could be more commanding for the head of a kingdom; none better chosen for noble prospects."

The centre has two distinct parts. North of the **Castle Rock**, the dignified, Grecian-style **New Town** was immaculately laid out during the Age of Reason, after the announcement of a plan to improve conditions in the city. The **Old Town**, on the other hand, with its tortuous alleys and tightly packed closes, is unrelentingly medieval, associated in popular imagination with its underworld lore of the schizophrenic Deacon Brodie, inspiration for Stevenson's *Dr Jekyll and Mr Hyde*, and the bodysnatchers Burke and Hare. Edinburgh earned its nickname of "Auld Reekie" for the smog and smell generated by the Old Town, which for centuries swam in sewage tipped out of the windows of cramped tenements.

Set on the crag which sweeps down from the towering fairytale **Castle** to the royal **Palace of Holyroodhouse**, the Old Town preserves all the key reminders of its role as a capital, while in contrast, a tantalizing glimpse of the wild beauty of Scotland's scenery can be had immediately beyond the palace in **Holyrood Park**, an extensive area of open countryside dominated by **Arthur's Seat**, the largest and most impressive of the volcanoes.

During the last two weeks of August and the first week of September, around a million visitors flock to the city for the **Edinburgh International Festival**, in fact a series of separate festivals that make up the largest arts extravaganza in the world. Among the many museums making the city one of the few places in Scotland worth visiting in the short grey winter days, the **National Gallery of Scotland** boasts as choice an array of Old Masters as is to be found anywhere, and its offshoot, the **Scottish National Gallery of Modern Art**, has Britain's oldest specialist collection of twentieth-century painting and sculpture.

On a less elevated theme, the city's distinctive howffs (pubs), allied to its brewing and distilling traditions, make it a great **drinking** city. The presence of three **universities**, plus several colleges, means that there is a youthful presence for most of the year – a welcome corrective to the stuffiness which is often regarded as Edinburgh's Achilles heel.

## Some history

It was during the **Dark Ages** that the name of Edinburgh – at least in its early forms of Dunedin or Din Eidyn ("fort of Eidyn") – first appeared. Castle Rock, a strategic fort atop one of the volcanoes, served as the nation's **southernmost border post** until 1018, when King Malcolm I established the River Tweed as the permanent frontier. In the reign of Malcolm Canmore the castle became one of the main seats of the court; and the town, which was given privileged status as a **royal burgh**, began to grow. In 1128 King David established Holyrood Abbey at the foot of the slope, later allowing its monks to found a separate burgh, known as **Canongate**.

Robert the Bruce granted Edinburgh a **new charter** in 1234, giving it jurisdiction over the nearby port of **Leith**, and during the following century the prosperity brought by foreign trade enabled the newly fortified city to establish itself as the permanent **capital of Scotland**. Under King James IV, the city enjoyed a short but brilliant **Renaissance era**, which saw not only the construction of a new palace alongside Holyrood Abbey, but also the granting of a royal charter to the College of Surgeons, the earliest in the city's long line of academic and professional bodies.

This period came to an abrupt end in 1513 with the calamitous defeat by the English at the Battle of Flodden, which led to several decades of political instability. In the 1540s, King Henry VIII's attempt to force a royal union with Scotland led to the sack of Edinburgh, prompting the Scots to turn to France: French troops arrived to defend the city, while the young queen Mary was despatched to Paris as the promised bride of the Dauphin. While the French occupiers succeeded in removing the English threat, they themselves antagonized the locals, who had become increasingly sympathetic to the ideals of the **Reformation**. When the radical preacher John Knox returned from exile in 1555, he quickly won over the city to his Calvinist message.

James VI's rule saw the foundation of the University of Edinburgh in 1582, but following the **Union of the Crowns** in 1603, the city was totally upstaged by London: although James promised to visit every three years, it was not until 1617 that he made his one and only return trip. In 1633 Charles I visited Edinburgh for his coronation, but soon afterwards precipitated a crisis by introducing episcopacy to the Church of Scotland, in the process making Edinburgh a bishopric for the first time. Fifty years of religious turmoil followed, culminating in the triumph of **presbyterianism**. Despite these vicissitudes, Edinburgh expanded throughout the seventeenth century and, constrained by its walls, was forced to build both upwards and inwards.

The **Union of the Parliaments** of 1707 dealt a further blow to Edinburgh's political prestige, though the guaranteed preservation of the national church and the legal and educational systems ensured that it was never relegated to a purely provincial role. On the contrary, it was in the second half of the eighteenth century that Edinburgh achieved the height of its intellectual influence, led by an outstanding group, including David Hume and Adam Smith. Around the same time, the city began to expand beyond its medieval boundaries, laying out a **New Town**, a masterpiece of the Neoclassical style.

**Industrialization** affected Edinburgh less than any other major city in the nation, and it never lost its white-collar character. Nevertheless, the city underwent an enormous **urban expansion** in the course of the century, annexing, among many other small burghs, the large port of Leith.

In 1947 Edinburgh was chosen to host the great **International Festival** which served as a symbol of the new peaceful European order; despite some hiccups, it has flourished ever since, in the process helping to make tourism a mainstay of the local economy. In 1975 the city carried out another territorial expansion, moving its boundaries westwards as far as the old burgh of South Queensferry and the Forth Bridges. Four years later, the inconclusive referendum on Scottish devolution robbed Edinburgh of the chance of reviving its role as a governmental capital; and Glasgow, previously the poor relation, began to overtake the city as a cultural centre, peaking in its status as European City of Culture in 1990. Despite these blows, however, Edinburgh remains a fascinating and complex place, whose character typifies that of a nation which has maintained its essential autonomy despite nearly three centuries of full political union with England.

The telephone code for Edinburgh is ☎031

# Orientation

Although Edinburgh occupies a large area relative to its population – less than half a million people – most places worth visiting lie within the city centre, which is easily explored on foot. This is divided clearly and unequivocally between the maze-like **Old Town**, which lies on and around the crag linking the Castle and the Palace, and the **New Town**, laid out in a symmetrical pattern on the undulating ground to the north. It's also worth venturing into the **outskirts**, which range from residential inner suburbs to formerly separate villages which still retain their own distinctive identities.

Orientation in Edinburgh is straightforward, particularly as most public transport services terminate on or near **Princes Street**, the city's main thoroughfare, which lies at the extreme southern end of the New Town, with the Old Town on the heights immediately to the rear. The city's compactness makes it easy to explore on foot, but if you want to travel out to the suburbs, or are staying outside the centre, the public transport system, although a little confusing, is reliable.

# Arrival

**Edinburgh International Airport** (☎333 1000) is at Turnhouse, seven miles west of the city centre, close to the start of the M8 motorway to Glasgow. Regular shuttle buses (£3) connect to **Waverley Station** in the town centre; taxis charge around £11 for the same journey. The station (☎556 2451) is the terminus for all mainline trains, conveniently situated at the eastern end of Princes Street in the New Town. The central exit takes you out on to Waverley Bridge, with Princes Street to the north and the Old Town to the south. The northern exit leads straight up the stairway to Princes Street itself, while the southern exit leads to Market Street, the outer fringe of the Old Town.

There's a second mainline stop, **Haymarket Station**, just under two miles west on the lines from Waverley to Glasgow, Fife and the Highlands, although this is only really of use if you're staying in the vicinity.

The **bus terminal** for local and inter-city services is on **St Andrew Square**, two minutes' walk from Waverley, on the opposite side of Princes Street. *SMT*'s shop (☎558 1616), at the northwestern corner of the station, keeps timetables and sells tickets for several of the confusing array of private bus operators.

# Information

Edinburgh's main **tourist office** is at 3 Princes Street beside the northern entrance to the station (July & Aug Mon–Sat 9am–8pm, Sun 11am–8pm; May, June & Sept Mon–Sat 9am–7pm, Sun 11am–7pm; April & Oct Mon–Sat 9am–6pm, Sun 11am–6pm; Nov–March Mon–Sat 9am–6pm; ☎557 1700) . Although inevitably flustered at the height of the season, it's efficiently run, with scores of free leaflets; when the office is closed, there's a 24-hour computerized information service at the door. The much smaller **airport branch** is in the main concourse, directly opposite Gate 5 (April–Oct Mon–Sat 8.30am–9.30pm, Sun 9.30am–9.30pm; Nov–March Mon–Fri 9am–6pm, Sat 9am–1pm, Sun 10am–2pm; ☎333 2167).

# City transport

Edinburgh is well served by **buses**, although even locals are confused by the consequences of deregulation, with several companies offering competing services along similar routes. Each bus stop lists the different companies together with the route numbers that stop there.

Most useful are the red buses operated by *Lothian Regional Transport*. Timetables and passes (a good investment at £8 for a week's unlimited travel, Sun–Sat, especially if you're staying far out, or want to explore the suburbs; passport photo needed) are available from their headquarters at 14 Queen Street (☎220 4111), or the ticket centre at 31 Waverley Bridge (☎225 8616). Otherwise, tickets have to be bought from the driver, for which you'll need exact change.

The green buses run by *Eastern Scottish* and the green and yellow buses of *Lowland Scottish* link the capital with outlying towns and villages. Most services depart from and terminate at the St Andrew Square bus station.

Although you can't hail **taxis** on the street, the city is well endowed with taxi ranks, especially around Waverley Bridge. Costs start at about £1 for the first 1000 yards and 15p for each additional 240 yards. For the phone numbers of the main local cab companies, see "Listings" at the end of this chapter.

It is emphatically *not* a good idea to take a **car** into central Edinburgh: despite the presence of several expensive multi-storey car parks, looking for somewhere to leave the car often involves long, fruitless searches. Bus lanes must be left clear during rush hours, and cars parked on yellow lines are regularly clamped or towed away, with a retrieval fee of £90. Most ticket and parking meter regulations cease at 5.30pm Monday to Friday, and at 1.30pm on Saturday.

# Accommodation

As befits its status as a top tourist city, Edinburgh has a larger and wider choice of **accommodation** than any other place in Britain outside London. The greatest number of places to stay can be found in the streets immediately north of Haymarket Station, Royal Terrace and the lower reaches of the New Town, and the inner suburbs of Bruntsfield and Newington, about a mile south of the West End and East End respectively.

In addition to Edinburgh's **hotels**, hundreds of **private houses** offer B&B deals at low rates, but in order to protect the guest house trade from excessive competition, they are only open between May and September. There is also a decent choice of both official and private **hostels**, and three **campsites** attached to caravan parks. Surprisingly, the wide range of **campus accommodation** is neither as cheap nor as convenient as might be expected. **Self-catering** is an alternative, extremely cost-effective for groups intending to stay a week or more, with some exceptionally enticing addresses available for let.

**Advance reservations** are very strongly recommended during the Festival: turning up on spec entails accepting whatever is left (which is unlikely to be good value) or else commuting from the suburbs. The **tourist office** (see previous page) send out accommodation lists for free, and can reserve any type of accommodation in advance for a non-refundable £3 fee: call in personally when you arrive or write in advance to Edinburgh Marketing Central Reservations Department, 3 Princes St, Edinburgh EH2 2QP (☎557 9655), stating require-

0        300yds

Royal Botanic Garden

Inverleith Park

INVERLEITH TERRACE

INVERLEITH ROW

GLENOGLE ROAD

HENDERSON ROW

STOCKBRIDGE

RAEBURN PLACE

BANK ROAD

ANN STREET

QUEENSBERRY ROAD

DEAN VILLAGE

Water of Leith

DEAN BRIDGE

BELFORD ROAD

Theatre Workshop

ST STEPHEN STREET

ROYAL CIRCUS

GREAT KING STREET

NEW TOWN

Gardens

Scottish National Portrait Gallery

Bus Station

Queen        Street

Georgian House

St Andrew & St George

QUEEN        STREET

Waverley Market

Scott Monument

West Register House

GEORGE        STREET

CHARLOTTE SQUARE

HILL STREET

YOUNG STREET

ROSE        STREET

Assembly Rooms

Royal Scottish Academy

East Princes

PRINCES        STREET

Street Gardens

West Princes Street Gardens

WEST END

MELVILLE STREET

Youth Hostel

St Mary's Episcopal Cathedral

PALMERSTON PLACE

COATES CRES

SHANDWICK PL

ATHOLL CRESCENT

St John
St Cuthbert

National Gallery of Scotland

St Giles

The Castle

OLD TOWN

Parliament House

KING'S STABLES

CASTLEHILL

Central Library

WEST MAITLAND ST

Traverse Theatre

LOTHIAN ROAD

JOHNSTON TERRACE

MORRISON STREET

Usher Hall

Royal Lyceum

Film House

WEST PORT

GRASSMARKET

Greyfriars Kirk

Haymarket Train Station

HAYMARKET

George Heriot's Hospital

LAURISTON PLACE

DALRY ROAD

FOUNTAINBRIDGE

TOLLCROSS

King's Theatre

◁ Forth Bridges

◁ SNG of Modern Art

◁ Airport, A8 Glasgow & Stirling

◁ Haymarket Terr

◁ A71 Kilmarnock

A702 Biggar, Carlisle ▽

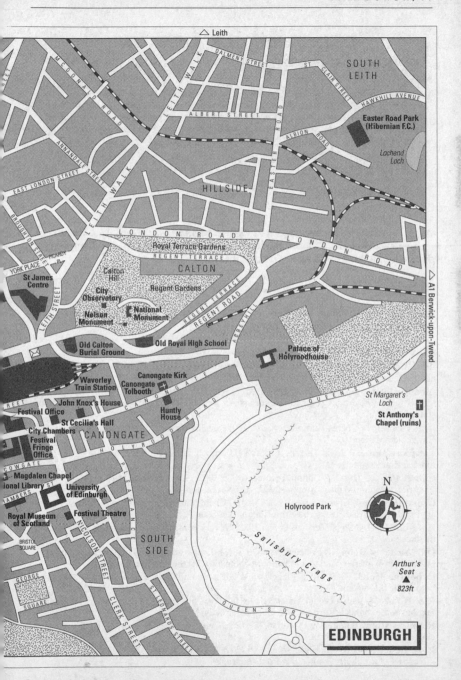

△ Leith

DALMENY STREET

SOUTH LEITH

HAWKHILL AVENUE

ALBERT STREET

Easter Road Park
(Hibernian F.C.)

*Lochend Loch*

HILLSIDE

LONDON ROAD

LONDON ROAD

Royal Terrace Gardens

REGENT TERRACE

CALTON

York Place

St James Centre

Calton Hill

City Observatory

Regent Gardens

Nelson Monument

National Monument

REGENT ROAD

△ A1 Berwick-upon-Tweed

Old Calton Burial Ground

Old Royal High School

Palace of Holyroodhouse

Waverley Train Station

Canongate Kirk

Canongate Tolbooth

CANONGATE

QUEEN'S DRIVE

St Margaret's Loch

John Knox's House

Festival Office

Huntly House

St Anthony's Chapel (ruins)

St Cecilia's Hall

City Chambers

CANONGATE

Festival Fringe Office

COWGATE

Magdalen Chapel

...ional Library

University of Edinburgh

Royal Museum of Scotland

Festival Theatre

Holyrood Park

BRISTOL SQUARE

N

SOUTH SIDE

*Salisbury Crags*

GEORGE SQUARE

NICOLSON STREET

CLERK STREET

*Arthur's Seat*
▲
*823ft*

ST LEONARD'S STREET

QUEEN'S DRIVE

**EDINBURGH**

ments. In Waverley Station the *Edinburgh Hotel and Guest House Association* runs an agency (Mon–Sat 7am–10pm, Sun 8am–10pm; ☎556 0030) which makes no charge for bookings with any of its members.

# Hotels

Although considerably more expensive than the guest houses, Edinburgh's **hotels** cover a reasonably wide range.

## New Town

**Ailsa Craig Hotel**, 24 Royal Terrace (☎556 6055). One of a clutch of good hotels on this elegant Georgian street overlooking a park. ⑤.

**Albany Hotel**, 39–43 Albany St (☎556 0397). Georgian listed building with many period features and comfortable rooms in a quiet street a couple of minutes' walk south of the bus station. ④.

**Argus Hotel**, 14 Coates Gardens (☎337 6159). Smallish rooms in a low-key hotel close to Haymarket Station. ④.

**Claymore Hotel**, 6 Royal Terrace (☎556 2693). Small, family-run hotel on one of the city's most desirable streets. ⑤.

**Clifton Private Hotel**, 1 Clifton Terrace (☎337 1002). Another family-run hotel, in roomy Victorian town house directly opposite Haymarket Station. ④.

**Grosvenor Hotel**, Grosvenor St (☎226 6001). Chain hotel retaining its old character; situated in the West End, just across from Haymarket Station. ⑥.

**Halcyon Hotel**, 8 Royal Terrace (☎556 1032). A very reasonably priced option, considering the location. ④.

**Old Waverley Hotel**, 43 Princes St (☎556 4648). Large, grand hotel in ideal location, right across from Waverley Station and with sweeping views of the city's skyline. ⑨.

**Osbourne Hotel**, 53–59 York Place (☎556 1012). Friendly place in a handy location just behind the bus station. ⑥.

**Ritz Hotel**, 14–18 Grosvenor St (☎337 4315). Posh five-storey hotel close to Haymarket Station. Some rooms feature antique four-poster beds. ⑥.

**Rothesay Hotel**, 8 Rothesay Place (☎225 4125). Quiet West End hotel in a Georgian terrace close to St Mary's Cathedral. ④.

**Roxburghe Hotel**, 38 Charlotte Square (☎225 3921). Characterful traditional hotel, right on the corner of Edinburgh's most beautiful square. ④.

**Royal British Hotel**, 20 Princes St (☎556 4901). Swanky hotel with a prime location on Edinburgh's main street, offering stunning views. ⑧.

**Royal Terrace Hotel**, 18 Royal Terrace (☎557 3222). On one of the city's handsomest Georgian streets, part of the eastern extension to the New Town. Has its own landscaped gardens, plus a leisure club with bathing pool. ⑧.

## South of the centre

**Braid Hills Hotel**, 134 Braid Rd (☎447 8888). Old-fashioned, Baronial-style hotel in a residential area up in the hills in the southern outskirts, with fine views. Ten minutes' drive from the city. ⑤.

**Bruntsfield Hotel**, 69–74 Bruntsfield Place (☎229 1393). Large hotel overlooking Bruntsfield Park, a mile south of Princes Street. ⑦.

**Donmaree Hotel**, 21 Mayfield Gardens (☎667 3641). Victorian mansion on the south side of the city, well known for its restaurant specializing in traditional Scottish food. ③.

**Prestonfield House Hotel**, Priestfield Rd (☎668 3346). Edinburgh's most eccentric hotel, a seventeenth-century mansion with opulent interiors set in its own park below Arthur's Seat. Just five rooms, only two of which have private facilities – historical values have not been sacrificed to modern comforts. Must book well in advance. ⑨.

**Teviotdale House Hotel**, 53 Grange Loan (☎667 4376). Peaceful non-smoking hotel, offering luxurious standards at moderate prices. Particularly renowned for the huge home-cooked Scottish breakfasts. ⑤.

**Thrums Private Hotel**, 14–15 Minto St (☎667 5545). Excellent hotel in large Georgian house with equally classy restaurant. ⑥.

## West of the centre

**Ellersly Country House Hotel**, 4 Ellersly Rd (☎337 6888). Edwardian country mansion set in walled garden in quiet suburban Corstorphine, between the city centre and the airport. Predominantly business clientele. ⑧.

**Merith House Hotel**, 2 Leith Links (☎554 5045). Overlooking Leith Links, about two miles from the centre. ③.

**Norton House Hotel**, Ingliston (☎333 1275). Country house owned by the Virgin group, set in extensive parkland a mile from the airport. ⑧.

# Guest houses

Edinburgh's innumerable **guest houses** are excellent value for money and far more personal places to stay than the larger city hotels.

## New Town

**Café Royal Guest House**, 5 W Register St (☎556 6894). Better known as a bar and restaurant, this is Edinburgh's most central guest house; the rooms are comfortable, and the location, down a side street just off the east end of Princes Street, could hardly be better. ②.

**Galloway Guest House**, 22 Dean Park Crescent (☎332 3672). Friendly, family-run place in the elegant setting of Stockbridge, within walking distance of the centre. ③.

**Marrakech Guest House**, 30 London St (☎556 4444). Small rooms in a residential street just a few minutes' walk south of the bus station. Superb Moroccan restaurant in the basement. ②.

**St Bernard's Guest House**, 22 St Bernard's Crescent (☎332 2339). Well located in Georgian Stockbridge. ④.

**Six Mary's Place**, Raeburn Place (☎332 8965). Collectively run, "alternative" guest house; has a no smoking policy, and offers excellent home-cooked vegetarian meals. ③.

**Stuart House**, 12 E Claremont St (☎557 9030). Refurbished Georgian house down in the eastern part of the New Town, a few minutes' walk from the bus station; no smoking. ⑤.

## South of the centre

**Arrandale House**, 28 Mayfield Gardens (☎667 6029). Good-value option among a large clutch of guest houses in Mayfield, a residential quarter about a mile from the centre. ③.

**International Guest House**, 37 Mayfield Gardens (☎667 2511). One of the best of the Mayfield guest houses, with comfortable, well-equipped rooms. ③.

**Mayfield Guest House**, 15–17 Mayfield Gardens (☎667 8049). One of Edinburgh's plushest guest houses, but still good value. ④.

**Meadows Guest House**, 17 Glengyle Terrace (☎229 9559). Quiet, relaxed place overlooking Bruntsfield Park, about a mile south of the West End. ④.

**Ravensneuk Guest House**, 11 Blacket Ave (☎667 5347). Good-value rooms set in a quiet conservation area, close to the Royal Commonwealth Pool and Holyrood Park. ③.

**Town House**, 65 Gilmore Place (☎229 1985). Victorian house close to the King's Theatre; no smoking. ③.

## Leith and Inverleith

**A-Haven Guest House**, 180 Ferry Rd (☎554 6559). Exceptionally friendly place; among the best of a number of guest houses on one of Edinburgh's main east–west arteries. ③.

**Ashlyn Guest House**, 42 Inverleith Row (☎552 2954). Right by the Botanical Gardens, and within walking distance of the centre. ③.

**Bonnington Guest House**, 202 Ferry Rd (☎554 7610). Comfortable, friendly guest house just down the road from the *A-Haven*. ④.

**Ravensdown Guest House**, 248 Ferry Rd (☎552 5438). Another place on Ferry Road, with fine panoramic view across Inverleith playing fields to the city centre. ②.

## East of the centre

**Joppa Turrets Guest House**, 1 Lower Joppa (☎669 5806). The place to come if you want an Edinburgh holiday by the sea: a quiet establishment right by the beach in Joppa, five miles east of the centre, close to bus routes #15, #26 and #86. ②.

# Self-catering apartments

**Glen House**, 22–26 Glen St (☎228 4043). Twelve apartments for rent in a large block just south of the city centre. Minimum stay three nights; open all year. Sleeps 2–7; £160–480 per week.

**National Trust for Scotland**, 5 Charlotte Square (☎243 9331). Has a two-room apartment in Gladstone's Land (the finest house on the Royal Mile) available for rent. Minimum period one week; open April–Oct only. Sleeps 2; costs from £180 per week.

**Royal Mile Enterprises**, c/o Vivien Andersen, 3 Doune Terrace (☎225 7189). Two apartments for rent in a historical tenement on the Royal Mile. Minimum stay three nights; open all year. Sleeps 2–4; £250–400 per week.

**West End Apartments**, c/o Brian Matheson, 2 Learmonth Terrace (☎332 0717 or 225 7900). Five apartments in West End town house. Minimum let two nights; open all year. Sleeps 2–6; £140–460 per week.

# Campus accommodation

**Heriot-Watt University Riccarton Campus**, Currie (☎449 5111 ext. 3113). Rather inconveniently sited at the extreme western finge of the city, but open all year. ④.

**Jewel and Esk Valley College**, 24 Milton Rd E (☎669 8461 ext. 292). Again the location, about five miles east of the centre, is not ideal, but is served directly by bus #44 and lies just beyond the terminus of bus #5. Open all year, except Dec. ③.

**Napier University**, 219 Colinton Rd (☎444 2266 ext. 4621). Reasonable location in the southern inner suburbs, but open Easter and July to mid-Sept only. ③.

**University of Edinburgh Pollock Halls of Residence**, 18 Holyrood Park Rd (☎667 1971). Unquestionably the best setting of any of the campuses, right beside the Royal Commonwealth Pool and Holyrood Park. Open Easter and late June to mid-Sept only. ④.

## Youth Hostels

**Belford Youth Hostel**, 6–8 Douglas Gardens (☎225 6209). Housed in a converted Arts and Crafts church just west of the centre, close to the Dean Village. Open all year; dorm beds and doubles.

**Bruntsfield Hostel**, 7 Bruntsfield Crescent (☎447 2994). Strictly run Grade 1 SYHA youth hostel, overlooking Bruntsfield Links a mile south of Princes Street; take bus #11, #15 or #16. 2am curfew; closed Jan.

**Christian Alliance Female Residence**, 14 Coates Crescent (☎225 3608). Clean, women-only hostel in an excellent West End location. No kitchen. Dorm beds and singles. Midnight curfew, extended to 1.30am during the Festival.

**Cowgate Tourist Hostel**, 112 Cowgate (☎226 2153). Basic, excellent value accommodation, in small apartments with kitchens, in the heart of the Old Town. Laundry facilities. July–Sept only; no curfew.

**Eglington Hostel**, 18 Eglington Crescent (☎337 1120). Grade 1 SYHA hostel west of the centre, near Haymarket Station; easier-going than its Bruntsfield counterpart. 2am curfew; closed Dec. Dorms only.

**High Street Hostel**, 8 Blackfriars St (☎557 3984). Privately run venture with room for 130 people, just off the Royal Mile. Slightly cramped, but its lively atmosphere makes up for it. Open 24hr, all year.

## Campsites

**Little France Caravan Site**, 219 Old Dalkeith Rd (☎666 2326). Three miles south of the centre, reached by bus #33, #82 or #89 from Princes Street. April–Sept.

**Mortonhall Caravan Park**, 38 Mortonhall Gate, Frogston Rd E (☎664 1533). Five miles out, near the Braid Hills; take bus #11 from Princes Street. March–Oct.

**Muirhouse Caravan Site**, Marine Drive, Silverknowes (☎312 6874). Pleasant campsite close to the shore in the western suburbs, a 20min ride from the centre by bus #14. April–Sept.

# The Old Town

The **OLD TOWN**, although only about a mile long and 300 yards wide, represents the total extent of the twin burghs of Edinburgh and Canongate for the first 650 years of their existence, and its general appearance and character remain indubitably medieval. Containing as it does the majority of the city's most famous tourist sights, it makes by far the best starting-point for your explorations.

In addition to the obvious goals of the **Castle**, the **Palace of Holyroodhouse** and **Holyrood Abbey**, there are scores of historic monuments along the length of the **Royal Mile** linking the two. Inevitably, much of the Old Town is sacrificed to hard-sell tourism, and can be uncomfortably crowded throughout the summer, especially during the Festival. A welcome antidote, and a reminder that the Old Town is by no means fossilized for the benefit of tourists, is provided by the area to the south, notably Chambers Street, location of the **Royal Museum of Scotland** and the **University of Edinburgh**.

While it's possible to cover the highlights of the Old Town in the course of a single day, a detailed visit requires several times as long. No matter how pressed you are, make sure to spare time for the wonderfully varied scenery and breathtaking vantage points of **Holyrood Park**, an extensive tract of open countryside on its eastern edge.

# The Castle

The history of Edinburgh, and indeed of Scotland, is indissolubly bound up with its **Castle** (April–Sept daily 9.30am–6pm; Oct–March 9.30am–5pm; £4) which dominates the city from its lofty seat atop an extinct volcanic rock. It requires no great imaginative feat to comprehend the strategic importance that underpinned the Castle's, and hence Edinburgh's, pre-eminence within Scotland: in the view from Princes Street, the north side rears high above an almost sheer rockface; the southern side is equally formidable, the western, where the rock rises in terraces, only marginally less so. Would-be attackers, like modern tourists, were forced to approach the castle from the crag to the east on which the Royal Mile runs down to Holyrood.

The Castle's many disparate styles reflect its many changes in usage, as well as advances in military architecture: the oldest surviving part is from the twelfth century, while the most recent additions date back to the 1920s. Nothing remains from its period as a seat of the Scottish court in the reign of Malcolm Canmore; indeed, having been lost to (and subsequently recaptured from) the English on several occasions, the defences were dismantled by the Scots themselves in 1313, and only rebuilt in 1356 when the return of King David II from captivity introduced a modicum of political stability. Thereafter, it gradually developed into Scotland's premier castle, with the dual function of fortress and royal palace. It last saw action in 1745, when the Young Pretender's forces, fresh from their victory at Prestonpans, made a half-hearted attempt to storm it. Subsequently, advances in weapon technology diminished its importance, but under the influence of the Romantic movement it came to be seen as a great national monument. A grandiose "improvement" scheme, which would have transformed it into a bloated nineteenth-century vision of the Middle Ages, was considered, but, perhaps fortunately, only a few elements of it were actually built.

### The Esplanade

The Castle is entered via the **Esplanade**, a parade ground laid out in the eighteenth century and enclosed a century later by ornamental walls, the southern one of which commands fine views towards the Pentland Hills. Each evening during the Festival, the Esplanade is the setting for the city's most shameless and spectacular demonstration of tourist kitsch, the Edinburgh Military Tattoo. An unfortunate side-effect of this is that the skyline is disfigured for virtually the entire summer by the grandstands needed to accommodate the spectators.

Dotted around are several military monuments, including an equestrian **statue of Field Marshal Earl Haig**, the controversial Edinburgh-born commander of the British forces in World War I, whose trench warfare strategy of sending men "over the top" led to previously undreamt-of casualties.

## The lower defences

The **Gatehouse** to the Castle is a Romantic-style addition of the 1880s, complete with the last drawbridge ever built in Scotland. It was later adorned with appropriately heroic-looking statues of Sir William Wallace and Robert the Bruce.

Rearing up behind is the most distinctive and impressive feature of the Castle's silhouette, the sixteenth-century **Half Moon Battery**, which marks the outer limit of the actual defences. Continuing uphill, you pass through the **Portcullis Gate**, a handsome Renaissance gateway of the same period, marred by the addition of a nineteenth-century upper storey equipped with anachronistic arrow slits rather than gunholes.

Beyond is the six-gun **Argyle Battery**, built in the eighteenth century by Major-General Wade, whose network of military roads and bridges still form an essential part of the transport infrastructure of the Highlands. Further west is **Mill's Mount Battery**, setting every weekday for a well-known Edinburgh ritual, the firing of the one o'clock gun – originally designed for the benefit of ships in the Firth of Forth, now used as a time signal by city centre office workers. Both batteries offer wonderful panoramic views over Princes Street and the New Town to the coastal towns and hills of Fife across the Forth.

Up the tortuously sloping road, the **Governor's House** is a 1740s mansion whose harled masonry and crow-stepped gables are archetypal features of vernacular Scottish architecture. It now serves as the officers' mess for members of the garrison, while the Governor himself lives in the northern side wing. Behind stands the largest single construction in the Castle complex, the **New Barracks**, built in the 1790s in an austere Neoclassical style. The road then snakes round towards the enclosed citadel at the uppermost point of Castle Rock, entered via the seventeenth-century **Foog's Gate**.

## St Margaret's Chapel

At the eastern end of the citadel, **St Margaret's Chapel** is the oldest surviving building in the Castle, and probably also in Edinburgh itself. Long secularized, this tiny Norman church was rediscovered last century and restored to an approximation of its original appearance. Externally, it is plain and severe, but the interior preserves an elaborate zigzag archway dividing the nave from the sanctuary. Although once believed to have been built by the saint herself, and mooted as the site of her death in 1093, its architectural style suggests that it actually dates from about thirty years later, and was thus probably built by King David I as a memorial to his mother.

The battlements in front of the chapel offer the best of all the Castle's panoramic views. They are interrupted by the **Lang Stairs**, which provide an alternative means of access from the Argyle Battery via the side of the Portcullis Gate. Continuing eastwards, you skirt the top of the Forewall and Half Moon Batteries, passing the 110-foot-deep **Castle Well** en route to **Crown Square**, the highest, most secure and most important section of the entire complex.

## The Palace

The eastern side of Crown Square is occupied by the **Palace**, a surprisingly unassuming block built round an octagonal stair turret heightened last century to bear the Castle's main flagpole. Begun in the 1430s, the Palace's present Renaissance appearance is thanks to King James IV, though it was remodelled for Mary,

Queen of Scots and her consort Henry, Lord Darnley, whose entwined initials (MAH), together with the date 1566, can be seen above one of the doorways. This gives access to a few historic rooms, the most interesting of which is the tiny panelled bedchamber at the extreme southeastern corner, where Mary gave birth to James VI. Along with the rest of the Palace, the room was remodelled for James' triumphant homecoming in 1617, though this was to be the last time it served as a royal residence.

Another section of the Palace has recently been refurbished with a detailed audio-visual presentation on the **Honours of Scotland**, the originals of which are housed in the Crown Room at the very end of the display. These magnificent crown jewels – the only pre-Restoration set in the United Kingdom – serve as one of the most potent images of Scotland's nationhood. They were last used for the Scottish-only coronation of Charles II in 1651, an event which provoked the wrath of Oliver Cromwell, who made exhaustive attempts to have the jewels melted down. Having narrowly escaped his clutches by being smuggled out of the Castle and hidden in a rural church, the jewels later served as symbols of the absent monarch at sittings of the Scottish parliament before being locked away in a chest following the Union of 1707. For over a century they were out of sight and eventually presumed lost, before being rediscovered in 1818 as a result of a search initiated by Sir Walter Scott.

Of the three pieces comprising the Honours, the oldest is the **sceptre**, which bears statuettes of the Virgin and Child, St James and St Andrew, rounded off by a polished globe of rock crystal: it was given to James IV in 1494 by Pope Alexander VI, and refashioned by Scottish craftsmen for James V. Even finer is the **sword**, a swaggering Italian High Renaissance masterpiece by the silversmith Domenico da Sutri, presented to James IV by the great artistic patron Pope Julius II. Both the hilt and the scabbard are engraved with Julius' personal emblem, showing the oak tree and its acorns, the symbols of the Risen Christ, together with dolphins, symbols of the Church. The jewel-encrusted **crown**, made for James V by the Scottish goldsmith James Mosman, incorporates the gold circlet worn by Robert the Bruce and is surmounted by an enamelled orb and cross.

## Around Crown Square

The south side of Crown Square is occupied by the **Great Hall**, built under James IV as a venue for banquets and other ceremonial occasions. Until 1639 the meeting-place of the Scottish Parliament, it later underwent the indignity of conversion and subdivision, firstly into a barracks, then a hospital. During this time, its hammerbeam roof – the earliest of three in the Old Town – was hidden from view. It was restored towards the end of last century, when the hall was decked out in the full-blown Romantic manner.

On the west side of the square, the eighteenth-century **Queen Anne Barracks** house part of the **Scottish United Services Museum**, with displays on each of the different Scottish military regiments, plus the navy and air force. Note the model of the ship *The Great George*, made by French prisoners incarcerated in the Castle during the eighteenth and early nineteenth centuries.

In 1755, the castle church of St Mary on the north side of the square was replaced by a barracks, which in turn was skilfully converted into the quietly reverential **Scottish National War Memorial** in honour of the 150,000 Scots who fell in World War I.

## The rest of the complex

From Crown Square, you can descend to the **Vaults**, a series of cavernous chambers erected by order of James IV to provide an even surface for the showpiece buildings above. They were later used as a prison for captured foreign nationals, who have bequeathed a rich legacy of graffiti. One of the rooms houses the famous fifteenth-century siege gun, **Mons Meg**, which when over two hundred years old, was still formidable enough to be described in Cromwell's inventory as "the great iron murderer, Muckle Meg". Its active life came to an ignominious end a few decades later when it exploded while firing a birthday salute to the future James VII.

Directly opposite the entrance to the Vaults is the **Military Prison**, built in 1842, when the design and function of jails was a major topic of public debate. The cells, though designed for solitary confinement, are less forbidding than might be expected. Finally, beyond the Governor's House, and overlooking the two-tier western defences, the late nineteenth-century **Hospital**, is a continuation of the Scottish United Services Museum.

# The Royal Mile

The **Royal Mile** is the name given to the ridge linking the Castle with Holyrood. Almost exactly a mile in length, it is divided into four separate streets – Castlehill, Lawnmarket, High Street and Canongate. From these, branching out in a herringbone pattern, a series of tightly packed closes and steep lanes are entered via archways known as pends. After the construction of the New Town, the Royal Mile degenerated into a notorious slum, but has since shaken off that reputation, becoming once again a highly desirable place to live. Although marred somewhat by rather too many overpriced shops, it is nonetheless among the most evocative parts of the city, and one that particularly rewards detailed exploration.

## Castlehill

The narrow uppermost stretch of the Royal Mile is known as **Castlehill**. On the side facing the Esplanade the pretty Art Nouveau **Witches' Fountain** commemorates the three-hundred-odd women burned at the spot on charges of sorcery, the last of whom died in 1722. Rising up behind is the picturesque **Ramsay Gardens**, centring on the octagonal **Goose Pie House**, home of the eighteenth-century poet Allan Ramsay, author of *The Gentle Shepherd* and father of the better-known portrait painter of the same name. The rest dates from the 1890s and was the brainchild of Patrick Geddes, a pioneer of the modern town-planning movement, who created thesedesirable apartments in an attempt to regenerate the Old Town.

At the top of the southern side of Castlehill, the so-called **Cannonball House** takes its name from the cannonball embedded in its masonry, which according to legend was the result of a poorly targeted shot fired by the Castle garrison at Bonnie Prince Charlie's encampment at Holyrood. The truth is far more prosaic: the ball marks the gravitation height of the city's first piped water supply. Alongside, the **Scotch Whisky Heritage Centre** (daily 10am–5pm, extended opening in high summer; £3.20) gives the lowdown on all aspects of Scotland's national beverage, featuring a gimmicky ride in a barrel through a series of historical tableaux, plus a film on aspects of production and blending. It's also worth popping into the shop, whose stock gives an idea of the sheer range and diversity of the drink, with dozens of different brands on sale.

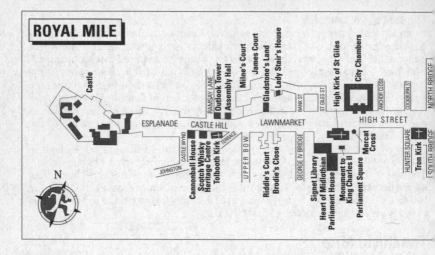

Across the road, the **Outlook Tower** (Mon–Fri 9.30am–6pm, Sat & Sun 10am–6pm; £2.70) has been one of Edinburgh's top tourist attractions since 1853, when the original seventeenth-century tenement was equipped with a **camera obscura**. It makes as good an introduction to the city as any: actual moving images are beamed on to a white table, accompanied by a running commentary. The viewing balcony is one of Edinburgh's best vantage points, and there are exhibitions on pinhole photography, holography, Victorian photographs of the city, and topographic paintings made between 1780 and 1860.

A few steps further on is the **Assembly Hall**, meeting-place of the annual General Assembly of the Church of Scotland, and, during the Festival, an extraordinarily effective venue for large-scale drama, normally staging the most ambitious event on the programme. It was built in 1859 for the breakaway Free Church; the established church previously met at the **Tolbooth Kirk** across the road. Stunningly sited at the foot of Castlehill, the Kirk is one of the most distinctive features of the Edinburgh skyline, thanks to its majestic spire, the highest in the city; sadly, it has lain disused since vacated by its Gaelic-speaking congregation in 1981, though various new roles have been mooted. The church's superb neo-Gothic detailing is due to Augustus Pugin, co-architect of the Houses of Parliament in London.

### Lawnmarket

Below the Tolbooth Kirk, the Royal Mile opens out into the much broader expanse of **Lawnmarket**, which, as its name suggests, was once a marketplace. At its northern end is the entry to **Milne's Court**, whose excellently restored tenements now serve as student residences, and immediately beyond, **James Court**, one of Edinburgh's most fashionable addresses prior to the advent of the New Town, with David Hume and James Boswell among those who lived there.

Back on Lawnmarket itself, **Gladstone's Land** (April–Oct Mon–Sat 10am–5pm, Sun 2–5pm; £2.40) takes its name from the merchant Thomas Gledstane (sic), who in 1617 acquired the modest existing dwelling on the site, transforming it into a magnificent six-storey mansion. The arcaded ground floor, the only

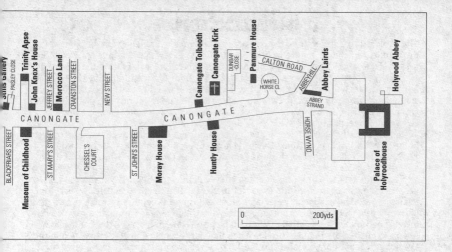

authentic example left of what was once a common feature of Royal Mile houses, has been restored to illustrate its original function as a shopping booth. Several other rooms have been kitted out in authentic period style to give an impression of the lifestyle of a well-to-do household of the late seventeenth century; the Painted Chamber, which takes its name from the decoration on its wooden ceiling and wall friezes, is particularly impressive. You can also stay here (see p.50).

A few paces further on, steps lead down to Lady Stair's Close, in which stands **Lady Stair's House** (Mon–Sat 10am–5/6pm; Sun 2–5pm during the Festival only; free), another fine seventeenth-century residence, albeit one subject to a considerable amount of Victorian refurbishment. It now serves as Edinburgh's literary museum, featuring a collection of personal mementoes of the three lions of Scottish literature – Robert Burns, Sir Walter Scott and Robert Louis Stevenson.

On the south side of Lawnmarket is **Riddle's Court**, actually a double courtyard, each with its own pend. Further down the street, **Brodie's Close** is named after the father of one of Edinburgh's most morbid characters, Deacon William Brodie, burglar by night, apparent pillar of society by day. He was hanged in 1788 on gallows of his own design, his ruse of trying to cheat death by secretly wearing an iron collar under his shirt having failed to save him.

### The High Kirk of St Giles

Across George IV Bridge, the **High Kirk of St Giles** (Mon–Sat 9am–5pm, extended opening in summer) closes off Parliament Square from the High Street. The sole parish church of medieval Edinburgh and where John Knox (see overleaf) launched and directed the Scottish Reformation, the Kirk is almost invariably referred to as a cathedral, although it has only been the seat of a bishop on two brief and unhappy occasions in the seventeenth century. According to one of the city's best-known legends, the attempt in 1637 to introduce the English prayer book, and thus episcopal government, so incensed a humble stallholder named Jenny Geddes that she hurled her stool at the preacher, prompting the rest of the congregation to chase the offending clergy out of the building. A tablet in the north aisle marks the spot from where she let rip.

## JOHN KNOX

The Protestant reformer **John Knox** has been alternately credited with, or blamed for, the distinctive national culture that emerged from the Calvinist Reformation, which has cast its shadow over Scottish history and the Scottish character right up to the present.

Little is known about Knox's early years: he was born between 1505 and 1514 in East Lothian, and trained for the priesthood at St Andrews University under John Major (sic), author of a *History of Great Britain* that advocated the union of Scotland and England. Ordained in 1540, Knox then served as a private tutor, in league with Scotland's first significant Protestant leader, **George Wishart** – and after Wishart was burnt at the stake for heresy in 1546, became involved with the group who carried out the revenge murder of the Scottish Primate, Cardinal David Beaton, subsequently taking over his castle in St Andrews. The following year, this was captured by the French, and Knox was carted off to work as a galley slave.

He was freed in 1548, as a result of the intervention of the English, who invited him to play an evangelizing role in the spread of their own Reformation. Following successful ministries in Berwick-upon-Tweed and Newcastle-upon-Tyne, Knox turned down the bishopric of Rochester, less from an intrinsic opposition to episcopacy than from a wish to avoid becoming embroiled in the turmoil he guessed would ensue if the Catholic Mary Tudor acceded to the English throne. When this duly happened in 1553, Knox fled to the Continent, ending up as minister to the English-speaking community in Geneva, which was then in the grip of the theocratic government of the Frenchman **Jean Calvin**. Knox was quickly won over to his radical version of Protestantism, declaring Geneva to be "the most perfect school of Christ since the days of the Apostles".

In exile, Knox was much preoccupied with the question of the influence wielded by political rulers, believing that the future of the Reformation in Europe was at risk because of the opposition of a few powerful sovereigns. This prompted him to write his most infamous treatise, *The First Blast of the Trumpet against the Monstruous Regiment of Women*, a specific attack on the three Catholic women then ruling Scotland, England and France, which has made his name synonymous with misogyny ever since.

When Knox was allowed to return to Scotland in 1555, he took over as spiritual leader of the Reformation, becoming minister of St Giles in Edinburgh, where he established a reputation as a charismatic preacher. However, the establishment of Protestantism as the official religion of Scotland in 1560 was dependent on the forging of an alliance with Elizabeth I, which Knox himself rigorously championed: the swift deployment of English troops against the French garrison in Edinburgh dealt a fatal blow to Franco-Spanish hopes of re-establishing Catholicism in both Scotland and England. Although the return of Mary, Queen of Scots the following year placed a Catholic monarch on the Scottish throne, reputedly Knox was always able to retain the upper hand in his famous disputes with her.

Before his death in 1572, Knox began mapping out the organization of the Scots Kirk, sweeping away all vestiges of episcopal control and giving laymen a role of unprecedented importance. He also proposed a nationwide education system, to be compulsory for the very young, and free for the poor; though lack of funds meant this could not be implemented in full. His final legacy was the posthumously published *History of the Reformation of Religion in the Realm of Scotland*, a justification of his life's work.

For all his considerable influence, Knox was not responsible for many of the features which have created the popular image of Scottish presbyterianism – and of Knox himself – as austere and joyless. A man of refined cultural tastes, he did not encourage the iconoclasm that destroyed so many of Scotland's churches and works of art: indeed, much of this was carried out by English hands. Nor did he promote the unbending Sabbatarianism, the obsessive work ethic or even the inflexible view of the doctrine of predestination favoured by his far more fanatical successors. Ironically, though, by fostering an irrevocable rift in the "Auld Alliance" with France, he did do more than anyone else to ensure that Scotland's future was to be linked irrevocably with that of England.

In the early nineteenth century, St Giles received a much-needed but over-drastic restoration, covering most of the Gothic exterior with a smooth stone coating that gives it a certain Georgian dignity while sacrificing its medieval character almost completely. The only part to survive this treatment is the late fifteenth-century tower, whose resplendent crown spire is formed by eight flying buttresses.The **interior** has survived in much better shape. Especially notable are the four massive piers supporting the tower, which date back, at least in part, to the church's Norman predecessor. In the nineteenth century, St Giles was adorned with a whole series of funerary monuments in order to give it the character of a national pantheon on the model of Westminster Abbey. It was also equipped with several Pre-Raphaelite stained-glass windows. The best of these, designed by Edward Burne-Jones and William Morris, showing Old Testament prophets and the Israelites crossing the River Jordan, can be seen on the facade wall of the **north aisle**. Alongside, the great **west window** is dedicated to Robbie Burns, which caused enormous controversy when commissioned in 1985 – as a hardened drinker and womanizer, the national bard was far from being an upholder of accepted presbyterian values.

At the southeastern corner of St Giles, with its own separate entrance on Parliament Square, the **Thistle Chapel** was built by Sir Robert Lorimer in 1911 as the private chapel of the sixteen knights of the Most Noble Order of the Thistle. Self-consciously derivative of St George's Chapel in Windsor, it's an exquisite piece of craftsmanship, with an elaborate ribbed vault, huge drooping bosses, and extravagantly ornate stalls.

## Parliament Square

The rest of **Parliament Square** is dominated by the continuous Neoclassical facades of the **Law Courts**, originally planned by Robert Adam. Because of a shortage of funds, the present exteriors were built to designs by Robert Reid, who faithfully quoted from Adam's architectural vocabulary without matching his flair. However, William Stark's **Signet Library**, which occupies the west side of the square, is one of the most beautiful interiors in Edinburgh, its sumptuous colonnaded hall a perfect embodiment of the ideals of the Age of Reason. Unfortunately it can only be seen by prior written application, except on very occasional open days.

Around the corner, facing the southern side of St Giles, is **Parliament House**, built in the 1630s for the Scottish Parliament, a role it maintained until the Union, when it passed into the hands of the legal fraternity. Today it is readily accessible during the week, used by lawyers and their clients for hushed conferrals in between court sittings. Inside, the most notable feature is the extravagant hammerbeam roof, and the delicately carved stone corbels from which it springs: in addition to some vicious grotesques, they include accurate depictions of several castles, including Edinburgh.

Outside on the square, an imposing equestrian **monument to King Charles II** depicts him in fetching Roman garb. Set in the pavement beside a bloated memorial to the fifth Duke of Buccleuch, a brickwork pattern known as the **Heart of Midlothian**, immortalized in Scott's novel of the same name, marks the site of the demolished Tolbooth. Passers-by traditionally spit on it for luck. Public proclamations have traditionally been read from the **Mercat Cross** at the back of St Giles. The present structure, adorned with coats-of-arms and topped by a sculpture of a unicorn, looks venerable enough, but most of it is little more than a hundred years old, a gift to the city from nineteenth-century prime minister, William Ewart Gladstone.

## High Street: the western block

The third section of the Royal Mile proper is known as **High Street**, and occupies two blocks on either side of the intersection between North Bridge and South Bridge. Directly opposite the Mercat Cross, the U-shaped **City Chambers** were designed by John Adam, brother of Robert, as the Royal Exchange. Local traders never warmed to the exchange, however, so the town council established its headquarters there instead. A little further down the street is **Anchor Close**, site of the printing works of William Smellie, who published the first-ever edition of the *Encyclopaedia Britannica* there in 1768.

Across the road is the **Tron Kirk**, best known as the favourite rendezvous for hardy Hogmanay revellers. The church was built in the 1630s to accommodate the presbyterian congregation ejected from St Giles when the latter became the seat of a bishop; the spire is an 1820s replacement for one destroyed by fire. For most of the last forty years, the church doors have remained firmly locked, but following a successful pilot scheme in the summer of 1993, it is due to open in summer 1994 as an orientation centre for the Old Town.

## High Street: the eastern block

Back on the northern side of High Street, beyond the intersection of North Bridge and South Bridge, the **Stills Gallery** (Tues–Sat 11am–5.30pm; free) hosts temporary exhibitions of the work of contemporary Scottish and international photographers. A few steps on is **Paisley Close**, above whose entrance is a bust of a youth with the inscription "Heave awa' chaps, I'm no' dead yet", uttered in 1861 by a boy trapped by rubble following the collapse of a tenement in the close, and who was subsequently dug out by rescue workers.

In Chalmers Close, just to the west, **Trinity Apse** is a poignant reminder of the fifteenth-century Holy Trinity Collegiate Church, formerly one of Edinburgh's most outstanding buildings, but demolished in 1848 to make way for an extension to Waverley Station. The stones were carefully numbered and stored on Calton Hill so that it could be reassembled at a later date, but many were pilfered before sufficient funds became available, and only the apse could be reconstructed on this new site. A few years ago, it was transformed into a **Brass Rubbing Centre** (Mon–Sat 10am–5/6pm, Sun 2–5pm during the Festival only; free), where you can rub your own impressions from Pictish crosses for around 40p.

The noisy **Museum of Childhood** (June–Sept Mon–Sat 10am–6pm; Oct–May Mon–Sat 10am–5pm, Sun 2–5pm during the Festival only; free) was, oddly enough, founded by an eccentric local councillor who disliked children. Although he claimed that the museum was a serious social archive for adults, and dedicated it to King Herod, it has always attracted swarms of kids, who delight in the dolls' houses, teddy bears, train sets, marionettes, and hosts of other paraphenalia.

Almost directly opposite, the impossibly picturesque **John Knox's House** (Mon–Sat 10am–4.30pm; £1.20) is the city's oldest surviving dwelling, dating from the sixteenth century. With its outside stairway, biblical motto, and sundial adorned with a statue of Moses, it gives a good impression of how the Royal Mile must have once looked. Whether or not it was ever really the home of Knox is debatable: he may have moved here for safety at the height of the religious troubles. The house did, however, once belong to goldsmith James Mosman, son of the designer of the Scottish crown, who was executed for his dogged loyalty to Knox's *bête noire*, Mary, Queen of Scots. The rather bare interiors, which give a good idea of the labyrinthine layout of Old Town houses, display explanatory material on Knox's life and career.

## Canongate

For over seven hundred years, the district through which Canongate runs was a burgh in its own right, officially separate from the capital. In recent decades, it has been the subject of some of the most ambitious restoration programmes in the Old Town, two notable examples of which can be seen at the top of the street. On the south side is the residential **Chessel's Court**, a mid-eighteenth-century development with fanciful Rococo chimneys; formerly the site of the Excise Office, scene of the robbery that led to the arrest and execution of Deacon Brodie. Over the road the **Morocco Land** is a reasonably faithful reproduction of an old tenement, incorporating the original bust of a Moor from which its name derived.

Dominated by a turreted steeple, the late sixteenth-century **Canongate Tolbooth** (Mon–Sat 10am–5/6pm, Sun 2–5pm during the Festival only; free), a little further down the north side of the street, has served both as the headquarters of the burgh administration and as a prison, and is now a museum devoted to the everyday life and work of Edinburgh people down the centuries. Next door, **Canongate Kirk** was built in the 1680s to house the congregation expelled from Holyrood Abbey when the latter was commandeered by James VII to serve as the chapel for the Order of the Thistle. It's a curiously archaic design, still Renaissance in outline, and built to a cruciform plan wholly at odds with the ideals and requirements of Protestant worship. Its churchyard, one of the city's most exclusive cemeteries, commands a superb view across to Calton Hill. Among those buried here is Robert Fergusson, regarded by some as Edinburgh's greatest poet, despite his death at the age of 24; his headstone was donated by Robert Burns, a fervent admirer, who also wrote the inscription.

Opposite the church, the local history museum in **Huntly House** (Mon–Sat 10am–5/6pm, Sun 2–5pm during the Festival only; free) includes a quirky array of old shop signs, some dating back to the eighteenth century, as well as displays on indigenous industries such as glass, silver, pottery and clockmaking, and on the dubious military career of Earl Haig. Also on view is the original version of the National Covenant of 1638; modern science has failed to resolve whether or not some of the signatories signed with their own blood, as tradition has it.

Among the several fine seventeenth-century mansions on the easternmost stretch of Canongate, **Panmure House** was for a time the home of Adam Smith, father of the science of political economy and unwitting guru of latter-day Conservatism. At the very foot of the street, the entrance to the residential **White Horse Close** was once the site of the inn from where stagecoaches began the journey to London. Stridently picturesque, it drips with all the most characteristic features of Scottish vernacular architecture, with crow-stepped gables, dormer windows, overhanging upper storeys and curving outside stairways.

# Holyrood

At the foot of Canongate lies **Holyrood**, Edinburgh's royal quarter, the **legend** of whose foundation in 1128 is described in a fifteenth-century manuscript which is still kept there. The story goes that King David I, son of Malcolm Canmore and St

### ADMISSION TO HOLYROOD

While Holyrood is an obligatory stop on any tour of Edinburgh, its continued royal status ensures that most of the grounds are permanently closed off, so that little of the exterior can be seen from ground level, while those few apartments that are open can only be viewed on hurried guided tours. In addition the buildings are closed to the public for long periods when taken over for state functions; you won't be able to visit in mid-winter, for a fortnight in the middle of May, and during the annual royal visit in the last two weeks in June and the first in July.

Margaret, went out hunting one day and was suddenly confronted by a stag who threw him from his horse and seemed ready to gore him. In desperation, the king tried to protect himself by grasping its antlers, but instead found himself holding a crucifix, whereupon the animal ran off. In a dream that night, he heard a voice commanding him to "make a house for Canons devoted to the Cross"; he duly obeyed, naming the abbey Holyrood, (rood being an alternative name for a cross). More likely, however, is that David, the most pious of all Scotland's monarchs, simply acquired a relic of the True Cross and decided to build a suitable home for it.

Holyrood soon became a favoured **royal residence**, its situation in a secluded valley making it far more agreeable than the draughty Castle. At first, monarchs lodged in the monastic guest house, for which a wing for the exclusive use of the court was constructed during the reign of James II. This was transformed into a full-blown palace for James IV, which in turn was replaced by a much larger building for Charles II, although he never actually lived there. Indeed, it was something of a white elephant until Queen Victoria started making regular trips to her northern kingdom, a custom that has been maintained by her successors.

## The precincts

On the north side of **Abbey Strand**, which forms a sort of processional way linking Canongate with Holyrood, Abbey Lairds is a four-storey sixteenth-century mansion which once served as a home for aristocratic debtors and is now occupied by royal flunkeys during the summer seat of the court.

Legend has it that Mary, Queen of Scots used to bathe in sweet white wine in the curious little turreted structure nearby known as **Queen Mary's Bath House**; it is more likely, however, that it was either a summer pavilion or a dovecot. Its architecture is mirrored in the **Croft an Righ**, a picturesque L-shaped house in a quiet, generally overlooked corner beside the eastern wall of the complex.

## The Palace of Holyroodhouse

In its present form, the **Palace of Holyroodhouse** (guided tours March–Oct Mon–Sat 9.30am–5.15pm, Sun 10am–4.30pm; Nov–Feb Mon–Sat 9.30am–3.45pm; £3) is largely a seventeenth-century creation, planned for Charles II. However, the towerhouse of the old palace was skilfully incorporated to form the northwestern block, with a virtual mirror image of it erected as a counterbalance at the other end. The three-storey **courtyard** is an early exercise in the Palladian style, exhibiting a punctiliously accurate knowledge of the main Classical orders to create a sense of absolute harmony and unity.

Inside, the **State Apartments**, as Charles II's palace is known, are decked out with oak panelling, tapestries, portraits and decorative paintings, all overshadowed by the magnificent white stucco **ceilings**, especially in the Morning Drawing Room. The most eye-catching chamber, however, is the **Great Gallery**, which takes up the entire first floor of the northern wing. During the 1745 sojourn of the Young Pretender this was the setting for a banquet, described in detail in Scott's novel *Waverley*, and it is still used for big ceremonial occasions. Along the walls are 89 portraits commissioned from the seventeenth-century Dutch artist Jacob de Wet to illustrate the royal lineage of Scotland from its mythical origins in the fourth century BC; the result is unintentionally hilarious, as it is clear that the artist's imagination was taxed to bursting point by the need to paint so many different facial types without having an inkling as to what the subjects actually looked like. In the adjacent **King's Closet**, de Wet's *The Finding of Moses* provides a Biblical link to the portraits, the Scottish royal family claiming descent from Scota, the Egyptian pharaoh's daughter who discovered Moses in the bullrushes.

The oldest parts of the palace, the **Historical Apartments**, are mainly of note for their associations with Mary, Queen of Scots, and in particular for the brutal murder, organized by her husband Lord Darnley, of her private secretary, David Rizzio, who was stabbed 56 times and dragged from the small closet, through the Queen's Bedchamber, and into the Outer Chamber. Until a few years ago, visitors were shown apparently indelible bloodstains on the floor of the latter, but these are now admitted to be fakes, and are covered up. A display cabinet in the same room shows some pieces of **needlework** woven by the deposed queen while in English captivity; another case has an outstanding **miniature portrait** of her by the French court painter François Clouet.

## Holyrood Abbey

At the end of the guided tour, you are left to look at leisure around the wonderfully evocative ruins of **Holyrood Abbey**. Of King David's original Norman church, the only surviving fragment is a doorway in the far southeastern corner. Most of the remainder dates from a late twelfth- and early thirteenth-century rebuilding in the early Gothic style.

The surviving parts of the **west front**, including one of the twin towers and the elaborately carved entrance portal, show how resplendent the abbey must once have been. Unfortunately, its sacking by the English in 1547, followed by the demolition of the transept and chancel during the Reformation, all but destroyed the building. Charles I attempted to restore some semblance of unity by ordering the erection of the great east window and a new stone roof, but the latter collapsed in 1768, causing grievous damage to the rest of the structure. By this time, the Canongate congregation had another place of worship, and schemes to rebuild the abbey were abandoned.

## Holyrood Park

**Holyrood Park** – or **Queen's Park** – a natural wilderness in the very heart of the modern city is unquestionably one of Edinburgh's main assets, as locals (though relatively few tourists) readily appreciate. Packed into an area no more than five miles in diameter is an amazing variety of landscapes – mountains, crags, moorland, marshes, glens, lochs and fields – representing something of a microcosm of Scotland's scenery. The **Queen's Drive** circumnavigates the park, enabling many of its features to be seen by car, though you really need to stroll around to appreciate it fully.

Opposite the southern gates of the Palace a pathway, nicknamed the Radical Road, traverses the ridge immediately below the **Salisbury Crags**, one of the main features of the Edinburgh skyline. Even though there is no path, you can walk along the top of the basalt crags, from where there are excellent views of the Palace of Holyroodhouse and Holyrood Abbey.

Following Queen's Drive in the other direction, you arrive at **St Margaret's Loch**, a nineteenth-century man-made pond, above which stand the scanty ruins of **St Anthony's Chapel**, another fine vantage point. From here, the road's loop is one-way only, ascending to **Dunsapie Loch**, another artificial stretch of water, which makes an excellent foil to the eponymous crag behind.

This is the usual starting-point for the ascent of **Arthur's Seat**, a majestic extinct volcano rising 823ft above sea level. The seat is Edinburgh's single most prominent landmark, resembling a huge crouched lion when seen from the west. The climb from Dunsapie, up a grassy slope, followed by a rocky path near the summit, is considerably less arduous than it looks, and is a fairly straightforward twenty-minute walk, though there are several other, somewhat longer and more taxing ways up from other points in the park. The views from the top are all you'd expect, covering the entire city and much of the Firth of Forth; on a clear day, you can even see the southernmost mountains of the Highlands. As there seems little reason to associate Arthur's Seat with the British king of the Holy Grail legends, no satisfactory story has emerged to explain its name.

Queen's Drive circles round to the foot of Salisbury Crags, from where the feline appearance of Arthur's Seat is particularly marked. The road then makes a sharp switchback, passing beneath **Samson's Ribs**, a group of basalt pillars strikingly reminiscent of the Hebridean island of Staffa (see *Argyll*). It continues on to **Duddingston Loch**, the only natural stretch of water in the park, now a bird sanctuary. Perched above it, just outside the park boundary, **Duddingston Kirk** dates back in part to the twelfth century and serves as the focus of one of the most unspoiled old villages within modern Edinburgh.

# The rest of the Old Town

Although most visitors to the Old Town understandably concentrate on the Royal Mile, the area has many other intriguing corners, none of which have so much as a hint of commercialism.

## Cowgate

Immediately south of the Royal Mile, and following a roughly parallel course, is **Cowgate**. One of Edinburgh's oldest surviving streets, it was also formerly one of the city's most prestigious addresses. However, the construction of the great **viaducts** linking the Old and New Towns entombed it below street level, condemning it to decay and neglect. In the last decade or so Cowgate has experienced something of a revival, though few tourists venture here and the contrast with the neighbouring Royal Mile remains stark.

At the corner with Niddry Street, which runs down from the eastern block of High Street, the unprepossessing **St Cecilia's Hall** (Wed & Sat 2–5pm; free) was built in the 1760s for the Musical Society of Edinburgh. Inside, Scotland's oldest and most beautiful concert room, oval in shape and set under a shallow dome, makes a perfect venue for concerts of Baroque and early music, held during the Festival and occasionally at other times of the year.

Towards the western end of Cowgate stands the **Magdalen Chapel**, a sixteenth-century almshouse under the jurisdiction of the Incorporation of Hammermen, a guild to which most Edinburgh workers, other than goldsmiths, belonged. A few years later, as one of the focal points of the Reformation, it was probably the setting for the first-ever General Assembly of the Church of Scotland. The Hammermen added a handsome tower and steeple in the 1620s, and later transformed the chapel into their guildhall, which was suitably adorned with fine ironwork. However, the main feature of the interior is the only significant pre-Reformation stained glass in Scotland still in its original location. That it escaped the iconoclasts is probably due to the fact that it is purely heraldic.

## Grassmarket and George IV Bridge

At its western end, Cowgate opens out into **Grassmarket**, which played an important role in the murkier aspects of Edinburgh's turbulent history. The public gallows were located here, and it was the scene of numerous riots and other disturbances down the centuries. The notorious duo William Burke and William Hare had their lair in a now-vanished close just off the western end of Grassmarket, luring to it victims whom they murdered with the object of selling their bodies to the eminent physician Robert Knox. Eventually, Hare betrayed his partner, who was duly executed in 1829, and Knox's career was finished off as a result. Today, Grassmarket is still pretty seamy, though the cluster of busy bars and restaurants along its northern side are evidence of a serious attempt to clean up its image.

At the northeastern corner of Grassmarket are five old tenements of the old **West Bow**, which formerly zigzagged up to the Royal Mile. The rest of this was replaced in the 1840s by the curving **Victoria Street**, an unusual two-tier thoroughfare, with arcaded shops below, and a pedestrian terrace above. This sweeps up to **George IV Bridge** and the **National Library of Scotland** which holds a rich collection of illuminated manuscripts, early printed books, historical documents, and the letters and papers of prominent Scottish literary figures, displayed in regularly changing thematic exhibitions (usually Mon–Sat 10am–5pm, Sun 2–5pm; free).

## Greyfriars and around

The **statue of Greyfriars Bobby** at the southwestern corner of **George IV Bridge** must rank as Edinburgh's most sentimental tourist attraction. Bobby was a Skye terrier acquired as a working dog by a police constable named John Gray. When the latter died in 1858, Bobby began a vigil on his grave which he maintained until he died fourteen years later. In the process, he became an Edinburgh celebrity, fed and cared for by locals who gave him a special collar (now in the Huntly House Museum) to prevent him being impounded as a stray. His statue, originally a fountain, was modelled from life, and erected soon after his death; his story has gained international renown, thanks to a spate of cloying books and tearjerking movies.

The grave Bobby mourned over is in the **Greyfriars Kirkyard**, which among its clutter of grandiose seventeenth- and eighteenth-century funerary monuments boasts the striking mausoleum of the Adam family of architects. Greyfriars is particularly associated with the long struggle to establish presbyterianism in Scotland: in 1638, it was the setting for the signing of the National Covenant, while in 1679 some 1200 Covenanters were imprisoned in the enclosure at the southwestern end of the yard. Set against the northern wall is the Martyrs'

Monument, a defiantly worded memorial commemorating all those who died in pursuit of the eventual victory.

The graveyard rather overshadows **Greyfriars Kirk** itself, completed in 1620 as the first new church in Edinburgh since the Reformation. It's a real oddball in both layout and design, having a nave and aisles but no chancel, and adopting the anachronistic architectural language of the friary that preceded it, complete with medieval-looking windows, arches and buttresses.

At the western end of Greyfriars Kirkyard is one of the most significant surviving portions of the **Flodden Wall**, the city fortifications erected in the wake of Scotland's disastrous military defeat of 1513. When open, the gateway beyond offers a short cut to **George Heriot's Hospital**, otherwise approached from Lauriston Place to the south. Founded as a home for poor boys by "Jinglin Geordie" Heriot, James VI's goldsmith, it is now one of Edinburgh's most prestigious fee-paying schools; although you can't go inside, you can wander round the quadrangle, whose array of towers, turrets, chimneys, carved doorways and traceried windows is one of the finest achievements of the Scottish Renaissance.

### The Royal Museum of Scotland

On the south side of Chambers Street, which runs east from Greyfriars Bobby, stands the **Royal Museum of Scotland** (Mon–Sat 10am–5pm, Sun 2–5pm; free), a dignified Venetian-style palace with a cast-iron interior modelled on that of the Crystal Palace in London. Intended as Scotland's answer to the museum complex in London's South Kensington, it contains an extraordinarily eclectic range of exhibits; the scope will be broader still after the completion of an annexe in 1998.

The **sculpture** in the lofty entrance hall begins with a superb Assyrian relief from the royal palace at Nimrud, and ranges via Classical Greece, Rome and Nubia to Buddhas from Japan and Burma and a totem pole from British Columbia. Also on the ground floor are collections of stuffed animals and birds, and a predominantly hands-on **technology** section featuring classic pieces of machinery of the Industrial Revolution. These include a double-action beam engine designed by James Watt in 1786; the *Wylam Dilly* of 1813, twin of the *Puffing Billy*; and the 1896 *Hawk Glider*, the earliest British flying machine. The 1862 watermill from Manchester is claimed to be the largest object to be found in any museum in Britain. Upstairs there's a fine array of Egyptian mummies, ceramics from ancient Greece to the present day, costumes, jewellery, natural history displays and a splendid selection of European decorative art ranging from early medieval liturgical objects via Limoges enamels and sixteenth-century German woodcarving to stunning **French silverware** made during the reign of Louis XIV. Finally, on the top floor, you'll come to a distinguished collection of historic scientific instruments, a small selection of arms and armour, plus sections on geology, fossils, ethnology, and the arts of Islam, Japan and China.

### The University of Edinburgh

Immediately alongside the Royal Museum is the earliest surviving part of the **University of Edinburgh**, variously referred to as Old College or Old Quad, although nowadays it houses only a few university departments; the main campus colonizes the streets and squares to the south.

Built to a design by Robert Adam, though not finished until after his death, it is arguably among his grandest and most inspired creations; the monumental entrance on South Bridge is perhaps his masterpiece.

The building was completed by Playfair, whose Upper Library now forms part of the **Talbot Rice Art Gallery** (Mon–Sat 10am–5pm; free) and provides an elegant setting for the display of the Torrie Collection, which includes many splendid seventeenth-century works from the Low Countries, with Teniers, Steen and van de Velde well represented. There are also some outstanding bronzes, notably the *Anatomical Horse* by an unknown Italian sculptor of the High Renaissance, and *Cain Killing Abel* by the Dutch Mannerist Adrian de Vries.

# The New Town

The **NEW TOWN**, itself well over two hundred years old, stands in total contrast to the Old Town: the layout is symmetrical, the streets broad and straight, and most of the buildings are Neoclassical. Originally intended to be residential, the entire area, right down to the names of its streets, is something of a celebration of the Union, which was then generally regarded as a proud development in Scotland's history. Today the New Town is the bustling hub of the city's professional, commercial and business life, dominated by shops, banks and offices.

The existence of the New Town is chiefly due to the vision of George Drummond, who made schemes for the expansion of the city soon after becoming Lord Provost in 1725. However, it was not until 1759, when the Nor' Loch below the Castle was drained, that work began. In 1766, following a public competition, a plan by a 22-year-old architect, James Craig, was chosen. Its gridiron pattern was perfectly matched to the site: the central George Street, flanked by showpiece squares, was laid out along the main ridge, with the parallel Princes Street and Queen Street on either side below. The last two were built up on one side only, so as not to block the spectacular views of the Old Town and Fife. Architects were accordingly afforded a wonderful opportunity to play with vistas and spatial relationships, particularly well exploited by Robert Adam, who contributed extensively to the later phases of the work. The First New Town, as the area covered by Craig's plan came to be known, received a whole series of extensions in the first few decades of the nineteenth century, all carefully in harmony with the Neoclassical idiom.

In many ways, the layout of the New Town is its own most remarkable sight, an extraordinary grouping of squares, circuses, terraces, crescents and parks with a few set-pieces such as **Register House**, the north frontage of **Charlotte Square** and the assemblage of curiosities on and around **Calton Hill**. However, it also contains an assortment of Victorian additions, notably the **Scott Monument**, as well as three of the city's most important public collections – the **National Gallery of Scotland**, the combined **Scottish National Portrait Gallery** and **Museum of Antiquities** and the **Scottish National Gallery of Modern Art**.

## Princes Street

Although only allocated a subsidiary role in the original plan of the New Town, **Princes Street** had developed into Edinburgh's principal thoroughfare by the middle of the last century, a role it has retained ever since. Its unobstructed views across to the Castle and the Old Town are undeniably magnificent – but have also made it the butt of Glaswegian jokes maintaining that, as it is only built down one side, it is only half a street. Indeed, without the views, Princes Street would lose much of its appeal; its northern side, dominated by ugly department stores, is almost always crowded with shoppers, and few of the original eighteenth-century buildings remain.

It was the coming of the railway, which follows a parallel course to the south, that sealed Princes Street's rise to prominence. The tracks are well concealed at the far end of the sunken **gardens** that replaced the Nor' Loch, which provide ample space to relax or picnic during the summer.

## The East End

**Register House** (Mon–Fri 10am–4pm; free), Princes Street's most distinguished building, is at its extreme northeastern corner, framing the perspective down North Bridge, and providing a good visual link between the Old and New Towns. Unfortunately, the majesty of the setting is marred by the **St James Centre** to the rear, a covered shopping arcade now regarded as the city's worst-ever planning blunder. Register House was designed in the 1770s by Robert Adam to hold Scotland's historic records, a function it has maintained ever since. Its exterior is a model of restrained Neoclassicism; the interior, centred on a glorious Roman rotunda, has a dome lavishly decorated with plasterwork and antique-style medallions.

Opposite is one of the few buildings on the south side of Princes Street, the **North British Hotel** or "NB" as it is popularly known, despite its re-designation as *The Balmoral* in a gesture of political correctness by its owners: North Britain was an alternative name for Scotland throughout the eighteenth and nineteenth centuries, but has been regarded by Scots as an affront ever since. Among the most luxurious hotels in the city, it has always been associated with the railway, and the timepiece on its bulky clock tower is always kept two minutes fast in order to encourage passengers to hurry to catch their trains. Alongside the hotel, the **Waverley Market** is a sensitive modern redevelopment that carefully avoided repeating the mistakes of the St James Centre. Its roof makes an excellent open-air piazza, a favourite haunt of street theatre groups and other performing artists during the Festival.

## The Scott Monument and the Royal Scottish Academy

Facing the Victorian shopping emporium *Jenners*, and set within East Princes Street Gardens, the 200ft-high **Scott Monument** (April–Sept Mon–Sat 9am–6pm; Oct–March 9am–3pm; £1) was erected by public subscription in memory of the writer within a few years of his death. The largest monument in the world to a man of letters, its magisterial, spire-like design is due to George Meikle Kemp, a carpenter and joiner whose only building this is: while it was still under construction, he stumbled into a canal one foggy evening and drowned. The architecture is closely modelled on Scott's beloved Melrose Abbey, while the rich sculptural decoration shows sixteen Scottish writers and 64 characters from the *Waverley* novels. Underneath the archway is a **statue** of Scott with his deerhound Maida, carved from a 30-ton block of Carrara marble.

The monument's blackened condition is a pity, and it was recently hidden under shrouds for two years while studies were carried out as to the possibility of cleaning it by sandblasting, a technique successfully applied on many of Edinburgh's other historic buildings. This exercise divided professional opinion, some believing the monument to be too slender to stand up to the treatment. As a result, the wraps have been removed, revealing some sample cleaned patches, and for the time being at least, you can ascend the narrow, twisting stairway to enjoy the superb view from the top platform.

The Princes Street Gardens are bisected by the **Mound**, which provides a road link between the Old and New Towns. Its name is an accurate description: it was formed in the 1780s by dumping piles of earth brought from the New Town's building plots. At the foot of the mound, Playfair's **Royal Scottish Academy** (Mon–Sat 10am–5pm, Sun 2–5pm; price varies) is a Grecian-style Doric temple used for temporary exhibitions, culminating during the Festival in a big international show, or a display of otherwise unseen Scottish art from the National Galleries. A few years back, the Academy was bequeathed the Borthwick-Norton collection of Old Masters, but at the time of writing legal complications meant that only four of these had been received – a pair of portraits by Gainsborough and single examples of Rubens and the rare Dutch landscape master Hercules Seghers, much admired by Rembrandt.

## The National Gallery of Scotland

To the rear of the Royal Scottish Academy the **National Gallery of Scotland** (Mon–Sat 10am–5pm, Sun 2–5pm; free) is another Playfair construction, built in the 1840s and now housing a choice display of Old Masters, many of which belong to the Duke of Sutherland.

A few years ago, the original Playfair rooms on the ground floor were controversially restored to their original appearance, with the pictures hung closely together, often on two levels, and intermingled with sculptures and *objets d'art* to produce a deliberately cluttered effect. Though individual works are frequently rearranged, the layout is broadly chronological, starting in the upper rooms above the entrance, and continuing clockwise around the ground floor. The upper part of the rear extension is devoted to smaller panels of the eighteenth and nineteenth centuries, while the basement contains the majority of the Scottish collection.

### EARLY NETHERLANDISH AND GERMAN WORKS

Among the gallery's most valuable treasures are the *Trinity Panels*, the remaining parts of the only surviving pre-Reformation altarpiece made for a Scottish church. Painted by **Hugo van der Goes** in the mid-fifteenth century, they were commissioned for the Holy Trinity Collegiate Church by its provost Edward Bonkil, who appears in company of organ-playing angels in the finest and best-preserved of the four panels. On the reverse sides are portraits of James III, his son (the future James IV) and Queen Margaret of Denmark. Their feebly characterized heads, which stand in jarring contrast to the superlative figures of the patron saints accompanying them, were modelled from life by an unknown local painter after the altar had been shipped to Edinburgh.

Of the later Netherlandish works, **Gerard David** is represented by the touchingly anecdotal *Three Legends of St Nicholas*, while the *Portrait of a Notary* by **Quentin Massys** is an excellent early example of Northern European assimilation of the forms and techniques of the Italian Renaissance. Many of his German contemporaries developed their own variations on this style, among them **Cranach**, by whom there is a splendidly erotic *Venus and Cupid*, and **Holbein**, whose *Allegory of the Old and New Testaments* is a Protestant tract painted for an English patron.

## ITALIAN RENAISSANCE WORKS

The Italian section includes a stupendous array of Renaissance masterpieces. Of these, *The Virgin Adoring the Child* is a beautiful composition set against a ruined architectural background shown in strict perspective: although known to have been painted in the workshop of the great Florentine sculptor **Andrea del Verrocchio**, its authorship remains a mystery. Equally graceful are the three works by **Raphael**, particularly *The Bridgewater Madonna* and the tondo of *The Holy Family with a Palm Tree*, whose striking luminosity, hidden for centuries under dirt and discoloured varnish, have been revealed to startling effect after recent restoration.

Of the four magnificent mythological scenes by **Titian**, the sensuous *Three Ages of Man*, an allegory of childhood, adulthood and old age, stands as one of the most accomplished compositions of his early period, while the later *Venus Anadyomene* ranks among the great nudes of Western art, notwithstanding its rough state of preservation. The companion pair of *Diana and Acteon* and *Diana and Calisto*, painted for Philip II of Spain, show the almost impressionistic freedom of his late style. A truly regal *Adoration of the Kings* by **Bassano**, a dramatic altarpiece of *The Descent from the Cross* by **Tintoretto**, and several works by **Veronese** complete a distinguished Venetian representation.

## SEVENTEENTH-CENTURY SOUTHERN EUROPEAN WORKS

Among the seventeenth-century works is the gallery's most important sculpture, **Bernini**'s *Bust of Monsignor Carlo Antonio dal Pozzo*. **El Greco**'s *A Fable*, painted during his early years in Italy, is a mysterious subject whose exact meaning is unclear, while *The Saviour of the World* is a typically intense, visionary image from his mature years in Spain. Indigenous Spanish art is represented by **Velázquez**'s *An Old Woman Cooking Eggs*, an astonishingly assured work for a lad of nineteen, and by **Zurbaran**'s *The Immaculate Conception*, part of his ambitious decorative scheme of the Carthusian monastery in Jerez. There are two small copper panels by the short-lived but enormously influential Rome-based German painter **Adam Elsheimer**; of these, *Il Contento*, showing Jupiter's descent to earth to punish the ungodly, is a *tour de force* of technical precision.

The series of *The Seven Sacraments* by **Poussin** are displayed in their own room, whose decor repeats some of the motifs of the paintings. Based on the artist's own extensive research into Biblical times, the set marks the first attempt to portray scenes from the life of Jesus and the early Christians in an authentic manner, rather than one overlaid by artistic conventions. The result is profoundly touching, with a myriad of imaginative and subtle details. Poussin's younger contemporary **Claude**, who likewise left France to live in Rome, is represented by his largest canvas, *Landscape with Apollo, the Muses and a River God*, which radiates his characteristically idealized vision of Classical antiquity.

## SEVENTEENTH-CENTURY FLEMISH AND DUTCH WORKS

**Rubens**' *The Feast of Herod* is an archetypal example of his grand manner, in which the gory subject matter is overshadowed by the vivacious depiction of the delights of the table. Like all his large works, it was executed with extensive studio assistance, whereas the three small *modellos*, including the highly finished *Adoration of the Shepherds*, are all from his own hand. The trio of large upright canvases by **Van Dyck** date from his early Genoese period; of these, *The Lomellini Family* shows his mastery at creating a definitive dynastic image.

Among the four canvases by **Rembrandt** is a poignant *Self-Portrait aged 51*, and the ripely suggestive *Woman in Bed*, which probably represents the Biblical figure of Sarah on her wedding night, waiting for her husband Tobias to put the devil to flight. *Christ in the House of Martha and Mary* is the largest and probably the earliest of the thirty-odd surviving paintings of **Vermeer**; as the only one with a religious subject, it inspired a notorious series of forgeries by Han van Meegeren. By **Hals** are a typical pair of portraits plus a brilliant caricature, *Verdonck*. There's also an excellent cross section of the specialist Dutch painters of the age, highlights being the mischievous *School for Boys and Girls* by **Jan Steen**, and the strangely haunting *Interior of the Church of St Bavo in Haarlem* by **Pieter Saenredam**, one of the gallery's most expensive purchases.

## EUROPEAN WORKS OF THE EIGHTEENTH AND NINETEENTH CENTURIES
Of the large-scale eighteenth-century works, **Tiepolo**'s *The Finding of Moses*, a gloriously bravura fantasy, stands out; despite its enormous size, it has lost a sizeable portion from the right-hand side. Other decorative compositions of the same period are **Goya**'s *The Doctor*, a cartoon for a tapestry design, and the three large upright pastoral scenes by **Boucher**. However, the gems of the French section are the smaller panels, in particular **Watteau**'s *Fêtes Vénitiennes*, an effervescent Rococo idyll, and **Chardin**'s *Vase of Flowers*, a copybook example of still-life painting.

There's also a superb group of Impressionist and Post-Impressionist masterpieces, including a particularly good cross section of the works of **Degas**, not least his seminal *Portrait of Diego Martelli*, depicting the Florentine critic who was one of the most fervent early champions of the movement. The three outstanding examples of **Gauguin**, set respectively in Brittany, Martinique and Tahiti, and **Cezanne**'s *The Tall Trees* – a clear forerunner of modern Abstraction.

## ENGLISH AND AMERICAN WORKS
Surprisingly, the gallery has relatively few English paintings, but they are of the highest class. **Hogarth**'s *Sarah Malcolm*, painted in Newgate Prison the day the murderess was executed, once belonged to Horace Walpole, who also commissioned **Reynolds**' *The Ladies Waldegrave*, a group portrait of his three great-nieces. **Gainsborough**'s *The Honourable Mrs Graham* is one of his most memorable society portraits, while **Constable** himself described *Dedham Vale* as being "perhaps my best". There are two prime Roman views by **Turner**, by whom the gallery owns a wonderful array of watercolours, faithfully displayed each January, when the light is at its weakest.

Even more unexpected than the scarcity of English works is the presence of some exceptional American canvases: **Benjamin West**'s collosal Romantic fantasy, *King Alexander III Rescued from a Stag*; **John Singer Sargent**'s virtuosic *Lady Agnew of Lochnaw*; and **Frederic Edwin Church**'s *View of Niagara Falls from the American Side*. The latter, having been kept in store for decades, was put back on display when the "rediscovery" of the artist in the late 1970s prompted astronomical bids from American museums keen to acquire the only work by the artist owned by a European gallery.

## SCOTTISH WORKS
On the face of it, the gallery's Scottish collection, which shows the entire gamut of Scottish painting from seventeenth-century portraiture to the Arts and Crafts movement, is something of an anticlimax. There are, however, some important

works displayed within a broad European context; **Gavin Hamilton**'s *Achilles Mourning the Death of Patrocolus*, for example, painted in Rome, is an unquestionably arresting image. **Allan Ramsay**, who became court painter to George III, is represented by his intimate *The Artist's Second Wife* and *Jean-Jacques Rousseau*, in which the philosopher is shown in Armenian costume.

Of **Sir Henry Raeburn**'s large portraits note the swaggering masculinity of *Sir John Sinclair* or *Colonel Alistair MacDonell of Glengarry*, both of whom are shown in full Highland dress. Raeburn's technical mastery was equally sure when working on a small scale, as shown in one of the gallery's most popular pictures, *The Rev Robert Walker Skating on Duddingston Loch*.

Other Scottish painters represented include the versatile **Sir David Wilkie**, whose huge history painting, *Sir David Baird Discovering the Body of Sultaun Tippo Saib*, is in marked contrast to the early documentary and genre scenes displayed in the basement, and **Alexander Nasmyth**, whose topographical views show Edinburgh before and during the building of the New Town.

# George Street

**George Street**, the city's chief financial thoroughfare, is the least prepossessing of the main streets of the First New Town, built up on both sides with a preponderance of unsympathetic development. At its eastern end is **St Andrew Square**, where a handsome town mansion is flanked by two graceful pavilions, the northern of which is designed by Robert Adam. This now houses the **Royal Bank of Scotland**, whose palatial mid-nineteenth-century banking hall is the most opulent in the city. On the south side of the street, the oval-shaped church of **St Andrew** (now known as St Andrew and St George) is chiefly famous as the scene of the 1843 Disruption led by Thomas Chalmers, which split the Church of Scotland in two.

At the western end of George Street, **Charlotte Square** was designed by Robert Adam in 1791, a year before his death. For the most part, his plans were faithfully implemented, an exception being the domed and porticoed church of St George, which was simplified on grounds of expense. Its interior was gutted in the 1960s and refurbished as **West Register House**; like its counterpart at the opposite end of Princes Street, it features changing documentary exhibitions (Mon–Fri 10am–4pm; free).

The **north side** of the square has deservedly become the most exclusive address in the city. No. 6 is the official residence of the Secretary of State for Scotland, while the upper storeys of no. 7 are the home of the Moderator of the General Assembly, the annually elected leader of the Church of Scotland. Restored by the National Trust for Scotland, the lower floors are open to the public under the name of the **Georgian House** (April–Oct Mon–Sat 10am–5pm, Sun 2–5pm; £2.80), whose contents give a good idea of what the house must have looked like during the period of the first owner, the head of the clan Lamont. The rooms are decked out in period furniture and hung with fine paintings, including portraits by Ramsay and Raeburn, seventeenth-century Dutch cabinet pictures, and a beautiful *Marriage of the Virgin* by El Greco's teacher, the Italian miniaturist Giulio Clovio. In the basement are the original wine cellar, lined with roughly made bins, and a kitchen, complete with an open fire for roasting, and a separate oven for baking.

# Queen Street

**Queen Street**, the last of the three main streets of the First New Town, is bordered to the north by gardens, and commands sweeping views across to Fife. Much the best preserved of the area's three main streets, its main attraction is its excellent gallery-cum-museum.

## The Scottish National Portrait Gallery and Museum of Antiquities

At the far eastern end of Queen Street is the **Scottish National Portrait Gallery**, which shares its premises with the **Museum of Antiquities**. The gallery building is itself a fascinating period piece, its red sandstone exterior, modelled on the Doge's Palace in Venice, is encrusted with statues of famous Scots – a theme taken up in the entrance hall, which has a mosaic-like frieze procession by William Hole of great figures from Scotland's past, with heroic murals by the same artist of stirring episodes from the nation's history adorning the balcony above.

### THE STEWART EXHIBITION

On the ground floor of the western wing an exhibition on the **Stewart dynasty** traces the history of the family from its origins as stewards (hence the name) to medieval royalty, via its zenith under James VI, who engineered the union with England, to its final demise under Bonnie Prince Charlie.

From the early periods, look out for two superb artefacts from the reign of Robert the Bruce, the **Kames Brooch** and the **Bute Mazer** (a large wooden bowl). An excellent collection of Mary, Queen of Scots memorabilia includes her **Penicuik Jewels** and a portrait by Rowland Lockey. The reign of Charles I is represented by several outstanding paintings by Flemish artists including **Daniel Mytens** and **Alexander Keirinox**, and there are fine official portraits of the later Stewart monarchs and members of their entourage. Mementoes of the Young Pretender include the ornate backsword and silver-mounted shield with which he fought at Culloden, and a Rococo **canteen** he left abandoned on the battlefield.

### THE PORTRAIT GALLERY

The floors above the Stewart exhibition are devoted to portraits, accompanied by potted biographies, of famous Scots – a definition stretched to include anyone with the slightest Scottish connection. From the seventeenth century, there's an excellent Van Dyck portrait of Charles Seton, second Earl of Dunfermline, and the tartan-clad Lord Mungo Murray, who died in the disastrous attempt to establish a Scottish colony in Panama. Eighteenth-century highlights include portraits of the philosopher-historian David Hume by Allan Ramsay, and the bard Robert Burns by his friend Alexander Nasmyth, and a varied group by Raeburn: subjects include Sir Walter Scott, the fiddler Niel Gow, and the artist himself. The star portrait from the nineteenth century is that of physician Sir Alexander Morison by his patient, the mad painter Richard Dadd – Edinburgh's fishing port of Newhaven is in the background.

### THE MUSEUM OF ANTIQUITIES

Ranged across three levels, objects in the Museum of Antiquities are displayed in a splendidly eclectic manner. The ground floor is, in the main, devoted to **Dark Age sculpture**, giving convincing proof of the vitality of artistic life among the tribes who later combined to form the Scottish kingdom: look out for the eighth-century Birsay Stone from Orkney, with its carvings of warriors; the ninth-century Hilton of Cadboll Stone from Easter Ross, whose main scene shows a woman riding side-saddle, and the twelfth-century **walrus ivory chessmen** from the island of Lewis. You can also see the **Deskford Carnyx**, a swine's head in brass which formed part of a Celtic war trumpet, and the so-called **Maiden**, Edinburgh's public guillotine from 1564 to 1710.

On the first floor, the **prehistoric and Viking collection** features excavations from a variety of sites beginning with the Neolithic settlement of Skara Brae in the Orkneys. Most of the artefacts are of specialist appeal only, but the Bronze Age Torrs Chamfrein, a war mask or drinking horn from around 200 BC and the Hunterston Brooch, an intricate piece of Viking jewellery, are eye-catching. Most striking of of all is the eighth-century St Ninian's Isle Treasure from the Shetlands, an ornamental set of Pictish silverware. The top floor is devoted to **Roman antiquities**, the most important of which are a milestone found at Ingliston, near the site of Edinburgh Airport; and the Traprain Treasure, a hoard of fourth- and fifth-century silver buried at Traprain Law near Haddington.

# Calton

Of the various extensions to the New Town, the most intriguing is **Calton**, which branches out from the eastern end of Princes Street and encircles a volcanic hill. The showpiece buildings all date from the time of the Napoleonic Wars or just after, and are intended as an ostentatious celebration of the British victory. While the predominantly Grecian architecture led to Calton being regarded as a Georgian Acropolis, it is, in fact, more of a shrine to local heroes.

**Waterloo Place** forms a ceremonial way from Princes Street to Calton Hill. On its southern side is the sombre **Old Calton Burial Ground**, in which you can see Robert Adam's plain, cylindrical memorial to David Hume and a monument, complete with a statue of Abraham Lincoln, to the Scots who died in the American Civil War. Hard up against the cemetery's eastern wall, perched above a sheer rockface, is a picturesque castellated building which many visitors arriving at Waverley Station below imagine to be Edinburgh Castle itself. In fact, it's the only surviving part of the **Calton Gaol**, once Edinburgh's main prison.

Further on, set majestically in a confined site below Calton Hill, is one of Edinburgh's greatest buildings. The **Grecian Old Royal High School** was built by Thomas Hamilton in the 1820s and housed Edinburgh's oldest school – *alma mater* to, among others, Robert Adam, Walter Scott and Alexander Graham Bell – until 1968. Earmarked in the 1970s as the home of the planned Scottish Assembly, the building was eventually put up for sale in 1993, while outside, diehard patiots mount a permanent vigil assailing passers-by with leaflets demanding home rule. Across the road, Hamilton also built the **Burns Monument**, a circular Corinthian temple modelled on the Monument to Lysicrates in Athens, as a memorial to the national bard.

Robert Louis Stevenson reckoned that **Calton Hill** was the best place to view Edinburgh: "since you can see the Castle, which you lose from the Castle, and Arthur's Seat, which you cannot see from Arthur's Seat." Though the panoramas from ground level are spectacular enough, those from the top of the **Nelson Monument** (April–Sept Mon 1–6pm, Tues–Sat 10am–6pm; Oct–March Mon–Sat 10am–3pm; £1) are even better. Begun just two years after Nelson's death at

Trafalgar, this is one of Edinburgh's oddest buildings, resembling a gigantic spyglass.

Alongside, the **National Monument** was begun in 1822 by Playfair to plans by the English architect Charles Cockerell. Had it been completed, it would have been a reasonably accurate replica of the Parthenon, but funds ran out with only twelve columns built. Various later schemes to finish it similarly foundered, earning it the nickname "Edinburgh's Disgrace". At the opposite side of the hill, the grandeur of Playfair's classical **Monument to Dougald Stewart** seems totally at odds with the stature of the man it commemorates: a now-forgotten Professor of Philosophy at the University.

Playfair also built the **City Observatory** for his uncle, the mathematician and astronomer John Playfair, whom he honoured in the cenotaph outside. Because of pollution and the advent of street lighting, which impaired views of the stars, the observatory proper had to be relocated to Blackford Hill before the end of the century, though the equipment here continues to be used by students. The small domed pavilion at the northeastern corner, an addition of the 1890s, now houses the **Edinburgh Experience** (July & Aug daily 10.30am–5pm; April–June, Sept & Oct Mon–Fri 2–5pm, Sat & Sun 10.30am–5pm; £1.70), a twenty-minute 3-D show on the city's history viewed through special glasses. At the opposite end of the complex is the **Old Observatory**, one of the few surviving buildings by James Craig, designer of the New Town.

# Elsewhere in the New Town

The **Northern New Town** was the earliest extension to the First New Town, begun in 1801. This has survived in far better shape than its predecessor: with the exception of one street, almost all of it is intact, and it has managed to preserve its predominantly residential character. One of the area's most intriguing buildings is the Neo-Norman **Mansfield Place Church**, designed in the late nineteenth century for the strange, now defunct Catholic Apostolic sect. Having lain redundant and neglected for three decades, it has suddenly acquired cult status, its preservation the current obsession of local conservation groups. The chief reason for this is its cycle of **murals** by the Dublin-born **Phoebe Traquair**, a leading light in the Scottish Arts and Crafts movement. She laboured for eight years on this decorative scheme, which has all the freshness and luminosity of a medieval manuscript, but desperately needs a thorough restoration to avert its already alarming decay. The church was open to the public throughout the summer of 1993, but its exact future remains uncertain.

## Dean Village and Stockbridge

Round the corner from Randolph Crescent, the four-arched **Dean Bridge**, a bravura feat of 1830s engineering by Thomas Telford, carries the main road high above Edinburgh's placid little river, the **Water of Leith**. Down to the left lies **Dean Village**, an old milling community that is one of central Edinburgh's most picturesque yet oddest corners, its atmosphere of terminal decay arrested by the conversion of some of the mills into yuppie flats.

**Stockbridge**, which straddles both sides of the Water of Leith on the other side of Dean Bridge, is another old village which has retained its distinctive identity, in spite of its absorption into the Georgian face of the New Town, and is particularly renowned for its antique shops and "alternative" outlets. The residential upper streets on the far side of the river were developed by Sir Henry Raeburn, who named the finest of them **Ann Street**, which after Charlotte Square is the most prestigious address in Edinburgh; alone among New Town streets, its houses each have a front garden.

## The West End

The western extension to the New Town was the last part to be built, deviating from the area's overriding Neoclassicism with a number of Victorian additions. Because of this, the huge **St Mary's Episcopal Cathedral**, an addition of the 1870s, is less intrusive than it would otherwise be, its three spires forming an eminently satifying landmark for the far end of the city centre. The last major work of Sir George Gilbert Scott, the cathedral is built in imitation of the Early English Gothic style and was, at the time of its construction, the most ambitious church built in Britain since the Reformation.

## The Scottish National Gallery of Modern Art

Set in spacious wooded grounds at the far northwestern fringe of the New Town, about ten minutes' walk from either the cathedral or Dean Village, the **Scottish National Gallery of Modern Art** (Mon–Sat 10am–5pm, Sun 2–5pm; free) was established in 1959 as the first collection in Britain devoted solely to twentieth-century painting and sculpture. The grounds serve as a sculpture park, featuring works by Jacob Epstein, Henry Moore, Barbara Hepworth and the Constructivist creations of the Edinburgh-born Eduardo Paolozzi. Inside, the display space is divided between temporary loan exhibitions and selections from the gallery's own holdings; the latter are arranged thematically, but are almost constantly moved around. What you get to see at any particular time is therefore a matter of chance, though the most important works are nearly always on view.

French painters are particularly well represented, beginning with **Bonnard's** *Lane at Vernonnet* and **Vuillard's** jewel-like *Two Seamstresses*, and by a few examples of the Fauves, notably **Matisse's** *The Painting Lesson* and **Derain's** dazzlingly brilliant *Collioure*; there's also a fine group of late canvases by **Leger**, notably *The Constructors*. Among some striking examples of German Expressionism are **Kirchner's** *Japanese Theatre*, **Feininger's** *Gelmeroda III*, and a wonderfully soulful wooden sculpture of a woman by **Barlach** entitled *The Terrible Year, 1937*. Highlights of the Surrealist section are **Magritte's** haunting *Black Flag*, **Miró's** seminal *Composition* and **Giacometti's** contorted *Woman with her Throat Cut*, while Cubism is represented by **Picasso's** *Soles* and **Braque's** *Candlestick*.

Of works by Americans, **Roy Lichtenstein's** *In the Car* is a fine example of his garish Pop-Art style, while **Duane Hanson's** fibre-glass *Tourists* is typically cruel. English artists on show include Sickert, Nicholson, Spencer, Freud and Hockney, but, as you'd expect, considerably more space is allocated to Scottish artists. Of particular note are the so-called Colourists – **Samuel John Peploe**, **J D Fergusson**, **Francis Cadell** and **George Leslie Hunter** – whose works are attracting fancy prices on the art market, as well as ever-growing posthumous critical acclaim. Although they did not form a recognizable school, they all worked in France and displayed considerable French influence in their warm, bright palettes. The gallery also shows works by many contemporary Scots, among them **John Bellany**, a portraitist of striking originality, and the "concrete poet" **Ian Hamilton Finlay**.

# The Suburbs

Edinburgh's principal sights are by no means confined to the city centre: indeed, at least three of its most popular tourist draws – the **Royal Botanic Garden**, the **Zoo** and the **Royal Observatory** – are out in the suburbs. Other major attractions in the outskirts include **Craigmillar Castle** and the southern hill ranges, the **Braids** and the **Pentlands**. Additionally, there are several districts with their own very distinct identity, among them the academic enclave of the **South Side**, the seaside resort of **Portobello** and the port of **Leith**.

## The Royal Botanic Garden

Just beyond the northern boundaries of the New Town, with entrances on Inverleith Row and Arboretum Place, is the seventy-acre site of the **Royal Botanic Garden** (May–Aug daily 10am–8pm; March, April, Sept & Oct daily 10am–6pm; Nov–Feb daily 10am–4pm; free), particularly renowned for the **rhododendrons,** which blaze out in a glorious patchwork of colours in April and May. In the heart of the grounds a group of hothouses designated the **Glasshouse Experience** (March–Oct daily 10am–5pm; Nov–Feb daily 10am–3.30pm; free, but £1.50 donation requested) display orchids, giant Amazonian water lilies, and a two-hundred-year-old West Indian palm tree. The last-named is in the elegant glass-topped Palm House, built in the 1850s.

## The South Side

The New Town was not the only mid-eighteenth-century expansion of Edinburgh: the city also spread in the opposite direction, creating a tenement suburb which became known as the **South Side**. Since the 1950s, this has developed into a lively academic quarter, having been progressively colonized by the mishmash of buildings that make up the University of Edinburgh.

On Nicolson Street, the southern extension of South Bridge, is **Surgeons' Hall**, a handsome Ionic temple built by Playfair as the headquarters of the Royal College of Surgeons. Most of it is accessible to the public only one day a year, an exception being the museum (Mon–Fri 10am–4pm; free) which has intriguing, if somewhat specialist exhibits on the history of medicine. Across the street is the site of the planned **Festival Theatre** (see p.94).

## The Southwest

The area southwest of the Old Town was formerly known as **Portsburgh**, a theoretically separate burgh outside the city walls that was nonetheless a virtual fiefdom of Edinburgh. Since the 1880s and the construction of the **Royal Lyceum Theatre** on Grindlay Street, the area has gradually developed into something of a theatre district. At its southern edge, the open parkland areas of **Meadows** and **Bruntsfield Links** mark the transition to Edinburgh's genteel Victorian villa suburbs. Prominent among these is **Morningside**, whose prim and proper outlook on life, accompanied by an appropriately plummy accent, was immortalized in Muriel Spark's *The Prime of Miss Jean Brodie*, and remains a favourite target for ridicule.

# Craigmillar Castle

**Craigmillar Castle** (April–Sept Mon–Sat 9.30am–6pm, Sun 2–6pm; Oct–March Mon–Wed & Sat 9.30am–4pm, Thurs 9.30am–noon, Sun 2–4pm; £1.20), where the murder of Lord Darnley, second husband of Mary, Queen of Scots, was plotted, lies in a green belt five miles southeast of the centre. It's one of the best-preserved medieval fortresses in Scotland, marred only by the proximity of the ugly council housing scheme of Craigmillar, one of Edinburgh's most deprived districts.

The oldest part of the complex is the L-shaped **tower house**, which dates back to the early 1600s: it remains substantially intact, and the great hall, with its resplendent late Gothic chimneypiece, is in good enough shape to be rented out for functions. A few decades after Craigmillar's completion, the tower house was surrounded by a quadrangular wall with cylindrical corner towers pierced by some of the earliest surviving gunholes in Britain. The west range was remodelled as an aristocratic mansion in the mid-seventeenth century, but its owners abandoned the place a hundred years later, leaving it to decay into picturesque ruin.

# The southern hills

The hills in Edinburgh's southern suburbs offer good, not overly demanding walking opportunities, with plenty of sweeping panoramic views. The **Royal Observatory** (April–Sept daily noon–5.30pm; Oct–March daily 1–5pm & 7–9pm; £1.50) stands at the top of Blackford Hill, just a short walk south of Morningside, or by buses #40 or #41 direct from the centre. The visitor centre here seeks to explain the mysteries of the solar system by means of models, videos and space photographs, and you also get to see the two main telescopes, which are put into operation during the winter evenings, the best time for a visit.

At the foot of the hill, the bird sanctuary of Blackford Pond is the starting point for the **Hermitage of Braid** nature trail, a lovely shady path along the course of the Braid Burn. The castellated eighteenth-century mansion along the route, after which the trail is named, now serves as an information centre. Immediately to the south are the **Braid Hills**, most of whose area is occupied by two golf courses, closed on alternate Sundays in order to allow access to walkers.

Further south are the **Pentland Hills**, a chain some eighteen miles long and five wide. The best entry point from within Edinburgh is **SWANSTON**, an unspoiled, highly exclusive hamlet of whitewashed thatched roof dwellings separated by almost a mile of farmland from the rest of the city. Robert Louis Stevenson (see opposite) spent his boyhood summers in Swanston Cottage, the largest of the houses, immortalizing it in the novel *St Ives*. To get a taste of the scenery of the Pentlands, follow the marked hiking trail to the artificial ski slope of **Hillend** to the east; this traverses two summits and passes the remains of an Iron Age fort in addition to offering outstanding views over Edinburgh and Fife. The lazy way into the range is to take the **chair lift** from Hillend itself (Mon–Sat 9.30am–9pm, Sun 9.30am–7pm; £1.45), which is connected with the city centre by buses #4 and #15.

# Portobello

Among Edinburgh's less expected assets is its **beach**, most of which falls within **PORTOBELLO**, once a lively **seaside resort** but now a forlorn kind of place, its funfairs and amusement arcades decidedly down-at-heel. Nonetheless, it retains a

## ROBERT LOUIS STEVENSON

Though **Robert Louis Stevenson** (1850–94) is often dismissed in highbrow academic circles for his deceptively simple manner, he was undoubtedly one of the best-loved writers of his generation, and one whose travelogues, novels, short stories and essays remain enormously popular a century after his death.

Born in Edinburgh into a distinguished family of engineers, Stevenson was a sickly child, with a solitary childhood dominated by his governess Alison "Cummie" Cunningham, who regaled him with tales drawn from Calvinist folklore. Sent to the university to study engineering, Stevenson rebelled against his upbringing by spending much of his time in the low-life howffs and brothels of the city, and eventually switching to law. Although called to the bar in 1875, by then he had decided to channel his energies into literature: while still a student, he had already made his mark as an **essayist**, and published in his lifetime over one hundred essays, ranging from lighthearted whimsy to trenchant political analysis. A set of topographical pieces about his native city was later collected together as *Edinburgh: Picturesque Notes*, these conjure up nicely its atmosphere, character and appearance – warts and all.

Stevenson's other early successes were two **travelogues**, *An Inland Voyage* and *Travels with a Donkey in the Cevennes*, kaleidoscopic jottings based on his journeys in France, where he went to escape Scotland's bad weather. It was there that he met Fanny Osbourne, an American ten years his senior, who was estranged from her husband and had two children in tow. His voyage to join her in San Francisco formed the basis for his most important factual work, *The Amateur Emigrant*, a vivid first-hand account of the great nineteenth-century European migration to the United States.

Having married the now-divorced Fanny, Stevenson began an elusive search for an agreeable climate that led to Switzerland, the French Riviera and the Scottish Highlands. He belatedly turned to the **novel**, achieving immediate acclaim in 1881 for *Treasure Island*, a highly moral adventure yarn that began as an entertainment for his stepson and future collaborator, Lloyd Osbourne. In 1886, his most famous **short story**, *Dr Jekyll and Mr Hyde*, despite its nominal London setting, offered a vivid evocation of Edinburgh's Old Town; an allegory of its dual personality of prosperity and squalour, and an analysis of its Calvinistic preoccupations with guilt and damnation. The same year saw the publication of the historical romance *Kidnapped*, a novel which exemplified his view that literature should seek above all to entertain.

In 1887 Stevenson left Britain for good, travelling first to the United States where he began one of his most ambitious novels, *The Master of Ballantrae*. A year later, he set sail for the South Seas, and eventually settled in Samoa; his last works include a number of stories with a local setting, such as the grimly realistic *The Ebb Tide* and *The Beach of Falesà*. However, Scotland continued to be his main inspiration: he wrote *Catriona* as a sequel to *Kidnapped*, and was at work on two more novels with Scottish settings, *St Ives* and *Weir of Hermiston*, a dark story of father-son confrontation, at the time of his sudden death from a brain haemorrage in 1894. He was buried on the top of Mount Vaea overlooking the Pacific Ocean, mourned by the islanders as a departed chieftain.

certain faded charm, and – on hot summer weekends at least – the promenade and the beach can be a mass of swimmers, sunbathers, surfers and pleasure boats. Portobello is about three miles east of the centre of town, and can be reached on buses #15, #26, #42 or #86.

# Leith

For several hundred years **LEITH** was separate from Edinburgh. As Scotland's major east coast port, it played a key role in the nation's history, even serving as the seat of government for a time, and in 1833 finally became a burgh in its own right. In 1920, however, it was incorporated into the capital, and in the decades that followed, went into seemingly terminal decline: the population dropped dramatically, and much of its centre was ripped out, to be replaced by grim housing schemes.

The 1980s, however, saw an astonishing turnaround. Against all the odds, a couple of waterfront bistros proved enormously successful; competitors followed apace, and by the end of the decade the port had acquired what's arguably the best concentration of restaurants and pubs in Edinburgh. The surviving historic monuments were spruced up, and a host of yuppified housing developments built or restored, earning the town the nickname of "Leith-sur-Mer".

To reach Leith from the city centre, take one of the many buses going down Leith Walk, near the top end of which is a statue of Sherlock Holmes, whose creator, Sir Arthur Conan Doyle, was born nearby. Otherwise, it's a brisk walk of around twenty minutes plus, or you can travel on from Portobello by bus #12.

### Around the port

While you're most likely to come to Leith for the bars and restaurants, the area itself warrants exploration; though the shipbuilding yards have gone, it remains an active port with a rough-edged character. Most of the showpiece Neoclassical buildings lie on or near **The Shore**, the tenement-lined road along the final stretch of the Water of Leith, just before it disgorges into the Firth of Forth. Note the former **Town Hall** on the parallel Constitution Street, now the headquarters of the local constabulary, immortalized in the tongue twister, "The Leith police dismisseth us". To the west, set back from The Shore, is **Lamb's House**, a seventeenth-century mansion comparable to Gladstone's Land in the Old Town. Built as the home of the prosperous merchant Andro Lamb, it currently functions as an old people's day centre.

Just east of the police station is the start of **Leith Links**, an area of predominantly flat parkland. Documentary evidence suggests that The Links was a golf course in the fifteenth century, giving rise to Leith's claim to be regarded as the birthplace of the sport: in 1744 its first written rules were drawn up here, ten years before they were formalized in St Andrews.

# The Zoo

Edinburgh's **Zoo** (April–Sept Mon–Sat 9am–6pm, Sun 9.30am–6pm; Oct–March Mon–Sat 9am–4.30pm, Sun 9.30am–4.30pm; £4.80) lies three miles west of Princes Street on an eighty-acre site on the slopes of Corstorphine Hill. Here you can see 1500 animals, including a number of endangered species such as white rhinos, red pandas, pygmy hippos and Madagascar tree boas. However, its chief claim to fame is its crowd of penguins (the largest number in captivity anywhere in the world), a legacy of Leith's whaling trade in the South Atlantic. The penguin parade, which takes place daily at 2pm from April to September, and on sunny October days, has gained something of a cult status.

# Lauriston Castle and Cramond

**Lauriston Castle** (40-min guided tours mid-June to mid-Sept Sat–Thurs 11am–5pm; April to mid-June & mid-Sept to end Oct Sat–Thurs 11am–1pm & 2–5pm; Nov–March Sat & Sun 2–4pm; £1.20) is a country mansion set in its own parkland overlooking the Firth of Forth, about five miles west of the centre. The original sixteenth-century tower house forms the centrepiece of what is otherwise a neo-Jacobean structure, which in 1902 became the retirement home of a prosperous local cabinet-maker. He decked out the interior with his private collection of furniture and antiques, which include Flemish tapestries and ornaments made of blue john from Derbyshire. The castle can be reached from the city centre by bus #41.

One mile further west, **CRAMOND** is one of the city's most atmospheric – and poshest – old villages. The enduring image of Cramond is of step-gabled whitewashed houses rising uphill from the waterfront, though it also boasts the foundations of a Roman fort, a medieval bridge and tower house, and a church, inn and mansion, all of the seventeenth century. At low tide it's possible to go across the causeway to the uninhabited **Cramond Island**, a haunt of sea birds.

# Dalmeny

In 1975, Edinburgh's boundaries were extended to include a number of towns and villages which were formerly part of West Lothian. Among them is **DALMENY**, a little west of Cramond and which can be reached directly from the city centre by bus or train. Another option is to take the coastal path from Cramond, which passes through the estate of **Dalmeny House** (May–Sept Sun 1–5.30pm, Mon & Tues noon–5.30pm; £3.40), the seat of the Earls of Rosebery. Built in 1815 by the English architect William Wilkins, it was the first stately home in Scotland in the neo-Gothic style, vividly evoking Tudor architecture in its picturesque turreted roofline, and in its fan vaults and hammerbeam ceilings. The family portraits include one of the fourth Earl (who commissioned the house) by Raeburn, and of the fifth Earl (the last British prime minister to govern from the House of Lords) by Millais; there are also likenesses of other famous society figures by Reynolds, Gainsborough and Lawrence. Among the furnishings are a set of tapestries made from cartoons by Goya, and the Rothschild Collection of eighteenth-century French furniture and *objets d'art*. There's also a fascinating collection of memorabilia of Napoleon Bonaparte – notably some items he used during his exile in St Helena – amassed by the fifth Earl, who wrote a biography of the French dictator.

Dalmeny **village** is a quiet community built around a spacious green. Its focal point is the mid-twelfth-century **St Cuthbert's Kirk**, a wonderful Norman church that has remained substantially intact. Although very weather-beaten, the south doorway is particularly notable for its illustrations of strange beasts. More vivaciously grotesque carvings can be seen inside on the chancel corbels and arch.

# South Queensferry and around

Less than a mile of countryside separates Dalmeny from **SOUTH QUEENSFERRY**, a compact little town used by Saint Margaret as a crossing point for her frequent trips between her palaces in Edinburgh and Dunfermline. The **High Street**, squeezed into the narrow gap between the seashore and the hillside above, is lined by a picturesque array of old buildings, among them an unusual two-tiered row of shops, the roofs of the lower level serving as the walkway for the upper storey.

Everything in South Queensferry is overshadowed, quite literally, by the two great bridges, each about a mile and a half in length, which traverse the Firth of Forth at its narrowest point. The cantilevered **Forth Rail Bridge**, built from 1883 to 1890 by Sir John Fowler and Benjamin Baker, ranks among the supreme achievements of Victorian engineering. Some fifty thousand tons of steel were used in the construction of a design that manages to exude grace as well as might. Derived from American models, the suspension format chosen for the **Forth Road Bridge** makes a perfect complement to the older structure. Erected between 1958 and 1964, it finally killed off the nine-hundred-year-old ferry, and attracts such a heavy volume of traffic that plans are afoot to build yet another bridge. It's well worth walking across its footpath to Fife (see *Central Scotland and Fife*) for the tremendous views of the Rail Bridge.

### Inchcolm

From South Queensferry's Hawes Pier, just west of the Rail Bridge, pleasure boats leave for a variety of cruises on the Forth (July to mid-Sept daily; Easter, May & June Sat & Sun; £5.75; ☎331 4857). Be sure to check in advance as sailings are always subject to cancellation in bad weather.

The most enticing destination is the island of **Inchcolm**, whose beautiful ruined **Abbey** was founded in 1123 by King Alexander I in gratitude for the hospitality he received from a hermit (whose cell survives at the northwestern corner of the island) when his ship was forced ashore in a storm. The best preserved medieval monastic complex in Scotland, the abbey's surviving buildings date from the thirteenth to the fifteenth centuries, and include a splendid octagonal chapter house. Although the church is almost totally delapidated, its tower can be ascended for a great aerial view of the island, which is populated by a variety of nesting birds and a colony of grey seals.

### Hopetoun House

Immediately beyond the western edge of South Queensferry, just over the West Lothian border, **Hopetoun House** (April–Oct daily 10am–5.30pm; £3.50) is one of Scotland's grandest stately homes. The original house was built at the turn of the eighteenth century for the first Earl of Hopetoun by Sir William Bruce, the architect of Holyroodhouse. A couple of decades later, it was engulfed in the enormous extension carried out by William Adam, whose curvaceous main facade and two projecting wings are superb examples of Roman Baroque pomp and swagger. The scale and lavishness of the Adam interiors, most of whose decoration was carried out after the architect's death by his sons, make for a stark contrast with the intimacy of those designed by Bruce. Particularly impressive are the Red and Yellow Drawing Rooms, with their splendid ceilings by the young Robert Adam. Among the house's furnishings are seventeenth-century tapestries, Meissen porcelain, and a distinguished collection of paintings, including portraits by Gainsborough, Ramsay and Raeburn.

# Midlothian

Immediately south of Edinburgh lies the old county of **MIDLOTHIAN**, once called Edinburghshire. It's one of the hilliest parts of the Central Lowlands, with the Pentland chain running down its western side, and the Moorfoots defining its boundary with the Borders to the south. Though predominantly rural, it contains a belt of former mining communities, which are struggling to come to terms with the recent decline of the industry. Such charms as it has are mostly low key, with the exception of the riotously ornate chapel at **Roslin**.

# Dalkeith and around

Despite its Victorian demeanour, **DALKEITH**, eight miles southeast of central Edinburgh – to which it is linked by very regular buses – grew up in the Middle Ages as a baronial burgh under the successive control of the Douglases and Buccleuchs. Today it's a bustling shopping centre, with an unusually broad High Street at its heart.

At the far end of the street is the entrance to **Dalkeith Country Park** (March–Oct daily 10am–6pm; £1.50), the estate of the Dukes of Buccleuch, whose seat, the early eighteenth-century **Dalkeith Palace**, can only be seen from the outside. You can, however, visit its one-time chapel, now the episcopalian parish church of **St Mary**, adorned inside with extremely rich furnishings. Further north, Robert Adam's **Montagu Bridge** straddles the River North Esk in a graceful arch; beyond are some derelict but once wonderfully grandiose garden follies.

A mile or so south of Dalkeith is **NEWTONGRANGE**, whose Lady Victoria Colliery is now open to the public as the **Scottish Mining Museum** (guided tours April–Sept daily 11am–3pm; £1.95), with a 1625-ft-deep shaft, and a winding tower powered by Scotland's largest steam engine. A series of nostalgic tableaux depict everyday life in the community.

# Roslin

The tranquil village of **ROSLIN** lies seven miles south of the centre of Edinburgh, from where it can be reached by city bus #15, or by regular *Eastern Scottish* services from St Andrew Square. An otherwise nondescript place, the village does boast the richly decorated late Gothic **Rosslyn Chapel** (April–Oct Mon–Sat 10am–5pm, Sun noon–5pm; £2). Only the choir, Lady Chapel and part of the transepts were built of what was intended to be a huge collegiate church dedicated to Saint Matthew: construction halted soon after the founder's death in 1484, and the vestry added to the facade nearly four hundred years later is the sole subsequent addition.

The outside of the chapel bristles with pinnacles, gargoyles, flying buttresses and canopies, while inside the foliage carving is particularly outstanding, with botanically accurate depictions of over a dozen different leaves and plants. Among them are cacti and Indian corn, providing fairly convincing evidence that the founder's grandfather, the daring sea adventurer Prince Henry of Orkney, did indeed, as legend has it, set foot in the New World a century before Columbus. The rich and subtle figurative sculptures have given Rosslyn the nickname of "a Bible in stone", though they're more allegorical than literal, with portrayals of the Dance of Death, the Seven Acts of Mercy and the Seven Deadly Sins.

The greatest and most original carving of all is the extraordinary knotted **Prentice Pillar** at the southeastern corner of the Lady Chapel. According to local legend, the pillar was made by an apprentice during the absence of the master mason, who killed him in a fit of jealousy on seeing the finished work. A tiny head of a man with a slashed forehead, set at the apex of the ceiling at the far northwestern corner of the building, is popularly supposed to represent the apprentice, his murderer the corresponding head at the opposite side. The entwined dragons at the foot are symbols of Satan, and were probably inspired by Norse mythology.

## THE EDINBURGH FESTIVAL

Founded in 1947 as a postwar act of faith in the new European order, the **Edinburgh Festival** is the largest cultural jamboree in the world, attracting an estimated million visitors to the city for the last three weeks of August, or the last fortnight of August and the first week of September. Although a vociferous local minority resents the disruption it causes, it now seems as much part of the fabric of Edinburgh as its Castle.

There are several separate festivals. The official **Edinburgh International Festival** is predominantly highbrow, with events performed by established world-class performers. Generally, up to four different themes are chosen to give some cohesion, though these by no means embrace every performance. The **music** programme is centred on piano, chamber and solo vocal recitals, which take place at 11am at the Queen's Hall, and on large-scale orchestral and choral concerts, mostly timed to start at 8pm in the Usher Hall. The **drama**, **opera** and **dance** events kick off at 7.30pm, with frequent matinees. There is usually at least one major **art exhibition** sponsored by the Festival; others are run concurrently but independently by, among others, the National Galleries and the City Arts Centre. The programme is published in April by the Edinburgh International Festival Society, 21 Market St, EH1 1BW (☎255 5756), and bookings begin shortly afterwards. **Prices** are generally reasonable, with low-cost tickets usually available for even the starriest events. All unsold tickets and returns are available from the venue thirty minutes before each performance. In the case of events that are heavily undersubscribed, tickets are sold half-price on the day from a temporary ticket booth at the Mound.

The **Festival Fringe** is a perfect complement to the official Festival. It remains true to its original ideals, whereby performers invite themselves and perform what they please. From the seven theatrical companies which performed in 1947, the Fringe has ballooned to such an extent that it is itself the largest single festival in the world, attracting thousands of performers, from student troupes to national theatre companies. Obviously, standards vary enormously, and many of the unknowns rely on self-publicity – taking to the streets to perform highlights from their show, or pressing leaflets into the hands of every passer-by. Performances go on round the clock: if so inclined, you could sit through twenty shows in a day. The full programme is usually available in June from the Festival Fringe Office, 180 High St, EH1 1QS (☎226 5257). Postal and telephone (☎226 5138) bookings can be made almost immediately afterwards; counter sales begin in early August.

The **Edinburgh Military Tattoo**, an unashamed display of the kilt and bagpipes view of Scottish culture, is held in a splendid setting on the Castle Esplanade. Pipes and drums form the kernel of the programme, with the lone piper towards the end; performing animals, gymnastic and daredevil displays, plus at least one guest regiment from abroad provide variety. Performances are held every weekday evening, and twice on Saturdays. Information and tickets are available from the Tattoo Office, 22 Market St, EH1 1QB (☎225 1188). Postal and telephone bookings can be made from January; the counter opens in early July.

The programme for the one-week **Edinburgh International Jazz Festival**, which begins at the same time as the Tattoo, is published about a month before the event and is available from the office at 116 Canongate, EH8 8DD (☎557 1642). The **Edinburgh International Film Festival** takes place during the first two weeks of the official Festival and Fringe, and features interviews and discussions with top directors, in addition to screenings. Tickets and information are available from the main venue, The Filmhouse, 88 Lothian Rd, EH3 9BZ (☎228 4051). The programme is usually ready by late June, when bookings start.

Held in odd-numbered years only, the **Edinburgh Book Festival** runs for roughly the same dates as the Film Festival, in the gardens of Charlotte Square. Hundreds of established authors from throughout the English-speaking world come to take part in readings, lectures, panel discussions and audience question-and-answer sessions. For further information, contact the Scottish Book Centre, 137 Dundee St, EH11 1BG (☎228 5444). Day tickets are available at the gate if you simply want to wander around; admission to specific events can be reserved in advance by post or telephone (☎225 1000) from the organizers.

# Cafés and restaurants

You can eat well in Edinburgh at almost any price, choosing from a wide range of cuisines. Although the city has nothing approaching the **café** society of other European capitals, if you fancy a snack, a series of good places serve cakes and sandwiches; for **lunch**, or if you feel like more substantial food, try a greasy fry-up at one of the many reliable diners.

Plenty of places specialize in **traditional Scottish cooking**, using fresh local produce, while the city's ethnic communities, despite their small size, have offered a lot to the **restaurant** scene, including some great **Italian** trattorias, and a host of excellent **Indian** restaurants serving regional dishes. In addition, the adaptation of home-grown ingredients to classic Gallic recipes is something the city does particularly well, resulting in a whole group of fabulous **French** restaurants. **Vegetarians** and vegans are well catered for, and there are plenty of **fish** specialists – seafood fans should make some attempt to get out to **Leith**, whose waterside restaurants serve consistently good food.

In choosing a place to eat, bear in mind that most pubs (which are covered in the following section) serve food, and that many have a restaurant attached. Edinburgh has a fairly high turnover of restaurants – some of impeccable repute have bitten the dust in the past few years – so don't be surprised if one or two of the listings have closed by the time you read this.

## Budget Food: cafés and diners

**Bell's Diner**, 7 St Stephen St (☎225 8116). Unpretentious little diner tucked away in Stockbridge. Good, inexpensive burgers, plus a wide choice of steaks and pancakes.

**Brattesani's**, 85–87 Newington Rd (☎667 5808). Typical Italo-Scottish chippie, with choice of sit-down or carry-out meals. South Side location. Daily 9.30am–midnight.

**Buffalo Grill**, 14 Chapel St (☎667 7427). Charcoal-grilled steaks are the speciality in this popular and busy diner facing the main university campus.

**Café–Patisserie Florentin**, 8–10 St Giles St (☎225 6267). French-style café whose extended opening hours make it a popular late-night rendezvous. Daily 7am–1am.

**Clarinda's**, 69 Canongate (☎557 1888). Spruce olde-worlde café serving home-cooked breakfasts and light lunches.

**Edinburgh Fudge House**, 197 Canongate (☎556 4172). Minimalist place serving snacks, sandwiches and cakes; notable for its huge range of delicious but pricy home-made fudges.

**Kinnell's**, 36 Victoria St (☎220 1150). Light snacks, and Edinburgh's biggest choice of teas and coffees.

**Laigh Kitchen**, 117a Hanover St (☎225 1552). Long-established, homely café with flagstone floor and cast-iron stoves. Good salads and soups, but best known for its wonderful home-baked scones and cakes.

**Lower Aisle**, in the High Kirk of St Giles, High St (☎225 5147). Light lunches in the crypt.

**Netherbow Café**, Netherbow Arts Centre, 43 High St (☎556 9579). Excellent wholefood snacks using produce from the café's own allotment.

**Queen's Hall Café**, 89 Clerk St (☎668 3456). Well-prepared salads, vegetarian dishes, soups and puddings; some decent wines and beers.

**Scottish National Gallery of Modern Art Café**, Belford Rd (☎332 8600). Far more than a standard refreshment stop for gallery visitors: many locals come here for lunch or a snack. Changing daily menu of salads, hot food and home baking. Second branch in the National Portrait Gallery building.

**Terrace Café**, in Royal Botanic Garden (☎552 0616). Superior spot offering stunning views of the city. Changing menu includes hot dishes, sandwiches and cakes.

## Scottish

**Dubh Prais**, 123b High St (☎557 5732). Basement restaurant offering innovative Scottish cuisine at affordable prices. Closed Sun & Mon.

**Howies**, 63 Dalry Rd (☎313 3334). Just beyond Haymarket, a brasserie-style variant of traditional Scottish cooking. Good-value lunch and dinner menus. There's a smaller South Side branch at 75 St Leonard's St (☎668 2917). Closed Mon lunch.

**Jacksons**, 209 High St (☎225 1793). Upmarket restaurant which turns the humble haggis into haute cuisine. Set lunches are among Edinburgh's best bargains at around £5; dinners are nearer £20. Closed Sat & Sun lunch.

**Keepers**, 13b Dundas St (☎556 5707). Game, steak and seafood are the specialities in this New Town basement. Very reasonably priced. Closed Sat lunch & Sun.

**Kelly's**, 46b W Richmond St (☎668 3847). South Side restaurant enjoying virtual cult status among Edinburgh foodies, serving modern Scottish food and scrumptious desserts. Closed Mon lunch & Sun.

**Martin's**, 70 Rose St N Lane (☎225 3106). The emphasis is on organic, unfarmed ingredients – salmon, venison, unpasteurized cheeses – in this long-established restaurant in an unlikely looking back street. Expensive, especially in the evenings. Closed Sun & Mon.

**The Vintner's Rooms**, 87 Giles St, Leith (☎554 6767). Splendid restaurant in a seventeenth-century warehouse. The bar in the cellar has a sombre, candlelit ambience and a coal fire; the ornate Rococo dining room serves expertly prepared food, especially strong on fish and Gallic dishes, using ingredients of the highest quality. Expensive, but well worth it.

**Witchery by the Castle**, 352 Castlehill (☎225 5613.) Tacky Halloween theme, but great Scottish food, especially fish. Set lunch £12.50; otherwise main courses £15 upwards. The wine list runs to some 250 choices.

## French

**L'Auberge**, 58 St Mary's St (☎556 5888). French nouvelle cuisine in a luxurious setting: a bit of a treat. Splurge on *Le Grand Menu Gourmand* at £30.

**La Bagatelle**, 22a Brougham Place (☎229 0869). Fine French food in an authentic atmosphere. Closed Sun.

**Café St Honoré**, 34 Thistle St Lane N W (☎226 2211). Brasserie serving good, inexpensive traditional French cooking, with fabulous pastries and coffee. Closed Sun.

**Chez Jules**, 1 Craigs Close (☎225 7007). Classic French food in fine, no-frills establishment. New Town branch at 61 Frederick St (☎225 7983). Closed Sun.

**La Cuisine d'Odile**, French Institute, 13 Randolph Crescent (☎225 5685). Inexpensive and popular French home-cooking in a West End basement. Lunch only; closed Sat & Sun.

**Le Marché Noir**, 2–4 Eyre Place (☎558 1608). In the Northern New Town, just off Dundas St. Adventurous Provençal menu, excellent wines and friendly hosts. Dinner about £25. Closed Sun.

**Pierre Victoire**, 10 Victoria St (☎225 1721), 38 Grassmarket (☎226 2442), 8 Union St (☎557 8451) and 5 Dock Place, Leith (☎555 6178). This ever-expanding group offers unmistakably French dining at affordable prices. Like the service, the food can be erratic, but is normally superb. Very popular so booking is almost mandatory. Each branch closes either Sun or Mon.

**Le Sept**, Old Fishmarket Close (☎225 5428). Brasserie upstairs and à la carte restaurant downstairs. Walk in and (if necessary) wait for the brasserie, but book for the restaurant.

## Italian

**Caprice Pizzerama**, 327 Leith Walk (☎554 1279). Enormous place, almost exactly halfway between Princes St and Leith. Specializes in giant pizzas baked in a wood-fired oven. Inexpensive.

**Cosmo's**, 58a N Castle St (☎226 6743). Straightforward, delicious Italian cuisine at long-established trattoria. Main courses start at around £10. Closed Sun & Mon.

**Giuliano's**, 18–19 Union Place (☎556 6590). Raucous trattoria across from the Playhouse, much favoured for family and office nights out. Does its best to conjure the full Italian atmosphere. Closes 2.30am.

**Lazio**, 95 Lothian Rd (☎229 7788). Pick of the family-run trattorias on a block appropriately dubbed "spaghetti lane". Moderately priced and particularly handy for a late-night meal after a show in the nearby theatre district. Closes 2am.

**Rafaelli**, 10–11 Randolph Place (☎225 6060). Classy ristorante in backstreet West End setting, with West End prices to match. Closed Sun.

**San Marco**, 107 Mary's Place (☎332 1569). Family-run Stockbridge pasta and pizza joint with fun atmosphere. Good value.

**Tinelli's**, 139 Easter Rd (☎652 1932). Small, moderately priced place, hidden away near the Hibernian FC ground, serving arguably the best North Italian food in Edinburgh. Geared mainly towards carnivores; does some pasta, but no pizza. Closed Sun & Mon.

**Vito's**, 55a Frederick St (☎225 5052). Bustling, quality Italian cooking at mid-range prices with the emphasis on seafood. Closed Sun.

## Spanish

**Igg's**, 15 Jeffrey St (☎557 8184). A Spanish-owned hybrid, offering tapas snacks and Mediterranean dishes, plus traditional Scottish food. Good lunchtime tapas selection for around a fiver. Closed Sun & Mon.

**Parador**, 26 William St (☎225 2973). A convincing mock-up of a Spanish bodega, with full restaurant menu as well as tapas. All-you-can-eat lunchtime buffet £6. Bar and tapas service 2–6.30pm only.

## Swiss

**Alp-Horn**, 167 Rose St (☎225 4787). Fondues, air-dried meats and wonderful desserts in this handy little restaurant just off Charlotte Square. Good value two-course lunches. Closed Sun.

**Denzlers**, 121 Constitution St, Leith (☎554 3268). Although it has moved premises a few times over the years, this has consistently ranked among Scotland's most highly praised restaurants. The ever-innovative menu is constantly changing, and prices are surprisingly reasonable, with most main courses under £10. Closed Sun & Mon.

## Indian

**Indian Cavalry Club**, 3 Atholl Place (☎228 3282). Upmarket, but moderately priced Indian restaurant with a pseudo-Raj decor and mildly spiced food.

**Kalpna**, 2 St Patrick Square (☎667 9890). Outstanding vegetarian restaurant, popular with students, serving authentic Gujarati dishes. On the southern continuation of Nicholson St. Portions are small, but it's inexpensive, especially for the lunch buffet. Closed Sun.

**Lancers**, 5 Hamilton Place (☎332 3444). Afficionados rate the curries at this moderately priced Stockbridge restaurant as the best in Scotland. Primarily Bengali and Punjabi.

**Raj**, 89–91a Henderson St, Leith (☎553 3980). An excellent ethnic alternative to the waterfront brasseries. Moderately priced Bangladeshi and North Indian dishes; few vegetarian choices.

**Shamiana**, 14 Brougham Place (☎229 5578). Established, first-class North Indian and Kashmiri cuisine in a tasteful environment located midway between the Kings and Lyceum theatres. One of the more expensive restaurants in this category, but well worth it.

**Spices**, 110 W Bow (☎225 1028). A spin-off of the long-established Kalpna (see above), but geared towards carnivores. Innovative Indian cooking with a few African choices. All-you-can-eat buffet lunches for around a fiver. Closed Sun.

**Suruchi**, 14a Nicholson St (☎556 6583). Popular establishment introducing genuine South Indian cooking to Scotland for the first time. The emphasis is on rice and vegetables, with a few splendid poultry dishes. Inexpensive; set lunch about £5.

**Verandah**, 17 Dalry Rd (☎337 5828). Predominantly Bangladeshi restaurant near Haymarket. Plain decor and moderately priced food; favourite haunt for visiting showbiz celebrities.

## Chinese and Southeast Asian

**Bamboo Garden**, 57a Frederick St (☎225 2382). Many of Edinburgh's Chinese community gather in this inexpensive place for great *dim sum* on Sunday lunchtime. Get the waiter to explain the choices rather than rely on the limited English-language menu.

**Buntoms**, 9–13 Nelson St (☎557 4344). First Thai restaurant in Scotland, and still as good as any of its competitors.

**Chinese Home Cooking**, 21 Argyle Place (☎229 4404). Tightly packed ground-floor front room in a tenement on the south side of the Meadows. The low-price, high-turnover Cantonese menu and the lack of a drinks licence make it impossible to spend more than a few pounds. Arrive early or book ahead. Evenings only.

**Kweilin**, 19–21 Dundas St (☎557 1752). Sleek Cantonese restaurant, with good food at moderate prices.

**Loon Fung**, 32 Grindlay St (☎229 5757), 2 Warriston Place (☎556 1781). The former, across the street from the Lyceum and the Usher Hall, has a strong line in fresh fish; the latter, something of a trail-blazer for Cantonese cuisine in Scotland, is near the eastern entrance to the Botanics. Both moderately priced.

**Singapore Sling**, 503 Lawnmarket (☎226 2826). Real fire-in-the-stomach inexpensive Singaporean and Malaysian cuisine in modest surroundings just down from the castle.

**Szechuan House**, 12 Leamington Place (☎229 4655). Authentically fiery and inexpensive Szechuan cuisine in basic surroundings near the King's Theatre. Closed Sun.

**Yee Kiang**, 42 Dalmeny St (☎554 5833). Homely little place, on a side street leading east off the middle of Leith Walk. Menu includes wonderful Pekinese specialities, notably duck. Closed Mon.

## North African

**Marrakech**, 30 London St (☎556 7293). Scotland's only Moroccan restaurant, very reasonably priced, dishing up superb and authentic *couscous*, and *tajine* plus a range of soups, superb fresh bread and pastries. Unlicensed, but you can take your own and there's no corkage charge.

**Phenecia**, 55–57 W Nicolson St (☎662 4493). Rockbottom prices at this basic food joint beside the main university campus. Basically Tunisian but draws on a variety of Mediterranean cuisines.

## Mexican

**Tex Mex**, 47 Hanover St (☎225 1796). Authentic, reasonably priced Tex-Mex food.

**Viva Mexico**, 10 Anchor Close (☎226 5145), 50 E Fountainbridge (☎228 4005). Inexpensive restaurants, with plenty of choice for vegetarians, and bargain options at lunchtimes.

## Brasseries

**44**, 44 Candlemaker's Row (☎220 3244). Good for both breakfast and à la carte dinners; reasonable prices.

**Maxies**, 32 West Nicolson St (☎667 0845). Large basement brasserie and wine bar with regular live music. Some vegetarian offerings. Popular with students and staff of nearby university. Closed Sun.

**Ship on the Shore**, 24–26 The Shore, Leith (☎555 0409). The homeliest and least expensive of the waterfront brasseries. Changing range of cask ales.

**The Shore**, 3 The Shore, Leith (☎553 5080). Bar-restaurant with good, moderately priced fish and decent wines. Great views at sunset, and live jazz and folk in the adjoining bar. Closed Sun.

**Skippers**, 1a Dock Place, Leith (☎554 1018). Across the Water of Leith from The Shore, with a vaguely nautical atmosphere and a superb – if expensive – fish-oriented menu that changes according to what's fresh. Closed Sun.

**Waterfront Wine Bar**, 1c Dock Place, Leith (☎554 7427). Housed in the former lock-keeper's cottage with outdoor seating overlooking the waterfront, this popular wine bar/restaurant serves moderately priced fish dishes and good wines.

## Seafood

**Café Royal Oyster Bar**, 17a W Register St (☎556 4124). Splendidly ornate Victorian interior featured in *Chariots of Fire*: look out for the stained-glass windows showing sportsmen. Classic seafood dishes, including freshly caught oysters, served in a civilized, chatty atmosphere. Expensive; be prepared to pay at least £30 for a full meal.
**Oyster Bar**, 10 Burgess St, Leith (☎554 6294), 6a Queen St (☎226 2530), 2 Calton Rd (☎557 2925) and 28 W Maitland St (☎225 3861). Lively, wood-panelled bars with a superb choice of cask beers and moderately priced fresh oysters.

## Vegetarian

**Black Bo's**, 57 Blackfriars St (☎557 6136). Non-meat diner with earthy atmosphere, moderate prices and friendly service. Open after 11pm for drinks only. Closed Sun.
**Helios Fountain**, 7 Grassmarket (☎229 7884). Tiny, unlicensed wholefood cafeteria in a book and crafts shop. Very inexpensive. Closed Sun.
**Henderson's**, 94 Hanover St (☎225 2131). Self-service vegetarian place, with adjacent bar. Freshly prepared hot dishes, plus a great choice of salads, soups, sweets and cheeses. An Edinburgh institution, so arrive early for lunch or be prepared to queue. Closed Sun.
**Pierre Lapin**, 32 W Nicolson St (☎668 4332). Drolly named vegetarian offshoot of the *Pierre Victoire* chain (see above), offering superb-value set menus. Closed Sun.
**Seeds**, 53 W Nicolson St (☎667 8673). Long-standing unlicensed café serving inventive soups, savouries and puddings, and a range of vegan food, to crowds of students from the nearby university.

# Pubs and bars

Many of Edinburgh's **pubs**, especially in the Old Town, have histories that stretch back centuries, while others, particularly in the New Town, are unaltered Victorian or Edwardian period pieces that rank among Edinburgh's most outstanding examples of interior design. Add in the plentiful supply of trendy modern bars, and there's a variety of styles and atmospheres to cater for all tastes. Many honest howffs stay open late, and during the Festival especially, it's no problem to find bars open till at least midnight.

Currently, Edinburgh has three **breweries**, including the giant Scottish and Newcastle (who produce *McEwan's* and *Younger's*). The small independent Caledonian Brewery uses old brewing techniques and equipment to produce some of the best beers in Britain, and there's also the tiny Rose Street Brewery with its own pub.

Edinburgh's main drinking strip is the near-legendary **Rose Street**, a pedestrianized lane of minimal visual appeal tucked between Princes Street and George Street. The ultimate Edinburgh pub crawl is to drink a half-pint in each of its dozen or so pubs – plus the two in West Register Street, its eastern continuation. Most of the **student pubs** are in and around Grassmarket, with a further batch on the South Side, an area overlooked by most tourists. **Leith** has a nicely varied crop of bars, ranging from the roughest type of spit-and-sawdust places to polished pseudo-Victoriana, while two of the city's best and most characterful pubs are further west along the seafront in **Newhaven**.

## The Royal Mile and around

**Deacon Brodie's Tavern**, 435 Lawnmarket. Named after the eighteenth-century city councillor who inspired Stevenson's Jekyll and Hyde, the pub is lined with murals that tell his life story. Busy bars on two floors; good lunches. Open until midnight.

**Doric Tavern**, 15 Market St. Favoured watering hole of journalists from the nearby *Scotsman* building. The downstairs *McGuffie's Tavern* is a traditional Edinburgh howff, while the upstairs restaurant is more of a brasserie-cum-wine bar.

**Ensign Ewart**, 521 Lawnmarket. Cosy, beamed bar with intimate alcoves. Being named after a hero of the Battle of Waterloo, and hung with military prints and paintings, it's appropriate that it's well patronized by members of the Castle garrison. Open until midnight.

**Hebrides Bar**, 17 Market St. Home from home for Edinburgh's Highland community: ceilidh atmosphere with lots of jigs, strathspeys and reels but no tartan kitsch.

**Malt Shovel**, 19 Cockburn St. Dimly lit, comfortable bar with an excellent range of cask beers and single malt whiskies. Pub lunches. Open until midnight Mon–Sat.

## The southern Old Town

**Bannermans**, 212 Cowgate. The best pub in the street, formerly a vintner's cellar, with a labyrinthine interior and good beer on tap. On weekdays, tasty veggie lunches at rockbottom prices; breakfasts available at weekends 11am–4pm. Open till 1am Mon–Sat.

**Bow Bar**, 80 West Bow. Old wood-panelled bar that recently won an award as the best drinkers' pub in Britain. Choose from among nearly 150 whiskies, an almost equally wide range of other spirits, and a changing selection of first-rate Scottish and English cask beers. Closed Sun.

**Cellar No.1**, 2 Chambers St. Lively stone-clad vault that doubles as a restaurant. Excellent wines by bottle or glass. Open until 1am.

**Fiddlers Arms**, 9–11 Grassmarket. Traditional bar serving excellent *McEwan's* 80 shilling. The walls are adorned with forlorn, stringless violins. Open late; closed Sun.

**Greyfriars Bobby**, 34 Candlemaker Row. Long-established favourite with both students and tourists, named after the statue outside. Lunch available.

**Last Drop**, 74–78 Grassmarket. "Drop" refers to the Edinburgh gallows, which were located in front, and whose former presence is symbolized in the red paintwork of the exterior. Cheapish pub food, and, like its competitors in the same block, patronized mainly by students.

**Oddfellows**, 14 Forrest Rd. Hip hangout for students and hard-up fashion victims. An amazing clutter of paraphernalia reflects the building's previous incarnation as a flea market.

**Preservation Hall**, 9 Victoria St. Converted church hall, with attractive bar and gantry. *McEwan's* 80 shilling and *Younger's No. 3* on tap. Open till midnight Mon–Wed, 1am Thurs, Fri & Sat. Closed Sun.

**Sandy Bell's**, 25 Forrest Rd. A folk music institution, hosting regular impromptu sessions. Small but busy with an impressive selection of beers and whiskies.

**Smugglers**, 3 Robertsons Close, Cowgate. Newish pub run for and by students. Specializes in imported beers and unorthodox bar food.

## The New Town

**Abbotsford**, 3 Rose St. Upscale pub whose original Victorian decor, complete with wood panelling and "island bar", is among the finest in the city. Good range of ales, including *Broughton Greenmantle*. Restaurant upstairs serves hearty Scottish food. Closed Sun.

**Café Royal**, 17 W Register St. The pub part of this stylish Victorian restaurant, the *Circle Bar*, is worth a visit for its decor alone, notably the huge elliptical "island" counter and the tiled portraits of renowned inventors. Open until midnight Thurs–Sat.

**Kenilworth**, 152–154 Rose St. Attractive high-ceilinged pub dating from 1899; has something of a gay tradition, though this is declining. Good Alloa beers, especially the *Arrol's* 70 shilling.

**Milne's Bar**, corner Rose St and Hanover St. Cellar bar once beloved of Edinburgh's literati, earning the nickname "The Poets' Pub" courtesy of Hugh MacDiarmid et al. Good range of cask beers, including *McEwan's* 80 shilling. Open Mon–Sat until midnight, Sun 7–11pm.

**Rose Street Brewery**, 55 Rose St. Edinburgh's only micro-brewery, whose equipment can be inspected in the upstairs restaurant; the two beers made there are also on tap in the ground-floor bar.

**Whigham's Wine Cellars**, 13 Hope St. Basement wine bar with French wine and fresh oysters amid lots of stone flagging and catacomb-like booths. Closed Sun; otherwise open till midnight.

## The Northern New Town and Stockbridge

**Baillie Bar**, 2 St Stephen St. Basement bar at corner of Edinburgh's most self-consciously bohemian street. English and Scottish ales, including some from the Caledonian Brewery.

**Kay's Bar**, 39 Jamaica St. Small, civilized one-time wine shop, warmed by a roaring log fire in winter. Fine cask ales. Closed Sun.

**Mathers**, 25 Broughton St. Relaxed, old-fashioned pub which attracts a mixed crowd. The best place in Edinburgh for stout, with *Guinness* and *Murphy's* on tap, as well as the local *Gillespie's*.

## The South Side

**Pear Tree House**, 36 W Nicolson St. Fine bar in eighteenth-century house with courtyard, one of Edinburgh's very few beer gardens. Decent bar lunches; open until midnight Thurs–Sat.

**Southsider**, 3–5 W Richmond St. Genuine local pub with a superb range of draught and imported bottled beers.

**Stewart's**, 14 Drummond St. A South Side institution since the beginning of the century, and seemingly little changed since then; popular with lecturers and students.

## Southwest of the Old Town

**Bennets Bar**, 8 Leven St, Tollcross. Edwardian pub with mahogany-set mirrors and Art Nouveau stained glass. Lunch daily except Sun. Packed in the evening, particularly when there's a show at the King's Theatre next door. Open until midnight Mon–Sat.

**Blue Blazer**, 2 Spittal St. Traditional Edinburgh howff with oak-clad bar and church pews. Closed Sun.

**Braidwood's**, 52 W Port. James Braidwood was the city's first firefighter, and this bar is based in an old Victorian fire station. Lunches recommended. Open until 1am.

**Canny Man's (Volunteer Arms)**, 237 Morningside Rd, Morningside. Atmospheric pub-museum adorned with anything that can be hung on the walls or from the ceiling. Open until midnight Mon–Sat.

## Leith

**Bay Horse**, 63 Henderson St. Elegant Edwardian bar with stained-glass windows and walls lined with black-and-white photographs of old Edinburgh and Leith.

**Central**, 7 Leith Walk. High-ceilinged bar that forms part of the long defunct Leith Central Station. A hardened drinker's den, it's worth visiting for a glimpse of the traditional rough side of Leith's character – one that prevails in spite of recent gentrification.

**Malt and Hops**, 45 The Shore. Real ale pub offering basic bar snacks.

**Port o' Leith**, 58 Constitution St. Good, honest local with nautical theme, much patronized by visiting sailors.

**Tattler**, 23 Commercial St. Pub-restaurant decked out in plush Victorian style. The award-winning bar meals are wonderful: high-quality Scottish food including fish, meat and poultry.

**Todd's Tap**, 42 Bernard St. Intimate pub that dates back to 1775, and is still preserved in its original state with a blazing log fire. Specializes in high-quality cask beers, mostly English.

## Newhaven

**Starbank Inn**, 64 Laverockbank Rd. Fine old stone-built pub overlooking the Forth with a high reputation for cask ales and bar food.

**Ye Olde Peacock Inn**, Lindsay Rd. Serves cheap, homely food, including the best fish and chips in the city. Advance reservations (☎552 8707) are advisable for the main bar and restaurant; otherwise try for a table in the small lounge. Be sure to see the gallery of prints of the pioneering Hill and Adamson calotypes of Newhaven fishwives.

## Elsewhere in the city

**Athletic Arms** (aka **The Gravediggers**), 1 Angle Park Terrace. Out in the western suburbs, near Tynecastle football ground and Murrayfield rugby stadium, the pub's nickname comes from the cemetery nearby. For decades, it has had the reputation of being Edinburgh's best pub for serious ale drinkers.

**Hawes Inn**, Newhalls Rd, S Queensferry. Famous old whitewashed tavern virtually under the Forth Rail Bridge, immortalized by Stevenson in *Kidnapped*. Bar serves a wide range of food and drink; the rambling complex also includes a hotel and upmarket restaurant (☎319 1120).

**Sheep Heid**, 43 The Causeway, Duddingston. Eighteenth-century inn with family atmosphere, making an ideal refreshment stop at the end of a tramp through Holyrood Park. Decent home-cooked meals are available at the bar, more substantial meals in the upstairs restaurant (☎661 1020).

# Nightlife

Inevitably, Edinburgh's **nightlife** is at its best during the Festival (see p.84), which can make the other 49 weeks of the year seem like one long anti-climax. However, by any normal standards, rather than by the misleading yardstick of the Festival, the city has a lot to offer, especially in the realm of **performing arts** and **concerts**.

**Nightclubs** don't offer anything startlingly original, but they serve their purpose, hosting a changing selection of one-nighters, while you can normally hear **live jazz**, **folk** and **rock** every evening in one or other of the city's pubs. For the really big rock events, ad hoc venues – such as the Castle Esplanade, Meadowbank Stadium or the exhibition halls of the Royal Highland Show at Ingliston – are often used.

The best way to find out **what's on** is to pick up a copy of *The List*, a fortnightly listings magazine covering both Edinburgh and Glasgow (£1.20). Alternatively, get hold of the *Edinburgh Evening News*, which appears daily except Sunday: its listings column gives details of performances in the city that day, hotels and bars included. **Tickets** and information on all events are available from the tourist office. Box offices of individual halls and theatres are likewise liberally supplied with promotional leaflets, and some are able to sell tickets for more than one venue.

# Nightclubs

**Buster Browns**, 25 Market St. Once the flashiest of the capital's funk spots, now less glamorous. Open till 3am.

**The Calton Studios**, 24 Calton Rd. Popular nightclub with regular gay night on Sat.

**The Cavendish**, W Tollcross. Packed out roots, ragga and reggae night on Sat.

**Century 2000**, 31 Lothian Rd. Probably the best of Edinburgh's big clubs, converted from a cinema. Open till 3am.

**Finsbury Park**, 3 S St Andrew St. Large lounge bar with small disco above. Open till 4am.

**Madisons**, Greenside Place, above the Playhouse Theatre. Goth rock, indie and subpop. Open till 3am. The *Sandino Club* plays latin dance music.

**Moray House Student Union**, Holyrood Rd. Popular Saturday club nights ranging from 1970s funk to wistful indie.

**Network**, 3 W Tollcross. Standard discotheque beloved of stags and hens. Upstairs in the *Mambo Club*, African rhythms till 3am.

**The Pelican**, 235 Cowgate. Variety of popular club nights in converted warehouse with two bars. Open till 3am.

**Red Hot Pepper Club**, 3 Semple St. Large disco. Open till 2am.

**The Venue**, 15 Calton Rd (☎557 3073). Small, intimate sweaty club popular with up-and-coming indie bands. Also used for a variety of hip one-nighters specializing in house, funk and reggae.

**Wilkie House**, 11 Cowgate. Popular rave spot, open till 4am.

## Gay clubs and bars

**Blue Oyster Club**, 96a Rose Street Lane S. The city's largest gay disco. Open Thurs–Sun 10pm–4am.

**Chapps**, 22 Greenside Place. Gay disco, Weds–Sun until 3am. Bar nightly.

**The Edge**, 37b George St. Regular gay nights at trendy central club.

**Laughing Duck**, 24 Howe St. One of Edinburgh's few predominantly gay bars, in the northern New Town, with regular music and cabaret evenings.

# Live music pubs and venues

**Café Royal**, 17 W Register St. Regular folk nights upstairs in one of the city's most famous bars.

**Negociants**, 45–47 Lothian St. Upstairs brasserie serves breakfast and lunch, plus Belgian fruit beers alongside more conventional booze. Downstairs bar hosts varied live bands. Popular with students. Open until 1am.

**Nicky Tam's**, 4 India Buildings, Victoria St. Very popular bar, especially with students. Dance venue downstairs; open till late.

**Nobles Bar**, 44a Constitution St, Leith. A standard of the local jazz scene, featuring live sessions six days a week in lovely Victorian pub with leaded glass windows and horseshoe bar. All-day Sunday breakfasts.

**Playhouse Theatre**, 18–22 Greenside Place (☎557 2590). Uncomfortable and soulless large concert hall used by hoary rock bands and new teen sensations.

**The Queen's Hall**, 37 Clerk St. Housed in a former church, with some pews still in place, hosting African, funk and rock bands, as well as smaller jazz and folk concerts.

**Rutland No.1**, 1 Rutland Place. Young, loud and fashionable venue with comfortable downstairs bar. Live music in the basement. Open till 2am.

# Theatre and comedy

**Assembly Rooms**, 54 George St (☎226 2428). Varied complex of small and large halls. Used all year, but really comes into its own during the Fringe, with large-scale drama productions and mainstream comedy.

**Bedlam Theatre**, 2a Forrest Rd (☎225 9893). Used predominantly by student groups and housed in a converted Victorian church.

**Festival Theatre**, Nicholson St. Due to open in summer 1994, the Festival Theatre will at long last provide the International Festival with a home of its own, ending the city's embarrassing lack of a venue suitable for staging grand opera and other theatrical spectaculars.

**Gilded Balloon Theatre**, 233 Cowgate (☎226 6550). Fringe festival comedy venue, noted for the Late 'n' Live (1–4am) slot which gives you the chance to see top comedians whose main show elsewhere may be booked out.

**King's Theatre**, 2 Leven St (☎228 5955). Stately Edwardian civic theatre that offers the most eclectic programme in the city: including opera, ballet, Shakespeare, pantomime and comedy.

**Leith Theatre**, 28 Ferry Rd (☎554 1508). The former Leith Town Hall, a regular standby for all kinds of performances, although the poor acoustics mean it is less used than it once was.

**Netherbow Arts Centre**, 43 High St (☎556 2647). Although the centre is run by the Church of Scotland, the emphasis in their adventurous year-round drama productions is more Scottish than religious.

**Playhouse Theatre**, 18–22 Greenside Place (☎557 2590). The most capacious theatre in Britain, formerly a cinema. Great venue for musicals and rock concerts.

**Pleasance Theatre**, 60 The Pleasance (☎556 6550). Fringe festival venue. Cobbled courtyard with stunning views across to Arthur's Seat and an array of auditoria used for a varied programme.

**Royal Lyceum Theatre**, 30 Grindlay St (☎229 9697). Fine Victorian civic theatre with compact auditorium. The city's leading year-round venue for mainstream drama.

**St Bride's Centre**, 10 Orwell Terrace (☎346 1405). Neo-Gothic church converted into an intimate stage that can be adapted for theatre in the round.

**Theatre Workshop**, 34 Hamilton Place (☎226 5425). Enticing programmes of international innovative theatre and performance art all year.

**Traverse Theatre**, 10 Cambridge St (☎228 1404). A byword in experimental theatrical circles, and unquestionably one of Britain's premier venues for new plays. Going from strength to strength in its new custom-built home beside the Usher Hall.

# Concert halls

**Queen's Hall**, 89 Clerk St (☎668 2019). Converted Georgian church with a capacity of around 800, though many seats have little or no view of the platform. Home base of both the Scottish Chamber Orchestra and Scottish Ensemble, and much favoured by jazz, blues and folk groups. Also hosts established comedians during the Fringe.

**Reid Concert Hall**, Bristo Square (☎650 4367). Narrow, steeply pitched Victorian hall owned by the university.

**St Cecilia's Hall**, corner of Cowgate and Niddry St (☎650 2805). A Georgian treasure that is again university-owned and not used as frequently as it deserves.

**Usher Hall**, corner of Lothian Rd and Grindlay St (☎228 1155). Edinburgh's main civic concert hall, seating over 2500. Excellent for choral and symphony concerts, but less apt for solo vocalists. The upper circle seats are cheapest and have the best acoustics; avoid the back of the grand tier and the stalls, where the sound is muffled by the overhanging balconies.

# Film

**Cameo**, 38 Home St (☎228 4141). Reruns and late nighters.

**Dominion**, 18 Newbattle Terrace (☎447 4771). Latest releases.

**Filmhouse**, 88 Lothian Rd (☎228 2688). Edinburgh's trendiest cinema.

**Odeon**, 7 Clerk St (☎667 7331). Five-screen cinema showing latest releases.

# Shopping

Despite the relentless advance of the big chains, central Edinburgh remains an enticing place for **shopping**, with many of its streets having their own distinctive character. **Princes Street**, though dominated by standard chain outlets, retains a number of independent emporia. At the eastern end is the **Waverley Market**, a glossy mall of specialist shops, while the middle section of **Rose Street** to the rear has a good array of small jewellers and trendy clothes shops. Along the **Royal Mile** there are several distinctly offbeat places among the tacky souvenir sellers, and in and around **Grassmarket** you'll find antique and arts and crafts shops plus some antiquarian booksellers. The main concentration of general, academic and remainder bookshops is in the area stretching from **South Bridge** to **George IV Bridge**.

The listings below place the emphasis on Scottish goods.

**Bagpipes** *Bagpipe Centre*, 49 Blackfriars St (☎557 3090); *Clan Bagpipes*, 13a James Court, Lawnmarket (☎225 2415); *Gillanders and McLeod*, 103 Whitehouse Loan, Bruntsfield (☎447 8863); *William Sinclair & Son*, 1 Madeira St, Leith (☎554 3489).

**Crafts** *Scotch House*, 39–41 Princes St (☎556 1252); *Scottish Experience*, 12 High St (☎557 9350).

**Food** *Baxters*, 122–124 Rose St (☎226 2202); *T.G. Willis*, 135 George St (☎225 2101).

**Haggis** *Charles MacSween & Son*, 130 Bruntsfield Place (☎229 1216) has an international reputation. Also makes a tasty vegetarian alternative.

**Tartan** *Kinloch Anderson*, corner of Commercial St and Dock St, Leith (☎555 1390). *James Pringle Woollen Mill*, 70 Bangor Rd, Leith (☎553 5161) has an archive computer which tells you if you're entitled to wear a clan tartan, and will give full historic information. *Geoffrey (Tailor)*, 57–59 High St (☎557 0256) and *Celtic Craft Centre*, 101 High St (☎556 3228) are two of many similar places on the Royal Mile.

**Tweed** *Romanes and Paterson*, 62 Princes St (☎225 4966) has tweeds, tartans and woollens.

**Whisky** *Lambert Brothers*, 9–11 Frederick St (☎225 4642); *Royal Mile Whiskies*, 379–381 High St (☎225 3383); *William Cadenhead*, 172 Canongate (☎556 5864).

**Woollen goods** *Bill Baber Knitwear*, 66 Grassmarket (☎225 3249) designs and makes the garments on the premises; *Ragamuffin*, 276 Canongate (☎557 6007) for Skye knitwear; *The Shetland Connection*, 491 Lawnmarket (☎225 3525) and *Simply Shetland*, 9 West Port (☎228 4578) for Shetland knitting wool, lace and cobweb. Further out, but selling splendid wools of all description, is *No. 2*, St Stephen St, Stockbridge.

# Listings

**Airlines** *British Airways*, 32 Frederick St (☎0345 222111). Other carriers handled by *Servisair*, Edinburgh Airport (☎344 3111).

**American Express**, 139 Princes St (☎225 9179).

**Banks** *Bank of Scotland*, The Mound (head office), 38 St Andrew Square, 64 George St, 141 Princes St; *Barclays*, 1 St Andrew Square; *Clydesdale*, 29 George St; *Lloyds*, 113–115 George St; *Midland*, 76 Hanover St; *NatWest*, 80 George St; *Royal Bank of Scotland*, 42 St Andrew Square (head office), 14 George St, 142–144 Princes St, 31 North Bridge; *TSB*, 28 Hanover St.

**Beer festivals** The *Caledonian Brewery*, 42 Slateford Rd runs its own German-style beer festival in June; the *Edinburgh Traditional Beer Festival*, with real ales from all over Britain, is held at Meadowbank Sports Stadium in October.

**Bike rental** *Central Cycles*, 13 Lochrin Place (☎228 6333); *Sandy Gilchrist Cycles*, 1 Cadzow Place (☎652 1760).

**Books** *Bauermeisters*, 19 George IV Bridge (☎226 5561). A row of separate shops (general and academic, music and stationery, paperbacks). *James Thin*, 53–59 South Bridge (☎556 6743) and 57 George St (☎225 4495). The first is a huge, rambling general and academic shop; the latter is smaller and more genteel, with a good café. *Waterstones*, 128 Princes St (☎226 2666), 13–14 Princes St (☎556 3034) and 83 George St (☎225 3436). All host regular literary events.

**Brewery tours** *Scottish and Newcastle*'s *Fountain Brewery*, Fountainbridge (☎229 9377 ext. 3015) offers tours Mon–Thurs at 10.15am and 2.15pm, Fri 10.15am only; £2.50. For morning tours, book directly with the brewery, for afternoon tours, with the main tourist office. In summer, the *Caledonian Brewery*, Slateford Rd (☎337 1286) runs daily tours: phone ahead to reserve a place.

**Car rental** *Arnold Clark*, Lochrin Place (☎228 4747); *Avis*, 100 Dalry Rd (☎337 6363); *Budget*, 111 Glasgow Rd (☎334 7740); *Carnies*, 46 Westfield Rd (☎346 4155); *Europcar*, 24 E London St (☎661 1252); *Hertz*, Waverley Station (☎557 5272); *Mitchells*, 32 Torphichen St (☎229 5384); *Thrifty Car Rental*, 24 Haymarket Terrace (☎313 1613).

**Chemist** *Boots*, 48 Shandwick Place (☎225 6757). Mon–Sat 8.45am–9pm, Sun 11am–4pm.

**Consulates** *Australia*, 80 Hanover St (☎226 6271); *Denmark*, 4 Royal Terrace (☎556 4043); *Germany*, 16 Eglinton Crescent (☎337 2323); *Italy*, 32 Melville St (☎226 3631); *Netherlands*, 113 Dundas St (☎550 5000); *Norway*, 86 George St (☎226 5701); *Poland*, 2 Kinnear Rd (☎552 1086); *Spain*, 63 N Castle St (☎220 1843); *Sweden*, 6 St John's Place (☎554 6631); *USA*, 3 Regent Terrace (☎556 8315).

**Exchange** *Thomas Cook* 79a Princes St (Mon–Fri 9am–5.30pm, Sat 9am–5pm; ☎220 4039); currency exchange bureaux in the main tourist office (Mon–Sat 9am–5.25pm) and in the accommodation office in Waverley Station (see "Arrival and Accommodation"). To change money after hours, try one of the swanky hotels – but expect to pay a hefty commission charge.

**Football** Edinburgh has two Scottish Premier Division teams, who are at home on alternate Saturdays. *Heart of Midlothian* (or *Hearts*) play at *Tynecastle Stadium*, Gorgie Rd, a couple of miles west of the centre; *Hibernian* (or *Hibs*) play at *Easter Road Stadium*, a similar distance east of the centre. Between them, the two clubs dominated Scottish football in the 1950s, but neither has won more than the odd trophy since, though one or the other periodically threatens to make a major breakthrough.

**Gay and lesbian contacts** *Gay Scotland*, 58a Broughton St (☎557 2625); *Gay Switchboard* (☎556 4049); *Lesbian Line* (☎557 0751).

**Genealogical research** *Scots Ancestry Research Society*, 29a Albany St (☎556 4220); *Scottish Geneaology Society*, 15 Victoria Terrace (☎220 3677); *Scottish Roots*, 57–59 High St (☎557 6550).

**Golf** Edinburgh is awash with fine golf courses, but most of them are private. The best public courses are the two on the *Braid Hills* (☎447 6666); others are *Carrick Knowe* (☎337 1096), *Craigentinny* (☎554 7501) and *Silverknowes* (☎336 3843).

**Guided tours** Most recommendable are the *Guide Friday* open-top buses, which depart from Waverley Station and cruise through the streets of the city, allowing you to get off and on at leisure. *Lothian Region Transport* have various coach tours leaving from Waverley Bridge, while several companies along the Royal Mile offer walking tours of the street.

**Helicopter trips** *Lakeside Helicopters*, Old Fire Station, Edinburgh Airport (☎339 2321) offers spectacular aerial sightseeing trips of the city for £39 per person, with a minimum of four people.

**Hospital** 24hr casualty department at the *Royal Infirmary*, 1 Lauriston Place (☎229 2477).

**Left luggage** Lockers available at Waverley Station and St Andrew Square bus station.

**Libraries** *Central Library*, George IV Bridge (Mon–Fri 9am–9pm, Sat 9am–1pm; ☎225 5584). In addition to the usual departments, there's a separate Scottish section, plus an Edinburgh Room which is a mine of information on the city. *National Library of Scotland*, George IV Bridge (Mon–Fri 9.30am–8.30pm, Sat 9.30am–1pm; ☎226 4531) is for research purposes only, though there are no formalities at its *Map Room*, 33 Salisbury Place (Mon–Fri 9.30am–5pm, Sat 9.30am–1pm).

**Maps** *Carson Clark*, 173 Canongate (☎556 4710) has wonderful antique maps, charts and globes. *Map Centre*, 51 York Place (☎557 3011) and the bookshops listed above for up-to-date maps.

**Motoring organizations** *AA*, 18–22 Melville St (☎225 3301); *RAC*, 35 Kinnaird Park (☎657 1122).

**Newspapers** *International Newsagent*, 351 High St (☎225 4827) has the best choice of foreign publications.

**Post office** 2–4 Waterloo Place (Mon–Fri 9.30am–5.30pm, Sat 9.30am–12.30pm; ☎550 8232).

**Rape crisis centre** ☎556 9437.

**Rugby** Scotland's international fixtures are played at *Murrayfield Stadium*, a couple of miles west of the city centre. Casual visitors will find tickets very hard to come by.

**Sports stadium** *Meadowbank Sports Centre and Stadium*, 139 London Rd (☎661 5351), setting for the Commonwealth Games of 1970 and 1986, is Edinburgh's main venue for most spectator and participatory sports. Facilities include an athletics track, a velodrome, and indoor halls.

**Taxis** *Capital Cabs* (☎220 0404), *Castle Cabs* (☎228 2555), *Central Taxis* (☎229 2468), *City Cabs* (☎228 1211).

**Travel agents** *Campus Travel* (student and youth specialist), 53 Forrest Rd (☎668 3303) and 5 Nicolson Square (☎225 6111); *Edinburgh Travel Centre* (student and youth specialist), 196 Rose St (☎226 2019), 92 South Clerk St (☎667 9488) and 3 Bristo Square (☎668 2221).

## travel details

### Trains

**Edinburgh** to: Aberdeen (hourly; 2hr 40min); Aviemore (2 daily; 3hr); Birmingham (6 daily; 4hr 30min); Crewe (6 daily; 3hr 30min); Dundee (hourly; 1hr 45min); Fort William (change at Glasgow; 3 daily; 4hr 55min); Glasgow (38 daily; 50min); Inverness (4 daily; 3hr 50min); Manchester (change at Preston; 6 daily; 3hr 30min); Newcastle upon Tyne (19 daily; 2hr 40min); Oban (change at Glasgow; 3 daily; 4hr 10min); Perth (12 daily; 1hr 15min); Stirling (every 30min; 45min); York (18 daily; 2hr 40min).

### Buses

Edinburgh St Andrew Square bus station to: Aberdeen (13 daily; express 3hr, standard 3hr 50min); Birmingham (2 daily; 6hr 50min); Campbeltown (3 daily; 6hr); Dundee (14 daily; express 1hr 25min, standard 2hr); Fort William (3 daily; 5hr); Glasgow (44 daily; 1hr 10min); Inverness (11 daily; express 3hr, standard 4hr); London (2 daily; 7hr 50min); Newcastle upon Tyne (4 daily; 3hr 15min); Oban (3 daily; 5hr); Perth (14 daily; 1hr 20min); Pitlochry (11 daily; 2hr); York (2 daily; 5hr).

# CHAPTER TWO

# SOUTHERN SCOTLAND

Although **Southern Scotland** doesn't have the high tourist profile of other areas of the country, in some ways the region is at its very heart. Its inhabitants bore the brunt of long wars with the English, its farms have fed Scotland's cities since industrialization, and two of the country's literary icons, **Sir Walter Scott** and **Robbie Burns**, lived and died here. The main roads, the fast routes from northern England to Glasgow and Edinburgh, bypass the best of the region, but if you make an effort to get off the highways, there's plenty to see, from the ruins of medieval castles and abbeys to well-preserved market towns and seaports set within a wild, hilly countryside.

Geographically, Southern Scotland is dominated by the **Southern Uplands**, a chain of flat-peaked hills and weather-beaten moorland punctuated by narrow glens, fast-flowing rivers and blue-black lochs extending south and west from an imaginary line drawn between Peebles and Jedburgh in Central Southern Scotland over to the Ayrshire coast. It's in the west, in **Galloway Forest Park**, that they are at their most dramatic, with peaks soaring over 2000ft, and crisscrossed by many popular **walking** trails.

North of the inhospitable **Cheviot Hills**, which straddle the border with England, a clutch of tiny towns in the **Tweed River Valley** form the nucleus of the windswept **Borders**, inspiration for countless folkloric ballads telling of bloody battles with the English and clashes between the notorious warring families, the Border Reivers. East of **Kelso**, one of four abbeys founded on the Borders by the medieval Canmore kings, the Tweed Valley widens to form the **Merse** basin, an area of tediously flat farmland that boasts a series of grand stately homes, principally **Floors Castle**, **Manderston** and **Mellerstain House**, which features the work of William Adam and his son, Robert.

North of the Tweed, a narrow band of foothills – the **Pentland**, **Moorfoot** and **Lammermuir** ranges – form the southern edge of the Central Lowlands. These Lowlands spread west beyond Edinburgh, but here they constitute the slender coastal plain of **East Lothian**, which rolls down towards a string of fine sandy beaches. Further east, the coastline becomes more rugged, its cliffs and rocky outcrops harbouring a series of ruined castles, and inland, the flatness of the terrain is interrupted by the occasional extinct volcano, inspiration for all sorts of ancient myths.

The gritty town of **Dumfries** is gateway to **Southwest Scotland**, where on the marshy **Solway coast** you can see the magnificent remains of **Caerlaverock Castle**. The **Ayrshire coast** also rewards a visit for its strong associations with Robert Burns, especially at Ayr and **Alloway**, the poet's birthplace.

For **getting around**, there's a **train** line along both coasts, and a good **bus** service between all the major towns and many of the villages, with supplementary tourist buses during the summer. The region is also excellent **walking** country; for the ambitious hiker there's the **Southern Upland Way,** a 212-mile path stretching from Portpatrick on the west to Cockburnspath on the east coast.

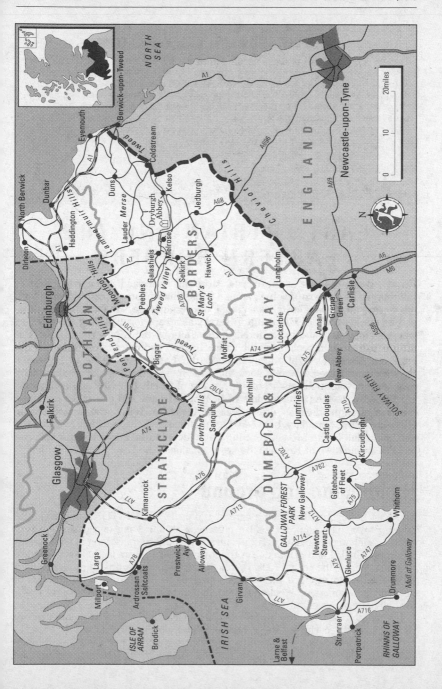

### · ACCOMMODATION PRICE CODES

Throughout this book, accommodation **prices** have been graded with the numbers below, according to the cost of the least expensive double room in high season. The bulk of the recommendations will fall in categories ② to ⑤; recommendations in the highest categories are limited to places that are especially attractive. Bear in mind that many of the swanky hotels often slash their tariffs at the weekend when the business types have gone home, and that many of the cheaper places will also have more expensive rooms. Note that in our accommodation listings price codes are not given for youth hostels – they all come into the lower end of the ① category.

| | | |
|---|---|---|
| ① under £20 | ④ £40–50 | ⑦ £70–80 |
| ② £20–30 | ⑤ £50–60 | ⑦ £80–100 |
| ③ £30–40 | ⑥ £60–70 | ⑧ over £100 |

# EAST LOTHIAN AND THE EASTERN BORDERS

**East Lothian** consists of the coastal strip and hinterland immediately east of Edinburgh. Its western reaches, around Musselburgh, are an easy day-trip from the capital; the remainder takes a couple of overnight stays to explore. The prosperous market town of **Haddington** serves as a base for exploring the interior, whose bumpy farmland is bordered to the south by the Lammermuir Hills. But most people make a beeline for the shore, the fifty-odd miles of coastline extending from **Aberlady** right round through the **Eastern Borders** to England's Berwick-upon-Tweed. There's something for most tastes here, from the sandy beaches and volcanic islets around the resort of **North Berwick** and neighbouring **Dirleton**, to the piercing cliffs of **St Abb's Head,** and a number of ruined medieval strongholds, most dramatically at **Tantallon**. Inland, the **Lammermuir Hills** cross the boundary between East Lothian and the Borders to form the northern edge of the Merse, centring on modest **Duns**. Further south still, the busy Georgian town of **Kelso** is the key attraction of the **Lower Tweed Valley**.

## Haddington and around

The East Lothian gentry keep a careful eye on **HADDINGTON**, their favourite country town. The compact centre preserves an intriguing ensemble of seventeenth- to nineteenth-century architectural styles where everything of any interest has been labelled and plaqued. Yet the town's staid appearance belies an innovative past. During the early 1700s, Haddington became a byword for modernization as its merchants supplied the district's progressive landowners with all sorts of new-fangled equipment, stock and seed, and in only a few decades utterly transformed Lothian agriculture.

Haddington was also the birthplace of **John Knox**, the fiery sixteenth-century religious reformer who led the Protestant assault on Scotland's Catholic Church. He laid the foundations of the Presbyterian movement, but is mainly remembered for his two tracts of 1558 entitled *Blasts of the Trumpet against the*

*Monstruous Regiment of Women*: a specific attack on Mary of Guise, regent of Scotland, Mary, queen of England, and Catherine de Medici. It didn't help him in his dealings with Queen Elizabeth I or Mary Stuart either.

Nowadays, a thorough exploration of Haddington takes two or three hours. Afterwards, consider a visit to **Lennoxlove House**, one of the area's more accessible stately homes, or venture a few miles south to the hamlet of **Gifford** on the edge of the Lammermuir Hills.

## The Town

Haddington's homogeneous centre is best approached from the west, where tree-trimmed **Court Street** ends suddenly with the stately stonework and dignified Venetian windows of the **Town House**, designed by William Adam in 1748. Close by, next door to a fine Italianate facade, the **Jane Welsh Carlyle House** (April–Sept Wed–Sat 2–5pm; 75p), childhood home of the wife of the essayist and historian Thomas Carlyle, has been restored to its early eighteenth-century appearance. Carrying straight on, the **High Street** is distinguished by its pastel-painted gables and quaint pends, a tad prettier than those in neighbouring **Market Street**. Keep an eye open, however, for **Mitchell's Close** on Market Street, a recently restored seventeenth-century close with crow-stepped gables, rubble masonry and the narrowest of staircase-towers.

Leaving the town centre to the east along High Street, it's a brief walk down Church Street – past the angular **Nungate Bridge** – to the hulking mass of **St Mary's Church**. Built close to the reedy River Tyne, the church dates from the fourteenth century, but it's a real hotch-potch of styles, the squat grey tower uneasy above clumsy buttressing and pinkish-ochre stone walls. Inside on the **Lauderdale Aisle** a munificent tomb features the best of Elizabethan alabaster carving, moustachioed knights and their ruffed ladies lying beneath a finely ornamented canopy. In stark contrast, a plain slab nearby is inscribed with Thomas Carlyle's beautiful tribute to his wife, who died on April 21, 1866.

## Practicalities

Fast and frequent **buses** connect Haddington with Edinburgh, fifteen miles to the west, and North Berwick on the east coast. All services stop on High Street. There's no **tourist office**, but orientation is easy and *A Walk around Haddington* (£1), detailing every building of any conceivable consequence, is available from local newsagents.

If you decide to **stay** the night, a clutch of central **B&Bs** include *Mrs Russell*, 4 High St (☎062082/2461; ②) and *Mrs Richards*, 19 Church St (☎062082/5663; ②). The *George Hotel*, High St (☎062082/3372; ④), is a reasonable alternative, whilst the luxurious *Browns' Hotel*, 1 West Rd (☎062082/2254; ⑦), occupies a fine Regency town house. **Monksmuir Caravan Park** (all year; ☎062086/0340), on the edge of town by the A1, also takes tents.

For **food**, *Defoe's*, inside the *George Hotel*, has a splendid display of mouth-watering cakes, while *The Carlyle* tea shop, across the street, serves good sandwiches. The best place for an evening meal is in the *Browns' Hotel* restaurant, where dinner is served at 7.30 each evening; or try the *Waterside Bistro*, on the far side of Nungate Bridge.

## Lennoxlove House and Gifford

One mile south of Haddington, rusticated **Lennoxlove House** (May–Sept Wed, Sat & Sun 2–5pm; £2) boasts much of the fine and applied art collection of the Duke of Hamilton. The hour-long tour takes in the usual oligarchic trappings – portraits of the family and their allies, French furniture, fancy porcelain and damask wall hangings – more unusual is the death mask of Mary, Queen of Scots, in the Great Hall.

A further three miles south along the B6369 lies tiny **GIFFORD**, whose tidy, eighteenth-century estate cottages slope up to a trim whitewashed church. The Reverend John Witherspoon, a signatory of the American Declaration of Independence, was born in the adjacent manse in 1723. Several footpaths set out across the surrounding red-soiled farmland for the burns, laws and moors of the Lammermuir Hills. Longer trails connect with the Southern Upland Way (see p.98).

Gifford has one good **B&B**, *Buffers*, Station Rd (April–Oct; ☎062081/455; ③), plus a brace of **hotels**: the garish *Goblin Ha'* (☎062081/244; ⑤) or the more traditional *Tweeddale Arms* (☎062081/240; ⑥).

# The east coast

Skirting the southern shore of the Firth of Forth before curving down along the North Sea Coast, that fifty-mile section of the **east coast** we've set apart from Edinburgh begins at **ABERLADY**, an elongated village just sixteen miles from the capital. Aberlady served as Haddington's port until its river silted up in the sixteenth century, and the pricy stained-glass windows of the **medieval church** act as a reminder of wealthier times. The salt marshes and sand dunes of the adjacent **Aberlady Bay Nature Reserve**, a bird watchers' haven, mark the site of the old harbour. From the reserve, it's a couple of miles to the modern villas and hotels of **GULLANE**, a disappointing location for the famous shoreline links of **Muirfield Golf Course**.

Things improve two miles east of Gullane with the genteel hamlet of **DIRLETON**, where a pair of triangular greens are bordered by tastefully restored cottages with thriving gardens. **Dirleton Castle** (April–Sept Mon–Sat 9.30am–6pm, Sun 2–6pm; Oct–March Mon–Sat 9.30am–4pm, Sun 2–4pm; £1.70) has lovely gardens too, leading to a volcanic knoll crowned by the Cromwell-shattered ruins. Scrambling round the castle is fun, and, if the weather's good, you can take the mile-long path from the church to the sandy beach. On the way, the **Yellowcraig Caravan Club Site** (April–Sept; ☎062085/217) is the only budget place to **stay**; the splendid *Open Arms Hotel* opposite the castle (☎062085/241; ⑨), on the other hand, has every luxury, including a fantastic restaurant serving moderate to expensive dinners from a varied and imaginative menu.

## North Berwick

**NORTH BERWICK** has an old-fashioned air, its guest houses and hotels extending along the shore in all their Victorian and Edwardian sobriety. Set within sight of two volcanic heaps – the **Bass Rock** and **North Berwick Law** – the resort's pair of wide and sandy **beaches** are the main attraction. These fall either side of a narrow headland-harbour that's an extension of the short main street, Victoria Road, itself an extension of Quality Street.

Little now remains of the original medieval town, but the fragmentary ruins of the **Auld Kirk**, next to the harbour, bear witness to one of the most extraordinary events of sixteenth-century Scotland. In 1590, while **King James VI** spent the summer in Denmark wooing his prospective wife, Francis Stuart, **Earl of Bothwell**, was plotting against him. On hearing of the king's imminent return, Bothwell, a keen practitioner of the "black arts", summoned the witches of Lothian to meet the Devil in the Auld Kirk. Bothwell turned up disguised as the Devil and instructed his two hundred acolytes to raise a storm that would shipwreck the king. To cast the spell, they opened a few graves and engaged in a little flagellation before kissing the bare buttocks of the "Devil" – reportedly "as cold as ice and as hard as iron" as it hung over the pulpit. Despite all these shenanigans, the king returned safely – when rumours reached him of Bothwell's treachery he refused to believe them, and the earl went unpunished, possibly because James was reassured by his failure. After all, if the Devil himself was unable to harm him, he must surely be blessed by God, a belief the monarch was later to elaborate as the "Divine Right of Kings".

## Bass Rock

Resembling a giant molar, the **Bass Rock** rises 350ft above the sea some three miles east of North Berwick. This massive chunk of basalt, formerly a prison, fortress and monastic retreat, is home to millions of nesting seabirds – among them razorbills, terns, puffins, guillemots, fulmars and gannets. Weather permitting, there are regular ninety-minute **boat trips** round the island from North Berwick harbour (Easter to early Oct daily 2–4pm; £3.20), but only Fred Marr (☎0620/2838) has landing rights: he charges £10 for an excursion that allows about four hours on the rock. It's not to everyone's taste: as William Dunbar, a fifteenth-century poet, described it,

> *The air was dirkit with the fowlis*
> *That cam with jammeris and with youlis*
> *With shrykking, shrieking, skyrmming scowlis*
> *And meikle noyis and showtes.*

## North Berwick Law

The other volcanic monolith, 613-foot-high **North Berwick Law**, is about an hour's walk from the beach: take Law Road off the High Street and follow the signs. On a clear day, the views out across the Firth of Forth make the effort worthwhile, and at the top you can see the remains of a Napoleonic watchtower and an arch made from the jawbone of a whale.

## Practicalities

It's ten minutes' walk east from North Berwick **train station**, with its frequent services from Berwick-upon-Tweed and Edinburgh, to the town centre along Abbey Road, Westgate and High Street. **Buses** from Edinburgh stop on the High Street and those from Haddington and Dunbar outside the **tourist office** on Quality Street (mid-April to May Mon–Sat 9am–6pm; June–Sept Mon–Sat 9am–6pm, Sun 11am–6pm; Oct to mid-April Mon–Thurs 9am–5pm, Fri 9am–4pm; ☎0620/2197). Here you can buy town maps, and, for a £1 booking fee, arrange accommodation; particularly useful in the height of summer.

There are several excellent **B&Bs** open from April to September. These include *Mrs Duns*, 20 Marmion Rd (☎0620/2066; ②), *Mrs McQueen*, 5 W Bay Rd (☎0620/4576; ②), and *Mrs Strachan*, 17 Beach Rd (☎0620/2241; ③). Out of season, try *Mrs Ralph*, 13 Westgate (☎0620/2782; ②), or *Mrs Gray*, 12 Marine Parade (☎0620/2884; ③). Alternatively, *Craigview*, 5 Beach Rd (☎0620/2257; ③), is a well-maintained **guest house**, and *Point Garry*, W Bay Rd (April–Oct; ☎0620/2380; ⑥), an upmarket **hotel**. The nearest **campsite**, *Rhodes Caravan Site* (April–Oct; ☎0620/3348), occupies a prime clifftop location a couple of miles east of the centre – take the Dunbar bus (Mon–Sat 6 daily, Sun 2 daily).

Several little places, such as *Ricky's*, Quality St, and *Buttercup*, High St, sell cheap **food**, but for an evening meal, try *Harding's*, 2 Station Rd (☎0620-4737; Wed–Sat only), which serves good food and wine from a daily changing menu.

# East of North Berwick

The melodramatic ruins of **Tantallon Castle** (April–Sept Mon–Sat 9.30am–6pm, Sun 2–6pm; Oct–March Mon–Wed & Sat 9.30am–4pm, Thurs 9.30am–noon, Sun 2–4pm; £1.70), three miles east of North Berwick, stand on the precipitous cliffs facing the Bass Rock. This pinkish sandstone edifice, with its imposing cylindrical towers, protected the powerful "Red" Douglases, Earls of Angus, from their enemies for over three hundred years, providing a secure base at the southern entrance to the Firth of Forth that was the envy of their rivals. With a sheer drop down to the sea on three sides and a sequence of moats and ditches on the fourth, the castle's desolate invincibility is daunting, especially when the wind howls over the remaining battlements and the surf crashes on the rocks far below. In fact, the setting is more striking than the ruins: Cromwell's army savaged the castle in 1651 and only the impressive fifty-foot-high and fourteen-foot-thick curtain wall has survived relatively intact. To reach Tantallon Castle from North Berwick, a fifteen-minute trip, take the Dunbar **bus** (Mon–Sat 6 daily, Sun 2 daily).

There's little to see at down-at-heel **DUNBAR**, twelve miles from North Berwick, though the double **harbour** remains a delightfully intricate affair of narrow channels, cobbled quays and roughened rocks, set beside the shattered remains of the once mighty castle. Incidentally, **John Muir**, the explorer and naturalist who created the United States national park system, was born in Dunbar, and his boyhood home, on the High Street, has been turned into a tiny **museum** (June–Sept Mon–Sat 11am–1pm & 2–5.30pm; Sun 2–5.30pm; free).

Good **bus** and **train** connections mean there's no reason to get stuck here, but if you do the **tourist office** on the High Street (mid-April to Sept Mon–Sat 9am–6pm, June–Sept also Sun 11am–6pm; Oct to mid-April Mon–Thurs 9am–5pm, Fri 9am–4pm; ☎0368/63353) will help with accommodation. For **food**, try the *William Smith Coffee Shop*, High St, or *The Cromwell* pub and bistro beside the harbour.

# St Abb's Head

Heading south from Dunbar, it's nine miles to tiny Cockburnspath where the Southern Upland Way reaches the coast. Nearby, the A1167/A1107 cuts off the main road for **ST ABBS**, a remote fishing village stuck onto the steepest of seashores. Flanked by jagged cliffs, St Abbs has a dramatic setting, but still manages to look a little grubby. Its redeeming feature is its proximity to **St Abb's Head Nature Reserve**, reached from the tea room and car park just half a mile back along the road. Owned by the National Trust for Scotland, this comprises two hundred acres of wild and rugged coastline with sheer, seabird-encrusted cliffs rising 300ft above the water. The main walking trail ends at the lighthouse, a mile or so from the car park, but it's possible to continue another three miles along the coast to the dramatically sited ruins of **Fast Castle**.

Three to four times daily the Dunbar to Berwick-upon-Tweed **bus** passes through Coldingham, where a **taxibus** service connects to St Abbs, a mile away. Buses south from St Abbs to Eyemouth run hourly. Coldingham has a **youth hostel** (April–Sept; ☎08907/71298; Grade 2); the best place to stay in St Abbs is the **Castle Rock Guest House**, with fine views out along the coast (Easter–Oct; ☎08907/71715; ③).

## Eyemouth

Almost the entire three and a half thousand population of **EYEMOUTH**, a few miles south of St Abbs, is dependent on the fishing industry. Consequently, the town's slender harbour is very much the focus of activity, its waters packed with deep sea and in-shore fleets and its quays strewn with tatters of old net, discarded fish and blood-spattered fish crates. If you want to get a feeling for the rough, macho edge that underpins this tight-knit community, pop into one of the harbourside pubs after a catch has been landed: try *The Whale Inn* or the *Contented Sole*.

Eyemouth's tiny centre, to the west of the harbour, is drearily modern, despite the town's medieval foundation. The **Eyemouth Museum**, in the Auld Kirk on the Market Place (April–June & Oct Mon–Sat 10am–4pm or 5pm; July & Aug Mon–Sat 9.30am–6pm, Sun 1–5.30pm; Sept Mon–Sat 10am–5pm, Sun 2–3.30pm; £1) is just about worth a visit for the **Eyemouth Tapestry**, commemorating the east coast fishing disaster of 1881 when a freak storm destroyed most of the in-shore fleet: 129 local men were lost, a tragedy of extraordinary proportions for a place of this size. Nearby, in the old **cemetery**, a stone memorial surmounted by a broken mast also pays tribute to the dead.

The elegant **Gunsgreen House**, standing alone on the far side of the harbour, was designed by Robert Adam in the 1750s. Despite its respectable appearance, in keeping with its present use by the golf club, the house was once used by smugglers, with secret passages and underground tunnels leading back into town. This illicit trade in tobacco and booze peaked in the eighteenth century, with local fishermen using their knowledge of the coast to regularly outwit the excise.

In the unlikely event you'll want to stay **overnight**, the **tourist office** (April–Oct; ☎08907/50678) has a small cache of **B&Bs**. Or you could try *The Hermitage*, Paxton Terrace (April–Sept; ☎08907/50324; ②). Leaving town, regular **bus** services run north along the coast and south across the border to Berwick-upon-Tweed, eight miles away.

# Duns, the Lammermuir Hills and Lauder

Heading inland from Eyemouth, the B6355 and then the A6105 cross the fertile farmland of the Merse to the little visited market town of **DUNS**. Jim Clark, the farmer-turned-motor racing ace, was born here and the **Jim Clark Room**, 44 Newtown St (Easter–Oct Mon–Sat 10am–1pm & 2–5pm, Sun 2–5pm; 50p) celebrates a brilliant career that ended with his death on the track at Hockenheim in

Germany in 1968. There's little else to do in Duns, but it's only twenty minutes' walk to the top of **Duns Law**: take Duns Castle Avenue and follow the signs. Most people make the trek up to the 714-foot-high summit for the view, some to see the **Covenanters' Stone**, marking the spot where Alexander Leslie's army camped in 1639. Leslie assembled his troops on the Law to watch for Charles I's mercenaries, who had been sent north to crush the Covenanters. In the event, the royalist army faded away without even forcing a battle, and the king, by refusing to accept defeat, took one more step towards the Civil War.

Duns is well connected by **bus** to all the major settlements of the east Borders, so you don't have to stay the night. However, the town does have half a dozen **B&Bs**, such as the centrally sited, *St Albans*, Clouds (☎0361/83285; ②). For a **drink** and a snack, try the *Whip and Saddle* pub in the main square.

### Around Duns: Manderston House

**Manderston House** (early May to Sept Thurs & Sun 2–5.30pm, plus some bank holidays; £3.90), two miles east of Duns on the A6105, is the very embodiment of Edwardian Britain. Between 1871 and 1905, the Miller family spent most of their herring and hemp fortune on turning their home into a prestigious country house, with no expense spared as architect John Kinross added entire suites of rooms in the Classical Revival style. It's certainly a staggering sight, from the intricate plasterwork ceilings to the inlaid marble floor in the hall and the extravagant silver staircase, the whole lot sumptuously furnished with trappings worthy of a new member of the aristocracy: James Miller married Eveline Curzon, the daughter of Lord Scarsdale, in 1893. When you've finished inside the house, stroll round the fifty-odd acres of garden, noted for their rhododendrons and azaleas.

# The Lammermuir Hills and Lauder

Leaving Duns to the north, it's about three miles to the edge of the **Lammermuir Hills**, a slender, east–west chain whose flat-topped summits and quiet streams are a favourite haunt of ramblers. The hills are criss-crossed with footpaths, some of which follow ancient carting and droving trails as they slice from north to south. In the other direction, tracking along the body of the Lammermuirs between Lauder in the west and Cockburnspath on the coast, is the **Southern Upland Way**. If you're keen to sample a portion, turn off the B6355 down the minor road to **Abbey St Bathans**, a hamlet beside the Whiteadder Water, where a pretty and undemanding ten-mile stretch of the trail leads down to the sea. Or you could carry on up to East Lothian's Gifford (see p.102), some twelve miles from Duns on the other side of the Lammermuirs.

It is also easy to join the Southern Upland Way on the western edge of the Lammermuir Hills in **LAUDER**, a grey market town twenty miles west of Duns on the A68. Lauder's only attraction is **Thirlestane Castle** (May, June & Sept Wed, Thurs & Sun 2–5pm; July & Aug Mon–Fri & Sun 2–5pm; £3), an imposing pile on the eastern edge of town: take the signposted footpath from Castle Wynd, just off the High Street. Owned by the Maitland family since the sixteenth century, the castle has been refashioned and remodelled on several occasions, but its impressive reddish turrets and castellated towers appear a cohesive whole nevertheless. The interior is disappointing, with little to see beyond the delicate plasterwork of the Restoration ceilings: most of the original furnishings were carted off to London in the 1840s to be replaced by inferior Victoriana.

# The Lower Tweed Valley

Rising in the hills far to the west, the River Tweed snakes its way across the Borders until it reaches the North Sea at Berwick-upon-Tweed. The eastern reaches of the river, constituting the **Lower Tweed Valley**, run from Kelso to the coast and for the most part form the boundary between Scotland and England. This is a gentle, rural landscape of farmland and wooded river banks where the occasional military ruin, usually on the south side of the border, serves as a reminder of more violent days. For the English, the east Borders were the quickest land route to the centre of Scotland and time and again they launched themselves north destroying everything in their way. Indeed, the English turned Berwick-upon-Tweed into one of the most heavily guarded frontier towns in northern Europe, and the massive fortifications survive today. The region also witnessed one of the most devastating of medieval battles when the Scots, under James IV, were decimated at **Flodden Field** in 1513. The heavily armoured Scottish noblemen got stuck in the mud at the bottom of a hill near Branxton, south of the border near Coldstream, and their over-long pikes and lances were simply no match for the shorter and sturdier English halberds.

Nowadays, the Lower Tweed Valley has one town of note, **Kelso**, a busy agricultural centre distinguished by the Georgian elegance of its main square and its proximity to a pair of stately homes. Perhaps surprisingly, Kelso is often visited for its abbey, even though the ruins of the colossal twelfth-century foundation, whose abbots claimed precedence over St Andrews, are scant indeed.

# Coldstream

Battered and bruised by traffic, tiny **COLDSTREAM** sits tight against the Tweed, its long main street part of the trunk road linking Newcastle across the border and Edinburgh. The town's only claim to fame is its association with the **Coldstream Guards**. General George Monck billeted his Cromwellian soldiers here in the winter of 1659–60, just before they were persuaded to discard their parliamentary allegiance and march on London to restore Charles II to the throne. Monck's regiment was thereafter recognized as the "Coldstream Guards" and the general became the first Duke of Albemarle – a handsome pay off for his timely change of heart. Oddly enough, in the sort of detail beloved of military historians, the Coldstreamers still sport the crownless tunic buttons they first wore as part of Cromwell's Model Army. The regiment's deeds are recorded in the **Coldstream Museum** (Easter–Oct Mon–Sat 10am–1pm & 2–5pm, Sun 2–5pm; 50p), on the Market Square, just off the High Street.

### Practicalities

Coldstream's **tourist office**, on the High Street near the obelisk (April–June & Sept Mon–Sat 10am–5pm, Sun 2–4pm; July & Aug Mon–Sat 10am–6pm, Sun 2–6pm; Oct Mon–Sat 10am–12.30pm & 1.30–4.30pm; ☎0890/882607), has a comprehensive supply of brochures and booklets on the Borders region as well as a list of **B&Bs**. The best of these is the beautifully kept Victorian villa, *Iolair*, on Victoria St, a side road about halfway along the High Street (☎0890/882084; ④). A cheaper alternative is *Pear Tree House*, 78 High St (☎0890/882452; ②). There is also a **campsite** (April–Sept; ☎0890/882333) in a field beside the Leet Water, a tributary of the Tweed, a couple of minutes' walk from the Market

Square. For **food**, try the *Besom Inn*, on the High Street at the foot of Victoria Street.

# Kelso and around

Compact **KELSO**, at the confluence of the Tweed and Teviot, grew up in the shadow of its abbey, once the richest and most powerful in Southern Scotland. The abbey was founded in 1128 during the reign of King David (1124–53), whose policy of encouraging the monastic orders had little to do with spirituality. The bishops and monks David established here, as well as at Melrose, Jedburgh and Dryburgh, were the frontiersmen of his kingdom, helping to advance his authority in areas of doubtful allegiance. This began a long period of relative stability across the region which enabled its abbeys to flourish, until frequent raids by the English, who savaged Kelso three times in the early sixteenth century, in 1522, 1544 and 1545. The last assault – part of the "Rough Wooing" led by the Earl of Hertford when the Scots refused to ratify a marriage treaty between Henry VIII's son and the infant Mary Stuart – was the worst, and the abbey never recovered. Such was the extent of the devastation – a combination of the raids and the Reformation – that the surviving ruins of **Kelso Abbey** (April–Dec Mon–Sat daylight hours, Sun afternoons; Jan–March ask for key at the tourist office; free) are disappointing: little more than a heavy central tower and supporting buttresses and scant memorial to the massive Romanesque original that took over eighty years to build. Just behind the abbey, notice the **Old Parish Church**, built in 1773 to an octagonal design that excited universal execration. "It is", wrote one contemporary, "a misshapen pile, the ugliest Parish Church in Scotland, but it is an excellent model for a circus."

From the abbey, it's a couple of minutes' walk along Bridge Street to the spacious **Market Square**, where the columns and pediments of the **Town Hall** are flanked by a splendid ensemble of three-storey eighteenth- and nineteenth-century pastel buildings. Beyond the general air of elegance, though, there's little to actually see.

Kelso has one other diversion. Leaving the Market Square along Roxburgh Street, take the alley down to the **Cobby Riverside Walk**, where a brief stroll leads to Floors Castle. En route, but hidden from view by the islet in the middle of the river, is the spot where the Teviot meets the Tweed. This junction has long been famous for its salmon fishing, with permits booked years in advance irrespective of the cost: currently £5000 per rod per week.

### Floors Castle

There's nothing medieval about **Floors Castle** (late April to June & Sept Mon–Thurs & Sun 10.30am–5.30pm; July & Aug daily 10.30am–5.30pm; Oct Wed & Sun 10.30am–4pm; £3.20), a vast castellated mansion overlooking the Tweed about a mile northwest of Kelso. The bulk of the building was designed by William Adam in the 1720s, and, picking through the Victorian modifications, much of the interior demonstrates his uncluttered style. Not that you'll see much of it: just ten rooms and a basement are open to the public. Highlights include Hendrick Danckerts' splendid panorama of Horse Guards Parade in the entrance hall; the Brussels tapestries in the ante and drawing rooms; paintings by Augustus John and Henri Matisse in the Needle Room; and all sorts of snuff boxes and cigarette cases in the gallery.

Floors remains privately owned, the property of the tenth Duke of Roxburghe, whose arrogant features can be seen in a variety of portraits. The duke is a close friend of royalty: it was here, apparently, that Prince Andrew proposed to Sarah Ferguson in 1986.

## Mellerstain House

**Mellerstain House** (May–Sept Mon–Fri & Sun 12.30–5pm; £3), six miles northwest of Kelso, represents the very best of the Adams' work: William designed the wings in 1725, and his son Robert the castellated centre fifty years later. Robert's love of columns, roundels and friezes culminates in a stunning sequence of plaster-moulded, plaster-shaded ceilings, from the looping symmetry of the library ceiling, adorned by medallion oil paintings of *Learning* and *Teaching* to the whimsical griffin and vase pattern in the drawing room. It takes about an hour to tour the house; afterwards you can wander the formal Edwardian gardens, which slope down to a lake.

## Practicalities

With good connections to Coldstream in the east and Melrose and Jedburgh to the west, Kelso **bus station** is on Roxburgh Street, a brief walk from the Market Square where you'll find the **tourist office** (April–June & Sept Mon–Sat 10am–5pm, Sun 2–4pm; July & Aug Mon–Sat 10am–6.30pm, Sun 2–6.30pm; Oct Mon–Sat 10am–4.30pm, Sun 2–4pm; ☎0573/223464).

The tourist office can provide you with a long list of **B&Bs**, two good choices being *Wester House*, 155 Roxburgh St (☎0573/225479; ②), and *Charlesfield*, Edenside Rd (☎0573/224583; ③). There's also one rather special **hotel**, *Ednam House*, on Bridge Street near the Market Square (☎0573/224168; ⑧), a splendid Georgian mansion whose gardens abut the Tweed. Kirk Yetholm **youth hostel** (late March to Sept; ☎0573/420631; Grade 2) is situated on the edge of the Cheviot Hills about six miles southeast of town along the B6352. There's a weekday bus service from Kelso to the hostel, which is also at the north end of the Pennine Way, the long-distance walking route that travels the length of northern England.

It's almost impossible to find anywhere to stay during Kelso's main **festivals**: the prestigious Border Union Dog Show in late June, the Border Union Agricultural Show in late July, the Kelso Rugby 7s in early September and the fascinating Ram Sales a week or so later.

For **food**, *Lombardi's Café*, on the square, sells cheap snacks and meals, as does the *Queen's Head*, Bridge St, though the *Ednam House* restaurant stands head and shoulders above the rest.

# CENTRAL SOUTHERN SCOTLAND

**Central Southern Scotland** encompasses a rough rectangle of land sandwiched between the Cheviot Hills on the English border and the chain of foothills – the Pentland and Moorfoot ranges – to the south of Edinburgh. The region incorporates some of the finest stretches of the **Southern Uplands,** with bare, rounded peaks and heathery hills punctuated by dales.

Most of the roads stick assiduously to the dales, and the main problem is finding a route that avoids endless to and froing. Whichever way you're travelling, be sure to take in the section of the **Tweed Valley** stretching from **Melrose** to **Peebles**, where you'll find a string of attractions, from the ruins of **Dryburgh** and **Melrose Abbey** to the eccentricities of Sir Walter Scott's mansion at **Abbotsford** and the intriguing Jacobite past of **Traquair House**. The extensive medieval remains of the abbey at **Jedburgh**, just south, also merit a visit.

Along with industrialized Selkirk and Galashiels, these towns form the heart of the **Borders** region, whose turbulent history was, until the Act of Union, characterized by endless clan warfare and Reivers' raids. Consequently, the countryside is strewn with ruined castles and keeps, while each major town celebrates its agitated past in the **Common Ridings**, when locals – especially the "Callants", the young men – dress up in period costume and ride out to check the burgh boundaries. It's a boisterous business, as is the local love of **Rugby Union**, which reaches a crescendo with the **Melrose 7s** tournament in April.

The Southern Uplands assume a wild aspect in **Liddesdale**, southwest of Jedburgh, and along the **Yarrow Water** and **Moffat Water** connecting Selkirk with Moffat. Choose either of these two routes for the scenery, using the old spa town of **Moffat** as a base.

Travelling around the region by **bus** takes some forethought: pick up timetables from any tourist office and plan your connections closely – it's often difficult to cross between valleys. Some relief is, however, provided by the *Harrier Scenic Bus Service*, which threads its way between the more noteworthy towns from early July to September: again, the tourist office has schedules.

# Melrose

Tucked in between the Tweed and the Eildon Hills, minuscule **MELROSE** is improbably quaint, its narrow streets trimmed by pretty little cottages and tweedy shops. At the foot of the town the pink- and ochre-tinted stone ruins of **Melrose Abbey** (April–Sept Mon–Sat 9.30am–6pm, Sun 2–6pm; Oct–March Mon–Sat 9.30am–4pm, Sun 2–4pm; £2) soar above the riverside surroundings. The abbey, founded in 1136 by David I, grew rich selling wool and hides to Flanders, but its prosperity was fragile: the English repeatedly razed Melrose, most viciously under Richard II in 1385 and the Earl of Hertford in 1545. Most of the present remains date from the intervening period, when extensive rebuilding abandoned the original austerity for an elaborate, Gothic style inspired by the abbeys of northern England.

The site is dominated by the **Abbey Church**, where the elegant window arches of the nave approach the **monk's choir**, whose grand piers are disfigured by the masonry of a later parish church. The adjacent **presbytery** is better preserved, its dignified lines illuminated by a magnificent Perpendicular window pointing piously high into the sky. Close by, in the **south transept**, another fine fifteenth-century window is surrounded by an undergrowth of delicate, foliate tracery sprouting over the window and beneath a cornice enlivened by angels playing musical instruments. This kind of finely carved detail is repeated everywhere you look; note two intriguing **gargoyles** outside – one a pig playing the bagpipes, the other a winged and calf-headed centaur.

The **Commendator's House** (same hours as the abbey), displays a mundane collection of ecclesiastical bric-a-brac in the house of the abbey's sixteenth-century lay administrators. Melrose's other museum, the **Trimontium Exhibition**, just off the Market Square (March–Oct daily 10am–12.30pm & 2–4.30pm; £1), is equally modest, with dioramas, models and the odd archeological find outlining the three Roman occupations of the region.

## Practicalities

**Buses** to Melrose stop in the Market Square, a brief walk from both the abbey ruins and the useful **tourist office** (April–June & Sept–Oct Mon–Sat 10am–5.30pm, Sun 1.30–5.30pm; July & Aug Mon–Sat 9.30am–6.30pm, Sun 1.30–6.30pm; ☎089682/2555).

Melrose has a clutch of **hotels**, notably the reasonably priced *Station Hotel* (☎089682/2038; ③), in the old train station on Palma Place, and the stately *George and Abbotsford*, High St (☎089682/2308; ⑥). There are also many excellent **B&Bs**, with some of the finest just a stone's throw from the abbey: try *Little Fordel*, Abbey St (☎089682/2206; ③), *Dunfermline House*, Buccleuch St (☎089682/2148; ③), or, best of all, *Braidwood*, Buccleuch St (☎089682/2488; ③). Other, cheaper places include *Orchard House*, High St (☎089682/2005; ②), and *Craigard*, Huntly Ave, near the foot of the High Street (☎089682/2041; ②). The town also has a **youth hostel** (March–Oct; ☎089682/2521; Grade 1), overlooking the abbey from beside the High Road; the **Gibson Caravan Park** (☎089682/2969) is just off the High Street.

Most of the better B&Bs serve reasonably priced **dinner** on request. Alternatively, the *Station Hotel* restaurant features an imaginative but affordable menu and busy *Burts Hotel*, on the Market Square, offers excellent bar meals, although their attitude to backpackers is a bit snooty. No such restrictions exist at *Haldane's Fish & Chip Shop*, just off the square, or at the nearby *Ship Inn*, the liveliest pub in town, especially on a Saturday afternoon after the Melrose Rugby Union team have played at home.

## Eildon Hills

From the centre of Melrose, it's a comfortable four-mile walk to the top of the **Eildon Hills**, the triple-peaked volcanic pile rearing up behind the town. The tourist office sells a leaflet detailing the hike, which follows Dingleton Road before cutting off to the left down the track that leads to the saddle between the peaks. To the right of the saddle are **Mid Hill**, the highest summit at 1385ft, and **Wester Hill**; to the left **North Hill** has the scant remains of an Iron Age Fort and a Roman signal station at the top. The hills have been associated with all sorts of legends, beginning with their creation by the wizard-cum-alchemist Michael Scot. It was here that the mystic Thomas the Rhymer received the gift of prophecy from the Faery Queen, and Arthur and his Knights are reckoned to lie asleep deep within the hills, victims of a powerful spell. There are several routes back to town; one cuts back to the river just east of Melrose at Newstead, the site of the important Roman fort of **Trimontium** (Three Hills), whose remains are on display in the National Museum, Edinburgh.

# Around Melrose

Melrose makes a great base for exploring the middle reaches of the **Tweed Valley**. The rich, forested scenery inspired Sir Walter Scott, and the area's most outstanding attractions – the elegiac ruins of **Dryburgh Abbey** and lonely **Smailholm Tower** – bear his mark. Perhaps fortunately, Scott died before the textile boom industrialized parts of the Tweed Valley, turning his beloved **Selkirk** and **Galashiels** into grotty mill towns.

A comprehensive network of **bus** services connects Melrose with its surroundings and footpaths line much of the river's length. *Gala Cycles*, 58 High St, Galashiels (☎0896/57587), rents mountain bikes.

## Dryburgh Abbey

Hidden away on a bend in the Tweed a few miles east of Melrose, the remains of **Dryburgh Abbey** (April–Sept Mon–Sat 9.30am–6pm, Sun 2–6pm; Oct–March Mon–Sat 9.30am–4pm, Sun 2–4pm; £2) occupy a superb position against a hilly backdrop, where ancient trees and wide lawns flatter the reddish hues of the stonework. The Premonstratensians, or White Canons, founded the abbey in the twelfth century, but they were never as successful – or apparently as devout – as their Cistercian neighbours in Melrose. Their chronicles detail interminable disputes about land and money – in one incident, a fourteenth-century canon called Marcus flattened the abbot with his fist. Later, the abbey attained its own folklore; Scott's *Minstrelsy* records the tale of a woman who lived in the vaults with a sprite called Fatlips. She only came out after dark to beg from her neighbours and was variously thought mad or demonic.

The abbey, demolished and rebuilt on several occasions, incorporates several architectural styles, beginning in the shattered **church** where the clumsy decoration of the main entrance contrasts with the spirited dog-tooth motif around the east processional doorway. The latter leads through to the **monastic buildings**, a two-storey ensemble that provides an insight into the lives of the monks. Bits and pieces of several rooms have survived, but the real highlight is the barrel-vaulted **chapter-house**, complete with low stone benches, grouped windows and carved arcade. The room was used by the monks for the daily reading of a chapter from either the Bible or their rule book, and was, as they prospered, draped with expensive hangings.

Finally, back in the church, the battered north transept contains the grave of **Sir Walter Scott**; nearby lies Field Marshal Haig, the World War I commander whose ineptitude cost thousands of soldiers' lives.

### Practicalities

There are several ways to get to **Dryburgh** from Melrose: if you're **driving**, the clearly signposted fifteen-minute route proceeds east along the A6091 and north up the A68 until the right turn that follows the back roads to the abbey. On the way, you'll pass **Scott's View** overlooking the Tweed Valley, where the writer and friends often picnicked; the scene inspired Joseph Turner's *Melrose 1831*, now on display in the National Gallery of Scotland (see p.69). Alternatively, the five-mile **walk** begins beside Melrose Abbey on the Priorswalk Footpath, which cuts across to Newstead. From here there's a choice of trails; the best loops along the banks of the Tweed between Ravenswood and the footbridge over to

Dryburgh. You can also take the Jedburgh **bus** (Mon–Sat hourly, Sun 5 daily; 10min) as far as Newtown St Boswells. Walk south from the village along the main road and take the first left down the mile-long lane that leads to the footbridge and Dryburgh. The only direct service is with the four-seater **post bus** (Mon–Fri 1 daily; 25min), but this doesn't make a return trip.

For overnight visits, Dryburgh has just one place to stay, the luxurious **Dryburgh Abbey Hotel** (☎0835/22261; ⑨), right next to the ruins.

## Smailholm Tower

Driving is the only way to reach the fifteenth-century **Smailholm Tower** (April–Sept Mon–Sat 9.30am–6pm, Sun 2–6pm; £1.50) perched on a rocky outcrop a few miles east of Dryburgh via the B6404. A remote and evocative fastness recalling Reivers' raids and border skirmishes, the tower was designed to withstand sudden attack: the rough rubble walls average 6ft thick and both the entrance – once guarded by a heavy door plus an iron yett (gate) – and the windows are disproportionately small. These were necessary precautions. On both sides of the border clans were engaged in endless feuds, a violent history that stirred the imagination of a "wee, sick laddie" who was brought here to live in 1773. The boy was Walter Scott and his epic poem *Marmion* resounds to the clamour of Smailholm's ancient quarrels:

> [The forayers], *home returning, fill'd the hall*
> *With revel, wassel-rout, and brawl.*
> *Methought that still with trump and clang,*
> *The gateway's broken arches rang;*
> *Methought grim features, seam'd with scars,*
> *Glared through the window's rusty bars.*

Inside, ignore the inept costumed models and press on up to the roof, where two narrow **wall-walks**, jammed between crow-stepped gables, provide panoramic views.

## Abbotsford House

**Abbotsford House** (mid-March to Oct Mon–Sat 10am–5pm, Sun 2–5pm; £2.20) was designed to satisfy the Romantic inclinations of Sir Walter Scott, who lived here from 1812 until his death twenty years later. Built on the site of a farmhouse Scott bought and subsequently demolished, Abbotsford took twelve years to evolve with the fanciful turrets and castellations of the Scots Baronial exterior incorporating copies of medieval originals: thus the entrance porch imitates that of Linlithgow Palace and the screen wall in the garden echoes Melrose Abbey's cloister. Scott was proud of his creation, writing to a friend "It is a kind of conundrum castle to be sure (which) pleases a fantastic person in style and manner".

Inside, visitors start in the wood-panelled **study**, with its small writing desk made of salvage from the Spanish Armada. The **library** boasts an extraordinary assortment of Scottish memorabilia, including Rob Roy's purse and *skene dhu* (knife), a lock of Bonnie Prince Charlie's hair and his *quaich* (drinking cup), Flora Macdonald's pocket book, the inlaid pearl crucifix that accompanied Mary, Queen of Scots to the scaffold, and even a piece of oatcake found in the pocket of a dead Highlander at Culloden. You can also see Henry Raeburn's famous portrait of

## SIR WALTER SCOTT

**Walter Scott** (1771–1832) was born in Edinburgh to a solidly bourgeois family whose roots were in Selkirkshire. As a child he was left lame by polio and his anxious parents sent him to recuperate at his grandfather's farm in Smailholm, where the boy's imagination was fired by his relatives' tales of derring-do, the violent history of the Borders retold amidst a rugged landscape that he spent long summer days exploring. Scott returned to Edinburgh to resume his education and take up a career in law, but his real interests remained elsewhere. Throughout the 1790s he transcribed hundreds of old Border ballads, publishing a three-volume collection entitled *Minstrelsy of the Scottish Borders* in 1802. An instant success, *Minstrelsy* was followed by Scott's own *Lay of the Last Minstrel*, a narrative poem whose strong story and rose-tinted regionalism proved very popular.

More poetry was to come, most successfully *Marmion* (1808) and *The Lady of the Lake* (1810), not to mention an eighteen-volume edition of the works of John Dryden and nineteen volumes of Jonathan Swift. However, despite having two paid jobs, one as the Sheriff-Depute of Selkirkshire, the other as clerk to the Court of Session in Edinburgh, his finances remained shaky. He had become a partner in a printing firm, which put him deeply into debt, not helped by the enormous sums he spent on his mansion, Abbotsford. From 1813, Scott was writing to pay the bills and thumped out a veritable flood of historical novels using his extensive knowledge of Scottish history and folklore. He produced his best work within the space of ten years: *Waverley* (1814), *The Antiquary* (1816), *Rob Roy* and the *The Heart of Midlothian* (both 1818) and, after he had exhausted his own country, two notable novels set in England, *Ivanhoe* (1819) and *Kenilworth* (1821). In 1824 he returned to Scottish tales with *Redgauntlet*, the last of his quality work.

A year later Scott's money problems reached crisis proportions after an economic crash bankrupted his printing business. Attempting to pay his creditors in full, he found the quality of his writing deteriorating with his increased speed and the effort broke his health. His last years were plagued by illness and in 1832 he died at Abbotsford and was buried within the ruins of Dryburgh Abbey.

Although Scott's interests were diverse, his historical novels mostly focused on the Jacobites, whose loyalty to the Stuarts had riven Scotland since the "Glorious Revolution" of 1688. That the nation was prepared to be entertained by such tales was essentially a matter of timing: by the 1760s it was clear the Jacobite cause was lost for good and Scotland, emerging from its isolated medievalism, had been firmly welded into the United Kingdom. Thus its turbulent history and independent spirit was safely in the past, and ripe for romancing – as shown by the arrival of King George IV in Edinburgh during 1822 decked out in Highland dress. Yet, for Sir Walter the romance was tinged with a genuine sense of loss. Loyal to the Hanoverians, he still grieved for Bonnie Prince Charlie; he welcomed a commercial Scotland but lamented the passing of feudal ties; and thus his heroes are transitional, fighting men of action superseded by bourgeois figures searching for a clear identity.

Although today many of Scott's works are out of print, Edinburgh University Press has recently begun a long-term project to issue proper critical editions of the *Waverley* novels for the first time, correcting hitherto heavily corrupted texts and restoring passages and endings that had been altered – often drastically – by the original publishers. See "Books" in *Contexts* for details of books by Scott currently in print.

Scott hanging in the **drawing room**; all sorts of armour and weapons, notably Rob Roy's sword, dagger and gun, in the **armoury**; and the barbaric-looking **entrance hall**, with elk and wild cattle skulls and a cast of the head of Robert the Bruce.

Abbotsford is sandwiched between the Tweed and the B6360, about three miles west of Melrose. The fast and frequent Melrose–Galashiels **bus** service provides easy access: ask for the Tweedbank island on the A6091 and walk up the road from there, for about ten minutes.

# Selkirk and around

Whichever way you're heading it's likely you'll pass through **SELKIRK**, a tatty town that spreads along the hillside above the Ettrick Water about six miles south of Abbotsford. At the west end of the High Street, off the Market Square, the **tourist office** (April–June & Sept Mon–Sat 10am–5pm, Sun 2–4pm; July & Aug Mon–Sat 10am–6.30pm, Sun 2–6.30pm; Oct Mon–Sat 10am–4.30pm, Sun 2–4pm; ☎0750/20054) is a good place to stock up with pamphlets and books. In the same building, **Halliwell's House Museum** (free) features an old-style hardware shop and an informative exhibit on the industrialization of the Tweed Valley, from the development of the first mills in the early nineteenth century to their slow decline after 1910. At the other end of the High Street, the statue of **Mungo Park**, the renowned explorer born in Selkirkshire in 1771, displays two finely cast bas reliefs depicting his exploits, which came to an end with his accidental drowning in 1805.

## Bowhill House

Three miles west of Selkirk, nineteenth-century **Bowhill House** (July Mon–Sat 1–4.30pm, Sun 2–6pm; £3) is the property of the Duke of Buccleuch and Queensberry, a seriously wealthy man. Beyond the mansion's grand stone facade is an outstanding collection of French antiques and European paintings: in the **dining room**, for example, there are portraits by Reynolds and Gainsborough and a Canaletto cityscape, while the **drawing room** boasts the only privately owned Leonardo da Vinci, the *Madonna with the Yarn-Winder*. Look out also for the **Scott Room**, which features another splendid portrait of Sir Walter by Henry Raeburn, and the **Monmouth Room**, commemorating James, Duke of Monmouth, the illegitimate son of Charles II, who married Anne of the Buccleuchs. After several years in exile, Monmouth returned to England when his father died in 1685, hoping to wrest the crown from James II. He was defeated at the battle of Sedgemoor in Somerset and subsequently sent to the scaffold: his execution shirt is on display.

The wooded hills of **Bowhill Country Park** (May to late Aug Mon–Thurs & Sat noon–5pm, Sun 2–6pm; £1), which adjoins the house, are criss-crossed by scenic footpaths and cycle trails. **Mountain bikes** can be rented in the Park Visitor Centre. Getting to Bowhill by **bus** is difficult: from July to late September, a once-weekly *Harrier Scenic Bus Service* leaves Selkirk (and Melrose) in the morning and returns in the afternoon; on weekdays there's also a bus from Selkirk in the early afternoon, but you'll have to walk back.

# The Tweed Valley: Galashiels to Peebles

There's a wide choice of routes on from Melrose; one of the more popular options is to travel eighteen miles west along the **Tweed Valley** to the pleasant country town of Peebles. On the way, savour the wooded scenery and drop into Traquair House, just off the main road at tiny Innerleithen. Public transport is no problem: frequent **buses** along the valley are supplemented by the seasonal *Harrier Scenic Bus Service*. Just west of Peebles, the River Tweed curves south towards Tweedsmuir, from where it's just a few miles further to Moffat (see p.122).

# Galashiels, Walkerburn and Traquair House

Four miles west of Melrose, it's probably best to avoid **GALASHIELS**, a bustling textile town spread along the valley of the Gala Water near its junction with the Tweed. You may, however, have to pass through the region's principal **bus station**, situated close to the main square. If you're delayed, have a cup of tea at the *Rowan Tree* on Bank Street, or collect leaflets and maps from the **tourist office** (April–Sept Mon–Sat 10am–5pm, Sun 1–3pm; Oct Mon–Sat 10am–12.30pm & 1.30–4.30pm) across the road.

## Walkerburn and Traquair House

West of Galashiels, tiny **WALKERBURN** is home to the **Museum of Woollen Textiles** (Mon–Sat 9am–5.30pm, April–Nov also Sun 11am–5pm; free). Some of the early wool and cloth patterns are of interest, but it won't be long before you're moving on. Peeping out from the trees three miles southwest of Walkerburn, **Traquair House** (Easter, May–June & Sept daily 1.30–5.30pm; July–Aug daily 10.30am–5.30pm; £3.50) is the oldest house in Scotland to have been continuously inhabited by the same family. In the tenth century, its first owner, **James**, first Earl of Traquair, inherited an elementary fortified tower, which his powerful descendants gradually converted into a mansion, visited, it is said, by 27 monarchs including Mary, Queen of Scots. Persistently Catholic, the family paid for their principles; the fifth Earl got two years in the Tower of London for his support of Bonnie Prince Charlie, Protestant mill workers repeatedly attacked their property, and by 1800 little remained of the family's once enormous estates – certainly not enough to fund any major rebuilding.

Traquair's main appeal is in its ancient shape and structure, from the twisting stone staircase to secret stairways and the hidden **Priest's Room**. Of the furniture and fittings, the carved oak door at the foot of the stairs is outstanding, as are the Dutch *trompe l'oeil* in the **Still Room** and the bright-yellow four-poster of the **King's Room**, with a bedspread embroidered by Mary, Queen of Scots. On the second floor, the **Museum Room** has an intriguing assortment of family documents and several fine examples of Jacobite or **Amen Glass**, inscribed with pictures of the Bonnie Prince or verses in his honour. Finally, walk down to the **Steekit Yetts**, or Bear Gates, associated with one of the more romantic legends of the '45. On his march south, Prince Charles Stuart popped in to visit his old ally at Traquair. As he left, the fifth Earl "Vowed [the gates] wad be opened nevermair till a Stuart king was crooned in Lunnon", and the family have kept his promise.

# Peebles

Straddling the Tweed, **PEEBLES** has a genteel, relaxing air, its wide High Street bordered by family-run stores. A stroll around town should include a visit to the **Tweeddale Museum** (summer Mon–Fri 10am–1pm & 2–5pm, Sat & Sun 2–5pm; winter Mon–Fri only; free), housed in the Chambers Institute on the High Street. William Chambers, a local worthy, presented the building to the town in 1859, complete with an art gallery dedicated to the enlightenment of his neighbours. He stuffed the place with casts of the world's most famous sculptures, and, although most were lost long ago, today's "Secret Room", once the Museum Room, boasts two handsome friezes: one a copy of the Elgin marbles taken from the Parthenon; the other of the *Triumph of Alexander*, originally cast in 1812 to honour Napoleon.

## Walks around Peebles

A series of **footpaths** snake through the surrounding hills with their rough-edged burns, bare peaks and deep woods. The main local tracks are listed in the *Popular Walks around Peebles* leaflet available from the tourist office. The five-mile-long *Sware Trail* is one of the easiest and most scenic, weaving west along the north bank of the river and looping back to the south. On the way, it passes **Neidpath Castle** (Easter–Sept Mon–Sat 11am–5pm, Sun 1–5pm; £1.50), a gaunt medieval tower house extensively remodelled in the seventeenth century, and the splendid skew **railway bridge**, part of the Glasgow line which was finished in 1850. Other, longer footpaths follow the old drove tracks, like the thirteen-mile haul to St Mary's Loch or the fourteen-mile route to Selkirk via Traquair House. For either of these, you'll need an Ordnance Survey map, a compass and proper hiking tackle. Alternatively, **mountain bikes** can be rented from the *Glentress Bike Centre* (Easter–Oct; ☎0721/722934), on the edge of Glentress forest two miles east of town. If you need four or more, they'll be delivered free within a ten-mile radius.

## Practicalities

**Buses** to Peebles stop outside the post office, a few doors down from the **tourist office** on the High Street (April–June Mon–Sat 10am–5pm, Sun 2–4pm; July–Aug Mon–Sat 9am–7pm, Sun 1–6pm; Sept Mon–Sat 10am–5.30pm, Sun 2–4pm; Oct 10am–4.30pm, Sun 2–4pm; Nov Mon–Sat 10am–12.30pm & 1.30–4.30pm; ☎0721/720138). Of the many **B&Bs** around the centre try *Mrs Kampman*, 12 Dukehaugh (☎0721/720118; ②), *Viewfield*, 1 Rosetta Rd (☎0721/721232; ②), or *Mrs Sked*, 21 Kirkland St (☎0721/720525; ②). The best of the more upmarket **hotels** is *The Park Hotel*, just east of town on the Innerleithen Road (☎0721/720451; ⑧). Cheaper alternatives include the central *Green Tree Hotel*, at 41 Eastgate (☎0721/720582; ⑤), and the *Kingsmuir Hotel*, south of the river on Springhill Rd (☎0721/720151; ⑥). The **Rosetta Caravan and Camping Park** (April–Oct; ☎0721/720770) is fifteen minutes' walk north of the High Street: take Old Town from the main bridge, follow the road round, turn right up Young Street and keep going.

For **food**, the *Crown Hotel*, on the High Street, features tasty daily specials, and the *Kingsmuir Hotel*, Springhill Rd, serves slightly more expensive but excellent bar meals. You should also sample the beers of the local Broughton brewery – *Old Jock*, *Greenmantle* or *Broughton Ale*.

# Jedburgh

**JEDBURGH** nestles in the valley of the Jed Water near its confluence with the Teviot out on the edge of the wild Cheviot Hills. During the interminable Anglo-Scottish Wars, it was the quintessential frontier town, a heavily garrisoned royal burgh incorporating a mighty castle and abbey. Though the **Castle** was destroyed by the Scots in 1409 its memory has been kept alive by local folklore: in 1285, for example, King Alexander III was celebrating his wedding feast in the Great Hall when a ghostly apparition predicted his untimely death and a bloody civil war; sure enough, he died in a hunting accident shortly afterwards and chaos ensued. Today the ruins of the **Abbey** are the main event, and Jedburgh's old town centre is often overwhelmed by tourists.

# The Town

The remains of **Jedburgh Abbey** (April–Sept Mon–Sat 9.30am–6pm, Sun 2–6pm; Oct–March Mon–Sat 9.30am–4pm, Sun 2–4pm; £2), right in the centre of town, date from the twelfth century. Benefiting from King David's patronage, the monks developed an extravagant complex on a sloping site next to the Jed Water, the monastic buildings standing beneath a huge red sandstone church. All went well until the late thirteenth century, when the power of the Scots kings waned after the death of Alexander III led to a prolonged civil war over the succession. The abbey was subsequently burnt and badly damaged on a number of occasions, the worst being inflicted by the English in 1544. The canons gamely repaired their buildings, but were unable to resist the Reformation and the monastery closed in 1560. However, the Abbey Church remained a parish kirk for another three centuries and has survived particularly well preserved.

Entry to the site is through the spanking new **Visitor Centre** at the bottom of the hill, whose explanation of the abbey's history uses both contemporary quotations and "mood music" – chanting monks and the like. Next to the centre are the scant remains of the cloister buildings; the **Abbey Church**, which lies on an east–west axis, is best entered from the west through a weathered Norman doorway with gables, arcading and ornamented windows. Behind the doorway lies the splendidly proportioned three-storeyed nave, a fine example of the transition from Norman to Gothic design, with pointed window arches surmounted by the round-headed arches of the triforium, which, in turn, support the lancet windows of the clerestory. This delicacy of form is, however, not matched at the east end of the church, where the squat central tower is underpinned by the monumental circular pillars and truncated arches of the earlier, twelfth-century choir.

It's a couple of minutes' walk from the abbey round to the tiny triangular **Market Place**. Up the hill from here, at the top of Castlegate, **Jedburgh Castle Jail Museum** (Easter–Sept Mon–Sat 10am–5pm, Sun 1–5pm; 70p) has a modest display on prison life in the nineteenth century. The prison buildings themselves are, for the period, remarkably comfortable, reflecting the influence of reformer John Howard. Finally, **Mary Queen of Scots' House** (Easter to mid-Nov daily 10am–5pm; £1.10), situated at the opposite end of the town centre, is something of a misnomer: it's true that Mary stayed here during the assizes of 1566, but there's precious little to see and the feeble attempt to unravel her complex life verges on farce. You can, however, see a copy of Mary's death mask and one of the few surviving portraits of the Earl of Bothwell.

# Practicalities

Jedburgh's **bus station**, next door to the abbey, is the starting point for a wide range of services around the Borders. Footsteps away on Murray's Green, the **tourist office** (April, May & Oct Mon–Sat 10am–5pm, Sun 2–5pm; June & Sept Mon–Sat 9.30am–5.30pm, Sun 1.30–5.30pm; July & Aug Mon–Sat 9am–7pm, Sun 10am–7pm; Nov–March Mon–Fri 10am–5pm; ☎0835/863435) has a vast array of written information and a comprehensive list of reasonably priced local **accommodation**. Try the excellent *Kenmore Bank Guest House*, Oxnam Rd (☎0835/ 862369; ④), the *Glenbank Country House Hotel*, Castlegate (☎0835/862258; ⑤), or the *Glenfriars Hotel*, The Friars (☎0835/862000; ⑥). Alternatively, there are several **B&Bs** along Castlegate, notably *Mrs Bathgate*, at no. 64 (April–Oct;

☎0835/862466; ②), *Mrs Hume*, at no. 48 (☎0835/862504; ②), and *Mrs Oliver*, at no. 75 (☎0835/863353; ②). The **Jedwater Caravan and Camping Park** (Easter to mid-Oct; ☎0835/84219) occupies a riverside site four miles south of town on the A68, while the **Elliot Park** campsite (April–Oct; ☎0835/863393) is beside the Edinburgh Road about a mile north of the centre.

Considering its heavy tourist trade, Jedburgh has surprisingly few **restaurants**. During the day, head for the *Brown Sugar* coffee bar, on the Market Place, which serves up good quality sandwiches, salads and cakes. At night, stick to the *Castlegate Restaurant*, Castlegate. **Jethart Snails**, a local speciality on sale everywhere, are sticky boiled sweets designed to corrupt the firmest of fillings.

### Jedburgh's festivals

Jedburgh is at its busiest during the town's two main **festivals**. The Common Riding, or **Callants' Festival**, takes place in the first two weeks of July, when the young people of the town – especially the lads – mount up and ride out to check the burgh boundaries, a reminder of more troubled days when Jedburgh was subject to English raids. In similar spirit, early February sees the day-long **Jedburgh Hand Ba'** game, an all-male affair between the "uppies" (those born above the Market Place) and "downies" (those born below). In theory the aim of the game is to get hay-stuffed leather balls – originally the heads of English men – from one end of town to the other, but there's more at stake than that: macho reputations are made and lost during the two, two-hour games.

# Teviotdale, Ewes Water and Liddesdale

If you're heading southwest from Jedburgh, there are two clearly defined routes. The first, along the A698 and A7, takes the dull way up **Teviotdale** to **Hawick**, before slipping through the dramatic uplands which stretch as far as the Dumfries boundary. Further south, **Fiddleton** marks the start of the **Ewes Water**, which straggles south to Canonbie on the English border.

The route down **Liddesdale** is slower but more picturesque, on a remote road flanked by dense forests, barren moors and secluded heaths. If you do come this way, stop off at solitary **Hermitage Castle**, a well-preserved fourteenth-century fortress.

The Jedburgh to Carlisle **bus** travels the length of Teviotdale and Ewes Water four to six times daily from Monday to Saturday; extra services link Jedburgh with Hawick, but there are no buses along the length of Liddesdale.

## Teviotdale and Ewes Water

Fourteen miles from Jedburgh is the unprepossessing mill town of **HAWICK** (pronounced "Hoyk"), its many factory outlets swarming with visitors and bearing witness to its history as centre of the region's knitwear and hosiery industry. To learn about the industry and the town in general, visit the **Hawick Museum and Art Gallery** (April–Sept Mon–Sat 10am–noon & 1–5pm, Sun 2–5pm; Oct–March Mon–Sat 1–4pm, Sun 2–4pm; 70p), near the town centre in Wilton Lodge Park.

Beyond Hawick, the scenery improves as the road twists its way south between the heathery hills edging the river. At Teviothead the road leaves the dale to cross over into Dumfries, where the **Ewes Water** strips down from Fiddleton to

**LANGHOLM**, a stone-built mill town at the confluence of the Esk, Ewes and Wauchope waters. The town, which flourished during the eighteenth-century textile boom, is now a quiet backwater. In 1892 this was the birthplace of the poet Hugh MacDiarmid, a co-founder of the Scottish National Party and a key player in the literary renaissance that fired the nationalist movement between the two world wars. MacDiarmid, born Christopher Murray Grieve, looked to the Scotland of the eighteenth century, lionizing Walter Scott and Robbie Burns while heaping scorn on the Anglicized gentry. This didn't go down well with the burghers of Langholm, who did their best to ignore the poet altogether. Indeed, when MacDiarmid died in 1978, at the age of 86, some of them even tried to prevent him being buried in the local churchyard.

There's no real reason to **stay** in Langholm, but if you need to, try the convenient *Eskdale Hotel* on the Market Place (☎03873/80357; ④), or *Langholm Guest House*, 81 High St (☎03873/81343; ③).

## On from Langholm

Four roads lead out of Langholm, but only one is of any charm – the narrow country lane that snakes its way east over the hills to **Newcastleton** in Liddesdale. Otherwise, choose between the dull thirty-mile journey west to **Dumfries** (see p.127); the far slower, and just as dreary trip northwest up **Eskdale** for (ultimately) Selkirk and the Tweed Valley; or the shorter journey south to **Gretna Green** (see p.121).

If you're travelling by **bus**, it takes about three hours to get to Dumfries, changing at Lockerbie, whilst Gretna Green can be reached via the Carlisle route. There aren't any services to Newcastleton or Selkirk.

# Liddesdale

Heading south out of Jedburgh on the A68, it's about a mile to the B6357, a narrow byroad that leads over the moors to the hamlet of Bonchester Bridge. From here, the road cuts south through Wauchope Forest and carries on into **Liddesdale**, whose wild beauty is at its most striking between Saughtree and Newcastleton. In between the two, take the turning to **Hermitage Castle** (April–Sept Mon–Sat 9.30am–6pm, Sun 2–6pm; Oct–March Sat 9.30am–4pm, Sun 2–4pm; £1.20), a bleak and forbidding fastness surrounded by all sorts of horrifying legends: one owner, William Douglas, starved his prisoners to death; whilst Lord de Soulis, another occupant, engaged the help of demons to fortify the castle against the king, Robert the Bruce. Soulis also drilled holes into the shoulders of his vassals, the better to yoke them to sledges of building materials, and Bruce became so tired of the complaints that he said "Boil him if you please, but let me hear no more of him". But Soulis had a pact with his demonic familiar, Redcap, that made him difficult to kill: "ropes could not bind him, nor steel weapons touch", so he met his end magically bound with ropes of sifted sand, wrapped in lead and slowly boiled.

From the outside, the castle remains an imposing structure, its heavy walls topped by stepped gables and a tidy corbelled parapet. However, the apparent homogeneity is deceptive: certain features were invented during a Victorian restoration, a confusing supplement to the ad hoc alterations that had already transformed the fourteenth-century original. The ruinous interior is a bit of a let-down, but look out for the tight Gothic doorways and gruesome dungeon.

It's a short journey on to **NEWCASTLETON**, a classic estate village built for the hand-loom weavers of the third Duke of Buccleuch in 1793. The gridiron streets fall either side of a long main road that connects three geometrically arranged squares – nice enough to while away the odd hour. You could even stay the night at the **Liddesdale Hotel** (☎03873/75255; ③) and sample some local trout or pheasant.

The road leaves Liddesdale ten miles southwest of Newcastleton at Canonbie. Around here, sandwiched between the **Esk** and the **Sark**, was what was known as the "**Debateable Land**", a pocket-sized territory claimed – but not controlled – by both England and Scotland from the fourteenth to the early eighteenth century. In the prevailing chaos, the Border Reivers flourished and famed outlaws like Kinmont Willie, Jock o' the Side and Clym of the Cleugh established fabulous reputations for acts of cruelty and kindness in equal measure. They could certainly die in style too: caught by James V, a chieftain named Johnnie Armstrong offered a colossal bribe and asked for a pardon; when this was refused and the noose was round his neck, he coolly disclaimed: "To seik het water beneath cauld ice, surely it is a great follie – I hae asked grace at a graceless face."

# Annandale: Gretna Green to Moffat

Cutting through **Annandale**, the M/A74 connects Carlisle with Glasgow. This is the fastest way to cross Southern Scotland but it's an unpleasantly busy road, jam-packed with trucks and lorries. You could break your journey by stopping off at **Gretna Green**, whose name is synonymous with elopements and fast-action weddings, before travelling the thirty miles north to the charming market town of **Moffat**, bypassed by the main road, which makes an ideal base for exploring the surrounding uplands. **Bus** services along Annandale are quick and frequent.

## Gretna to Lockerbie

There's not much to the twin villages of **GRETNA GREEN** and **GRETNA** except their curious history, the result of the quirks of the British legal system. Up until 1754 English couples could buy a quick and secret wedding at London's Fleet Prison, bribing imprisoned clerics with small amounts of money. The Hardwicke Marriage Act brought an end to this seedy wheeze, enforcing the requirement of a licence and a church ceremony. However, in Scotland, a marriage declaration made before two witnesses remained legal. The conse-quences of this difference in the law verged on farce: hundreds of runaway couples dashed north to Scotland, their weddings witnessed by just about anyone who came to hand – ferrymen, farmers, tollgate keepers and even self-styled "priests" who set up their own "marriage houses".

Gretna and Gretna Green, due to their position beside the border on the main turnpike-road to Edinburgh, became the most popular destination for the fugi-tives, but, even in emergency, class distinctions were maintained: the better-off headed for the staging post at Gretna Hall, the rest gravitated towards Gretna Green. The first "priest" was the redoubtable Joseph Paisley, a twenty-five-stone goliath who gave a certain style to the ceremony by straightening a horseshoe, a show of strength rather than a symbolic act, but one that led to stories of Gretna weddings being performed over the blacksmith's anvil, although this is, in fact, a comparatively recent custom. Both villages boomed until the marriage laws were further amended in 1856, but some business continued right down to 1940, when marriage by declaration was made illegal.

Today, the **Old Blacksmith's Shop**, next to the **tourist office** on the east side of the A74, is a tacky place stuffed with souvenirs and a handful of marital mementoes. On the other side of the road, roughly half a mile away, the rather more genteel **Blacksmith's Shop and Museum at Gretna Hall** (50p entrance) has another modest collection of bygones. You can still "get married" at Gretna, although the ceremony has no legal force.

There are lots of places **to stay** in and around Gretna and Gretna Green. The tourist office has the full list, but the nicest options are to be found in Gretna: try the *Surrone Guest House*, Annan Rd (☎0461/38341; ④), or *The Beeches*, Loanwath Rd (☎0461/37448; closed Dec; ③), which has just two (non-smoking) rooms.

### Ecclefechan and Lockerbie

It's about nine miles from Gretna to the tidy hamlet of **ECCLEFECHAN**, birthplace of the historian and essayist Thomas Carlyle. His old home, the whitewashed **Arched House** (April to late Oct daily noon–5pm; £1.50), is now a tiny museum, featuring among the personal memorabilia a bronze cast of his hands, old smoking caps and his cradle. Perhaps surprisingly, there's little here to indicate either the man's stern demeanour or his Calvinist roots.

The quiet country town of **LOCKERBIE**, seventeen miles from Gretna, was catapulted into the headlines on Wednesday December 21, 1988, when a Pan-Am Jumbo Jet, flying from Frankfurt to New York via Heathrow, was blown up by a terrorist bomb concealed in a transistor radio. All the crew and passengers died and the plane's fragments crashed down on Lockerbie, killing a further eleven. Those who planted the bomb, apparently Arab terrorists now resident in Libya, are still to be brought to book. The local people have set up a Remembrance Garden on the outskirts of town, but this is no place for the casual visitor.

# Moffat

Encircled by hills and dales, **MOFFAT** is a good-looking market town, its wide and elegant **High Street** lined with simple brick cottages and grand Georgian mansions. The latter hark back to the eighteenth century, when Moffat was briefly a modish spa, its sulphur springs attracting the rich and famous. One disappointed customer suggested they smelt of bilge-water – but they were good enough for luminaries Robbie Burns and James Boswell, who came to "wash off the scurvy spots".

Moffat is no longer such a fashionable spot, but while you're here take a look at the John Adam-designed **Moffat House Hotel** and the neighbouring **Colvin Fountain**, whose sturdy bronze ram was accidentally cast without any ears. Close by, the dark shadows of the **Black Bull** pub once quartered John Graham of Claverhouse as he planned his persecution of the Covenanters on behalf of Charles II. For details of the town's history, pop into the **museum** (Easter–Sept Mon, Tues & Thurs–Sat 10.30am–1pm & 2.30–5pm, Sun 2.30–5pm; 50p).The **Sulphurous Well** that made Moffat famous is a two-mile walk away from the centre: take Well Street and turn right along Well Road. There's little to see, but you'll certainly notice the smell.

## Practicalities

**Buses** to Moffat drop passengers on the High Street near the **tourist office** (April–June, Sept & Oct daily 10am–5pm; July & Aug daily 10am–6pm; ☎0683/ 20620), which has all the usual information plus a helpful compendium of local walks. The best **hotel** in town is the opulent *Moffat House Hotel*, on the High Street (☎0683/21288; ⑦). Other High Street alternatives include the palatable *Buccleuch Arms* (☎0683/20003; ⑤) and the basic *Star Hotel* (☎0683/20156; ④). For **B&Bs** try along Beechgrove, a five-minute walk from the town centre: head north along the High Street, continue down Academy Road, and it's the turning beside Moffat Academy. Here you'll find *Mrs Murray* at no. 12 (☎0683/20538; Feb–Nov; ②), *Mrs Pirie* at no. 23 (☎0683/20550; March–Oct; ②), *Gilbert House* (☎0683/20050; ③) and *Springbank* (☎0683/20070; Feb–Nov; ②). The **Hammerland's Farm camping and caravan site** (☎0683/20436; March–Oct) sits beside the Selkirk Road, about half a mile east of Moffat.

The *Buccleuch Arms* serves the finest **bar meals** in town, while further up the High Street, the *Valle Verde Trattoria* has filling, very cheap pizzas, and *Pacitti's* café serves great coffee and average snacks. You might also want to try the local treat, **Moffat toffee**.

# Around Moffat

From Moffat, there are three beautiful routes you can take through the most dramatic parts of the Southern Uplands. Of the three, the finest is the A708 between Moffat and Selkirk (see p.115), via **Moffat Water** and **Yarrow Water**. On the way, the Grey Mare's Tail Waterfall provides the opportunity for an exhilarating ramble and St Mary's Loch gives easy access to an especially stimulating section of the Southern Upland Way. Further west, the second route uses the A701, which climbs over the hills at the head of Annandale, cuts down **Tweeddale**, and joins the Tweed Valley near Peebles (see p.116). The third option begins at Elvanfoot, where the B7040 leaves the main road to cross the **Lowther Hills**. Passing through the former lead mining villages of **Leadhills** and **Wanlockhead**, this road reaches Nithsdale north of Drumlanrig Castle (see p.128).

Travelling these routes by **bus** remains difficult. The only service along the A708 is the *Harrier Scenic Bus*, which runs from Moffat to Melrose once weekly between July and late September. The *Harrier* also links Moffat and Peebles via the A701 once weekly during the summer. The only way to reach Leadhills and Wanlockhead is on the once- or twice-daily service from Sanquhar in Nithsdale.

## Moffat Water and Yarrow Water

Heading northeast from Moffat, the A708 snakes its way through the forests and hills along the lower stretches of **Moffat Water**. Before long the road climbs to wilder terrain, tracking along the bottom of a gloomy gully surrounded by desolate moorland. Beyond, ten miles from town, the two-hundred-foot **Grey Mare's Tail Waterfall** tumbles down a rocky crevasse – one of Dumfries' best-known beauty spots. Maintained by the National Trust for Scotland, the base of the falls is approached by a precipitous footpath along the stream, a ten-minute clamber each way from the road. There's a longer hike too, up the other bank, past the head of the falls, and on to remote **Loch Skeen**.

Back on the road, and crossing over into the Borders, it's a few miles further to the pair of icy lakes that mark the start of **Yarrow Water**. Tiny **Loch of the Lowes** to the south and the larger **St Mary's Loch** to the north are separated by a slender isthmus and magnificently set beneath the surrounding hills. This spot was popular with the nineteenth-century Scottish literati, especially Walter Scott and his friend James Hogg, the "Shepherd poet of Ettrick", who gathered to chew the fat at **Tibbie Shiels Inn** on the isthmus. The inn takes its name from Isabella Shiel, a formidable and, by all accounts, amusing woman who ruled the place till her death in 1878 at the age of 96. Today, the inn (☎0750/42231; ⑤) is a famous watering hole on the Southern Upland Way, but the rooms are pretty dire. For a short and enjoyable walk, follow the footpath from the inn along the east side of St Mary's Loch into **Bowerhope forest**. Alternatively, the Southern Upland Way heads across the moors north to Traquair House and south to the Ettrick Water Valley, both strenuous hikes that require an Ordnance Survey map and a compass.

East of St Mary's Loch, the A708 follows the course of the Yarrow Water down to Selkirk, about seventeen miles away. You can stay en route at the Broadmeadows **youth hostel** (April–Sept; ☎0750/76262; Grade 3) in **Yarrowford**, five miles from Selkirk.

# Tweeddale

Just north of Moffat, the A701 ascends the west side of **Annandale** to skirt the impressive box-canyon at its head. Best viewed from the road about six miles from town, the gorge – the **Devil's Beef Tub** – takes its name from the days when rustling Reivers hid their herds here. Walter Scott described the place aptly: "It looks as if four hills were laying their heads together to shut out daylight from the dark hollow place between them". The gorge was also a suitably secret spot for persecuted Covenanters during Charles II's "Killing Times".

Beyond the Tub, the road crosses over into **Tweeddale** and soon reaches tiny **Tweedsmuir**, where you could, as an alternative route, take the right turn over the Tweedsmuir Hills before returning to St Mary's Loch (see above). Keeping to the A701, widening Tweeddale loses much of its scenic appeal long before it reaches the village of **BROUGHTON**. Here, there's a modest **museum** (May–Sept Mon–Sat 2–5pm; 50p) in honour of novelist John Buchan, who spent his childhood holidays in the district.

# The Lowther Hills

West of Moffat, sandwiched between the M/A74 and Nithsdale, the **Lowther Hills** offer a wild landscape of tightly clustered peaks, bare until the heather blooms, hiding fast-flowing burns and narrow valleys – a dramatic terrain once known as "God's Treasure House" on account of its gold and silver ores. These mineral deposits were much sought after by the impoverished kings of Scotland, who banned their export and claimed a monopoly – draconian measures that only encouraged smuggling. There was lead here too, mined from Roman times right up to the 1950s, and used in the manufacture of pottery and glass.

### Leadhills and Wanlockhead

Twenty-one miles north of Moffat, tiny **LEADHILLS** is a forlorn place in a now forgotten corner of Strathclyde. The terraced cottages of this classic "company town" were built by the mine owners for their employees, but the boom years ended in the 1830s, since when the village has been left to wither away.

A couple of miles away, over the boundary in Dumfries, remote and windswept **WANLOCKHEAD** is even smaller than its neighbour, and, at 1500ft, is the highest village in Scotland. It shares Leadhills' mining history, but Wanlockhead's attempts to lure the tourists, have made the villages very different. The **Scottish Lead Mining Museum** (Easter to mid-Oct daily 11am–4pm; £1.80) deserves a good hour or two, beginning with the spruce **Visitor Centre**, which traces the development of the industry and its workforce. Afterwards, highlights of the open-air site include a guided tour of the underground **Loch Nell Mine** and of a couple of restored miners' cottages. There's also a rare example of a wooden **beam engine** and all sorts of industrial bits and pieces, mostly dating from the late 1950s when government grants sponsored a brief revival in lead mining; the earlier workings were closed in the 1930s. Sometimes the eighteenth-century **library** is open too, its books purchased from the voluntary subscriptions of its members: at its height, the library had a stock of two thousand volumes.

Wanlockhead straddles the Southern Upland Way, and is thus blessed with a **youth hostel** (April–Sept; ☎0659/74252; Grade 2), sited in the old mine surgeon's house. The Visitor Centre has the details of a couple of cheap **B&Bs**, or you can go straight to *Belton House* (☎0659/74487; ①).

# Biggar and around

**BIGGAR**, a somewhat staid town twelve miles northeast of Abington, warrants an hour or two, starting at the **Moat Park Heritage Centre** (Easter–Oct Mon–Sat 10am–5pm, Sun 2–5pm; £1.50), which occupies a grand neo-Romanesque church near the foot of Kirkstyle, off the High Street. Inside, a well-presented exhibition traces the history of Upper Clydesdale, and on the upper floor you can see a display of extraordinary table covers made by local tailor Menzies Moffat (1828–1907). Don't miss the banquet-size Royal Crimean Hero Tablecloth, which sets a cartoon strip of notable figures alongside scenes from Scottish country life. Biggar has three other museums. The nearest, the **Gladstone Court Museum** (Easter–Oct Mon–Sat 10am–12.30pm & 2–5pm, Sun 2–5pm; £1), across Kirkstyle on North Back Road, boasts a shop-lined Victorian street illustrating different aspects of nineteenth-century life, from the telephone exchange and classroom to the bank and the cobblers. Returning to Kirkstyle, walk over the hill to the footpath beside Biggar burn. To the right is the **Greenhill Covenanters' Museum** (Easter to mid-Oct daily 2–5pm; 50p), which attempts to explore the development of the Covenanting movement and the religious conflicts that ensued. To the left along the burn lies **Biggar Gasworks Museum** (June to late Sept daily 2–5pm; July & Aug Sun also noon–5pm; free). Before North Sea gas was piped across the UK, small coal-based gasworks like this one were common. Most were demolished in the 1970s, but Biggar's has survived and even manages to look quite spick and span.

Back up the High Street, the **sundial** outside the tourist office is the work of local poet-artist Ian Hamilton **Finlay**, a founder of the "concrete poetry" movement; you can see more of his work in the National Gallery of Modern Art in Edinburgh.

## Practicalities

Regular **bus** services to Biggar arrive from a wide range of towns including Edinburgh, Peebles, Moffat and Dumfries. They stop on Biggar High Street, near the **tourist office** (Easter–June & Sept to mid-Oct Mon–Sat 10am–5pm, Sun 11am–5pm; July & Aug Mon–Sat 9am–7pm, Sun 11am–5pm; ☎0899/21066). There's a **B&B**, *Mrs Bolton* at 59 North Back Rd (☎0899/20659; ②), a stone's throw away. For **food**, both the *Elphinstone Hotel* and the *Crown*, on the main street, have tasty daily specials.

## Around Biggar

Six miles southwest of Biggar, near the village of Thankerton, the solitary peak of **Tinto Hill** was the site of Druidic festivals in honour of the sun-god Baal, or Bel. It's relatively easy to walk the footpath up to the 2320-foot-high summit, from where the views are splendid – you'll also see a Druidic Circle and a Bronze Age burial cairn. A regular **bus** links Biggar with Thankerton.

Just north of town lie the southern extremities of the **Pentland Hills**, the narrow belt of upland extending into the suburbs of Edinburgh. The hills are best visited from the capital, but the pretty little village of **WEST LINTON**, straddling the Lyne Water twelve miles from Biggar, gives ready access to several rambles across the neighbouring hills. If you decide **to stay** the night, try the *Rae Martin Hotel* (☎0968/60464; ④).

# THE SOUTHWEST

Up until the eleventh century the whole of **Southwest Scotland** was known as Galloway, where independent chieftains maintained close contacts with the Vikings rather than the Scots. Gradually, this autonomy was whittled away and by the late thirteenth century the region, which comprises the rough triangle of land between the Solway Firth, the Firth of Clyde and the stretch from Dumfries to Kilmarnock, was integrated into Scotland. Indeed, it was here that both Robert the Bruce and William Wallace launched their wars against the English. Later on, from around the seventeenth century, the ports of the Solway Coast prospered with the expansion of local shipping routes over to Ireland, and, later still, the towns along the Firth of Clyde benefited from the industrialization of Glasgow. The region subsequently experienced economic decline as trade routes changed, turning busy ports into sleepy backwaters, and these days Southwest Scotland is agreeably laid-back, not crossed by motorway and – with most travellers skipping past on their way to the Highlands and islands – suffering little of the tourist crush familiar further north.

**Robert Burns** lived and died in this part of Scotland, a fact much exploited by the tourist offices. The **Burns Heritage Trail**, a motorist's route across much of the region, passes every conceivable place with which he had any connection, but frankly, unless you're particularly devoted, stick to the Burns sights in **Dumfries** and Ayr.

Extending southwest of Dumfries, the low-lying **Solway Coast** boasts a handful of splendid medieval ruins, principally **Caerlaverock Castle** and **Sweetheart Abbey**. Criss-crossed by walking trails that cater for every level of athleticism and any amount of time, the **Galloway Hills** rise just to the north of the coast, their beautiful moors, mountains, lakes and rivers centred on the 150,000-acre

**Galloway Forest Park**. After this the **Ayrshire Coast** is something of a disappointment with the exception of Victorian **Ayr**, noteworthy for its Burns attractions and beach, and the district's other main resort, **Largs**, with its agreeable setting between hills and sea.

Travelling the region by **bus** presents few problems and there's a good **train** service from Glasgow along the Ayrshire coast to Stranraer. It's also easy to travel on from Southwest Scotland by **ferry**, from Stranraer to Belfast and Larne, in Northern Ireland, and from the port of Ardrossan, north of Ayr, to the Isle of Arran, where you can hopscotch on up the Western Isles.

# Dumfries and around

With a population of thirty thousand, bustling **DUMFRIES** crowds the banks of the River Nith a few miles from the Solway Firth. Long known as the "Queen of the South", the town flourished as a medieval seaport and trading centre, its success attracting the attention of many English armies. The invaders managed to polish off most of the early settlement in 1448, 1536 and again in 1570, but Dumfries survived to prosper with its light industries supplying the agricultural hinterland. The town planners of the 1960s badly damaged the town, reducing it to an architectural hotch-potch, with the graceful fifteenth-century lines of Dervorgilla Bridge set next to faceless concrete council estates. Nevertheless, the town makes a good base for exploring the Solway coast, and is at least worth a visit for its associations with Robert Burns, who spent the last five years of his life here.

## The Town

Hemmed in by the river to the north and west, the snout-shaped centre of Dumfries radiates out from the pedestrianized **High Street**, which runs roughly parallel to the Nith. At its northern edge is the **Burns Statue**, a fanciful piece of Victorian frippery featuring the great man holding a poesy in one hand, whilst the other clutches at his heart. They haven't forgotten his faithful hound either, who lies curled around his feet.

Heading south down High Street, it's a couple of minutes' walk to **Midsteeple**, the old prison-cum-courthouse, and the narrow alley that leads to the smoky, oak-panelled *Globe Inn,* one of Burns' favourite drinking spots, and still a tavern. Back on the High Street, the **Burns' House** (Easter–Sept Mon–Sat 10am–1pm & 2–5pm, Sun 2–5pm; Oct–Easter Tues–Sat only; 70p) is a simple sandstone building where the poet died of rheumatic heart disease in 1796. Inside, there's an incidental collection of Burns' memorabilia – manuscripts, letters and the like – and one of the bedroom windows bears his signature, scratched with his diamond ring.

Burns was buried in a simple grave beside **St Michael's Church**, a monstrous eighteenth-century heap situated just south of his house. Just twenty years later, though, he was dug up and moved across the graveyard to a purpose-built Neoclassical **Mausoleum**, whose bright white columns hide a statue of Burns being accosted by the Poetic Muse. The subject matter may be mawkish, but the execution is excellent – notice the hang of the bonnet and the twist of the trousers. All around, in contrasting brownstone, stand the tombstones of the town's bourgeoisie, including many of the poet's friends; a plan indicates exactly where each is interred.

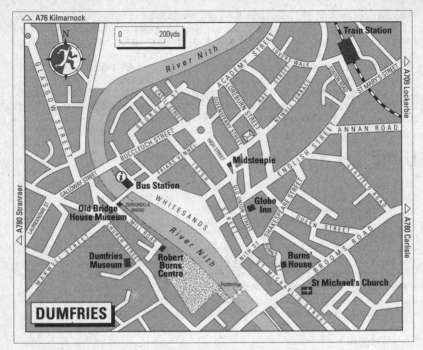

From the mausoleum, saunter back along the Nith and cross Dervorgilla Bridge to the **Old Bridge House Museum** (April–Sept Mon–Sat 10am–1pm & 2–5pm, Sun 2–5pm; free) of Victorian bric-a-brac and the **Robert Burns Centre** (April–Sept Mon–Sat 10am–8pm, Sun 2–5pm; Oct–March Tues–Sat 10am–1pm & 2–5pm; free), sited in an old water mill, which concentrates on the poet's years in Dumfries. On the hill above, occupying an eighteenth-century windmill, the **Dumfries Museum** (April–Sept Mon–Sat 10am–1pm & 2–5pm, Sun 2–5pm; Oct–March Tues–Sat only; free) traces the region's natural and human history and features a **camera obscura** on its top floor (April–Sept only; 70p).

### Drumlanrig Castle
**Drumlanrig Castle** (May to late Aug Mon–Wed & Fri–Sat 11am–5pm, Sun 1–5pm; £2.50) is not in fact a castle, but a massive, many turreted seventeenth-century mansion near the village of **THORNHILL**, eighteen miles north of Dumfries. The interior is stuffed with priceless paintings, including Rembrandt's *Old Woman Reading*, and the usual cacophony of antique furnishings and fittings, the property of the Duke of Buccleuch and Queensberry.

## Practicalities

Dumfries **train station**, on the east side of town, is a five-minute walk from the centre. The **bus station** stands at the top of Whitesands beside the River Nith on the west edge of the centre, next door to the **tourist office** (Nov–March Mon–

Sat 10–1pm & 2–5pm; April–June, Sept & Oct daily 10am–5pm; July & Aug daily 10am–6pm; ☎0387/53862) where they will book accommodation for a ten percent refundable deposit.

There are lots of **guest houses** and **B&Bs** in the villas clustered round the train station, including *Morton Villa*, 28 Lovers Walk (☎0387/55825; ②); *Cairndoon*, 14 Newall Terrace (☎0387/56991; ②); *Lindean*, 50 Rae St (☎0387/51888; ②); and *Redlands Guest House*, 54 Rae St (☎0387/68382; ②). For a more distinctive setting try along Kenmure Terrace, which overlooks the Nith from beside the footbridge below the Burns Centre. There are several choices, but *The Haven*, at no. 1 (☎0387/51281; ③), should be your first port of call. If you're looking for a **hotel**, head for Laurieknowe, a five- to ten-minute walk from the bus station. Here, the best options are the *Edenbank Hotel* (☎0387/52759; ⑥), and the *Dalston Hotel*, no. 5 (☎0387/54422; ⑥).

The cheapest **meals** in town are provided by the popular *YMCA* café, on Castle Street near the Burns Statue. Nearby, the *Hole in the Wa'* **pub**, down an alley opposite *Woolworth's* on the High Street sells reasonable bar food. If you want a pub with more atmosphere, however, you should make your way instead to the *Globe Inn*, a great place for a drink and a snack.

The *Nithsdale Cycle Centre*, Rosefield Mills, Troqueer Rd (☎0387/54870), offers **mountain bike rental**, useful for reaching the nearby Solway coast.

# Around Dumfries: the east Solway coast

The magnificent **Caerlaverock Castle** and the fine early Christian cross at **Ruthwell** are set on the shores of the Solway Firth southeast of Dumfries, from where a regular bus service runs to both.

### Caerlaverock Castle and Wildlife Centre

The remote and lichen-stained **Caerlaverock Castle** (April–Sept Mon–Sat 9.30am–6pm, Sun 2–6pm; Oct–March Mon–Sat 9.30am–4pm, Sun 2–4pm; £1.70), forms a dramatic triangle with a mighty gatehouse at the apex. It clearly impressed medieval chroniclers. During the siege of 1300, Edward I's balladeer, Walter of Exeter, commented "In shape it was like a shield, for it had but three sides round it, with a tower at each corner . . . and good ditches filled right up to the brim with water. And I think you will never see a more finely situated castle".

Nowadays, close inspection reveals several phases of construction, which reflect Caerlaverock's turbulent past: time and again, the castle was attacked and slighted, each subsequent rebuilding further modifying the late thirteenth-century original. For instance, the fifteenth-century machicolations of the gatehouse top earlier towers that are themselves studded with wide-mouthed gunports from around 1590. This confusion of styles continues inside, where the gracious Renaissance facade of the **Nithsdale Apartments** was added by the first earl in 1634. Nithsdale didn't get much value for money: just six years later he was forced to surrender his castle to the Covenanters, who proceeded to wreck the place. It was never inhabited again.

From the castle it's about a mile to the **Caerlaverock Wildlife and Wetlands Centre** (daily 10am–5pm; £2.95), 1400 acres of protected salt-marsh and mud-flat, equipped with screened approaches that link the main observatory to a score of well-situated birdwatchers' hides. The area is famous for the twelve thousand or so Barnacle Geese which return here in winter. Between May and August, when the geese are away, walkers along a wetlands trail may glimpse the rare Natterjack Toad.

## The Ruthwell Cross

From the nature reserve it's about seven miles to the village of **RUTHWELL**, on the northern edge of which is the minor Dumfries–Annan road, the B724, where you should turn down the short, signposted lane to the modest country church. The keys are kept at one of the houses at the bottom of the lane; just look for the notice. Inside the church is the **Ruthwell Cross**, an extraordinary early Christian monument dating from the late seventh century when Galloway was ruled by the Northumbrians. The eighteen-foot-high Cross reveals a striking diversity of influences, with Germanic and Roman Catholic decoration and, running round the edge, a poem written in both runic figures and Northumbrian dialect. But it's the Biblical carvings on the main face that really catch the eye, notably Mary Magdalene washing the feet of Jesus.

There's no real reason to **stay**, but the *Kirkland Country House Hotel* (☎038787/284; ④) is a comfortable establishment next door to the church.

# The Solway coast to the Galloway Hills

The creeks, bays and peninsulas of the **Solway coast** string along the Solway Firth, a shallow estuary wedged between Scotland and England. Edged by tidal marsh and mud bank, much of the shoreline is flat and somewhat tedious, but there are some fine stretches, where rocky bays shelter beneath wooded hills, most notably at **Rockcliffe**, about twenty miles west of Dumfries. **Kirkcudbright** and **Gatehouse of Fleet** were once bustling ports thronged with sailing ships, but they were bypassed by the Victorian train network and so slipped into economic decline which in effect preserved their handsome eighteenth- and early nineteenth-century town houses and workers' cottages. Both these towns are popular with tourists, as are **Sweetheart Abbey**, whose splendid Gothic remains are near Dumfries, and **Threave Castle**, a gaunt tower house outside Castle Douglas.

Within comfortable striking distance of the coast are the **Galloway Hills**, whose forested knolls and grassy peaks flank lochs and tumbling burns – classic Southern Upland scenery, with scores of trails within **Galloway Forest Park**.

## Sweetheart Abbey

**NEW ABBEY**, a tidy hamlet eight miles south of Dumfries, is home to the red sandstone ruins of **Sweetheart Abbey** (April–Sept Mon–Sat 9.30am–6pm, Sun 2–6pm; Oct–March Mon–Wed 9.30am–4pm, Thurs 9.30am–12.30pm, Sat 9.30am–4pm, Sun 2–4pm; £1). Founded by Cistercians in 1273, Sweetheart takes its name from the obsessive behaviour of its patron, Dervorgilla de Balliol, who carried her husband's embalmed heart around with her for the last sixteen years of her life. The site is dominated by the remains of the **Abbey Church**, a massive structure that abandons the austere simplicity of earlier Cistercian foundations. The grand, high-pointed window arches of the nave, set beneath the elaborate clerestory, draw the eye to a mighty central tower with a battlemented parapet and flamboyant corbels. The opulent style reflects the monks' wealth, born of their skill in turning the wastes and swamps of Solway into productive farmland.

After the abbey, pop into the *Abbey Cottage* tearooms next door for a great cup of coffee and a piece of homemade cake. **To stay** in the village, try the *Criffel Inn*, 2 The Square (☎038785/244; ④).

## The Colvend coast: Rockcliffe

To the south of Sweetheart, the **Colvend coast** is a six-mile-long, low-key holiday strip extending north from Sandyhills to Dalbeattie. In the middle, nestling round a beautiful cove, is **ROCKCLIFFE**, where there are some great walks. At low tide you can waddle out across the mud-flats to **Rough Island**, a humpy twenty-acre bird sanctuary owned by the National Trust for Scotland, though it's out of bounds in May and June when the Terns and Oyster Catchers are nesting. Alternatively, you can hike up the coast a mile or so to the **Mote of Mark**, a Celtic hill fort, and continue another couple of miles to the village of **Kippford**, once a ship-repair centre, and now the home of the yachting brigade. From here, it's a few minutes to the **Rough Firth** causeway, a more reliable route to Rough Island.

Rockcliffe has a reasonable range of **accommodation**, but note that advance reservations are recommended at most places during the summer. There's the attractive *Albany B&B* (☎055663/355; ③), right on the seafront, and several cottages available for rental by the week: try *Westlin* (April–Oct; ☎055663/212), overlooking the bay, which sleeps four for between £140 and £200, or the charming *Port Donnell* cottage rented out by the National Trust for Scotland (details from head office in Edinburgh, ☎031/226 5922). The only **hotel**, the grand *Barons Craig* (April–Oct; ☎055663/225; ⑨), occupies a splendid Victorian mansion on the hill above the bay.

## Around Castle Douglas

The eighteenth-century streets of **CASTLE DOUGLAS**, eleven miles north of Rockcliffe, were designed by the town's owner, William Douglas, a local lad who made a fortune trading in the West Indies. Douglas had ambitious plans to turn his town into a prosperous industrial and commercial centre, but, like his scheme to create an extensive Galloway canal system, it didn't quite work.

You'll only need to hang around town long enough to get your bearings as the district's two attractions are situated well outside the centre. Beginning from the **bus station**, at the west end of the long main drag, King Street – the **tourist office** (April–Oct daily; ☎0556/2611) is at the other end – it's about a mile's walk west along the A75 to **Threave Garden** (daily 9am–sunset; £2.80), a magnificent spread of flowers and woodland, where the National Trust's School of Horticulture is based. The garden is best visited in the springtime for its splendid blaze of daffodils, and the **Visitor Centre** (April–Oct daily 9am–5.30pm) provides some background on some of the garden's more exotic species, where they came from and who brought them back.

Returning to the main road, continue west for another half mile and turn right down the lane which leads to the River Dee, where a boat takes visitors over to **Threave Castle** (April–Sept Mon–Sat 9.30am–6pm, Sun 2–6pm; £1.20 including ferry), a stern-looking, fourteenth-century fortified tower house on a flat, grassy islet in the middle of the river. The castle was built by a Black Douglas, Archibald the Grim, who earned his sobriquet by hanging his victims from the large corbel – the "gallows knob" – that sticks out above the doorway. The Covenanters wrecked the place in 1640, and it's stood abandoned ever since.

# Kirkcudbright

KIRKCUDBRIGHT (pronounced "Kirkcoobrie"), hugging the banks of the Dee ten miles southwest of Castle Douglas, has a good-looking **harbourside** with a medley of complementary architectures: simple brick cottages sharing space with medieval pends, Georgian villas and Victorian town houses. This is the setting for **McLellan's Castle** (April–Sept Mon–Sat 9.30am–6pm, Sun 2–6pm; Oct–March Sat 9.30am–4pm, Sun 2–4pm; £1), a sullen, pink-flecked hulk towering above the water. Go inside for a look around the sombre interior and keep an eye out for the laird's lug, or peephole, behind the fireplace of the Great Hall. The stronghold was built during the 1580s for Sir Thomas McLellan, now buried in neighbouring **Greyfriars Church** (daily 9am–6pm; free), where the man's tomb is an eccentrically crude attempt at Neoclassicism – it even incorporates parts of someone else's gravestone.

Close by, on the L-shaped High Street, **Broughton House** (Easter to mid-Oct Mon & Wed–Sat 11am–1pm & 2–5pm, Sun 2–5pm; £1.50) was once the home of Edward Hornel, an important member of the late nineteenth-century Scottish art establishment. Hornel and his buddies established a self-regarding artists' colony in Kirkcudbright, and some of their work is on display here. It's all pretty modest stuff, but Hornel's paintings of Japan, a country he often visited, are bright and cheery – a bit like the **Japanese garden** he designed to the rear of the house.

Don't miss the **Stewartry Museum** on St Mary's Street (Easter & Oct Mon–Sat 11am–4pm; May, June & Sept Mon–Sat 11am–5pm; July & Aug Mon–Sat 11am–7.30pm, Sun 2–5pm; Nov–Easter Sat only 11am–4pm; £1), where, packed into a purpose-built Victorian building, hundreds of local exhibits illuminate the life and times of the Solway Coast. It's an extraordinary collection, cabinets crammed with anything from glass bottles, weaving equipment, pipes, pictures and postcards to stuffed birds, pickled fish and the tri-cornered hats once worn by town officials. There are also examples of book jackets designed by Jessie King and E. A. Taylor, two of Hornel's coterie, and a small feature on **John Paul Jones** (1747–92), an early hero of the US navy. Born in nearby Kirkbean, "John Paul", as he was christened, went to sea on the slavers before captaining his own vessel from Kirkcudbright. At the age of 23, he was accused of killing a crew-member, Mungo Maxwell, and imprisoned in Kirkcudbright tolbooth. Released on bail, Jones escaped punishment by claiming that Maxwell had died of the fever, and to escape the stigma, emigrated to Virginia in 1773. Two years later, under the assumed name of Jones, John Paul was appointed first lieutenant of the *Alfred*, a frigate in the new American navy. In 1778, he turned up in the Solway to kidnap the Earl of Selkirk, but satisfied himself with pillaging the family silver instead – though he did repent and return the treasure forthwith.

## Practicalities

**Buses** to Kirkcudbright stop by the harbourside, next to the **tourist office** (April–June & Sept–Oct daily 10am–5pm; July & Aug daily 10am–6pm; ☎0557/30494), where you can get help finding accommodation, a service you will probably need in high season. The town has several quality **hotels** – among them the *Gladstone House*, 48 High St (☎0557/31734; ④), or the *Selkirk Arms*, just up the road (☎0557/30402; ⑤). For a convenient **B&B**, walk over to Castle Street where there's the *Castle Guest House* at no. 16 (Feb–Nov; ☎0557/30204; ③), and *Mrs*

*Mitchell* at no. 7 (April–Oct; ☎0577/30502). You could also try along Millburn Street – follow the High Street onto St Mary's Place and it's the first turning on the left – at *Mrs Mcllwraith*, no. 22 (Feb–Nov; ☎0557/30056; ②) or *Millburn House* (☎0577/30926; ③). The **Silvercraigs Caravan and Camping Site** (Easter to mid-Oct; ☎0557/30123) is located on a bluff overlooking town at the end of St Mary's Place, five to ten minutes' walk from the centre.

Kirkcudbright is light on **restaurants**, but the *Selkirk Arms* serves excellent bar meals and snacks. The *Solway Tide* tearoom, opposite the tourist office, is good value; for a drink, the *Masonic Arms* on Castle Street, pulls a reasonable pint.

## Around Kirkcudbright

In summer there are regular sea angling and sightseeing **boat trips** from Kircudbright harbour. Popular **walks** include the five-mile round trip up the Dee to **Tongland Power Station** (May–Sept Mon–Sat guided tours 4 times daily; £1; bookings ☎0557/30114), whose turbines and generators are housed in a striking Art Deco building. Another option is the five-mile trek southeast along narrow country roads to **DUNDRENNAN**, an appealing little village hiding the grey-stone ruins of **Dundrennan Abbey**. Enough remains of this twelfth-century foundation to be able to appreciate its architectural simplicity, in contrast to the more ornate style adopted by its daughter house, Sweetheart at New Abbey (see p.130). **Bus** service #501 connects Kirkcudbright and Dundrennan six days a week. (Mon–Fri 4 daily, Sat 2 daily).

# Gatehouse of Fleet

The quiet streets of **GATEHOUSE OF FLEET**, easily reached by bus from Kirkcudbright ten miles to the west, give no clue that for James Murray, the eighteenth-century laird, this spot was to become the "Glasgow" of the Solway Coast – a centre of the cotton industry whose profits had already made him immeasurably rich. Yorkshire mill owners provided the industrial expertise, imported engineers designed aqueducts to improve the water supply, and dispossessed crofters – and their children – yielded the labour. Between 1760 and 1790, Murray achieved much success, but his custom-built town failed to match its better placed rivals. By 1850 the boom was over, the mills slipped into disrepair, and nowadays tiny Gatehouse is sustained by tourism and forestry.

It's the country setting that appeals rather than any particular sight, but there are some fine Georgian houses along the High Street, which also has an incongruous, granite clock tower and the **Mill on the Fleet Museum** (April–Oct daily 10am–5.30pm; £2.50), gallantly tracing the history of Gatehouse and Galloway from inside an old bobbin mill. The **tourist office** nearby (April–Oct daily 10am–5pm; ☎0557/814212) sells an excellent leaflet on local **walks**, the best of which loops south through the forests beside the Water of Fleet river and on towards the Solway Firth. En route, you can't miss James Murray's country mansion, converted into the sumptuous **Cally Palace Hotel** (☎0557/814341; ⑨). More affordable places **to stay** in Gatehouse include the attractive *Murray Arms Hotel* (☎0557/814207; ⑦), the homely *Bobbin Guest House* (☎0557/814229; ③) and the *Bay Horse B&B* (April–Oct; ☎0557/814073; ③). The *Murray Arms* offers delicious **meals** and the *Bobbin Coffee Shop*, on the High Street, is good value too.

# Newton Stewart and Glen Trool

To the west of Gatehouse, the A75 skirts the mud flats of Wigtown Bay before cutting up to **NEWTON STEWART**, an unassuming market town beside the River Cree, famous for its salmon and trout fishing. The excellent **Creebridge House Hotel** (☎0671/2121; ⑦), in an old hunting lodge near the main bridge, arranges permits for around £10 per day, can provide personal gillies (guides) for a further £20 daily, and at a pinch they'll even rent you all the tackle. The hotel **restaurant** is great too – try the fish or the homemade pies.

With its plentiful supply of accommodation (see below) and good bus connections along the A75, Newton Stewart has also become a popular base for **hikers** heading for the nearby **Galloway Hills**, most of which are enclosed within **Galloway Forest Park**. Many hikers aim for the park's **Glen Trool** by following the A714 north for about ten miles to Bargrennan, where a narrow lane twists the five miles over to the glen's **Loch Trool**. From here, there's a choice of magnificent hiking trails, as well as lesser tracks laid out by the forestry commission. Several longer routes curve round the grassy peaks and icy lochs of the Awful Hand and Dungeon ranges, whilst another includes part of the **Southern Upland Way**, which threads through the Minnigaff hills to Clatteringshaws Loch, beside the A712. This is the road that links Newton Stewart with New Galloway.

For the more adventurous trails, you'll need to be properly equipped; the Newton Stewart **tourist office** (April–Oct daily 10am–5pm; ☎0671/2431), on the main street opposite the bus station, has bags of helpful literature. If you mean business, be sure to buy the Ordnance Survey maps and *The Galloway Hills: A Walker's Paradise* by George Brittain (£2.50). Reaching Loch Trool by **bus** is a bit of a pain: service #517 makes the twenty-minute trip to Glentrool Village between two and three times daily, but you have to walk the final four miles.

The tourist office will provide a full list of local **accommodation** and book a bed on your behalf. In town, the cheapest choice is the convenient Minnigaff **youth hostel** (April–Sept; ☎0671/2211; Grade 3), or – setting aside the *Creebridge House Hotel* – you could try along Corvisel Road, where there's *Lynwood* (☎0671/2074; ②) and *Kilwarlin* (April–Oct; ☎0671/3047; ②). Alternatively, **Caldons Campsite** (April–Oct; ☎0671/2420) is near the car park at the western tip of Loch Trool.

# The Queen's Way: New Galloway and The Glenkens

The twenty-mile stretch from Newton Stewart to New Galloway, known as the **Queen's Way**, cuts through the southern periphery of **Galloway Forest Park**, a landscape of glassy lochs, wooded hills and bare, rounded peaks. You'll pass all sorts of **hiking trails**, some the gentlest of strolls, others long-distance treks. For a short walk, stop at the **Talnotry Campsite** (April–Oct; ☎0671/2420), about five miles from Newton Stewart, where the forestry commission have laid out three trails between two and four miles long: each delves into the pine forests beside the road, crossing gorges and burns. A few miles further on is **Clatteringshaws Loch**, a reservoir surrounded by pine forest, with a footpath running right round. This connects with the Southern Upland Way as it meanders north towards the **Rhinns of Kells**, the bumpy range marking the park's eastern boundary.

From the lake, it's seven miles further to **NEW GALLOWAY**, nestling in the river valley at the northern tip of Loch Ken. Although little more than one long street lined by neat and attractive stone houses, it provides further access to the Southern Upland Way and the Rhinns of Kells, as does the neighbouring village of **DALRY**, a couple of miles upstream. New Galloway is in the valley of **The Glenkens**, which extends south to Castle Douglas via Loch Ken, and north along the river as far as **Carsphairn**, a desolate hamlet surrounded by wild moors.

### Practicalities

Connecting with services from Dumfries and Kirkcudbright, the fast and frequent Castle Douglas to Ayr **bus** stops in New Galloway. There's no official tourist office, but **The Smithy Teashop** (March–May & Oct daily 10am–6pm; June–Sept daily 10am–9pm), on the High Street, provides all the essential information. The village has many **hotels** and **B&Bs** strung along the main drag, try the agreeable *Leamington Hotel* (closed Nov; ☎06442/327; ④), or *The Smithy* itself (March–Oct; ☎06442/269; ②), which also serves excellent meals. If you want to stay in **Dalry**, head for the *Lochinvar Hotel* (☎06443/210; ④). The nearest **youth hostel**, *Kendoon* (mid-May to Sept; no phone; Grade 3), is five miles north of Dalry, near the Southern Upland Way. It's also about fifteen minutes' walk from the A713; if you're travelling there on the Castle Douglas–Ayr bus, ask the driver to tell you when to get off.

# The Machars

**The Machars**, the name given to the peninsula of flat farmland south of Newton Stewart, is a neglected part of the coastline, with an abandoned, disconsolate air. Just six miles off the A75 is **WIGTOWN**, an unassuming country town whose spacious main street and square occupy a hill above Wigtown Bay. It's a five-minute walk from the square to the tidal flats below, where a simple stone obelisk commemorates two Covenanter martyrs, Margaret McLachlan and Margaret Wilson. In 1685, the two women were tied to stakes on the flats and drowned by the rising tide.

## Whithorn

From Wigtown it's a further eleven miles south to **WHITHORN**, with a sloping, airy high street of pastel-painted cottages. This one-horse town occupies an important place in Scottish history, for it was here in 397 AD that **Saint Ninian** founded the first Christian church north of Hadrian's Wall. Ninian daubed his tiny building in white plaster and called it **Candida Casa**, translated as "Hwiterne", hence Whithorn, by his Pictish neighbours. Ninian's life is shrouded in mystery, but he does seem to have been raised in Galloway and he was a key figure in the Christianization of his country. Indeed, his tomb became a popular place of pilgrimage and, in the twelfth century, a priory was built to service the shrine.

Halfway down the main street, the **Whithorn Dig** (early April to Oct daily 10.30am–5pm; £2.50) exploits these ecclesiastical connections. A high-tech video gives background details and a handful of archeological finds serve as an introduction for a stroll round the dig. Be sure to take up the complimentary guide service – you won't make much sense of the complex sequence of ruins without one. Beyond the dig neither the meagre remains of the priory and the original site of Candida Casa are as diverting as the adjacent **Whithorn Museum** (April–Sept Mon–Sat 9.30am–6pm, Sun 2–6pm; Oct–March Sat 9.30am–4pm, Sun 2–4pm; £1.20). Its assortment of early Christian memorials includes a series of standing crosses and headstones, the earliest being the Latinus Stone of 450 AD.

The pilgrims who crossed the Solway to visit St Ninian's shrine landed at the **ISLE OF WHITHORN**, three miles south of Whithorn. Not, in fact, an island at all, it's a bedraggled seaport hiding the minuscule remains of the thirteenth-century **St Ninian's Chapel**.

### Glenluce Abbey and Castle Kennedy Gardens

It's fourteen miles from Whithorn to the turning for **Glenluce Abbey** (April–Sept Mon–Sat 9.30am–6pm, Sun 2–6pm; Oct–March Sat 9.30am–4pm, Sun 2–4pm; £1; no buses), whose ruins lie in a gentle valley a couple of miles off the main road. Founded in 1192, Glenluce prospered from the diligence of its Cistercian monks, who drained the surrounding marshes, creating prime farmland. The brothers' fifteenth-century Chapter House has survived pretty much intact, and with its ribbed vault ceiling generates the clearest of acoustics – opera singers practise here. Notice too, the green man motif carved into the corbels and bosses. Popularized in the twelfth century, these grotesques have human or cat-like faces, with large, glaring eyes, frowning foreheads, and prominent teeth or fangs. All (hence the name) have greenery sprouting from their faces, a feature that originated with pagan leaf masks and the Celtic concept of fertility.

The thirteenth-century wizard and alchemist **Michael Scot** lived here, supposedly luring the plague into a secret vault where he promptly imprisoned it. Scot, one-time magician to the court of the Emperor Frederick in Sicily, appears in Dante's *Inferno*.

Seven miles from Glenluce and three miles east of Stranraer, **Castle Kennedy Gardens** (April–Sept daily 10am–5pm; £1.80) flank the shattered, ivy-clad remains of a medieval fortress, situated on a narrow isthmus between two lochs. The gardens are famous for their monkey puzzle trees, magnolias and rhododendrons.

# The Rhinns of Galloway

West of the Machars the **Rhinns of Galloway** is a hilly, hammer-shaped peninsula at the end of the Solway Coast, encompassing two contrasting towns, the grimy port of **Stranraer**, where there are regular ferries over to Northern Ireland, and the beguiling resort of **Portpatrick**, the western terminus of the Southern Upland Way. Between the two, a string of tiny farming villages lead down to the **Mull of Galloway**, the windswept headland at the southwest tip of Scotland.

## Stranraer

It's hard to be kind about **STRANRAER**. However, if you're heading to (or coming from) Northern Ireland you may well have to pass through, and at least everything's convenient. The **train station** adjoins the **Sealink ferry terminal** on the East Pier, where boats depart for Larne; a couple of minutes' walk away, on Port Rodie, small green stands pass for the town's **bus station;** and nearby, further round the bay, **Seacat Hovercraft** services leave from the West Pier to Belfast.

While you're waiting for a ferry, a walk along the dishevelled main street, variously Charlotte, George and High streets, takes in Stranraer's one specific attraction, a medieval tower which is all that remains of the **Castle of St John** (April–Sept Mon–Sat 10am–1pm & 2–5pm; 60p). Inside, an exhibition traces the history of the castle down to its use as a police station and prison in the nineteenth century. The old exercise yard is on the roof.

Stranraer has plenty of basic snack bars, but it's well worth paying a little extra to enjoy a **meal** at the *Apéritif*, just up the hill from the bus station along Bellevilla Road. If you're stranded, the **tourist office** (April–Oct daily 10am–5pm) will arrange accommodation, or you can try *Fernlea*, Lewis St (☎0776/3037; ③). The *Aird Donald Camp & Caravan Park* (☎0776/2025) is ten minutes' walk east of the town centre along London Road.

## Portpatrick and south

Perched on the west shore of the Rhinns, the pastel-shaded houses of **PORTPATRICK** spread over the craggy coast above the slender harbour. Until the mid-nineteenth century, when sailing ships were replaced by steamboats, this was the main embarkation point for Northern Ireland, with coal, cotton and British troops heading in one direction, Ulster cattle and linen in the other. Nowadays, Portpatrick is a quiet resort enjoyed for its rugged scenery and coastal hikes, as well as excellent **sea fishing**. There are daily trips in summer, costing £7 for three hours, £15 for seven.

Portpatrick has several good **hotels** and **guest houses**, the best of which are the *Portpatrick Hotel* (☎0776/81333; ⑧), occupying a grand Edwardian mansion above the harbour, and the comfortable *Carlton Guest House*, on South Crescent (☎0776/81253; ③). For a **meal** and a **drink**, head on down to the *Crown* pub, near the lighthouse.

### South to the Mull of Galloway

The remoter reaches of the Rhinns of Galloway, extending about twenty miles south from Portpatrick, consist of gorse-covered hills and pastureland crossed by narrow country lanes and dotted with farming hamlets. Of the two shorelines, the west has a sharper, rockier aspect and it's here, near the village of Port Logan, you'll find the **Logan Botanic Garden** (mid-March to Oct daily 10am–6pm; £1.50), an outpost of Edinburgh's Royal Botanic Garden. There are three main areas; a peat garden, a woodland and a walled garden noted for its tree ferns and cabbage palms (the Gulf Stream keeps the Rhinns almost completely free of frost in a climate that can support subtropical species).

It's a further twelve miles south to the **Mull of Galloway**, a bleak and precipitous headland where wheeling birds and whistling winds circle a bright whitewashed lighthouse. On clear days you can see over to Cumbria and Ireland.

# The South Ayrshire coast

Fifty miles from top to bottom, the **South Ayrshire Coast**, stretched out between Stranraer and Ayr, is easily seen from the A77 coastal road, which leaves Stranraer to trim thirty miles of low, rocky shore before reaching **Girvan**, a brash seaside resort where boats depart for **Ailsa Craig**, out in the Firth of Clyde. Back on shore, the A77 presses on through the village of **Turnberry**, home to one of the world's most famous golf courses, where the A719 branches off for eighteenth-century **Culzean Castle** (pronounced "Cullane"). From the castle, it's twelve miles further to **Ayr**. There's a reasonable **bus** service along the coast, a better one between Culzean and Ayr – plus a rail line that runs from Stranraer to Girvan, Maybole and Ayr.

## Girvan and Ailsa Craig

Set beneath a ridge of grassy hills, **GIRVAN** is at its prettiest round the harbour, a narrow slit beside the Girvan Water. On either side are ancient stone cottages, the homes of local fishermen, and, for a moment, it's possible to ignore the amusement arcades and seaside tat elsewhere in town. From late May to September **boats** leave the harbour for the ten-mile excursion west to the **Ailsa Craig**, "Fairy Rock" in Gaelic – though the island looks more like an enormous muffin than a place of enchantment. With its jagged cliffs and 1114-foot-high summit, Ailsa Craig is a privately owned bird sanctuary that's home to thousands of gannets. The best time to make the trip is at the end of May and in June when the fledglings are trying to fly. Boats are not allowed to land and the cruise, lasting about two hours and operating between three and seven times a week, costs £7; ring the boat owner, Tony Wass, on ☎0294/833724, for up-to-date details.

There are regular **bus** services from Stranraer and Ayr to Girvan, which is also on the Glasgow–Stranraer **train** line. If you decide to stay overnight, the **tourist office** (Easter–June & Sept daily 10am–5pm; July & Aug daily 10am–7pm; early Oct Mon–Fri 10am–4pm, Sat & Sun noon–4pm) has a full list of **accommodation**, or try along the seafront, at the *Thistleneuk Guest House*, 19 Louisa Drive (☎0465/2137; ③).

## Culzean Castle

Designed by Robert Adam, **Culzean Castle** (April to late Oct daily 10.30am–5.30pm; £3.30) and the surrounding **country park** (daily 9am–sunset; £5 per car, pedestrians free) are Ayrshire's premier tourist attractions. The best place to start is at the **Visitor Centre**, located in the modernized Home Farm buildings of 1777. Here, you can pick up free maps – as well as wildlife leaflets – that help you get your bearings, the layout of the place being rather confusing. From here, it's a few minutes' walk over to the **Castle**, whose towers and turrets rise high above the sea cliffs. Nothing remains of the original fifteenth-century structure, since, in 1777, the tenth Earl of Cassillis commissioned Robert Adam to remodel the family home.

The work took fifteen years to complete, and, although the exterior, with its arrow slits and battlements, preserves a medieval aspect, the interior exemplifies the harmonious classical designs Adam loved. On the ground floor, the subtle greens of the old eating room are enlivened by basket-of-fruit plasterwork along the curtain cornices, and the chimneypiece is decorated with trailing vine leaves and grapes. There's the brilliantly conceived oval staircase, where three tiers of Corinthian and Ionic columns add height and perspective, while the sweep of the stairs and the ironwork balustrade give a sense of movement, and on the upper floor, the carefully contrived decor of the circular saloon deliberately contrasts with the natural land and seascapes on view through the windows. Next door, a set of photographs celebrate President Eisenhower's association with Culzean; Ike stayed here on several occasions and the National Guest Flat, on the top floor, was given to him by the Kennedys for his lifetime. Nowadays, it's used by the very wealthy as a holiday apartment and is closed to the public.

Leave time for an exploration of the **country park**, whose 565 acres spread out along the seashore. Criss-crossed by footpaths, the park's varied terrain incorporates woodland, cliffs, a beach and a walled garden, whose blooms are at their best in July and August.

# Ayr and around

With a population of around fifty thousand, **AYR**, the largest town on the Firth of Clyde coast, was an important seaport and trading centre for many centuries, and rivalled Glasgow in size and significance right up until the late seventeenth century. In recognition, Cromwell made it a centre of his administration and built an enormous fortress here, long since destroyed. With the relative decline of its seaborne trade, Ayr developed as a market town, praised by Robert Burns, who was born in the neighbouring village of **Alloway** (see p.141), for its "honest men and bonny lasses". In the nineteenth century, Ayr became a popular resort for middle-class Victorians, with a new town of wide streets and boulevards built behind the beach immediately southwest of the old town. Nowadays, Ayr is both Ayrshire's commercial centre and a holiday resort, its long sandy beach (and prestigious racecourse) attracting hundreds of Scotland's city dwellers.

## The Town

The cramped, sometimes seedy streets and alleys of Ayr's **old town** occupy a wedge-shaped parcel of land between Sandgate to Alloway Place in the west, and the south bank of the treacly River Ayr to the east. Almost all the medieval buildings were knocked down by the Victorians, but the **Auld Brig**, with its cobbles and sturdy breakwaters, has survived from the thirteenth century. The bridge was saved by Robert Burns, or rather his poem *Twa Brigs*, which made it too famous to demolish; an international appeal raised the capital necessary for its refurbishment in 1907.

The bridge connects with the High Street near the Kirk Port, a narrow lane leading to the **Auld Kirk** (July & Aug Tues & Thurs only), the church funded by Cromwell as recompense for the one he incorporated into his stronghold. At the lych gate, a plan of the graveyard shows where many of Burns' friends are buried. Notice also the mort-safe (heavy grating) on the wall of the lych gate. Placed over newly dug graves, these mort-safes were a sort of early nineteenth-century corpse security system meant to deter body snatchers at a time when dead bodies – no questions asked – were swiftly bought up by medical schools. The church's dark and gloomy interior retains the original pulpit. Retracing your steps past the Kirk Port, take the next left down pedestrianized Newmarket Street, leading onto Sandgate, with the elegant spire of the **Town Buildings**, down towards the New Bridge.

Extending southwest of Sandgate to the Esplanade and the **beach**, the wide, gridiron streets of the Victorian **new town** contrast with the crowded lanes of old Ayr. It was the opening of the Glasgow to Ayr railway line in 1840 that brought the first major influx of holidaymakers and Ayr remains a busy resort today, with many visitors heading for the plethora of trim guest houses concentrated around **Wellington Square**, whose terraces flank the impressive County Buildings dating from 1820. The new town extends north towards the river, with its comfortable villas spreading over the old perimeter of Cromwell's fort. It's here, off Bruce Crescent, you'll find **St John's Tower**, all that's left of the church Cromwell used as his armoury.

## Practicalities

Ayr **train station** is less than ten minutes' walk east of the town centre. Nearby, at the foot of Sandgate, is the **bus station**, past the **tourist office**, at no. 39 (Mon–Fri 9.15am-5pm, 7pm in July & Aug; Easter to mid-Oct also Sat & Sun 10am–5pm, 7pm in July & Aug; ☎0292/284196). They can help with accommodation, a particularly useful service at the height of the season and during important race meetings.

At other times, head straight for the cluster of **hotels** and **guest houses** around Wellington Square, a couple of minutes' walk south of Sandgate along Alloway Place. In particular, try along Queen's Terrace where, among others, there's the *Dargil Guest House* at no. 7 (☎0292/261955; ②), *Queens* at no. 10 (☎0292/265618; ②), and the *Daviot*, no. 12 (☎0292/269678; ②). The *Arrandale Hotel* is close by at 2–4 Cassillis St (☎0292/289959; ③) and fifteen minutes' walk further south the Ayr **youth hostel** is on Craigweil Road (March–Oct; ☎0292/262322; Grade 1), near the beach. The *Heads of Ayr Leisure Park* (March–Nov; ☎0292/442269), five miles south of town along the coastal A719, accepts caravans and tents.

All three guest houses listed serve reasonable evening **meals**, but if you're determined to venture out, head for Newmarket Street and the *Wee Windaes*, where you can get good fish dishes. For a drink, try the *Tam O'Shanter*, on the High Street, a pub-cum-museum decked out with Burns memorabilia.

# Alloway

There's little else but Burnsiana in the small village of **ALLOWAY**, a key stop on the **Burns Heritage Trail** (see p.126) fifteen minutes south of Ayr by bus #61 (Mon–Sat 6 daily). Get off at the whitewashed **Burns Cottage and Museum** (April, May, Sept & Oct Mon–Sat 10am–5pm, Sun 2–5pm; June–Aug Mon–Sat 9am–6pm, Sun 10am–5pm; Nov–March Mon–Sat 10am–4pm; £1.80, ticket includes entry to Burns Monument) for a peep at the poet's birthplace, a dark and dank, long thatched cottage where animals and people lived under the same roof. The two-room museum boasts all sorts of memorabilia – the family Bible, letters and manuscripts – plus a potted history of his life, illuminated by contemporaneous quotes.

The modern, faceless **Land O'Burns Visitor Centre** (daily 10am–5.30pm), a few minutes further down the road, is for the most part a souvenir shop selling a good selection of books about, and works of, Burns, though it does show a video (50p) that provides helpful background information on mid-eighteenth-century Ayrshire.

Across the road from here are the plain, roofless ruins of **Alloway Church**, where Robert's father William is buried. Burns set much of his poem *Tam o'Shanter* here. Tam, having got drunk in Ayr, passes "By Alloway's auld haunted kirk" and stumbles across a witches' dance, from which he's forced to fly for his life over the **Brig o' Doon**, a hump-backed bridge.

> *But hornpipes, jigs, strathspeys and reels,*
> *Put life and mettle in their heels.*
> *A winnock-bunker in the east,* [window recess]
> *There sat auld Nick, in shape o' beast;*
> *A towzie tyke, black, grim and large,* [shaggy dog]
> *To gie them music was his charge:*
> *He screw'd the pipes and gart them skirl* [made; scream]
> *Till roof and rafters a' did dirl.* [vibrate]

Across the street from the church the thirteenth-century bridge still stands, curving gracefully over the river below the **Burns Monument** (April–Oct only, same hours & ticket as Cottage), a striking Neoclassical temple in a small leafy garden.

## ROBERT BURNS

The first of seven children, **Robert Burns**, the national poet of Scotland, was born in Alloway on January 25, 1759. His father, William, was employed as a gardener until 1766 when he became a tenant farmer at Mount Oliphant, near Alloway, moving to Lochlie farm, Tarbolton, eleven years later. A series of bad harvests and the demands of the landlord's estate manager bankrupted the family, and William died almost penniless in 1784. These events had a profound effect on Robert, leaving him with an antipathy towards political authority and a hatred of the landowning classes.

With the death of his father, Robert became head of the family and they moved again, this time to a farm at Mossgiel, near Mauchline. Burns had already begun writing poetry and prose at Lochlie, recording incidental thoughts in his *First Commonplace Book*, but it was here at Mossgiel that he began to write in earnest, and his first volume, *Poems Chiefly in the Scottish Dialect*, was published in Kilmarnock in 1786. The book proved immensely popular, celebrated by ordinary Scots and Edinburgh literati alike, with the satirical trilogy *Holy Willie's Prayer*, *The Holy Fair* and *Address to the Deil* attracting particular attention. The object of Burns' poetic scorn was the kirk, whose ministers had obliged him to appear in church to be publicly condemned for fornication – a commonplace punishment in those days.

Burns spent the winter of 1786–87 in the capital, lionized by the literary establishment. Despite his success, however, he felt trapped, unable to make enough money from writing to leave farming. He was also in a political snare, fraternizing with the elite, but with radical views and pseudo-Jacobite nationalism that constantly landed him in trouble. His frequent recourse was to play the part of the unlettered ploughman-poet, the noble savage who might be excused his impetuous outbursts and hectic womanizing.

Burns had, however, made useful contacts in Edinburgh and as a consequence was recruited to collect, write and rearrange two volumes of songs set to traditional Scottish tunes. These volumes, James Johnson's *Scots Musical Museum* and George Thomson's *Select Scottish Airs*, contain the bulk of his songwriting, and it's on them that Burns' international reputation rests with works like *Auld Lang Syne*, *Scots, wha hae*, *Coming through the Rye* and *Green Grow the Rushes, O*. At this time too, though poetry now took second place, he produced two excellent poems; *Tam o' Shanter* and a republican tract, *A Man's a Man for a' that*.

In 1788, Burns married Jean Armour and moved to Ellisland Farm, near Dumfries. The following year, he was appointed excise officer and could at last leave farming, moving to Dumfries in 1791. Burns' years of comfort were short-lived, however. His years of labour on the farm, allied to a rheumatic fever, damaged his heart, and he died in Dumfries on July 21, 1796, aged 37.

Burns' work, inspired by a romantic nationalism and tinged with a wry wit, has made him a potent symbol of "Scottishness". Ignoring the Anglophile preferences of the Edinburgh elite, he wrote in Scots vernacular about the country he loved, an exuberant celebration that filled a need in a nation culturally colonized by England. Today Burns Clubs all over the world mark every anniversary of the poet's birthday with the Burns' Supper, complete with Scottish totems – haggis, piper and whisky bottle.

# The North Ayrshire coast

The **North Ayrshire coast** extends some thirty-odd miles from Ayr up to **Largs,** by far the area's most agreeable resort. Getting there, however, along the busy coastal road, is something of an aesthetic ordeal: leaving Ayr, the road trims the outskirts of Prestwick, the site of an international airport, before bypassing **Troon**, a desultory resort with a seaside golf course. **IRVINE** is a grim industrial settlement that was once the principal port for Glasgow, whose highlight is the **Scottish Maritime Museum** (April–Oct daily 10am–5pm; £1.50) down at the old harbour, a couple of miles southwest of the town centre. The assortment of craft moored to the museum docks include a dredger, a fishing skiff, a lifeboat, a tug and a "puffer" boat, the last used as an inshore supply vessel along the Clyde and between the islands. The history of the puffers forms part of the museum's well-presented display on Clydeside shipping.

Eight miles inland from Irvine, **KILMARNOCK** is a shabby manufacturing town that's the home of **Johnnie Walker** whisky. There are guided tours of the bottling plant, on Hill Street near the train station, on weekdays from April to October (☎0563/23401 for times).

North from Irvine, it's just eight miles to **ARDROSSAN**, where ferries leave for Brodick on the Isle of Arran (see p.263), and another twelve miles to Largs, from where you can catch a ferry across to the nearby island of **Great Cumbrae**, a subdued but popular holiday spot.

# Largs and Great Cumbrae

Tucked in between the hills and the sea, **LARGS** remains a traditional family resort, its guest houses and B&Bs spreading out behind an elongated promenade. There's a tiny pier too, set beside an unpretentious town centre that conceals one real surprise: **Skelmorlie Aisle** (June–Aug Mon–Sat 9.30am–6pm, Sun 2–6pm; £1), a Renaissance gem hidden away beside the old graveyard off Main Street. Once the north transept of a larger church, the aisle was converted into a mausoleum for Sir Robert Montgomerie, a local bigwig, in 1636. Carved by Scottish masons following Italian patterns, the tomb is decorated with Montgomerie's monogram and arms as well as symbols of mortality such as the skull, winged hour-glass and inverted torch. Up above, the intricate paintwork of the barrel-vaulted ceiling includes the signs of the zodiac, biblical figures and texts, and the legendary coats of arms of the tribes of Israel.

Back outside on the promenade, it's about a mile south along the shoreline footpath to the **Pencil Monument**, a modern obelisk commemorating the Battle of Largs of 1263. The battle was actually an accident, forced on King Hakon's Vikings when their longships were blown ashore by a gale. The invaders were attacked by the Scots as they struggled through the surf, and, although both sides claimed victory, the Norwegians did retreat north, and abandoned their territorial claims to the Western Isles three years later.

## Practicalities

There are excellent connections to Ayr and Glasgow from Largs' **train** and adjacent **bus station**, situated on Main Street, a short stroll from the pier where **ferries** leave for Great Cumbrae. Beside the pier the **tourist office** (Easter to mid-Oct Mon–Fri 9am–5pm, Sat & Sun 10am–5pm, July & Aug closes 7pm; mid-Oct to Easter Mon–Fri 9am–5pm; ☎0475/530753) has heaps of free literature and will help with accommodation. There are lots of **guest houses** and **B&Bs**, including a cluster along Aubery Crescent, a short side street overlooking the coast a few minutes' walk north of the pier. Choose from the *Old Rectory B&B* at no. 2 (☎0475/674405; ②), the *MacPherson's B&B* at no. 10 (April–Sept; ☎0475/672313; ②), and the *Ardmore Guest House*, no. 16 (April–Oct; ☎0475/672516; ②). Alternatively, half a mile south of the centre on Broomfields is the *Elderslie* (☎0475/686460; ④), the best **hotel**. *Skelmorlie Mains Campsite* (March–Oct; ☎0475/520794) lies about three miles north of town up along the coast.

For **food**, the *Green Shutter Tearoom*, along the seafront just south of the pier, serves excellent food and the *Bagel Basket*, Main St, is cheap and simple. *Nardini's*, on the Promenade near the pier, serves breakfast, fish suppers and splendid ice cream in a pure, unadulterated 1950s decor.

## Great Cumbrae Island

Just offshore from Largs lies **Great Cumbrae**, a plump, hilly island roughly four miles long and half as wide. The only settlement of any size is **MILLPORT**, which curves around an attractive hilly bay on the south coast. The town possesses Britain's smallest cathedral, the **Cathedral of The Isles**, which was completed in 1851 to a design by William Butterfield, an enthusiastic member of the high-church Oxford Movement and one of the leading Gothic revival architects of the day. A mile or so away, along the south shore to the east, is the **Marine Biological Station** (Mon–Fri 9.30am–12.15pm & 2–4.15pm, June–Sept also Sat) of the universities of Glasgow and London. The aquarium is excellent, but you're more likely to remember the view of the nuclear power station and iron ore terminal back on the mainland. Get away from this depressing sight by heading inland either on foot or by bike to enjoy the peaceful countryside. **Bike rental** is available in Millport from *Mapes* on Guildford Street (☎0475/530444).

It takes ten minutes for the **ferry** to cross from Largs to the island's northeast tip, where a connecting **bus** travels on to Millport. The ferries run hourly, so there's no need to overnight on the island, but if you decide to stay over in the summer, be sure to book a room beforehand at Largs' tourist office. Incidentally, Little Cumbrae, the islet opposite Millport, is privately owned.

## travel details

### Trains

**Ayr** to: Glasgow (3 daily; 1hr 20min); Stranraer (3 daily; 50min).

**Dumfries** to: Carlisle (4 daily; 35min); Kilmarnock (4 daily; 1hr 5min).

**Edinburgh** to: Dunbar (hourly; 20min); Musselburgh (hourly; 10min); North Berwick (hourly; 30min).

**Glasgow** to: Ardrossan Harbour (3–5 daily; 50min); Ayr (3 daily; 1hr 20min); Carlisle (4 daily; 2hr 15min); Dumfries (4 daily; 1hr 40min); Kilmarnock (4 daily; 35min); Largs (hourly; 1hr); Stranraer (3 daily; 2hr 10min).

**Kilmarnock** to: Carlisle (4 daily; 1hr 40min); Dumfries (4 daily; 1hr 5min).

**Largs** to: Glasgow (hourly; 1hr).

**Stranraer** to: Ayr (3 daily; 50min).

### Buses

**Ayr** to: Culzean Castle (hourly; 25min); Girvan (hourly; 1hr); Stranraer (3 daily; 2hr); Glasgow (1 express daily, 1hr 15min), New Galloway (Mon–

Sat 2 daily; 2hr); Castle Douglas (Mon–Sat 2 daily; 2hr 30min).

**Dumfries** to: Caerlaverock (Mon–Sat 3 daily; 35min); Castle Douglas (4 daily; 30min); Gatehouse of Fleet (4 daily; 1hr); Newton Stewart (4 daily; 1hr 20min); Stranraer (4 daily; 2hr); Kirkcudbright (2 daily; 1hr 10min); Gretna (6 daily; 1hr); Carlisle (6 daily; 1hr 40min); Lockerbie (hourly; 35min); Rockcliffe (2 daily; 1hr 10min); Thornhill (6 daily; 30min); Sanquhar (4 daily; 50min); Edinburgh (45min/3hr).

**Edinburgh** to: Aberlady (every 30min; 45min); Dirleton (every 30min; 1hr); North Berwick (every 30min; 1hr 10min); Haddington (3–4 daily; 1hr 5min); Dunbar (3–4 daily; 1hr 30min); Eyemouth (3–4 daily; 2hr 40min); Berwick-upon-Tweed (3–4 daily; 3hr); Jedburgh (5 daily; 2hr); Peebles (6–8 daily; 1hr 50min); Galashiels (6–8 daily; 1hr 50min); Melrose (6–8 daily; 2hr 15min).

**Galashiels** to: Berwick-upon-Tweed (3–5 daily; 1hr 40min); Selkirk (3–5 daily; 15min); Hawick (3–5 daily; 35min); Langholm (3–5 daily; 1hr 15min); Canonbie (3–5 daily; 1hr 25min); Carlisle (3–5 daily; 2hr).

**Haddington** to: Gifford (4–9 daily; 15min); North Berwick (4–9 daily; 40min).

**Jedburgh** to: Hawick (1 daily; 40min); Kelso (3–6 daily; 30min).

**Kelso** to: Coldstream (5 daily; 20min).

**Leadhills** to: Wanlockhead (2 daily; 5min).

**Lockerbie** to: Langholm (Mon–Sat 1 daily; 1hr 15min).

**Melrose** to: Duns (3–7 daily; 50min); Eyemouth (1hr 20min); Galashiels (every 30min; 15min); Hawick (Mon–Sat 3 daily; 50min); Jedburgh (hourly; 30min); Kelso (8 daily; 35min); Lauder (2–4 daily; 40min); Peebles (hourly; 1hr 10min); Selkirk (Mon –Sat hourly, Sun 3 daily; 20min).

**Moffat** to: Dumfries (7 daily; 35min); Lockerbie (2–4 daily; 40min).

**Newton Stewart** to: Ayr (1–3 daily; 2hr 15min); Bargrennan (1–3 daily; 20min); Glentrool (1–3 daily; 25min); Girvan (1–3 daily; 1hr 20min); Stranraer (2 daily; 40min); Wigtown (2–4 daily; 15min); Whithorn (2–4 daily; 50min); Isle of Whithorn (2–4 daily; 1hr).

**Peebles** to: Biggar (4–6 daily; 40min).

**Selkirk** to: Carlisle (hourly; 2hr); Hawick (hourly; 20min); Langholm (hourly; 1hr).

**Stranraer** to: Portpatrick (5 daily; 25min); Port Logan (1–2 daily; 35min); Drummore (1–2 daily; 45min).

## Ferries

**To Arran**: Ardrossan–Brodick (up to 6 daily; 55min).

**To Great Cumbrae Island**: Largs–Millport (hourly; 10min).

**To Larne**: Stranraer–Larne (5–10 daily; 2hr 20min).

**To Belfast**: Stranraer–Belfast (hydrofoil 4–5 daily; 1hr 30min).

# CHAPTER THREE

# GLASGOW AND THE CLYDE

R ejuvenated, upbeat **Glasgow**, Scotland's largest city, has not enjoyed the best of reputations. Once an industrial giant set on the banks of the mighty River Clyde, today it can initially seem a grey and depressing place, with the M8 motorway screeching through the centre and a fringe of crumbling slums on its outskirts. However, in recent years Glasgow has undergone a remarkable overhaul, set in motion in the 1980s by a self-promotion campaign featuring a fat yellow creature called Mr Happy, beaming beatifically that "Glasgow's Miles Better". The city proceeded to generate a brisk tourist trade, reaching a climax after beating Paris, Athens and Amsterdam to the title of European City of Culture in 1990.

The epithet is apt; Glasgow has some of the best-financed and most imaginative museums and art galleries in Britain – among them the showcase **Burrell Collection** of art and antiquities – and nearly all of them are free. There's also a robust social scene and nightlife that, partly due to the generous Scottish licensing laws, feels more European than British. Its **architecture** is some of the most striking in the nation, from the restored eighteenth-century warehouses of the Merchant City to the hulking Victorian prosperity of George Square. Most distinctive of all is the work of local luminary Charles Rennie Mackintosh; whose elegantly streamlined Art Nouveau designs appear all over the city, reaching their apotheosis in the **School of Art**.

Despite all the upbeat hype, however, Glasgow's gentrification has passed by deprived inner-city areas such as the **East End**, home of the **Barras market** and some solidly change-resistant pubs, which stand incongruously close to the sandblasted facades of the **Merchant City**. And indeed, the glossy new image has been met with some ambivalence among large sections of its populace, not least the loosely organized "Workers' City" discussion group, which includes authors James Kelman and Jeff Torrington, who aim to promote Glasgow's rich working-class and socialist traditions.

For visitors, one of the tangible effects of Glasgow's socialism is the city's longstanding belief in the power of popular culture. Main attractions include the **People's Palace** – one of Britain's most celebratory social history museums – founded in 1898 to extol ordinary lives and achievements, and the **Citizens' Theatre**, formed in 1942 by playwright James Bridie to promote indigenous work for local people who might never previously have visited a theatre, and whose innovative productions still cost next to nothing to see. In addition, Glasgow's **Mayfest**, with its roots in the traditional working-class spring celebrations, has grown to become Britain's second largest arts bash after the Edinburgh festival.

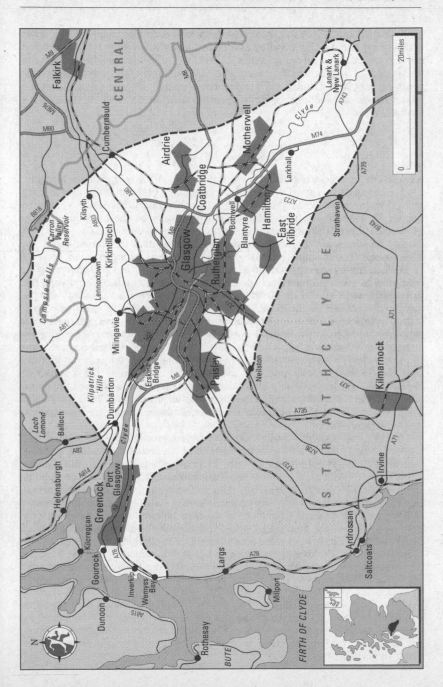

Quite apart from all its attractions, Glasgow also makes an excellent base from which to explore the **Clyde valley and coast**, made easy by the region's reliable rail service. Of the small communities in the Clyde valley, **Lanark** is probably the best-suited for overnight stays, as well as being the home of the remarkable eighteenth-century **New Lanark** mills and workers' village. Beyond that, most of the inland towns (as well as the coastal resorts) are best approached as day trips from Glasgow.

# GLASGOW

**GLASGOW**'s earliest **history**, like so much else in this surprisingly romantic city, is obscured in a swirl of myth. It is generally agreed that the first settlers arrived in the sixth century to join Christian missionary **Kentigern** – later to become St Mungo – in his newly founded monastery on the banks of the tiny Molendinar Burn. The city's name is said to derive from the Celtic *Glas-cu*, which loosely translates as "the dear, green place" – a tag that the tourist board are keen to exploit as an antidote to the sooty images of popular imagination.

William the Lionheart gave the town an official charter in 1175, after which it continued to grow in importance, peaking in the mid-fifteenth century when the **university** was founded on Kentigern's site – the second in Scotland after St Andrew's. This led to the establishment of an archbishopric, and hence city status, in 1492, and, due to its situation on a large, navigable river, Glasgow soon expanded into a major **industrial port**. The first cargo of tobacco from Virginia offloaded in Glasgow in 1674, and the 1707 Act of Union between Scotland and England – despite demonstrations against it in Glasgow – led to a boom in trade with the colonies until American independence. Following the **Industrial Revolution** and James Watt's innovations in steam power, coal from the abundant seams of Lanarkshire fuelled the ironworks all around the Clyde, worked by the cheap hands of the Highlanders and, later, those fleeing the Irish potato famine of the 1840s.

The Victorian age transformed Glasgow beyond recognition. The population boomed from 77,000 in 1801 to nearly 800,000 at the end of the century, and new tenement blocks swept into the suburbs in an attempt to cope with the choking influxes of people. Two vast and stately **International Exhibitions** were held in 1888 and 1901 to showcase the city and its industries to the outside world, necessitating the construction of huge civic monoliths such as the Kelvingrove Art Gallery and the Council Chambers in George Square. At this time Glasgow became known as the **"Second City of the Empire"** – a curious epithet for a place that today rarely acknowledges second place in anything

By the turn of the **twentieth century**, Glasgow's industries had been honed into one massive shipbuilding culture. Everything from tugboats to transatlantic liners were fashioned out of sheet metal in the yards that straddled the Clyde from Gourock to Rutherglen.

In the harsh economic climate of the 1930s, however, unemployment spiralled, and Glasgow could do little to counter its popular image as a city dominated by inebriate violence and, having absorbed vast numbers of Irish emigrants, sectarian tensions. The **Gorbals** area in particular became notorious as one of the worst slums in Europe.

The city's violent image has never been helped by the depth of animosity between its two great rival football teams: the Catholic **Celtic** and Protestant **Rangers**, whose warring armies of fans clash with monotonous regularity, despite the token signing in 1989 of Catholic Mo Johnston from Celtic to the hostile terraces of Ibrox, Rangers' great fortress in the south of the city.

However, in the Eighties, the promotion campaign began, snowballing towards the 1988 **Garden Festival** and year-long party as **European City of Culture** in 1990. Today Glasgow no longer needs such artificial boosts to its credibility. Edinburgh may still be the official capital of Scotland, but Glasgow and its people are rightfully confident that their city has finally broken through into the big league.

> The telephone code for Glasgow and the Clyde is ☎041

# Orientation

Glasgow is a sprawling place, built upon some punishingly steep hills, and with no really obvious **centre**. However, as most transport services converge on the area around Argyle Street and, 200yd to the north, George Square, this pocket of the city is the most obvious candidate for city-centre status. However, the name, when it is used, refers to a far larger swathe that stretches from **Charing Cross** underground station and the M8 in the west through to **Glasgow Green** in the **East End**. Outside the city centre, the **West End**, home to Glasgow University and some great museums, is roughly defined as the area west of the M8 motorway. The Gorbals and Govan, neither of which hold much for the visitor, lie south of the Clyde, as does the area known as **South Side**, a relaxed version of the West End, boasting the excellent Burrell Collection. To reach and explore South Side you'll need your own car or to take a taxi – none of the sights are within walking distance of the centre, and public transport connections are complicated.

# Arrival

Glasgow's **airport** (☎887 1111) is out at Abbotsinch, eight miles southwest of the city. To get into town, take *Citylink* bus #500 (£2), which runs to **Buchanan Street** (☎332 9191) bus station, three streets north of George Square, every twenty minutes during the day. You could also take *Clydeside 2000* bus #60 or #80 (every 10min during the day) to Paisley Gilmour Street train station, and from there a fast train into **Glasgow Central**, where trains from anywhere south of Glasgow arrive.

Central station sits over Argyle Street, one of the city's main shopping thoroughfares. A **shuttle bus** (60p) from the front entrance on Gordon Street makes four trips per hour between here and **Queen Street station**, at the corner of George Square, for trains to Edinburgh and the north. The walk between the two takes about ten minutes.

All long-distance buses arrive at Buchanan Street station, while suburban and city buses pull into **Anderston** (☎248 7432) bus station, north of Argyle Street on the western edge of the city centre.

# Information

The city's excellent **tourist office** is at 35 St Vincent Place just off George Square (July–Sept Mon–Sat 9am–9pm, Sun 10am–6pm; Oct–May Mon–Sat 9am–6pm; ☎204 4400). Aside from providing a particularly wide array of maps, leaflets and souvenirs, they also offer a free accommodation-booking service. A couple of hundred yards south down Buchanan Street over the St Enoch Underground station sits the neo-Gothic hut of the **Strathclyde Travel Centre** (Mon–Sat 9.30am–5.30pm; ☎226 4826), where you can pick up sheaves of maps, leaflets and timetables. Their comprehensive and colour-coded *Visitors' Transport Guide* is the best free map of the city centre and West End, but if you're staying for longer, or want to explore the tiny streets and alleys that are invariably airbrushed off the tourist maps, it's probably worth investing in a *Geographia Street Atlas* (£2.75).

# City transport

For exploring any one part of the city, **walking** is an ideal way of getting around, although it can be tough negotiating the steep hills. However, as the main sights are scattered – the West End, for example, is a good thirty-minute walk from the centre – you'll need to use the comprehensive and easy **public transport** system.

The best way to get between the city centre, southern suburbs and the West End is to use the city's **Underground**, whose stations are marked with a large U. Affectionately known as the "Clockwork Orange" (there's only one, circular route and the trains are a garish bright orange), the service is extremely easy to use. There's a flat fare of 50p, or you can buy a **day ticket** for £1.50. Unfortunately, however, the whole system shuts down at 11.30pm between Monday and Saturday and at 6pm on Sunday.

If you're travelling beyond the city centre or the West End, you may need to use the **bus** and **train** networks. Since deregulation, the city has been besieged with a horde of bus companies in hot competition. The biggest are *Strathclyde Transport*, whose buses can be identified from their orange livery, and *Kelvin Central Buses*, which are blue and white. If it gets too confusing, pick up the *Visitors' Transport Guide* (see above).

The suburban train network is swift and convenient. The suburbs south of the Clyde are connected to Glasgow Central mainline station, while trains from Queen Street head into the northeast. The grim but functional **cross-city line**, which runs beneath Argyle Street (and includes a low-level stop below Central station), connects northwestern destinations with southeastern districts as far out as Lanark. Trains on both the Queen Street and Central station lines go as far as **Partick** station, west of the city centre; this is also an Underground stop.

There is no day ticket that combines bus, rail and Underground in Glasgow alone, but if you are in the city for at least a week, it's worth investing in a **Zonecard**, which covers all public transport networks, and is valid for seven days or a month. Costs depend on the number of zones that you want to travel through – a two-zone card, for example, which gets you from Partick in the west to Rutherglen in the east, and as far as the Burrell Collection in the south, will set you back £8.30. This central two-zone core (divided by the Clyde) is ringed with a further six zones around its edge. Ask at the Strathclyde Travel Centre for help to demystify the system. There is also an **all-Strathclyde day pass**, which covers all the transport networks in the region and costs £6 for one adult and up to two children, or £11 for two adults and up to four children, although you'd need to spend a very busy day sightseeing to make it worthwhile.

Should you want to avoid public transport altogether, you can hail black **taxis**, which run all day and night, from the pavement. There are taxi ranks at Central and Queen Street train stations and Buchanan Street and Anderson bus stations. As an example, the fare from Central to Pollok Park and the Burrell Collection, a journey of about three miles, costs £5.

As for **driving**, with the M8 motorway running right through the heart of the city, Glasgow is one of the country's most car-friendly cities, with plenty of parking meters, and 24-hour multi-storey car parks at Waterloo Street, Anderston Cross, Mitchell Street, Oswald Street and Cambridge Street.

# Accommodation

There's a good range of **accommodation** in Glasgow, from an excellent youth hostel in the leafy West End through to some top international hotels in the city centre. Most of the guest accommodation is located in the city centre, the West End or down in the southern suburb of Queen's Park. Glasgow's speciality is its profusion of converted Victorian townhouses, well located in the middle of town, many of which are now privately run B&Bs that offer excellent value for money.

During Mayfest or in summer it's worth **booking ahead** to ensure a good room – at any time of year the **tourist office** will do their utmost to secure you somewhere to stay.

## Hotels and B&Bs

There are some very good **hotels and B&Bs** spread throughout the city centre and, in particular, the West End. South Side, too, particularly around Queen's Park, with its legion of reasonably priced accommodation, makes a good base. Some of the city's classier hotels drop their prices dramatically at the weekend in order to fill their rooms when businesspeople have fled the city. Details of these weekend breaks are gathered in a brochure published by the tourist office.

---

### ACCOMMODATION PRICE CODES

Throughout this book, accommodation **prices** have been graded with the numbers below, according to the cost of the least expensive double room in high season. The bulk of the recommendations will fall in categories ② to ⑤; recommendations in the highest categories are limited to places that are especially attractive. Bear in mind that many of the swanky hotels often slash their tariffs at the weekend when the business types have gone home, and that many of the cheaper places will also have more expensive rooms. Note that in our accommodation listings price codes are not given for youth hostels – they all come into the lower end of the ① category.

| | | |
|---|---|---|
| ① under £20 | ④ £40–50 | ⑦ £70–80 |
| ② £20–30 | ⑤ £50–60 | ⑦ £80–100 |
| ③ £30–40 | ⑥ £60–70 | ⑧ over £100 |

## City centre

**Babbity Bowster**, 16–18 Blackfriars St (☎552 5055). A traditional and very lively hotel, bar and restaurant that makes much of its Scottishness, with haggis and neaps and tatties permanently on the menu. ③.

**Baird Hall**, 460 Sauchiehall St (☎553 4148). Lavish Art Deco building that belies the functional, ex-student rooms. All the same, it's well situated for the School of Art and the upper end of Sauchiehall Street. ③.

**Carrick Hotel**, 377–383 Argyle St (☎248 2355). One of the cheapest large chain hotels in the city centre. Dependable rooms, if not very original decor. ④.

**Central Hotel**, Gordon St (☎221 9680). Imposing, comfortable hotel, with its own leisure centre, in the heart of the action near the stations. ⑤.

**Copthorne Hotel**, George Square (☎332 6711). Large and impressive hotel occupying the entire northwestern corner of the central George Square. Popular bar in the ground floor glass verandah. ⑥.

**Enterprize Hotel**, 144 Renfrew St (☎332 8095). A small, family town house in a quiet area near Cowcaddens Underground station. ③.

**Hampton Court Hotel**, 230 Renfrew St (☎332 6623 or 5885). Low-key and fairly small Victorian house conversion, well placed for the School of Art and Sauchiehall Street. ②.

**Marriott**, Argyle St (☎226 5577). Large and luxurious chain hotel with excellent food and popular health centre. Ask for a room out of earshot of the M8. Considerable reductions available at weekends. ⑦.

**Rab Ha's**, 83 Hutcheson St (☎553 1545). Beautiful and highly individual hotel-cum-restaurant in swish Merchant City. They only have a few rooms, so booking is essential. ⑤.

**Town House Hotel**, Nelson Mandela Place, 54 W George St (☎332 3320). Sumptuously converted sandstone block with a tweedy air. Well situated for nightlife. ⑤.

**Victorian House**, 212 Renfrew St (☎332 0129). Large and friendly terraced guest house, with some of the cheapest rooms in the city centre. ③.

**Willow Hotel**, 228 Renfrew St (☎332 2332 or 7075). Well-converted Victorian town house on the north side of the city centre. ③.

## West End

**Alamo Guest House**, 46 Gray St (☎339 2395). Good value, family-run boarding house next to Kelvingrove Park. Small but comfortable rooms. ②.

**Ambassador Hotel**, 7 Kelvin Drive (☎946 1018). Smallish, family-run hotel in lovely surroundings next to the River Kelvin and Botanical Gardens. ③.

**Argyll Lodge**, 969 Sauchiehall St (☎334 7802). Deservedly busy guest house with only a handful of rooms, on the fringes of the West End. ②.

**Chez Nous**, 33 Hillhead St (☎334 2977). Roomy guest house in the heart of the West End. Especially accommodating and good value for single travellers. ②.

**Hamilton House Hotel**, 2–4 Hamilton Park Ave (☎334 1510). Small and chintzy, but squeaky clean, set off the Great Western Road, ten minutes' walk from the shops and restaurants of Byres Road. ③.

**Heritage Hotel**, 6 Belgrave Terrace (☎337 1379). Compact hotel fashioned out of one of the Great Western Road's elegant terraces. Near Byres Road and the Botanical Gardens. ③.

**Hillhead Hotel**, 32 Cecil St (☎339 7733). Quiet and welcoming hotel only a couple of minutes' stroll from Hillhead Underground and the excellent local pubs and restaurants. ③.

**Hillview Guest House**, 18 Hillhead St (☎334 5585). Unassuming and peaceful small hotel near the university and the Byres Road. ③.

**Kelvin Park Lorne Hotel**, 923 Sauchiehall St (☎334 4891). Well-priced rooms in a dependable, if slightly sterile, international hotel environment. ⑤.

**Kelvin View**, 411 N Woodside Rd (☎339 8257). Welcoming B&B near Kelvin Bridge Underground station. ③.

**One Devonshire Gardens**, 1 Devonshire Gardens, Great Western Rd (☎339 2001). Although it's a 10-min walk up the Great Western Road from the Botanical Gardens, the hotel and its expensive gourmet restaurant are among the city's finest. ⑦.

**Smith's Hotel**, 963 Sauchiehall St (☎339 6363). Slightly scruffy, but cheap and cheerful. ②.

## South Side

**Boswell Hotel**, 27 Mansionhouse Rd (☎632 9812). Informal and relaxing Queen's Park hotel with a superb real-ale bar, and regular folk and jazz nights. ④.

**Ewington Hotel**, 132 Queen's Drive (☎422 2030). Comfortable and peaceful family-run hotel facing Queen's Park. Excellent, moderately priced subterranean restaurant. ⑤.

**Glades Guest House**, 142 Albert Rd (☎423 4911). Friendly B&B in excellent situation, near Queen's Park and good transport routes. ③.

**Mrs Black**, 19 Myrtle Park (☎423 8014). Quiet B&B in suburban surroundings. ②.

**Queen's Park Hotel**, 10 Balvicar Rd (☎423 1123). Faintly shabby, but very welcoming and with a crowd of regular visitors. Good views over the hill of Queen's Park. ③.

## Self-catering and campus accommodation

**University of Glasgow** (☎945 1636 or 330 5385). Call the former number for B&B rooms all over town (③); the latter for low-priced self-catering rooms and flats during the student vacations.

**University of Strathclyde** .Various sites, most of which are gathered around the cathedral. Vacation lets (③) and self-catering flats for between four and six people are available near the main campus in Rottenrow (☎553 4148). The rooms in their **Graduate Business School**, Cathedral Street, are better (and pricier) than many city hotels (☎553 6000; ⑤).

**YMCA**, 33 Petershill Drive, Balornock (☎558 6166). Clean, if rather lifeless self-catering flats sleeping between four and six people available from April to Sept. Three miles northeast of the city centre, a 10-min walk from Barnhill Underground station. No dorms.

## Youth hostel

**Glasgow Youth Hostel**, 7–8 Park Terrace (☎332 3004). Grade 1 hostel nuzzled deep in the splendour of the West End. A 10-min walk south from Kelvinbridge Underground station, or take #11 and #44 *Strathclyde Transport* bus from the city centre, after which it's a short stroll west up Woodlands Road. Very popular, so book in advance.

## Campsite

**Craigendmuir Park**, Campsie View, Stepps (☎779 4159). The only campsite within a decent distance of Glasgow, four miles northeast of the city centre, a 15-min walk from Stepps Underground station. Only ten pitches.

# The City

Glasgow's enormous city centre is ranged across the north bank of the River Clyde. At its geographical centre is **George Square**, a nineteenth-century municipal showpiece crowned by the enormous City Chambers at the eastern end. Behind the City Chambers lies one of the 1980s greatest marketing successes, the **Merchant City**, an area of massive gentrification that sits uneasily side by side with the down-at-heel **East End**. The oldest part of the city, around the **Cathedral**, lies to the immediate north of the East End.

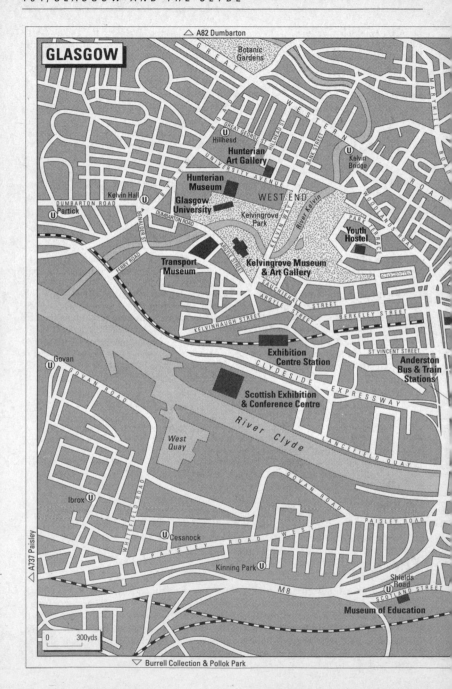

△ A82 Dumbarton

# GLASGOW

Botanic Gardens

Ⓤ Hillhead

**Hunterian Art Gallery**

**Hunterian Museum**

**Glasgow University**

Kelvin Hall

Ⓤ Kelvin Bridge

DUMBARTON ROAD

Ⓤ Partick

DUMBARTON ROAD

WEST END

Kelvingrove Park

River Kelvin

**Youth Hostel**

**Transport Museum**

ARGYLE STREET

**Kelvingrove Museum & Art Gallery**

SAUCHIEHALL STREET

ARGYLE STREET

KELVINHAUGH STREET

BERKELEY STREET

ST VINCENT STREET

**Exhibition Centre Station**

CLYDESIDE EXPRESSWAY

**Anderston Bus & Train Stations**

Ⓤ Govan

GOVAN ROAD

**Scottish Exhibition & Conference Centre**

River Clyde

LANCEFIELD QUAY

West Quay

Ⓤ Ibrox

GOVAN ROAD

PAISLEY ROAD

WHITEFIELD ROAD

PAISLEY ROAD WEST

Ⓤ Cessnock

Ⓤ Kinning Park

M8

Shields Road Ⓤ

SCOTLAND STREET

**Museum of Education**

△ A737 Paisley

0    300yds

▽ Burrell Collection & Pollok Park

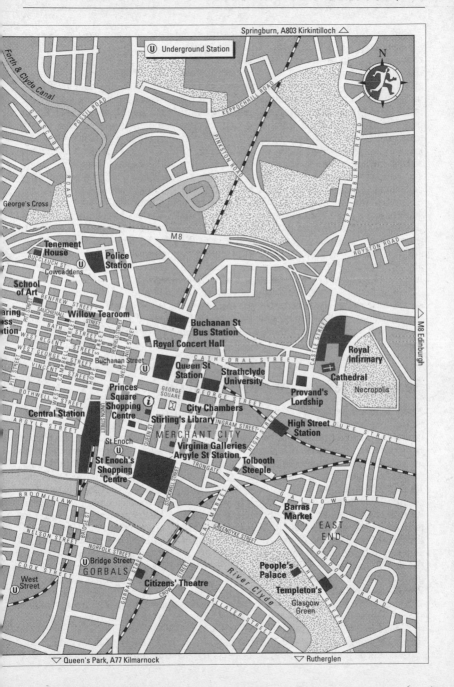

Springburn, A803 Kirkintilloch △

Ⓤ Underground Station

N

Forth & Clyde Canal

George's Cross

M8 Edinburgh △

M8

ROYSTON ROAD

SPRINGBURN ROAD

KEPPOCHILL ROAD

PINKSTON ROAD

GARSCUBE ROAD

POSSIL ROAD

Tenement
House
BUCCLEUCH ST
Cowcaddens Ⓤ

Police
Station

School
of Art

aring
ess
tion

Willow Tearoom

Buchanan St
Bus Station

Royal Concert Hall

Royal
Infirmary

CATHEDRAL STREET

CASTLE STREET

Cathedral

Necropolis

Buchanan Street

Queen St
Station

Strathclyde
University

Provand's
Lordship

GEORGE
SQUARE

GEORGE STREET

Princes
Square
Shopping
Centre

City Chambers

Stirling's Library

High Street
Station

Central Station

St Enoch Ⓤ

ARGYLE STREET

MERCHANT CITY

INGRAM STREET

HIGH STREET

DUKE STREET

Virginia Galleries
Argyle St Station

St Enoch's
Shopping
Centre

TRONGATE

Tolbooth
Steeple

GALLOWGATE

BROOMIELAW

STOCKWELL STREET

Barras
Market

EAST
END

NELSON STREET

BRIDGE STREET

SALTMARKET

GREENDYKE STREET

LONDON ROAD

GLASGOW GREEN

COOK STREET

Bridge Street Ⓤ

GORBALS

NORFOLK STREET

River Clyde

People's
Palace

West
Street Ⓤ

Citizens' Theatre

CROWN STREET

Templeton's

BALLATER STREET

Glasgow
Green

Still in the city centre, Glasgow's commercial core spreads west of George Square, built on a vast, quasi-American grid system, with ruler-straight wide roads soaring up severe hills to grand, sandblasted buildings – the part of the city that John Betjeman called "the greatest Victorian city in the world". The main shopping areas here are **Argyle Street**, running parallel to the river east–west underneath Central train station, and **Buchanan Street**, which crosses it and leads up to the pedestrianized shopping thoroughfare, **Sauchiehall Street**. Lying between the commercial bustle of Argyle and Sauchiehall streets, and to the immediate west of Buchanan Street, are the contours of an ice-age drumlin, now known as **Blythswood Hill**. The confusing grid of streets piled on its slopes seems curiously deserted, in comparison with the bustling shopping streets surrounding the area on three sides, with sparse commercial activity and only the occasional pub or sandwich bar to break the grey facades of countless offices.

Outside the city centre, the **West End** begins just over a mile west of Central station, and covers most of the area west of the M8. In the nineteenth century, as the East End tumbled into poverty, the West End ascended the social scales with great speed, a process crowned by the arrival of the **University**. Today, this is still very much the student quarter of Glasgow, exuding a decorously well-heeled air, with graceful, tree-lined avenues, parks and cheap, wacky shops and cafés. It's also well connected with the city centre by Underground.

Not as genteel as the West End, nor as raffishly downbeat as the East End, the **south side** of the city is nevertheless also worth a visit – though you may want to bypass the scruffy and infamous suburbs of **Govan** and the **Gorbals**, immediately south of the Clyde, for leafy enclaves such as **Queen's Park**, further out, which is home to the national football stadium, Hampden Park. The main attraction south of the river, though, has to be **Pollok Park** and the Burrell Collection.

# George Square and the Merchant City

Now hemmed in by speeding traffic, the ponderous architecture of **George Square** reflects the sober pomposity of Glasgow's Victorian age. Rising high above the centre of the square is an eighty-foot column topped with Sir Walter Scott, although his links with Glasgow were, at best, sketchy. Haphazardly dotted around the great writer's plinth are a number of gloomy statues of assorted luminaries, ranging incongruously from Queen Victoria to Scots heroes such as James Watt and wee Robbie Burns. The florid splendour of the **City Chambers**, opened by Queen Victoria in 1888, occupies the entire eastern end of the square. Its intricately detailed facade includes high-minded friezes typical of the era: the four nations (England, Ireland, Scotland, Wales) of the then United Kingdom at the feet of the throned queen, the British colonies and allegorical figures representing Religion, Virtue and Knowledge. It's worth taking a free guided tour (Mon–Fri 10.30am & 2.30pm; ☎227 4017) of the labyrinthine interior if only to gawp at the acres of intricate gold leaf, Italian marble, Wedgwood ceilings and Rococo trimmings.

Equally opulent is the **Merchant's House** opposite Queen Street station (May–Sept Mon–Fri 10am–4pm; free), where the ostentatious Banqueting Hall and silk-lined Directors' Room are highlights. Queen Street leads south to the Royal Exchange Square and the graceful Corinthian **Stirling Library**, built for tobacco lord William Cunninghame in 1780 as the most ostentatious of the

Glasgow merchants' homes. Since then it has served as the city's Royal Exchange and central library, and refurbishment is currently under way to give it a new lease of life as the city's Museum of Modern Art, due to open in 1996.

## Merchant City

The grid of streets that lies immediately east of the City Chambers is known as the **Merchant City**, an area of eighteenth-century warehouses and homes once bustling with cotton, tobacco and sugar traders, which in the last decade or so has been sandblasted and swabbed clean with greater enthusiasm and municipal money than any other part of Glasgow in an attempt to bring residents back into the city centre. The cost of living here is prohibitive for most people, however, and many of the gracious warehouses remain smothered with "To let" signs. The whole place bristles with the trappings of the 1980s, with expensive designers displaying an exquisite handful of their wares alongside bijou bars and cafés, and there's a slightly phoney atmosphere – some of the buildings are literally no more than original facades, held in place with vast struts like a film set, with mock period buildings in construction behind – but as a whole the Merchant City avoids tumbling into tasteless parody by virtue of its simple elegance.

The streets in the Merchant City deserve at least gentle perusal – especially towards dusk when traffic has died down and floodlights bathe the elegant and scrubbed porticos in a range of colours. Look out for the delicate white spire of the National Trust for Scotland's regional headquarters, **Hutcheson's Hall**, at 158 Ingram St (Mon–Fri 9am–5pm, Sat 10am–4pm). The NTS have a shop on the ground floor and visitors can see the ornately decorated hall upstairs. Almost opposite, on Glassford Street, the Robert Adam-designed **Trades House** (Mon–Fri 10am–5pm; free) is easily distinguished by its neat, green copper dome. Built for the purpose in 1794, it still functions as the headquarters of the Glasgow trade guilds, fourteen societies of well-to-do city merchants first incorporated in 1605, and the forerunners of the trade unions. Initially these included a Bakers' Guild, and societies for Hammermen, Gardeners, Bonnet Makers, Wrights and Weavers, although they have since become little more than proto-masonic lodges for men from all sections of Glasgow's business community. The former civic pride and status of the guilds is still evident, however, from the rich assortment of carvings and stained-glass windows, with a lively pictorial representation of the different trades in the silk frieze around the walls of the first-floor banqueting hall.

On Virginia Street, parallel to Glassford Street, the **Virginia Galleries** sit behind the intricately wrought iron gate of no 33. Formerly the city's nineteenth-century tobacco and sugar trading house, the graceful market hall is now a sedate place, filled with upmarket antique shops and some good jewellery stalls.

# From Trongate to the East End

Until 1846, **Glasgow Cross** – the junction of **Trongate**, Gallowgate and the High Street – was the city's principal intersection, until the construction of the new train station near George Square shifted the city's emphasis west. The turreted seventeenth-century **Tolbooth Steeple** still stands here, although the rest of the building has long since disappeared, and today the stern tower is little more than a traffic hazard at a busy junction. Further east, down Gallowgate, beyond the train lines, lies the downbeat world of the **EAST END**, the area that perhaps most closely corresponds to the general perception of Glasgow, its pitted streets surrounded by wasteland, with a few isolated pubs, tatty shops and cafés sitting amid the dereliction. It's hard to believe that the glossy Merchant City is only a few blocks to the west.

Three hundred yards down either London Road or Gallowgate, **The Barras** is Glasgow's largest and most popular weekend market. Shiny new red iron gates announce its official entrance, but boundaries are breached as the stalls – selling household goods, bric-a-brac, clothes and records – spill out into the surrounding cobbled streets. The fast-talking traders provide a lot of fun, and there are plenty of bargains to be had, but you'll be in doughty competition with locals.

Between London Road and the River Clyde are the scruffy open spaces of **Glasgow Green**. Reputedly the oldest public park in Britain, the Green has been common land since at least 1178, when it was first mentioned in records. Glaswegians hold it very dear, considering it to be an immortal link between themselves and their ancestors, for whom a stroll on the Green was a favourite Sunday afternoon jaunt. It has also been the site of many of the city's major political demonstrations; in the 1930s the authorities planted huge flowerbeds to cut down the crowds amassing to listen to the radical oratory. Various memorials (some in tatty states of disrepair) are dotted around the lawns: the 146-foot **Nelson Monument**, the ornate – but derelict – terracotta **Doulton Fountain**, rising like a wedding cake to the pinnacle where the forlorn Queen Victoria oversees her crumbling Empire, and the coy monument extolling the evils of drink and the glory of God that was erected by the nineteenth-century Temperance movement – today, quite a meeting place for local drunks.

## The People's Palace

On the northern end of Glasgow Green, the **People's Palace** (Mon–Sat 10am–5pm, Sun 11am–5pm; free) is a wonderfully haphazard evocation of the city's history. This squat, red-brick Victorian building (with a vast semi-circular glasshouse tacked on the back) was purpose-built as a museum back in 1898 – almost a century before the rest of the country caught on to the fashion for social history collections.

On the ground floor, the medieval city and its first skirmishes with the fiendish English are represented through recreated monastic rooms, pictures and captions, leading into an exhibition of period interiors removed from Stockwell Mansion, the city's last seventeenth-century building, demolished in 1976 after spending its final years as the *Bonny Bingo Hall*. Also on this level is an exhibition about eighteenth-century Glaswegian merchants, complete with smug portraits of tobacco lords and their picture-perfect families. The upper floor is more appealing, a rag-bag collection of nostalgia-soaked ephemera from the lives of ordinary nineteenth- and twentieth-century Glaswegians, which includes exhibits on John Maclean, the most notorious of the Red Clydesiders (members of a radical Independent Labour Party formed in the economic slump post-World War I) who became consul to the Bolshevik government in 1918; music-hall mementoes; shipbuilding exhibits; pro- and anti-suffragette propaganda, and Billy Connolly's legendary 1975 banana boots. The glasshouse at the back of the palace is the **Winter Gardens**, whose café, water garden, twittering birds and assorted tropical plants and shrubs make a pleasant place in which to pass an hour or so.

A hundred yards across the road from the People's Palace you can see the riotously intricate orange and blue Venetian-style facade of **Templeton's Carpet Factory**, built in 1889. William Leiper, Templeton's architect, is said to have modelled his industrial cathedral on the Doge's Palace in Venice; today it houses a centre for small businesses.

# Around the Cathedral

Rising north up the hill from the Tolbooth Steeple at Glasgow Cross is Glasgow's **High Street**. In British cities, the name is commonly associated with the busiest central thoroughfare, and it's a surprise to see how forlorn and dilapidated Glasgow's version is, long superseded by the grander boulevards further west. The High Street leads up to the **Cathedral**, on the site of Glasgow's original settlement.

### Glasgow Cathedral

Built in 1136, destroyed in 1192 and rebuilt soon after, the stumpy-spired **Glasgow Cathedral** (April–Sept Mon–Sat 9.30am–1pm & 2–6pm, Sun 2–5pm; Oct–March Mon–Sat 9.30am–1pm & 2–4pm, Sun 2–4pm) was not completed until the late fifteenth century, with the final reconstruction of the chapter house and the aisle designed by Robert Blacader, the city's first archbishop. Thanks to the intervention of the city guilds, it is the only Scottish mainland cathedral to have escaped the hands of religious reformers in the sixteenth century. The cathedral is dedicated to the city's patron saint and reputed founder, St Mungo, about whom four popular stories are frequently told – they even make an appearance on the city's coat of arms. These involve a bird that he brought back to life, the bell with which he summoned the faithful to prayer, a tree that he managed to spontaneously combust and a fish that he caught with a repentant adulterous queen's ring on its tongue.

Because of the sloping ground on which it is built, at its east end the cathedral is effectively on two levels, the crypt actually part of the "lower church". On entering, you arrive in the impressively lofty nave of the upper church, with the lower church entirely hidden from view. Most of this **upper church** was completed under the direction of Bishop William de Bondington (1233–58), although later design elements came from Blacader. Either side of the nave, the narrow **aisles** are illuminated by vivid stained-glass windows, most of which date from this century. Threadbare Union flags and military pennants hang listlessly beneath them, serving as a reminder that the cathedral is very much a part of the Unionist Protestant tradition. Beyond the nave, the **choir** is hidden from view by the curtained stone pulpit, making the interior feel a great deal smaller than might be expected from the outside. In the choir's northeastern corner, a small door leads into the cathedral's gloomy **sacristy**, in which Glasgow University was first founded over five hundred years ago. Wooden boards mounted on the walls detail the alternating Roman Catholic and Protestant clergy of the cathedral, testimony to the turbulence and fluctuations of the Church in Scotland.

Two sets of steps from the nave lead down into the **lower church**, where you'll see the dark and musty **chapel** surrounding the tomb of St Mungo. The saint's relics were removed in the late Middle Ages, although the tomb still forms the centrepiece. The chapel itself is one of the most glorious examples of medieval architecture in Scotland, best seen in the delicate fan vaulting rising up from the thicket of cool stone columns. Scots designer Robert Stewart was commissioned in 1979 to produce a tapestry detailing the four myths of St Mungo, which can be illuminated using the button at the bottom of the north-side stairs to reveal its swirl of browns and oranges. Also in the lower church, the spaciously light **Blacader Aisle** was originally built as a two-storey extension; today only this lower section survives, where the bright, and frequently gory, medieval ceiling bosses stand out superbly against the simple whitewashed vaulting.

Outside, the atmospheric **Necropolis** forms a hilly *Hammer Horror* backdrop to the cathedral, its Doric columns, gloomy catacombs and Neoclassical temples reflecting the vanity of the nineteenth-century industrialists buried here. From the summit, next to the column topped with an indignant John Knox, there are superb views over the cathedral and its surrounding area.

### Cathedral Square

Back in Cathedral Square, the new **St Mungo Museum of Religious Life and Art** (Mon–Sat 10am–5pm, Sun 11am–5pm; free) focusses on objects, beliefs and art from Christianity, Buddhism, Judaism, Islam, Hinduism and Sikhism. Portrayals of Hindu gods are juxtaposed with the stunning Salvador Dali painting *Christ upon the Cross* – moved here from Kelvingrove Art Gallery – a magnetic picture that draws the viewer into its morose depths. In additon to the main exhibition is a small collection of photographs, papers and archive material looking at religion in Glasgow, the power and zealotry of the nineteenth-century Temperance movement, Christian missionaries and local boy, David Livingstone, in particular. Outside is Britain's only permanent Zen Buddhist garden.

Across the square, the oldest house in the city, the **Provand's Lordship** (Mon–Sat 10am–5pm, Sun 11am–5pm; free) dates from 1471, and has been used, among other things, as an ecclesiastical residence and an inn. Many of the rooms have been kitted out with period furniture, including a recreation of the fifteenth-century chamber of cathedral clerk Cuthbert Simon, who is seen as a contemplative bewigged wax dummy living in comparative luxury for the age.

As a reminder of the manse's earthier history, the upper floor contains cuttings and pictures telling interesting tales of assorted lowlife characters, such as notorious drunkards, match-sellers and prostitutes of eighteenth- and nineteenth-century Glasgow.

## From Buchanan Street to Sauchiehall Street

The huge grid of streets that runs from just west of George Square, over Buchanan Street and to the M8 a mile to the west, is home to Glasgow's main shopping district as well as its financial and business corporations, piling up the punishing slopes of drumlins shaped by the receding glaciers of the last ice age. The **St Enoch Shopping Centre**, south of George Square, sandwiched between Argyle and Howard streets, is a huge, lofty glass pyramid built around a redundant train station. Among the glossy shops and piped muzak the centre's most unusual feature is its **ice rink** (☎221 5835) complete with cappuccino bar. A short walk north, on Buchanan Street, **Princes Square**, hollowed out of the innards of a soft sandstone building, is another shopping centre, albeit one of the most stylish and imaginative in the country. The interior, all recherché Art Deco and ornate ironwork, has lots of pricy, highly fashionable shops, the whole place set to a soothing background of classical music.

At the northern end of Buchanan Street, where it intersects with the eastern end of Sauchiehall Street, lies the £29 million **Royal Concert Hall**, given a prime city perspective but failing miserably to excite much attention. It looks like a hybrid of a car park and a power station, with three huge flagpoles protruding to proclaim that this is, in fact, a building of note. The showpiece hall plays host to world-class musical events (see p.158), while the lobbies are used for temporary art exhibitions. These can be seen for free, or you can take a guided tour of the huge hall and its backstage areas (Mon–Fri 1, 2 & 3pm; £1.50; ☎332 6633).

Sauchiehall Street runs in a straight line west past dull and half-empty shopping malls, leading to a few of the city's most interesting sights. Charles Rennie Mackintosh fans should head for the **Willow Tearoom**, at 217 Sauchiehall St, a faithful reconstruction of an eaterie created by the architect for Kate Cranston, one of his few contemporary supporters in the city. The distinctively high-backed silver-and-purple chairs and all the fittings and trimmings – right down to the teaspoons and menu cards – were designed by Mackintosh; tea is served here until 5pm.

A couple of footsteps west are the **McLellan Galleries,** 270 Sauchiehall St (Mon–Sat 10am–5pm, Thurs until 8pm, Sun noon–5pm; charges for some exhibitions), recently restored after a severe fire in 1985. Despite its inauspicious frontage, inside the building is as soothing an example of classical architecture as

## CHARLES RENNIE MACKINTOSH

No Glaswegian artist has attained higher status than Charles Rennie Mackintosh (1868–1928). Although he came from a large, working-class family who did little to encourage his artistic ambitions, Mackintosh gained a place at the Glasgow School of Art to study architecture, developing his highly idiosyncratic style of mixing Scottish Baronial with Gothic, Art Nouveau and modern designs, to which he added startling uses of light, shade and dark. His first big break came when fellow Glaswegian Kate Cranston commissioned him to design the decor and furniture for her tea rooms in Buchanan Street (1896). As nothing was too small or insignificant to escape Mackintosh's attention, he designed the cutlery, chairs, napkin holders and stained glass, transforming the humble tea room into an art arena. Today you can take tea in another of his commissions for Cranston, the _Willow Tearoom_ in Sauchiehall Street.

In his time Mackintosh's designs were seen as frivolous, pretentious and "too modern" – assessments that were to dog the artist in Glasgow as long as he stayed there. Fortunately, the few supporters he did have were in positions to help the young man's career, among them Francis Newbery, the School of Art's comparatively new principal in Mackintosh's student days. When the School needed new premises in 1896, Newbery persuaded the governors to go with the design submitted by their 28-year-old ex-student. However, the chorus of disapproval from press critics only swelled on his execution of the design; ironically, this is now rightfully considered to be his greatest work.

Mackintosh's fastidiousness – insisting that he should have total control over both the larger architectural plans and the interior design – gained him a reputation as an awkward artist, easily given to losing his temper at the lack of vision and courage in others. It won him few friends and lamentably few commissions, especially in his native city, and ultimately, Mackintosh and his artist wife Margaret decided to quit "philistine" Glasgow for the more comfortable surroundings of Suffolk and then London.

Since the years following World War II, Mackintosh's ideas have become fashionable, giving rise to a certain amount of ersatz "Mockintosh" in his home city, with the distinctive lettering and small design features used time and again by shops, pubs and businesses. Fortunately, there are also plenty of examples of the genuine article, making the city something of a pilgrimage centre for art and design students from all over the world.

anywhere in the city. A grand staircase sweeps you up into the main exhibition space, lit naturally by beautiful pedimented windows. There is no permanent display; the McLellan specializes in imaginative touring and temporary exhibitions, many of which have local themes – in recent years, anything from new Glaswegian art to an eccentric display of the city's rubbish. For relentlessly avant garde art and culture, stroll down the same side of Sauchiehall Street to no. 350 and the **Centre for Contemporary Arts** (Mon–Sat 11am–6pm; free), with its eclectically internationalist exhibitions and performances, trendy café and bar.

## Glasgow School of Art

Rising above Sauchiehall Street to the north is one of the city centre's steepest hills, where Dalhousie Street and Scott Street veer up to Renfrew Street and, at no. 167, Charles Rennie Mackintosh's **Glasgow School of Art** (guided tours Mon–Fri 11am & 2pm, Sat 10.30am; extra tours April–Sept; £2; booking advised; ☎332 9797) – one of the most prestigious in the country, with such notable alumni as Robert Colquhoun and Robert Macbryde and, more recently, Steven Campbell, Ken Currie and Robbie Coltrane. Widely considered to be the pinnacle of Mackintosh's work, the school is a characteristically angular building of warm sandstone which, due to financial constraints, had to be constructed in two sections (1897–99 and 1907–09). There's a clear change in the architect's style from the earlier severity of the mock-Baronial east wing to the softer lines of the western half.

The only way to see the school is by taking one of the student-led daily guided tours, the extent of which are dependent on curricular activities. You can, however, be sure of seeing at least some of the differences between the two halves and a handful of the most impressive rooms. All over the school, from the roof to the stairwells, Mackintosh's unique touches – light Oriental reliefs, tall-backed chairs and stylized Celtic illuminations – recur like leitmotifs. Even before entering the building up the gently curving stairway, you cannot fail to be struck by the soaring height of the north-facing windows, which light the art studios and were designed, in the architect's inimitable style, to combine aesthetics with practicality.

In the main entrance hall, the school shop sells tour tickets and a good selection of Mackintosh books, posters and cards. Hanging in the hall stairwell is the artist's highly personal wrought-iron version of the "bird, bell, tree, ring and fish" design from the legend of St Mungo. The stairs lead up to the **Director's Room**, where the rounded lines of the central table and arched window contrast with the starkly angular chairs, cupboard and writing desk. You'll see excellent examples of his early furniture in the tranquil **Mackintosh Room**, flooded with soft, natural light, while the **Furniture Gallery**, tucked up in the eaves, shelters an Aladdin's cave of designs that weren't able to be housed elsewhere in the school – numerous tall-backed chairs, a semi-circular settle designed for the *Willow Tea Rooms*, domino tables, a chest of drawers with highlighted silver panels and two bedroom suites. Around the room are mounted building designs and a model of the *House for an Art Lover*, which Mackintosh submitted to a German competition in 1901. In recent years, this project – which never saw the light of day in Mackintosh's lifetime – was resuscitated after Glasgow city council donated a corner of Bellahouston Park for the house's construction. The building, to be constructed exactly to Mackintosh's specifications, was supposed to have opened for the 1990 City of Culture beanfeast, although wrangling and financial difficulties have left it still incomplete.

You can peer down from the Furniture Gallery into the school's most spectacular room, the glorious two-storey **Library** below. Here, sombre oak panelling is set against angular lights adorned with primary colours, dangling down in seemingly random clusters. The dark bookcases sit precisely in their fitted alcoves, while of the furniture, the most unusual feature is the central periodical desk, whose oval central strut displays perfect and quite beautiful symmetry.

## The Tenement House

Just a few hundred yards northwest of the School of Art – albeit on the other side of the sheer hill that rises and falls down to Buccleuch Street – is the **Tenement House** at no. 145 (April–Oct daily 2–5pm; Nov–March Sat & Sun 2–4pm; NTS; £1.60). This is the perfectly preserved home of the habitually hoarding Agnes Toward, who moved here with her mother in 1911, changing nothing and throwing very little out until she was hospitalized in 1965. On the ground floor, the National Trust for Scotland have constructed a fascinating display on the development of the humble tenement block as the bedrock of urban Scottish housing, with a display of relics – ration books, letters, bills, holiday snaps and so forth – from Miss Toward's life. Upstairs you have to ring the doorbell to enter the living quarters, which give every impression of still being inhabited, with a roaring hearth and range, kitchen utensils, recess beds, framed religious tracts and sewing machine all untouched. The only major change since Miss Toward left has been the reinstallation of the flickering gas lamps she would have used in the early days.

# The West End

The urbane veneer of the **WEST END**, an area which contains many of the city's premier museums, seems a galaxy away from Glasgow's raw image. In the 1800s, the city's focus moved west as wealthy merchants established huge estates away from the soot and grime of city life, and in 1870 the ancient university was moved from its cramped home near the cathedral to a spacious new site overlooking the River Kelvin. Elegant housing swiftly followed, the Kelvingrove Art Gallery was built to house the 1888 International Exhibition, and in 1896 the Glasgow District Subway – today's Underground – started its circuitous shuffle from here to the city centre.

The hub of life in this part of Glasgow is **Byres Road**, running down from the straight Great Western Road past Hillhead Underground station. Shops, restaurants, cafés, some enticing pubs and hordes of roving young people, including thousands of students, give the area a certain panache. Even the tenements here look upmarket, blasted in a sunny red sandstone that evokes an English seaside resort more than a Glaswegian suburb.

Straddling the banks of the cleaned up River Kelvin, the slopes, trees and statues of **Kelvingrove Park** are framed by a backdrop of the Gothic towers and turrets of **Glasgow University** and the **Kelvingrove Museum and Art Gallery**, off Argyle Street in the park.

### Kelvingrove Museum and Art Gallery

Founded on donations from the city's chief industrialists, the huge, redbrick fantasy castle of **Kelvingrove Museum and Art Gallery** (Mon–Sun 11am–5pm; free) is a brash statement of Glasgow's nineteenth-century self-confidence. On the ground floor, a fairly dusty hall contains the **Scottish Natural History** display, together with an unremarkable exhibition of European and Scottish weapons.

However, it's the art collections, the majority of which are upstairs, that are of most interest. The **Scottish Gallery** houses works from the eighteenth and nineteenth centuries, with a glut of Victorian paintings depicting great moments of Scottish history. In this category is James Hamilton's magnificent *Massacre of Glencoe 1692*, portraying a stoic and strong Macdonald clan comforting wailing women as their village is razed to the ground. The gallery also houses late nineteenth-century works by many of the **Glasgow Boys**, among which richly hued works by George Henry and Edward Hornel amply demonstrate their bold experimentation with Japanese art techniques and styles. The **Modern Gallery** begins with the late nineteenth century and a fine collection of Impressionists, from Signac's calming *The Seine at Herblay*, through Renoir, Monet, Sisley and Degas' *Dancers on a Beach*, to Van Gogh's bullish portrait of Glasgow art dealer *Alexander Reid*. Van Gogh and Reid shared rooms together in Paris, during which time Reid bought up works by the burgeoning Impressionists and took them back to Scotland – the collection you see in the Kelvingrove today is largely attributable to him. Twentieth-century paintings in the Modern Gallery include works by Glasgow School of Art graduates Colquhoun and Macbryde, and William Strang's coolly piercing portrait of Vita Sackville-West gazing out from under the rim of an oversized red hat.

The gallery of the **Classical Tradition** is an educative trot from the Florentine and Venetian schools of the fifteenth century right through to twentieth-century Modernism. Although the Italian collection is fairly small, it includes splendid works by Renaissance artists Filippino Lippi and Sandro Botticelli, and features Giorgione's emotionally wrought *The Adulteress Brought Before Christ*. Paintings from the Dutch school of the seventeenth and eighteenth centuries are divided between this gallery and its counterpoint, the Realist Tradition. Among the Classical works is one of the gallery's most revered pieces, Rembrandt's *The Man in Armour*, a beautifully quiet painting of a single figure, whose armour catches the soft yellow light against a contrastingly murky background. The Classical tradition is brought up to date by the vigorous bronze scuplture of *Perseus Arming* by the precociously brilliant Victorian Alfred Gilbert, whose most celebrated work is the statue of Eros in London's Piccadilly Circus.

## THE GLASGOW BOYS

Glasgow's much-trumpeted artistic renaissance is rooted in the city's cultural history and its long-standing feud with Edinburgh. The Scottish capital ruled the national artistic consciousness until the 1870s, when a group of disgruntled Glaswegians began to experiment with lavish colours, liberally splashing paint across the canvas. The content and concerns of the paintings, often showing peasant life and work, were as offensive as the style of painting to the effete art establishment, as, until then, most of Glasgow's public art collections had been accrued by wealthy tobacco lords and merchants. Derisively nicknamed the **Glasgow Boys**, only in later years did their work come to be seen as quintessentially Glaswegian, and reclaimed with considerable pride. Today, works by the group – including Joseph Crawhall, Edward Hornel, Arthur Melville and chief protagonist James Guthrie – occupy pride of place in most of the city's public galleries.

The gallery of the **Realist Tradition** includes a few more French Impressionists such as Corot and the stippled style of Camille Pissaro. Landscapes feature large, most famously in Constable's expansive view over *Hampstead Heath*, Horatio McCulloch's *Glencoe* and Glasgow Boy James Guthrie's magnificent 1834 twin views from Ben Lomond. His powerfully sombre *Highland Funeral* brings a personal element into the epic Scottish landscape, its distant sliver of watery winter sun barely illuminating the grim faces of the mourners and the dirty grey snow underfoot.

## The Transport Museum

The twin-towered **Kelvin Hall** is home to the excellent and enormous city **Transport Museum**, a collection of trains, cars, trams, circus caravans and prams, along with an array of old Glaswegian ephemera, whose entrance is in Bunhouse Road (Mon–Sat 10am–5pm, Sun 11am–5pm; free). Near the entrance, "Kelvin Street" is a recreated 1950s cobbled street featuring an old Italian coffee shop, butchers (complete with plastic meat joints dangling in the window), a bakers (where labels claim that the buns were provided by the university's taxidermy department) and an old-time Underground station. A cinema shows fascinating films – mostly on themes based loosely around transport – of old Glasgow life, with crackly footage of Sauchiehall Street packed solid with trams and shoppers and hordes of pasty-faced Glaswegians setting off for their annual jaunts down the coast. Nearby, the Super X simulator (£1.50) rocks the nauseous viewer around in time with videoed skiing, white-water rafting and other stomach-churning activities. The Clyde Room displays intricate models of ships forged in Glasgow's yards – everything from tiny schooners to ostentatious ocean liners such as the *QE2*.

## Glasgow University

Dominating the West End skyline, the gloomy turreted tower of Glasgow's **University**, designed by Sir Gilbert Scott in the mid-nineteenth century, overlooks the glades of the River Kelvin. Access to the main buildings and museums is from University Avenue, running east from Byres Road. In the dark neo-Gothic pile under the tower you'll find the **University Visitors Centre** (Mon–Fri 9.30am–5pm), which, as well as giving information for potential students, distributes leaflets about the various university buildings and the statues around the campus.

Next door to the University Visitor Centre, the collection of the **Hunterian Museum** (Mon–Sat 9.30am–5pm; free), Scotland's oldest public museum dating back to 1807, was donated to the university by ex-student William Hunter, a pathologist and anatomist whose eclectic tastes form the basis of a fairly dry, but frequently diverting zoological and archeological museum. Exhibitions include Scotland's only dinosaur, a look at the Romans in Scotland – the chilly farthest outpost of a massive empire – and a vast coin collection .

On the other side of University Avenue is Hunter's more frequently visited bequest: the **Hunterian Art Gallery** (Mon–Sat 9.30am–5pm; free), best known for its works by James Abbott McNeil Whistler – only Washington DC has a larger collection. Whistler's breathy landscapes are less compelling than his portraits of women, which give his subjects a resolute strength in addition to their fey and occasionally winsome qualities: look out especially for the trio of full-length portraits, *Pink and Silver – the Pretty Scamp*, *Pink and Gold – the Tulip* and *Red and Black – the Fan*.

The gallery's other major collection is of nineteenth- and twentieth-century Scottish art, including the quasi-Impressionist Scottish landscapes of William McTaggart, their bold, broad brush strokes remaining acutely sensitive to delicate patterns of light. McTaggart was a forerunner of the Glasgow Boys movement, represented here by E A Walton – especially in the spirited portrait of his wife – W Y McGregor, Sir David Murray, James Guthrie and Edward Hornel's sweeping, extravagantly colourful canvasses that mix Oriental and Scottish styles with bold panache. A small selection of French Impressionists includes Corot's soothing *Distant View of Corbeil* and works by Boudin and Pissaro.

A side gallery leads to the **Mackintosh House**, a recreation of the interior of the now-demolished Glasgow home of Margaret and Charles Rennie Mackintosh. An introductory display contains photographs of the original house sliding irrevocably into terminal decay, from where you are lead into an exquisitely cool interior that contains over sixty pieces of Mackintosh furniture on three floors. Among the highlights are the Studio Drawing Room, whose cream and white furnishings are bathed in expansive pools of natural light, and the Japanese-influenced guest bedroom in dazzling, monochrome geometrics.

### The Botanic Gardens

At the top of Byres Road, where it meets the Great Western Road, is the main entrance to the **Botanic Gardens** (gardens daily 7am–dusk; Kibble Palace summer daily 10am–4.45pm; winter closes 4.15pm; Main Range glasshouses summer Mon–Sat 1pm–4.45pm, Sun noon–4.45pm; winter closes 4.15pm). The best-known glasshouse here, the hulking, domed Kibble Palace – originally known as the Crystal Palace – was built in 1863 for wealthy landowner John Kibble's estate on the shores of Loch Long, where it stood for ten years, before he decided to transport it into Glasgow, drawing it up the Clyde on a vast raft pulled by a steamer. It remained for over twenty years on this spot, used not as a greenhouse but as a Victorian pleasure palace, before the gardens' owners put a stop to the drunken revels that wreaked havoc with the lawns and plant beds. Today the palace is far more sedate, housing a damp, musty collection of swaying palms from around the world. The smell is much sweeter on entering the Main Range glasshouse, home to lurid and blooming flowers and plants – including stunning orchids, cacti, ferns and tropical fruit – luxuriating in the humidity. Quite apart from the main glasshouses, the Botanic Gardens have some beautifully remote paths that weave and dive along the closely wooded banks of the gorged River Kelvin.

### Scottish Exhibition and Conference Centre

Half a mile south of Kelvinbridge, beyond the expressway and not strictly part of the West End, the harshly relandscaped **Scottish Exhibition and Conference Centre (SECC)**, down by the riverside on the other side of the Clydeside Expressway, was built in 1985 to kick-start the revival of the Riverbank – two vast adjoining red and grey sheds that make a dutifully utilitarian venue for travelling fairs, mega-concerts and anonymous bars and cafés. The gleaming hotel alongside and the expensive restaurants in the nearby rotunda – one of two access shafts to a long-closed tunnel under the Clyde – have been reasonably successful, but the rotunda's twin on the opposite bank, the **Dome of Discovery**, once a hands-on science museum and showpiece of the 1988 Glasgow Garden Festival site, is an example of what happens when the money runs out. Indeed it's hard to believe today that this wasteground, spattered with empty bottles and used syringes, was the focus of one of Britain's most ambitious urban renewal projects; when the festival ended, the gardens rotted and the museum closed. Perhaps most poignant of all is the redundant pedestrian Bell's Bridge that connects the two banks – opened for the Garden Festival and closed a couple of years later.

# South of the Clyde

The southern bank of the Clyde, facing the city centre, is home to the notoriously deprived districts of **Govan**, a community yet to find its niche after the shipbuilding slump, and the **Gorbals**, synonymous with the razor gangs of old. On the southern side of Govan the vast bowl of **Ibrox**, home to the rigidly Protestant Rangers football team, proudly displays the Union flag. This Unionist fortress was totally overhauled following the disaster on January 2, 1971, when 66 fans died after a match against bitter arch-rivals Celtic – a stand collapsed as hundreds of early-leavers stampeded back into the stadium after an unlikely last-minute goal.

Inner-city decay fades into altogether gentler and more salubrious suburbs, commonly referred to as **South Side**. These include Queen's Park, a residential area home to Hampden Park football stadium, and the rural landscape of **Pollok Park**, three miles southwest of the city centre, which contains two of Glasgow's major museums: the **Burrell Collection** and **Pollok House**. Buses #34 and #34A from Govan Underground station set down outside the gate nearest to the Burrell. Slightly farther to walk is the route from the Pollokshaws West station (don't confuse with Pollokshields West), served by regular trains from Glasgow Central and nearby bus stops on the Pollokshaws Road: *Clydeside* buses #10 and #11 or *Strathclyde* buses #45 and #48 from Union Street. However, as Pollok Park is only three miles from the city centre, taking a taxi to the Burrell is probably less complicated.

## The Burrell Collection

The lifetime collection of shipping magnate Sir William Burrell (1861–1958), the outstanding **Burrell Collection** (Mon–Sat 10am–5pm, Sun 11am–5pm; free) is, for some, the principal reason for visiting Glasgow. Unlike many other art collectors, Sir William's only real criterion for buying a piece was whether he liked it or not, enabling him to buy many "unfashionable" works, which cost comparatively little, and subsequently proved their worth. He wanted to leave his collection of art, sculpture and antiquities for public display, but stipulated in 1943 that they should be housed "in a rural setting far removed from the atmospheric pollution of urban conurbations, not less than sixteen miles from the Royal Exchange". For decades, these conditions proved too difficult to meet, with few open spaces available and a pall of industrial smoke ruling out any city site. However, by the late 1960s, after the nationwide Clean Air Act had reduced pollution, and the vast sweeping land of Pollok Park, previously privately owned, had been donated to the city, plans began for a new, purpose-built gallery, which finally opened in 1983. Today the simplicity and clean lines of the Burrell building are its greatest assets, with large picture windows giving sweeping views over woodland and serving as a tranquil backdrop to the objects inside. The sculpture and antiques are on the ground level, arranged in six sections that overlap and occasionally backtrack, while a mezzanine above displays most of the paintings.

On entering the building, the most striking piece, by virtue of sheer size, is the Warwick Vase, a huge bowl containing fragments of a second century AD vase from Hadrian's Villa in Tivoli. Next to it are the first of a series of sinewy and naturalistic Rodin sculptures, among them *The Thinker*, *A Call to Arms* and the painfully realistic *Man with a Broken Nose*. Beyond the entrance hall, on three sides of a courtyard, are a trio of dark and sombre panelled rooms re-erected in faithful detail from the Burrells' Hutton Castle home, their heavy tapestries, antique furniture and fireplaces displaying the same eclectic taste as the rest of the collection.

From the courtyard, leading up to the picture windows, the **Ancient Civilizations** collection – a catch-all title for Greek, Roman and earlier artefacts – includes an exquisite mosaic Roman cockerel from the first century BC and a four-thousand-year-old Mesopotamian lion's head. The bulk of it is Egyptian, however, with rows of inscrutable gods and kings. Nearby, also illuminated by the enormous windows, the **Oriental Art** forms nearly one quarter of the complete collection, ranging from Neolithic jades through bronze vessels and Tang funerary horses to cloisonné. The earliest piece, from around the second century BC, is a lovable earthenware watchdog from the Han Dynasty, but most dominant is the serene fifteenth-century *Iohan* (disciple of Buddha), who sits cross-legged and contemplative up against the window and the trees of Pollok Park. Near-Eastern art is also represented, in a dazzling array of turquoise- and cobalt-decorated jugs, and a swathe of intricate carpets.

Burrell considered his **Medieval and Post-medieval European Art,** which encompasses silverware, glass, textiles and sculpture, to be the most valuable part of his collection. Ranged across a maze of small galleries, the most impressive sections are the sympathetically lit stained glass – note the homely image of a man warming his toes by the fire – and the hundreds of tapestries, among them the fifteenth-century riotous *Peasants Hunting Rabbits with Ferrets*. Among the church art and reliquary are simple thirteenth-century Spanish wooden images and cool fifteenth-century English alabaster, while a trio of period interiors, interrupted by an exhibition of fragile, antique lace, cover the Gothic, Elizabethan, and seventeenth- and eighteenth-century eras. In the latter you can see selections from Burrell's vast art collection, the highlight of which is one of Rembrandt's evocative early self-portraits (1632).

Of the other paintings on the ground floor are some key nineteenth-century French works, amongst them Géricault's stunning evocation of equine power in his *Prancing Grey Horse*, Degas' more subtle but equally forceful *Jockeys in the Rain*, Manet's sweeping still life, *The Ham*, and pieces by Boudin, Corot, Cézanne and Pissaro.

Upstairs, the cramped, and comparatively gloomy mezzanine is probably the least satisfactory section of the gallery, not the best setting for its sparkling array of paintings. These include further pieces from the French Impressionists, and a good selection of work from the Glasgow Boys. Honorary Glasgow Boy, Joseph Crawhall, who was in fact from Newcastle-upon-Tyne, is probably the best represented, with a selection of his tender and precise animal portraits.

## Pollok House and Haggs Castle

A quarter of a mile away down rutted tracks lies the lovely eighteenth-century **Pollok House** (Mon–Sat 10am–5pm, Sun 11am–5pm; free), the manor of the Pollok Park estate and once home of the Maxwell family, local lords and owners of most of southern Glasgow until well into this century. Designed by William

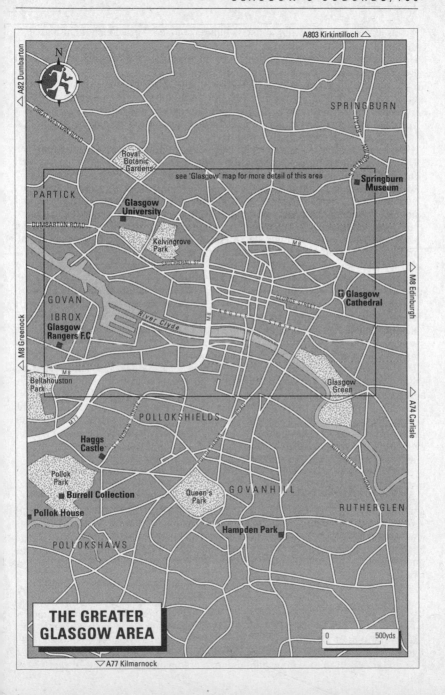

A803 Kirkintilloch △

A82 Dumbarton ◁

N

GREAT WESTERN ROAD

SPRINGBURN

Royal
Botanic
Gardens

see 'Glasgow' map for more detail of this area

■ Springburn
Museum

PARTICK

**Glasgow
University**

DUMBARTON ROAD

Kelvingrove
Park

SAUCHIEHALL ST

M8

◁ M8 Greenock

GOVAN

IBROX

**Glasgow
Rangers F.C**

River Clyde

GEORGE STREET

M8

✝**Glasgow
Cathedral**

▷ M8 Edinburgh

M8

Bellahouston
Park

M77

POLLOKSHIELDS

Glasgow
Green

▷ A74 Carlisle

**Haggs
Castle**

Pollok
Park

■**Burrell Collection**

Queen's
Park

GOVANHILL

RUTHERGLEN

■**Pollok House**

**Hampden Park** ■

POLLOKSHAWS

**THE GREATER
GLASGOW AREA**

0 _____ 500yds

▽A77 Kilmarnock

Adam in the mid-1700s, the house is typical of its age: graciously light and sturdily built, looking out onto the pristine raked and parterre gardens, whose stylized daintiness contrasts with the heavy Spanish paintings inside, among them two El Greco portraits and works by Murillo and Goya.

The house itself is, however, like so many stately homes, a little sterile, a series of plush period rooms whose ornate furniture you view from behind red sash cordons, and only the servants' quarters downstairs catch the imagination – a virtually untouched labyrinth of tiled Victorian parlours and corridors that includes a good tearoom in the old kitchen.

Close to the eastern entrances to Pollok Park, **Haggs Castle** on St Andrew's Drive (Mon–Sat 10am–5pm, Sun 11am–5pm; free) was built in 1685 as a Maxwell family Baronial hall, the precursor to the far more ornate Pollok House. Today the stark grey turrets and impenetrable stone walls conceal a historical museum, which, although aimed squarely at children, is passably entertaining for people of any age. Some of the rooms have been decked out with figures and tableaux of the Maxwell family at home, others turned over to interactive exhibitions looking at Scottish history – including an unusually clear explanation of the history and importance of Mary, Queen of Scots.

### Scotland Street School Museum of Education

A mile and a half northeast of the Burrell Collection is another great Mackintosh monument, the **Scotland Street School Museum of Education** (Mon–Fri 10am–5pm, Sun 2–5pm; free), slap opposite the Shields Road Underground station. Opened as a school in 1906 to Mackintosh's distinctively angular design, it closed in 1979, since when it has been refurbished as a vastly entertaining education museum, housing a fascinating collection of memorabilia related to life in the classroom. There are reconstructed classrooms from the Victorian, Edwardian, World War II and 1960s eras, as well as changing rooms, a primitive domestic science room and re-creations of a headmaster's office, the school matron's sanitorium and a janitor's lair. If you visit during term time, you will probably get the chance to watch a period lesson going on with local schoolkids struggling to understand their ink blotters, gas masks and archly unsympathetic teachers. Even the faint smell of antiseptic will conjure up memories of scuffed knees and playground tantrums.

# The outskirts

Thanks to extensive local government reorganization, most notably in the mid-1970s, Glasgow's boundaries have extended ever outwards to incorporate an increasingly sprawling urban area fringed by vast concrete housing estates – notably **Easterhouse** next to the M8 in the east and **Castlemilk** at the foot of the hills in the south – unserviced, largely neglected neighbourhoods that represent the worst horrors of post-war planning.

The city has also absorbed a number of formerly separate communities that still struggle to maintain their autonomy. **RUTHERGLEN**, four miles southeast of the city centre, is the most notable – the oldest burgh in Scotland (a full five hundred years older than Glasgow), and still harbouring deep resentment about its absorption in 1975 into the anonymous suburbs of its upstart neighbour. It's a feeling reflected in the small town **museum** in King Street (Mon–Fri 10am–5pm, Sun 11am–5pm; free), a good antidote to the rampant Glaswegiania of every other city museum, chronicling the history of the burgh and its constant struggles against Glasgow. The bigger city's desire to annexe Rutherglen had been simmering for centuries – a 1658 document from the town council to the Scots parliament complains that Rutherglen was "...in a very mean and low condition these many years bygone by reason of its contiguity with the City of Glasgow, who has all the Commerce and Trading in those parts, so that their Ancient Royal Burgh is likely to decay and ruin". Four trains per hour leave from Glasgow Central low-level station for the ten-minute journey to Rutherglen.

Two miles to the north of the city centre another museum attempts to tell the story of a similar, once independent community. Trains leave Queen Street station every thirty minutes for **SPRINGBURN** and the **Springburn Museum**, Atlas Square (Mon–Fri 10.30am–5pm, Sat 10am–4.30pm, Sun 2–5pm; free), which aims to recount the life of this seemingly anonymous suburb as the once largest rail engineering yard in Europe. The tight-knit glory days are now long gone, and Springburn's tale makes painfully familiar reading. Pictures recall the community up to the 1950s and its wholesale redevelopment in the 1960s, squeezed into dreadful tower blocks that ended up as student accommodation.

# Cafés and restaurants

Glasgow's renaissance has seen an explosion in fine restaurants, European-style bars and cafés, which, in additon to its diverse and ethnically mixed population, make eating possibilities in Glasgow pretty wide. For **budget food**, Glasgow's cafés range from the cheapest, greasiest cholesterol-hole through to bars offering reasonable snacks all day, and frequently into the evening.

The city's **restaurants** cover an impressively international spectrum – incorporating unusual cuisines such as Catalan and Irish along with more familiar dishes from France, Italy, India and China. Traditional **Scottish cuisine** has become very trendy in recent years, with an upsurge in the number of places, covering most price ranges, that serve local specialities. There are few exclusively **vegetarian** restaurants, but most places – especially around the Merchant City – have good, imaginative vegetarian choices.

Predominantly due to the large local student population, the best area for cheap, stylish restaurants and cafés, and bars serving food is around Hillhead Underground station on Byres Road in the **West End**, where the restaurants along **Ashton Lane** dish out unreservedly good food. On the other side of Byres Road from the station, **Ruthven Lane** is home to several lively theme restaurants which try desperately to outdo each other with cheap happy hours. In other areas of the city, as a rule of thumb, the **East End** is where you are most likely to find greasy spoon cafes; the **Merchant City** contains the largest concentration of designer brasseries and some very pricy restaurants, while **Buchanan and Sauchiehall streets** feature the big restaurant and fast-food chains. Unlike in staid Edinburgh, where a lot of places close on Sunday, most of Glasgow's restaurants are open seven days a week.

## Budget food: cafés, diners and pubs

**Back Alley**, 8 Ruthven Lane (☎334 7165). Glasgow's best burger joint, worlds away from fast-food glop. Enormous burgers, smothered in assorted toppings, to be washed down with good beer and finished off with calorific puddings. Moderately priced, with an early evening happy hour.

**Boswell Hotel**, 27 Mansionhouse Rd, Queen's Park (☎632 9812). Unusually cheap and extensive bar food menu with some offbeat house specialities – a good complement to the wide selection of real ales. Regular live music.

**Café Gondolfi**, 64 Albion St (☎552 6813). Trendy Merchant City café-bar that attracts hordes of posing beauties, although the down-to-earth, moderate menu is mainly comprised of standard pasta, salads, chilli and so forth.

**California Gourmet**, 291 Byres Rd. Daytime American ice cream and sandwich bar.

**Chimmy Chungas**, 499 Great Western Rd (☎334 0884). Loud and popular Tex-Mex bar and café that is good for anything from a light snack through to a full blow-out.

**Delifrance**, 119–121 Sauchiehall St (☎353 2700). French café with take-away service, serving cheap and authentic food. Daytime only in winter, open until around 9pm during the summer.

**Fratelli Sarti**, 133 Wellington St. Authentic daytime Italian deli. Closed Sun.

**Granary**, 82 Howard St, by St Enoch's Shopping Centre (☎226 3770). Daytime-only vegetarian café with some excellent-value vegetable patés, salads and hot meals. Closed Sun.

**Grosvenor Café**, 35 Ashton Lane (☎357 3268). Small traditional Italo-Scots café tucked behind Hillhead Underground station with a diehard clientele, addicted to the no-nonsense food (pizzas, fried food, burgers) served at unbelievably low prices. Slightly more upmarket menu in the evening, although even this is an astonishing bargain. Closed Sun, & Mon evenings.

**Jimmy's**, 1 Victoria Rd (☎423 4820). Splendid fish-and-chip shop serving deliciously fresh battered salmon, haddock, sole, salmon and plaice, seven days a week until 11pm.

**Jinty McGinty's**, 21–29 Ashton Lane. Wood-panelled and frosted-glassed Irish pub that, as well as serving excellent stout, maintains a small menu of Irish favourites such as bacon and cabbage, steak and Guinness pie or hearty soups.

**Junkanoo**, 11 Hope St, near Central station (☎248 4055). Boisterous and inexpensive Latin American bar that successfully, and unusually, combines a pleasant drinking atmosphere with some great food, with tapas and chilli looming large. Closed Sun.

**October Café**, top floor, Princes Square Shopping Centre. A variety of different foods, including some vegetarian options, served all day and into the night on the wraparound verandah peering down into the swish designer shopping paradise. Closed Sun.

**Sloans**, Argyll Arcade, off Argyle St (☎221 8917). Huge pub-cum-restaurant serving well-cooked food such as pasta and steaks in surroundings that become increasingly like a riotous Victorian gin palace the further up the building you rise.

**Tramway Theatre**, Albert Drive, off Pollokshaws Rd. Good daytime (and evening when there's a performance) café and bar with a smallish menu of trendy treats.

**Willow Tea Room**, 217 Sauchiehall St (☎332 0521). Refined elevenses, lunches and afternoon tea in Mackintosh-designed splendour.

## Scottish

**Babbity Bowster**, 16–18 Blackfriars St (☎552 5505).Trendy yet relaxed Merchant City bar on the ground level serving excellent Scottish food – anything from hearty broths to haggis, salmon and kippers. The restaurant upstairs is pricier, and more sedate, serving venison, fresh fish and the like. Open till midnight.

**Buttery**, 652 Argyll St (☎221 8188). A fine, if slightly snooty, restaurant serving lavish, imaginative and expensive food, with lots of tarted-up traditional Scottish dishes. Closed Sun.

**Crannog**, 28 Cheapside St (☎221 1727). Excellent seafood restaurant tucked away underneath the vast motorway bridge. Much of the food, which is very reasonably priced compared with other city seafood joints, is caught by the restaurant and smoked on the premises. Also has a good vegetarian selection. Closed Sun.

**Ewington**, at the *Ewington Hotel*, 132 Queen's Drive (☎423 1152). Facing Queen's Park, this sedate suburban hotel has a cellar restaurant whose very pink and flouncy decor is compensated for by the fine mix of moderately priced traditional Scottish and Continental cuisine.

**Rogano**, 11 Exchange Place (☎248 4055). Although the food here is not solely Scottish, the Rogano is a Glasgow institution, an absolutely superb but shockingly expensive fish restaurant decked out inside as an authentic replica of the 1930s Cunard liner, the *Queen Mary*. Café Rogano, in the basement, is cheaper but not so deliciously ostentatious. Both closed Sun.

**Ubiquitous Chip**, 12 Ashton Lane (☎334 5007). Splendid West End restaurant with a covered patio that resembles an indoor forest. Glasgow's most delicious Scottish food – game, seafood and local cheeses, and occasionally oatmeal ice cream and venison haggis. Expensive.

## Italian

**Di Maggio's**, 61 Ruthven Lane (☎334 8560). Inexpensive, extremely popular West End pizzeria and pasta joint, usually packed solid with bargain-hungry students. Frantic atmosphere with occasional live music. There's another less studenty branch South Side at 1038 Pollokshaws Rd, Queen's Park (☎632 4194), offering the same selection of gargantuan pizzas and hefty pasta dishes.

**Enzo's Trattoria Marida**, 221 St Andrew's Rd, E Pollokshields (☎429 4604). Cosy, reasonable and traditional trattoria in an unlikely setting, with a few imaginative Italian dishes tucked among the standard pastas and pizzas.

**Fire Station**, 33 Ingram St (☎552 2929). Merchant City restaurant housed in a huge old fire station, dating from 1900, walled with municipal cast-off marble tiling. The excellent menu, especially the pasta and the indulgent puddings, is moderately priced, and they offer a wide choice of beer and wine.

**Joe's Garage**, 52 Bank St, next to Glasgow University Union (☎339 4507). Offers a fairly predictable range of pizza and pasta, but the food is good, inexpensive and there's no corkage charge for bringing your own wine. The imaginative chef's specials are worth a try.

**O'Sole Mio**, 32 Bath St (☎331 1397). A superb, and easily affordable, city-centre restaurant that offers a wide-ranging choice from some unusual pasta dishes, as well as pizzas from their log-fired oven.

**PJ's Pastaria**, Maryfield House, Ruthven Lane (☎339 0932). Old farmhouse converted into a popular West End haunt, serving huge portions of well-known and more unusual dishes – spaghetti in a beef and Guinness sauce, for example. Inexpensive, and cheaper still in the early evening, when various happy hours offer dishes at half-price.

## Spanish

**Barcelona**, 16 Byres Rd, West End (☎357 0994). Avowedly Catalan, as opposed to Spanish, although the casual observer might be hard pushed to tell the difference. Expensive, but good, with a menu ranging from tapas to exquisitely cooked fresh fish and seafood, served in friendly whitewashed surroundings. Closed Sun & Mon.

## Indian

**Ashoka**, 19 Ashton Lane (☎357 5904). Moderately priced Dhosa house and Indian restaurant, popular with local students.

**Balbir's Vegetarian Ashoka**, 141 Elderslie Rd (☎248 4407). Inexpensive Indian vegetarian restaurant serving huge portions to a horde of regulars.

**Koh-i-noor**, 235 North St, Charing Cross (☎221 1555). Good-value range of diverse Indian dishes, especially notable for its highly reasonable Sunday brunches.

**Shalimar**, 23–25 Gibson St, near Glasgow University (☎339 6453). Mixed clientele who appreciate the extensive, and very reasonable, standard Indian restaurant menu.

## Chinese and Southeast Asian

**Blossom**, 80 Miller St, Merchant City (☎221 1292). In a city not terribly well blessed with Chinese restaurants, this is undoubtedly one of the best, with a well-priced and wide-ranging menu that includes an unusually good number of vegetarian options.

**Gourmet House**, 19 Ashton Lane (☎334 3229). Moderately priced Cantonese restaurant with especially good fresh fish dishes, served in gaudy red surroundings.

**Loon Fung**, 417 Sauchiehall St (332 1477). Great *dim sum* and inexpensive vegetarian set meals.

**Mata Hari**, 17 W. Princes St (☎332 9789). Deservedly popular Malaysian restaurant with some unusual – and highly spicy – dishes on the moderately priced menu. Closed Sun.

## Vegetarian

**Basil's**, 184 Dumbarton Rd (☎337 1416). The best of Glasgow's solely vegetarian and vegan places; a stylish, if not inexpensive, small West End co-op restaurant with some boldly imaginative dishes, organic wines and speciality liqueurs.

**Cul de Sac**, 44 Ashton Lane (☎336 4749). Beautiful creperie and brasserie that, although not exclusively meatless, offers some of the best vegetarian options around.

# Pubs and bars

Not so many years ago, Glasgow's rough image was inextricably associated with its **pubs**, widely thought of as no-go areas for any visitor. Although much of this reputation was overexaggerated, there was an element of truth in it. Nowadays, however, you're just as likely to spend an evening in a succession of open and airy café-bars as in a dark, dangerous, nicotine-stained pub. The centre has an admirable range of reliable watering holes; if you tire of the glossy **Merchant City**, head for the **East End**, where a fair number of local spit-and-sawdust places make a welcome change. All in all, though, the liveliest area, once again, has to be the **West End**, its good cross section of pubs and bars matching its great restaurants.

## City centre

**Babbity Bowster**, 18 Blackfriars St. Arty hangout at the heart of the Merchant City.

**Bay Horse**, 19 Bath St. Ordinary Glasgow pub, serving malt whisky, pies and peas.

**Brahms and Liszt**, 71 Renfield St. Candlelit cellar bar that takes great pride in its beer selection, some of which is available by the jug. Great atmosphere, but gets very crowded.

**Buzzy Wares**, Princes Square Shopping Centre. Glossy bar popular at weekends as a pre-club stop.

**Cairns Bar**, 5–12 Miller St. Unpretentious, very central pub popular with Glaswegians and serving a wide range of ales and whiskies.

**Chadfield**, 158 Bath St. Peaceful pub which makes an enjoyable respite from the loud and boisterous bars in which Glasgow seems to specialize.

**Corn Exchange**, 88 Gordon St. Slap opposite Central station, this fairly new bar has successfully recreated the feel of a traditional Victorian Glaswegian pub.

**The Griffin**, 226 Bath St. Friendly, if faintly tacky, three-bar pub with a firm crowd of devotees and regulars – mostly students.

**Horseshoe Bar**, 17 Drury St. Traditional old pub, reputedly Glasgow's busiest – loud, frantic and great fun, with a very mixed clientele. Karaoke upstairs, with a downstairs bar for quiet conversation.

**The Maltman**, 61 Renfield St. Busy three-bar pub with a regular penchant for live and recorded jazz, which sits well with their selection of over one hundred malt whiskies.

**Nico's**, 375–379 Sauchiehall St. The best of all Glasgow's recently opened chic new café-bars. Trendy without being painfully so, the ambience strives towards a French flavour – prices, especially for the bottled beer, are steep.

**Phileas Fogg**, 73 Bath St. Popular with young business people, this stylish bar fills out with a more interesting crowd later in the evening.

**Rock Garden**, 73 Queen St. Nostalgia-soaked bar that serves as a focus for Glasgow's rock music heritage – hence the large portraits of local musical luminaries that adorn the walls. A bit cramped, but a fun atmosphere.

**Saracen Head**, Gallowgate (opposite the Barras market). Unchanged East End pub that offers an enjoyably beery, sawdust-floored wallow. Look out for the tax demand from Robbie Burns displayed on the wall, from the days when he was the local tax officer.

**Scotia Bar**, 112 Stockwell St. Laid-back bar popular with writers and other tortured souls, including leading lights in the Workers' City group. Occasional live folk music – Billy Connolly began his career here, telling jokes in between singing folk songs.

**Ten**, Mitchell Lane. In a tiny street connecting Buchanan and Mitchell streets, *Ten* was designed by the same crew as Manchester's legendary *Hacienda* club. As you'd expect, it's suitably chic, although with a healthy dose of Glaswegian humour to take off the posey edge.

**Victoria Bar**, 157–159 Bridgegate. Basic, folksy pub serving a wide selection of real ales.

## West End

**The Aragon**, 131 Byres Rd. Old-fashioned bar with mixed crowd. The main attraction here is the vast beer selection, which includes European fruit beers and weekly guest ales.

**Bonham's**, 194 Byres Rd. Tall, spacious bar with splendid stained-glass windows. Popular, arty, and serving reasonable daytime food.

**The Halt**, 106 Woodlands Rd. Great beer and a vast selection of whiskies in this relaxed music pub. Regular live jazz.

**Mitchell's**, 157 North St. Next to the domed Mitchell's Library, a heavily panelled pub with a scholarly atmosphere. Good beer and an excellent refuge.

**Partick Tavern**, 163–169 Dumbarton Rd. Traditional pub serving good Scottish food in a refreshingly untrendy atmosphere.

**Reid's of Pertyck**, 80 Dumbarton Rd. A world apart from the student haunts nearby, this genuinely friendly working-class stronghold has walls that read like a city social history treatise, with lots of old photographs and faded memorabilia.

**Tennent's**, 191 Byres Rd. No-nonsense, beery den, a refreshing antidote to all the designer paradises nearby. Large and very popular, especially with real ale afficianados.

**Uisge Beatha**, 232 Woodlands Rd. The plain frontage broken only by the bar's name in small green neon letters is far from indicative of the eclectic insides, where a trendy and lively crowd relish in the recreated Scottish atmosphere – all kilts, piped music and stripped wood. The name, by the way, is Gaelic for "water of life", or whisky.

**Whistler's Mother**, 116–122 Byres Rd. Combines an elegant restaurant with the more basic bar, which is deservedly popular with students and legions of young people. Great decor that doesn't sacrifice comfort for style.

## South Side

**Athena Taverna**, 780 Pollokshaws Rd. Quiet real ale haven near Queen's Park Underground station.

**Boswell Hotel**, 27 Mansionhouse Rd. Lively Queen's Park pub with great atmosphere and occasional live music. Good selection of real ales, including some unusually potent local brews. Fine bar food (see p.172).

# Nightlife

Glasgow's City of Culture tag resulted in a great liberalization of the city's licensing laws, which transformed the **clubbing** scene alomost overnight. Since then, however, many of these laws have been repealed, and, at the time of writing, there is outrage at a new by-law decreeing that no one is to be allowed into a bar or club after midnight. Considering that many clubs were licensed until 6am a couple of years ago, encouraging club-hopping, the new rules are, in the view of many, absurdly draconian.

Most of Glasgow's nightclubs are in the heart of the main shopping areas off Argyle and Buchanan streets, many of them within walking distance of each other. Establishments are pretty mixed, and although there's still a stack of outdated mega-discos with endless chart pap and rigorous dress codes, the last couple of years has seen the arrival of far more stylish haunts. Opening hours hover from around 9pm to 3am, and cover charges are reasonable – expect to pay around £5 for entry at the weekend, with drinks usually about thirty percent more expensive than in the pubs.

The city's traditional breadth of art, theatre, film and music is undeniably impressive, especially during **Mayfest,** Glasgow's most concentrated splurge of cultural activity. The majority of the larger theatres, cinemas and showpiece music halls are around the shopping streets of the city centre, while the West End is home to student-oriented venues such as the quirky *Grosvenor* cinema. The city's two trendiest theatres, the *Citizens'* and the *Tramway*, are South Side. You can find details of the city's events in the *Glasgow Herald* or *Evening Times* newspapers, or the fortnightly listings magazine, *The List* (£1.20), which also covers Edinburgh. To book **tickets** for theatre productions or big concerts, phone the *Ticket Centre* (☎227 5511) or call in at their headquarters at City Hall, Candleriggs, on the Trongate end of Argyle Street (phone bookings Mon–Sat 9am–9pm, Sun noon–5pm; office Mon–Sat 10am–6.30pm, Sun noon–5pm).

## Nightclubs

**The Cotton Club**, 5 Scott St (☎332 0712). Friendly club with a variety of one-nighters including Club Havana, one Sunday a month, playing salsa and flamenco and offering free dance lessons.

**Fury Murray's**, 96 Maxwell St (☎221 6511). Student-oriented and lively, with music spanning from the 1960s to rave and techno.

**Mayfair**, 490 Sauchiehall St (☎332 3872). Medium-sized club at the heavier end of the rock spectrum.

**Riverside Club**, Fox Rd, off Clyde St (☎248 3144). Regular weekend ceilidh that gets absolutely packed out with good-natured, drunken Scottish dancers. Great fun, with a live band and callers involving everyone from seasoned ceilidh dancers to visiting novices. Get there early (8–9pm) to ensure a place.

**Sub Club**, 22 Jamaica St (☎248 4600). Nightclub aimed squarely at the ravier end of the market. Weekend nights are very trendy.

**The Tunnel**, 84 Mitchell St (☎204 1000). Fabulously stylish club with arty decor – the gents' toilet has cascading waterfall walls. Gay night on Mon.

**The Volcano**, 15 Benalder St (☎337 1100). The major club in the West End, drawing in hordes of students. An eclectic selection of specialist music nights in the week and just a damn good boogie at the weekends.

## Gay clubs and bars

**Austin's**, 183 Hope St. Dingy but lively central cellar bar, with a mainly male — and fairly cruisey – crowd of all ages.

**Bennett's**, 90 Glassford St (☎552 5761). Glasgow's main gay club, predominantly male, fairly old-fashioned but enjoyable nonetheless. Straight nights on Tues.

**Club Xchange**, Royal Exchange Square (☎204 4599). *Bennett's* biggest rival, this mixed gay club is funkier and more upbeat.

**The Court Bar**, 69 Hutcheson St. Quiet backstreet pub near George Square, mixed in daytimes and gay in the evenings. Friendlier, and less self-conscious, than most of Glasgow's gay pubs.

**Del Monica's**, 68 Virginia St. Glasgow's liveliest and most stylish gay bar, very near George Square, with a mixed and hedonistic crowd.

**The Waterloo Bar**, 306 Argyle St. Very central, garish but enjoyable bar, which gets packed at weekends. Mainly men.

## Live music pubs and venues

**Barrowlands**, 244 Gallowgate (☎552 4601). Legendary East End dance hall, complete with spinning glitterball, that hosts some of the sweatiest, liveliest gigs you will ever encounter. Has a capacity of a couple of thousand, so tends to attract bands that are just breaking into the big time.

**Curlers**, 256 Byres Rd. Smooth pub that hosts mid-week jazz and blues.

**King Tut's Wah Wah Hut**, 272a St Vincent St. One of the city's best programmes of bands at this splendid live music pub. Good bar downstairs if you want to sit out the sweaty gig above.

**Scotia Bar**, 112 Stockwell St. The folkies' favourite, a mellow musical pub that acts as a magnet for folk players and followers. Regular live gigs and frequent jam sessions.

**Solid Rock Café**, 19 Hope St. Glasgow's top rock pub.

## Theatre and comedy

**The Arches**, 30 Midland St (☎221 9736). Trendy base for performances by touring theatre groups.

**Blackfriars**, 45 Albion Rd (☎552 5924). The city's premier comedy and cabaret venue, renowned for its good-value Saturday night line-ups. In the Merchant City.

**Centre for Contemporary Arts**, 346 Sauchiehall St (☎332 7521). Radical theatre, dance and art.

**Citizens' Theatre**, 119 Gorbals St (☎429 0022). Glasgow's infamous theatre that grew from working-class roots to become one of the most respected, and adventurous, theatres in Britain. Three stages, with bargain prices for students and the unemployed, together with free preview nights.

**King's Theatre**, 297 Bath St (☎227 5511). Mainstream shows and comedy, south of Sauchiehall Street.

**Mitchell Theatre**, 6 Granville St (☎221 3198). Enjoyable venue for touring groups.

**Old Athenaeum**, 179 Buchanan St (☎332 2333). A smallish base for the *Scottish Youth Theatre*, as well as for visiting companies and stand-up comedians.

**Tramway Theatre**, 25 Albert Drive, off Pollokshaws Rd (☎225 5511). Good venue for experimental theatre, dance, music and regular art exhibitions.

**Tron Theatre**, 63 Trongate (☎552 4267). Varied repertoire of mainstream and experimental productions from visiting companies, together with one of the city's most laid-back bars.

## Concert halls

**Royal Concert Hall**, 2 Sauchiehall St (☎227 5511). Big-name rock and soul stars, orchestras and opera companies.

**Scottish Exhibition & Conference Centre**, Finnieston Quay (☎248 3000). Soulless and overpriced huge shed with the acoustics and atmosphere of an aircraft hangar, but, unfortunately, the only venue in Glasgow (often the only venue in Scotland) visited by the megastars on their world tours.

**Theatre Royal**, Hope St (☎332 9000). Opulent home of the Scottish Opera and regular host to visiting classical orchestras, opera companies, theatre blockbusters and occasional comedy.

## Film

**Cannon**, 326 Sauchiehall St (☎332 9513). Five-screen mainstream multiplex.

**City Centre Odeon**, 56 Renfield St (☎332 3413). Multi-screen cinema with similar programming to the Cannon.

**Glasgow Film Theatre**, 12 Rose St (☎332 6535). The city's main art house and independent cinema.

**Grosvenor**, Ashton Lane (☎339 4298). Eclectic mix of repertory, mainstream and arthouse movies on two screens in this tiny West End alley. Occasional theme nights and frequent lates for local students.

# Listings

**Airlines** *Aer Lingus*, 19 Dixon St (☎248 4121); *British Airways*, 66 Gordon St( ☎332 9666); *Icelandair*, Glasgow Airport (☎889 1001); *Loganair*, Glasgow Airport (☎889 1311); *Lufthansa*, 78 St Vincent St (☎221 7132); *Northwest*, 38 Renfield St (☎226 4175); *Qantas*, 39 St Vincent St (☎226 3955).

**Airport enquiries** ☎887 1111.

**American Express** ☎221 4366

**Banks** *Bank of Scotland*, 65 Gordon St, 110 St Vincent St, 63 Waterloo St, 235 Sauchiehall St and 55 Bath St; *Clydesdale Bank*, 14 Bothwell St, 7 St Enoch Square, 91 Buchanan St, 344 Argyle St and 134 W George St; *Royal Bank of Scotland*, 22 St Enoch Square, 76 Gordon St, 140 St Vincent St and 393 Sauchiehall St. English banks in Glasgow include *Barclays*, 90 St Vincent St; *Lloyds*, 12 Bothwell St and *National Westminster*, 14 Blythswood Square.

**Books** *John Smith's*, 57 St Vincent St and *Waterstone's*, 132 Union St, both have extensive local studies sections.

**Car rental** *Arnold Clark*, 10 Vinnicomb St (☎334 9501); *Avis*, 161 North St (☎221 2827); *Budget*, 101 Waterloo St (☎226 4141); *Hertz*, 106 Waterloo St (☎248 7733). Car rental firms at the **airport** include *Avis* (☎887 2261); *Budget* (☎887 0501); *Eurodollar* (☎887 7915); *Europcar* (☎887 0414); *Hertz* (☎887 2451); *Swan National* (☎887 7915).

**Chemist** *Sinclair's*, 693 Great Western Rd (daily 9am–9pm; ☎339 0012) and at Central station (Mon–Sat 8am–8pm, Sun noon–6pm; ☎248 1002).

**Coach enquiries** For *Scottish Citylink* and *National Express* call ☎332 9191.

**Consulates** *Canada*, 151 St Vincent St (☎221 4415); *Italy*, 170 Hope St (☎332 4297); *Netherlands*, 102 Hope St (☎221 0605); *Norway*, 80 Oswald St (☎204 1353); *Spain*, 389 Argyle St (☎221 6943); *Sweden*, 288 Clyde St (☎221 7845).

**Exchange** Outside banking hours you can change money at *Thomas Cook* in Central station (Mon–Fri 8am–7pm, Sat 8am–8pm, Sun 10am–6pm; ☎204 4496).

**Football** Of the two big Glasgow teams, you can see *Celtic* at *Celtic Park*, 95 Kerrydale St, off A749 London Rd (☎556 2611), and bitter opponents *Rangers* at the mighty *Ibrox* stadium, Edminston Drive (☎427 8000). Glasgow's other, lesser teams include *Partick Thistle* in *Firhill stadium*, Firhill Rd (☎945 4811) or, on the South Side, lowly *Queen's Park* at the national stadium *Hampden Park*, Mount Florida (☎632 1275).

**Gay and lesbian contacts** *Lesbian and Gay Switchboard* (daily 7–10pm; ☎221 8372), *Lesbian Line* (Weds 7–10pm; ☎353 3117).

**Hospital** 24-hr casualty department at the *Royal Infirmary*, 84 Castle St (☎552 3535).

**Left luggage** Lockers available at Buchanan St bus station and staffed offices at both Central (Mon–Sat 6.30am–11pm, Sun 7.30am–11pm) and Queen St (Mon–Sat 7am–10pm, Sun 10am–6pm) train stations.

**Police** Cranstonhill Police Station, 945 Argyle St (☎248 3042) and Stewart St station, Cowcaddens (☎332 1113).

**Post office** George Square (Mon–Fri 9am–5.30pm, Sat 9am–noon; ☎248 2882), with branch offices at 85–89 Bothwell St, 216 Hope St and 533 Sauchiehall St.

**Taxis** *TOA Taxis* (☎332 7070).

**Train enquiries** ☎204 2844

**Travel agents** *Campus Travel*, The Hub, Hillhead St (☎357 0608); 90 John St (☎552 2867). *Glasgow Flight Centre*, 143 W Regent St (☎221 8989).

# THE CLYDE

The temptation to speed through the **Clyde valley** is considerable, especially since the raw beauty of the Highlands, the islands and lakes of Argyll and the urbane sophistication of Edinburgh are all within easy reach of the city. Although many of the towns and villages surrounding Glasgow are decidedly missable, a few receive far fewer visitors than they deserve, tarnished with the frequently redundant image of dejected industrial towns clinging to the coat tails of Glasgow.

From Glasgow regular trains dip down the southern bank of the Clyde to **Paisley**, where the distinctive cloth pattern gained its name, before heading up to the Firth of Clyde. Along the northern bank, the train rattles through some of Glasgow's oldest shipbuilding communities before arriving in the ancient Strathclyde capital of **Dumbarton**, whose twin-peaked **castle** dominates the flat estuary for miles around.

Heading southeast out of Glasgow, the river's industrial landscape gives way to a far more attractive scenery of gorges and towering castles. Here you can see the stoic town of **Lanark**, where eighteenth-century philanthropists built their model workers' community around the mills of **New Lanark**, and the spectacular **Falls of Clyde**, a mile upstream.

North of the city lies some wonderful upland countryside. Trains terminate at tiny **Milngavie**, which makes great play of its status as the start of the long-distance walk, the **West Highland Way**. Nearby is the rolling beauty of the **Campsie Fells**, providing excellent walking and stunning views down onto Glasgow and the glinting river that runs through it (see *Central Scotland and Fife* for the full story on all this).

# The Firth of Clyde

The shipbuilding industry forged the **Firth of Clyde**. This is still evident today in the numerous yards that pepper the banks as you head west out of the city, especially in the north Clyde communities of **Clydebank**, **Yoker** and **Dalmuir**. The A82 and the rail line run along this northern bank, hemmed in to the shore by the **Kilpatrick Hills** that rise menacingly above.

These days, the two riverbanks are connected by the concrete parabola of the **Erskine bridge**, dominating the landscape in a way that even Dumbarton Castle has never managed. The bridge disgorges its traffic onto the M8, which runs straight down south to the textile centre of **Paisley** – billed rather meaninglessly as "Scotland's largest town". In the other direction, the M8/A8 and the main train line cling to the shipyard-lined estuary edge, passing the shipbuilding centre of **Greenock**, the old-fashioned seaside resort of **Gourock**, and **Wemyss Bay**, the ferry port for Argyll and Bute. Of the three, Greenock is by far the most interesting, with an excellent town museum that examines the life and achievements of local boy James Watt.

# Paisley

Founded in the twelfth century as a monastic settlement around an abbey, **PAISLEY** expanded rapidly after the eighteenth century as a linen manufacturing town, specializing in the production of highly fashionable imitation Kashmiri shawls. Paisley quickly eclipsed other British centres producing the cloth, eventually lending its name to the swirling pine cone design.

South of the train station, down Gilmour or Smithills streets lies the bridge over the White Cart Water and the borough's ponderous **Town Hall**, seemingly built back-to-front as its municipal clock and mismatched double towers loom incongruously over the river instead of facing onto the town. Opposite the town hall, the **Abbey** was built on the site of the town's original settlement but was massively rebuilt in the Victorian age. The unattractive, fat grey facade of the church does little justice to the rampantly Unionist interior, which is tall, spacious and elaborately decorated. The elongated choir, rebuilt extensively throughout the last two centuries, is illuminated by jewel-coloured stained glass from a variety of ages and styles. The abbey's oldest monument is the tenth-century Celtic cross of St Barochan, which lurks like a gnarled old bone at the eastern end of the north aisle.

Paisley's tatty **High Street** leads from the town hall to the west and towards two churches that make far more of an impression on the town's skyline than the modest abbey. The steep cobbles of Church Hill rise away from the High Street up to the grand steps and five-stage spire of the **High Church**, while beyond the civic museum at the bottom of the High Street, the **Thomas Coates Memorial Church** (May–Sept Mon, Wed & Fri 2–4pm) is a Victorian masterpiece of hugely overstated grandeur. Sitting squat like a giant red predator waiting to pounce, the church is one of the most opulent Baptist centres in Britain, with huge tower-top buttresses and an interior of seemingly endless marble and alabaster.

Between the two churches, Paisley's civic **Museum and Art Gallery** (Mon–Sat 10am–5pm; free) shelters behind pompous Ionic columns which face the grim buildings of Paisley University. The local history section, nearest the entrance, contains an enjoyable selection of newspaper clippings, old song sheets and some good photographs of the 1860s, when the town's abbey was rebuilt. You can also see grainy photos of the "Teetotal Tower", built in the 1840s as a warning to the townsfolk against the evils of the hard stuff. The most popular part of the museum, which deals with the growth and development of the Paisley pattern and shawls, shows the familiar pine cone (or teardrop) pattern, from its simplistic beginnings to elaborate later incarnations. You can also see an old Jacquard loom, which, when introduced in the 1820s, revolutionized the weaving process, speeding it up and enabling a dozen different colours to be printed on one shawl. The exhibition also includes an interesting look at the lives of the early weavers and the inhospitable conditions under which they worked.

### Practicalities

Regular **trains** from Glasgow Central connect with Paisley's Gilmour Street station in the centre of town. Four buses per hour leave Gilmour Street forecourt for Glasgow Airport, two miles north of the town. The **tourist office** (June–Sept

Mon–Sat 9am–6pm; Oct–May Mon–Fri 9am–1pm & 2–5pm; ☎889 0711) is in the town hall. Few people bother to stay in Paisley, except those catching an early flight, and **accommodation** in the town tends to be overpriced. If you do need to stay, the spacious *Rockfield Hotel* at 125 Renfrew Rd (☎889 6182; ⑤) is the nicest alternative. **B&Bs** include *Clabern*, 88 Renfrew Rd (☎889 6194; ③) and *Greenlaw*, 12 Greenlaw Drive, off the Glasgow road (☎889 5359; ②). Lunchtime and evening bar **meals**, together with reasonably convivial atmospheres, can be found in *Gabriel's Bar* at 33 Gauze St, near the abbey, and the *Bankhouse* on Gilmour St, almost next to the station.

# From Port Glasgow to Wemyss Bay

**PORT GLASGOW** is the first of a string of unprepossessing towns that sprawl along the southern coast of the Firth of Clyde. A small fishing village until 1688, when the burghers of Glasgow bought it and developed it as their main harbour, it's a grim place, with nothing to detain you. The train line splits here, one branch heading north along the industrialized coast and the other heading inland before curving round to the ferry port at Wemyss Bay.

### North of Port Glasgow

**GREENOCK** was the site of the first dock on the Clyde, founded in 1711, and the community has grown on the back of shipping ever since. Despite its ranks of anonymous tower blocks and dreary shopping centres, the town still retains a few features of interest.

From the Central train station, it's a short walk down the hill to **Cathcart Square**, where an exuberant 245-foot Victorian tower looms high over the Council House, home of the **tourist office** (Mon–Fri 8.45am–4.45pm, Sat 9.30am–12.30pm; ☎0475/24400). On the dockside, reached by crossing the dual carriageway behind the square, the Neoclassical **Custom House** has a lively museum (Mon–Fri 9.30am–12.30pm & 1.30–4pm; £1) of the work of the Customs and Excise departments, with a display on illicit whisky distilleries and a computer game in which you search a ship for contraband. From the dock in front, tens of thousands of nineteenth-century emigrants felt their last grain of Scottish soil before departing for the New World.

Greenock's town centre has been disfigured by astonishingly unsympathetic developments. More attractive, and indicative of the town's wealthy past, is the western side of town, with its mock-Baronial houses, graceful churches and quiet, tree-lined avenues. This area can be reached either via Greenock West station, or by taking a ten-minute walk up the High Street from the Council House. One hundred yards from the well-proportioned **George Square**, just behind Greenock West station, the **Mclean Museum and Art Gallery** in Union St (Mon–Sat 10am–noon & 1–5pm; free) contains pictures and contemporary records of the life and achievements of Greenock-born James Watt, prominent eighteenth-century industrialist and pioneer of steam power, as well as featuring exhibits on the local shipbuilding industry and other local trades. The upper gallery houses a curious exhibition that purports to show the district's internationalism through its trading links, with a random selection of oddments from, among others, Japan, Papua New Guinea, India, China and Egypt.

On the train line between Greenock and Gourock, **Fort Matilda** station perches below **Lyle Hill**, an invigorating 450-foot climb that is well worth the effort for the astounding views over the purple mountains of Argyll and the creeks and lochs spilling off the Firth of Clyde. West of here lies the dowdy old resort of **GOUROCK**, from where *CalMac* ferries (☎0475/33755) head across to Dunoon and Kilcreggan on the Cowal peninsula (see *Argyll*). Generations of Glaswegians have holidayed here, and today the place is a familiar seaside mix of paint-peeling hotels, amusement arcades and cheap, steamy cafes. There's also an enjoyable seafront swimming pool with a spectacular backdrop of the Argyll mountains. The **tourist office** (April–Oct Mon–Sat 10am–5pm) is in a garish yellow building shaped like a steam kettle (as a reminder of the district's link with James Watt), in the train station car park.

### South of Port Glasgow

The southern branch of the train line from Port Glasgow heads inland, clipping the edge of Greenock before curling around the mountains and moors, playing a flirtatious game of peek-a-boo with the Clyde estuary. The terminus station, at **WEMYSS BAY**, is a startling wrought-iron and glass reminder of the great glory days, when thousands of Glaswegians would alight for their steamer trip "doon the watter". Today, Wemyss Bay station is far quieter, as the ferries chug their way from its exit over to Rothesay, capital of the Island of Bute (see *Argyll*).

# Dumbarton

Despite having been founded in about the fifth century, today the town of **DUMBARTON** is a brutal concrete sprawl, fulfilling every last hellish cliché about post-war planning and architecture. Avoid the town itself – though *Talking Heads* fans might be interested to know that David Byrne, of big suits fame, was born here – and head one mile southeast to the two-thousand-year-old **Dumbarton Castle** (April–Sept Mon–Sat 9.30am–6pm, Sun 2–6pm; Oct–March Mon–Wed & Sat 9.30–11.45am & 1.30–4pm, Thurs 9.30–11.45am, Sun 2–4pm; £1), sitting almost intact atop a twin plug of volcanic rock overlooking the Clyde. The castle is best reached from Dumbarton East train station, from where you turn right and take the second left, Victoria Street, continuing straight for just over half a mile. As a natural site, Dumbarton Rock could not be bettered – surrounded by water on three sides and with commanding views. First founded as a Roman fort, the structure was expanded in the fifth century by the Damnonii tribe, and remained Strathclyde's capital until its absorption into the greater kingdom of Scotland in 1034. The castle then became a royal seat, from which Mary, Queen of Scots sailed for France to marry Henri II's son in 1548, and to which she was attempting to escape when she and her troops were defeated twenty years later at the Battle of Langside. Since the 1600s, the castle has been used as a garrison and artillery fortress to guard the approaches to Glasgow – most of the current buildings date from this period.

The solid eighteenth-century Governor's House lies at the base of the rock, from where you enter the castle complex proper by climbing the steep steps up into the narrow cleft between the two rocks, crowned by the oldest structure in the complex, a fourteenth-century portcullis arch. Vertiginous steps ascend to each peak – to see both you must climb more than five hundred steps. The eastern rock is the highest, with a windy summit that affords excellent views over to the lakes, rivers and mountains beyond Dumbarton town.

# The Clyde valley

The landscape becomes more rural as the River Clyde heads east out of Glasgow, passing the last of a string of shipbuilding yards in Rutherglen, and crisscrossing the M74 as both river and road head southeast into Lanarkshire. Less than ten miles from central Glasgow, **Bothwell Castle** lies about a mile northeast from the **Blantyre** tenement in which explorer David Livingstone was born. Two miles further upstream, the valley's largest settlements, **Motherwell** and **Hamilton**, straddle either side of the river and motorway. Motherwell is a depressed town, hard hit by the closure of its steel works in 1992, and although Hamilton fancies itself as more upscale, there is little for the visitor in either place. Sandwiched between the two, the enormous **Strathclyde Country Park** features a glassy two-hundred-acre man-made loch, the focus of many sports and outdoor pursuits.

From here the river winds through lush market gardens and orchards that bloom far below the austere lines of **Craignethan Castle**, before passing beneath the sturdy little town of **Lanark**, probably the best base from which to explore the valley. **New Lanark**, on the riverbank, is a remarkable planned village dreamed up by eighteenth-century industrialists, David Dale and his son-in-law, Robert Owen.

## From Blantyre to Craignethan Castle

**BLANTYRE**, now a colourless suburb of Hamilton, was a remote Clydeside hamlet when explorer and missionary David Livingstone was born there in 1813. Regular trains from Glasgow Central low-level station stop at Blantyre station, from where a right turn brings you to a quiet country lane. The entire tenement block at the bottom of the lane, now painted a brilliant white, has been taken over by the **David Livingstone Centre** (Mon–Sat 10am–6pm, Sun 2–6pm; £1.70), exploring his life from early years as a mill worker up until his death in 1873 searching for the source of the River Nile. In 1813, the block consisted of twenty-four one-room tenements, each occupied by an entire family. Today the Livingstone family room shows the claustrophobic conditions under which he was brought up; all the others feature slightly defensive exhibitions on the missionary movement with tableaux of scenes from his life in Africa, including the infamous meeting with Stanley. The Africa Pavilion, made up of a group of thatched huts donated by the government of Malawi, houses changing exhibitions on African themes.

A mile or so from Blantyre, **Bothwell Castle** (April–Sept daily 9.30am–6pm; Oct–March Sat–Wed 9.30am–4pm, Thurs 9.30am–12.30pm; £1) is one of Scotland's most dramatic citadels, a great red sandstone bulk looming high above a loop in the river. The oldest section is the solid *donjon*, or circular tower, at the western end, built by the Moray family in the late 1200s to protect themselves against the English king Edward I during the Scottish wars of independence. Such was the might of the castle, Edward only finally succeeded in capturing it in September 1301 after ordering the construction and deployment of a vast siege engine, wheeled from Glasgow to Bothwell in order to lob huge stones at the castle walls. Over the next two centuries, the castle changed hands numerous times and was added to by each successive owner, with the last section, the Great Hall, in the grassy inner courtyard. Despite its jigsaw construction, the overwhelming sense today is of the almost impenetrable strength of the castle, its solid red towers – whose walls reach almost 16ft thick in places – standing firm centuries after their construction.

Kelvin Central bus #250 shuttles between Glasgow's Anderston bus station and Hamilton, dropping off on the Bothwell Road, near the castle entrance. By car, it is best approached from the B7071 Bothwell–Uddingston road.

The section of the Clyde Valley southeast from Hamilton to Lanark has appropriately become known as "Greenhouse Glen", where the winding road, lined with small stone villages and inordinate numbers of garden centres, gives occasional glimpses of the river through the trees. Buses #17 and #217 from Hamilton and Lanark stop off at **CROSSFORD**, five miles short of Lanark, where the River Nethan forks off from the Clyde. From here you can either climb a difficult mile through the wooded Nethan valley up to the gaunt clifftop ruins of **Craignethan Castle** (April–Sept daily 9.30am–6.30pm; March & Oct daily 9.30am–4.30pm; £1), or, if driving, take the extremely tortuous three-mile signposted route. The last major castle to be built in Scotland, Craignethan was constructed by Sir James Hamilton of Finnart, Master of Works to James V, in 1530. Hamilton, inspired by new styles of artillery fortification in Italy, built a unique *caponier*, a dank vault wedged into the dry moat between the two sections of the castle. From here, defenders could spray the ditch with small arms fire from behind the safety of walls 5ft thick. It was from Craignethan, owned by Mary, Queen of Scots loyalist James Hamilton, that the queen left on May 13, 1568, ultimately for defeat at Langside, followed by exile and imprisonment in England. The castle, like so many others in Scotland, is said to be inhabited by her ghost, as Craignethan was probably the last time she was ever amongst true friends. Whatever the truth, Craignethan does have a spooky quality about it, its stillness only interrupted by the shriek of circling crows. The most intact parts of the castle are the gloomy *caponier* and the musty cellars underneath the vast main tower, from which gun holders still protrude.

## Lanark and New Lanark

The neat little market town of **LANARK** is an old and distinguished burgh, sitting in the purple hills high above the River Clyde, its rooftops and spires visible for miles around. Beyond the world's oldest bell, cast in 1130 and visible in the Georgian Church of St Nicholas, there's little to see in town and most people make their way to **NEW LANARK** (daily 11am–5pm; £2.45), a mile below the main town on Braxfield Road.

Although New Lanark is served by an hourly bus from the train station, it's a walkable, if steep, journey down, and well worth it for the views. The first sight of the village, hidden away down in the gorge, is unforgettable: large broken curving walls of honeyed warehouses and tenements, built in a Palladian style, lined up along the turbulent river's edge. The community was founded by David Dale and Richard Arkwright in 1785 to harness the power of the Clyde waterfalls in their cotton-spinning industry, but it was Dale's son-in-law, Robert Owen, who revolutionized the social side of the experiment in 1798, creating a "village of unity". Believing the welfare of the workers to be crucial to industrial success, Owen built adult educational facilities, the world's first day nursery and playground, and schools in which dancing and music were obligatory subjects and there was no punishment or reward.

The Neoclassical building at the very heart of the village was opened by Owen in 1816 under the utopian title of **The Institute for the Formation of Character**. With a library, chapel and dance hall, the Institute became the main focus of town, and today you can see an introductory video about the village and its founders in the spacious congegational hall. Of the three vast old mill buildings open to visitors, one houses the **Annie McLeod Experience**, where a chairlift whisks visitors through a social history of life in the village from the imaginary perspective of a young mill girl. With a plethora of special effects – low light diffused through aromatic fog, holograms and lasers – the ten-minute journey portrays honest and unsentimental pictures of life in the community. Of the other exhibits in the mills you can see huge spinning wheels and contemporaneous children's games.

The village itself is just as fascinating: everything, from the co-operative store to the workers' tenements and workshops, was built in an attempt to prove that industrialism need not be unaesthetic. A path along the Clyde from the village leads past the small falls of spumy green water on which the project was first founded, past the Bonnington hydro-electric power station, and to the major **Falls of Clyde**, where at the stunning tree-fringed **Corra Linn** the river plunges 90ft in three tumultuous stages.

## Practicalities

By **train**, Lanark is the terminus on the line from Glasgow Central station. The town's **tourist office** (April–Sept Mon–Fri 9am–7pm, Sat 10am–7pm, Sun 11am–6pm; Oct–March Mon–Fri 9am–5pm, Sat 10am–5pm; ☎0555/661661) is housed in a circular building in the Horsemarket, next to Gateway, 100yd to the west of the station. **Accommodation** varies from the spectacular wooded surroundings of the *Cartland Bridge Hotel* on the town's edge just off the A73 Glasgow Road (☎0555/664426; ⑥) to faintly seedy town centre pubs such as the *Royal Oak*, opposite the train station at 34–35 Bannatyne St (☎0555/65895; ②). **B&Bs** include *Mrs Hamilton*, 49 West Port, the continuation of the High Street (☎0555/663663; ②) and *Mrs Gair's*, 10 Park Place (☎0555/664403; ②). There are plenty of cheap **cafés** and take-aways on the High Street, and some more pricy Indian and Italian **restaurants** along Wellgate. The rather posh *Clydesdale Hotel*, at 15 Bloomgate, serves bar meals in the cellar bar until 9.30pm, while the far less pretentious *Crown Tavern*, a quiet drinking haunt in Hope Street, serves reasonable food until 10pm. Other good local pubs include the *Horse and Jockey* in the High Street or the *Wallace Cave* in Bloomgate. Young people congregate in the *Woodpecker Inn*, tucked behind the High Street off the tiny Wide Close alley.

## travel details

**Trains**

**Glasgow Central** to: Ardrossan (hourly; 45min); Ayr (every 30min; 50min); Birmingham (5 daily; 4hr 30min); Blantyre (every 30min; 20min); Carlisle (7 daily; 2hr 25min); Crewe (7 daily; 3hr 15min); East Kilbride (every 30min Mon–Sat; 30min); Gourock (every 30min; 47min); Greenock (every 30min; 40min); Hamilton (every 30min; 25min); Kilmarnock (hourly; 40min); Lanark (hourly Mon–Sat; 50min); Largs (hourly; 1hr); London (8 daily; 5hr 45min); Manchester (2 daily; 3hr 50min); Motherwell (every 20min; 30min); Newcastle-upon-Tyne (8 daily; 2hr 30min); Paisley (every 15min; 10min); Port Glasgow (every 15min; 25min); Queen's Park (every 15min; 6min); Rutherglen (every 20min; 10min); Stranraer

(5 daily; 2hr 10min); Wemyss Bay (hourly; 55min); York (8 daily; 3hr 30min).

**Glasgow Queen Street** to: Aberdeen (hourly; 2hr 35min); Aviemore (5 daily; 2hr 40min); Balloch (every 30min Mon–Sat; 45min); Dumbarton (every 20min; 25min); Dundee (hourly; 1hr 20min); Edinburgh (every 30min; 50min); Fort William (3 daily; 3hr 40min); Helensburgh (every 30min; 45min); Inverness (5 daily; 3hr 25min); Mallaig (3 daily; 5hr 15min); Milngavie (every 30min Mon–Sat; 22min); Oban (3 daily; 3hr); Perth (hourly; 1hr); Springburn (every 30min Mon–Sat; 13min); Stirling (hourly; 30min).

**Buses**

**Glasgow** to: Aberdeen (12 daily; 4hr); Aviemore (hourly; 3hr 30min); Campbeltown (3 daily; 4hr 20min); Dundee (hourly; 2hr 15mins); Edinburgh (hourly; 1hr 15min); Fort William (5 daily; 3hr); Glencoe (5 daily; 2hr 30min); Inverness (hourly; 4–5hr); Kyle of Lochalsh (5 daily; 5hr); Lochgilpead (3 daily; 2hr 40min); Loch Lomond (hourly; 45min); London (5 daily; 7hr 30min); Newcastle-upon-Tyne (1 daily; 4hr); Oban (3 daily; 3hr); Perth (hourly; 1hr 35min); Pitlochry (hourly; 2hr 20min); Portree (5 daily; 6hr); Stirling (hourly; 45min); York (1 daily; 6hr 30min).

# CHAPTER FOUR

# CENTRAL SCOTLAND AND FIFE

L ying immediately north of both Edinburgh and Glasgow, **Central Scotland** is a heavily visited area, combining many of the physical and cultural attributes for which the nation is commonly known. The region encompasses much of the great Highland Boundary Fault – the geological dislocation which runs from **Dumbarton**, north of Glasgow on the west coast, up to Stonehaven, south of Aberdeen on the east coast – and the scenery ranges from snow-capped peaks, heather-covered hills and steep-sided glens to frothy rivers and dark lochs. The landscape begins gently, in the little-known **Campsie Fells**, becoming more dramatic as you move further north to the wild and wonderful **Trossachs** and **Ochil Hills**, which together stretch as far west as the banks of **Loch Lomond** and as far east as **Loch Leven**.

At the heart of Central Scotland, packed above a dull, industrial waste, is venerable **Stirling**, historically one of the most important bridging points across the River Forth and site of two of the most important battles fought during the **Wars of Independence**. In the eighteenth century the town was again besieged due to its location, and its strategic importance led to various involvements with the Jacobite rebellions of 1715 and 1745, before Bonnie Prince Charlie captured it on his march south to tackle the Hanoverians.

The geography and history of the region caught the imagination of Sir Walter Scott, who took so much delight in the tales of local clansman **Rob Roy** MacGregor, the notorious seventeenth-century Scottish Robin Hood, that he set them down in writing in his novel of the same name. Thanks to his – and William Wordsworth's – effusive praise, Queen Victoria deigned to visit, and so the area was placed firmly on the map.

Tacked onto the eastern side of the Ochils like a child under arm is tiny **Fife**, the only one of Scotland's seven original kingdoms to survive relatively intact. Neither Norse nor Norman influence found its way to this independent corner, and nine and a half centuries later, when the government at Westminster redrew local boundaries in 1975, the Fifers stuck to their guns and successfully opposed the changes. Here you'll find coastal fishing villages and sandy beaches and the self-assured town of **St Andrews**, inextricably linked in the public consciousness with golf. The game arrived from France in the fifteenth century, went through various modifications, and by the time the world-famous Royal and Ancient Golf Club was established in the eighteenth century, was not dissimilar – high stakes aside – to the sport played today.

N

HIGHLAND

Glen Spean

GRAMPI

Dalwhinnie

A9

Loch Ericht

Loch Errochty

Glen Errochty

Blair Atholl

Rannoch Forest

Rannoch Station

Kinloch Rannoch

Loch Tummel

Loch Rannoch

A82

Rannoch Moor

Glen Lyon

Aberfeldy

Kenmore

Loch Tay

Glen Almond

A85

Killin

Crianlarich

Ben More 1174ft

A85

Loch Voll

Lochearnhead

Loch Earn

Ben Vorlich 985ft

Comrie

Crieff

Strathearn

CENTRAL

Loch Katrine

Loch Lubnaig

Ben Ledi 878ft

The Trossachs

Callander

Ben Lomond 974ft

Duke's Pass

Loch Drunkie

Aberfoyle

A81

Dunblane

A91

QUEEN ELIZABETH FOREST PARK

Loch of Menteith

Forth

A811

Kippen

Alloa

Stirling

Loch Lomond

A82

Drymen

Fintry Hills

Kincardine Bridge

Fintry

M80

Denny

Campsie Fells

Falki

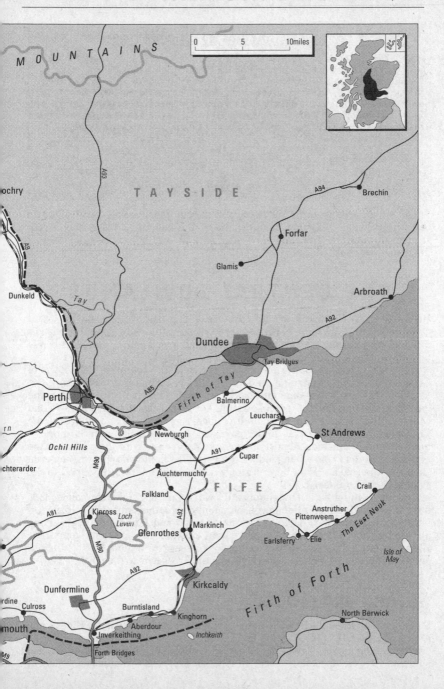

MOUNTAINS

0    5    10miles

...ochry

TAYSIDE

A93

A94    Brechin

Forfar

Glamis

Dunkeld    Tay

Arbroath

A92

Dundee

Tay Bridges

Perth    A85    Firth of Tay    Balmerino

Leuchars

Newburgh    St Andrews

Ochil Hills    A91    Cupar

...rn

...chterarder    Auchtermuchty    FIFE    Crail

M90    Falkland    Anstruther
Pittenweem

A91    Kinross    Loch    Markinch
Leven    A92
Glenrothes    The East Neuk

Earlsferry    Elie
Isle of
May

A92    Kirkcaldy

Firth of Forth

Dunfermline    Burntisland
...dine    Culross    Kinghorn    North Berwick
...mouth    Aberdour    Inchkeith

M9    Inverkeithing
Forth Bridges

---

**ACCOMMODATION PRICE CODES**

Throughout this book, accommodation **prices** have been graded with the numbers below, according to the cost of the least expensive double room in high season. The bulk of the recommendations will fall in categories ② to ⑤; recommendations in the highest categories are limited to places that are especially attractive. Bear in mind that many of the swanky hotels often slash their tariffs at the weekend when the business types have gone home, and that many of the cheaper places will also have more expensive rooms. Note that in our accommodation listings price codes are not given for youth hostels – they all come into the lower end of the ① category.

| | | |
|---|---|---|
| ① under £20 | ④ £40–50 | ⑦ £70–80 |
| ② £20–30 | ⑤ £50–60 | ⑦ £80–100 |
| ③ £30–40 | ⑥ £60–70 | ⑧ over £100 |

---

The whole area is easily accessed, and easy to **get around**. Scotland's two main train lines – Glasgow to Inverness and Edinburgh to Aberdeen – cut straight through the area, and good intercity and local bus services connect all the main towns and villages.

---

# THE CENTRAL LOWLANDS

Historically, the **Central Lowlands** are one of the most strategically important areas in Scotland. With the Forth and Clyde rivers cutting into Central Scotland's east and west coasts, the narrow passage of land in between, at one point barely fifty miles across, forms a vital link between north and south.

Historically, because of the inhospitable terrain of the **Campsie Fells** north of Glasgow, the easiest passage through the heart of Scotland was via **Stirling**. The situation isn't altogether different today, and you'll find that Stirling makes the best base for exploring the area in general. The town is an attraction in itself, and within an hour's drive lie a range of diversions, from the hills and villages of the **Trossachs** to the palace at **Linlithgow** and the banks of **Loch Lomond** – touristy on the west side, almost untouched on the east. With the decline of the region's important coal mining industry, tourism has come into its own, and even skiing is a possibility from here: it's only a couple of hours up the road to the slopes at Aviemore (see p.354).

**Access** to the area is straightforward, with good bus and train connections from Glasgow, Perth and Edinburgh, although during the summer the roads fast become congested with daytrippers from Glasgow and Edinburgh, and walking and cycling holidays are likely to prove more rewarding than driving tours. The **Glasgow–Loch Lomond–Killin cycleway** crosses the region, linking Balloch and Glasgow in the south and Aberfoyle and the Trossachs to the north.

---

## Stirling and around

Straddling the River Forth a few miles upstream from the estuary at Kincardine, at first glance **STIRLING** seems like a smaller version of Edinburgh. With its cragtop castle, steep, cobbled streets and mixed community of locals and students, it's an appealing place, despite lacking the cosmopolitan edge of

Edinburgh or Glasgow. It's historic too, due to its former importance as a much coveted river crossing, but – geographically trapped between Scotland's two main cities – Stirling remains at heart decidedly provincial.

The town was the scene of some of the most significant developments in the evolution of the Scottish nation. It was here that the Scots under William Wallace defeated the English at the **Battle of Stirling Bridge** in 1297, only to fight – and win again – under Robert the Bruce just a couple of miles away at the **Battle of Bannockburn** in 1314. Stirling Castle was the favoured residence of the Stuart monarchy, and in 1543 was the setting for the coronation of the young Mary, future Queen of Scots.

Today Stirling no longer enjoys such national political status, and is known instead for its two draws of **Stirling Castle** – just as beautiful as its Edinburgh counterpart – and the lofty **Wallace Monument**, a mammoth Victorian monolith high on Abbey Craig to the northeast. The **University**, also, has helped to maintain Stirling's profile.

The town is at its liveliest during the summer, with buskers and street artists jostling for performing space in the pedestrianized centre. If you get decent weather – which isn't all that uncommon despite the proliferation of surrounding hills – there's very much a holiday air about the place, with kids rushing around the castle ramparts, backpackers struggling up the steep hill to the youth hostel, and students – many of whom choose to stay here over the summer – spilling out of the cafés.

## Arrival and information

The **bus** (☎0786/473763) and **train stations** (☎0786/464754) are next to each other in the centre of town on Goosecroft Road. To reach the town centre from the bus station cut through the monstrous 1960s Thistle Shopping Centre opposite to reach the main drag, Port Street. From the train station, walk up Station Road opposite and turn left at the mini-roundabout. Stirling's **tourist office** is in the heart of the town centre at 41 Dumbarton Rd (Mon–Sat 9am–8pm, Sun 9am–7.30pm; ☎0786/475019). This is the main office for Loch Lomond, Stirling and the Trossachs, with a wide range of books, maps and leaflets, and a free accommodation-booking service. Because of Stirling's compact size – barely five miles from the centre to the outermost fringes – sightseeing is best done on foot.

## Accommodation

If you're in Stirling between May and October, you'll need to book a room by lunchtime at the latest on the day of arrival, or you're likely to be stranded. The tourist office carries details of **accommodation**; most of the **B&Bs** are concentrated in the residential area nearby. Rooms go fast at the comfortable and clean *Woodside Guest House*, directly opposite the tourist office at 4 Back Walk (☎0786/475470; ①); a little further up Dumbarton Road the *Garfield Hotel*, 12 Victoria Square (☎0786/473730; ③) is a family-run Victorian town house, serving hearty breakfasts. The cheapest option is the spanking new **youth hostel** in a converted church on St John St (☎0786/473442; Grade 1). Situated at the top of town (a mountainous trek with a backpack), all rooms have en suite showers and toilets, and you get a free continental breakfast. There's a **campsite** three miles east of town, off the A91 road to St Andrews (April–Oct; ☎0786/474947).

If you arrive late in the day, and there are no other options, or if you prefer to stay out of town, try the **campus accommodation** at Stirling University (☎0786/ 467140 or 467146; ②) a couple of miles north of the town centre. Regular buses leave from Murray Place, at the end of the main street (last service 10.53pm Mon–Sat). Also on campus, the new *Stirling Management Centre* (☎0786/451666; ④), is pricier, but as popular with tourists as with the conference guests towards whom it was originally aimed, with luxurious, en suite rooms giving atmospheric, mist-drenched views of the Wallace Monument.

# The Town

Stirling evolved from the top down, starting with its castle and gradually spreading south and east onto the low-lying flood plain. At the centre of the original **Old Town**, Broad Street was the main thoroughfare, with St John Street running more or less parallel, and St Mary's Wynd forming part of the original route to Stirling Bridge below. In the eighteenth and nineteenth centuries, as the threat of attack decreased, the centre of commercial life crept down towards the River Forth, with the modern town – commonly called the **Lower Town** – growing on the edge of the plain over which the castle has traditionally stood guard.

### Stirling Castle and the Old Town

In its early days, **Stirling Castle** (April–Sept Mon–Sat 9.30am–5.15pm, Sun 10.30am–4.45pm; Oct–March Mon–Sat 9.30am–4.20pm, Sun 12.30–3.35pm; HS; £2.50) must have presented would-be invaders with a formidable challenge. Its impregnability is most daunting when you approach the town from the west, from where the sheer, 250-foot drop down the side of the crag is most obvious. The rock was first fortified during the Iron Age, though what you see now dates largely from the fifteenth and sixteenth centuries.

The **visitor centre** (hours as castle) on the esplanade shows an introductory film giving a potted history of the castle, but the best place to get an impression of its gradual expansion is in the courtyard known as the **Upper Square**, surrounded by the splendidly Gothic fifteenth-century **Great Hall**, complete with fireplaces and hammerbeam roof, and the **Palace**, built roughly one hundred years later. The palace has a wonderful facade – note the ornate Renaissance stonework and grotesque carved figures – while inside, in the otherwise bare royal apartments, various monarchs are depicted in the **Stirling Heads**, a collection of intricately carved wooden medallions. Also in the courtyard is the **Chapel Royal** , where Mary, Queen of Scots was crowned at the age of nine months – the chapel was rebuilt in 1594, but you can trace the outline of the old structure by following the darker shaded stones in the courtyard.

The castle is now the headquarters of the regiment of the Argyll and Sutherland Highlanders, whose **museum** houses a magnificent collection of well-polished silver, as well as a diverse selection of memorabilia, including seemingly endless Victoria crosses won by the regiment.

Leaving the castle, head downhill into the old centre of Stirling, fortified behind the massive, whinstone boulders of the **town walls**, built in the mid-sixteenth century and intended to ward off the advances of Henry VIII, who had set his sights on the young Mary as a wife for his son, Edward. The walls now constitute some of the best-preserved town defences in Scotland, and can be traced by following the path known as **Back Walk**. This circular walkway was

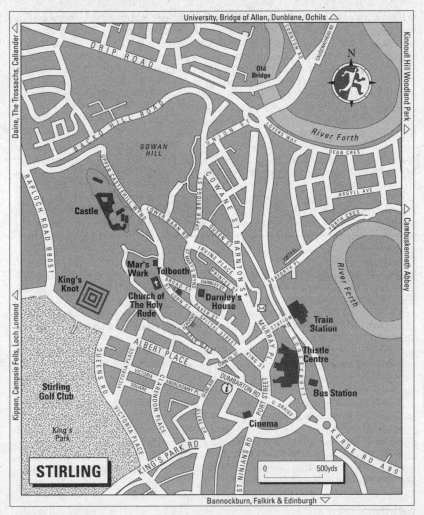

University, Bridge of Allan, Dunblane, Ochils △

N

DRIP ROAD

Old Bridge

River Forth

BACK O HILL ROAD

UNION ST

LOVERS WAY

GOWAN HILL

DEAN CRES

RAPLOCH ROAD B8051

UPPER CASTLEHILL WYND

LOWER BARN RD

COWANE ST

UPPER BRIDGE S

QUEEN ST

BARNTON ST

ARGYLL AVE

Castle

FORTH CRES

IRVINE PLACE

River Forth

Mar's Wark

Tolbooth

PRINCES ST

King's Knot

DARNLEY ST

Church of The Holy Rude

Darnley's House

BROAD ST

ST JOHN ST

BAKER ST

SPITTAL STREET

PORT STREET

MURRAY PL

SEAFORTH PL

STATION RD

GOOSECROFT

Train Station

Thistle Centre

ALBERT PLACE

QUEENS RD

VICTORIA PLACE

VICTORIA SQUARE

CLARENDON PLACE

ABERCROMBY PL

GLEBE AVE

CORN EX ST

KING ST

PORT STREET

GOOSECROFT RD

Bus Station

Stirling Golf Club

DUMBARTON RD

GLEBE CR

U GRAIGS

Cinema

KERSE RD A90

King's Park

VICTORIA PLACE

KING'S PARK RD

ST NINIANS RD

**STIRLING**

0        500yds

◁ Daine, The Trossachs, Callander

◁ Kippen, Campsie Fells, Loch Lomond

Kinnoull Hill Woodland Park ▷

Cambuskenneth Abbey ▷

Bannockburn, Falkirk & Edinburgh ▽

built in the eighteenth century and in the upper reaches encircles the castle, taut along the edge of the crag, offering panoramic views of the surrounding countryside.

The richly decorated facade at the top of Broad Street on Castle Wynd hides the dilapidated **Mar's Wark**, a would-be palace which the first Earl of Mar, Regent of Scotland and hereditary Keeper of Stirling Castle, started in 1570. His dream house was never to be realized, however, for he died two years later and what had been built was left to ruin, its degeneration speeded up by extensive damage during the 1745 Jacobite Rebellion. Behind here is the **Church of the Holy Rude** (May–Sept Mon–Fri 10am–5pm, Sunday service), a fine medieval structure, the oldest parts of which, including the impressive oak hammerbeam roof, date from the early fifteenth century. Go in during the day and imagine the ceremony that was held here in 1567 for the coronation of the infant James VI – later the first monarch of the United Kingdom – and come back in the evening to the spooky graveyard, from where you can watch dreamy sunsets. Just south of the church on the edge of the crag, the grand E-shaped **Guildhall** was built as a 1649 almshouse for "decayed [unsuccessful] members of the Guild of Merchants". Above the entrance, John Cowane, the wealthy merchant who founded the hospital, is commemorated in a statue which, it is said, comes alive at Hogmanay.

**Broad Street** was the site of the marketplace and centre of the medieval town. Many of its buildings have been restored in recent years, and work is still going on to preserve what remains. Down here, past the **Mercat Cross** (the unicorn on top is known, inexplicably, as "the puggy"), the **Tolbooth**, on the corner with Jail Wynd, was built in 1705 by Sir William Bruce, who designed the Palace of Holyrood House in Edinburgh. It was used as both a courthouse and, after 1809, a prison, from where the unfortunate were led to execution in the street outside. **Darnley's House**, at the bottom of Broad Street, was where Mary, Queen of Scots' husband is believed to have lodged while she lorded it up in the castle; it is now a touristy coffee shop.

### The Lower Town

The further downhill you go in Stirling's Lower Town, the more recent the buildings become. Follow St John Street into Spittal Street, and then on down into King Street, where austere Victorian facades block the sun from the cobbled road. Stirling's main **shopping** area is down here, along Port Street and Murray Place, while the **Smith Art Gallery and Museum** (April–Oct Tues–Sat 10.30am–5pm, Sun 2–5pm; Nov–March Tues–Fri noon–5pm, Sat 10.30am–5pm, Sun 2–5pm) is a short walk west up Dumbarton Road. Founded in 1874 with a legacy from local painter and collector Thomas Stuart Smith, it houses a permanent exhibition relating the history of Stirling, and a range of changing displays of arts and crafts, contemporary art and photography.

The **Old Bridge** over the Forth lies on the edge of the town centre, about a fifteen-minute walk from the northern end of Murray Place. Although once the most important river crossing in Scotland – the lowest bridging point on the Forth until the new bridge was built in 1831 – it now stands virtually forgotten, an almost incidental reminder of Stirling's former importance. An earlier, wooden **bridge** nearby was the focus of the Battle of Stirling Bridge in 1297, where William Wallace defeated the English.

## Eating

The best bet for **budget food** in Stirling is to head for the town's numerous pubs. At the top of town, *No. 39*, 39 Broad St, next to the Tolbooth Theatre, serves filling pub grub for under a fiver, including a better-than-average selection of vegetarian dishes, in a quietly respectable atmosphere. Alternatives to pub food include the tiny *Caruso*, on Upper Craigs, which offers a good value, three-course set menu (variations on onion soup, T-bone steak and pudding), although individual orders work out to be more expensive. Also on Upper Craigs, *The Arches* at nos. 35–37 and *All That Jazz* at no. 9 are both inexpensive and popular: the former for its bar lunches, high teas and lively cocktail bar, the latter for its "Deep South Specialities", served in what was formerly one of the town's oldest grain and seed warehouses. Another good option is *Littlejohns*, 52 Port St (☎0786/463222), which boasts moderately priced burgers, pasta and chilli, and intriguing wall fixtures (toy trains, old violins, sepia-stained photographs). For a more upmarket meal, try *The Heritage*, 16 Allan Park (☎0786/73660), where fine Scottish produce is served with a distinctly French touch.

## Nightlife

Entertainment in Stirling revolves around its **pubs** and **bars**. The lively *Barnton Bar and Bistro* on Barnton St caters for the student crowd, serving a good selection of beers and not bad snacks in a setting of wrought-iron and marble tables, picture mirrors and decorative ceiling cornices. Also popular with students is the real ale at the *Settle Inn*, 91 St Mary's Wynd. This is Stirling's oldest ale house, built in 1733 with a barrel-vaulted roof, and has a patina that testifies to centuries of smoking and drinking.

If you're staying at the university, try *The Birds and the Bees*, Easter Cornton Rd (turn left opposite the garage just before the Causewayhead roundabout). Occupying a converted farmstead, it is an odd but appealing mixture – they play **boules** out the back at weekends and the bar seats are eccentric make-believe stuffed sheep. Tasty pub food is served in the bar area, and there is a good, but more expensive restaurant at the side. You can hear **live music** – anything from salsa and punk to r'n'b – at *CJ's*, 52 Cowane St, which also dishes out an intriguing blend of African and Italian food.

The main venue for **theatre** and **film** is the excellent *MacRobert Arts Centre* (☎0786/461081) on the university campus (see below), which shows a good selection of drama and mainstream and art-house films.

## Around Stirling

North of Stirling, a ten-minute walk from the Victorian spa town of **BRIDGE OF ALLAN, Stirling University** was until 1992 (when colleges and polytechnics acquired university status), the youngest university in Scotland, and once one of the most radical. Though the architecture is typically utilitarian, the landscaped grounds are undeniably beautiful – resplendent with daffodils in spring, rhododendrons along the sides of the artificial Airthrey Loch in summer, and the rich colours of the Ochil Hills as a backdrop in autumn. Stranded on the northern edge, **Airthrey Castle** (closed to the public) is a prepossessing nineteenth-century affair built by Robert Adam, which now houses Radio Airthrey, the student broadcasting station. Frequent buses run to the university from Murray Place in Stirling.

Overlooking the university from one mile to the southwest is the prominent **Wallace Monument** (April–Oct daily 10am–5pm; July–Aug 9am–6pm; £2.35), an ugly, rocket-like tribute to Sir William Wallace ("the hammer and scourge of the English") built in 1861–9. It was from the nearby Wallace's Pass that the Scottish hero led his troops down to defeat the English at the Battle of Stirling Bridge in 1297. Informative exhibits inside the monument include Wallace's long steel sword, swathed in tartan, and the Hall of (Scottish) Heroes, a row of stern white marble busts featuring John Knox and Adam Smith, among many, less significant others. If you can manage the climb – 246 spiral steps up – there are superb views across to Fife and Ben Lomond from the top of the 220-foot tower.

A woodland path weaves its way from the monument to the ruins of **Cambuskenneth Abbey**, about a mile east of Stirling (ruin open April–Sept, grounds all year; HS; free). Founded in 1147 by David I on the site of an Augustinian settlement, the abbey is distinguished by its twelfth-century bell-tower, though there's little else to see there now. Its history, however, makes it worth a brief look; the Scots parliament met here in 1326 to pledge allegiance to Robert the Bruce's son David, and James III (1451–88) and his wife, Queen Margaret of Denmark, are both buried in the grounds, their graves marked by a nineteenth-century monument.

Frequent trains, and buses #58 or #258 make the fifteen-minute journey to **DUNBLANE**, four miles north of Stirling. This small, attractive town has been an ecclesiastical centre since the seventh century, when the Celts founded the Church of St Blane here. **Dunblane Cathedral** (April–Sept Mon–Sat 9.30am–12.30pm & 1.30–6pm, Sun 2–6pm; Oct–March Mon–Sat 9.30am–12.30pm & 1.30–4pm, Sun 2–4pm; HS; free) dates from the thirteenth century, and restoration work carried out a century ago has returned the cathedral to its Gothic splendour. Inside, note the delicate blue-purple stained glass, and the exquisitely carved pews, screen and choir stalls, all crafted in the early twentieth century. The cathedral stands serenely among a clutch of old-world buildings, among them the seventeenth-century Dean's House, which houses the tiny cathedral **museum** (June–Sept Mon–Sat 10.30am–12.30pm & 1.30–4.30pm) with exhibits on local history.

High in the Ochil Hills east of Dunblane are the wild, windswept moors of **Sheriffmuir**, where the Earl of Mar fought the crown forces in 1715. The only access to the area is by car up steep, single-track roads, but the splendid hills are worth the effort. At the top, pop into the Sheriffmuir **pub**, sitting in glorious isolation, which serves food and is a popular watering hole during the summer months.

In the opposite direction, five miles northwest of Stirling (take buses #59 and #211, which run daily except Sun), **Blair Drummond Safari Park** (April–Oct daily 10am–4.30pm; £5.50), is an attempt to recreate the African bush and Limpopo. The only wildlife park in Scotland, it's good for a family day out, with everything from big cats to sea lions, and a 3-D cinema and performing clown for good measure.

**DOUNE**, eight miles northwest of Stirling, is a sleepy village which belies its violent past. The ruined, fourteenth-century **Castle** (April–Sept Mon–Sat 9.30am–6pm, Sun 2–6pm; Oct–March Mon–Weds & Sat 9.30am–1pm, Sun 2–4pm; HS; £1.75) is a marvellous old pile standing on a small hill in a bend of the River Teith. Built by Robert, Duke of Albany, it eventually ended up in the hands of the Earls of Moray (whose descendants still own it), following the execution of the Albany family by James I. In the sixteenth century it belonged to the second earl, James Stewart – son of James V and half-brother of Mary, Queen of Scots – who has been immortalized in the ballad the *Bonnie Earl of Moray*. Today the most prominent features of the castle are its mighty 95-foot gatehouse, with its spacious vaulted rooms, and the kitchens, complete with medieval rubbish chute.

The present earl has a fabulous collection of flash vintage cars, which are on show one mile northwest of town in the **Doune Motor Museum** (April–Oct daily 10am–5pm; £2.50) off the A84. Among the examples of gleaming paintwork and tanned upholstery you can see legendary models of Bentley, Lagonda, Jaguar, Aston Martin and the second oldest Rolls Royce in the world. To get to

Doune from Stirling, take bus #59 or #259 which leave hourly, or every two hours on Sunday.

A couple of miles south of Stirling, just north of the village of **BANNOCKBURN** the **Bannockburn Heritage Centre** (April–Oct daily 10am–6pm; NTS; £1.50) is situated close to where Robert the Bruce won his mighty victory over the English at the **Battle of Bannockburn** on June 24, 1314. It was this battle, the climax of the Wars of Independence, which united the Scots under Bruce and led to independence under the Declaration of Arbroath (1320) and the Treaty of Northampton (1328).

Outside, a concrete rotunda encloses a cairn near the spot where Bruce planted his standard after beating Edward II. Of the original bore stone, only a fragment remains, safely on display in the visitor centre. Over-eager visitors used to chip pieces off, and the final straw came when a particularly zealous enthusiast attempted to blast enough of it away to make two curling stones. Pondering the scene is an equestrian statue of Bruce, on the spot from where he is said to have commanded the battle, which was fought on the boggy carse down towards the burn.

# The Campsie Fells

The hills southwest of Stirling are the **Campsie Fells**, a range often overlooked in the rush to reach the more spectacular Trossachs. They're worth a detour, though, if you've got the time, boasting a gentle landscape and several quiet, understated villages.

The southern route around the region winds along the northern edges of Glasgow's commuter belt, where almost every view is spoilt by industrial blight. Branch off into the hills beyond **LENNOXTOWN**, however, and the hills are interrupted by nothing but sheep and waterfalls, the roads narrow and winding, and there are few signs of habitation. In winter it's an eerie sight, with the mists rolling in from the moors. The northern section of the Fells, across the flat plain to the west of Stirling, is even more appealing, particularly once you cut up into the hills beyond the village of **KIPPEN**.

Hikers might want to follow the Campsie Fells Trail, which links the Campsie villages (details from Stirling's tourist office). Otherwise, plenty of **buses** run through the region from Stirling (#10, #107, #210, 3 or 4 daily, fewer at weekends), and from Monday to Saturday a postbus service operates from **Denny**, roughly five miles south of Stirling (reached from Stirling bus station on buses #39, #81, #81A). The postbus stops at Fintry, from where two buses daily (except Sun) head on to Balfron at the other end of the Fells.

### Fintry

The key settlement in the Campsie Fells is **FINTRY**, a picture-postcard village at the head of Strathendrick valley and at the centre of the Campsie Fells Trail, that is a regular winner of the "Best Kept Small Village in Scotland" award. There are a couple of **places to stay**: if you're feeling flush, stop off at *Culcreuch Castle Hotel* (☎036086/228; ⑥), a fourteenth-century country house on the northern side of the village; if you're not, try the *Clachan Hotel* (☎036086/237; ③), a seventeenth-century hostelry next to the kirk at the east end of town, which does pub food and B&B.

## Drymen

At the western end of the Fells, all roads meet at the small town of **DRYMEN**, which sits peacefully on the hills overlooking the winding Endrick water as it nears Loch Lomond. Rob Roy used to come here to collect protection money from local cattle owners for the security he and his "watch" provided against potential attack by marauding Highlanders. Although there's nothing to actually do in the village, its reputation as the "gateway to east Loch Lomondside" means it gets extremely busy during the summer. Ten miles southeast of town in the Blane Valley, Lang Brothers' **Glengoyne Distillery** (April–Nov Mon–Fri 10.30am–4pm, Sat 11am–1.30pm; £2) offers interesting guided tours – although the snooty staff don't make it worth going out of your way for unless it's the only distillery you're likely to visit.

# Loch Lomond

**Loch Lomond** – the largest stretch of fresh water in Britain – is almost as famous as Loch Ness, thanks to the ballad about its "bonnie, bonnie banks", the epitome of the Scottish folk song. However, all is not bonnie at the loch nowadays, especially on its overdeveloped west side, fringed by the A82; on the water itself, speedboats tear up and down on summer weekends, destroying the tranquility which so impressed the likes of Queen Victoria, the Wordsworths and Sir Walter Scott.

Nevertheless, the west bank of the loch is a beautiful stretch of water, and despite the crowds, gives better views than the heavily wooded east side. **LUSS,** the setting for the enormously popular Scottish TV soap *Take the High Road*, is the prettiest village, though its picturesque streets can become unbearably crowded in summer. **BALLOCH**, a brash holiday resort at the loch's southern tip, is the place to head for if you want to take a boat trip; various operators offer cruises around the 33 islands scattered near the shore.

The tranquil east bank is far better for walking than the west, and can only be traversed in its entirety by the West Highland Way footpath, from where you can head on through **Queen Elizabeth Forest Park** (see p.206), or take the stiff three-hour hike from **ROWARDENNAN** to the summit of Ben Lomond (3192ft), the most southerly of Scotland's "Munros", and subject of the Scottish proverb "Leave Ben Lomond where it stands" – just let things be.

## Practicalities

The West Highland **train** – the line from Glasgow to Mallaig, with a branchline to Oban – joins the loch seventeen miles north of Balloch at **TARBET**, and has one other station eight miles further on at **ARDLUI**, at the mountain-framed head of the loch. There are plenty of **buses** along the shore from Balloch.

Loch Lomond's **tourist office** (April–June, Sept & Oct daily 10am–5.30pm; July & Aug 9.30am–7.30pm; ☎0389/53533) is above the marina in Balloch; they'll reserve a room for you without charge at one of the many local **B&Bs**. A couple of miles up the west side of the loch at minuscule **ARDEN** is Scotland's most beautiful **youth hostel**: a turreted building complete with ghost (March–Nov; Fri & Sat rest of year; ☎0389/85226; Grade 1). There's another youth hostel at **INVERBEG** (March–Nov; ☎043686/635; Grade 3). Caravan parks abound on the west side of the loch; tents are best pitched at the secluded Forestry Commission **campsite** (April–Sept; ☎036087/234) two miles south of Rowardennan on the east bank.

Passenger ferries cross between Inverbeg and Rowardennan, where there is an eponymous **hotel** (☎036087/259; ⑤) and another **youth hostel** (March–Oct & New Year; ☎036087/259; Grade 1).

As for **eating**, on the west side of the loch the *Inverbeg Inn*, signposted off the A82, is the most convenient place to stop, with tasty bar snacks and outdoor seating from which to view the loch. It also has a few comfortable rooms (☎0436/86678; ⑤). On the east side, there's little option but to take a picnic.

# The Forth Valley

The **Forth Valley** stetches some forty miles southeast of Stirling along the Firth of Forth. The area has long been known for its industry, most historically for the famous – but now redundant – Carron Ironworks near Falkirk, which began in 1760 by manufacturing "carronades" (small cannons) for Nelson's fleet, and more recently for BP's petrochemical plant at Grangemouth. Consequently, it is often bypassed by visitors, despite the attraction of Linlithgow Palace near Falkirk.

If you reach the area from the east, across the Kincardine Bridge, you may want to pop into the signposted **tourist office** at Pine'N'Oak Layby, Kincardine Bridge (April–May Mon–Sat 11am-5pm, Sun 1-5pm; June–Aug Mon–Sun 10am–6pm; Sept Mon–Sat 11am–5pm, Sun 1–5pm; ☎0324/831422).

## Falkirk and around

**FALKIRK**, the Forth Valley's main commercial centre, was the site of two major battles, one in 1298, when William Wallace fell victim to the English under Edward I, and the other in 1746, when Bonnie Prince Charlie, retreating northwards, sent the Hanoverians packing in one of his last victories over government troops. Traditionally a livestock centre, Falkirk was transformed in the eighteenth century from a rural into an industrial town by the construction of first the Forth and Clyde Canal, allowing easy access to Glasgow, and then the Edinburgh and Glasgow Union Canal, which continued the route through to Edinburgh. Only twenty years later, however, the trains arrived, and the canals became obsolete.

If you've got time to spare, stop off here for a few hours. The town today is a busy local shopping centre, with its own **museum** on Orchard Street (Mon–Fri 10am–12.30pm & 1.30–5pm; free) telling the town's story from Roman times. In Callendar Park, Bonnie Prince Charlie is said to have stayed at **Callendar House** (Mon–Sat 10am–5pm, plus April–Sept Sun 2–5pm; HS; free), owned by the staunchly Jacobite Livingston family and which today recreates "upstairs-downstairs" life from the early nineteenth century, complete with costumed interpreters demonstrating traditional cooking methods. In the area surrounding Falkirk, the wide network of old industrial **canals** offers good opportunities for boating, canoeing and strolling.

If you've got your own transport, get out to **BONNYBRIDGE**, five miles west of Falkirk. Here you'll see **Rough Castle**, one of the forts which were built at two-mile intervals along the entire length of the Roman **Antonine Wall,** built in AD 142. In the opposite direction, the industrial town of **GRANGEMOUTH** sits at the edge of the Forth, its industrial chimneys spewing out smoke visible for miles around. If industrial heritage is your scene, then come to the **museum** here (Mon–Sat 2–5pm; free), otherwise give it a miss.

**The Pineapple** (garden open all year), north of Falkirk on the A905 (turn off onto the B9124), qualifies as one of Scotland's most exotic and eccentric buildings, a 45-foot high stone pineapple built as a garden folly by an unknown architect in 1761. The surrounding buildings were heated by hot air from well-stoked furnaces and used for growing pineapples. The folly is now owned by the National Trust for Scotland, and the outhouses can be rented for holidays through the Landmark Trust (☎0628/825920).

## Practicalities

Regular **trains** run from Glasgow Queen Street, Edinburgh and Stirling to Falkirk Grahamston Station (as opposed to Falkirk High Station, which is further from the centre), from where it's a five-minute walk to the **tourist office**, 2–4 Glebe St (April–May daily 9.30am–6pm; June–July Sun–Thurs 9.30am–6pm, Fri & Sat 9am–6pm; Aug daily 9.30am–8pm; Sept–Oct daily 9.30am–6pm; Nov–March Mon, Tues & Thurs–Sat 9.30am–12.30pm & 1.30–5pm; ☎0324/20244). If you want to **stay**, the modern *Stakis Falkirk Park Hotel*, Camelon Rd (☎0324/28331; ③), at the west end of town overlooking Dollar Park, is your best bet, with comfortable, luxurious rooms.

You can **eat** great Mexican food and hear **live music** and cabaret at *Behind the Wall*, 14 Melville St, a brasserie-style café with a beer garden. There's more cabaret at *The Three Kings*, Wester Shieldhill (☎0324/21743), which serves moderately priced Scottish food and traditional Sunday high teas.

# Linlithgow

Roughly equidistant (fifteen miles) between Falkirk and Edinburgh is the ancient royal burgh of **LINLITHGOW**, a residential town on the main train routes from Edinburgh to both Glasgow Queen Street and Stirling, whose quiet air of domesticity belies an historic past. The town itself has largely kept its medieval layout, but development since the 1960s has sadly stripped it of some fine buildings, notably close to the **Town Hall** and **Cross** – the former marketplace – on the long High Street.

You should head straight for **Linlithgow Palace** (April–Sept 9.30am–6pm & Sun 2–6pm; Oct–March 9.30am–12.30pm & 1.30–4pm, Sun 2–4pm; £1.50), a well-preserved fifteenth-century ruin romantically located on the edge of Linlithgow Loch and associated with some of Scotland's best-known historical figures – including the ubiquitous Mary, Queen of Scots, who was born here in 1542.

A royal manor house is believed to have existed on this site since the time of David I. Fire razed the manor in 1424, after which James I began construction of the present palace, a process which continued through two centuries and the reign of no fewer than eight monarchs. Today you can see roofless remains of various bedchambers and corridors, but most impressive is the massive **Great Hall** with a grand, ornate fireplace. Detailed plaques and noticeboards explain the construction and history of the palace. Bonnie Prince Charlie is said to have arranged for the octagonal, Gothic/Renaissance **fountain** in the inner courtyard – with its wonderfully intricate figures and medallion heads – to flow with wine during his stay, and a forlorn Queen Margaret (Tudor) sat patiently in what was once the **cap room**, gazing in vain for the return of her husband from the fields of Flodden in 1513.

**St Michael's Church,** adjacent to the palace, is one of Scotland's largest pre-Reformation churches, consecrated in the thirteenth century. The present building was completed three hundred years later, with the exception of the hugely incongruous aluminium spire, tacked on in 1946. Inside, decorative wood carving around the pulpit depicts queens Margaret, Mary and Victoria.

The only other thing to see in Linlithgow is its section of the **Union Canal**, the 31-mile artery opened in 1822 which linked Edinburgh with Glasgow via Falkirk. On summer weekends the Linlithgow Union Canal Society runs short trips on the *Victoria*, a diesel-powered replica of a Victorian steam packet boat. The boat departs from the Manse Road canal basin, uphill from the train station at the southern end of town (☎0506/842575; 60p). A walk along the canal towpath leads eventually to the centre of Edinburgh, but involves negotiating a path across a section of the Edinburgh ring road.

## Practicalities

Frequent **buses** between Stirling and Edinburgh stop at the Cross, while the **train station** is at the southern end of town. From the train station head downhill for the High Street, where the **tourist office** is in the Burgh Halls building at the Cross (April–July daily 10am–6pm; Aug daily 10am–8pm; Sept daily 10am–6pm; Oct–March Thurs–Mon 11am–4pm; ☎0506/844600).

*The Star and Garter*, 1 High St (☎0506/845485; ③), at the east end of town, is a comfortable old coaching inn that also serves tasty inexpensive **bar meals**. At the opposite end of the High Street the smaller *West Port Hotel*, 18–20 West Port (☎0506/847456; ②), is more basic but has a popular **bar** downstairs which also serves good food. The Victorian *Pardovan House* is an excellent **B&B** (May–Sept; ☎0506/834219; ①) at Philipstoun, a couple of miles west of Linlithgow, or you could try the friendly *Belsyde Farm*, Lanark Rd (☎0506/842098; ①), a late eighteenth-century house on a sheep and cattle farm beside the Union Canal.

For **camping**, the only official site in the area is at the fully serviced **Beecraigs Caravan Park** (April–Sept; ☎0506/844516) about four miles south of town, and part of the larger Beecraigs Country Park. There are only 36 pitches, however, so get there early or telephone first.

# Around Linlithgow

The small hillside town of **BO'NESS**, roughly four miles north of Linlithgow – which has traditionally looked down its nose at its pint-sized neighbour – sprawls in a less than genteel fashion down to the Forth, where a riverside path is separated from the road by a strip of scrub. On a clear day there are good views across the Forth to Culross (see p.209). The **Bo'ness and Kinneil train**, which has its headquarters at the old station at the eastern end of the waterfront road, is Scotland's largest vintage train centre, and on summer weekends (July & Aug daily; April–Oct Sat & Sun; ☎0506/822298) runs lovingly kept steam trains to Birkhill, just over three miles away. A small **tourist office** operates at Hamilton's Cottage (May–September daily 9am–5pm; ☎0506/826626), but if you can't find it – even some of the locals don't know it's there – then ask at the post office on the waterfront road. If you want to **stay the night**, try the *Richmond Park Hotel*, 26 Linlithgow Rd, Bo'ness (☎0506/823213; ④) which offers comfortable rooms in a recently extended Victorian house, set in its own grounds and with good views across the Forth to the Fife hills. The moderately priced **restaurant** serves a good choice of dishes, including some vegetarian, and the airy conservatory is a popular place to drink.

Further down the coast from Bo'ness and four miles northeast of Linlithgow, boldly positioned on a rocky promontory in the Forth, lies the village of **BLACKNESS**, once Linlithgow's seaport but now known for the fifteenth-century **Blackness Castle** (April–Sept Mon–Sat 9.30am–6.30pm, Sun 2–6pm; Oct–March Mon–Sat 9.30am–4.30pm, Sun 2–4.30pm, closed Thurs pm & Fri in winter; £1.20), which, after the Treaty of Union in 1707, was one of only four in Scotland to be garrisoned. Said to be built in the shape of a galleon, the castle offers grand views of the Forth bridges from the narrow gun slits in its northern tower.

General Tam Dalyell, the seventeenth-century Scottish royalist, spent part of his youth at the **House of the Binns** (Easter weekend & May–Sept daily except Fri 2–5pm; NTS; £2.80), occupying a hilltop site about two miles east of Linlithgow. Inside you can see ornate plaster ceilings and family relics not much changed since Tam's day, though a touch of rot was discovered in 1993, and restoration work is underway, so opening hours may be erratic.

# The Ochils and Loch Leven

The rugged **Ochil Hills** stretch for roughly forty miles southeast of Stirling, along the northern side of the Firth of Forth, forming a steep-faced range which drops down to the floodplain of the Forth Valley and is sliced by a series of deep-cut, richly wooded glens. Although they provide a dramatic backdrop for the region's towns, villages and castles, this is gentler country than, say, the Trossachs, with the hills gradually giving way to the pastoral landscape of Fife.

The area has been at the centre of Scotland's wool production for centuries, rivalled only by the Borders. The cottage industry of the district of **Clackmannan**, immediately southeast of Stirling, capitalized on the technological advances of the industrial revolution and by the mid-nineteenth century there were over thirty mills in the space of half as many miles.

Recent times have seen a change in the industry, with the old family firms and hand-knitters unable to compete with modern technology. Nonetheless, you can still see traditional producers working in shops and private houses, especially on the **Mill Heritage Trail** that links the main towns, historic sites and modern mill shops. A glimpse of a different past is offered by various fortified tower houses – the Clackmannan area was a convenient base from which the country's powerful families could keep abreast of developments at the Royal Court at Stirling. None of them are open to the public, but substantial remains can still be seen at the Bruce house at Clackmannan and the Erskine's at **Alloa**.

## The Ochil Hillfoots

Three miles or so northeast of Stirling, the small community of **BLAIRLOGIE** sits amidst orchards and gardens below a private castle. **Logie Old Kirk**, a ruined church and graveyard dating from the late seventeenth century, occupies an attractive site by Logie Burn. Immediately to the rear looms **Dumyat** (pronounced "Dum-eye-at"), which offers spectacular views from its 1376foot summit.

**MENSTRIE**, a mile east, is noted these days for **Menstrie Castle** (open by appointment with the NTS Perth office, ☎0738/31296), a much-restored, sixteenth-century stone-built mansion on Castle Road, which is totally at odds with the ugly housing estate that now hems it in. The castle was the birthplace of Sir William Alexander, later first Earl of Stirling, who in 1621 set off to found a Scots colony in Nova Scotia. There's little to actually see now, but an exhibition room displays the coats-of-arms of the 109 subsequent baronets of Nova Scotia.

As well as a strong tradition of weaving, **ALVA**, five miles further on, was also known for its silver mining – an industry long since gone. From here you can follow **Alva Glen**, a hearty walk dipping down through the hills, which takes in a number of waterfalls. **TILLICOULTRY**, the next town, lies at the heart of the Mill Trail, and its **Clock Mill Centre**, Upper Mill St (April–Oct 10am–5pm; July–Aug until 6pm) traces the development of the weaving industry through an audio-visual presentation and an exhibition of traditional materials. Local craftspeople beaver away upstairs like elves in a grotto. The centre also houses a **tourist office** (same hours; ☎0259/752176).

Nestling in a fold of the Ochils on the northern bank of the small River Devon where mountain waters rush off the hills, **DOLLAR** is the most affluent of the hillfoot towns. Its Academy, founded in 1820 with a substantial bequest from local lad John MacNabb, has become one of Scotland's most respected private schools – the pupils and staff of which account for around a third of the town's population. Above the town, the dramatic chasm of **Dollar Glen** is commanded by **Castle Campbell** (April–Sept Mon–Sat 9.30am–6pm, Sun 2–6pm; Oct–March Mon–Wed 9.30am–4pm, Sun 2–4pm, closed Thurs pm; NTS & HS; £1.50), formerly, and still unofficially, known as Castle Gloom – a fine and evocative tag but, prosaically, a derivation of an old Gaelic name. A one-mile road leads up from the main street, but it is very narrow, very steep, and stops short of the castle, with only limited parking at the top. Most of the structure dates from the late fifteenth century, when it was built by Colin Campbell, first Earl of Argyll, but there are also a number of later additions, including a splendid, vaulted seventeenth-century arch-way. The tower is the oldest part of the castle, and still relatively intact; look out for the trap door to the castle dungeon in front of the fireplace in the Great Hall. John Knox is said to have preached on the hillside outside the castle in 1556.

## The Devon Valley

Beyond Dollar, the A91 leads through the hills to Kinross and the **Devon Valley**, passing through the hamlets of **Pool o' Muckhart** and **Yetts o' Muckhart**, and running along the southern edge of the valley. There is no train line, but a good **bus** service operates between Stirling and Kinross, with less-frequent local services winding their way through the surrounding hills.

The scenic A823 cuts up from Pool o' Muckhart through the glen itself, where there is a **campsite** just beyond the village of **GLENDEVON**. The road continues from here to **Gleneagles**, with its famous eponymous hotel and golf course (see p.35).

In the other direction, south of Pool o' Muckhart, the same road crosses the River Devon at **Rumbling Bridge** – effectively two bridges; the newer one, built in the early nineteenth century, sweeping over the top of the old one, which dates from 1713. The observation point offers breathtaking views of the magnificent, 120-foot-deep **gorge**, and you can follow a shady path along the river, through the lush vegetation flourishing in the damp, limestone walls of the chasm.

## Kinross and Loch Leven

Although still by no means a large place, **KINROSS** has been transformed in the last couple of decades by the construction of the M90 Edinburgh–Perth motorway. The old village is still there, at the southern end of the main street, but apart from the views of Loch Leven, its charm has been eroded by amorphous splodges of modern housing which threaten to nudge it into the loch itself. The best time to visit is on Sunday, when the stalls of a large and lively **covered market** spring up on the southern edge of town, pulling in crowds who come to rifle through anything from kitsch ornaments to leather jackets.

During the summer a **ferry** departs regularly to ply the trout-filled waters of **Loch Leven**. In recent years the loch has become a National Nature Reserve and the location of international fishing competitions, and it also features **Castle Island**, where Mary, Queen of Scots was imprisoned for eleven months in 1567–68. On the island, the ruined fourteenth-century Douglas **Castle** (April–Sept Mon–Sat 9.30am–7pm, Sun 2–7pm; Oct–March Mon–Sat 9.30am–4pm, Sun 2–4pm; HS; £2) stands forlorn, little more than a tower. Nevertheless, it's easy to imagine the isolation of the incarcerated Mary, who is believed to have miscarried twins while here. She managed to charm the eighteen-year-old son of Lady Douglas into helping her escape by stealing the castle keys, securing a boat in which to row ashore, locking the castle gates behind him and throwing the keys into the loch, from where they were retrieved three centuries later.

# The Trossachs

Like Loch Lomond, the **Trossachs** straddle the boundary between Highland and Lowland and boast a magnificent diversity of scenery, with dramatic peaks and mysterious, forest-covered slopes that live up to every image ever produced of Scotland's wild land. This is Rob Roy country, where every waterfall, hidden cave and barely discernible path was at one time frequented by the seventeenth-century Scottish hero who led the Clan Macgregor, appearing out of the misty Highlands to raid cattle and sheep, before disappearing without trace into the hills he made his own. Strictly speaking, the name "The Trossachs" originally referred only to the wooded glen between Loch Katrine and Loch Achray, but today it is usually taken as being the whole area between Callander in the east and Queen Elizabeth Forest Park in the west. Its real meaning, however, remains

---

### ROB ROY

The story of Rob Roy (meaning "Red Robert" in Gaelic) is the stuff of legends. Born into the feisty Clan Gregor in 1671, he swapped his peaceful occupation as a herdsman for a turbulent life striving against those, in particular the powerful Duke of Montrose, who had outlawed the clan for their warring ways. Rallying the Macgregors, he would lead them in raiding parties down out of the glens to plunder the richer farmlands of the Carse of Stirling.

A proud leader, he revelled in clan life and in daring escapades of cattle rustling and protection rackets, and has come to be regarded as a Scottish Robin Hood due to his sympathies with the poor. Although captured three times, on each occasion he escaped back to his people. He died in 1734 and is buried in Balquhidder churchyard with his wife, Mary, and two of his four sons.

anybody's guess, though it is normally translated as either "bristly country" or "crossing place".

The Trossachs' high tourist profile was largely attributable in the early days to Sir Walter Scott, whose *The Lady of the Lake* and *Rob Roy* were set in and around the area. Since then, neither the popularity – nor beauty – of the region have waned, and in high season the place is jam-packed. Autumn is a better time to come, when the hills are blanketed in rich, rusty colours and the crowds are that much thinner.

# Aberfoyle and Lake of Menteith

Like Brigadoon waking once a year from a mist-shrouded slumber, the sleepy little town of **ABERFOYLE** dusts itself down each summer for the annual influx of tourists that make it one of Scotland's key holiday destinations. Its position on the western edge of the Trossachs is ideal, with **Loch Ard Forest** and **Queen Elizabeth Forest Park** stretching across to **Ben Lomond** and **Loch Lomond** to the west, and the forests of the Trossachs crowding around the lower slopes of **Ben Venue** and **Ben Ledi** to the north.

Don't come here for lively nightlife or entertainment, but for a good, healthy blast of the outdoors. The town itself is well equipped to lodge and feed visitors (though booking is recommended), and is an excellent base for walking and pony-trekking, or simply wandering the hills. About four miles west towards Doune, the **Lake of Menteith** is a superb fly-fishing centre and Scotland's only lake (as opposed to loch), so named due to an historic mix-up with the word *laigh*, the Scots for "low-lying ground", which applied to the whole area. The atmospheric **Inchmaholme Priory** still stands on one of three islands on the lake. A ruined Augustinian monastery dating from 1238, the priory has kept part of its roof, as well as its chapter house, and gives a good impression of medieval monastic life. The young Mary, Queen of Scots was sent here for safety in 1547 – not the last island on which she was to be confined – before leaving for France to escape the reach of Henry VIII. A ferry runs from the northeastern corner of the lake to the abbey (weather permitting) between April and September (Mon–Sat 9.30am–5pm, Sun 2–5pm, returning at 7pm).

## Practicalities

Regular **buses** from Stirling to Aberfoyle pull into the car park on Main Street. The **tourist office**, directly next door, has full details of local accommodation, sights and outdoor activities (April–Sept; ☎0877/382352). Next door is the **Scottish Wool Centre**, selling all the usual jumpers and woolly toys – a popular stop-off point with tour buses.

For **accommodation** and **food**, try the *Covenanter's Inn* (☎0877/382347; ③) at the northern end of town (turn left across the bridge and it's up behind the trees on the right), an irresistible warren of a place. The bedrooms are different shapes and sizes and public rooms vary from a small, welcoming library to a spacious bar, wood-panelled restaurant and games room – tartan-carpeted throughout. At the top of town, the *Inverard Hotel*, Loch Ard Rd (☎08772/382229; ②) is a large country house with well-furnished rooms and good views over the River Forth and the hills beyond. A step down in price, both the *Old Coach House Inn* (☎0877/382822; ①) and *The Forth Inn* (☎0877/382372; ②) on Main Street offer basic but adequate rooms. There are also scores of **B&B**s located throughout the town and dotted around the surrounding countryside, among them *Cabrach*, at the end of Main Street (☎0877/382379; ②), a quiet family home with a pleasant garden.

A couple of miles south of Aberfoyle on the edge of Queen Elizabeth Forest Park, *Cobleland Campsite* (☎0877/382392 or 383) is run by the Forestry Commission: it covers five acres of woodland by the River Forth (little more than a stream here) and has one hundred pitches. Further south is the family-run *Trossachs Holiday Park* (☎0877/382614) – twice the size, but with fewer pitches. Both sites are open from April to October, and both offer **bikes** for rent.

# Duke's Pass

Even if you have to walk it, don't miss the trip from Aberfoyle to Callander along the **Duke's Pass** (so called because it once belonged to the Duke of Montrose), which weaves its way through the **Queen Elizabeth Forest Park**. A **bus** runs through the pass from Aberfoyle to Callander.

The A821 twists up out of Aberfoyle, following the contours of the hills and snaking back on itself in tortuous bends. About half-way up is the Queen Elizabeth Forest Park **Visitor Centre** (mid-March to mid-Oct daily 10am–6pm), which details the local fauna and flora. From here various marked paths wind through the forests giving splendid views over the lowlands and surrounding hills. About a mile further on, a track to the right marks the start of the **Achray Forest Drive**, a worthwhile excursion by car or foot which leads through the forest and along the western shore of **Loch Drunkie**, before rejoining the main road. After another couple of miles, a road branches off to the left, leading to the southern end of **Loch Katrine** at the foot of **Ben Venue** (2370ft), from where the historic steamer, the SS *Sir Walter Scott*, has been plying the waters since 1900, chugging up the loch to Stronachlachar and the wild Rob Roy country of Glenogle (mid-April to late Sept Sun–Fri 3 times daily, Sat twice daily; £3).

The final leg of the pass is along the tranquil shores of **Loch Venachar** at the southern foot of Ben Ledi. Look out for the small **Callander Kirk** in a lovely setting at the edge of the loch, where services are still held on the first Sunday of each month at 3pm – presumably because it takes all morning (or month) to get there.

---

### QUEEN ELIZABETH FOREST PARK

Covering 75,000 acres on the edge of the Highlands, **Queen Elizabeth Forest Park** is a spectacular tract of wilderness incorporating **Loch Lomond**, **Loch Ard**, **Loch Achray** and **Loch Lubnaig**, as well as **Ben Venue** and **Ben A'an** and **Ben Ledi**. Managed by the Forestry Commission, it is used partly for leisure and recreation and is criss-crossed by way-marked paths and trails, including part of the **West Highland Way** and, on the southern side, access to **Ben Lomond** (3,192ft/974m). Among its varied wildlife habitats are the forests north of Balmaha, which are home to red and roe deer, as well as wild goats. The park **visitor centre** is just outside **Aberfoyle** in the Trossachs (see above).

**Accommodation** in the park is available at two **campsites** – one on the banks of Loch Lomond at Cashel (Rowardennan), and the other beside the River Forth at Cobleland, south of Aberfoyle. There are also **log cabins** on the shores of Loch Lubnaig in Strathyre (south of Lochearnhead, see p.208). To book cabins call ☎031/334 0303.

Full details about the park are available from the **Forestry Commission**: Aberfoyle, Stirling FK8 3UX (☎08772/383) and the **Countryside Ranger Service**: Central Regional Council, Planning Department, Viewforth, Stirling FK7 2ED (☎0786/473111 ext 390).

# Callander

**CALLANDER**, on the eastern edge of the Trossachs, sits quietly on the banks of the River Teith roughly ten miles north of Doune, at the southern end of the **Pass of Leny**, one of the key routes into the Highlands. Larger than Aberfoyle on the western side of the Trossachs, it is an even more popular summer holiday base and a convenient springboard for exploring the surrounding area. Its wide main street recalls the influence of the military architects who designed the town after Bonnie Prince Charlie's Jacobite Rebellion of 1745.

Callander first came to fame during the so-called "Scottish Enlightenment" of the eighteenth and nineteenth centuries, when the glowing reports given by Sir Walter Scott and William Wordsworth prompted the first tourists to venture into the wilds by horse-drawn carriage. Development was given a boost when Queen Victoria chose to visit, and then by the arrival of the train – long since closed – in the 1860s.

The rural community of today has not been slow to capitalize on its appeal, and there is a plethora of restaurants and tearooms, antique shops and secondhand book stores, and shops selling local woollens and crafts. The chief formal attraction is the **Rob Roy and Trossachs Visitor Centre** at Ancaster Square on the main street (March–May & Oct–Dec daily 10am–5pm; June & Sept daily 9am–6pm; July & Aug daily 9am–7pm; £1.70), which has historical displays about the area and its favourite hero – although if you've been touring for several days already, you're likely to have had your fill of him by now.

## Practicalities

Callander's **tourist office** is in the Rob Roy and Trossachs Visitor Centre (same hours; ☎0877/30342); they'll book accommodation for you if you want to **stay**. Good choices include *Arden Guest House*, Bracklinn Rd (☎0877/30235; ③), a Victorian house in its own gardens with good views of the surrounding countryside, and *Arran Lodge*, Leny Rd, on the western outskirts of town (☎0877/30976; ③), a small, neat house in well laid-out gardens on the banks of the River Teith. For more luxury, try the *Roman Camp Hotel*, signposted off Callander's main street (☎0877/30003; ⑤), a seventeenth-century country house in twenty-acre gardens beside the river. Despite its popularity, there are few good **restaurants** in Callander. The best place is in the *Roman Camp Hotel*, which serves splendid Scottish produce in refined surroundings, or you could try the Canadian-owned *Lade Inn* at **KILMAHOG**, a couple of miles west of town, where you'll find good barbecues and grills, along with a good selection of wines, whiskies and beers.

# On to Lochearnhead

On each side of Callander pleasant and less-than-arduous walks wind through a wooded gorge to the **Falls of Leny** to the north and **Bracklinn Falls** to the south – both distances of only a mile or so. Longer **walks** of varying degrees of exertion thread their way through the surrounding countryside, the most challenging being that to the summit of **Ben Ledi** (2857ft), which should only be undertaken by serious hikers.

North of town, you can also walk the six-mile **Callander to Strathyre Cycleway**, which forms part of the network of cycleways between the Highlands and Glasgow. The route is based on the old Caledonian train line to Oban, which closed in 1965, and runs along the western side of **Loch Lubnaig**. To the north, Rob Roy is buried in the small yard behind the ruined church at tiny **BALQUHIDDER**, where he died in 1734. Oddly enough, considering the Rob Roy fever that plagues the region, his grave – marked by a rough stone marked with a sword, cross and a man with a dog – is remarkably underplayed.

Watersports are the lifeforce of the village of **LOCHEARNHEAD**, which is scattered around the western head of its eponymous loch, a substantial body of water running east into Perthshire and fed by waters off the slopes of **Ben Vorlich** (3201ft) to the south. A more impressive stretch of water is **Loch Tay**, about fifteen miles north of Callander, which points northeastwards like a four-teen-mile finger towards Aberfeldy (see p.232).

# FIFE

The Kingdom of **FIFE**, designated such by the Picts in the fourth century, is a small area (barely fifty miles at its widest points), but one which has a definite identity, inextricably bound with the waters which surround it on three sides – the Tay to the north, the Forth to the south, and the cold North Sea to the east. That the Fifers managed to retain their "Kingdom" when local government was reorganized in 1973, and that they will probably do so again when local boundaries are redrawn in the next year or two, is perhaps testimony to their will.

Despite its size, Fife encompasses several different areas, with a marked difference between the semi-industrial south and the rural north. In the **south**, the recent closure of the coal mines has left local communities floundering to regain a foothold, and the squeeze on the fishing industry up the coast may well lead to further decline; in the meantime many of the villages have capitalized on their unpretentious appeal and welcomed tourism in a way that has enhanced rather than degraded their natural assets.

**Central Fife** is dominated in the south by **Kirkcaldy**, the region's largest town, and in the north by **Cupar**, Fife's capital. Although only twenty miles separate the two, they couldn't be more different: the former is something of an industrial blackspot in an otherwise green area, while the latter is an endearing market town surrounded by the rolling scenery for which the area is known.

Tourism and agriculture are the economic mainstays of the **northeast** corner of Fife, where the landscape varies from the gentle hills in the rural hinterland, to the windswept cliffs, rocky bays and sandy beaches on which scenes from the film *Chariots of Fire* were shot. The fishing industry is still prominent, as seen in a series of ancient villages lining the shore of the East Neuk, while **St Andrews**, Scotland's oldest university town, home to the world-famous Royal and Ancient Golf club is on the northeast coast. Development here has been cautious, and the hills and hamlets of the surrounding area retain a slow, not unappealingly old-fashioned feel.

The main transport route through the region is the M90 from Edinburgh to Perth, which edges Fife's western boundary. The coastal route is more attractive, however, and also affords relatively easy access into the centre of the area. The train line follows the coast as far north as Kirkcaldy and then cuts inland, towards Dundee. Exploration of the eastern and western fringes by public transport – even getting to St Andrews – requires some thought as there is no train service and buses are few and far between.

# The south coast

Although the **south coast** of Fife is predominantly industrial – with everything from cottage industries to the refitting of nuclear submarines – thankfully only a small part has been blighted by insensitive development. Even in the old coal-mining areas, disused pits and left-over slag heaps have either been well camouflaged through landscaping or put to alternative use as recreation areas.

It was from **Dunfermline**, now a major shopping and administrative centre, that Queen Margaret ousted the Celtic Church from Scotland in the eleventh century. Her son, David I, founded an abbey here in the twelfth century, which, as it grew, acquired vast stretches of land from miles around, and today, even though the lands no longer belong to the town, Dunfermline remains the chief town and the focus of the coast.

Fife is linked to Edinburgh by the two **Forth bridges**. You used to be able to take guided walks across the historic rail bridge, whose boldness of concept was all the more remarkable for coming so hard on the heels of the Tay Bridge disaster of 1879 (see p.222); today, however, you'll have to be satisfied with seeing it from a train or a boat (for more on the Forth bridges see *Edinburgh*).

## West of the bridges

The area north of the Forth bridges is historic, but not scenic. Both the shipyards at **Inverkeithing** and the naval dockyard at **Rosyth** blot the landscape like aggravated sores, although both have played a vital part in the area's development, the former dismantling ships, the latter putting them together.

The A985 heads west along the Forth before approaching **CULROSS** (pronounced "Cooros"). One of Scotland's most picturesque settlements, the village began in the fifth century with the arrival of St Serf on the northern side of the Forth at "Holly Point", or Culenros, and is said to be the birthplace of St Kentigern, who travelled west and founded Glasgow. The village today is in excellent condition, thanks to the work of the NTS, who have been restoring its white-washed, red-tiled buildings since 1932.

Make your first stop the **National Trust Visitor Centre** (Easter weekend & May–Sept daily 11am–1pm & 2–5pm), in the Town House in the village centre on the main road, for an excellent introduction to the burgh's detailed history. The focal point of the community is the rusty-coloured **Culross Palace**, built by wealthy coal merchant George Bruce in the late sixteenth century and not a palace at all – its name comes from the Latin *palatium*, or "hall", and it is, in fact, just an overgrown house, with lots of small rooms and connecting passageways. Inside, the main features are the painted ceilings and pine panelling; outside, its dormer windows and crow-stepped gables dominate the walled court in which it stands.

A cobbled alleyway known as **Back Causeway**, complete with raised central aisle formerly used by noblemen to separate them from the commoners, leads up behind the Town House to the **Study** (May–Sept Sat & Sun 2–4pm; £2), a restored house which takes its name from the small room at the top of the corbelled projecting tower, which is reached by a turnpike stair. Built in 1610, its oak panelling in Dutch Renaissance style dates from around twenty years later. Further up the hill lie the remains of **Culross Abbey**, a thirteenth-century ruin originally founded by Cistercian monks on land given to the Church – in return for a greater chance of salvation – by the Earl of Fife in 1217. Sadly, little remains to be seen of either the abbey, or of the monk's way of life, which revolved around the export of wool from their famous flocks of sheep and the extraction of coal from huge surface mines.

Beyond Culross, the B9037 continues to **Kincardine**, where the **Kincardine Bridge** provides a second crossing point over the Forth before the Old Bridge at Stirling.

# Dunfermline

Scotland's capital until the Union of the Crowns in 1603, **DUNFERMLINE** lies seven miles east of Culross. This "auld, grey toun" is built on a hill, dominated by the abbey and ruined palace at the top. Up until the late nineteenth century, Dunfermline was one of Scotland's foremost linen producers, as well as a major coal-mining centre, and today the town is a busy place, its ever-increasing sprawl attesting to its booming economy.

Dunfermline began in the eleventh century, when **Malcolm III** (Canmore) offered a refuge to Edgar Atheling and his family, heir to the English throne, who were fleeing the Norman Conquest. Malcolm married Edgar's sister, the Catholic Margaret, in 1070, and in so doing started a process of reformation which ultimately supplanted the Celtic Church. So horrified was Margaret by Scots ways that in 1072 she began building a Benedictine priory, the remains of which can still be seen beneath the nave of the present church. Her son, **David I**, founded the abbey the following century, but the entire complex was left a ruin by Edward I in 1304. **Robert the Bruce** helped rebuild the abbey, and was buried here 25 years later, although his body went undiscovered until building began on a new parish church in 1821. His heart lies in Melrose Abbey in Southern Scotland (see p.110).

## The Town

Dunfermline's **centre**, at the top of the hill around the abbey, holds an appeal of its own, with its narrow, cobbled streets, pedestrianized shopping areas and gargoyle-adorned buildings. One of the best of these, the **city chambers** building on the corner of Bridge Street and Bruce Street, is a fine example of the Gothic Revival style fashionable in the late nineteenth century. Among the ornate porticoes and grotesques of dragons and winged serpents which adorn the exterior are the sculpted heads of Robert the Bruce, Malcolm Canmore, Queen Margaret and Queen Elizabeth I.

All that is left of **Dunfermline Abbey** (April–Sept Mon–Sat 9.30am–6.30pm, Sun 2–6.30pm; Oct–March Mon–Wed & Sat 9.30am–4.30pm, Thurs & Sun 2–4.30pm) is the twelfth-century nave of the medieval monastic church and the nineteenth-century parish church. A plaque beneath the pulpit marks the spot where Robert the Bruce's remains were laid to rest for the second time, while Malcolm and his queen, Margaret, who died of grief three days after her husband in 1093, have a shrine outside. The enormous stonework graffiti, "King Robert the Bruce", at the top of the tower is attributable to an over-excited architect thrilled by the discovery of Bruce's remains.

The guest house from Margaret's Benedictine monastery, south of the abbey, became the **Palace** (same hours) in the sixteenth century under James VI, who gave both it and the abbey to his consort, Queen Anne of Denmark. Charles I, the last monarch to be born in Scotland, came into the world here in 1600. All that is left of it today is a long, sandstone facade, especially impressive when silhouetted against the evening sky. The four redundant walls next to the palace are those of the refectory, connected via the gatehouse to the kitchen, which was tacked on at the palace's eastern end.

**Pittencrieff Park**, known to locals as "the Glen", covers a huge area in the centre of town. Bordering the ruined palace, the 76-acre park used to be owned by the Lairds of Pittencrieff, whose 1610 estate house still stands within the grounds. In 1902, however, the entire plot was purchased by a local boy, the rags-to-riches American industrialist Andrew Carnegie, who donated it to his home town. This was just as much sweet revenge as beneficent public spiritedness: the young Carnegie had been banned from the estate according to a former laird's edict that no Morrison would pass through the gates. Since his mother had been a Morrison, Carnegie could do little but gaze through the bars on the one day a year that the estate was open to the rest of the public. Today **Pittencrieff House** (May–Oct daily except Tues; free) displays exhibits on local history, the glasshouses are filled with exotic blooms, and the Pavilion coffee shop offers refreshment. In the centre of the park are the remains – little more than the foundations – of **Malcolm Canmore's Tower**, where the king stayed before he married Margaret. Dunfermline – meaning "fort by the crooked pool" – takes its name from the tower's location: "Dun" meaning hill or fort, "Fearum" bent or crooked, and "Lin" (or "Lyne/Line") a pool or running water.

Just beyond the southeast corner of the park, the modest little cottage at the bottom of St Margaret Street is **Andrew Carnegie's Birthplace** (April–Oct Mon–Sat 11am–5pm, Sun 2–5pm; Nov–March daily 2–4pm; free). The son of a weaver, the young Carnegie (1835–1919) lived upstairs with his family, while the room below housed his father's loom shop. Following the family's emigration to America in 1848, he worked on the railroads before becoming involved with the iron and then the steel industries. One success followed another and by the time he sold his companies in 1901, he was a steel baron worth millions. His house today, an ordinary two-up two-down, has been preserved as it was at the end of the last century, and the adjacent Memorial Hall details his life and work.

### Practicalities

Dunfermline's **train station** is southeast of the centre, halfway down the long hill of St Margaret's Drive. It's about fifteen minutes up the hill from here to the **tourist office**, in Abbot House, Maygate (May–Sept; ☎0383/720999). From the **bus station**, cut through the upstairs floor of the shopping centre and then turn right along the High Street – about a five-minute walk. If you do want to **stay overnight** in Dunfermline, options include the comfortable *Davaar House Hotel*, 126 Grieve St (☎0383/721886; ②), in a tastefully furnished Victorian town house. As **eating** goes, there's really little choice, though the *Auld Toll Tavern*, 119–121 St Leonards St (☎0383/721489), is well known for its good, inexpensive pub grub.

# East of the bridges

Fife's south coast curves sharply northwards at the mouth of the River Forth, exposing the towns and villages to an icy east wind that somewhat undermines the sunshine image of their beaches. If you're driving, it's tempting once you've crossed the river to beat a path directly north up the M90 motorway. If you've got the time, though, or fancy an alternative route to St Andrews, cut off to the west along the A921, following the train line as it clings to the northern shore of the mouth of the Forth. Here you'll find a straggle of Fife fishing communities which have depended on the crop of the sea for centuries, and now make popular holiday spots.

## North Queensferry

Cowering beneath the bridges is **NORTH QUEENSFERRY**, a small fishing village, which, until the opening of the road bridge, was the northern landing point of the ferry across the Forth, and a nineteenth-century bathing resort. Built on a rocky outcrop, the place is comparatively well preserved for somewhere which takes such a battering from the elements, and there are good views across the Forth and of the bridges, particularly the rail bridge, the massive spans of which loom frighteningly large from such close range. Also here is the new **Deep-Sea World** (daily 9.30am–5pm; £3.50), a huge aquarium that boasts the world's largest underwater viewing tunnel, through which you glide on a moving walkway while sharks, conger eels and all manner of creatures from the deep swim nonchalantly past.

## Inverkeithing

The North Queensferry peninsula gives way to Inverkeithing Bay and **INVERKEITHING**, a medieval watering place established by David I in the twelfth century and granted a charter by William I around 1165, thanks to its strategic location and safe harbour. Modern Inverkeithing is unprepossessing, with lumpen housing estates sprawling around the old town centre, where the broad main street shows the town's more attractive side. The **Parish Church of St Peter** on Church Street began as a wooden Celtic church before Queen Margaret set to work, and ended up as a Norman stone structure bequeathed to Dunfermline Abbey in 1139. The oldest part of it today is the fifteenth-century tower, the rest having been razed by fire in 1825.

## Aberdour

Beyond Inverkeithing, **ABERDOUR** clings tight to the walls of its **Castle** (April–Sept Mon–Wed & Sat 9.30am–6.30pm, Sun 2–6.30pm; Oct–March closes 4.30pm; 60p) at the southern end of the main street. The oldest part of the castle is the fourteenth-century tower, the other buildings having been added in the sixteenth and seventeenth centuries, including the well-preserved dovecote. **St Fillan's Church**, also in the castle grounds, dates from the twelfth century, with a few fifteenth-century additions, such as the porch, and has managed to preserve its medieval atmosphere, despite restoration from total dereliction earlier this century. Beyond the castle there's little to see apart from the town's popular **silver sands** beach, which, along with its watersports, golf and sailing, has earned Aberdour the rather optimistic tourist board soubriquet the "Fife Riviera".

If you want to **stay** you could do worse than the friendly *Aberdour Hotel* on the High Street (☎0383/860325; ②), which also has an inexpensive **restaurant** downstairs. Alternatively, head for *Hawkcraig House*, Hawkcraig Point (☎0383/860335; ①), a good B&B in an old ferryman's house overlooking the harbour.

## Burntisland

From Aberdour it's three miles to the large holiday resort of **BURNTISLAND**. The busy High Street runs the length of the waterfront, hemmed in by buildings at the western end, where you'll find the unkempt **train station**. Offices now occupy **Rossend Castle**, beyond the west end of the High Street, which was first built in the early twelfth century. Today's structure dates from around 1554 and, despite its long history – including a visit from Mary, Queen of Scots and the subsequent discovery of Pierre de Chastelard, an eager French poet, in her bedchamber – it is not open to the public. Incidentally, Chastelard, having been warned once already about hiding in the young queen's private rooms at Holyrood Palace, was whisked to St Andrews where, proclaiming "Adieu, thou most beautiful and most cruel Princess in the world", he was promptly executed.

Burntisland's **tourist office** is at 4 Kirkgate (April–Sept Mon–Thurs 9am–5pm, Fri–Sat 9am–4.30pm; Oct–March Mon–Thurs 9am–5pm, Fri 9am–4.30pm; ☎0592/872667). Although almost every house along the Links, just beyond the High Street, sports a **B&B** sign, the choice of **hotels** is limited to four. The *Inchview Hotel*, 69 Kinghorn Rd (☎0592/872239; ③) in a listed Georgian building looking out across the sea, and *Kingswood Hotel*, Kinghorn Rd (☎0592/872329; ③) are the most comfortable. The latter, in a leafy road just north of town, will also organize fishing and shooting trips for guests, and offers tasty bar meals, high teas and dinners. Other **eating** options include the *Charene Hotel*, 241 High St, for cheap lunches, afternoon teas, traditional Scottish high teas and dinners, with a limited vegetarian selection. *The Smugglers Inn*, 14 Harbour Place, does light snacks and bar meals.

## Kinghorn

Shortly before reaching **KINGHORN**, the coastal road from Burntisland passes a **Celtic Cross** commemorating Alexander III, the last of the Celtic kings, who plunged over the cliff near here one night in 1286, after his horse stumbled. There has been a settlement at Kinghorn since ancient times, and today it is a popular holiday centre, not too crowded, with few formal attractions but a good beach. The ugly brown pebble-dashed **parish church**, looking over the beach and whipped by wintry winds at the land's edge, dates from 1894, though the site had been used as a church for centuries before that and the small graveyard – a popular place with local genealogists – is filled with lichen-covered, semi-legible tombstones from the eighteenth century. At the opposite (southern) end of town, a hill lined with Spanish-style villas leads down to the waterfront and the beach at **Pettycur Bay**, where fishing boats cluster round the small harbour and brightly coloured lobster nets dot the sands.

Regular trains from Edinburgh and Dundee arrive at Kinghorn's **train station**, just off the High Street. The best place to stay is *The Longboat Inn*, 107 Pettycur Rd (☎0592/890625; ②), overlooking the River Forth, just above the beach at Pettycur Bay. Ask for a room with a balcony, from where you'll get good views across to Edinburgh and the Lothians. Decent **bar meals** are available in the wine bar and full meals in the moderately priced **restaurant**.

# Kirkcaldy and around

Scattered across the hills as they roll down to the edge of the North Sea, **KIRKCALDY** (pronounced "Kirkcawdy") is familiarly known as "The Lang Toun" for its four-mile-long esplanade which stretches the length of the waterfront. The esplanade was built in 1922–23 – not just to hold back the sea, but also to alleviate unemployment – and runs parallel for part of the way with the shorter

High Street. If you're here in April, you'll see the historic **Links Market**, a funfair that dates back to 1305, before the settlement was passed over to the monks of Dunfermline Abbey.

Incidentally, though there's little to show for it today, architect brothers Robert and James Adam were born in Kirkcaldy, as was the eighteenth-century scholar, philosopher and political economist Adam Smith, whose *Inquiry into the Nature and Causes of the Wealth of Nations* (1776) remains in print.

# The Town

Kirkcaldy doesn't hold a great deal of interest for the visitor, but a stroll along the promenade is pleasant on a sunny day, and there's a larger range of shops in the town centre than you'll find anywhere else between Edinburgh and Dundee. The town's history is chronicled in its **Museum and Art Gallery** (Mon–Sat 11am–5pm, Sun 2–5pm; free) in the colourful War Memorial Gardens between the train and bus stations. The museum covers everything from archeological discoveries to the tradition of the local Wemyss Ware pottery and the evolution of the present town. Established in 1925, in the past 70 years the gallery has built up its collection to around 300 works by some of Scotland's finest painters from the late eighteenth century onwards, including works by Sir David Wilkie, Samuel Peploe and Sir Henry Raeburn. For a town which is known primarily for linoleum production and whose reputation is firmly rooted in the prosaic, the art gallery is an unexpected boon.

Just beyond the northern end of the waterfront, Ravenscraig Park is the site of the substantial ruin of **Ravenscraig Castle**, a thick-walled, fifteenth-century defence post, which occupies a lovely spot above a beach. The castle looks out over the Forth, and is flanked on either side by a flight of steps – the inspiration, apparently, for the title of John Buchan's novel, *The 39 Steps*. Sir Walter Scott also found this a place worthy of comment, using it as a setting for the story of "lovely Rosabella" in *The Lay of the Last Minstrel*.

Beyond Kirkcaldy lies the old suburb of **DYSART**, where tall ships once arrived bringing cargo from the Netherlands, setting off again with coal, beer, salt and fish. Well restored, and retaining historic street names such as Hot Pot Wynd (after the hot pans used for salt evaporation), it's an atmospheric place of narrow alleyways and picturesque old buildings. In Rectory Lane, the birthplace of John McDouall Stuart (who in 1861–62 became the first man to cross Australia from the south to the north) now holds the **McDouall Stuart Museum** (June–Aug Mon–Sat 2–5pm; NTS; free), giving an account of his emigration to Australia in 1838 and his subsequent adventures.

### Practicalities

Kirkcaldy's **train** and **bus stations** are in the upper part of town – keep heading downhill to get to the centre. For the **tourist office**, 19 Whytecauseway (April–Sept daily 10am–6pm; Oct–March Mon–Thurs 9am–5pm, Fri 9am–4.30pm; ☎0592/267775), follow the road for about ten minutes around to the right from the bus station. If you have to stay in Kirkcaldy, the office's accommodation booking service is a life-saver; there are few places to stay, and the layout of the town away from the centre is not easy to follow because of the way it falls across the hillside. In Kirkcaldy itself the *Parkway Hotel*, Abbotshall Rd (☎0592/262143; ④), offers smart rooms and traditional breakfasts, while the smaller, more refined *Dunnikier House Hotel*, Dunnikier Park, Dunnikier Way (☎0592/268393; ⑥), serves fine local food and is set in pleasant grounds. The *Strathearn Hotel*, 2 Wishart Place, on Dysart Rd (☎0592/52210; ⑤), is a welcoming place set in its own gardens, a couple of miles north of the centre of town. You can get cheaper rooms along the road in Dysart, at the *Royal Hotel*, Townhead (☎0592/54112; ①), which occupies one of the village's historic buildings.

For **snacks**, the *Gifthouse and Coffeeshop*, 23–25 Tolbooth St, serves good old-fashioned home baking, and *Olivers*, 151 High St, does sandwiches, baked potatoes, pizzas and salad. You can get reasonable pasta and pizza from *Mamma Mia's*, on Nicol St, while the *Strathearn Hotel*, is not a bad choice for moderately priced grills and steaks.

## Around Kirkcaldy

Inland from Kirkcaldy, the old **mining towns** of Cowdenbeath, Kelty, Lochgelly and Cardenden huddle together, their fires virtually extinguished by a blanket of economic depression. These are neglected places, and indeed are rarely even seen by visitors shooting up to St Andrews on the coastal route or zooming along the M90 from Edinburgh to Perth. Take the train, however, and you'll weave through this forlorn stretch as the line leaves the coast and heads inland to Perth.

Ten miles inland from Kirkcaldy, **GLENROTHES** is a new town in much the same mould as any other. Stark, concrete and utilitarian, it is the European head-quarters of the Californian company *Hughes Micoelectronics*, who, along with similar operations, have given the town much-needed wealth and self-confidence. Only a short time ago, a sign at Markinch train station to the west (Glenrothes' nearest station) boldly announced "Welcome to Glenrothes, the Capital of Fife". So outraged at this audacity were the residents of Cupar, Fife's real capital for centuries, that the sign had to be removed.

# The Howe of Fife

Completely different from the industrial landscape of Kirkcaldy and Glenrothes, the **Howe of Fife**, lying north of Glenrothes, is a low-lying stretch of ground ("howe") lying at the foot of the twin peaks of the heather-swathed **Lomond Hills** – West Lomond (1696ft) and East Lomond (1378ft). Frequent buses run throughout the area, with regular services threading their way towards Dundee from Kirkcaldy. The train also comes this way, stopping at Cupar and Leuchars before crossing the Tay Bridge to Dundee.

## Falkland

Nestling in the lower slopes of East Lomond, the narrow streets of **FALKLAND** are lined with well-preserved sixteenth-century buildings. The village grew up around **Falkand Palace** (April–Sept Mon–Sat 10am–6pm, Sun 2–6pm; Oct closes 5pm; NTS; £3, gardens only £2), a fourteenth-century stronghold which originally belonged to the Macduffs, the Earls of Fife, but which passed in the fifteenth century to the Stuarts, who made it their hunting lodge. Charles II stayed here in

1650, when he was in Scotland for his coronation, but after the Jacobite rising of 1715 the palace was left to ruin, remaining so until the late nineteenth century when the keepership was acquired by the third Marquess of Bute. He restored the palace entirely, and today it is a stunning example of early Renaissance architecture, complete with corbelled parapet, mullioned windows, round towers and massive walls. A forty-minute tour takes in a cross section of public and private rooms in the south and east wings. The former is better preserved and includes the stately drawing room, the Chapel Royal (still used for Mass) and the Tapestry Gallery, swathed with splendid seventeenth-century Flemish hangings. Outside, the gardens are also worth a look, their well-stocked herbaceous borders lining a pristine lawn, and with the oldest tennis court in Britain – built in 1539 for James V.

When not playing tennis, the royal guests at Falkland would hunt deer and wild boar in the forests which then covered the Howe of Fife, stretching towards Cupar, ten miles northeast. There are still deer here today, at the **Scottish Deer Centre** (April–Oct daily 10am–5pm; July & Aug closes 6pm; £3.25), three miles west of Cupar on the A91, which specializes in the rearing of red deer, and is also home to species of sika, fallow and reindeer. It's a good place for children, who can pet the tamer animals, and there are play and picnic areas and guided nature trails.

If you want to **stay the night** in Falkland, there's a **youth hostel**, Back Wynd (March–Oct; Nov–Feb Sat only; ☎0337/57710; Grade 3), and the *Hunting Lodge Hotel*, High St (☎0337/57226; ②).

# Cupar

Straddling the small River Eden and surrounded by gentle hills, **CUPAR**, the capital of Fife, has retained much of its medieval character – and its self-confident air – from the days when it was a bustling market centre, and a livestock auction is still held here every week. In 1276 Alexander III held an assembly here, bringing together the Church, aristocracy and local burgesses in an early form of Scottish parliament. For his troubles he subsequently became the butt of Sir David Lindsay's biting play, *Ane Pleasant Satyre of the Thrie Estaitis* (1535), one of the first great Scottish dramas.

Situated at the centre of Fife's road network, Cupar's main street, part of the main road from Edinburgh to St Andrews, is plagued with thundering traffic. The **Mercat Cross**, stranded in the midst of the lorries and cars which speed through the centre, now consists of salvaged sections of the seventeenth-century original, following its destruction by an errant lorry a couple of years ago.

One of the best reasons for stopping off at Cupar is to visit the **Hill of Tarvit** (April Sat & Sun 2–6pm; May–Oct daily 2–6pm; NTS; £2.80; gardens open all year daily 10am–sunset; £1), an Edwardian mansion two miles south of town. The estate was formerly the home of Sir John Scott, who built the five-storey **Scotstarvit Tower**, three quarters of a mile west of the present house, in the seventeenth century (keys available from house during season only). This L-shaped tower house now stands opposite the mansion, which was designed by Sir Robert Lorimer earlier this century. The entire estate was bequeathed to the NTS in 1949, and the house contains an enviable collection of eighteenth-century Chippendale and French furniture, Dutch paintings, Chinese porcelain, and a restored Edwardian laundry.

## Practicalities

Cupar's **tourist office** (June & Sept Mon–Sat 9.30am–5.30pm, Sun 2–5pm; July–Aug Mon–Sat 9.30am–5.30pm, Sun 11am–5pm; ☎0334/52874) operates during the summer from a cabin in the oddly named Fluthers car park at the eastern end of town. If you want to stay, try the friendly *Eden House Hotel*, 2 Pitscottie Rd (☎0334/52510; ④), which also serves excellent inexpensive Scottish food. The best hotels, however, are out of the centre: *Balbirnie House Hotel*, Balbirnie Park (☎0592/610066, ⑨), is a magnificent old mansion five miles southwest of Cupar, complete with 416 acres of parkland and prices to match. Roughly five miles north of Cupar in **LETHAM**, the *Fernie Castle Hotel* (☎0337/81381; ⑤) occupies a real castle and offers bar meals as well as a more expensive à la carte menu.

## Ceres

Unusually for Scotland, **CERES**, two miles east of the Hill of Tarvit, is set around a village green. Occupying several well-preserved seventeenth-century buildings is the **Fife Folk Museum** (April–Oct Sun–Thurs 2.15–5pm; £1.30), which exhibits all manner of historical farming and agricultural paraphernalia. The pillory that used to restrain miscreants on market days still stands at the entrance of the old burgh tollbooth.

# St Andrews

Confident, poised and well groomed, **ST ANDREWS**, Scotland's oldest university town and something of a pigrimage centre for golfers from all over the world, stares out to sea like a ponderous sage from above its wide bay on the northeastern coast of Fife. It's often referred to in tourist literature as "the Oxford or Cambridge of the North", and indeed, like Cambridge, by and large St Andrews *is* its university.

The town was founded, pretty much by accident, in the fourth century. Saint Rule – or Regulus – a custodian of the bones of Saint Andrew on the Greek island of Patras, had a vision in which an angel ordered him to carry five of the saint's bones to the western edge of the world, where he was to build a city in his honour. The conscientious courier duly set off, but was shipwrecked on the rocks close to the present harbour. Struggling ashore with his precious burden, he built a shrine to the saint on what subsequently became the site of the cathedral. In time, Saint Andrew became Scotland's patron saint and the town its ecclesiastical capital.

Local residents are proud of their town, considering themselves a cut above their rural kinfolk in northeast Fife. Indeed, St Andrews would not be the place it is without such pride, for it's thanks to a strong and well-informed local conservation lobby that so many of the original buildings have survived. Almost the entire centre consists of listed buildings, and the ruined castle and cathedral have all but been rebuilt in the efforts to preserve their remains. If you're here in August, make sure to get to the **Lammas Fair**, Scotland's oldest surviving medieval market, complete with town crier. The other main event in the St Andrews calendar is the **Kate Kennedy Pageant**, usually held in April, which involves an all-male procession of students taking to the streets dressed as characters associated with the university, from Kate Kennedy herself, niece of one of the university founders, to Mary, Queen of Scots.

# Arrival and information

St Andrews is not on the train line. The nearest **train station** is on the Edinburgh–Dundee–Aberdeen line at **Leuchars**, five miles northwest across the River Eden, from where regular (but not always connecting) buses make the fifteen-minute trip into town. The price of the rail ticket to Leuchars does not include the bus trip to St Andrews. Frequent **buses** from Edinburgh and Dundee terminate at the bus station on City Road at the west end of Market Street. The **tourist office**, 78 South St (Mon–Fri 9.30am–1pm & 2–5pm, Sat 2–5pm; ☎0334/72021), holds comprehensive information about St Andrews and northeast Fife.

If you're **driving**, the town's fiendish **parking** system requires vouchers which you can get from the tourist office and some local shops. Scratch out the month, day, date and hour from the card, display it in your car, and cross your fingers that you've worked it out correctly.

# Accommodation

Although **rooms** in St Andrews cost more than in the surrounding area, they often get booked up in the summer, when reserving ahead is strongly recommended. Most of the **guest houses** are around Murray Place and Murray Park between The Scores and North Street. On North Street, try *Aslar House* at no. 120 (☎0334/73460; ②) or *Cadzow Guest House* at no. 58 (☎0334/76933; ②). Between June and September, the **university** (☎0334/72281 or 77641; ① and ②) offers about two hundred rooms in various locations, all on a B&B basis with dinner optional. More upmarket are the various **hotels** lining The Scores, beyond the eastern end of the Old (golf) Course, overlooking the bay. The *St Andrews Golf Hotel*, at no. 40 (☎0334/72611; ⑤) occupies a three-storey town house, with chintzy, comfortable bedrooms – those at the front have great views – and the dining room serves delicious local produce with an extensive international wine list.

As you come into town from Leuchars, you'll see the entrance to the swanky *Rusacks Hotel*, 16 Pilmour Links (☎0334/74321; ⑥) on the left. From the airy lobby to its spacious rooms, this is an elegant place whose old-fashioned style is in keeping with the town's air of respectability. A little further up the road is the *Tudor Inn*, 129 North St (☎0334/74906; ③) – its uncharacteristic black-and-white Tudor facade more English than Scottish. Although less luxurious than the above hotels, this is good value as long as you're not sleeping above the noisy downstairs bar.

# The Town

St Andrews is best absorbed by wandering the streets. The centre still follows the medieval layout, with its three main streets, North Street, South Street and Market Street, running west to east towards the ruined Gothic cathedral and dotted with some of the original university buildings from the fifteenth century. Narrow alleys connect the cobbled streets, attic windows and gable ends shape the rooftops, and here and there you'll see old wooden doors with heavy knockers and black iron hinges.

Once the largest in Scotland, today the ruined **St Andrew's Cathedral** (April–Sept Mon–Sat 9.30am–6pm, Sun 2–6pm; £1.20; grounds only Sun am), at the east

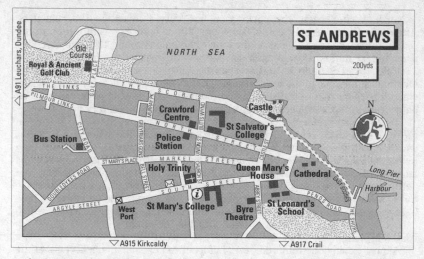

end of town, gives only an idea of its former importance. The cathedral was founded in 1160, but not consecrated until 1318, in the presence of Robert the Bruce. It survived in good condition until June 5, 1559, when the Reformation took its toll and supporters of John Knox, fresh from a rousing meeting, plundered it and left it to ruin.

Standing above the harbour where the land drops to the sea, the cathedral site can be a blustery place, with the wind whistling through the great east window and down the stretch of turf that was once the central aisle. In front of the window a slab is all that remains of the high altar, where the relics of St Andrew were once enshrined. Previously, it is believed that they were kept in **St Rule's Tower** (same hours and ticket as cathedral), the austere Romanesque monolith next to the cathedral, which was built as part of an abbey in 1130. From the top of the tower (a climb of 157 steps), there's a good view of the town and surroundings, and of the remains of the monastic buildings which made up the priory. Surrounding the entire complex is a sturdy wall dating from the sixteenth century, over half a mile long and with three gateways.

Southwest of the cathedral enclosure lies **the Pends**, a huge fourteenth-century vaulted gatehouse which marked the main entrance to the priory, and from where the road leads down to the harbour, passing prim **St Leonard's**, one of Scotland's leading private schools for girls. The sixteenth-century, rubble-stonework building on the right as you go through the Pends is **Queen Mary's House**, where she is believed to have stayed in 1563. The house was restored in 1927 and is now used as the school library.

Down at the **harbour**, gulls screech above the fishing boats, keeping an eye on the lobster nets strewn along the quay. If you come here on a Sunday morning, you'll see students parading down the long pier, red gowns billowing in the wind, in a time-honoured after-church walk. The beach, **East Sands**, is a popular stretch, although it's cool in summer, and positively biting in winter. A path leads south from the far end of the beach, climbing up the hill past the caravan site and cutting through the gorse; this makes a pleasant walk on a sunny day, taking in hidden coves and caves.

North of the beach, the rocky coastline curves inland to the ruined **St Andrew's Castle** (April–Sept 9.30am–6pm, Sun 2–6pm; £1), with a drop to the sea on three sides and a moat on the fourth. Founded around 1200 and extended over the centuries, it was built as part of the palace of the Bishops and Archbishops of St Andrews and was consequently the scene of some fairly grim incidents at the time of the Reformation. There's not a great deal left of the castle, since it fell into ruin in the seventeenth century, and most of what can be seen dates from the sixteenth century, apart from the fourteenth-century Fore Tower.

The Protestant reformer George Wishart was burned at the stake in front of the castle in 1545, as an incumbent Cardinal Beaton, the notorious Catholic, watched with glee. Wishart had been a friend of John Knox's, and it wasn't long before fellow reformers sought vengeance for his death. Less than three months later, Cardinal Beaton was stabbed to death and his body displayed from the battlements before being dropped into the "bottle dungeon", a 24foot pit hewn out of solid rock which can still be seen in the Sea Tower. The perpetrators then held the castle for over a year, and during that time dug the secret passage which can be entered from the ditch in front. Outside the castle, the initials "GW" are carved in stone.

Almost exactly one hundred years before these events, it is believed that the young James I spent time here with his tutor, Bishop James Kennedy, founder of **St Andrew's University**, established in 1410 as a school attached to the Augustinian priory of the cathedral. The first building was on the site of the Old University Library and by the end of the Middle Ages three colleges had been built: St Salvator's (1450), St Leonard's (1512) and St Mary's (1537). At the time of the Reformation, St Mary's became a seminary of Protestant theology, and today it houses the university's Faculty of Divinity. The **quad** here has beautiful gardens and some magnificent old trees, perfect for flopping under on a warm day.

St Andrews' status as a world-renowned **golf** centre is particulary obvious as you enter the town from the west, where the approach road runs adjacent to the famous **Old Course**. At the eastern end of the course lies the strictly private **clubhouse**, a stolid, square building dating from 1854. The first British Open Championship was held here in 1873, having been inaugurated in 1860 at Prestwick in Ayrshire, and since then, the British Open is held here regularly, pulling in enormous crowds. The eighteenth hole of the Old Course is immediately in front of the clubhouse, and has been officially christened the "Tom Morris", after one of the world's most famous golfers. Pictures of Nick Faldo, Jack Nicklaus and other golfing greats, along with clubs and a variety of memorabilia which they donated, are displayed in the admirable **British Golf Museum** on Bruce Embankment, along the waterfront below the clubhouse (Jan–Feb Thurs–Mon 11am–3pm; March–April Thurs–Tues 10am–5pm; May–Oct daily 10am–5.30pm; Nov Thurs–Tues 10am–4pm; Dec Thurs–Mon 11am–3pm; £3). There are also plenty of hands-on exhibits, including computers, video screens and footage of British Open championships, tracing the development of golf through the centuries.

If you've got kids in tow you may want to visit the huge **Sea Life Centre** on The Scores, at the west end of town close to the golf museum (daily 10am–6pm; July & Aug closes 9pm; £3.90), which examines marine life of all shapes and sizes with displays, live exhibits, observation pools and underwater walkways. Also good for kids is the fifty-acre **Craigtoun Country Park** (April–Oct daily

---

**GOLF**

St Andrew's **Royal and Ancient Golf Club** (or "R&A") is the governing body for golf the world over, dating back to a meeting of 22 of the local gentry in 1754, who founded the Society of St Andrews Golfers. It acquired its current title after King William IV agreed to be the society's patron in 1834.

The game itself has been played here since the fifteenth century. Those early days were instrumental in establishing Scotland as the home of golf, for the rules were distinguished from those in the French game by the fact that participants had to manoeuvre the ball into a hole, rather than hit an above-ground target. (Early French versions were, in fact, more like croquet.) The game developed, acquiring popularity along the way – even Mary, Queen of Scots was known to have the occasional round. It was not without its opponents, however, particularly James II who, in 1457, banned his subjects from playing since it was distracting them from archery practice.

---

10.30am–5.30pm; £1.50), a couple of miles southwest of town on the B939. As well as several landscaped gardens there is a miniature train, trampolines, boating, crazy golf and picnic areas, while a country fair is held here each May with craft stalls, wildlife exhibits, and showjumping displays.

## Eating and drinking

St Andrews has no shortage of **restaurants** and **cafés**. In town, the trusty *Littlejohns*, at the east end of Market Street, serves hearty burgers and steaks, and *The Vine Leaf Restaurant*, St Mary's Place (☎0334/77497) is known for its well-priced, quality dishes made from local produce, in particular a good range of seafood.

Both *Brambles*, 5 College St, and *The Merchant's House*, 49 South St, offer inexpensive home baking, while the *Victoria Café*, 1 St Mary's Place, serves lighter snacks such as baked potatoes and toasted sandwiches. This is a popular student haunt, and a good place in which to have a few drinks in the evening. Similarly, *Ma Belle's*, 40 The Scores, in the basement of the *St Andrews Golf Hotel*, is a lively pub serving cheap food and catering for locals as much as students. The basement bar underneath the *Rusacks Hotel*, 16 Pilmour Links, also fills up quickly. Here you can collapse in large leather armchairs and sofas, study the book-spines in the shelves painted on the wall, or have a game of snooker.

For truly great food, at a price, head for the *Peat Inn* (☎033484/206), five miles south of town on the A915 and then one mile west on the B940. This is one of Britain's top restaurants, serving a varied menu of local specialities. The dining area is intimate without being cramped, and a three-course meal – perhaps featuring noisettes of venison or roast monkfish – will set you back at least £35 per head.

# Around St Andrews

There are two main excursion areas from St Andrews. The most popular is the **East Neuk**, stretching from Fife Ness to Largo Bay; the other is the **Tay coast**, north of St Andrews, running around Fife's northeast headland and along the Tay estuary almost to Perth.

## The East Neuk

South of St Andrews, the **East Neuk** (*Neuk* is Scots for "corner") is a region of quaint fishing villages, all crow-stepped gables and tiled rooves. The best beaches are at the resorts of **ELIE** and **EARLSFERRY** which lie next to each other about twelve miles south of St Andrews.

The villages between St Andrews and Elie fall into two distinct types: either scattered higgledy-piggledy up the hillside like **ST MONANS**, between Pittenweem and Elie, or neatly lined along the harbour like **ANSTRUTHER**, between Crail and Pittenweem. Anstruther is home to the wonderfully unpretentious **Scottish Fisheries Museum** (April–Oct 10am–5.30pm, Sun 11am–5pm; Nov–March 10am–4.30pm, Sun 2–4.30pm; £1.80), quite in keeping with the no-frills integrity of the area in general. Set in a complex of sixteenth- to nineteenth-century buildings on a total of eighteen different floors, it chronicles the history of the fishing and whaling industries in ingenious displays. Moored in the harbour outside is the **North Carr Lightship** (Easter–Oct daily 11am–5pm; £1.40), which for almost 45 years served off Fife Ness. Have a look around to get a feeling of life on board. A **tourist office** operates from the fisheries museum during the summer.

The current lighthouse, erected in 1816 by Robert Louis Stevenson's grandfather, is several miles offshore from Anstruther on the rugged **Isle of May**, where you can also see the remains of Scotland's first lighthouse, built in 1636, which burned coals as a beacon. The island is now a nature reserve and bird sanctuary, and can be reached by boat from Anstruther (May–Sept; ☎0333/310103). Between April and July the dramatic seacliffs are covered with breeding kittiwakes, razorbills, guillemots and shags, while inland there are thousands of puffins and eider duck. Grey seals also make the occasional appearance. Check up on departure times, as crossings vary according to weather and tide, and allow between three and five hours for a round trip: an hour each way, and a couple of hours there. Take plenty of warm, waterproof clothing.

## The Tay coast

Looking across to Dundee and Perthshire, the **Tay coast**, a peaceful wedge of rural hinterland on the edge of the River Tay, offers little in the way of specific attractions, but a lot of undiscovered hideaways. Gentle hills fringe the shore, sheltering the villages – several of which only acquired running water and street lights in the past decade or two – that lie in the dips and hollows along the coast.

**LEUCHARS**, north of St Andrews, is known for its RAF base, from where low-flying jets screech over the hills, appearing out of nowhere and sending sheep, cows and horses galloping out for shelter. Romantic **Earlshall Castle**, just east of Leuchars (Easter & May–Sept daily 2–6pm; £2.90), is the home of the Baron and Baroness of Earlshall, whose ancestor, Sir William Bruce, built the castle in 1546. Antique armour, Jacobite relics, and coats of arms fill the imposing fortress, which is surrounded by splendid grounds, including an organic, Victorian walled garden.

Northeast of Leuchars, **Tentsmuir Forest** occupies the northeasternmost point of the Fife headland, and is also a nature reserve with a good beach and peaceful woodland walks – so peaceful that you would never guess it's only five miles or so from the **Tay bridges** and Dundee just the other side (80p toll charge on the road bridge). The current Tay **rail bridge** is the second to span the river on this spot, the first having collapsed in a terrifying disaster during a storm on

December 28, 1879, which claimed the lives of around one hundred people in a train crossing the bridge at the time. The event was recorded by the notoriously bad poet, William McGonagall, who has gone down in history as responsible for some of the most banal verse ever written, including some memorably trite rhyme about the disaster:

*So the train mov'd slowly along the Bridge of Tay,*
*Until it was about midway,*
*Then the central girders with a crash gave way,*
*And down went the train and passengers into the Tay!*
*The storm Fiend did loudly bray,*
*Because ninety lives had been taken away,*
*On the last Sabbath day of 1879,*
*Which will be remember'd for a very long time.*

There's a **camping** and **caravan** site at **TAYPORT**, a popular resort a couple of miles east of the bridge, from where one of Scotland's oldest ferries once ran across the river. Here the "silvery Tay" more than justifies this traditional description, shimmering in the light whatever the season. There are good views across the river from the shingly cove at **BALMERINO**, a quaint hamlet five miles further on, just below the ruin of **Balmerino Abbey** (daily dawn–dusk; NTS; 50p), surrounded by venerable old trees, including an enormous gnarled Spanish chestnut, which has stood here for centuries. The Cistercian abbey was founded in 1229, built by monks from the abbey at Melrose in the Borders. Destroyed by the English in 1547, reconstruction work was halted for good by the Reformation.

**Lindores Abbey**, seven miles or so further along the coast, dates from the century before and was a Benedictine settlement. The west tower still stands, silhouetted against the sky, and there are views down to nearby **NEWBURGH**, stunning on a summer evening, with the setting sun lighting up the mudflats below and skimming across the Tay. Newburgh itself is a fairly quiet, slightly rough-edged place. Originally a fishing village, it evolved due to its proximity to the abbey, and is now known for the admirable **Laing Museum** (April–Sept Mon–Fri 11am–6pm, Sat & Sun 2–5pm; Oct–March Wed & Thurs noon–4pm, Sun 2–5pm; free). The collection, donated by the banker and historian Dr Alexander Laing in 1892, includes a fine array of antiques and geological specimens gathered from the surrounding area.

# PERTH AND THE HIGHLANDS

Genteel **Perthshire**, the domain of Scotland's country-club set, is an area of scenic valleys and glens, rushing rivers, and peaceful lochs. First settled over eight thousand years ago, it was taken by the Romans and then the Picts, before Celtic missionaries established themselves here, enjoying the amenable climate, fertile soil and ideal defensive and trading location.

The region of **Strathearn** marks Scotland's geographical transition from Lowland to Highland. Its key town is the port of **Perth**, which for centuries has benefitted from its inland position on the River Tay. Salmon, wool and, by the sixteenth century, whisky – *Bell's, Dewar's* and the *Famous Grouse* whiskies all hail from this area – were exported from here, while a major import was Bordeaux claret.

**Northwest Perthshire** is a place of magnificent beauty, where the snow-capped peaks of soaring mountains fall away down forested slopes to long, deep lochs on the valley floor. The area is dominated by the western Grampian Mountains, a mighty range which controls transport routes, influences the weather and tolerates little development.

**Transport** connections in the region are at their best if you head straight north from Perth, along the train line to Inverness, but buses – albeit often infrequent – also trail the more remote areas. Keep asking at bus stations for details of services, as the further you get from the main villages the less definitive timetables become.

# Perth

Surrounded by fertile agricultural land and beautiful scenery, **PERTH** – for several centuries Scotland's capital – was voted by the *Daily Record* in 1990 the town in Britain which provided the best quality of life. Viewed from the hills to the south, Perth still justifies Sir Walter Scott's glowing description of it in the opening pages of his novel *The Fair Maid of Perth*. Lying on the River Tay, it spreads down the hills to the south and east and across the low-lying ground to the west.

During the reign of James I this was the meeting place of Parliament on several occasions, but its glory was short-lived when the king was murdered here in 1437. During the Reformation, on May 11, 1559, John Knox preached his rousing sermon here, in St John's Church, which led to the destruction of the town's four monasteries. Despite decline in the seventeenth century, the community expanded in the eighteenth and has prospered ever since – today it's a finance centre and important market town, and, despite the destruction of many of its older buildings, has retained the air of a bustling county town. Its long history as a livestock trading centre is continued throughout the year, notably with the Aberdeen Angus shows and sales in February and October, and the Perthshire Agricultural Show in August; and grain, malt and timber are still shipped out regularly from the harbour at the southern end of town. The most testing event in the town's recent history was the flooding of the centre in early 1993, when, following particularly heavy rains, the Tay burst its banks, filling the streets with several feet of water and bringing local life to a standstill.

## Arrival, information and accommodation

Perth is on the main train line north from Edinburgh and Glasgow: the **bus** and **train stations** are on opposite sides of the road at the west end of town where Marshall Place runs into Leonard Street. The **tourist office**, 45 High St (Mon–Sat 9am–5pm; ☎0738/38353), is a ten-minute walk away.

Of the numerous **hotels** in Perth's town centre, try the *Station Hotel*, on Leonard Street (☎0738/24141; ④), right by the station, which vies for customers with the slightly smaller *Queens Hotel* (☎0738/25471; ④) immediately opposite. Both are traditional places, with comfortable bedrooms and spacious public rooms. The *Salutation Hotel*, 34 South St (☎0738/30066; ③), claims – not without some justification – to be one of Scotland's oldest hotels, having been established in 1699. Large-scale refurbishment in 1992 has left the place spick and span.

There are **B&Bs** and guest houses all over town, notably on the approach roads from Crieff and Perth. In the centre, Marshall Place, overlooking the South

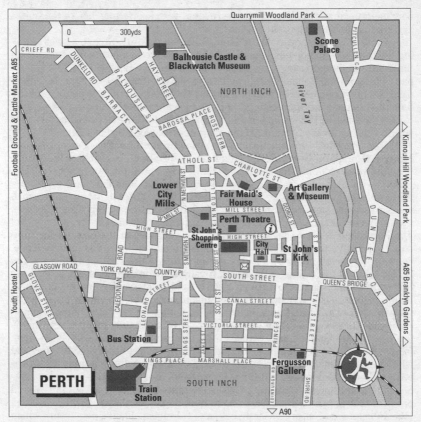

Inch, is the place to look. Of the many possibilities along here *Kinnaird House*, 5 Marshall Place (☎0738/28021; ②) offers a warm welcome in a lovely town house, with well-equipped en suite rooms. On the other side of the river, at *Ballabeg*, 14 Keir St (☎0738/20434; ①), you'll feel like one of the family as soon as you walk in. Rooms are spacious and comfortable, but facilities are shared. The **youth hostel** is housed in an impressive old mansion at 107 Glasgow Rd (☎0738/23658; Grade 1) beyond the west end of York Place.

## The Town

Perth's compact **centre** occupies a small area on the west bank of the Tay. Only the middle section of the High Street is pedestrianized, and the rest of the streets are busy with traffic, so it's best to explore on foot. Two large areas of green parkland, known as the North and South Inch, flank the centre. The **North Inch** was the site of the Battle of the Clans in 1396, in which thirty men from each of the clans Chattan and Quhele (pronounced "Kay") met in a battle which was later vividly captured by Scott in *The Fair Maid of Perth*, while the **South Inch** was the public meeting place for witch-burning in the seventeenth century. Both are now used for more civilized public recreation, with sports matches to the north, and boating and putting to the south.

A good variety of shops line the **High Street** and **South Street**, as well as filling **St John's** shopping centre on King Edward Street. Opposite the entrance to the centre is the imposing **City Hall**, which is used by Scotland's politicians for party conferences. Behind here lies **St John's Kirk** (daily 10am–noon & 2–4pm; free), founded by David I in 1126, although the present building dates from the fifteenth century and was restored to house a war memorial chapel designed by Robert Lorimer in 1923–8. It was in St John's that John Knox preached his fiery sermon calling for the "purging of the churches from idolatry" in 1559.

Across the High Street from St John's, in the north of the centre, the **Fair Maid's House**, on North Port, behind Charlotte Street, is arguably the town's best-known attraction (Mon–Sat 10am–5pm), now housing a twee craft shop and gallery with changing craft and jewellery exhibitions. Standing on the site of a thirteenth-century monastery, this cottage of weathered stone with small windows and an outside staircase was the setting chosen by Sir Walter Scott as the house of Simon Glover, father of the virginal Catherine Glover, in his novel *The Fair Maid of Perth*. Set in Perth in turbulent times at the close of the fourteenth century, the novel tells a traditional story of love, war and revenge, centring on the attempts by various worthies to win the hand of Catherine, the "Fair Maid". In the course of the novel, royalty and commoners clash under King Robert III, and Catherine is stolen away and held captive in the palace at Falkland, before Hal o' Wynd, a local smith and armourer, eventually takes her as his wife after chasing off Conachar of the clan Quhele at the Battle of the Clans.

Despite its story, there's little to actually see at the house; more interesting is the nearby **Art Gallery and Museum** on George Street (Mon–Sat 10am–5pm; free), which features exhibits on local history, art, natural history, archeology and whisky, and gives a good impression of local life through the centuries. In similar vein, at **Lower City Mills**, W Mill St (Easter–Oct Mon–Sat 10am–5pm; also July–Sept Sat & Sun noon–5pm; Nov–March Mon–Sat 10am–4pm; £1.50), a restored oatmeal mill driven by a massive waterwheel recalls Victorian Perth. The excellent **Fergusson Gallery**, Marshall Place (Mon–Sat 10am–5pm; free), which opened at the end of 1991 in the Round House, is probably the most interesting of Perth's museums, housed in a domed circular structure at the edge of the Tay which used to house the waterworks. Today it holds the works of J D Fergusson, the Edinburgh-born artist who was one of the few British painters to witness the developments in art in Paris in the first decade of the twentieth century. Closely associated with friends and fellow artists Samuel Peploe, F C B Caddell and Leslie Hunter (known now as the Scottish Colourists), he was also close friends with Charles Rennie Mackintosh, whom he first met while living in London in 1917. On his death, Fergusson bequeathed his works to his wife, who established the Fergusson Art Foundation and donated the collection to Perth and Kinross District Council in 1991.

North of the town centre, and adjacent to the North Inch, the elegantly restored Georgian terraces beyond the Fair Maid's House give way to newer buildings, which have gradually encroached on the former territory of the fifteenth-century **Balhousie Castle**, off Hay Street (summer Mon–Fri 10am–4.30pm, Sun 2–4.30pm; winter closes 3.30pm; free). The castle sits incongruously in a peaceful residential area and has been restored in Scots Baronial style with turrets and crow-stepped gables. Originally the home of the Earls of Kinnoull, who have lent their name to Kinnoull Hill across the Tay to the east of Perth, it now houses the headquarters and **museum of the Black Watch**. This historic regiment – whose name refers to the dark colour of their tartan – was formed in 1739, having been built up by General Wade earlier in the century, who employed groups of Highlanders to keep the peace. The museum chronicles its history through a good display of paintings, uniforms, documents, weapons and photographs.

## Around Perth

A number of attractions lie around Perth. To the north, on the Inveralmond Industrial Estate, are the **Caithness Glass** factory (April–Sept Mon–Sat 9am–5pm, Sun 11am–5pm; Oct–March Mon–Sat 9am–5pm, Sun 1pm–5pm; free) and **John Dewar's and Sons** whisky distillery (guided tours Mon–Thurs 10am, 11.15am, 2pm & 3.15pm, Fri 10am & 11.15am; free; book ahead on ☎0738/21231). The former has a viewing area where you can watch glass-blowing; tours of *Dewar's* are excellent, and as usual give you the chance to drink the end product. To get to the industrial estate take bus #5, #6 or #10 from Mill Street in Perth.

For outdoor distractions, head for **Bell's Cherrybank Gardens** (May–Oct daily 9am–5pm; £1), west of the centre, where you'll find eighteen acres of well-kept gardens, including the largest collection of heathers in Britain, interspersed with a waterfall, pools, aviary and children's play area. If it's a pleasant day, this is a good place to bring the kids. On the other side of the Tay, the **Branklyn Gardens**, Dundee Rd (March–Oct daily 9.30am–sunset; NTS; £2), comprise an astonishing collection of Alpine plants, spread across a compact two acres of hillside. Looking over the gardens from the north is **Kinnoull Hill**, which also offers splendid views of Perth, the Tay and the surrounding area from its 783-foot summit (a 20-min walk from the car park on Braes Road). Pick up a leaflet from Perth's tourist office for details of the hill's various woodland walks.

## Eating and drinking

There are plenty of **restaurants** in Perth. In the moderate price range, *Littlejohns*, 65 S Methven St, serves hearty steaks, burgers and nachos and has a good selection of vegetarian dishes, but is nonetheless having to work hard to keep up with *Pacos*, 16 St John's Place, a newer upstart rival which manages to do it better. For fresh local produce and a more upmarket atmosphere, try *The Bridges*, 70 Tay St (☎0738/25484; closed Mon), an intimate little place down by the river. The bar lunches are cheaper than the full-blown evening meals. If you want a quick, inexpensive day-time bite, coffee shops such as *Brambles*, 11 Princes St, and *Willows*, 12 St John's Place, dish up filling, home-cooked snacks, while *Strangeways*, 24 George St, is a bistro and lively night-time wine bar.

# North of Perth

Situated a couple of miles north of Perth on the eastern side of the Tay, **Scone Palace** (pronounced "Scoon") is worth every penny of the admission charge levied by its owners, the Earl and Countess of Mansfield, whose family have owned it for almost four centuries (Easter–Oct Mon–Sat 9.30am–5pm, Sun

---

## THE STONE OF DESTINY

Legend has it that the Stone of Destiny (also called the Stone of Scone) was "Jacob's Pillow", on which he dreamed of the ladder of angels from earth to heaven. Its real history is obscure, but it is known that it it was moved from Ireland to Dunadd by missionaries, and thence to Dunstaffnage, from where Kenneth MacAlpine, king of the Dalriada Scots, brought it to the abbey at Scone in 838. There it remained for almost five hundred years, used as a coronation throne on which all Kings of Scotland were crowned.

In 1296, an over-eager Edward I stole what he believed to be the Stone and installed it at Westminster Abbey. Apart from a brief interlude in 1950, when Scottish nationalists stole it back again and hid it in Arbroath for several months, it has been there ever since.

Speculation surrounds the authenticity of the Stone at Westminster, for the original is said to have been intricately carved, while the one seen today is a plain block of sandstone. Many believe that the canny monks at Scone palmed this off onto the English king and that the real Stone of Destiny lies hidden in an underground chamber, its whereabouts a mystery to all but a chosen few.

---

1.30pm–5pm; July & Aug 10am–5pm; £4). As soon as it comes into view at the end of its long, tree-flanked driveway, its appeal is evident. The two-storey building is stately but not overpowering; it is far more a home than an untouchable state monument, and the rooms inside, although full of priceless antiques and lavish furnishings, feel lived in and used.

Restored in the nineteenth century, the palace today consists of a sixteenth-century core surrounded by earlier buildings, most built of red sandstone, complete with battlements and the original gateway. The abbey that stood here in the sixteenth century, and where all Scottish kings until James I were crowned, was one of those destroyed following John Knox's sermon in Perth. In the extensive grounds which surround the palace lies the Moot Hill, which was once the site of the famous Coronation Stone of Destiny (see above).

Inside, a good selection of sumptuous rooms are open to visitors, including the library, which has exchanged its books in favour of an outstanding collection of porcelain, one of the foremost in the world, with items by Meissen, Sèvres, Chelsea, Derby and Worcester. Look out too for the beautiful papier mâché Vernis Martin, dishes once carried when travelling, Marie-Antoinette's writing desk, and John Zoffany's exquisite portrait of the *Lady Elizabeth Murray* (daughter of the second earl) *with Dido*. You could easily spend at least a morning here, enjoying the gardens with strutting peacocks, livestock areas with Highland cattle, picnic area, donkey park, children's play area and a grand and fragrant pine garden, which was started in 1848 with exotic conifers. Bus #7 runs from South Street in Perth to Scone every twenty minutes; #26 and #46 make the same journey every hour (at 6min past).

### Huntingtower Castle

Not quite as grand as Scone, but nonetheless worth a visit, is **Huntingtower Castle** (April–Sept Mon–Sat 9.30am–6.30pm, Sun 2–6.30pm; Oct–March Mon–Thurs & Sat 9.30am–4.30pm, Sun 2–4.30pm; £1.20), three miles northwest of Perth. Two three-storey towers formed the original fifteenth- and sixteenth-century tower house, and these were linked in the seventeenth century by a range to provide more room. Formerly known as Ruthven Castle, it was here that the Raid of Ruthven took place in 1582, when the sixteen-year-old James VI, at the request of William, fourth Earl of Ruthven, came to the castle only to be held captive by a group of conspirators demanding the dismissal of favoured royal advisers. The plot failed and the young James was released ten months later. Today the castle's chief attractions are its splendid sixteenth-century painted walls and ceilings – you'll see them in the main hall in the east tower. To reach the castle take bus #15 from Scott Street in Perth.

## Dunkeld

**DUNKELD**, twelve miles further on up the A9, was proclaimed Scotland's eccle-siastical capital by Kenneth MacAlpine in 850. Its position straddling the "Highland Line" – the southern boundary of the Grampian Mountains – made it a favoured meeting place for Highland and Lowland cultures, but in 1689 it was burned to the ground by the Cameronians – fighting for William of Orange – in an effort to flush out troops of the Stuart monarch, James VII. Subsequent rebuilding, however, has created one of the area's most delightful communities, and it's well worth at least a brief stop to view its whitewashed houses and historic cathedral. The seasonal **tourist office** is at The Cross in the town centre (April–June Mon–Sat 9am–6pm, Sun 11am–5pm; July–Aug Mon–Sat 9am–8pm, Sun 11am–8pm; Sept–Oct Mon–Sat 9.30am–5.30pm, Sun 2–5pm; Nov Sat 10am–5pm, Sun 2–5pm; ☎0350/727688).

Dunkeld's **cathedral** is on the northern side of town, in an idyllic setting amidst lawns and trees on the east bank of the Tay. Construction began in 1318 and continued through two centuries, but the building was more or less ruined at the time of the Reformation. The present structure, in Gothic and Norman style, consists of the fourteenth-century choir and the fifteenth-century nave. The choir was restored in 1600 (and several times since) and now serves as the parish church, while the nave remains roofless apart from the clock tower. Inside, note the leper's peep near the pulpit in the north wall, through which lepers could receive the sacrament without contact with the congregation.

Dunkeld is linked to its sister community, **BIRNAM**, by Thomas Telford's seven-arched bridge of 1809. This little village has a place in history thanks to Shakespeare, for it was on "Dunsinane Hill" to the southeast that Macbeth lived in his castle, claiming proudly "Till Byrnane wood remove to Dunsinane,/I cannot taint with Feare ...", only to be told by a messenger:

*As I did stand my watch upon the Hill,*
*I look'd toward Byrnane, and anon me thought*
*The Wood began to move ...*
*Within this three Mile may you see it coming.*
*I say a moving grove...*

Several centuries later another literary personality, Beatrix Potter, drew inspi-ration from the area, recalling her childhood holidays here when penning the *Peter Rabbit* stories.

# Strathearn

**Strathearn** – the valley of the River Earn – stretches west of Perth, across to **Loch Earn** and the watersports centre at **Lochearnhead**. Agricola was here around two thousand years ago, trying to establish a foothold in the Highlands, while later on the area was frequented by Bonnie Prince Charlie and Rob Roy, both bound up in the north–south struggle between Highlands and Lowlands.

In the south, the small town of **AUCHTERARDER** sees its fair share of visitors, many of whom come to play golf at the swanky **Gleneagles Hotel** nearby (☎0764/662231; ⑨). The area between the two makes a pleasant, slow drive if you've got both a car and time, but there is little here in the way of specific attractions. There is a **tourist office** on the High Street (Mon–Fri 9.30–1.30pm; ☎0764/663450).

The northern part of the valley is more attractive, all routes converging on the old spa town of **CRIEFF**, of which William McGonagall declaimed:

> *Ye lover of the picturesque if ye wish to drown your grief*
> *Take my advice and visit the ancient town of Crieff*

Crieff is, undoubtedly, in a lovely position on a south-facing slope of the Grampian foothills. Cattle traders used to come here in the eighteenth century, since this was a good location – between Highland and Lowland – for buying and selling livestock, but Crieff really came into its own with the arrival of the train in 1856. Shortly after that, Morrison's Academy, now one of Scotland's most respected schools, took in its first pupils, and in 1868 the grand old *Crieff Hydro* (☎0764/2401; ④) opened its doors – still the nicest place to stay in town, despite being dry (of alcohol). There's nothing to do here nowadays, but you'll find it a pleasant mixture of Edwardian and Victorian houses, with a busy little centre which still retains something of the atmosphere of the former spa town. The **Crieff Visitor Centre** (daily 9.30am–5pm) is a "craftsy" place, crammed with pottery and paperweights. The **tourist office** is in the town hall on the High Street (Mon–Fri 9.30am–5pm, Sat 9.30am–1.30pm; ☎0764/652578).

From Crieff, it's a short drive or a twenty-minute walk to the **Glenturret Distillery** (March–Dec Mon–Sat 9.30am–6pm, Sun noon–6pm, last tour 4.30pm; Jan–Feb Mon–Fri 11.30am–4pm, last tour 2.30pm; free), just off the A85 to Comrie. To get there on public transport, catch any bus going to Crieff, Comrie or St Fillans and ask the driver to drop you at the bottom of the Glenturret Distillery road, from where it's a five-minute walk. This is Scotland's oldest distillery, established in 1775, and a good one to visit, if only for its splendidly isolated location.

## Comrie

**COMRIE**, a pretty conservation village another five miles along the River Earn, has the dubious distinction of being the location where more seismological tremors have been recorded than anywhere else in Britain, due to its position on the Highland Boundary Fault. Earthquake readings are still taken at **Earthquake House**, about six hundred yards off the A85, on the south side of the river. The building itself is not open to the public, but there are information panels outside, and if you're really keen you can look through the windows at a model of the world's first seismometer, set up here in 1874.

If you've got children with you, an excellent place to take them is the **Auchingarrich Wildlife Centre** (daily 10am–dusk), a couple of miles south of Comrie on the B827. Recently established in a blustery hillside location, it covers one hundred acres and provides lots of opportunities to pet the animals.

# Around Loch Tay

The mountains and valleys of **Glenalmond**, north of Strathearn, give way to the fourteen-mile-long, freshwater **Loch Tay**, a stunning stretch of water dominated by moody **Ben Lawers** (3984ft), Perthshire's highest mountain, immediately north, from the top of which there are incredible views towards both the Atlantic and the North Sea. The climb up – which should not be tackled without all the right equipment – takes around three hours from the NTS **visitor centre** (Easter–Sept daily 10am–5pm; £1.50; ☎0567/820399), which is at 1300ft and reached by a track off the A827 along the northern side of Loch Tay. The centre carries information on the rare Alpine flora found here.

## Breadalbane

The mountains of **Breadalbane** (pronounced "Bread-*al*bane"), named after the Earls of Breadalbane, loom over the southern end of Loch Tay. Glens Lochay and Dochart curve into the north and south respectively from the small town of **KILLIN**, where the River Dochart comes rushing out of the hills and down the frothy **Falls of Dochart**, before disgorging into Loch Tay. There's little to do in Killin itself, but it does make a convenient base for some of the region's best walks. One of the most appealing places to stay is the *Dall Lodge Hotel*, Main St (☎056782/0217; ③), which the owner, who lives in the Far East, has filled with all manner of exotic bits and pieces. The dining room serves fine local produce. There is also a **youth hostel** (April–Oct; ☎05672/546; Grade 2), in an old country house just beyond the northern end of the village.

Beyond Breadalbane, the mountains tumble down into **Glen Lyon**, where, legend has it, the Celtic warrior Fingal built twelve castles. Access to the glen – at 34 miles long, generally regarded as the longest enclosed glen in Scotland – is usually impossible in winter, but the narrow roads are passable in summer. You can either take the road from Killin up to the **Ben Lawers Visitor Centre**, four miles up Loch Tay, and continue going, or take the road from Fortingall, which is a couple of miles north of the loch's northern end. The two roads join up, making a round trip possible, but bear in mind there is no road through the mountains to Loch Rannoch further north. **FORTINGALL** itself is little more than a handful of thatched cottages, although locals make much of their three-thousand-year-old yew tree – believed (by them at least) to be the oldest living thing in Europe. The village also lays claim to being the birthplace of Pontius Pilate, reputedly the son of a Roman officer stationed here.

On a slight promontory at Loch Tay's northern end and overlooking the River Tay, **KENMORE**'s whitewashed houses and well-tended gardens cluster around the gate to **Taymouth Castle** – built by the Campbells of Glenorchy in the early nineteenth century and now a private golf club. The village's sporting reputation is due partly to various boat rental places around this end of the loch, and also to **Croft-na-Caber** (☎0887/830588), an impressive **outdoor pursuits** complex on the southern side of the loch, which offers waterskiing, fishing, hill walking, cross-country skiing, sledging and various forms of shooting. The complex also offers comfortable **accommodation** in either its own hotel (☎0887/830236; ⑤) or in well-equipped chalets overlooking the loch. You don't have to stay here to use the facilities, however, and tuition or equipment rental is available by the hour, half-day, full day or longer. As an example of prices, a day's sailing or wind-surfing instruction costs around £40. You can also stay at the overwhelmingly Scottish *Kenmore Hotel*, in the village square (☎0887/830205; ⑤), which is the descendant of Scotland's oldest inn, established here in 1572. Even if you don't stay, stop off for a meal or drink.

ABERFELDY, a largely Victorian town six miles or so further on, makes a good base for exploring the area. The **tourist office** at The Square in the town centre (summer Mon–Sat 9am–5pm, Sun noon–4pm; winter Mon, Tues & Thurs – Sat 10am–2pm; ☎0887/820276) gives details of the so-called Locus Project, a local initiative which has devised a series of looped trails that take in all the main sights.

Aberfeldy sits at the point where the Urlar Burn – lined by the silver birch trees celebrated by Robert Burns in his poem *The Birks of Aberfeldy* – flows into the River Tay. The Tay is spanned by **Wade's Bridge**, built by General Wade in 1733 during his efforts to control the trouble in the Highlands, and, with its hump-back and four arches, regarded as one of the general's finest remaining crossing points. Overlooking the bridge from the south end is the **Black Watch Monument**, a pensive, kilted soldier, erected in 1887 to commemorate the peace-keeping troop of Highlanders gathered together by Wade in 1739.

The small town centre is a busy mixture of craft and tourist shops, its main attraction the early nineteenth-century **Aberfeldy Water Mill** (Easter–Oct Mon–Sat 10am–5.30pm, Sun noon–5.30pm; £1.50), a superbly restored mill, which harnesses the water of the Urlar to turn the wheel that stone-grinds the oatmeal in the traditional Scottish way.

One mile west of Aberfeldy, across Wade's Bridge, **Castle Menzies** (April–Sept Mon–Fri 10.30am–5pm, Sun 2–5pm; £2) is an imposing, Z-shaped, sixteenth-century tower house, which until the middle of this century was the chief seat of the Clan Menzies. With the demise of the Menzies line the castle was taken over by the Menzies Clan Society, who since 1971 have been involved in the lengthy process of restoring it. Now the interior, with its wide stone staircase, is refreshingly free of fixtures and fittings, with structural attributes such as the plasterwork ceilings laid open for perusal.

If you want to **stay** in Aberfeldy, *Moness House Hotel and Country Club*, Crieff Rd (☎0887/820446; ③), occupies a whitewashed country house and offers luxurious self-catering cottages, as well as fishing, golf and watersports. *Guinach House*, By the Birks (☎0887/820251; ③), in pleasant grounds near the famous silver birches, is a tastefully decorated house converted into a small hotel, with a good dining room. Of the various smaller establishments, *Tigh'n Ellean Guest House*, Taybridge Drive (☎0887/820109; ①), and *Handa*, Taybridge Rd (☎0887/820334; ①), both offer quality B&B.

# Pitlochry

Surrounded by hills just north of the confluence of the Tummel and Tay rivers at Ballinluig, **PITLOCHRY** spreads itself gracefully along the eastern shore of the Tummel, on the lower slopes of Ben Vrackie (2733ft). Even after General Wade built one of his first roads through here in the early eighteenth century, Pitlochry remained little more than a village. Queen Victoria's visit in 1842 helped to put the area on the map, but it wasn't until the end of the century that Pitlochry started to come into its own, establishing itself as a popular holiday centre.

# Practicalities

Access to Pitlochry is easy by public transport, thanks to its position on the main train line to Inverness, and regular buses running from Perth. The **bus** stop and the **train** station are on Station Road, at the north end of town, ten minutes' walk from the town centre and the **tourist office**, 22 Atholl Road (Mon–Fri 9am–1pm & 2–5pm, Sat 9.30am–1.30pm; ☎0796/472215). The office has details of attractions in the surrounding area, and also offers an **accommodation** booking service.

  *Birchwood Hotel*, E Moulin Rd (☎0796/472477; ④), occupies a lovely Victorian country house at the top of town, set in four acres of grounds, and has a particularly good restaurant. Close by, the friendly *Castlebeigh House*, 10 Knockard Rd (☎0796/472925; ③), has good views from the bedrooms. Further along the road, the much pricier *Pitlochry Hydro*, Knockard Rd (☎0796/472666; ⑥) looks out over the Tummel Valley. In the town centre, there are a number of cheaper hotels along the main street, including the comfortable *McKays Hotel*, 138 Atholl Rd (☎0796/473888; ②), and many guest houses and **B&Bs**, at the top of town – most notably *Whinrigg*, Aldour, Perth Rd (☎0796/472330; ①), with magnificent views across the valley, and *Comar House*, Strathview Terrace (☎0796/473531; ②). The **youth hostel** (☎0796/472308; Grade 1) is on Knockard Road at the top of town.

  Despite its popularity, Pitlochry is pitifully short of **restaurants**, and the best bet is to try any of the local hostelries along the main street. If you're out of town to the north, stop in at the *Atholl Arms Hotel*, Blair Atholl (☎079681/205; ③), which does good afternoon teas and bar meals.

# The Town

Pitlochry's busy main street is a constant flurry of traffic, locals and tourists. Beyond the train bridge at the southern end of the main street is Bells' **Blair Atholl Distillery**, Perth Rd (Mon–Sat 9.30am–4pm, Easter–Sept also Sun noon–4pm), where the excellent visitor centre illustrates the process involved in making the Blair Atholl Malt. Whisky has been produced on this site since 1798, in which time production has been stepped up to around two million litres a year, making this only a medium-sized distillery.

  A perfect contrast to the Blair Atholl is the **Edradour Distillery** (March–Oct daily 9.30am–5pm; Nov–Feb Mon–Sat 10.30am–4pm), Scotland's smallest, in an idyllic position tucked into the hills a couple of miles east of Pitlochry. A whistle-stop audio-visual presentation covering more than 250 years of production precedes the tour of the distillery itself.

  On the western edge of Pitlochry, just across the river, lies Scotland's renowned "Theatre in the Hills", the **Pitlochry Festival Theatre** (☎0796/472680). Originally set up in 1951, the theatre started in a tent on the site of what is now the town curling rink, before moving to the banks of the river in 1981. Backstage tours (£2.50; booking advised) run through the day, while a variety of productions – both mainstream and offbeat – are staged in the evening.

  A short stroll upstream from the theatre is the **Pitlochry Power Station and Dam**, a massive concrete wall which harnesses the water of the man-made Loch Faskally, just north of the town, for hydro-electric power. Although the visitor centre (April–Oct daily 9.40am–5.30pm) explains the ins and outs of it all, the main attraction here, apart from the views up the loch, is the **salmon ladder**, up which the salmon leap on their annual migration – a sight not to be missed.

# Loch Tummel and Loch Rannoch

Between Pitlochry and Loch Ericht lies a sparsely populated, ever-changing panorama of mountains, moors, lochs and glens. Venturing into the hills is difficult without a car – unless you're walking – but infrequent local buses do run from Pitlochry to the outlying communities in the surrounding area, and the train to Inverness runs parallel to the A9.

West of Pitlochry, the B8019 twists and turns along the Grampian mountainsides, overlooking **Loch Tummel** and then **Loch Rannoch**. These two lochs, celebrated by Harry Lauder in his famous song *The Road to the Isles*, are joined by Dunalastair Water, which narrows to become the River Tummel at the western end of the loch of the same name. This is a spectacular stretch of countryside and one which deserves leisurely exploration. **Queen's View** at the eastern end of Loch Tummel is a fabulous vantage point, looking down the loch across the hills to the misty peak of Schiehallion (3520ft), the "Fairy Mountain", whose mass was used in early experiments to judge the weight of the Earth. The Forestry Commission's **visitor centre** (April–Oct daily 9.30am–5pm) interprets the fauna and flora of the area, and also has a café.

Beyond Loch Tummel, **KINLOCH RANNOCH** marks the eastern end of Loch Rannoch. This small community is popular with backpackers, who stock up at the local store before taking to the hills again. The road follows the loch to its end and then heads six miles further into the desolation of **Rannoch Moor**, where **Rannoch Station**, a lonely outpost on the Glasgow to Fort William West Highland train, marks the end of the line. The only way back is by the same road as far as Loch Rannoch, where it's possible – but not always advisable, depending on conditions – to return on a (very) minor road along the south side of the lochs. The round trip is roughly seventy miles.

# Blair Atholl to Loch Ericht

Four miles north of Pitlochry the road cuts through the **Pass of Killiecrankie**, a breathtaking wooded gorge which falls away to the River Garry below. This dramatic setting was the site of the **Battle of Killicrankie** in 1689, when the Jacobites quashed the forces of General Mackay. Legend has it that one soldier of the Crown, fleeing for his life, made a miraculous jump across the eighteen-foot **Soldier's Leap**, an impossibly wide chasm half-way up the gorge. Queen Victoria, visiting here 160 years later, contented herself with recording the beauty of the area in her diary. Exhibits at the slick NTS **visitor centre** (May–Oct daily 9.30am–5.30pm; 50p) recall the battle and examine the gorge in detail.

Before leading the Jacobites into battle, Graham of Claverhouse, Viscount ("Bonnie") Dundee, had seized **Blair Castle** (April–Oct daily 10am–6pm; £3), three miles up the road at Blair Atholl. Seat of the Atholl dukedom, this white-washed, turreted castle, surrounded by parkland and dating from 1269, presents an impressive sight as you approach up the drive. A piper may be playing in front of the castle: he is one of the Atholl Highlanders, a select group retained by the duke as his private army – a privilege afforded to him by Queen Victoria, who stayed here in the nineteenth century. Today the duke is the only British subject allowed to maintain his own force.

A total of 32 rooms are open for inspection, and display a selection of paintings, furniture, plasterwork and the like that is sumptous in the extreme. The Tapestry Room, on the top floor of the original Cumming's Tower, is hung with Brussels tapestries and contains an outrageous four-poster bed, topped with vases of ostrich feathers which originally came from the first duke's suite at Holyrood Palace in Edinburgh. The Ballroom, also, with its timber roof, antlers and melange of portraits, is Baronial Scotland at its best. The castle also has a self-service restaurant, and a **caravan park** in the grounds.

Beyond Blair Atholl, the A9 follows the line of **Glen Garry** and the River Garry through the Grampian Mountains. The road climbs continuously, sweeping past the eastern end of **Glen Errochty**, on towards the barren **Pass of Drummochter** and to the bleak little village of Dalwhinnie at the northern end of **Loch Ericht**. The scenery is marvellous all the way, but there is literally nothing here apart from the mountains and moors.

## travel details

### Trains

**Falkirk High** to: Edinburgh (every 30min; 30min); Glasgow Queen Street (every 30min; 25min); Linlithgow (hourly; 8min).

**Kirkcaldy** to: Aberdeen (hourly; 2hr); Dundee (hourly; 40min or 1hr); Edinburgh (24 daily; 40min); Perth (7 daily; 40min); Pitlochry (3 direct daily; 1hr 15min; 4 indirect, change at Perth; 1hr 25min).

**Linlithgow** to: Edinburgh (hourly; 20min); Falkirk High (hourly; 10min); Glasgow Queen Street (hourly; 30min).

**Perth** to: Aberdeen (hourly; 1hr 40min); Dundee (hourly; 25min); Edinburgh (9 daily; 1hr 25min); Glasgow Queen Street (hourly; 1hr 5min); Kirkcaldy (7 daily; 40min); Pitlochry (8 daily; 30min).

**Pitlochry** to: Edinburgh (5 daily; 2hr); Glasgow Queen Street (3 daily; 1hr 45min); Kirkcaldy (4 direct daily; 1hr 15min; 1 indirect, change at Perth; 1hr 45min); Perth (8 daily; 30min); Stirling (3 daily; 1hr 10min).

**Stirling** to: Aberdeen (hourly; 2hr 15min); Dundee (hourly; 1hr); Edinburgh (hourly; 1hr); Falkirk High (hourly; 20min); Glasgow Queen Street (hourly; 30min); Linlithgow (hourly; 35min); Perth (hourly; 30min); Pitlochry (5 daily; 1hr 15min).

### Buses

**Bo'ness** to: Edinburgh (5 daily; 45min); Stirling (3 daily; 35min).

**Dundee** to: Glenrothes (7 daily; 1hr 10min); St Andrews (every 30 min; 35min); Kirkcaldy (7 daily; 1hr 35min); Stirling (9 daily; 1hr 30min).

**Dunfermline** to: Edinburgh (2 daily; 40min); Glenrothes (15 daily; 1hr 5min); Kirkcaldy (every 30min; 1hr); St Andrews (11 daily; 2hrs).

**Glenrothes** to: Dundee (7 daily; 1hr 10min); Dunfermline (12 daily; 1hr 10min); Kirkcaldy (hourly; 20min); St Andrews (7 daily; 40min).

**Kirkcaldy** to: Dundee (16 daily; 1hr 10min); Dunfermline (hourly; 1hr); Glenrothes (hourly; 20min); St Andrews (16 daily; 50min).

**Perth** to: Dunblane (every 30 min; 35min); Dunfermline (every 30 min; 50min); Edinburgh (12 daily; 1hr 20min); Glasgow (20 daily; 1hr 35min); Gleneagles (12 daily; 25min); Inverness (3 daily; 2hr 30min); London (4 daily; 9hrs); Stirling (18 daily; 50min).

**St Andrews** to: Dundee (every 30min; 40min); Dunfermline (Mon–Sat 13 daily; 1hr 40min); Edinburgh (12 daily; 2hr); Glasgow (6 daily; 2hr 50min); Glenrothes (hourly; 45min); Kirkcaldy (16 daily; 1hr); Stirling (6 daily; 2hr).

**Stirling** to: Aberfoyle (4 daily; 50min); Bo'ness (3 daily; 35 min); Callander (11 daily; 45min); Dollar (2 daily; 50min); Doune (14 daily; 30min); Dunblane (15 daily; 1hr 15min); Dundee (9 daily; 1hr 30min); Dunfermline (13 daily; 50min); Edinburgh (hourly; 1hr 35min); Falkirk (every 45min; 30min); Glasgow (34 daily; 1hr 10min); Gleneagles (16 daily; 30min); Inverness (2 daily; 3hr 30min); Killin (2 daily; 2hr); Linlithgow (hourly; 1hr); Lochearnhead (2 daily; 1hr 40min); Perth (15 daily; 50min); Pitlochry (2 daily; 1hr 30min); St Andrews (6 daily; 2hr).

# CHAPTER FIVE

# ARGYLL

C ut off for centuries from the rest of Scotland by the mountains and sea lochs that characterize the region, **Argyll** remains remote and sparsely populated, its scatter of offshore islands forming part of the Inner Hebridean archipelago (the remaining Hebrides are dealt with in *Skye and the Western Isles*). The region's name derives from *Araghaidal*, which translates as "Boundary of the Gaels", the Irish Celts who settled here in the fifth century AD, and whose **kingdom of Dalriada** embraced much of what is now Argyll. Known to the Romans as *Scotti* – hence Scotland – it was the Irish Celts who promoted Celtic Christianity from centres such as Iona, and whose Gaelic language eventually became the national tongue.

After a brief period of Norse invasion and settlement, the islands (and the peninsula of Kintyre) fell to the immensely powerful Somerled, who became King of the Hebrides and Lord of Argyll in the twelfth century. Somerled's successors, the MacDonalds, established Islay as their headquarters in the 1200s, but were in turn dislodged by Robert the Bruce. Of Bruce's allies, it was the **Campbells** who benefitted most from the MacDonalds' demise, and eventually, as the dukes of Argyll, gained control of the entire area – even today they remain one of the largest landowners in the region.

In the aftermath of the Jacobean uprisings, the islands of Argyll, like the rest of the Highlands, were devastated by the **Clearances**, with thousands of crofters evicted from their homes in order to make room for profitable sheep-farming – "the white plague" – and cattle rearing. Today the traditional industries remain under threat, leaving the region ever more dependent on tourism and a steady influx of new settlers to keep things going, while Gaelic, once the language of the majority in Argyll, retains only a tenuous hold on the outlying islands of Islay, Coll and Tiree – all officially part of Scotland's *Gàidhealtachd,* or Gaelic-speaking areas. Even the name Argyll disappeared in the redrawing of the county boundaries, being subsumed into the amorphous mass of Strathclyde, which includes the old Lowland counties of Ayrshire, Lanarkshire, Renfrewshire and also Glasgow.

Geographically, as well as culturally, this is a transitional area between Highland and Lowland, boasting a rich variety of scenery, from lush, subtropical gardens warmed by the Gulf Stream to flat and treeless islands far out in the Atlantic. It's in the folds and twists of the countryside and the views out to the islands, that the strengths and beauties of mainland Argyll lie – though the one area of man-made sights you shouldn't miss is the cluster of **Celtic and prehistoric sites** near Kilmartin. Of the mainland towns, **Oban** is by far the largest, yet its population barely exceeds seven thousand, while the prettiest, **Inveraray**, boasts a mere four hundred inhabitants.

The eastern duo of **Bute** and **Arran** – once a separate county in their own right – are the most popular of Argyll's islands, the latter justifiably so, with spectacular scenery ranging from the granite peaks of the north to the Lowland pasture of the south. Of the other Hebridean islands covered in this chapter, mountainous **Mull**

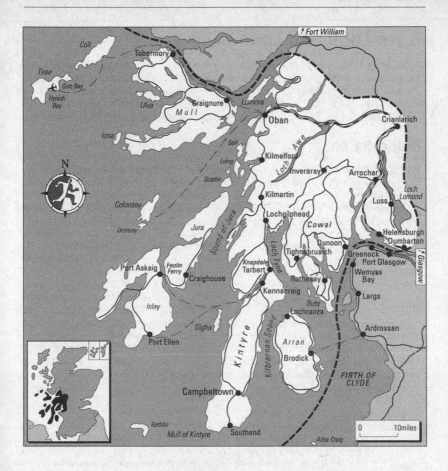

is the most visited, though it is large enough to absorb the crowds, many of whom are only passing through en route to the tiny isle of **Iona**, a centre of Christian culture since the sixth century. **Islay**, best known for its distinctive malt whiskies, is fairly quiet even in the height of summer, as is neighbouring **Jura**, which offers excellent walking opportunities. And for those seeking still more solitude, there are the remote islands of **Tiree** and **Coll**, which, although swept with fierce winds, boast more sunny days than anywhere else in Scotland.

It's on Argyll's west coast that the unpredictability of the **weather** can really affect your holiday. If you can, avoid July and August when the crowds on Mull, Iona and Arran are at their densest – there's no guarantee the weather will be any better than during the rest of the year, when you might have more chance of avoiding the persistent Scottish midge.

All accommodation prices in this book are coded ①–⑨: see p.22 for a full explanation

# Gare Loch and Loch Long

Apart from Helensburgh, there's little to see along the shores of **Gare Loch** and **Loch Long**, which are littered with decaying industrial remains, including the Trident nuclear submarine base at Faslane on Gare Loch and the oil tanks at Finnart on Loch Long. Only occasionally is it possible to glimpse the "unspeakably beautiful" landscape described by eighteenth-century travellers.

## Helensburgh

**HELENSBURGH** is a smart, Georgian grid-plan settlement laid out in an imitation of Edinburgh's New Town. In the eighteenth century it was a well-to-do commuter town for Glasgow and a seaside resort, whose bathing-master, **Henry Bell**, invented one of the first steamboats, the *Comet*, to transport Glaswegians here and back. Today Helensburgh is a stop on the route of the *Waverley*, the last sea-going paddle steamer in the world, which does a zigzag tour of the lochs of Argyll throughout the summer (pick up a timetable from the tourist office).

The inventor of TV, John Logie Baird, was born here, as was Charles Rennie Mackintosh, who in 1902 was commissioned by the Glaswegian publisher Walter Blackie to design **Hill House** (April–Dec daily 1–5pm; NTS £2.80), on Upper Colquhoun Street. Without doubt the best surviving example of Mackintosh's domestic architecture, the house – right down to light fittings – is stamped with his very personal interpretation of Art Nouveau, characterized by his sparing use of colour and stylized floral patterns. The effect is occasionally overwhelming – it's difficult to imagine actually living in such an environment – yet it is precisely Mackintosh's attention to detail that makes the place so special. After exploring the house, head for the kitchen quarters, which have been sensitively transformed into a tearoom.

### Practicalities

Hill House is a good twenty-minute walk from the lochside up Sinclair Street, or just five minutes from Helensburgh Upper train station. The **tourist office** is on the ground floor of the clocktower on the lochside (April–Oct daily 9.30am–7pm; ☎0436/72642). **Accommodation** options include the luxurious *Commodore*, 112–117 W Clyde St (☎0436/76924; ⑤), or the smaller *Imperial*, at no. 12–14 (☎0436/76924; ③); there are also **B&Bs** such as *Kyra*, at no. 100 (☎0436/75576; ②), and *Ashfield*, 38 William St (☎0436/72259; ②).

# Cowal and Bute

The **Cowal peninsula**, formed by Loch Fyne and Loch Long and shaped like a giant claw, is the most visited part of Argyll. The landscape here is extremely varied, ranging from the Highland peaks of the Argyll Forest Park in the north, to the gentle low-lying coastline of the southwest, but most visitors confine themselves to the area around **Dunoon** in the east, leaving the rest of the countryside relatively undisturbed. The island of **Bute** is in many ways simply an extension of the peninsula, from which it is separated by the merest slither of water; its chief town, **Rothesay**, rivals Dunoon as the major seaside resort on the Clyde.

# Argyll Forest Park

**Argyll Forest Park** stretches from Loch Lomond south as far as Holy Loch, providing the most exhilarating scenery on the peninsula. The park includes the **Arrochar Alps**, north of Glen Croe, whose Munros offer some of the best climbing in Argyll: Ben Ime (3318ft) is the tallest of the range, The Cobbler (2891ft) easily the most distinctive – all are for experienced walkers only. Less threatening are the peaks south of Glen Croe, between Loch Goil and and Loch Long, known as **Argyll's Bowling Green** – no ironic nickname but a corruption of the Gaelic *Baile na Greine* (Sunny Hamlet). At the other end of the scale, there are several gentle forest walks clearly laid out by the Forestry Commission.

Approaching from Glasgow by road, you enter the park from **ARROCHAR**, at the head of Loch Long. The village itself is ordinary enough, but the setting is dramatic, and it makes a convenient base for exploring the northern section of the park. There's a **train station**, a mile or so up the Tarbet road, and numerous **hotels** and **B&Bs** – try the *Lochside Guest House* (☎03012/467; ②) or the lovely *Ferry Cottage* (☎03012/428; ③). Two miles beyond Arrochar at **ARDGARTAN**, there's a lochside Forestry Commission **campsite** (mid-March to Oct; ☎03012/293), and a **youth hostel** (☎03012/362; Grade 1).

## Loch Goil, Loch Eck and Holy Loch

Wherever you're heading on Cowal, you're forced to climb **Glen Croe**, a strategic hill pass whose saddle is called for obvious reasons Rest-and-be-Thankful. Here the road forks, with the B828 heading down to **LOCHGOILHEAD**. The setting is difficult to beat, but the village has been upstaged by the **Drimsynie Leisure Centre**, a giant holiday complex a mile to the west, notable for its **European Sheep and Wool Centre** (Mon–Fri 11am, 1 & 3pm, Sat & Sun 1 & 3pm; £2) which hosts sheep shearing and sheep dog shows and its own Miss World-style sheep contest. A road tracks the west side of the loch, petering out after five miles at the ruins of **Carrick Castle**, built around 1400 and used as a hunting lodge by James IV.

To explore any more of Cowal, it's necessary to continue from the Rest-and-be-Thankful down the grand Highland sweep of **Glen Kinglas** to the banks of Loch Fyne. From here the A815 heads southwest to Strachur before heading inland to **Loch Eck**, an exceptionally narrow freshwater loch, squeezed between steeply banked woods. Halfway down, there's a rugged, scenic road off to the pretty village of **ARDENTINNY** on the west side of Loch Long, which boasts the finest sandy beach on Cowal. There's just one **hotel**, the *Ardentinny* (☎036981/209; ④), plus a smattering of **B&Bs** and the *Glenfinart* **caravan park** (April–Oct; ☎036981/256) – though this only has limited space.

At the southern tip of Loch Eck are the **Younger Botanic Gardens** (mid-March to Oct daily 10am–6pm; £1.50), an offshoot of Edinburgh's Royal Botanic Gardens, especially striking for its avenue of Great Redwoods, planted in 1863 and now over 100ft high. You could combine a visit here with one of the most popular of the park's forest walks, the rocky ravine of **Puck's Glen**; the walk begins from the car park a mile south of the gardens (1hr 30min round trip). Another mile further on, **Holy Loch** is Cowal's most densely populated area, whose economy received an unexpected setback in 1991 when the Polaris base ended its thirty-year presence here.

# Dunoon

In the nineteenth century, Cowal's capital, **DUNOON**, grew from a mere village to a major Clyde seaside resort; it is still a favourite holiday spot for Glaswegians, who arrive here by ferry from Gourock. Apart from its practical uses – Cowal's only **tourist office** is on Alexandra Parade (Mon–Fri 9.30am–5pm, Sat–Sun 10am–5pm; ☎0369/3785) and there are plenty of **B&Bs** – there's little to tempt you to linger. The shorter, more frequent of the two **ferry crossings** across the Clyde to Dunoon is the half-hourly *Western Ferries* service to Hunter's Quay, a mile north of the town centre; *CalMac* have the prime position, however, on the main pier.

If you're just passing through and need to **stay** the night, look no further than the centrally located *Caledonian* on George Street (☎0369/2176; ②); around Hunter's Quay, try *Foxbank* on Marine Parade (☎0369/3858; ②). Plusher accommodation can be had at the *Argyll* on Argyll Street (☎0369/3858; ⑤), or the highly reputable *Ardfillayne*, West Bay (☎0369/2267; ⑦). The nearest **campsite** is *Cot House* at Kilmun (April–Oct; ☎036984/351), on the north side of Holy Loch, or else there's the *Stratheck* site by the Botanical Gardens (April–Oct; ☎036984/472). *Chatters*, 85 John St, is Dunoon's best restaurant, offering delicious Loch Fyne seafood. The **Cowal Highland Gathering**, one of Scotland's largest pipe band competitions, is held here on the last weekend in August.

# Southwest Cowal

The mellow landscape of **southwest Cowal**, in complete contrast to the bustle of Dunoon or the Highland grandeur of the forest, becomes immediate as soon as you head west to Loch Striven, where, from either side, there are few more beautiful sights than the **Kyles of Bute**, the thin slithers of water which separate the bleak bulk of north Bute from Cowal.

**COLINTRAIVE**, on the eastern Kyle, marks the narrowest point in the Kyles – barely more than a couple of hundred yards – and is the place from which the small *CalMac* car ferry to Bute departs. However, the most popular spots from which to appreciate the Kyles are the twin villages of **TIGHNABRUAICH**, which has a **youth hostel** (☎0700811/622; Grade 2), and its smaller, more attractive neighbour, **KAMES**. On the seafront, the *Kames Hotel* (☎0700811/489; ③) has wonderful views over the Kyles, as does the *Piermount* (☎0700811/218; ②).

The Kyles can get busy in July and August, but you can escape the crowds head up Cowal's deserted west coast, overlooking Loch Fyne. The one brief glimpse of habitation is the whitewashed hamlet of **KILFINAN**, set back from a sandy bay seven miles by road from Tighnabruaich, with just one, expensive hotel, the *Kilfinan* (☎0700/82201; ⑥). Further up the coast there was once a ferry link to Lochgilphead from **OTTER FERRY**, its name not derived from the furry beast but from the Gaelic *Oitir* (sandbank), which juts out a mile or so into Loch Fyne. If you're heading for Knapdale, Kintyre or Islay, you can avoid the long haul up Loch Fyne by using the **ferry service to Tarbert** from Portavadie (July & Aug only).

# Isle of Bute

Thanks to its consistently mild climate and the ferry link with Wemyss Bay (see p.182), the island of **Bute** has been a popular holiday and convalescence spot for Clydesiders – particularly the elderly – for over a century. Even considering the island's small size (fifteen miles long and up to five miles wide) you can escape the crowds; most of its inhabitants are centred around the two wide bays on the east coast of the island.

Bute's one and only town, **ROTHESAY**, is a long-established resort, set in a wide sweeping bay, backed by green hills, with a classic promenade, pagoda-style Winter Gardens and a pier whose gents' lavatories, built in 1899, have been declared a national treasure. Rothesay also boasts the impressive moated ruins of **Rothesay Castle** (April–Sept Mon–Sat 9.30am–6pm, Sun 2–6pm; Oct–March closes 4pm; £1.20), hidden amid the town's backstreets but signposted from the pier. Built in the twelfth century, it was twice captured by the Vikings in the 1400s; such vulnerability was the reasoning behind the unusual, almost circular curtain wall, which features four big drum towers, of which only one remains fully intact.

Of the rest of the island, the north is hilly, uninhabited and little visited, and **KILCHATTAN**, on the southern tip, is where you should head if you want to relax by the sea. The early history of the island is recalled at **St Blane's Chapel**, a twelfth-century ruin beautifully situated in open countryside two miles south of Kilchattan, and at **St Ninian's Point**, five miles west of Rothesay, where the ruins of a sixth-century chapel overlook a fine sandy strand and the uninhabited island of **Inchmarnock**. For the best overall view of the island, take a walk up **Canada Hill** above the freshwater Loch Fad, which all but divides the island in two.

## Practicalities

Rothesay's **tourist office**, 15 Victoria St (summer daily 9am–5pm; winter Mon–Thurs 9am–5.30pm, Fri 9am–5pm; ☎0700/502 151) can help with accommodation, though there's no shortage of B&Bs along the seafront from Rothesay to Port Banntyne. The grandest **place to stay** is the giant, former spa sanatorium *Glenburn Hotel*, Glenburn Rd (☎0700/502 500; ⑤), others like the *Commodore* at 12 Battery Place (☎0700/502 178; ③) or the distinctive-looking *Glendale*, at no. 20 (☎0700/502 329; ②), both up E Princes Street, are more modest. For **bike rental**, try *Calder Bros*, 7 Bridge St or the *Bute Electrical Centre*, E Princes St.

Apart from the plush *Queen's Restaurant* in the *Victoria Hotel* on Victoria Street, **food** options are limited to pasta and steak at *Oliver's*, also on Victoria Street, or the simple dishes served at the Winter Gardens bistro on the prom. Bute holds its own **Highland Games** on the last weekend in August, plus a newly established international **folk festival** on the last weekend in July, and a mainly trad-**jazz festival** during May Bank Holiday.

# Inveraray and around

A classic example of an eighteenth-century planned town, **INVERARAY** was built on the site of a ruined fishing village in 1745 by the third Duke of Argyll, head of the powerful Campbell clan, in order to distance his newly rebuilt castle from hoi polloi in the town and to establish a commercial and legal centre for the region. Today Inveraray, an absolute set-piece of Scottish Georgian architecture, has a truly memorable setting, the brilliant white arches of Front Street reflected in the still waters of Loch Fyne, which separate it from the Cowal peninsula.

# The Town

Squeezed onto a headland some distance from the duke's new castle, there's not much more to Inveraray's "New Town" than its distinctive **Main Street**, flanked by whitewashed terraces, whose window casements are picked out in black. At the top of the street, the road divides to circumnavigate the town's Neoclassical church, originally built in two parts: the southern half served the Gaelic-speaking community, while the northern half (still in use) served those who spoke English.

East of the church is **Inveraray Jail** (April–Oct daily 9.30am–6pm; Nov–March daily 10am–5pm; £2.50), whose attractive Georgian courthouse and grim prison-blocks ceased to function in the 1930s. The jail is now an imaginative and thoroughly enjoyable museum, which graphically recounts conditions from medieval times up until the nineteenth century. You can also sit in the beautiful semi-circular court house and listen to the trial of a farmer accused of fraud.

During the replanning of the town, the **Inveraray Cross** was moved to its present position at the other end of Main Street by the loch, while another cross from Tiree was placed in the castle gardens; both date from the fifteenth century and feature intricate figural scenes. For a panoramic view of the town, castle and loch, you can climb the **Bell Tower** (May–Sept 10am–1pm & 2–5pm, Sun 2–5pm; free) of All Saints' Church, accessible through the screen arches on Front Street, and built as a war memorial to the fallen Campbells by the tenth Duke of Argyll.

Slightly removed from the New Town, to the north, the mock-Gothic **Inveraray Castle** (April–June, Sept & Oct Mon–Thurs & Sat 10am–1pm & 2–6pm, Sun 1–6pm; July & Aug Mon–Sat 10am–6pm, Sun 1–6pm; £3) remains the family home of the Duke of Argyll. Built in 1745 by the third duke, it was given a touch of the Loire with the addition of dormer windows and conical roofs in the nineteenth century. Inside, the most startling feature is the armoury hall, whose displays of weaponry – supplied to the Campbells to put down the Jacobites – rise through several storeys. Gracing the castle's extensive grounds is one of three elegant bridges built during the relandscaping of Inveraray (the other two are on the road from Glen Kinglas), while the **Combined Operations Museum** (same times as castle; £1) in the old stables recalls the wartime role of Inveraray as a training centre for the D-Day landings, during which over half a million troops practised secret amphibious manoeuvres around Loch Fyne.

## Auchindrain Folk Museum

Six miles southwest of Inveraray, the **Auchindrain Folk Museum** (Easter–Sept daily 10am–5pm; £2.20), is in fact an old township of around twenty thatched buildings packed full of domestic memorabilia to give an idea of life here before the Clearances, and before the planning of towns like neighbouring Inveraray. Demonstrations are held of the old "run rig" strip-farming methods used in the eighteenth and nineteenth centuries, and the informative visitor centre has a good bookshop and a tearoom.

## Practicalities

The **tourist office** is on Front Street (Mon–Fri 10am–1pm & 2–5pm; ☎0499/ 2063), as is the town's chief **hotel**, the historic *Great Inn* (April–Oct ☎0499/2466; ④). There's a **B&B** on Main Street East, and a couple beyond the petrol station on the Campbeltown road: *Arch House* (☎0499/2289; ②) and *Glen Eynord* (☎0499/2031; ②). The **youth hostel** (☎0499/2454; Grade 2) is just up the Oban road. The old Royal Navy base, two miles down the A83, is now the *Argyll Caravan Park* (☎0499/2285). With a population of just four hundred, Inveraray is understandably a little short on **nightlife**; the bar of the *George Hotel* (☎0499/2111) in the middle of town is the liveliest spot, while for coffee, cakes and **full meals** most people head for the *Great Inn* .

The best place to sample Loch Fyne's delicious fresh fish is six miles back up the A83 towards Glasgow at the *Loch Fyne Oyster Bar* (☎0499/6264), which offers a variety of oak-smoked seafood at reasonable prices; the shop sells picnic supplies.

# Loch Awe

Legend has it that **Loch Awe** – at over twenty-five miles in length, the longest stretch of freshwater in the country – was created by a witch and inhabited by a monster even more gruesome than the one at Loch Ness. Dotted around the north of the loch, where it's joined by the A819 from Inveraray to Oban, are several tiny islands which now sport picturesque ruins; on **Inishail** you can see a crumbling thirteenth-century chapel which once served as a burial ground for the MacArthur clan; the ruined castle on **Fraoch Eilean** dates from the same period. Before moving to Inveraray in 1746, the Campbells had their headquarters at the fifteenth-century **Kilchurn Castle**, strategically situated on a rocky spit – once an island – at the head of the loch. Now one of Argyll's most photogenic lochside ruins, Kilchurn has been abandoned to the elements since being struck by lightning in the 1760s.

If you have time to linger, it's worth seeking out two interesting churches in the area. The first is the unusual octagonal **Dalmally parish church**, built in the early nineteenth century and set on high ground above the River Lochy beyond the village itself, two miles east of Kilchurn. The second, **St Conan's Church** in the village of **LOCHAWE**, a mile or so west of Kilchurn, was designed in the early part of this century by a Campbell, whose foray into every style from Roman to Norman manages somehow to meld successfully.

### Cruachan Power Station and the Pass of Brander

Further on, gorged into the giant granite bulk of Ben Cruachan (3695ft), is the underground **Cruachan Power Station** (daily 9am–4.30pm; £1.80), built in 1965. A mildly interesting half-hour guided tour sets off every hour from the visitors' centre by the loch, taking you to a viewing platform above the generating room deep inside the mountain. Using the water from an artificial loch high up on Ben Cruachan to drive the turbines, the power station can become fully operational in less than two minutes, supplying electricity during surges on the National Grid. Sadly it takes ten percent more electricity to pump the water back up into the artificial loch, so the station only manages to make a profit by buying cheap off-peak power and selling during daytime peak demand. If you're keen to go, make sure you get there before the queues start to form as they do during the summer.

In order to maintain the right level of water in Loch Awe itself, a dam was built at the mouth of the loch, which then had to be fitted with a special lift to transport the salmon – for which the loch is justly famous – upriver to spawn. From the dam, the

River Awe squeezes through the mountains via the gloomy **Pass of Brander** (which means "ambush" in Gaelic), where Robert the Bruce put to flight the MacDougall clan, cutting them down as they fought with one another to cross the river and escape. As you begin to approach Loch Etive, a sign to the right invites you to visit the *Inverawe Fisheries and Smokery*, where you can buy traditionally smoked local fish and mussels, or picnic while you admire the view over the loch.

# Oban and around

The solidly Victorian resort of **OBAN** enjoys a superb setting – the island of Kerrera providing its bay with a natural shelter – distinguished by a bizarre granite amphitheatre, dramatically lit at night, on the hilltop above the town. Despite a population of just seven thousand, it's by far the largest port in northwest Scotland, the largest place in Argyll, and the main departure point for many of the Hebrides. If you arrive late, or are catching an early ferry, you may well find yourself staying the night (though there's no real need otherwise); if you're staying elsewhere, it's a useful base for wet-weather activities and shopping, although it does get uncomfortably crowded in the summer.

### The Town

The only real sight in Oban is the town's landmark, **McCaig's Folly**, a stiff ten-minute climb from the quayside. An imitation of the Coliseum in Rome, it was the brainchild of a local banker a century ago, who had the twin aims of alleviating unemployment among the local stonemasons and creating a family mausoleum. Work never progressed further than the exterior walls before McCaig died, but the folly provides a wonderful seaward panorama, particularly at sunset. Equally beautiful evening views can be had by walking along the northern shore of the bay, past the modern, Catholic **St Columba Cathedral**, to the rocky ruins of **Dunollie Castle**, a MacDougall stronghold on a very ancient site, successfully defended by the laird's Jacobite wife during the 1715 uprising but abandoned after 1745.

You can pass a few hours watching the bustling harbour life; or, if the weather's bad, check out the glass-blowers working at the furnaces of the **Caithness Glassworks**, in the new, somewhat pretentiously named Oban Experience Centre by the train station. You can also take a 45-minute guided tour of the **Oban Distillery** (Mon–Fri 9.30am–5pm; Easter–Oct also Sat; £2), in the centre of town off George Street, which ends with a dram of whisky. **The World in Miniature** (April–Oct daily 10am–6pm; £1.50), on the north pier, contains an assortment of minute "dolls' house" rooms, with even a couple of mini-Charles Rennie Mackintosh interiors to admire.

### Practicalities

The *CalMac* **ferry terminal** for the islands is a stone's throw from the **train station**, itself adjacent to the **bus terminus**. A host of private **boat operators** can be found around the harbour, particularly along its northern side: their excursions – direct to the castles of Mull, to Staffa and the Treshnish Islands – are worth considering, particularly if you're pushed for time, or have no transport. Alternatively, you can rent a **bike** from *Oban Cycles*, 9 Craigard Rd, or a **boat** from *Borroboats*, on the Gallanach Road.

The **tourist office** (summer Mon–Sat 9.15am–8.45pm, Sun 10am–5pm; shorter hours the rest of year; ☎0631/63122) is tucked away on Argyll Square just east of the bus station; a £1 fee is charged for finding **accommodation**. Should you wish to look for yourself, there's a whole host of grandiose Victorian **hotels** to choose from on the quayside, ranging from the *Columba* (☎0631/62183; ⑥) on the north pier to the *Palace* (☎0631/622 294; ⑦) on George Street, plus dozens of **B&Bs** on Dunollie Road beyond George Street – try *Glendale* (☎0631/63877; ②) or *Glengorm* (☎0631/65361; ②) – and on Ardconnel Road, just below McCaig's Tower. The **youth hostel** (☎0631/62025; Grade 1) is on the Esplanade, just beyond the cathedral, and there's an **independent hostel** run by Jeremy Ingles at 21 Aird's Crescent (☎0631/65065; ①). The nearest **campsite** is about three miles north at Ganavan Sands (☎0631/62179).

The best **restaurant** in town is the *Waterfront* (☎0631/63110), between the train station and the quay, which does both bar food and à la carte meals. The town's **fish-and-chip** shops are also better than average; try *Onorio's* on George Street. Oban's one and only good **pub** is the *Oban Inn* opposite the north pier, with a classic dark-wood-and-brass bar downstairs and food in the lounge upstairs.

# Around Oban

There are a few, palpably low-key attractions around Oban – good if it's raining and you have kids in tow, but not otherwise worth going out of your way for. A couple of miles east of Oban, up Glencruitten Road, the **Rare Breeds Farm Park** (late March–Sept daily 10am–5.30pm; mid-June to Aug closes 7.30pm; £2.50) displays rare but indigenous species of deer, cattle, sheep and so forth – with a children's corner where they can meet the baby animals. Less compelling for kids is the **Salmon Centre**, seven miles south of Oban; for £2 you can view the cages out in the loch. The real reason for coming here, though, is to sample the wonderful seafood in the farm's excellent restaurant.

**Dunstaffnage Castle** (April–Sept Mon–Sat 9.30am–6pm, Sun 2–6pm; £1.50), two miles up the coast from Oban, has even less to offer for children or adults. The curtain wall battlements are safe and fun to climb and give out views across to Lismore, Appin and Morvern, but there's not much else to get excited about this old MacDougall fort, which was later handed over to the Campbells. Visible from the castle is the Connel cantilever bridge which crosses the sea cataract at the mouth of Loch Etive, taking you onto the hammerhead peninsula of Benderloch ("the hill between two lochs"). On its northern shores, overlooking Loch Creran, is **Barcaldine Castle**, an early seventeenth-century Campbell towerhouse, recently modernized and privately owned but occasionally open to the public (☎0631172/214).

Since the weather in this part of Scotland can be bad at almost any time of the year, it's also as well to know about the **Sea Life Centre** (Feb–Nov daily 10am–6pm; Dec & Jan Sat & Sun only; £3), situated along Loch Creran on the A828. Here you can see locally caught sea creatures at close quarters – look out for the octopus and stingray – before they are returned to the sea at the end of the season.

Having circumnavigated the loch, you enter the district of **Appin**, setting for Robert Louis Stevenson's *Kidnapped*, a fictionalized account of the murder of Colin Campbell by one of the disenfranchized Stewart clan. The name Appin derives from the Gaelic *Abthaine*, meaning "Lands belonging to the Abbey", in this case the one of Lismore, which is still linked to Port Appin by a passenger ferry. One of Argyll's most romantic ruined castles, **Castle Stalker** occupies an island just north of Port Appin. Built by the Stewarts, it was taken by the Campbells on two occasions, but is now in private ownership and being restored; phone ☎08832/3994 to enquire about visits.

## Kerrera

**Gallanach**, two miles down the coast from Oban, is the ferry departure point for the low-lying island of **Kerrera**, which shelters Oban harbour from the worst of the westerly winds. Measuring just five by two miles, it is easily explored on foot, and gives panoramic views from its highest point – 600ft above the sea – over to Mull, the Slate Islands, Lismore, Jura and beyond. However, as the island has a total population of less than twenty, you should bring your own food and drink with you. The passenger-only ferry (Mon–Sat only) lands at **Port Kerrera**. If the weather's fine and you feel like lazing by the sea, head for the island's finest sandy beach, **Slatrach Bay**, just one mile west of the ferry slip. Otherwise, the most rewarding trail is down to **Gylen Castle**, a cliff-top ruin on the south coast, built in 1582 by the MacDougalls and burnt to the ground by the Covenanter General Leslie in the Civil War. You can head to the ferry back via the Drove Road, where cattle from Mull and other islands were once herded to be swum across the sound to market in Oban.

## Lismore

Legend has it that Saints Columba and Moluag both fancied the skinny island of **Lismore** as a missionary base, but as they raced towards it Moluag cut off his finger and threw it ashore ahead of Columba, claiming the land for himself. Lismore is undoubtedly one of the most fertile of the Inner Hebrides – its name, coined by Moluag himself, derives from the Gaelic *lios mór* meaning "sacred enclosure" – and at one time it supported more than one thousand inhabitants. The population today is about a quarter of that size.

Of Moluag's sixth-century foundation nothing remains, but in 1236 the island became the seat of the Bishop of Argyll, and shortly afterwards the diminutive **Cathedral of St Moluag** was built at **CLACHAN**, a mile and a half north of the main village of Achnacroish. The remnants of the cathedral are now incorporated into the parish church, which, though much altered, exhibits elements of the original medieval building. East of the church, **Tirefour Castle**, a circular stone fort over two thousand years old, occupies a commanding position and boasts walls over almost 10ft thick in places. West of Clachan are the much more recent ruins of **Castle Coeffin**, an old MacDougall fortress, once haunted by the ghost of Bheothail, sister of the Norse prince Caiffen. Two other places worth exploring are **Salen**, an abandoned quarry village on the west coast, and the ruins of **Achadun Castle**, in the southwest, where the bishops are thought to have resided.

There are two **ferries** serving Lismore; a *CalMac* car ferry from Oban to Achnacroish (Mon–Sat twice daily; 50min), and a shorter passenger-only crossing from Port Appin to the island's north point (Mon–Sat every 2hr; 15min). **Accommodation** on the island is limited to the *Isle of Lismore Guest House* (②), a couple of B&Bs – try *Ach-na-Croish* (☎063176/241; ②) or the self-catering cottages at *Bailuachraidh Farm* (☎063176/213).

# The Slate Islands and the Garvellachs

Eight miles south of Oban on the A816, a road heads off west to a small group of islands commonly called the **Slate Islands**, which at their peak in the mid-nineteenth century quarried over nine million slates annually. Today they're almost entirely depopulated, and an inevitable air of melancholy hangs over them, but their dramatic setting amid crashing waves make them a good day trip.

## Seil

The most northerly of the group is the **Isle of Seil**, separated from the mainland by the thinnest of sea channels and spanned by Thomas Telford's elegant hump-backed **Clachan Bridge**, known as the "only bridge over the Atlantic". The main village on Seil is **ELLANBEICH**, its neat white terrraces of workers' cottages crouching below the black cliffs of Dùn Mór on the westernmost tip of the island. This was once the tiny island of Eilean a'Beithich, separated from the mainland by a narrow channel until the intensive slate quarrying succeeded in silting it up. Confusingly it's often referred to by the same name as the nearby island of Easdale, since they formed an interdependent community based exclusively around the slate industry.

## Easdale

**Easdale** remains an island, though the few hundred yards which separate it from Ellanbeich have constantly to be dredged to keep the channel open. On the eve of a great storm of November 23, 1881, Easdale, less than a mile across at any one point, enjoyed a population of 452. That night, waves engulfed the island and flooded the quarries – the island never really recovered and by 1960 the population was reduced to seven. Recently many of the old cottages have been restored, some as holiday homes, others sold to new families. The **museum** (April–Oct daily 10.30am–4.30pm; £1), near the main square, has a useful historical map of the island, which you can walk round in about half an hour. A **ferry** runs on demand (April–Sept Mon–Sat 7.30am–9pm, Sun 10.30am–5pm), and there's a nice **tea-room** near the quayside, plus a **B&B** further inland (☎08523/438; ②).

## Luing

At the southern tip of Seil a summer car ferry (Mon–Sat 8am–6pm) crosses the narrow, treacherous Cuan Sound to the **Isle of Luing**, a long, thin, fertile island which once supported a population of six hundred crofting families. During the Clearances the population was drastically reduced to make way for cattle; the island is still renowned for its beef and has cultivated a successful new crossbreed.

In **CULLIPOOL**, the main village, quarrying ceased in 1965, and the place now relies on tourism and lobster fishing. You can take a boat trip across the treacherous Sound of Luing, to abandoned **Belnahua**, the most northerly of the group of islands offshore. Luing's only other village, **TOBERONOCHY**, lies on the more sheltered west coast, three miles southwest of Cullipool, its distinctive white cottages, as on the other islands, built by the slate company in 1805.

## Scarba and the Garvellachs

**Scarba** is the largest of the islands around Luing, a brooding 1500-foot hulk of slate, inhospitable and wild – the few families who once lived here had all left by the mid-nineteenth century. To the south, the raging **Gulf of Corrievreckan** is site of one of the world's most spectacular whirlpools, thought to be caused by a rocky pinnacle which lies below the sea. It remains calm only for an hour or two at high and low tide; at flood tide, accompanied by a westerly wind, water shoots deafeningly some 20ft up in the air. Inevitably there are numerous legends about the place, which is known as *Coire Bhreacain* (Speckled Cauldron) in Gaelic, concerning *Cailleach*, the Celtic storm goddess.

Boat trips from Oban and Toberonochy and the Cuan Sound on Luing visit a string of uninhabited islands west of Luing, known collectively as the **Garvellachs**. Their name derives from the largest of the group, Garbh Eileach (Rough Rock), which was inhabited as recently as fifty years ago. The most northerly, Dùn Chonnuill, contains the remains of an old fort thought to have belonged to Conal of Dalriada, and Eileach an Naoimh (Holy Isle), the most southerly of the group, is where the Celtic missionary Brendan the Navigator founded a community in 542, some twenty years before Columba landed on Iona. Nothing survives from Brendan's day, but there are a few ninth-century remains, among them a double-beehive cell and a grave enclosure. For some reason many people believe that the island is Hinba, Columba's legendary secret retreat, where he buried his mother.

# Mull

The second largest of the Inner Hebrides, **MULL** is by far the most accessible – just forty minutes away from Oban by daily ferry. First impressions largely depend on the weather, for without the sun the large tracts of moorland, particularly around the island's highest peak, Ben More, can appear bleak and unwelcoming. There are, however, areas of more gentle pastoral scenery around Dervaig and Salen in the north, and the indented west coast varies from the sandy beaches around Calgary to the cliffs of Loch na Keal. The most common mistake is to try and "do" the island in a day or two: Mull is a place that will grow on you only if you have the time and patience to explore.

Historically, crofting, whisky distilling and fishing supported the islanders (Muileachs), but the population decreased dramatically in the nineteenth century due to the Clearances and the potato famine. Happily on Mull, it is a trend that has been reversed, with a large influx of settlers from elsewhere in the country. One of the main reasons for this resurgence is of course mass tourism, although oddly enough, there are very few large hotels or campsites, and B&Bs still dominate the accommodation scene. Public transport is limited, and the roads are exclusively single-track, which can cause serious congestion in summer.

## Around Craignure

**CRAIGNURE** is the main entry point to Mull, linked to Oban by several car ferries daily; a faster, less frequent car ferry service crosses from Lochaline on the Morvern peninsula (see p.363) to Fishnish, six miles northwest of Craignure. Fishnish is just a slipway and Craignure itself is little more than a scattering of cottages, though there is a **tourist office** (Mon & Fri 9am–5.30pm, Tues–Thurs & Sat 9.45am–6.45pm; July & Aug also Sun 10.45am–6.45pm; ☎06802/377), a couple of **guesthouses**, a **campsite**, plus the occasional bus connection with Tobermory and a **bike rental** outlet (☎06802/487).

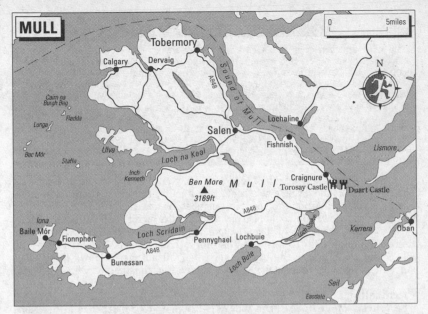

Two castles lie immediately to the east of Craignure. The first, **Torosay Castle** (mid-April to mid-Oct daily 10.30am–6.30pm; £3.50), is linked to Craignure by the narrow gauge *Mull Rail* link (summer only). The magnificent garden (daily 9am–7pm; £1.50) with its avenue of eighteenth-century statues and views over to neighbouring Duart, is the highlight; the house itself, in the full-blown mid-nineteenth-century Scottish Baronial style, is stuffed with junk relating to the present owners, the little-known Guthries, all of it amusingly captioned but of no particular interest. Lacking the gardens, but on a much more aesthetic spit of rock, fifteen minutes' walk east of Torosay, **Duart Castle** (May–Sept daily 10.30am–6pm; £2) is a real medieval fortress, the headquarters of the once-powerful MacLean clan until the late seventeenth century when it was left to rot by the Campbells; only in 1911 did the MacLeans manage to buy it back. You can peek in the dungeons and ascend the ramparts, but the castle is seen to best advantage from the ferry.

Both Torosay and Duart are inundated with visitors in the high season – not so **LOCHBUIE**, a peaceful, sandy bay ten miles or so southwest of Craignure. The shore is dominated by the fifteenth-century ivy-strewn ruins of **Moy Castle**, an old MacLaine stronghold, and north of the castle is one of the few **stone circles** in the west of Scotland.

## Tobermory

Mull's chief town, **TOBERMORY**, is easily the most attractive fishing port on the west coast of Scotland, its clusters of brightly-coloured houses and boats sheltering in a bay backed by a steep bluff. Founded in 1788 by the British Fisheries Society – the upper town is a classic grid-plan village – it never really took off as a fishing port and only survived due to the steady influx of crofters evicted from other parts of the island during the Clearances.

### THE TOBERMORY TREASURE

The most dramatic event in Tobermory's history was in 1588 when a ship from the Spanish Armada sank in mysterious circumstances while having repairs done to its sails and rigging. The story goes that one of the MacLeans of Duart was taken prisoner, but when the ship weighed anchor, he made his way to the powder magazine and blew it up. However, several versions of the story exist, and even the identity of the ship is in dispute: some say it was the treasure-laden Spanish galleon *Florida*, while others assert that it was the *San Juan de Sicilia*, a troop carrier for the Spanish Armada. Whatever the truth, the possibility of precious sunken booty at the bottom of Tobermory harbour has fired the greed of numerous lairds and kings – as recently as the 1950s Royal Navy divers were engaged by the Duke of Argyll in the seemingly futile activity of diving for treasure.

If you're staying any length of time on Mull, you're bound to end up here – for one thing, it has the island's sole bank. But practicalities aside, there's little to do beside watch the harbour go about its business, or take a stroll to the upper town to admire the view. You could also pay a visit to the small **Mull Museum** (Mon–Fri 10.30am–4.30pm, Sat 10.30am–1.30pm; 50p), on the main street. Alternatively, there's the minuscule **Tobermory Distillery** (Easter–Sept Mon–Fri 10am–4pm; £2) at the south end of the bay, founded in 1795 but closed down three times since then. Recently reopened, it offers a guided tour finishing off with a tasting.

### Practicalities

The **tourist office** (daily 9am–1pm & 2–5.30pm; ☎0688/2182) is in the same building as the *CalMac* ticket office at the northern end of the harbour; while you're there, be sure to pick up the free Mull listings broadsheet *Round & About*. If you're looking for **bike rental**, head for *Tom-a'Mhuillin* on the Salen road.

The tourist office can book you into a **B&B** for a £1 fee – not a bad idea since many places are a stiff climb from the harbour. There are, however, several on the main street – try *Failte* (☎0688/2495; ②) or the *Tobermory Hotel* (☎0688/2091; ⑤) – though these tend to fill up early. The island's **youth hostel** is also on the main street (☎0688/2481; Grade 3). The grand Victorian *Western Isles Hotel* (☎0688/2012; ⑥) overlooks the bay, as do several of the cheaper B&Bs on Argyll Terrace such as *Kilmory* (☎0688/2232; ②) or *Ivybank* (☎0688/2250; ②). The nearest **campsite** is by the Mishnish lochs on the Dervaig road.

For **eating**, it's best to avoid the places on the main street. Tobermory's best restaurant is the *Strongarbh House* (☎0688/2328), situated behind the *Western Isles Hotel*. The lively bar of the *Mishnish*, on the main street, is the local hangout, and the focus of Mull's annual **Traditional Music Festival**, a feast of Gaelic folk music held on the last weekend in April.

## Along the coast

The soft crofting countryside west of Tobermory, beyond the Mishnish lochs, provides some of the most beguiling scenery on the island. The main village, **DERVAIG**, with its pencil-shaped church spire and spick and span cottages, nestles beside a narrow sea loch just eight miles southwest of Tobermory. Dervaig is home to the underfunded *Mull Little Theatre*, one of the smallest professional theatres in the world, which puts on an adventurous season of plays adapted for just two resident actors (May–Sept; booking advised ☎06884/245). Charles Dickens once stayed at the *Ardbeg House* (☎06884/254; ③), still the best hotel in town; other options include *Antuim Farm* (☎06884/230; ②) or the vegetarian *Glenbellart* (☎06884/282; ③). Pricy pre-theatre dinners are available from the *Druimard Country House* (☎06884/345). From Dervaig, the road continues across country to **CALGARY**, once a thriving crofting community, now an idyllic holiday spot boasting Mull's finest sandy bay, but with self-catering accommodation only.

## Ulva
Barely a hundred yards of sea separate Mull from the island of **Ulva**, which had its heyday in the early nineteenth century, exporting huge quantities of kelp for glass and soap production. The population peaked at around five hundred, before the kelp industry collapsed and the 1847 potato famine hit; nowadays barely twenty people live here. A small passenger-only ferry to Ulva is available on demand (mid-April to mid–Oct Mon–Fri 8am–5pm; June–Aug also Sun; £2 return). *The Boathouse*, near the ferry slip, sells sandwiches and fresh oysters, and features a display on the history of the island. There's no accommodation, but with permission from the present owners (☎06885/226), you can camp rough overnight.

## Staffa and the Treshnish Isles
Five miles southwest of Ulva, **Staffa** is the most romantic and dramatic of Scotland's many uninhabited islands. On its south side, the perpendicular rockface features an imposing series of black basalt columns, known as the Collonade, which have been cut by the sea into cathedralesque caverns, most notably **Fingal's Cave**. The Vikings knew about the island – the name derives from their word for "Island of Staves" – but it wasn't until 1772 that it was "discovered" by the world. Turner painted it, Wordsworth and Keats explored it, but Mendelssohn's *Die Fingalshölle*, inspired by the sounds of the sea-wracked caves he heard on a visit here in 1829, did most to popularize the place. The geological explanation for these polygonal basalt organ pipes is that they were created by a massive subterranean explosion some sixty million years ago. A huge mass of molten basalt ejaculated onto land and, as it cooled, solidified into what are, essentially, crystals. Of course, confronted with such artistry, most visitors have found it difficult to believe that their origin is entirely natural – indeed, the various Celtic folk tales, which link the phenomenon with the Giant's Causeway in Ireland, are certainly more appealing. To get to Staffa, join one of the many boat trips from Oban, Ulva Ferry, Dervaig and Fionnphort, weather permitting (return trip for around £10).

Several boat trips combine a visit to Staffa with a tour of the archipelago of uninhabited rocky islets that make up the **Treshnish Isles** northwest of Staffa. The most distinctive is **Bac Mór**, shaped like a puritan's hat and popularly dubbed the Dutchman's Cap, while **Lunga**, the largest island, is visited for its wildlife; it is a nesting place for auks and puffins, and an autumn breeding ground for grey seals. One of the northerly islands, **Cairn na Burgh Beg**, has the remains of a ruined castle, which served as a lookout post for the lords of the Isles and was last garrisoned in the Civil War.

## Ben More and the Ross of Mull
Round the coast from Ulva Ferry, the road hugs the shores of Loch na Keal, which almost splits Mull in two. South of the loch rise the terraced slopes of **Ben More** (3169ft), a mighty extinct volcano. Beyond Derryguaig, the road carves through the sheer cliffs before heading south past the Gribun rocks which face the tiny island of **Inch Kenneth**, once owned by the Mitford family. There are great views

out to Staffa and the Treshnish Isles as the road climbs over the pass to Loch Scribain, where it joins the equally dramatic Glen More road from Craignure.

Stretching for twenty miles west of the road junction as far as Iona is the rocky peninsula known as the **Ross of Mull,** which, like much of Scotland, appears blissfully tranquil in good weather, and desolate and bleak in bad. Most visitors simply drive through the Ross en route to Iona, but given that accommodation is severely limited on Iona, it's worth staying here. The *Pennyghael Hotel* (☎06814 205/288; ⑥), overlooking Loch Scridain, is a luxury option; **BUNESSAN,** roughly two thirds of the way along the Ross, has more choice with the *Assapol Country House* (☎06817/258; ④) and B&Bs such as *Ardtun House* (☎06817/264; ②). **FIONNPHORT**, facing Iona, is the least attractive place to stay, but offers many B&Bs; try *Seaview* (☎06817/235; ②) or *Bruach Mhor* (☎06817/276; ②), which caters for vegetarians and vegans.

# Iona

Minutes away from the southwestern tip of Mull, **IONA**, although just three miles long and no more than a mile wide, manages to encapsulate all the enchantment and mystique of the Hebrides. It is frequently tagged "the cradle of Christianity": Saint Columba arrived here from Ireland in 563 and established a monastery which was responsible for the conversion of more or less all of pagan Scotland as well as much of northern England. This history and the island's splendid isolation have lent it a peculiar religiosity; in the words of Dr Johnson, "that man is little to be envied ... whose piety would not grow warmer among the ruins of Iona". Today, however, the island can barely cope with its thousands of daytrippers, so to appreciate the special atmosphere and to have time to see the whole island, including the often overlooked west coast, you should plan on staying at least one night.

## Some history

Legend has it that **Saint Columba** (Colum), born in Donegal in 521 AD, was a direct descendant of the Irish king, Niall of the Nine Hostages. A scholar and soldier priest, who founded numerous monasteries in Ireland, he became involved in a bloody dispute with the king when he refused to hand over a psalm book copied illegally from the original owned by St Finian of Moville. At the Battle of Cooldrumman, Columba's forces won, though with great loss of life; repenting this bloodshed, he went into exile with twelve other monks, eventually settling on Iona in 563. The modern Gaelic name for the island is *I Chaluim Chille* (Island of Columba's Church), often abbreviated simply to *I* (Gaelic for "island"). Columba's miraculous feats included defeating the Loch Ness monster and banishing snakes (and, some say, frogs) from the island.

During his lifetime, Iona enjoyed a great deal of autonomy from Rome, establishing a specifically Celtic Christian tradition. Missionaries were sent out to the rest of Scotland and parts of England and Iona quickly became a respected seat of learning and artistry; the monks compiled a vast library of intricately illuminated manuscripts – most famously the *Book of Kells* – while the masons excelled in carving peculiarly intricate crosses. Two factors were instrumental in the demise of the Celtic tradition: relentless pressure from the established Church, and a series of Viking raids which culminated in the massacre of 68 monks on the sands of Martyrs' Bay in 803.

By the twelfth century, Iona had become a more conventional centre for the Benedictine order, and its masons enjoyed a second flowering of stone carving before the complex was ransacked during the Reformation as a bastion of the papal Church. Although plans were drawn up at various times to turn the abbey into a Cathedral of the Isles, nothing came of it until its then owner, the Duke of Argyll, donated the abbey buildings to a trust who had restored the abbey church for worship by 1910. Iona's modern resurgence began in 1938, when George MacLeod, a minister from Glasgow, established a group of priests, students and artisans to begin rebuilding the remainder of the monastic buildings. What began as a male, Gaelic-speaking, strictly Presbyterian community is now mostly a lay, mixed and ecumenical retreat. The entire abbey complex has now been successfully restored and the island, apart from the church land and a few crofts, now belongs to the National Trust for Scotland.

# Baile Mór

The ferry from Fionnphort stops at the island's main village, **BAILE MÓR** (literally "large village"), which is in fact little more than a single terrace of cottages facing the red sandstone rocks. Just inland, the ruins of a small **Augustinian nunnery** are built of the same red sandstone. Founded in around 1200, the nunnery fell into disrepair after the Reformation and, if nothing else, gives you an idea of the state of the present-day abbey before it was restored. At a bend in the road just beyond the nunnery stands the fifteenth-century **MacLean's Cross**, a fine example of the distinctive, flowing, three-leaved foliage of the Iona school. To the north is the **Iona Heritage Centre** (Mon 10.30am–4.30pm, Tues–Sat 9.30am–4.30pm; £1), with displays on the history of the island housed in a manse, built, like the nearby parish church, by the ubiquitous Thomas Telford.

## The Abbey

No buildings remain from Columba's time: the present **Abbey** dates from the arrival of the Benedictines in around 1200, was extensively rebuilt in the fifteenth and sixteenth centuries, and restored virtually wholesale in the 1900s. Adjoining the facade is a small steep-roofed chamber, believed to be St Columba's grave, now a small chapel. The three high crosses in front of the abbey date from the eighth to tenth centuries, and are decorated with the Pictish serpent-and-boss and Celtic spirals for which Iona's early Christian masons were renowned. For reasons of sanitation, the cloisters were placed, contrary to the norm, on the north side of the church (where running water was available to flush away the monkish faeces); entirely reconstructed in the late 1950s, they now shelter a useful historical account of the abbey's development through photos and text.

South of the abbey is Iona's oldest building, **St Oran's Chapel**, with a Norman door dating from the eleventh century. It stands at the centre of the sacred burial ground, *Reilig Odhráin*, which is said to contain the graves of numerous kings of Norway, Ireland and Scotland including Shakespeare's Duncan and Macbeth. Archeological evidence has failed to back this up; it's about as likely as the legend that the chapel could only be completed through human sacrifice. Oran, one of the older monks in Columba's entourage, apparently volunteered to be buried alive, and was found to have survived the ordeal when the grave was opened a few days later. Declaring that he had seen hell and it wasn't all bad, he was promptly re-interred for blasphemy. The best of the early Christian gravestones and medieval effigies which once lay in the *Reilig Odhráin* are now the chief exhibits of the **Abbey Museum** in the old infirmary behind the abbey.

## Possible walks

In many ways the landscape of Iona – low-lying, treeless with white sandy coves backed by machair – is more reminiscent of the distant islands of Coll and Tiree than it is of neighbouring Mull. Few tourists bother to stray from Baile Mór, yet in high season there is no better way to appreciate Iona's solitary beauty.

Perhaps the easiest jaunt is up **Dùn I**, Iona's only real hill, which rises to the north of the abbey to a height of 300ft – a great place to wander at dawn or dusk. The west coast has some great sandy beaches; the **Camus Cul an Taibh** (Bay at the Back of the Ocean) by the golf course is the longest. More sheltered is the tiny bay on the south coast, Port na Curaich, also known as **Columba's Bay**, thought to be where the saint first landed and dotted with over fifty small cairns. More difficult to reach is the **disused marble quarry** at Rubha na Carraig Géire, on the southeasternmost point of Iona. Quarried intermittently for several centuries, it was finally closed down in 1914; much of the old equipment still visible rusting away by the shore.

## Practicalities

There's no **tourist office** on Iona, and, as demand far exceeds supply, you should organize **accommodation** in advance. Of the island's two, fairly pricy hotels, the *Argyll* (☎06817/334; ⑨) is the nicer. B&Bs are cheaper but fill up quickly: try *Cruachan* (☎06817/523; ②), *Finlay Ross* (☎06817/357; ②) or *Seaview* (☎06817/373; ②); for longer stays, self-catering is available on Bishop's Walk (☎06817/329). If you want to stay with the Iona Community, contact the MacLeod Centre (☎06817/404) – you must be prepared to participate fully in the daily activities, prayers and religious services. **Camping** is possible with the crofter's permission. Visitors are not allowed to bring cars onto the island, but **bikes** can be rented from *Finlay Ross*. The Iona Community also organizes **guided walks** around the island (March–Oct Wed 10.15am).

**Food** options are limited to hotel restaurants (the *Argyll* is particularly good) or the *Martyrs' Bay* restaurant by the pier. The coffee house (daily 11am–4.30pm) run by the Iona Community just west of the abbey serves homemade soup and delicious cakes.

# Coll and Tiree

**Coll** and **Tiree** are among the most isolated of the Inner Hebrides, and if anything have more in common with the outlying Western Isles than with their closest neighbour, Mull. Each one roughly twelve miles long and three miles wide, both are low-lying, treeless and exceptionally windy, with white sandy beaches and the highest sunshine records in Scotland. Like most of the Hebrides, they were once ruled by Vikings, and didn't pass into Scottish hands until the thirteenth century; both were eventually sold to the Duke of Argyll, in whose estate they remain. Nominally at least, both islands are part of the *Gàidhealtachd* or Gaelic-speaking area of the Hebrides, but the percentage of English-speaking newcomers is rising steadily.

The *CalMac* ferry from Oban calls at Coll and Tiree three times a week throughout the year – more frequently in July and August – which means you should plan on staying at least two nights. Tiree also has an **airport** with more or less daily flights to and from Glasgow.

# Coll

The fish-shaped island of **Coll** (population 150) lies less than seven miles off the coast of Mull. The *CalMac* ferry drops off at **ARINAGOUR** on the western shore of Loch Eatharna, where you'll find the island's post office, petrol pump, two shops, a laundrette and a nine-hole golf course to the northwest. The island's two **hotels** overlook the bay: the *Isle of Coll* (☎08793/334; ④) and the more modern *Tigh-na-Mara* (☎08793/354; ③), which also offers **bike rental**. There's self-catering in Arinagour (☎08793/373), and a couple of **B&Bs** in **ACHA**, two miles west of Arinagour – *Acha House* (☎08793/339; ②) and *Achamore* (☎08793/430; ③). For a change from hotel food, try the *Coll Bistro* (Easter–Oct) in Arinagour's main street, which serves delicious lobster and Mull salmon, as well as venison and beef.

On the southwestern coast there are two edifices – Coll's only formal attractions – both known as **Breacachadh Castle**, built by the MacLeans. The oldest, at the head of Loch Breacacha, is a fifteenth-century towerhouse with an additional curtain wall, recently restored and in private hands; the "new castle", northwest, is made up of a central block built around 1750 and two side-pavilions added a century later. Among the first visitors were Dr Johnson and Boswell, who stayed here after a storm forced them to take refuge en route to Mull. The island's **campsite** (☎08793/374) is on Breacachadh Bay, in the old walled gardens of the castle.

There's little else to see, though you could take a walk over the strip of **giant sand dunes** which link the westernmost tip of Coll with the rest of the island; wander along to **Ben Hogh** – at 339ft, Coll's highest point – or take a look at the **Cairns of Coll**, a series of prehistoric mounds which rise out of the sea off the northern coastline around Bousd and Sorisdale.

# Tiree

**Tiree**, as its Gaelic name *Tìr Iodh* (Land of Corn) suggests, was once known as the breadbasket of the Inner Hebrides, thanks to its acres of rich machair. Nowadays crofting and tourism are the main sources of income for the resident population of eight hundred, and every June the windswept sandy beaches attract large numbers of windsurfers for an international competition.

The *CalMac* ferry calls at **SCARINISH**, on a headland to the west of the great sandy sweep, the *Tràigh Mhór*, of **Gott Bay**. The village has a post office, general store, pub and bank, and a petrol pump by the pier. Of the two **hotels**, the *Tiree Lodge* (☎08792/353; ③), a mile or so along Gott Bay, has the edge over the *Scarinish* (☎08792/308; ③), overlooking the old harbour.

It's just one mile across the island from Gott to Vaul Bay, on the north coast, where the well-preserved remains of a dry-stone broch, **Dun Mor** – dating from the first century BC – lie hidden in the rocks to the west of the bay. From here it's another two miles west along the coast to the *Clach a'Choire* or **Ringing Stone**, a huge boulder decorated with mysterious prehistoric markings, which when struck with a stone gives out a musical sound. The story goes that should the Ringing Stone ever be broken in two, Tiree will sink beneth the waves. A mile further west you come to the *Balephetrish Guest House* (☎08792/353; ③), overlooking the lovely **Balephetrish Bay**.

The most intriguing sights lie in the bulging western half of the island. Tiree's highest hill, **Ben Hynish** (463ft), is unfortunately occupied by a "golf ball" radar station which tracks incoming transatlantic flights; the views from the top, though, are great. Below Ben Hynish is the abandoned **Hynish harbour**, designed by Robert Stevenson in the 1830s, with an ingenious reservoir to prevent silting. **Skerryvore Lighthouse** lies on a sea-swept reef some twelve miles southwest of Tiree. The signal tower, by the row of lightkeepers' houses, has been turned into a **museum** which tells the history of the Herculean effort required to erect this 140-ft lighthouse which was last manned in 1954. The best place to get a glimpse of Skerryvore is from the spectacular headland of **Kenavara** (*Ceann a'Mhara*), two miles southwest of Barrapol, whose cliffs are home to literally thousands of sea birds, including fulmar, kittiwakes, shags and cormorants; the island of Barra is also visible on the northern horizon.

The only transport around the island is the **post bus** which calls at all the main settlements. Otherwise, you'll need to make use of the **bike rental** facilities at the *Tiree Lodge* on Gott Bay. There are no official campsites, but **camping** is allowed with the crofter's permission. As for eating, just north of Barrapoll, the *Glassary Guest House* (☎08792/684; ③) serves local lamb, beef and carrageen seaweed pudding, and offers accommodation too.

# Colonsay and Oronsay

Isolated between Mull and Islay, the craggy hills of **Colonsay** support the occasional patch of woodland, a bewildering array of plant and birdlife, wild goats and rabbits, and one of the finest tropical gardens in Scotland at **Colonsay House**. Although the number of self-catering cottages is steadily increasing, with no camping or caravanning and just one hotel, there's no fear of mass tourism taking over.

The *CalMac* ferry terminal (3 weekly from Oban; 2hr 30min) is at **SCALASAIG**, on the west coast, where there's a post office, a store and *Seaview* (☎09512/315; ③), one of three B&Bs on the island. Colonsay's **hotel**, the *Isle of Colonsay* (☎09512/316; ③), is in **KILORAN**, the other main settlement, two miles north of Scalasaig inland. Giant breakers roll in from the Atlantic across Kiloran Bay, Colonsay's most impressive white sandy beach to the west of Kiloran itself, though the shell beach at Balnahard, a mile further north, is more deserted. The island's west coast forms a sharp escarpment, at its most spectacular just west of Kiloran around Beinn Bhreac (456ft).

**Oronsay**, half a mile to the south, is only an island when the tide is in, and, as you can't stay overnight, is basically just a daytrip from Colonsay. The two are separated by the "Strand", a mile of tidal mudflats which act as a causeway for three hours or so at low tide; check locally for current timings. Although legends (and etymology) link saints Columba and Oran with both Colonsay and Oronsay, the ruins of the **Oronsay Priory** date back only as far as the fourteenth century. Abandoned since the Reformation, you can still see the original church and cloisters, and the Oronsay Cross, a superb example of late medieval artistry from Iona. There are also over thirty graveslabs in the Prior's House, though you'll need a torch to inspect them properly.

# Mid-Argyll

**Mid-Argyll** is a vague term which loosely describes the central wedge of land south of Oban and north of Kintyre, extending west from Loch Fyne to the Atlantic. The highlights of this gently undulating scenery lie along the sharply indented west coast, in particular the rich Celtic remains in the Kilmartin valley, one of the most important prehistoric sites in Scotland.

## Kilmartin and Dunadd

In the uneventful one-street village of **KILMARTIN** the nineteenth-century **Church** (April–Sept 9.30am–7pm) shelters the **Kilmartin Crosses**: one depicts Christ on each side and dates from the tenth century, the other, slightly more recent, is smothered with intricate Celtic knotting. You can also see an interesting collection of medieval graveslabs of the Malcolm chiefs in a separate enclosure in the graveyard. Kilmartin's castle is ruined beyond recognition; head instead for **Carnasserie Castle**, on a high ridge a mile up the road. Built in the 1560s, it represents the transition between fully fortified castles and later mansion houses, and has several original fireplaces, gun-loops and shot-holes.

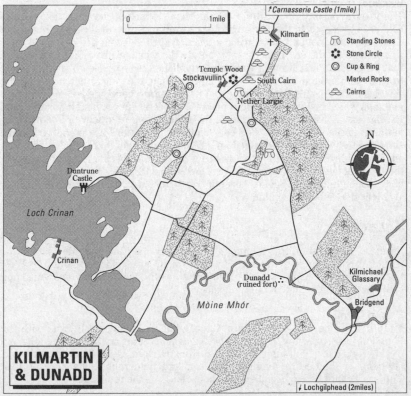

The **Kilmartin valley**, fanning out south of the village, is one of the most important prehistoric sites in Scotland. The most significant relic is the **linear cemetery**, where several cairns are aligned for more than two miles, beginning just south of Kilmartin. Whether these represent the successive burials of a ruling family or chieftains, nobody can be sure. The best view of the cemetery's configuration is from the Bronze Age Mid-Cairn, but the Neolithic South Cairn, dating from around 3000 BC, is by far the oldest and the most impressive, with its large chambered tomb roofed by giant slabs.

Close to the Mid-Cairn, in a small copse, the **Templewood** stone circles were the architectural focus of burials in the area from Neolithic times. Visible to the south are the impressively cup-marked **Nether Largie standing stones**, the largest of which looms over 10ft high. **Cup- and ring-marked rocks** are a recurrent feature of prehistoric sites in the Kilmartin valley and elsewhere in Argyll. There are many theories as to their origin: some see them as Pictish symbols, others as African death symbols, primitive solar calendars and so on.

The most extensive markings are at **Achnabreck**, off the A816 towards Lochgilphead, but there are other well-preserved rocks in **Slockavullin**, a mile or so west of Temple Wood.

### Dunadd

The marshy plain of *Mòine Mhór* (Great Moss), which opens up to the south of Kilmartin, is home to the Iron Age fort of **Dunadd**, one of the most important Celtic sites in Scotland, occupying a distinctive 176-foot high rocky knoll once surrounded by the sea but currently beside the winding River Add. It was here that Fergus, the first King of Dalriada, established his royal seat, having arrived from Ireland around 500 AD. Its strategic position, the craggy defences and the view from the top are all impressive, but it's the **stone carvings** between the twin summits which make Dunadd so remarkable: several lines of inscription in ogam, (an ancient alphabet of Irish origin), the faint outline of a boar, a hollowed-out footprint and a small basin. The boar and the inscriptions are probably Pictish, since the fort was clearly occupied long before Fergus got there, but the footprint and basin have been interpreted as being part of the royal coronation rituals of the kings of Dalriada. It is thought that the Stone of Destiny was used at Dunadd before being moved to Scone Palace in Perthshire (see p.227) and eventually to Westminster Abbey in London.

# Knapdale

Forested **Knapdale** forms a buffer zone between the Kintyre peninsula and the rest of Argyll bounded to the north by the Crinan Canal, and to the south by West Loch Tarbert. Its name is said to derive from the Norse *knapp dalr*, meaning something like "the land of hills and valleys".

### Crinan Canal

In 1801 the nine-mile-long **Crinan Canal** opened, linking Loch Fyne with the Sound of Jura across the bottom of the *Mòine Mhór*, thus cutting out the long and treacherous journey around the Mull of Kintyre. John Rennie's original design, although an impressive engineering feat, had numerous faults and by 1816 Thomas Telford had to be called in to take charge of the renovations.

The largest concentration of locks – there are fifteen in total – is around Cairnbaan, but the best place to view the canal in action is at **CRINAN**, the picturesque fishing port at the western end of the canal. Crinan's tiny harbour is, for the moment at least, still home to a small fishing fleet, though the majority of the traffic on the canal itself is now made up of pleasure boats. Every room in the *Crinan Hotel* (☎054683/261; ⑨) looks across Loch Crinan to the Sound of Jura – one of the most beautiful views in Scotland; if this is beyond your means, there are some infinitely cheaper but less well-appointed B&Bs. For lunch, the bar meals at the *Crinan* are superb, with tables outside from which you can watch the harbour. Tea and calorific cakes can be had from *Lock 16* right on the quayside.

### Knapdale Forest and Loch Sween
South of the canal, **Knapdale Forest**, planted in the 1930s, stretches virtually uninterrupted from coast to coast, across hills sprinkled with tiny lochs. The Forestry Commission have set out several lovely forest walks, the easiest of which is the three-mile route around **Loch Coille-Bharr**, which begins from a bend in the B8025 to Tayvallich. The other walk, although half a mile shorter, is more strenuous, starting from the B841 which runs along the canal and ascending the peak of **Dunardry** (702ft). Shortest of the lot is the circular, mile-long path which takes you deep into the forest just past Achanamara.

Six miles south of Achanamara, on the shores of Loch Sween is the "Key of Knapdale", **Castle Sween**, in ruins since 1647. The tranquility and beauty of the setting is unfortunately spoiled by the nearby caravan park, an eyesore which makes a visit here pretty depressing. You're better off continuing south to the thirteenth-century **Kilmory Chapel**, also ruined but with a new roof protecting the medieval graveslabs and the well-preserved MacMillan's Cross, an eight-feet-high fifteenth-century Celtic cross showing the crucifixion on one side, and a hunting scene on the other.

### Lochgilphead
The regional hub of the towns along the east coast of Knapdale is **LOCHGILPHEAD**, a planned town in the same vein as Inveraray, but without the pristine whitewashed terraces or the mountainous backdrop. If you're staying in the area, you're bound to find yourself here at some point, as Lochgilphead has the only bank and supermarket for miles.

**Rooms** at the *Stag*, Argyll St (☎054660/2496; ⑥) are overpriced; alternatives include the *Argyll,* Lochnell St (☎054660/2221; ④), or *Kilmory House*, Paterson St (☎054660/3658; ②). Alternatively, you could ask at the **tourist office**, 27 Lochnell St (April–Oct Mon–Sat 9.30am–6.30pm, Sun 11am–5pm; ☎054660/2344). *The Smiddy*, on Smithy Lane, does the best **home cooking** in town.

# Kintyre

But for the mile-long isthmus between West and East Loch Tarbert, **KINTYRE** (from the Gaelic *Ceann Tire*, "Head of Land") would be an island. Indeed, in the eleventh century, when the Scottish king, Malcolm Canmore, told Magnus Barefoot, King of Norway, he could lay claim to any island he could navigate his boat round, Magnus succeeded in dragging his boat across the Tarbert isthmus and added the peninsula to his Hebridean kingdom. After the Wars of the Covenant, when the vast majority of the population and property was wiped out by a combination of the 1647 plague coupled with the destructive attentions of the Earl of Argyll, Kintyre became a virtual desert until the earl began his policy of transplanting Gaelic-speaking Lowlanders to the region.

**Getting around** Kintyre without your own transport is very difficult. One bus goes from Glasgow daily to Kintyre's main town, Campbeltown, calling at Tarbert. If you're driving, the new west coast road is extremely fast, whereas the single-track east coast road takes more than twice as long.

# Tarbert

A distinctive rocket-like church steeple heralds the fishing village of **TARBERT** (in Gaelic *Tairbeart*, meaning Isthmus), sheltering an attractive little bay backed by rugged hills. Tarbert's herring industry was mentioned in the Annals of Ulster as far back as 836 AD – though right now the future of the local fishing industry is under threat from EC quotas, as the participants in the 1993 Tarbert Regatta discovered when they found themselves blockaded by a local fishermen's protest.

Other than shop and watch life go by in the harbour, there's little to do in Tarbert. Of Robert the Bruce's fourteenth-century **Castle** above the town, there are now only scant remains, though the view from the overgrown rubble makes a trip up here worthwhile. If you need to **stay**, there's the *Columba* on the waterfront (☎0880/820 808; ③), or *Springside* B&B on Pier Rd (☎0880/820 413; ②). The **tourist office** (daily 9am–1pm & 2–5pm; ☎0880/820 429) is on the harbour. If you're just looking for a fill-up, the **bar snacks** at the *Islay Frigate Hotel* on the harbour should suffice, but for some of the best fish or seafood in the whole of Argyll, head for *The Anchorage*, unforgettable not least for its eccentric proprietor.

One reason you might find yourself staying in Tarbert is its proximity to no fewer than four **ferry terminals**. The nearest is the new *CalMac* service east to Portavadie on the Cowal peninsula, which runs in July and August only. The busiest terminal is just under eight miles south at **Kennacraig** which runs daily sailings to Islay all year round; further south is the Gigha ferry from Tayintoan, and on the opposite coast the Claonaig ferry to Arran runs only from April to October.

# Isle of Gigha

The island of **Gigha** (pronounced "Geeya", with a hard "g"), just three miles off the west coast of Kintyre, is a low-lying, fertile island, whose distinctive fruit-shaped cheese is now one of its main exports. Like many of the smaller Hebrides, having been sold by its original lairds, the MacNeils, Gigha is frequently put on the market with little regard for its 120 or so inhabitants, who have to endure these periods of instability as best they can.

The ferry from Tayinloan, 23 miles south of Tarbert, deposits you at **ARDMINISH**, where you'll find the post office and shop, and the *Gigha Hotel*, (see below) which does really good bar meals. Tea, coffee and cakes are best taken by the shore at the *Boathouse* (May–Sept) which overlooks the ferry pier. The only sights, as such, are the **Achamore Gardens**, one mile south of Ardminish. Established by the first post-war owner, Sir James Horlick of hot drink fame, they are best seen in early summer, ablaze with rhododendrons and azaleas.

Gigha is so small – six miles by one – that most visitors come here just for the day. However, it is possible to **stay**, either at the *McSporrans*, in the old post office (☎05835/251; ③), or the *Gigha Hotel* (☎05835/254; ⑥), which also has self-catering flats dotted over the island and offers **bike rental**. Caravans and camping are not allowed on Gigha.

# The west coast

Kintyre's bleak **west coast** ranks among the most exposed stretches of coastline in Argyll. The Atlantic pounds the monotonous shoreline, while the persistent westerly wind forces the trees against the hillside. That said, there are numerous deserted sandy beaches to enjoy with great views over to Gigha, Islay, Jura and even Ireland – though, as always in Scotland, everything depends upon the weather. Apart from the luxury late-Victorian *Balinakill Country House* at Clachan (☎08804/206; ⑥), accommodation along the coast is limited to the odd B&B, but there are several blustery **campsites**: the one in **Rhunahaorine**, two miles north of Tayinloan (☎05834/263) is near a long stretch of sandy beach, as is the one at **Muasdale** (☎05832/234), and further south at **Machrihanish** (☎058681/366). One of the few places to eat along the coast is the *North Beachmore Farm*, signposted off the A83 south of Tayinloan, which gives superb views over the coast, and serves good, low-priced meals, tea and cakes.

The **Killean Church**, three miles south of Tayinloan, is one of the few conventional sights on the entire coast, a ruined twelfth-century edifice whose graveyard contains some unusual, carved, medieval graveslabs. **Glenbarr Abbey** (daily except Tues 10am–6pm; £2) is an eighteenth-century laird's house filled with tedious memorabilia about the once powerful MacAlister clan, now reduced to augmenting their income by opening up their house to the trickle of tourists that pass this way. Still, there are plenty of musty old sofas to lounge around in, a tearoom and attractive grounds which provide a brief respite from the Atlantic winds.

The only major development along this coast is at **MACHRIHANISH**, at the southern end of the longest continuous stretch of sand in Argyll. Once a thriving, salt-producing and coal-mining town, Machrihanish now survives solely on tourism. Consequently, there are several B&Bs – try *East Drumlemble Farm* (☎058681/220; ②) – and a hotel, as well as the campsite listed above. To get to Machrihanish, the road takes a detour through Campbeltown itself, in order to skirt the flat and fertile landscape known as the Laggan.

# Campbeltown

There's little to recommend **CAMPBELTOWN** beyond its setting, in a deep bay sheltered by Davaar Island and the surrounding hills. However, with a population of 6500, it is the second largest town in Argyll after Oban, and if you're staying in the southern half of Kintyre, is the best place to stock up on supplies. Renamed in the seventeenth century by the Earl of Argyll – a Campbell – when it became one of the main points for immigration from the Lowlands, Campbeltown's heyday was the Victorian era when shipbuilding was going strong, coal was shipped by canal from Drumlemble, the fishing fleet was vast and Campbeltown Loch was said to be made of whisky.

Indeed, nineteenth-century visitors to Campbeltown found the place engulfed in a thick fog of pungent peat smoke from the town's 34 **whisky distilleries**. Nowadays, only the *Glen Scotia* and *Springbank* distilleries are left to maintain this regional sub-group of single malt whiskies which is distinct from Highland, Islay or Lowland varieties (see p.27 in *Basics* for more on whisky). Neither distillery is keen on encouraging visitors, however, and the town's one sight is the **Campbeltown Cross**, a fourteenth-century blue-green cross with figural scenes and spirals of Celtic knotting, which presides over the main roundabout on the quayside. Also on the harbour is the "**Wee Picture House**", a dinky little Art Deco cinema on Hall Street, built in 1913 and still going strong.

Perhaps most rewarding is the trip to **Davaar Island**, linked to the peninsula at low tide by a mile-long bank of shoal or *dòirlinn* as it's known in Gaelic. You'll need to find out the times of the tides from the tourist office before setting out; you have around six hours in which to make the return journey from Kildalloig Point. Used for grazing, but no longer inhabited, the main attraction on Davaar, besides the wealth of rock flora, is the cave painting of the crucifixion executed in secret by local artist, Archibald MacKinnon, in 1887, and touched up by the same man after he'd owned up in 1934, a year before he died at the age of 85.

### Practicalities

Campbeltown's **tourist office** on the Old Quay (Mon–Fri 9am–5pm; ☎0586/552 056), can help with accommodation. The *Royal Hotel*, on Main Street (☎0586/552 017; ④), is a big, traditional, Victorian hotel; the *Whitehill* on Witchburn Road (☎0586/552 117; ④) is more modest, and cheaper still is the *Westbank Guest House* on Dell Road (☎0586/553 660; ③). There are few **places to eat** in town, unless you're prepared to fork out for an expensive meal with all the trimmings in the *White Hart Hotel* on Main Street, or *Seafield Hotel* on Kilkerran Road.

# Southend and the Mull of Kintyre

Travelling south from Campbeltown to the bulbous, hilly end of Kintyre takes you through some of the most spectacular scenery on the whole peninsula. Consequently, **SOUTHEND** itself, one of those bleak, blustery spots beloved of fixed caravan sites, comes as something of a disappointment. It does have a sandy beach, but even so, the nicest spot for swimming is **Macharioch Bay**, three miles east, which looks out to distant Ailsa Craig in the Firth of Clyde.

Out to sea, but closer to Southend, is **Dunaverty Rock**, where a force of three hundred Royalists were massacred by the Covenanting army of the Earl of Argyll in 1647 despite having surrendered voluntarily. Below the cliffs to the west of Southend, a ruined thirteenth-century chapel marks the alleged arrival point of Saint Columba prior to his trip to Iona, and on a rocky knoll nearby a pair of footprints carved into the rock are known as "Columba's footprints", though only one is actually of ancient origin.

Most people venture south of Campbeltown to make a pilgrimage to the **Mull of Kintyre** – the nearest Britain gets to Ireland, whose coastline, just twelve miles away, is visible on clear days. Although the Mull was made famous by the mawkish number-one hit by one-time local resident, Paul McCartney, with the help of the Campbeltown Pipe Band, there's nothing specifically to see in this godforsaken storm-racked spot but the view. The roads up to the "**Gap**" (1150ft)

– where you must leave your car – and down to the lighthouse, itself 300ft above the ocean waves, are terrifyingly precipitous.

There are few places to **stay** in this remote region. Southend's only hotel is currently closed; try instead *Ormsary Farm* (☎058683/665; ②), also in Southend.

## The east coast

Compared to the west coast, the **east coast** of Kintyre has marginally more to offer in the way of conventional sights, though you need to have a fair amount of time on your hands if you are to drive the thirty-odd miles up to Skipness on the slow, winding, single-track B842.

The ruins of **Saddell Abbey**, a Cistercian foundation thought to have been founded by Somerled in 1160, lie ten miles up the coast from Campbeltown. The remains are not exactly impressive, but they do shelter a collection of medieval graveslabs decorated with full-scale relief figures of knights.

A little further north, the fishing village of **CARRADALE** is the only place of any size on the east coast and something of a holiday resort. The village itself is drab, but the sandy bay on which it's situated makes up for it. There are a couple of hotels – the *Ashbank* (☎05833/650; ③) is the best value – and several B&Bs, including *Mains Farm* (☎05833/216; ②), and a **campsite** (Easter–Sept; ☎05833/665).

The B842 ends twelve miles north of Carradale at **CLAONAIG**, little more than a slipway for the summer car ferry to Arran. Beyond here, a dead-end road winds its way along the shore a few miles further north to **SKIPNESS**, where the considerable ruins of an enormous thirteenth-century castle and a chapel look out across the Kilbrannan Sound to Arran. You can sit outside and admire both, whilst enjoying fresh oysters, mussels and the like from the excellent seafood cabin at *Skipness House*, which also offers accommodation in a family home (☎08806/207; ⑦).

# Arran

Shaped like a kidney bean, **Arran** is the most southerly of the Scottish islands. The Highland–Lowland dividing line passes right through its centre – hence the tourist board's aphorism about "Scotland in miniature" – leaving the northern half underpopulated, mountainous and bleak, while the lush southern half enjoys a milder climate. Despite its immense popularity, the tourists, like the population, tend to stick to the southeastern quarter of the island, leaving the west and the north relatively undisturbed.

Although tourism is now by far the most important industry, at twenty miles in length, Arran is large enough to have a life of its own. Although the history of the Clearances on Arran, set in motion by the local lairds, the dukes of Hamilton, is as depressing as elsewhere in the Highlands, in recent years it has not suffered from the depopulation which has plagued other, more remote islands.

**Transport** is good: daily **buses** circle the island (Brodick tourist office has timetables) and in summer there are two **ferry services**, one from Ardrossan in Ayrshire to Brodick, and a smaller ferry from Claonaig on the remote Kintyre peninsula to Lochranza in the north.

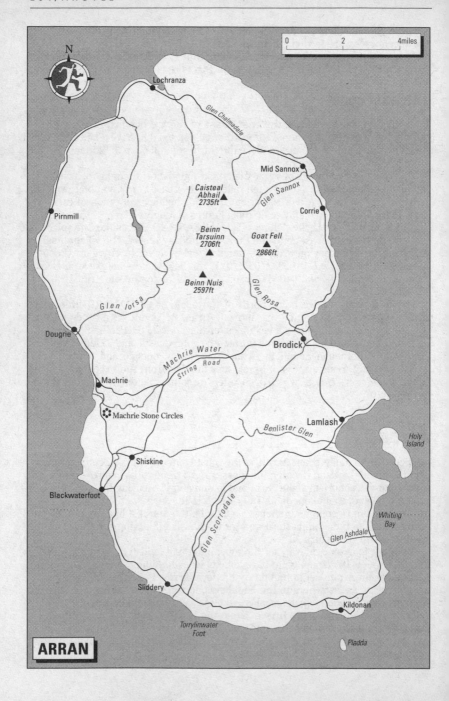

0    2    4miles

Lochranza

*Glen Chalmadale*

Mid Sannox

*Glen Sannox*

Corrie

Caisteal
*Abhail*
2735ft ▲

Pirnmill

Beinn
*Tarsuinn*
2706ft
▲

*Goat Fell*
▲
2866ft.

*Glen Rosa*

▲
*Beinn Nuis*
2597ft

*Glen Iorsa*

Dougrie

Brodick

*Machrie Water*

*String Road*

Machrie

Holy
Island

:::Machrie Stone Circles

Lamlash

*Benlister Glen*

Shiskine

Blackwaterfoot

*Glen Scorrodale*

*Whiting
Bay*

*Glen Ashdale*

Sliddery

Kildonan

*Torrylinwater
Foot*

*Pladda*

**ARRAN**

# Brodick

Although the resort of **BRODICK** is a place of very little charm, it does at least have a grand setting in a wide, sandy bay set against a backdrop of granite mountains. Its development as a tourist resort on the Clyde was held back for a long time by its elitist owners, the dukes of Hamilton, though nowadays, as the island's capital and main communication hub, Brodick is by far the busiest town on Arran.

In their day, the dukes lived at **Brodick Castle** (Easter to mid-Oct daily 1–5pm; NTS; £3.50), on a steep bank on the north side of the bay. The interior is for the dedicated period furniture buff only; more accessible are the views over Brodick Bay, from the flower-filled walled grounds (same hours; £2) and the very good tearooms. The **Arran Heritage Museum** (Easter–Oct Mon–Sat 9am–5pm; £1), is a somewhat dry collection of old tools and furniture in a converted crofter's farm halfway between the castle and the town centre – really only worth visiting to escape from bad weather.

## Practicalities

Unless you've got to catch an early-morning ferry, there's very little reason to stay in Brodick. There are, however, plenty of rooms close to the ferry terminal, in old Victorian hotels such as the *Douglas* (☎0770/302 155; ⑥) as well as more modest places like the *Glencloy Farmhouse* (☎0770/302 351; ④). Of the many B&Bs, try the *Belvedere*, on Alma Road (☎0770/302 397; ②); the nearest **campsite** is *Glenrosa* (April–Oct; ☎0770/302 380), a mile or so north of the town centre, off the String Road. The only **restaurant** which really stands out in Brodick is *Creelers*, a superb seafood restaurant by the Arran Heritage Museum on the road to the castle. The **tourist office** (July & Aug daily 9am–7.30pm; progressively shorter hours the rest of the year; ☎0770/302 401) is by the *CalMac* pier, with reams of information on bus and ferry services, accommodation and every kind of activity on the island from pony-trekking to paragliding. You can **rent bikes** from *Brodick Cycles*, opposite the village hall, or from *Mini-Golf Cycle Hire* near the pier.

# The south

The southern half of Arran is less spectacular, and less forbidding than the north; the land is more fertile, and for that reason the vast majority of the population lives here. The tourist industry has followed them, though with considerably less justification.

## Lamlash and the south coast

With its distinctive Edwardian architecture and mild climate **LAMLASH** epitomizes the sedate charm of southeast Arran. Its major drawback is its bay, which is made up not of sand but of boulder-strewn mudflats. You can take a boat out to the slug-shaped hump of **Holy Island** which shelters the bay, and was recently bought by a group of Tibetan Buddhists who plan to set up a meditation centre there – providing you don't dawdle, it's possible to scramble up to the top of Mullach Mòr (1030ft), the island's highest point, and still catch the last ferry back.

If you want to **stay** in style, head for the *Glenisle Hotel* (April–Oct; ☎0770/600 258; ④), or the much smaller *Lilybank Hotel* (☎0770/600 230; ③); cheaper B&Bs such as *Douglas Villa* (☎0770/600 261; ②) are easy enough to find, and

*Middleton's* **campsite** (April to mid-Oct; ☎0770/600 255) is just five minutes' walk north of the centre. The best **restaurant** in Lamlash is undoubtedly the *Carraig Mhor* near the pier (☎0770/600 453), which offers an exclusive and expensive menu featuring fresh local game, fish and seafood.

Although it has been an established Clydeside resort for over a century now, **WHITING BAY**, four miles south of Lamlash, is actually pretty characterless. However, there are plenty of places to stay, among them the *Royal Hotel* (☎0770/ 7286; ③), *Viewbank*, (☎0770/7326; ③) or *Silverhill North* (☎0770/7414; ②), and a **youth hostel** (☎07707/339; Grade 2). Elsewhere the easiest point of access to the sea is at **KILDONAN**, a small village off the main road, with just one hotel, *Drimla Lodge* (☎0770/82296; ③), the odd B&B like *Dippen House* (☎0770/82223; ②), and a campsite (☎0770/82210). There's a nice sandy beach below the village, and, at its east end, a ruined castle looking out to Pladda.

### Blackwaterfoot and Machrie

**BLACKWATERFOOT**, on the western end of the Strong Road that bisects the island, is less a Clyde-style resort than a genuine Hebridean fishing village, and, like Lochranza, is a good place to escape the worst of Arran's summer crowds. If you want to stay, there's the Victorian *Blackwaterfoot Hotel* (March–Oct; ☎077086/202; ③) and plenty of cheaper B&Bs: try *Midmar* (☎077086/413; ③), *Parkhouse* (☎077086/392; ②), or *Broombrae* (☎077086/435; ②), a mile or so south of town in Kilpatrick.

North of Blackwaterfoot is the wide expanse of **Machrie Moor**, which boasts a wealth of Bronze Age sites. No fewer than six **stone circles** sit east of the main road; although many of them barely break the peat's surface, the tallest surviving monolith is over 18ft high. The most striking configuration is at Fingal's Cauldron Seat, with two concentric circles of granite boulders; legend has it that Fingal tied his dog to one of them while cooking at his cauldron. Incidentally, **King's Cave**, two miles along the coast from Blackwaterfoot, is where Robert the Bruce is thought to have encountered the famously patient arachnid, while hiding during his final bid to free Scotland in 1306.

# The north

The desolate north half of Arran – effectively the Highland part – features bare granite peaks, the occasional golden eagle and miles of unspoilt scenery, within reach only to those prepared to do some serious hiking. Arran's most accessible peak is also the island's highest, **Goat Fell** (2866ft) – from the Gaelic, *Goath*, meaning "windy" – which can be ascended in just three hours from Brodick, though it's a strenuous hike. From Goat Fell, experienced walkers can follow the horeshoe of craggy summits and descend either from the saddle below Beinn Tarsuinn (2706ft) or from Beinn Nuis (2597ft).

Another good base for hiking is the pretty little seaside village of **CORRIE**, six miles north of Brodick, where a procession of pristine cottages line the road to Lochranza. There are numerous self-catering flats, as well as a couple of hotels and B&Bs: try *Blackrock Guest House* (☎0770/81282; ③). At Sannox, two miles north, the road leaves the shoreline and climbs steeply, giving breathtaking views over to the scree-strewn slopes around Caisteal Abhail (2735ft). If you make this journey around dusk, be sure to pause in **Glen Chalmadale**, on the other side of the pass, to catch a glimpse of the red deer who come down to pasture by the water.

The ruined castle which occupies the mudflats of the bay, and the gloomy north-facing slopes of the mountains which frame it, make for one of the most spectacular settings on the island – yet **LOCHRANZA**, despite being the only place of any size in this sparsely populated area, attracts far fewer visitors than Arran's southern resorts. Nevertheless, there's a **tourist office** by the *CalMac* pier (mid-May to Sept Mon–Sat 9.30am–5pm; ☎0770/83320), a **youth hostel** (☎0770/830 631; Grade 2) overlooking the castle, and a well-equipped **campsite** (Easter–Oct; ☎0770 83273) by the golf course on the Brodick Road. Plusher **accommodation** can be had from the *Apple Lodge Hotel* (☎0770/83229; ③), the *Lochranza Hotel* (☎0770/83223; ③), or *Belvaren* B&B (☎0770/83647; ②).

# Islay and Jura

**Islay** (pronounced "eye-ler") is famous for one thing – single malt whisky. The smoky, peaty, pungent quality of Islay whisky is unique, recognizable even to the untutored palette, and seven of the eight distilleries that still function lay on free guided tours, ending with the customary complimentary tipple. Yet despite the fame of its whiskies, Islay remains relatively undiscovered, much as Skye and Mull were some twenty years ago. Part of the reason, no doubt, is that it takes a pricy, two-hour ferry journey from Kennacraig on Kintyre to reach the island; and once there, you'll find no luxury hotels or fancy restaurants.

In medieval times, Islay was the political centre of the Hebrides, with Finlagan Castle, near Port Askaig, the seat of the MacDonalds, lords of the Isles. As an official part of the *Gàidhealtachd*, you'll see bi-lingual signs in Bowmore, Port Charlotte and elsewhere. The sedate towns and villages you see on Islay today, however, date from the planned settlements founded by the Campbells in the late eighteenth and early nineteenth centuries. Apart from whisky, the other great draw is the birdlife, in particular, the scores of white-fronted and barnacle geese who winter here.

The long whale-shaped island of **Jura** – or, to be more accurate the distinctive Paps of Jura (smooth mountains so-called because of their breast-like shape) – seems to dominate every view off the coast of Argyll. It's one of the most forbidding and dramatic of the Inner Hebrides, a huge land mass with just one road struggling up the eastern coast, and only one cluster of human habitation, in the southeast corner of the island.

## Port Ellen and the south

Notwithstanding the daily ferry from Kennacraig, **PORT ELLEN**, on the island of **Islay,** is a sleepy little place, laid out as a planned village in 1821 and named after the wife of the founder. The neat terraces along the harbour are pretty enough, but the bay is dominated by the now disused whisky distillery – the smell of malt which wafts across the harbour comes from the modern plant just off the Bowmore road. As well as the two hotels, the *Trout Fly* restaurant has **rooms** (☎0496/2204; ③), or you could try any of the B&Bs on Frederick Crescent. There's **youth hostel** accommodation at the *Kintra Outdoor Centre* (☎0496/2051; ①), three miles northwest of Port Ellen, at the southern tip of Laggan Bay. For further information about the southern half of Islay, check out the ad hoc **tourist office** based in a caravan beside the *White Hart Hotel*.

From Port Ellen, a dead-end road heads off east along the coastline, passing three functioning distilleries in as many miles. First comes **Laphroaig distillery** (closed July & Aug; ☎0496/2418) which produces the most uncompromisingly smoky of the Islay whiskies. As every bottle of Laphroaig tells you, translated from the Gaelic the name means "the beautiful hollow by the broad bay", and, true enough, the whitewashed distillery is indeed in a gorgeous setting by the sea. The **Lagavulin distillery** (☎0496/2400), a mile down the road, produces a superb sixteen-year old single malt, while the **Ardbeg distillery**, another mile on, sports the traditional pagoda-style roofs of the malting houses – though sadly it's one of the few not to encourage visitors. Each tour offers a free taster, but a bottle of the stuff is no cheaper at source, so expect to pay at least £20.

Armed with a bottle of your choice, you could do worse than head down to the shoreline just beyond Lagavulin and have a tot or two beside **Dunyvaig Castle** (*Dùn Naomhaig*), a romantic ruin on a promontory looking out to the tiny isle of Texa. You can stay at *Tigh na Suil* **B&B** (☎0496/2483; ②), or three miles further along the rapidly deteriorating road at *The Kennels* (☎0496/2149; ②). A mile beyond this, the simple thirteenth-century **Kildalton Chapel** boasts a wonderful eighth-century Celtic cross made from the local "bluestone", which is, in fact, a rich bottle-green. The quality of the scenes matches any to be found on the crosses carved by the monks in Iona: Mary and child are on one side with what look like elephants on the other.

The nub of land west of Port Ellen is known as **The Oa**. This windswept and inhospitable landscape, much loved by illicit whisky distillers and smugglers over the centuries, culminates in some pretty awesome cliffs around the Mull of Oa, inhabited by, among others, golden eagles and choughs. The road disintegrates around **Lower Killeyan**, and you'll have to walk the last mile to the cliff's edge, where a monument was erected by the US government in memory of the 266 men who died when HMS *Tuscania* was torpedoed and sank seven miles offshore in February 1918.

North of Port Ellen, between the seven-mile-long strand of Laggan Bay and the mountains of the southeast, lies the **Duich Moss** peat bog, a favoured feeding-ground for white-fronted and barnacle geese. As the peat is also one of the crucial ingredients which flavours malt whisky, some years ago the area became the subject of a heated dispute between environmentalists and locals. To the uninitiated, the bog is nondescript, enlivened only by the large Norse earthworks of **Dun Nosebridge** which rises above the River Laggan.

# Bowmore and the Rhinns of Islay

**BOWMORE**, Islay's administrative capital, was founded as a planned village in 1768 to replace the village of Kilarrow which was deemed by the local laird to be too close to his own residence. It's a striking place, laid out in a grid plan rather like Inveraray, with the main street climbing up the hill in a straight line from the pier on Loch Indaan to the town's crowning landmark, the **Round Church**. A little to the west of the main street is **Bowmore distillery** (guided tours Mon–Fri from 10am; Sat & Sun phone ☎049681/671), the first of the legal Islay distilleries, founded in 1779 and still occupying its original buildings.

Islay's only official **tourist office** is in Bowmore (Mon–Sat 9am–1pm & 2–5.30pm; ☎049681/254), and can help you find accommodation anywhere on Islay

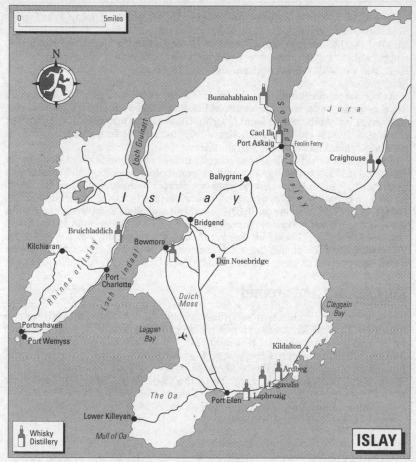

Whisky Distillery

**ISLAY**

or Jura. In Bowmore itself, there are several **hotels**, the nicest of which is the *Lochside* on Shore Street (☎049681/244; ④). Alternatively, there's *Lambeth House* on Jamieson Street (☎049681/597; ③). For **food**, head for the *Harbour Inn*, on Main Street, where you can sample the local prawns and warm yourself by a peat fire, or settle down to some homely food at *The Cottage*, further up on the same side of the street.

North of Bowmore, the RSPB reserve on the mudflats of **Loch Gruinart** aims to encourage the geese to winter here rather than on the valuable peat bogs at Duich Moss, and in summer this is a good place to spot lapwings, snipes and redshanks. A little further along the A847, the **Bruichladdich distillery** (☎049685/221) is Scotland's most westerly whisky producer, and enjoys a wonderful location overlooking Loch Indaal.

**PORT CHARLOTTE**, named after the founder's mother, is generally agreed to be Islay's prettiest village, its immaculate cottages hugging the sandy shores of

Loch Indaal. East of the village, the imaginative **Museum of Islay Life** (April–Sept Mon–Sat 10am–5pm; Sun 2–5pm; Oct–March Mon–Fri 10am–4.30pm; £1.50), has a kids' corner, a good library of books about the island, and tantalizing snippets about eighteenth-century illegal whisky distillers. If you pop across the road, you can visit the **Islay Creamery** and buy some of the island's distinctive hard cheese.

As for **accommodation**, the *Lochindaal Hotel* (☎049685/202; ③) is currently the only hotel, but among the scores of B&Bs are the wonderful *Taigh-na-Creag*, 7 Shore St (☎049685/261; ③) and *Craigfad Guest House*(☎049685/244; ③) as well as a **youth hostel** (☎049685/385; Grade 2). The *Croft Kitchen*, near the museum, serves hot meals including vegetarian dishes.

The coastal road culminates seven miles south of Port Charlotte at **PORTNAHAVEN**, a fishing and crofting community since the early nineteenth century. The familiar Hebridean cottages wrap themselves around the steep banks of a deep bay; in the distance, you can see Portnahaven's twin settlement, **PORT WEMYSS**, a mile south. There are few amenities in this isolated part of Islay, but you'll get **rooms** at *Glenview House* on Church Street in Portnahaven (☎049686/303; ②). Those in search of still more solitude should head for *Tormisdale Croft* (no phone; ②), a B&B across the moor on the road to Kilchiaran which serves organic home cooking and has welcoming peat and driftwood fires.

# Port Askaig and around

Islay's other ferry connection with the mainland, and its sole link with Jura, is from **PORT ASKAIG**, a scattering of buildings which tumble down a little cove by the narrowest section of the Sound of Islay. The *Port Askaig Hotel* (☎049684/245; ⑤) by the pier is one of the best on the island, with views over to the Paps of Jura; there are cheaper B&Bs to choose from, too. A short walk north along the shore from Port Askaig will bring you to the **Caol Ila distillery** (guided tours Mon–Fri; ☎049684/207), named after the Sound of Islay (*Caol Ila*) which it overlooks. **Bunnahabhainn distillery** (guided tours Mon–Fri; ☎049684/646) is a couple of miles further up the coast.

# Jura

Twenty-eight miles long and eight miles wide, **Jura** is one of the wildest and most mountainous of the Inner Hebrides, its entire west coast uninhabited and inaccessible except to the dedicated walker. The island's name derives from the Norse for "Deer Island", and, appropriately enough, the current deer population outnumbers humans by twenty-five to one. The island's landmarks are the famous **Paps of Jura**, though there are, somewhat confusingly, three Paps, the tallest of which is Beinn an Oìr (2571ft).

Anything that happens on Jura happens in **CRAIGHOUSE**. *Western Ferries* run a regular service from Port Askaig to Feolin Ferry, eight miles away. **Craighouse distillery** (☎049682/240), which looks out across Small Isles Bay to the mainland of Knapdale, is the island's only industry besides crofting and tourism, and welcomes visitors. The one hotel, the *Jura Hotel* (☎049682/243; ⑤), is supplemented by a smattering of B&Bs, such as the *Fish Farm House* (☎049682/304; ③) or *Mrs Woodhouse* at 7 Woodside (☎049682/379; ②).

In April 1946 Eric Blair (better known by his pen name of **George Orwell**), suffering badly from TB and intending to give himself "six months' quiet" in which to write his novel, *1984,* moved to a remote farmhouse called Barnhill, on the northern tip of Jura. He lived out a spartan existence there for two years but was forced to return to London shortly before his death. The house, 23 miles north of Craighouse up an increasingly poor road, is as remote today as it was in Orwell's day, and sadly there is no access to the interior.

## travel details

**Trains**

**Glasgow** to: Oban (Mon–Sat 3 daily; Sun 2 daily; 3hr).

**Buses**

**Glasgow** to: Campbeltown (3 daily; 4hr 20min); Inveraray (up to 5 daily; 1hr 40min); Kennacraig (3 daily; 3hr 30min); Lochgilphead (3 daily; 1hr 40min); Oban (3 daily; 3hr); Tarbert (3 daily; 3hr 15min).

**Kennacraig** to: Claonaig (1 daily except Wed; 15min); Glasgow (3 daily; 3hr 30min); Tarbert (1 daily; 10min).

**Tarbert** to: Claonaig (schooldays only; 1 daily; 25min); Glasgow (3 daily; 3hr 15min); Kennacraig (1 daily; 10min).

**Car ferries** (summer timetable)

**To Arran**: Ardrossan–Brodick (up to 6 daily; 55min); Claonaig–Lochranza (10 daily; 30min).

**To Bute**: Wemyss Bay–Rothesay (10 daily; 30min); Colintraive–Rhubodach (frequently; 5min).

**To Coll**: Oban–Coll (up to 5 weekly; 3hr)

**To Colonsay:** Oban–Colonsay (3 weekly; 2hr 10min); Kennacraig–Colonsay (1 weekly; 2hr 45min).

**To Islay**: Kennacraig–Port Ellen (up to 2 daily; 2hr 15min); Kennacraig–Port Askaig (1 daily; 2hr).

**To Lismore**: Oban–Lismore (Mon–Sat 2 daily; 50min)

**To Mull**: Oban–Craignure (5–7 daily; 40min); Lochaline–Fishnish (every 45min; 15min); Oban–Tobermory (3 weekly; 1hr 30min); Kilchoan–Tobermory (10 daily; 35min).

**To Tiree**: Oban–Tiree (up to 5 weekly; 4hr 15min).

**Flights**

**Glasgow** to: Campbeltown (Mon–Fri 2 daily; 30min); Islay (Mon–Fri 2 daily; Sat 1 daily; 35min); Tiree (Mon–Sat 1 daily; 45min).

# CHAPTER SIX

# SKYE AND THE WESTERN ISLES

A procession of Hebridean islands, islets and reefs off the northwest shore of Scotland, **Skye and the Western Isles** between them boast some of the country's most alluring scenery. It's here that the turbulent seas of the Atlantic smash up against an extravagant shoreline hundreds of miles long, a geologically complex terrain whose rough rocks and mighty seacliffs are interrupted by a thousand sheltered bays and, in the far west, a long line of sweeping sandy beaches. The islands' interiors are equally dramatic, a series of formidable mountain ranges soaring high above great chunks of boggy peat moor, a barren wilderness enclosing a host of tiny lakes, or lochans.

Skye and the Western Isles were first settled by Neolithic farming peoples in around 4500 BC. They lived along the coast, where they are remembered by scores of incidental remains, from passage graves through to stone circles – most famously at **Callanish** on Lewis. This was the kingdom of the **Scotti**, whose language was the precursor of modern **Gaelic**, still spoken in many areas today.

After Culloden, and with the onset of the Clearances, the isolation of the Western Isles and the Small Isles especially exposed them to the whims and fancies of the various merchants and aristocrats who caught "island fever" and bought them up. Time and again, from the mid-eighteenth century onwards, both the land and its people were sold to the highest bidder. Some proprietors were relatively progressive – like **Lord Leverhulme**, who tried to turn Lewis into a centre of the fishing industry in the 1920s – while others were autocratic – **George Bullough** wanted Rhum to be an Edwardian hunting park – but always the islanders were powerless and almost everywhere they were driven from their ancestral homes, robbing them of their particular sense of place. However, their language survived, ensuring a degree of cultural continuity, especially in the Western Isles, where even today, though locals will speak to visitors in English, the road signs are almost exclusively in Gaelic.

Aficionados of this part of Scotland swear that each island has its own distinct character, and that is to some extent true, although you can split the grouping quite neatly into two. **Skye** and the so-called **Small Isles** – the improbably named **Canna**, **Rhum**, **Eigg** and **Muck** – are part of the Inner Hebrides, which also include the islands of Argyll (see *Argyll*). Beyond Skye, across the unpredictable waters of the Minch, lie the Outer Hebrides, otherwise known as the **Western Isles**, a 130-mile-long archipelago stretching from **Lewis** and **Harris** in the north – in fact a single island, just about joined by a narrow isthmus – to the uninhabited islets below **Barra** in the south.

Although this area is one of the most popular holiday spots in Scotland, the crowds only become oppressive on Skye, and even here, most visitors stick to a

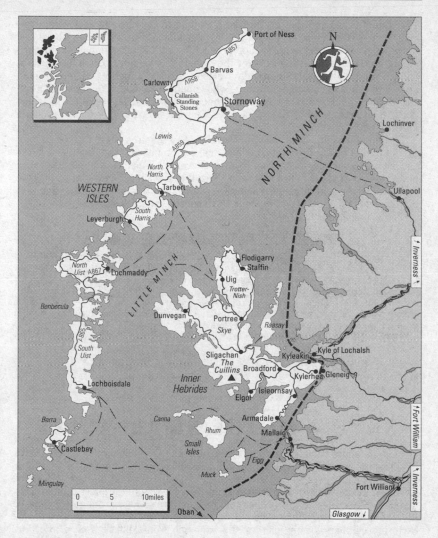

well-trodden sequence of roadside sights that leaves the rest of the island unaffected. The main attraction, the spectacular scenery, is best explored on **foot**, following the scores of paths that range from the simplest of cross-country strolls to arduous treks. There are three obvious areas of outstanding natural beauty to aim for: on Skye the harsh peaks of the **Cuillins** and the mountains of the **Trotternish peninsula**, both of which attract hundreds of walkers and mountaineers, and out on the Western Isles, the mountains of **South Harris**, together with the splendid sandy beaches that string along the Atlantic seaboard beneath them.

The tourist world and that of the islanders tend to be mutually exclusive, especially in the Western Isles, one of the last bastions of Gaelic culture. There are, however, ways to meet people – not so much by sitting in the pubs than by staying in the B&Bs and getting to know the owners. You could, too, join the locals at church, where visitors are generally welcome. This is a highly religious region, dotted with numerous tiny churches, whose denominations differ from island to island. In general terms, the south is predominantly Catholic, while the Calvinist north is a stronghold of the strict Free Church of Scotland – more familiarly known as the "Wee Frees".

Travelling around Skye and the Western Isles requires some degree of forethought. The *CalMac* **ferries** run to a complicated timetable, and the **bus** services are patchy to say the least. Also, in accordance with Calvinist dogma, the entire public transport system closes down on **Sunday**. You should consider visiting the Hebrides in the spring or early autumn, rather than the height of the summer, both to avoid the crowds and to elude the attentions of the pesky **midge**.

---

### ACCOMMODATION PRICE CODES

Throughout this book, accommodation **prices** have been graded with the numbers below, according to the cost of the least expensive double room in high season. The bulk of the recommendations will fall in categories ② to ⑤; recommendations in the highest categories are limited to places that are especially attractive. Bear in mind that many of the swanky hotels often slash their tariffs at the weekend when the business types have gone home, and that many of the cheaper places will also have more expensive rooms. Note that in our accommodation listings price codes are not given for youth hostels – they all come into the lower end of the ① category.

| | | |
|---|---|---|
| ① under £20 | ④ £40–50 | ⑦ £70–80 |
| ② £20–30 | ⑤ £50–60 | ⑦ £80–100 |
| ③ £30–40 | ⑥ £60–70 | ⑧ over £100 |

---

# SKYE AND THE SMALL ISLES

Despite its unpredictable weather – justifiably, the Gaelic name for **Skye**, *Eilean a' Cheo*, means "Island of Mist" – tourism has been an important part of the island's economy ever since 1897, when the train line pushed through to Kyle of Lochalsh in the western Highlands. From here, it was the briefest of boat trips across to Skye, and the Edwardian bourgeoisie were soon swarming over to walk its mountains, whose beauty had been proclaimed by an earlier generation of Victorian climbers. Many visitors still approach from Mallaig (see p.365), but crossing the sea to Skye will soon, however, be unnecessary: much to the consternation of many islanders, work on a road bridge spanning the Kyle of Lochalsh is already underway.

By far the most dramatic areas of the islands are the clustered peaks of **The Cuillins** and the striking rock formations of the **Trotternish** peninsula, both of which offer powerfully beautiful land- and seascapes. Between the two, curved around a pretty bay, lies **Portree**, the island's only town and a convenient place to break your journey.

**Canna**, with its high basalt cliffs, is the prettiest of the **Small Isles**, while the outstanding built attraction is **Rhum**'s remarkable Kinloch Castle, once the home

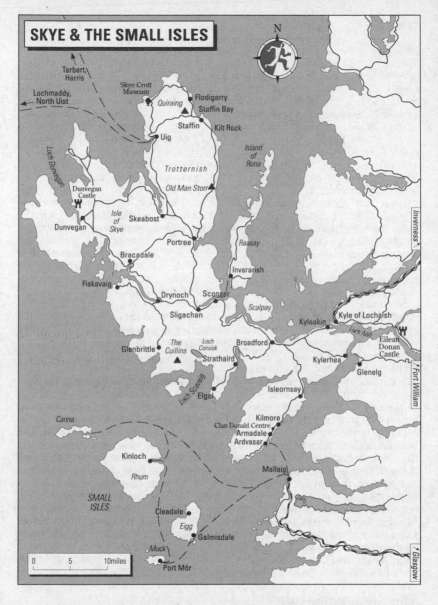

## SKYE & THE SMALL ISLES

Tarbert,
Harris

Lochmaddy,
North Uist

Loch Dunvegan

Skye Croft
Museum

Quiraing

Flodigarry

Staffin Bay

Staffin

Kilt Rock

Uig

Island
of
Rona

*Trotternish*

Old Man Storr

Dunvegan
Castle

*Isle
of
Skye*

Skeabost

Dunvegan

Portree

*Raasay*

Bracadale

Invararish

Fiskavaig

Drynoch

Sconser

*Scalpay*

Sligachan

Kyleakin

Kyle of Lochalsh

Loch Alsh

Glenbrittle

*The
Cuillins*

Loch
Coruisk

Broadford

Eilean
Donan
Castle

Strathaird

Kylerhea

Loch Scavaig

Elgol

Isleornsay

Glenelg

Canna

Kilmore

Clan Donald Centre

Armadale

Ardvasar

Kinloch

Mallaig

*Rhum*

*SMALL
ISLES*

Cleadale

*Eigg*

Galmisdale

*Muck*

Port Mór

Inverness

Fort William

Glasgow

0     5     10miles

of the island's owner, George Bullough, and now a swanky hotel. Cheaper accommodation is also available on Rhum, as it is on the other islands, but it's essential you reserve a bed before you catch the ferry – on all but Rhum, it's usually booked up months in advance.

# Skye

Jutting out from the mainland like a giant wing, the bare and bony promontories of **Skye** fringe a deeply indented coastline that makes the island never more than twenty-five, sometimes as little as seven, miles wide. Linked by an extensive road system, almost all Skye's scattered settlements cling to the shore. The fastest and busiest section of road follows the 33 miles from **Kyleakin** on the east coast, past minuscule **Sconser** – from where a car **ferry** crosses to the nearby mountainous island of **Raasay**, a finger of land some fourteen miles long and, at most, four miles wide – before heading to the small town of **Portree**. Portree's tourist office has easily the best selection of booklets on walking on the island, and the town makes an ideal base for day trips north into and around the **Trotternish**, a thumb-shaped peninsula sliced down the middle by the extraordinary rock formations of the jagged Trotternish ridge.

Back near Sconser, beside Skye's main road junction, the grimly commercial *Sligachan Hotel* is a popular starting point for walks into the **Cuillins**. From the hotel the A850 heads on to Portree, while the A863 cuts across to the west coast, passing, after six miles, the turning for the narrow vein of **Glen Brittle**, and another series of hiking trails off into the Cuillins. The west coast is something of an anticlimax, a gentle, repetitive shoreline which ends at **Dunvegan**, whose only redeeming feature is Dunvegan Castle, a mostly nineteenth-century structure that's long been the seat of the chieftains of the MacLeods.

Skye has several substantial **campsites**, five official and several independent **youth hostels** – all of which recommend advance bookings from mid-July to the end of August – and a string of great **hotels**. Most visitors arrive by car, as the **bus** services, while adequate between the villages, peter out in the more remote areas.

### Getting to Skye and the Islands

Most visitors still reach Skye via **Kyle of Lochalsh**, linked to Inverness by train, using the car ferry which shuttles back and forth to **Kyleakin**, on the western tip of the island. However, this part of Skye is pretty dull, and the more scenic approach – and the only way to get to the **Small Isles** – is from the **ferry** port of **Mallaig**, further south (see p.365). Linked by **train** with Glasgow, the Mallaig boat takes thirty minutes to cross to **Armadale**, on the gentle southern slopes of the Sleat peninsula. A third option is the privately operated car **ferry** which leaves the mainland at Glenelg, about thirty miles south from Kyle of Lochalsh, to arrive at **Kylerhea**, from where the road heads north towards Kyleakin.

If you're carrying on to the Western Isles, it's 57 miles from Armadale to the opposite end of Skye, where **ferries** leave **Uig** for Tarbert, on Harris. From Mallaig, the round-trip passenger **ferry** crossing to the rocky and frugal **Small Isles** takes about seven hours, and far longer in rough weather. The boat sometimes bypasses **Muck**, the smallest of the group, but it drops by the other three, **Eigg**, **Rhum** and **Canna**, once every Monday, Wednesday and Friday, and twice on Saturdays, when the sailing times make a day trip perfectly feasible.

# The Sleat peninsula

**ARMADALE** is an elongated hamlet stretching along the wooded shoreline of the **Sleat peninsula**. About half a mile from the jetty you'll find the **Clan Donald Visitor Centre** (Easter–late Oct daily 10am–5pm; gardens open all year; £3), whose handsome forty-acre gardens surround the nineteenth-century remains of **Armadale Castle**. Part of the castle has been turned into a **museum** that traces the history of the Gaels, concentrating on medieval times when the Donalds were the Lords of the Isles. It's well done, and the sound effects – savage clanging swords and battle songs – just about compensate for the lack of original artefacts. For more substantial information, you'll have to return to the refurbished stable block beside the entrance, where the bookshop carries a wide range of Scottish history books.

From Monday to Friday during the summer, there are regular **buses** from Armadale to Broadford and a once-daily service direct to Portree, but to move on at the weekend you'll have to hitch. Armadale has a **youth hostel** (late March–Sept; ☎0471/4260; Grade 2), off the main road near the seashore, a signposted ten-minute walk from the pier. The hostel rents **bikes** and has a small store.

Travelling northeast from Armadale, it's eight miles to the narrow country lane which leads the few hundred yards down to **ISLEORNSAY**, a secluded little village of ancient whitewashed cottages that was once Skye's main fishing port. With the mountains of the mainland on the horizon, the views out across the bay are wonderful, overlooking a necklace of seaweed-encrusted islets and a trim lighthouse, built by Robert Louis Stevenson's father. You can stay at the mid-nineteenth-century *Isle Ornsay Hotel* (☎0471/3332; ④), which also serves great seafood. Try and get a room in the main hotel building rather than the modern, soulless annexe.

## Kyleakin and Broadford

The tidy hamlet of **KYLEAKIN** lies along the flat shoreline beside the narrow channel separating Skye and Kyle of Lochalsh. There's nothing much to see or do here – you're well advised to just keep going – but you could have a quick look at the scant remains of **Castle Moil**, poking out into the straits on top of a diminutive rocky knoll. If you're marooned, the **youth hostel** (Feb–Nov; ☎0599/4585; Grade 1) is a couple of hundred yards from the ferry dock, and close by, *Mrs MacLennan*, 16 Kyleside (☎0599/4468; ②), is one of the cheapest of a long line of **B&Bs**.

Heading west out of Kyleakin, you'll spy the first piers of the bridge that will soon connect Skye with the mainland on your way to the island's second largest village, charmless **BROADFORD**, whose mile-long main street curves round a wide bay, with a **youth hostel** on the west shore (March–Oct; ☎0471/822442; Grade 2). From Broadford, there are regular **buses** to Portree and Kyleakin, and an occasional service to Elgol, fourteen miles to the west along the Strathaird peninsula – a journey that makes a grand cycle ride: **bikes** can be rented near the Broadford youth hostel from *Fairwinds Guest House* (April–Oct; ☎0471/822270). The **tourist office** (April–May & mid-Sept to Oct Mon–Sat 9am–1pm & 2–5.30pm; June to mid-Sept Mon–Sat 9am–7pm; ☎0471/822361) is also just a few minutes' walk from the hostel, next door to the garage on the main road.

## Elgol and Loch Coruisk

The only reason to visit the desparate-looking village of **ELGOL**, eight miles west of Broadford, is to take the boat trip, which bobs its way up **Loch Scavaig** once or twice daily throughout the season, to the tight entrance of **Loch Coruisk**. Arguably Scotland's wildest loch, this needle-like shaft of water, less than two miles long and only a couple of hundred yards wide, lies in the shadow of the highest peaks of the Cuillins, a wonderfully dramatic landscape. The excursion takes an hour or so and costs £5 – for details of sailing times, ring the skipper, Donald MacKinnon (☎0471/6244). Elgol itself is pretty dismal, but it does have a couple of **B&Bs**: try *Mrs MacKinnon*, at 4 Drinen (☎0471/6255; ②), or *Strathaird House* (☎0471/6269; ③), above a tiny bay four miles back towards Broadford. The latter is close to the start of one of the finest **walking trails** in Skye, the eight-mile round trip over the hills to **Camasunary** bay, at the foot of Glen Sligachan in the Cuillins. The path is easy to follow and not too steep, climbing over the shoulder of Am Mam for the first couple of miles, to reveal a stunningly beautiful view of the mountains with the islands of Soay, Rhum and Canna lying out to sea.

The only public transport along the Elgol road is the **post bus**, which leaves Broadford every weekday morning and returns in the afternoon to connect with – in theory at least – the Loch Coruisk boat; check up-to-date times and details at Broadford tourist office.

# Raasay

Travelling west from Broadford, with the Red Cuillins to the left of you and the sea to the right, it's thirteen miles to **SCONSER**, where a car **ferry** (£1.50 one-way, £2.40 day-return) leaves six times daily, except Sunday, for the small isle of **Raasay**. Though it takes only fifteen minutes to cross to the island, which offers great walks across its bleak and barren hills, Raasay remains well off the tourist trail. Once the property of the Jacobite MacLeods of Raasay, and practically destroyed by government troops in the 1760s, the island experienced a brief boom in the 1910s with the development of an iron ore mine. Today, however, now the mine's closed, it's a peaceful spot whose population – of just 150 – is concentrated in **INVERARISH** and **CLACHAN**, two tiny villages set within thick woods on the island's southwest coast.

The ferry docks at the southern tip of the island, an easy fifteen-minute walk from Inverarish and a further half mile from Clachan's **Raasay Outdoor Centre**, which occupies the grand Georgian mansion built by the MacLeods in the late 1740s to be all but ruined by government troops twenty years later. Today the place is being restored, and offers comfortable accommodation in tastefully bohemian rooms (March–Oct; ☎0478/62266; ③). You can also **camp** in the grounds, rent **mountain bikes** and join in the centre's activity programme – anything from sailing, windsurfing and canoeing, through to climbing and hill walking – for a daily cost of £25. Close by, there are comfortable rooms at the likeably old-fashioned *Isle of Raasay Hotel* (☎0478/62222; ⑤), which sits above the seashore looking out over Skye; they also serve delicious traditional Scottish food.

The grounds of the Outdoor Centre slope down to Clachan's tiny **harbour**, which is overlooked, from the top of a lumpy knoll, by two weathered stone mermaids with intimidating biceps. To the north, along the coast, lies the hamlet of **OSKAIG**, from where a rough track cuts up the steep hillside to reach, by turning right at the road, an isolated **youth hostel** (mid-May to Sept; ☎0478/62240; Grade 3).

Most of the rest of Raasay is starkly barren, a rugged and rocky terrain of sandstone in the south and gneiss in the north, with the most obvious feature being the curiously truncated basalt cap on top of **Dun Caan** – at 1456ft, Raasay's highest mountain. There's a strenuous and sometimes hard-to-follow trail to the peak, a splendid five-mile trek up through the forest and along the burn behind Inverarish. The quickest return is made down the northwest slope of Dun Caan, but – by going a couple of miles further – you can get back to the ferry along the southeast shore, passing the occasional abandoned crofters' village.

# The Cuillins

Back on Skye, about three miles southwest of Sconser, the *Sligachan Hotel* (April–Nov; ☎0478/650204; ④) and its adjacent campsite are the most popular starting points for hikes into the neighbouring **Cuillins**, whose sharp snow-capped peaks rise mirage-like from the flatness of the surrounding terrain. The hotel is at the top of **Glen Sligachan**, which stretches south down to the sea dividing the granite of the **Red Cuillins** from the dark, coarse-grained gabbro of the **Black Cuillins**, to the right. The track along the glen is one of Skye's most popular walks, leading the eight miles to **Camasunary** bay. A tougher route leaves the glen to climb over the hills to lochs Coruisk and Scavaig – though you can avoid the steep descent down to the lakes by taking a secondary path to the magnificent vantage point on the slopes of *Sgurr na Stri*.

Stony **Glen Brittle**, edging the western peaks of the Black Cuillins, is a favourite for climbers and serious walkers, who congregate at the **youth hostel**, nine miles south of the main Dunvegan road (late March–Sept; ☎047842/278; Grade 2). During the summer, there's one bus a day from Portree to both the hostel and Glen Brittle **campsite** (April–Sept; ☎047022/206), a mile or so further south behind the wide sandy beach at the foot of the glen. Both the youth hostel and the campsite have grocery stores, the only ones for miles.

From the valley a score of difficult and strenuous trails lead into the **Black Cuillins**, a rough circle of peaks that, rising to about 3000ft, surround Loch Coruisk. There are easier walks too, such as the five-mile round trip from the campsite to **Coire Lagan**, a crystal-cold lochan squeezed in among the sternest of rock faces.

### Dunvegan
After the Glen Brittle turning, the main road slips across bare rounded hills to skirt the bony seacliffs and stacks of the west coast near Struan and its tiny neighbour **ULLINISH**, where you'll find the remote *Ullinish Lodge Hotel* (Easter–Oct; ☎047072/214; ⑤). From here, it's about ten miles to **DUNVEGAN**, an unappealing place strung out along the east shore of the sea loch of the same name. Just beyond the village, **Dunvegan Castle** (April–Oct Mon–Sat 10am–5.30pm & Sun 1–5.30pm; £3.80) perches on top of a rocky outcrop, a greying, rectangular fortress sandwiched between the sea and several acres of beautifully maintained gardens. There's been a castle here since the thirteenth century, but the present structure mostly dates from the 1840s when the twenty-fifth Chief of the MacLeods had the building modernized, creating the uniform battlements and dummy pepperpot turrets you see today. In medieval times, the castle could only be entered from the sea, and the mighty warships of the MacLeods were famous throughout Scotland, but now a bridge spans the old moat, leading to a small, unassuming entrance.

The stately rooms of the interior – about half a dozen are open to the public – sport all sorts of clannish trinkets, including a drinking horn, which each new chief was supposed to drain at one draught "without setting down or falling down", and an intriguing display on the remote archipelago of St Kilda, flung far out west of North Uist, and long the fiefdom of the MacLeods. You can also see a portrait of Dr Johnson, who visited the castle in 1773, and a lock of hair from the head of Bonnie Prince Charlie, but most intriguing of all are the battered remnants of the **Fairy Flag** in the drawing room. Made in Syria or Rhodes between the fourth and sixth century AD, the silken flag may have been the battle standard of the Norwegian king, Harald Hardrada, who had been the commander of the imperial guard in Constantinople. Hardrada died trying to seize the English throne at the Battle of Stamford Bridge in 1066, his flag alleg- edly carried back to Skye by his Gaelic boatmen. More fancifully, MacLeod family tradition asserts that the flag was the gift of the fairies, blessed with the power to protect the clan in times of danger – and as late as World War II, MacLeod pilots carried pictures of it for luck.

From the jetty outside the castle there are regular seal-spotting **boat trips** (Mon–Sat; 30min; £3.20) out along Loch Dunvegan, as well as longer and less frequent sea cruises (£6.50).

It's unlikely you'll want to stay in Dunvegan, but there are several reasonably priced **hotels** and **B&Bs** dotted along the main road, including the family-owned *Tables Hotel* (☎047022/404; ③). The Dunvegan **campsite** (April–Sept; ☎047022/ 206) is about half a mile east of the village out towards Portree. In the opposite direction, out on the west coast, are some of Skye's most fearsome sea cliffs, with blustery footpaths leading to the dramatically sited lighthouse on **Neist Point** and to the sheer thousand-foot **Biod an Athair** at the mouth of Loch Dunvegan.

# Portree

Originally known as Kiltaraglen, **PORTREE** (*Port-an-Righ*, Port of the King) takes its name from the state visit James V made in 1540 to assert his authority over the chieftains of Skye. The village only began to expand in the late eight- eenth century, when it became the island's administrative and commercial centre, and today the most prepossessing part of this small town is the harbour, a deep cliff-edged indentation filled with colourful fishing boats and circled by the restau- rants and guest houses of Beaumont Crescent. **Boat trips** leave the pier for excursions out along the Sound of Raasay three times daily from April to October – the trip takes two hours and costs £6 per person.

The harbour is bordered by **The Lump**, a steep and stumpy peninsula that was once the site of public hangings, the unfortunates dragged from the neighbouring jail-cum-courthouse that now houses the tourist office. Up above the harbour is the spick and span town centre, built around Sommerled Square, with its banks, pubs and churches. A mile or so out of town on the Sligachan road, Skye's **Heritage Centre**, or *Dualchas an Eilein* (April–Oct daily 9am–9pm; Nov–March daily 9am– 6pm; £3.50) displays a collection of dioramas and videos that trace the troubled history of the island – an enjoyable way to pass a couple of hours if it's raining.

## Practicalities
**Buses** to Portree arrive in Sommerled Square, from where it's a couple of minutes walk along Wentworth and Bank streets to the **tourist office** (April–May & mid-Sept to Oct Mon–Sat 9am–5.30pm; June to mid-Sept Mon–Sat 9am–7pm; Nov–March Mon–Fri 9am–5pm; ☎0478/2137), who will, for a £1 fee, book accom-

modation for you – especially useful at the height of the season. They also have bus timetables and the island's best selection of maps and guides. The tourist office has the details of local **car rental** firms too, among them *Ewen MacRae*, at the BP station about a mile out of town on Dunvegan Road (☎0478/2554).

Portree has a good range of comfortable and convenient, if rather pricy, **hotels**, including the *Caledonian*, on Wentworth Street (☎0478/2641; ④); *The Kings Haven*, overlooking the harbour at 11 Bosville Terrace (☎0478/2290; ④); and the converted fishermen's houses of the *Rosedale Hotel*, which has splendid views out to sea from Beaumont Crescent (☎0478/3131; ⑥). There are plenty of **B&Bs**, too, several of which are clustered on and around the harbour: try *Craiglockhart Guest House*, Beaumont Crescent (☎0478/2233; ③), or, on Bosville Terrace, the *Harbour View* (☎0478/2069; ③) and the *Coolin View Guest House* (☎0478/2300; ④). Torvaig **campsite** (April–Oct; ☎0478/2209) lies a mile and a half north of town on the A855 Staffin road.

The best **restaurant** in town is the *Ben Tianavaig Bistro*, 5 Bosville Terrace (☎0478/2152; closed Mon), where a full meal will set you back about £8, a little more if you choose fresh seafood. Other good choices are the restaurant in the *Rosedale Hotel*, and, for a budget feast, the fish and chip shop out towards the pier on Quay Street.

# The Trotternish peninsula

Protruding twenty miles north from Portree, the **Trotternish peninsula** boasts some of the island's finest scenery, its narrow coastal shelf overshadowed by the wizened basalt of the Trotternish ridge, whose pinnacles and pillars are at their most eccentric in the **Quiraing**, above Staffin Bay.

An occasional bus service along the road encircling the peninsula gives access to almost all the coast. About six miles north of Portree, the **Old Man of Storr** is a distinctive, pear-shaped column of rock, which along with its neighbours is part of a massive landslip, with huge blocks of stone continuing to occasionally break off the cliff face above and slide downhill. At 165ft, the Old Man is a real challenge for climbers – less difficult is the brief and boggy footpath up to the column from the car park beside the main road. Eight miles further north, there's another car park for the **Kilt Rock**, whose tube-like, basaltic columns rise precipitously from the sea.

From the Kilt Rock, it's a couple of miles to one of the island's best **B&Bs**, *Quiraing Lodge* (☎0470/62330; ③). Set in an acre of well-tended garden a few minutes' walk from the main road, overlooking Staffin Bay and loomed over by the scowling mass of the Quiraing, the *Lodge* serves delicious vegetarian food and also rents bikes. Another excellent base for exploring the Quiraing is the tiny hamlet of **FLODIGARRY**, three miles further north. Here, the exquisite *Flodigarry Country House Hotel* (☎0470/52203; ④), with its lovely wrought-iron loggia and partly castellated walls, sits tight between the mountains and the fossil-strewn beach. Behind the hotel is the cottage where local heroine Flora MacDonald and her family lived from 1751 to 1759, though currently it's not open to the public on anything like a regular basis. The hotel restaurant, concentrating on local produce, is superb, if pricy – light lunches and snacks are available at the bar, a favourite haunt of residents from the neat and tidy independent *Dun Flodigarry Hostel* (☎047052/212), a couple of minutes' walk away.

From Flodigarry, a well-beaten track leads into the savage rock formations of the **Quiraing**, passing a series of lochans and mighty pinnacles on its way to the Table, a great sunken platform where Victorian ramblers picnicked and played cricket. Even if the weather's foul, you can get a good impression of the Quiraing by crossing the peninsula via the minor road that starts near Quiraing Lodge and ends up at Uig (see below).

Beyond Flodigarry, the road veers west, rounding the tip of the Trotternish ridge before reaching **DUNTULUM**, whose heyday as a major MacDonald powerbase is recalled by the shattered remains of a headland **fortress**. The swanky *Duntulum Castle Hotel* (Easter–Oct; ☎0470/52213; ⑤) is next door.

Heading down the west shore of the Trotternish, it's two miles to the cluster of restored thatched houses that make up the **Skye Museum of Island Life** (April–Oct daily 9am–6pm; £1.25), though the emphasis here is strictly on tartan kitsch and the museum shop. Behind the museum up the hill is **Flora MacDonald**'s grave, inscribed with a simple, contemporaneous tribute by Dr Johnson. A further four miles south is the ferry port of **UIG**, which curves its way round a horseshoe-shaped bay. Uig **campsite** (April–Oct; ☎0470/42360) is by the shore near the dock, while the **youth hostel** (April–Oct; ☎0470/42211; Grade 2) is on the south side of the village. Nearby, at the other end of the accommodation spectrum, the *Uig Hotel* (Easter to mid-Oct; ☎0470/42205; ⑤) serves up great home-made food.

# The Small Isles

In the 1740s, the chief of the Clanranalds, long the leading local family among the **Small Isles** southwest of Skye, introduced the **potato** to the islands. The consequences were as dramatic as they were unforeseen. The success of the crop and its nutritional value – when grown in conjunction with traditional cereals – eliminated famine at a stroke, prompting a population explosion. In 1750, there were just one thousand islanders, but by 1800 their numbers had almost doubled.

At first, the problem of overcrowding was camouflaged by the **kelp** boom, in which the islanders were employed, and the islands' owners made a fortune, gathering and burning local seaweed to sell for use in the manufacture of gunpowder, soap and glass. But the economic bubble burst with the end of the Napoleonic Wars and, to maintain their profit margins, the owners resorted to drastic action. Alexander Maclean sold **Rhum** as grazing land for sheep, got quotations for shipping its people to Nova Scotia, and gave them a year's notice to quit. He also cleared **Muck** to graze cattle, as did the MacNeills on **Canna**. Only on **Eigg** was some compassion shown; the new owner, a certain Hugh MacPherson, who bought the island from the Clanranalds in 1827, actually gave some of his tenants extended leases.

Since the Clearances each of the islands has been bought and sold several times, though only Eigg and Muck are now in private hands. The other islands were bequeathed to national agencies, Rhum passing to the Nature Conservancy Council in 1957, and Canna to the NTS in 1981.

At eight miles square, **Rhum** is the largest and most visited of the group, possessing a cluster of formidable volcanic peaks south of **Kinloch,** the island's only village. The bumpy, basaltic terrain of **Canna** deserves at least a day trip, offering wonderful walking opportunities and a calming sense of isolation typical of all the Small Isles.

# Rhum

Loch Scresort, the pencil-thin harbour of **Rhum**, is too shallow to take the ferry from Mallaig, so incomers have to hop off onto the island tender, which lands them just a few minutes' walk along the shore from **KINLOCH**. There's nothing much to see in this unassuming village, until you reach the elongated arcades and squat turrets of **Kinloch Castle**, a reddish sandstone edifice completed in 1901 and now maintained as a hotel. It's an odd-looking place, a hesitant attempt at the Gothic style, but the interior, past the main hall draped with animal skins and a forest of antlers, is extraordinary, packed with the knick-knacks collected by a self-made millionaire, one Sir George Bullough, who used the place as a part-time hunting lodge. If you're not staying, ask the manager to show you around – Bullough, keen to impress his guests, not only paid a piper to play at every sunset, but also had an orchestrion, an electrically driven barrel organ, crammed in under the stairs to grind out an eccentric mixture of pre-dinner tunes – *The Ride of the Valkyries* and *Ma Blushin Rosie*, among others, are still played. The *pièce de resistance*, though, has to be Bullough's Edwardian **shower**, whose six dials, on the hooded head-piece, fire high-pressure water from every angle imaginable. Outside, but long gone, great glasshouses once sheltered tropical trees, and heated pools were stocked with turtles and alligators, though these were eventually removed at the insistence of the terrified staff.

The year before the construction of his house was completed, Bullough had, at his own expense, sent a hospital ship to the Boer War. He was rewarded with a knighthood, but, as the grandson of a Lancashire weaver, was still kept at arm's length by the aristocracy, who mocked both him and the unlettered taste of his castle. Hurt, Sir George began to keep strangers off the island and the house was barely used when he died in 1939.

If you can't afford to stay at the *Kinloch Castle Hotel* (☎0687/2037; ⑦), where rates include a superb dinner and breakfast, there's also a thirty-bed independent **youth hostel** behind the hotel, in the old servants' quarters. The hostel's bistro dishes up good-value meals. Other accommodation options in Kinloch include several cheap and simple **bothies** rented by the Nature Conservancy Council and **camping** on the foreshore near the jetty (reservations for both ☎0687/2026). The council's resident warden will advise on local **walks** too, the most dramatic being the trail along the southern shoreline beneath the mountain peaks.

# Canna, Muck and Eigg

On Saturdays, the Mallaig boat's first port of call is **Canna**, whose horn-shaped harbour shelters the main settlement of the same name. For visitors, the chief pastime is walking; from the dock it's about a mile across a grassy basalt plateau to the bony seacliffs of the north shore, and just five miles to the buffeted western tip of the island, where you can spy, some seven miles offshore, the **Heiskeir of Canna**, a curious mass of stone columns sticking up 30ft above the water. If you want to stay on the island, the only place is the NTS-owned *Tighard*, half a mile from the jetty, which sleeps a maximum of ten people and costs £300 per week, rising to £500 in July and August. Booking forms are available from *Holiday Cottages*, National Trust for Scotland, 5 Charlotte Square, Edinburgh (☎031/226 5922). Remember, however, that there are no shops on Canna, so you must bring your own supplies.

Canna supports the tiniest of populations, who croft the land and fish the sea, as do the inhabitants of low-lying **Muck**, whose name derives from *muc*, the Gaelic for "pig" – much to the irritation of earlier lairds who preferred to call it the "Isle of Monk", because it had briefly belonged to the medieval church. Frankly, there's no real reason to stay here, but it is possible – the island Estate Office takes bookings for a handful of double rooms (☎0687/2365; ②).

Last of all, **Eigg**, measuring five miles by three, is distinguished by a brooding mile-long ridge of columnar basalt that reaches a height of 1290ft straight above the crofting hamlet of **GALMISDALE** and provides a splendid walk, with fine views over the sea to Rhum. The only place to stay on Eigg is the refurbished, three-bedroomed croft house, *Lageorna*, (☎0687/82405; ①, or ② full board).

# THE WESTERN ISLES

The wild and windy **Western Isles** vaunt a strikingly hostile mix of landscapes. The interior of the northernmost island, **Lewis**, is mostly peat moor, a barren and marshy tract that gives way abruptly to the bare peaks of **North Harris**. Across a narrow isthmus lies **South Harris**, presenting some of the finest scenery in Scotland, with wide sandy beaches trimming the Atlantic in full view of the mountains and a rough boulder-strewn interior lying to the east. Further south still, a string of tiny, flatter islets, mainly **North Uist**, **Benbecula**, **South Uist** and **Barra**, offer breezy beaches, whose fine sands front a narrow band of boggy farmland, which, in turn, is mostly bordered by a lower range of hills to the east.

In direct contrast to their wonderful landscapes, the Western Isles claim only the scrawniest of villages, unhappy-looking places that straggle out along the elementary road system. Only **Tarbert**, on Harris, and **Lochmaddy**, on North Uist, sustain a modicum of charm; **Stornoway**, Lewis's only town, is eminently unappealing. Many visitors, walkers and nature watchers forsake the settlements altogether and retreat to secluded cottages and B&Bs – though this is difficult without your own transport.

The islands' six official **youth hostels** – there are also several independents – are geared up for the outdoor life, occupying remote locations on or near the coast. Four of these are run by the *Gatliff Hebridean Hostels Trust*, who have renovated several old crofters' cottages. None of these have phones, you can't book in advance, and, although each has a simple kitchen, you have to take your own food. If you're after a little more comfort, then the islands have a generous sprinkling of reasonably priced **B&Bs** and **guest houses** – many of which are a lot more elegant than the hotels.

Although travelling around the islands is time-consuming, for many people this is part of their charm. A series of inter-island causeways makes it possible to drive from one end of the Western Isles to the other with just two interruptions – the *CalMac* **ferry** trip from Harris to North Uist, and the one from South Uist to Barra. A couple of smaller companies operate additional inter-island routes, some of them connecting with the islands' distinctly low-key **bus** service – though you should certainly not count on an onward bus connection when you arrive.

There are two other peculiarities worth mentioning. First, the road signs are almost exclusively in **Gaelic**, and, particularly if you're driving, it's well worth buying the bilingual **Western Isles Leisure Map**, available at most of the tourist

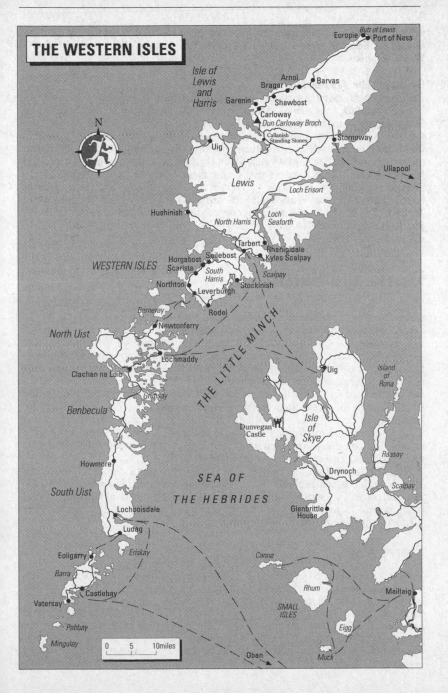

# THE WESTERN ISLES

*Isle of Lewis and Harris*

Eoropie
Butt of Lewis
Port of Ness

Arnol
Barvas
Bragar
Garenin
Shawbost
Carloway
Dun Carloway Broch
Callanish Standing Stones
Stornoway
Uig

*Lewis*

Loch Erisort

Ullapool

Hushinish

*North Harris*

Loch Seaforth

Tarbert
Rhenigidale
Seilebost
Kyles Scalpay
Horgabost
Scarista
*South Harris*
Scalpay
Northton
Stockinish
Leverburgh

*WESTERN ISLES*

Berneray
Rodel

Newtonferry

*North Uist*
Lochmaddy

Uig
*Island of Rona*

Clachan na Luib

*Grimsay*

*Benbecula*
Dunvegan Castle
*Isle of Skye*

*THE LITTLE MINCH*

Howmore
*Raasay*

*South Uist*
Drynoch

*SEA OF*
*Scalpay*

Lochboisdale
*THE HEBRIDES*

Glenbrittle House

Ludag
*Eriskay*
Eoligarry
*Canna*
*Barra*
*Rhum*
Maillaig
Castlebay
Vatersay
*SMALL*
*ISLES*
*Pabbay*
*Eigg*
*Mingulay*

0    5    10miles

Oban
*Muck*

offices. Secondly, although several local companies – but none of the big multinationals – offer **car rental**, you're not permitted to take their vehicles off the Western Isles.

### Getting to the Western Isles

*British Airways* operates fast and frequent **flights** from Glasgow to Stornoway on Lewis. *Loganair* have small planes flying from Stornoway to Benbecula and Barra, where there are flights direct to and from Glasgow. But be warned, the weather conditions on the islands are notoriously changeable, making Loganair's flights both prone to delay and sometimes stomach-churningly bumpy. On Barra, the other complication is that you land on the beach, so the timetable is adjusted with the tides. *CalMac* **car ferries** run from Ullapool in the Highlands to Stornoway; from Uig, on Skye, to Tarbert and Lochmaddy; and from Oban to South Uist and Barra. There's also an **inter-island ferry** from Lochmaddy to Tarbert. The smaller companies operate passenger ferries from Leverburgh, on South Harris, to Newton Ferry, North Uist; and from Ludag, South Uist to Eoligarry, on Barra.

# Lewis and Harris

Many of the 21,000 inhabitants of **Lewis** live in the crofting and fishing villages along the west coast, between **Callanish** and **Port of Ness**, 34 miles away on the island's northern tip. On this coast you'll find the islands' best preserved prehistoric remains – at **Carloway** and **Callanish** – as well as a smattering of ancient crofters' houses in various stages of abandonment. The shoreline is for the most part fairly flat and quite dull, although the **Butt of Lewis**, a group of rough rocks near Port of Ness, are a dramatic exception.

Most visitors use **Stornoway**, on the east coast, as a base for exploring the island, though this presents problems if you're travelling by bus. There's a regular service to Port of Ness and Tarbert, and although the most obvious excursion – the 45-mile round trip from Stornoway to Callanish, Carloway, Arnol and back – is almost impossible to complete by public transport, the tourist office's minibus tours make the trip on most days during the season.

Heading south from Stornoway, the mountains mark the start of **North Harris**, an inhospitable chunk of land extending west from Loch Seaforth to the Atlantic coast. On **South Harris**, you'll find the ferry port of **Tarbert**, giving ready access to superb hiking country and an easy excursion to **Rodel**, near **Leverburgh**, with its twelfth-century church.

## Stornoway

For centuries life in **STORNOWAY** (*Steornabhagh*) has focused on its harbour, whose deep and sheltered waters were thronged with coastal steamers and fishing boats in their nineteenth-century heyday. Today, the catch is landed on the mainland, and, despite the comings and goings of the Ullapool ferry, the harbour is a shadow of its former commercial self. The port's west bank is covered by the wooded grounds of **Lews Castle**, a nineteenth-century Gothic pomposity now turned into a technical college, while Stornoway's modern centre, packed between the harbour and the Bayhead River, is little more than a string of tatty shops and rough-edged bars. There's little to see, though you could drop by the town hall, on the harbour front, where the **An Lanntair Art Gallery** (Mon–Sat 10am–5.30pm; free) features the work of local artists.

### Practicalities

The best thing about Stornoway is the convenience of its services. The island's **airport** is just four miles east of the town centre, a £4 taxi ride away, and the **ferry** terminal is only a couple of minutes' walk along the harbour front from the **bus station**. You can get the timetables of the area's most useful bus routes from the nearby **tourist office**, 26 Cromwell St (mid-Oct to late March Mon–Fri 9am–5pm; April to mid-Oct Mon–Sat 9am–6pm; ☎0851/703088), who also sell the tickets for the £5-per-person minibus **trips** to Callanish, Carloway and Arnol; failing that taxis cost around £30 for a maximum of four people.

The tourist office will also, for a £1 booking fee, fix you up with local **accommodation** (for out-of-town reservations they charge £2.50). If you prefer to look for yourself, try the **B&Bs** along Matheson Road: *Mrs C. Macleod*, at no. 19 (☎0851/704180; ②), and *Mrs A. Macleod*, at no. 12 (☎0851/702673; ③), are both good. Other convenient options include *Mrs MacMillan*, 64 Keith St (☎0851/704815; ②), and *Mrs Skinner*, 29 Francis St (☎0851/703482; ③). Stornoway has two independent **youth hostels**, one a basic affair about five minutes' walk from the ferry at 47 Keith St (☎0851/703628; ①), the other, the *Bayble Bunkhouse* (☎0851/870863; ①), has dormitory beds eight miles east of town in **UPPER BAYBLE** (*Pabail Uarach*) – call ahead if you need them to come and collect you from Stornoway. The nearest **campsite**, the *Laxdale Caravan Site* (☎0851/703234), lies a couple of miles out of town beside the road to Barvas, on Laxdale Lane in **LAXDALE** (*Lacasdal*). Two of the more established of Stornoway's several **car rental** firms are *Arnol Motors*, Arnol (☎0851/71548) and *Mackinnon Self-Drive*, 18 Inaclete Rd (☎0851/702984). *Alex Dan Cycle Centre*, 67 Kenneth St (Mon–Sat 9am–6pm; ☎0851/704025 or 702934), rents **mountain bikes**.

As for **food**, you can get tasty snacks and lunches from the *An Lanntair Art Gallery*'s coffee shop, while *John MacIver's* fish and chip shop, 6 Church St, is one of several similar places. The *Fisherman Cafeteria* (Mon–Fri 8am–5pm) serves good-value, filling meals in the *National Mission to Deep Sea Fishermen* building on North Beach Street, while the *Crown Hotel*, nearby on Castle Street, serves huge main courses as part of their evening menu – the fish, especially, is delicious. Stornoway's hotels have the busiest **bars**: try either the *County Hotel*, 14 Francis St, or the *Royal Hotel*, Cromwell St.

# Callanish, Carloway, Arnol and Port of Ness

West of Stornoway, the road crosses the **moorland** of the interior, an empty wilderness marked by innumerable peat diggings. The moors were once covered by forests, but these disappeared long ago, leaving a smothering deposit of peat that is, on average, 5ft thick. The islanders cut the peat in the spring, turning it over and leaving it stacked in the open air to dry, returning in summer to collect the dried sods, which remain the island's main source of domestic fuel.

After sixteen miles, you reach the **Callanish Standing Stones**, whose monoliths – nearly fifty of them – occupy a dramatic lochside setting near the road on the edge of the village of **CALLANISH** (*Calanais*). There's been years of heated debate about the origin and function of the Standing Stones – slabs of wizened and finely-grained gneiss up to 15ft high – though almost everyone agrees that they were lugged here by Neolithic peoples between 3000 and 1500 BC. It's also obvious that the planning and construction of the site – as well as several other lesser circles nearby – was spread over many generations. Such an endeavour could, it's been argued, only be prompted by the desire to predict the seasonal cycle upon which these early farmers were entirely dependent, and indeed, many of the stones are aligned with the position of the sun and the stars. This rational explanation, based on clear evidence that this part of Lewis was once a fertile farming area, dismisses as coincidence the ground plan of the site, which resembles a colossal Celtic cross, and explains away the central burial chamber as a later addition of no special significance. These two features have, however, fuelled all sorts of mystic mumbo-jumbo, from tales of alien intervention to gory suggestions of human sacrifice.

The crofter's cottage adjacent to the Standing Stones has been refurbished as a **tea shop**, and nearby, beside the village post office, is the **B&B** of *Mrs Cathy Crossley*, 24 Callanish (March–Oct; ☎0851/72236; ②); there's another, just as good, at no. 27 (March–Oct; ☎0851/72392; ②).

## Carloway Broch and Arnol's Island Blackhouse

From the Standing Stones, it's six miles to the sprawling hamlet of **DOUNE CARLOWAY** (*Dun Charlabhaigh*), where **Carloway Broch** perches on top of a conspicuous rocky outcrop overlooking the sea about 400yd from the road. Scotland's Atlantic coast is strewn with the remains of over five hundred brochs, or fortified towers, but this is one of the best preserved, its drystone circular walls reaching a height of over 30ft on the seaward side. The broch consists of two concentric walls, the inner one perpendicular, the outer one slanting inwards, the two originally fastened together by roughly hewn flagstones, which also served as look-out galleries reached via a narrow stairwell. The only entrance to the roofless inner yard is through a low doorway set beside a crude and cramped guard cell. Like the Standing Stones, there have been all sorts of theories about the purpose of the brochs, which date from between 100 BC and 100 AD; the most likely explanation is that they were built to provide protection from Roman slave traders.

Doune Carloway is the first of a trio of roadside hamlets that take the name Carloway, the others being **CARLOWAY** (*Charlabhaigh*) and then **UPPER CARLOWAY** (*Mullach Charlabhaigh*). This becomes confusing as each village runs into the other, but it's Carloway you want for the mile-long turning down to the remote coastal settlement of **GARENIN**, where one of the old thatched crofters' houses has been opened as a primitive **youth hostel** (May–Dec; no phone; Grade 3). The nearest store is back in Carloway.

Returning to the main road, it's about five miles north along the coast to **BRAGAR** (*Bragar*), where you'll spot a stark arch formed by the jawbone of a blue whale. The spear sticking through the bone is the harpoon that killed the mighty beast way back in 1919. A further two miles brings you to the village of **ARNOL**, which meanders down towards the sea. Here, the crofters' modern concrete houses sit surrounded by the abandoned stone cottages and enclosures of their forebears, while a rusting assortment of discarded cars and vans gives the place a depressingly uncared-for air.

On the far side of the village, about a mile from the main road, is the **Island Blackhouse** (April–Sept Mon–Sat 9.30am–6.30pm; Oct–March Mon–Sat 9.30am–

4pm; £1.50), which dates from the 1870s and was inhabited right up until 1964. Built low against the wind, the house's thick walls are made up of an inner and outer layer of loose stone on either side of a central core of earth, a traditional type of construction which attracted the soubriquet "blackhouse" around 1850, when buildings with single-thickness walls were introduced to Lewis from the mainland and were commonly called "white houses" (*tigh geal*) by the locals – even though they weren't all white. Thus traditional dwellings came to be called "blackhouses" (*tigh dubh*).

The Island Blackhouse is typical of its type, with a chimney-less roof overlaid with grassy sods and oat-straw thatch, lashed down with fishnets and ropes. Beneath, a simple system of wooden tie-beams supports the roof, which covers both the living quarters and the attached byre and barn. The post-war wallpaper inside has been removed to reveal the sooty roof rafters above the living room, where, in the centre of the stone and clay floor, the peat fire was the focal point of the house. As one of the children described her house in a school essay of the 1950s, "During winter, many neighbours come in each night. We form a circle round the fire and discuss many subjects...The Blackhouse is definitely the cosiest you can find".

## Port of Ness

At **BARVAS** (*Barabhas*) you can either head across the moors for the twelve-mile return journey to Stornoway, or continue north along the coast another fifteen miles, passing a string of crofting villages en route to the remote village **PORT OF NESS** (*Port Nis*), nestled round its tiny harbour. Each September, local hunters set sail from here for **Sulisgeir**, thirty miles offshore, to harvest the young gannets (*gugas*) that nest high up on the islet's seacliffs. It's a dangerous activity, but then, for some reason unknown to outsiders, boiled gannet and potato is a favourite Lewis dish.

From Port of Ness, a minor road heads two miles north to the hamlet of **EUROPIE** (*Eoropaidh*) and the **Church of Saint Moluag** (*Teampull Mholuaidh*), an austere stone structure dating from the twelfth century. In the seventeenth century, the traveller Martin Martin noted "[everyone went to church] and then [after] standing silent for a little time, one of them gave a signal ... and immediately all went into the fields, where they fell a drinking their Ale and spent the remainder of the Night in Dancing and Singing". Unfortunately, services today aren't quite as stimulating as they used to be.

From Europie, a narrow road twists north to the bleak and blustery tip of the island, the **Butt of Lewis** (*Rubha Robhanais*), where a lighthouse sticks up above a desolate seashore alive with a cacophany of sea birds.

Several **B&Bs** line the main road between Barvas and Port of Ness: one of the most comfortable is the *Harbour View Guest House* (☎0851/81735; ③), located in an old boat builder's house overlooking the Port of Ness harbour; the home-cooked food is good here too.

# North and South Harris

South of Stornaway the road bumps through the peat moors of Lewis where it follows the dramatic shores of the fjord-like **Loch Seaforth** to meet the bulging, pyramidical mountains of **North Harris**. This bitter terrain offers but the barest of vegetation, with the occasional cluster of crofters' houses sitting in the shadow of a host of pointed peaks, anywhere between 1000ft and 2500ft high. Eventually, the road finds a way to thread across the range, sneaking over a boulder-strewn saddle beneath mighty *Sgaoth Aird* and its lesser neighbours, to twist down to the ferry port of **TARBERT** (*Tairbeart*), sheltered in a green valley on the narrow isthmus between two lochs at the point where North and South Harris meet. There's nothing much to the place – just a few terraces sloping up from the dock – but you could do worse than stay at the easy-going, old-fashioned *Harris Hotel* (☎0859/2154; ⑤), five minutes' walk from the ferry. Cheaper, equally convenient places to stay include the *Allan Cottage Guest House* (☎0859/2146; ③), in the old telephone exchange, and a couple of nearby **B&Bs**, *Rockcliffe* (☎0859/2386; ③) and *Dunard* (☎0859/2340; ③). Excellent, reasonably priced **food** is served at both the *Harris Hotel* and the *Allan Cottage*.

Beside the ferry terminal, Tarbert **tourist office** (April to mid-Oct Mon–Sat 9am–5pm; summer also Tues, Thurs & Sat 8–9pm; ☎0859/2011) will arrange accommodation and has a full set of bus timetables, but its real value is as a source of information on local walks. There are many possible routes, but a particular favourite is the six-mile trek over to the Gatliff Trust's **youth hostel** (no phone; Grade 3) in the lonely coastal hamlet of **RHENIGIDALE** (*Reinigeadal*). To reach the hostel, walk east from Tarbert down the road to **Kyles Scalpay** (*Caolas Scalphaigh*), and, after two miles, watch for the sign marking the start of the trail, near the lay-by. The path threads its way through the peaks of the craggy promontory that lies trapped between Loch Seaforth and East Loch Tarbert. It's a magnificent hike, with superb views out along the coast and over the mountains, but you'll need to be properly equipped and should allow three hours for the one-way trip.

Another possibility is the six-mile trek south to **Stockinish youth hostel** (April–Sept; ☎0859/83373; Grade 3) in **KYLES STOCKINISH** (*Caolas Stocinis*), on South Harris. The trek serves as a good introduction to the island's rough and rocky southeast coast, and the hostel, overlooking the coast, is a good base for further walks. It is also accessible by road. Booking ahead is advised in late July and August.

Tarbert tourist office also have the addresses of local weavers who will show you how they make **"Harris Tweed"** – not a picturesque cottage industry, as it's sometimes presented, but a vital part of the local economy with a well-organized and unionized workforce. Traditionally the tweed was made by local women to clothe their families, with each woman responsible for the entire process, from the washing and scouring of the wool through to its colouring, spinning, weaving and finishing. However, in the mid-nineteenth century, a local landowner, the Countess of Dunmore, started to sell surplus cloth to her aristocratic friends, thus forming the genesis of the modern industry, which now employs about four hundred mill workers and a further seven hundred and fifty weavers – though demand, and employment, fluctuates wildly as fashions change. To earn the official Harris Tweed trademark, the fabric has to be hand-woven on the Outer Hebrides from 100 percent pure new Scottish wool, although other parts of the manufacturing process take place in the local mills.

In recent years, there has been a revival of traditional tweed-making techniques, with several small producers, like *Clo Mor* at 1 Liceasto (☎0859/83364), in the village of **LIKISTO** (*Liceasto*), about four miles south of Tarbert, religiously following old methods. One of the more interesting aspects of the process is the use of indigenous plants and bushes to dye the cloth. Yellow comes from rocket and broom, green from heather, grey and black from iris and oak, and, most popular of all, reddish brown from crotal, a flat grey lichen scraped off rocks.

## Scarista, Leverburgh and Rodel

Heading into **South Harris** from Tarbert, the main road snakes its way west across the lunar interior to emerge, after ten miles, at the hamlet of **SEILEBOST**, and the first of a chain of sweeping sandy **beaches** that stretches for nine miles south along the Atlantic coast. Both here, and at the neighbouring villages of **HORGABOST** and **SCARISTA** (*Sgarasta*), the scenery is stunning, the golden sands set against the rounded peaks of the mountains to the north and the islet-studded sea to the west. Nobody bothers much if you camp or park down on the dune-edged beach; alternatively, you can find shelter at the **B&Bs** and **guest houses** dotted along the road. Good-value B&Bs include *Mrs MacLennan*, 1 Horgabost (April–Oct; ☎0859/85246; ③), and *Mrs MacDonald*, at 6 Horgabost (☎0859/ 85215; ②). The swankiest accommodation is at *Scarista House* (April–Oct; ☎0859/85238; ⑧), which looks out to sea from above the beach.

In the lee of the sharp headland bordering Harris's last beach is the crofters' village of **NORTHTON** (*Taobh Tuath*), where the road veers to the east to trim the island's south shore, reaching the ugly sprawl of **LEVERBURGH** (*An T-ob*)* after a couple of miles. From a jetty about a mile south of the main road, a passenger **ferry** (summer Mon–Sat 2 daily; other times 3 weekly; £3; sailing times from Tarbert tourist office or call Donald Macaskill ☎0876/7230) leaves for **Berneray** (*Bearnaraigh*), a low-lying islet eight miles in circumference, with yet another excellent sandy beach. If you want to stay, the island has the **B&B** of *Mrs MacLeod* (☎08767/254; ②), and a simple Gatliff Trust **youth hostel** (no phone; Grade 3), in a pair of thatched cottages two miles from the dock, right round Bays Loch. You could conceivably head on to North Uist on the Leverburgh ferry, though it's a highly inconvenient way of getting there.

Back on South Harris, it's just three miles southeast from Leverburgh to the old port of **RODEL** (*Roghadal*), where a smattering of ancient stone houses lie among the hillocks surrounding the dilapidated harbour. On top of one of these grassy humps, with sheep grazing in the graveyard, is the castellated tower and thick-walled nave of the church of **St Clement's**. Dating from the 1520s, the church's gloomy interior is distinguished by its wall-tombs, notably that of the founder, Alasdair Crotach, whose heavily weathered effigy lies beneath an intriguing cartoon strip of vernacular and religious scenes – elemental representations of, amongst others, a stag hunt, the Holy Trinity, St Michael, and the Devil weighing the souls of the dead.

You can visit Rodel by **bus** from Tarbert: a morning service runs twice weekly along the east coast via Stockinish, with the return bus leaving from Leverburgh (for points along the west coast) a little under two hours later. There's nowhere to stay in Rodel, and the nearest **B&Bs** are back in dreary Leverburgh, strung out along a two-mile stretch of the main road: in emergencies, try the **B&B** at *Garryknowe*, Ferry Rd (April–Oct; ☎0859/82246; ②), not too far from the Berneray jetty, or struggle back the extra three miles to the bayside village of **NORTHTON** (Taobh Tuath), where there's the B&B of *Mrs Morrison*, at no. 39 (April–Sept; ☎0859/82228; ②).

# The Uists, Benbecula and Barra

After the stunning scenery of North and South Harris, the string of fairly flat islands that make up the southern half of the Western Isles cannot help but be something of an anticlimax, but for their vast sandy **beaches**, which extend – almost without interruption – right along the Atlantic coast.

Approached from Harris, the first island is **North Uist**. The ferry from Leverburgh to Berneray finishes its journey at **Newton Ferry** (*Port Nan Long*), but it makes little sense to take this route; the only public transport on from here is the post bus, an occasional service whose times you should check at Tarbert tourist office – Newton Ferry is a desperately lonely place to get stuck.

Far more convenient is to take either the mainland or the Tarbert **ferry**, which dock at the principal village, **Lochmaddy** on the east coast. This is easily the most appealing of the island's settlements, and despite being some distance away from the beach, its clutch of good youth hostels and one hotel make it the best base for exploring the area.

It's 45 miles from Lochmaddy to grotty **Lochboisdale**, the **ferry** port for the seven-hour trip to Oban, via **Castlebay**, the only significant settlement on the island of **Barra**. Here the grand beaches of the seaboard finally fade away to a chain of uninhabited rocky islets that includes the formidable cliffs of **Mingulay** (*Miu' Laigh*), inhabited with countless sea birds.

Public transport round the southern islands is pretty poor; the most frequent **bus** service links Lochmaddy with Lochboisdale.

## Lochmaddy and North Uist

Over half the surface area of **North Uist** (*Uibhist a Tuath*) – seventeen miles long and thirteen miles wide – is covered by water, creating a distinctive lochan-studded landscape best seen from the boat as it pulls into **LOCHMADDY** (*Loch na Madadh*) harbour. The village itself occupies a narrow, bumpy promontory that stretches a mile or so inland, and, although there's nothing special to see, a wander along the tortuous coast can be fun when the midges aren't out. Lochmaddy has a couple of convenient **B&Bs** – the *Old Courthouse* (☎0876/3358; ③), and the *Old Bank House* (☎0876/3275; ③), as well as two **youth hostels**. The **official** one is *Ostram House* (mid-May to Sept; ☎0876/3368; Grade 2), half a mile from the docks – just follow the signs. Nearby, the **independent** hostel in the *Uist Outdoor Centre* (☎0876/3480; ①) offers four-person bunk rooms. A few minutes' walk from the jetty is the spick and span *Lochmaddy Hotel* (☎0876/3331; ⑥), whose restaurant serves outstanding seafood. The hotel rents out boats and sells fishing permits for brown trout, sea trout and salmon. Nearby, the **tourist office** (mid-April to mid-Oct Mon–Sat 9am–5pm; ☎0876/3321) has local bus and ferry timetables.

There's a choice of routes out of Lochmaddy. The uneventful A867 cuts straight across the lochans and peat moors of the interior to reach the west coast at **Clachan na Luib**, just eight miles away. The other, longer route heads north, skirting the shoreline of North Uist for 25 miles before it also joins the A867 at Clachan na Luib. On the way, it leaves the boggy east coast to slip past a couple of wide and sandy river estuaries before reaching the rolling hills that slope down to the sea in the northwest corner of the island. It's around here, about seventeen miles from Lochmaddy, that you'll find a modest stone tower erected as a summer house in the 1830s. A footpath leads down from the road to the tower and the rocky shoreline beyond, at **Griminish Point**, the closest landfall to St Kilda – which is sometimes visible on the horizon.

# Benbecula, South Uist and Barra

South of Clachan na Luib, a series of causeways trim the west edge of **Grimsay** (*Griomasaigh*) on the way to **Benbecula** (*Bienn na Faoghla*), a dull and dishevelled island from where Bonnie Prince Charlie and Flora MacDonald sailed "over the sea to Skye" in 1746. After the Battle of Culloden, the prince spent no less than 157 days on the run, criss-crossing the Highlands and islands in his desperate attempt to elude the Hanoverians and escape back to France. On South Uist (*Uibhist a Deas*) he met the 23-year-old Flora, who was persuaded by either his beauty or her relatives – depending on which account you believe – to disguise Charles as a servant girl and smuggle him over to Skye, a perilous undertaking considering the stormy weather and the warships patrolling the Minch. Before they parted, over in Portree, the prince gave her a lock of his hair and, kissing her on the forehead, declared "For all that has happened, Madam, I hope we shall meet in St James' yet". They never did, and the exiled prince drank himself to an early grave, whilst his rescuer was soon forgiven and pardoned, to die a farmer on Skye in 1790.

Beyond Benbecula, the island of **South Uist** boasts some of the region's finest beaches, a necklace of gold and grey sand strung twenty miles from one end of the island to the other. A whole series of country lanes lead west from the main road to the old crofters' villages that straggle along the coast, but – although the paths are rarely more than three miles long – it's surprisingly easy to get lost, tramping round in circles before you stumble upon the shore. This is not the case, however, at **HOWMORE** (*Tobha Mor*), with its easy mile-long walk from the main road to the gorgeous beach. The village is the prettiest place for miles, the shattered ruins of its medieval chapel and burial ground standing near a cluster of neat little blackhouses, one of which the Gatliff Trust operates as a **youth hostel** (no phone; ungraded).

South of Howmore, the main road passes the cairn that marks the birthplace of Flora MacDonald and continues to the depressing port of **LOCHBOISDALE** (*Loch Baghasdail*). Arriving here late at night on the boat from Oban (or Castlebay) is a grim experience, but at least you can get your head down beside the **tourist office** (Easter to mid-Oct Mon–Sat 9am–1pm & 2–5pm; also open to meet the night ferry; ☎0878/4286), to wait for the morning's buses. There are also several **B&Bs** within comfortable walking distance of the dock: try *Bayview* (March–Oct; ☎0878/4329; ②), or *Mrs Steele*, 18 Kenneth Drive (Feb–Nov; ☎0878/4394; ②). You'd be well advised to book accommodation here in advance.

If you're heading on down to the island of **Barra** (*Barraigh*) from South Uist, there's an alternative to the *CalMac* ferry. Buses (2 daily; 30min) leave Lochboisdale for nearby **Ludag**, from where there's an occasional passenger **ferry** over to the **Eoligarry** jetty, on the route of the Barra **post bus**. Also from Ludag, a frequent **car ferry** slips across to the hilly island of **Eriskay** (*Eiriosgaigh*), where in 1941 the SS *Politician* and its cargo of 24,000 cases of whisky sank on its way from Liverpool to Jamaica, inspiring Compton Mackenzie's book – and the Ealing Comedy – *Whisky Galore!*. Lochboisdale's tourist office has details of ferry sailing times.

Just four miles wide and eight miles long, tiny **Barra** has only one settlement of any size, the old herring port of **CASTLEBAY** (*Bagh a Chaisteil*), which curves around the barren hills of a wide bay on the south side of the island. The main **ferry** docks here, passing the sturdy walls of the islet-fortress of **Kisimul Castle** (Wed, Fri & Sat 2–5pm; £2), the traditional home of the chief of the Macneil clan. The 45th chieftain, Robert Lister Macneil, restored the castle to something of its medieval appearance in the 1960s, making a visit just about worth the effort. But most people come to Barra for the peace and quiet, walking across the hilly interior or making the twelve-mile excursion right round the island by road, passing the low-lying grasslands of the west or the rocky bays of the east coast to reach the sandy beaches beyond.

Near the jetty, the **tourist office** (April to mid-Oct Mon–Sat 9am–1pm & 2–5pm; also open for late ferry arrivals; ☎0871/4336) will advise on walking routes; they also have details of accommodation, including several cheap **B&Bs** clustered in and around Castlebay – try *Tigh-na-Mara* (May–Oct; ☎0871/4304; ②), or *Grianamul* (April–Oct; ☎0871/4416; ②) – as well as a modest **hotel**, the *Craigard* (☎0871/4200; ④). *Barra Cycle Hire*, 29 St Brendan Rd, in Castlebay (☎0871/4284), rents **mountain bikes**.

## Mingulay and St Kilda

George MacLeod at the *Isle of Barra Hotel* (☎0871/4383) and Ray Burnett of *Celtic Quests*, The Old Schoolhouse, Torlum, Benbecula (☎0870/602334) organize frequent sea trips to the seacliffs of **Mingulay**. Ray also arranges full-scale, but infrequent, expeditions out across the Atlantic to the nature reserves on the NTS-owned **St Kilda** archipelago, roughly forty miles northwest of Barra. The last inhabitants of **Hirta**, St Kilda's main island, were evacuated at their own request in 1930, ending several hundred years of a peculiarly harsh existence – well recorded in Tom Steel's *The Life and Death of St Kilda*. Today, presuming you can get permission from the NTS to land – even tour operators have to negotiate long and hard – you can visit their old village, recently restored by volunteers, and struggle up the massive cliffs, where the islanders once caught puffins, young fulmars and gannets.

## travel details

**Trains**

**Glasgow** to: Mallaig (Mon–Sat 3 daily, Sun 1 daily; 5hr 10min); Oban (2–3 daily, 3hr).

**Inverness** to: Kyle of Lochalsh (Mon–Sat 3 daily; 2hr 30min).

**Buses**

**Broadford** to: Elgol (postbus; 1 daily; 45min).

**Castlebay** to: Eoligarry jetty (postbus; 1–2 daily; 1hr).

**Glasgow** to: Broadford (2–4 daily; 5hr 30min); Kyleakin (2–4 daily; 5hr 15min); Portree (2–4 daily; 6hr 10min); Sconser (2–4 daily; 5hr 45min); Uig (2–4 daily; 6hr 35min).

**Lochmaddy** to: Lochboisdale (Mon–Sat 1 daily; 2hr).

**Portree** to: Armadale (1 daily; 1hr 30min); Carbost (Mon–Fri 2–3 daily; 35min); Duntulum (Mon–Sat 1–3 daily; 50min; Dunvegan Castle (Mon–Fri 1–3 daily; 50min); Edinburgh (2–3 daily; 6hr 30min); Inverness (2–3 daily; 3hr 15min); Sligachan (Mon–Fri 2–3 daily; 20min); Uig (1–4 daily; 25min).

**Stornoway** to: Callanish (Mon–Sat 1 daily; 1hr); Carloway (Mon–Sat 1 daily; 1hr 20min); Port of Ness (Mon–Sat 1–3 daily; 1hr 20min); Tarbert (Mon–Sat 3–6 daily; 1hr 30min).

**Tarbert** to: Leverburgh (Mon–Sat 1 daily; 1hr 30min); Northton (Mon–Sat 1 daily; 1hr 35min); Rodel (Mon–Sat 1 daily; 1hr 20min); Stockinish (Mon–Sat 1 daily; 30min).

## Ferries

**To Skye**: Glenelg–Kylerhea (privately run shuttle; April & May Mon–Sat 9am–6pm; June–late Sept Mon–Sat 9am–6pm & Sun 10am–5pm; 15min); Kyle of Lochalsh–Kyleakin (daily, inc. Sun, shuttle service 7.30am–9.45pm; thereafter every 30min through the night subject to demand; 5min); Mallaig–Armadale (4 daily; 30min).

**To Raasay**: Sconser–Raasay (6 daily; 15min).

**To the Small Isles**: Mallaig–Canna (5 weekly; 4hr); Mallaig–Eigg (5 weekly; 1hr 30min); Mallaig–Muck (3 weekly; 4hr 30min); Mallaig–Rhum (5 weekly; 3hr).

**To Lewis**: Ullapool–Stornoway (3 daily; 3hr 30min).

**To Harris**: Uig–Tarbert (1–2 daily; 1hr 45min).

**To North Uist**: Tarbert–Lochmaddy (1–2 daily; 1hr 55min); Uig–Lochmaddy (1–2 daily inc Sun; 1hr 45min).

**To South Uist**: Oban–Lochboisdale (1 daily; 7hr).

**To Barra**: Oban–Castlebay (1 daily; 5hr).

## Flights

**Benbecula** to: Barra (4 weekly; 20min).

**Glasgow** to: Barra (1 daily; 1hr); Benbecula (Mon–Sat 1 daily; 1hr); Stornoway (Mon–Fri 3 daily, Sat 2 daily; 1hr 45min).

**Inverness** to: Stornoway (1–2 daily; 40min).

**London** to: Benbecula (Mon–Sat 1 daily; 3hr); Stornoway (Mon–Sat 2 daily; 2hr 45min).

**Stornoway** to: Benbecula (4 weekly; 35min); Barra (4 weekly; 1hr 10min).

# CHAPTER SEVEN

# NORTHEAST SCOTLAND

A large triangle of land thrusting into the North Sea from a line drawn roughly from Perth up to Nairn, just east of Inverness, the **northeast** of Scotland takes in most of the county of **Tayside** to the south, and, beyond the Grampian Mountains, the entire **Grampian** region. Geographically it's a diverse area, in the south made up predominatly of undulating farmland, but, north of the Firth of Tay, giving way to wooded glens, mountains and increasingly harsh land fringed by a dramatic coast of cliffs and long sandy beaches.

The northeast was the southern kingdom of the **Picts**, reminders of whom remain in the form of symbolic carved stones such as those at **Meigle**. As a remote, self-contained area, cut off from the centres of major power in the south, it never grew particularly prosperous, and a few feuding and intermarrying families, such as the Gordons, the Keiths and the Irvines, grew to wield disproportionate influence, building the region's many **castles** and religious buildings and developing and planning its towns.

Although much of the region remains economically deprived, parts have, however, been transformed recently by the discovery of oil in the North Sea, particularly **Aberdeen**, Scotland's third largest city. Aberdeen is the region's most stimulating urban centre, a fast, relatively sophisticated city that continues to ride on the crest of the oil boom. In stark contrast, **Dundee**, the next largest metropolis in the area, is a drab and rather depressed place, though it does make a good base for visiting nearby **Glamis Castle**, famous from Shakespeare's *Macbeth*. Close by, a little way up the Angus coast, lie the historically important towns of **Arbroath**, where Robert the Bruce was declared King of Scotland, and **Montrose**, where Edward I was forced to sign over his kingdom. Inland, the **Angus glens** cut picturesquely through the hills, their villages, such as **Blairgowrie** and **Kirremuir**, perfect centres for hikers and skiers.

North of the glens, **Deeside** is a wild, unspoilt tract of land made famous by the royal family, who have favoured **Balmoral** as one of their prime residences since Queen Victoria fell in love with the place back in the nineteenth century. Beyond, the **Don Valley** is less visited, although it does generate something of a tourist season in the winter, when keen skiiers head for the **Lecht** area; while **Speyside**, a little way west, is a tranquil region best-known for its numerous distilleries – Scotland's premier whisky-producing region. Despite the blots of **Peterhead** and **Fraserburgh**, the route further north, around the northeast coast, fringed with mighty oil rigs, offers the best of **Grampian**, with rugged cliffs and remote fishing villages, barely sheltered from the ferocious elements.

Northeast Scotland is well served by an extensive road network, with the A92 following the coast from Dundee to Aberdeen and beyond, while the area north and east of Aberdeen is dissected by a series of efficient routes. Trains from the south stop at Dundee and Aberdeen, and other towns on the coast. Inland, there is one branch line from Aberdeen northwest to Elgin, Nairn and on to Inverness.

# DUNDEE AND ANGUS

The predominantly agricultural region of **Angus**, east of the A9 and north of the Firth of Tay, is best visited for its countryside and pretty cliff-lined coast, for despite its undeniable energy, **Dundee**, Scotland's fourth largest city, sitting beside the Tay river on the area's southern outskirts, is not particularly inspiring.

In the north of the region, the vast sweep of the **Angus glens** is overlooked by the Grampian Mountains. There's hardly a loch in sight, but the heather-covered hills laced with rushing rivers and dotted with deserted crofters' cottages are still as close to pure Scottish countryside as you could expect. The region's market towns and villages, like **Kirremuir**, are sleepy places, in the main unspoilt by tourist crowds who tend to head further west for the Highlands proper.

## Dundee

At first sight, **DUNDEE** is a grim place. Sitting on the banks of the Tay, in the nineteenth century it was Britain's main processor of jute – the world's most important vegetable fibre after cotton. Today, however, it's a depressed town, overshadowed by its northerly neighbour, Aberdeen.

Even prior to its Victorian heyday, Dundee was a town of considerable importance. It was here in 1309 that Robert the Bruce was proclaimed the lawful King of Scots, and during the Reformation it earned itself a reputation for tolerance, sheltering leading figures such as George Wishart and John Knox. In the seventeenth century, the town was destroyed by the Royalists *and* Cromwell's army during the Civil War; later the Stuart Viscount Dundee, who was granted the city for his services to the crown after the Restoration, razed the place to the ground in the Battle of Killiecrankie. Dundee picked itself up in the 1700s, its train and harbour links making it a major centre for shipbuilding, whaling and the manufacture of jute, although little investment was ploughed back into the city.

Despite a burst of prosperity after World War II, there's little left to show today of Dundee's former glory. Its centre has been ripped to pieces with ugly soulless shopping malls, and its outskirts display all the worst of 1970s estate architecture. Except for the significant student population, there's a dearth of young people, who are forced to head for employment elsewhere.

Nevertheless, Dundee is a refreshingly unpretentious city, which makes a lot of D C Thomson, the local publishing group that produces the timelessly popular *Beano* and *Dandy* comics, as well as the *Sunday Post*. It was also, oddly enough, where marmalade was invented in the nineteenth century by a local housewife determined not to let a cargo of Seville oranges go to waste; giving rise to the saying that Dundee was built on three Js – jam, jute and journalism. Local sights, like the new development for **RRS Discovery**, and the **McManus Art Galleries**, put a brave face on a city that has little to smile about.

> The telephone code for Dundee is ☎0382

# Arrival, information and city transport

Dundee's **airport** (☎643242) is situated five minutes' drive west from the city centre. There are no buses but a taxi will only set you back about £2. By **train**, Taybridge Station is on South Union Street (☎28046) about three hundred yards south of the city centre, near the River Tay. Long-distance **buses** arrive at the Seagate bus station (☎28345) – head a couple of hundred yards west along Seagate to reach the centre.

Dundee's very helpful **tourist office** is right in the centre of things at 4 City Square (May, June & Sept Mon–Sat 8.30am–8pm, Sun 11am–8pm; July & Aug Mon–Sat 8.30am–9pm, Sun 11am–9pm; Jan–April & Oct–Dec Mon–Fri 9am–6pm, Sat 10am–4pm; ☎27723) and sells train and bus tickets as well as booking accommodation. You can also pick up the free monthly *What's On* listings magazine here, detailing local events and exhibitions.

Dundee's centre is pretty compact, and you won't have much need for **public transport**. You might need a bus if you're staying out at Broughty Ferry (see below); local **buses** operate from along the High Street and around the Albert Square area – for information call ☎201121. The journey costs 65p. Taxi ranks are dotted around City Square or you could call ☎69333.

# Accommodation

There's nowhere in Dundee that really stands out as a place to stay – decent **accommodation** is only just beginning to shape up in a city that has only relatively recently discovered tourism. There isn't a youth hostel, and the cheapest beds are available in summer at vacated student residences. Rooms out at Broughty Ferry may prove marginally cheaper if you don't mind a twenty-minute bus ride into the city – #8, #10 and #12 leave from outside *Littlewoods* in the centre of town.

The tourist office charge ten percent of the first night's tariff for booking accommodation, which is then reimbursed by the hotel.

### Hotels

**Carlton House Hotel**, 2 Dalgleish Rd (☎462056). Comfortable rooms in central, nineteenth-century building. Rates include breakfast. ③.

**Shaftesbury Hotel**, 1 Hyndford St (☎69216). A converted jute merchant's house in a residential area very near town. ③.

**Strathdon Hotel**, 277 Perth Rd (☎65648). Family-run hotel in the west end of Dundee. The rooms are good, and the food is even better – breakfast is included and 3-course dinner without wine costs around £15. ④.

**Queens Hotel**, 160 Nethergate (☎22515). Friendly, old hotel with grand sweeping staircase and good views of the Tay. ⑤.

**Woodlands Hotel**, 13 Panmure Terrace, Broughty Ferry (☎480033). Smart townhouse in a back street of this Dundee suburb. ④.

## Guest houses and B&Bs

**Cullaig Guest House**, Upper Constitution St (☎22154). Victorian town house right in the centre. ②.

**Errolbank Guest House**, 9 Dalgleish Rd (☎462118). Good views of the Tay. Some rooms with bathrooms. ②.

**Fisherman's Tavern**, 12 Fort St, Broughty Ferry (☎7594). Rooms above a pub with decent food and over 30 malt whiskies. ②.

**Hillside**, 43 Constitution St (☎23443). Homely, central B&B with three, welcoming rooms. ③.

**Kemback Guest House**, 8 McGill St (☎461273). Right in the middle of town, with TVs in every room. ②.

## Campus accommodation

**Duncan of Jordanstone College of Art**, Perth Rd (☎23261). Flats or shared cottage in leafy campus. Early July to mid-Sept only. ②.

**University of Dundee** (☎23181). Self-catering flats on and off campus and B&B accommodation in the halls of residence – try for Chalmers Hall right on the High Street. Open March, April and July–Sept only. Includes use of university swimming pool and sports centre. ②.

# The City

The best approach to Dundee is across the mile-and-a-half-long **Tay Bridge** from Fife. Offering a tremendous panorama of the city huddled along the river's banks, the bridge is also a symbol of the city's economic difficulties, in a constant state of disrepair. The bridge is also home to over a million pairs of starlings – watch them circle at dusk.

Dundee's city centre, around **City Square**, is lined with the same mundane mass of chain stores that you see in high streets all over Britain, and it's best to walk north from here along Reform Street, to the much more attractive **Albert Square**, fringed with unspoiled Victorian buildings and the **McManus Art Galleries and Museum** (Mon–Sat 10am–5pm; free). This gives an admirable overview of Dundee's past, with excellent displays on prehistoric life in the area – including an Iron Age ring ditch house and Pictish carved stones – and the city's industrial history, spanning everything from the three Js to the Tay Bridge disaster. The "Here's Tae Dundee" gallery is the most intriguing, with photos and mock-ups telling a social history of the town – everything from death masks of locally hanged criminals to a mahogany bar rescued from two old city pubs. Upstairs, the **Albert Hall** with its church-like wood-beamed ceiling, holds some wonderful classical sculpture and a whole array of silver and furniture – check out the Cumberland table at which the Duke of Cumberland signed the death warrants of captured Jacobites after the Battle of Culloden, and an exquisite golden snuff mill from 1725. Don't miss the museum's red-walled **Victoria**

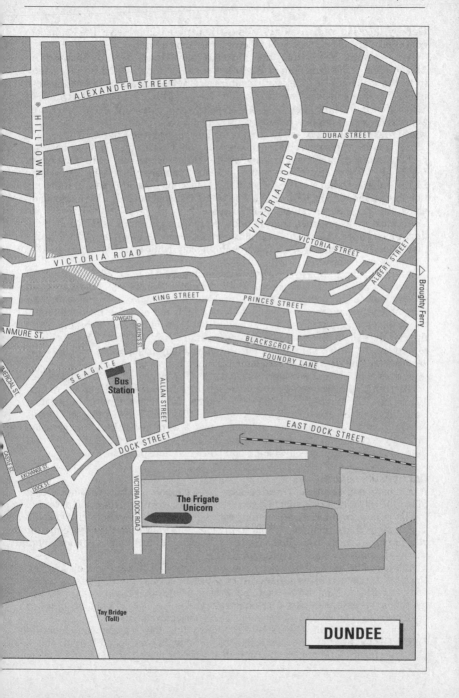

ALEXANDER STREET

HILLTOWN

DURA STREET

VICTORIA ROAD

VICTORIA STREET

ALBERT STREET

△ Broughty Ferry

VICTORIA ROAD

KING STREET

PRINCES STREET

COWGATE

QUEENS ST.

ANMURE ST.

BLACKSCROFT

FOUNDRY LANE

SEAGATE

**Bus Station**

ALLAN STREET

MERCIAL ST.

EAST DOCK STREET

DOCK STREET

CASTLE ST.

EXCHANGE ST.

DOCK ST.

VICTORIA DOCK ROAD

**The Frigate Unicorn**

**Tay Bridge (Toll)**

**DUNDEE**

**Gallery**, heaving with paintings – most notably an impressive Pre-Raphaelite collection – and glass cases full of Victorian art and ceramics.

Across Ward Road from the museum, the **Howff Burial Ground** on Meadowside (daily 9am–5pm or dusk) has some great carved tombstones dating from the sixteenth to nineteenth centuries. Originally gardens belonging to a monastery, the land was given to Dundee for burials in 1564 by Mary, Queen of Scots. Nearby is the run-of-the-mill **Barrack Street Museum** (Mon–Sat 10am–5pm; free), with a motley collection of stuffed local wildlife – the skeleton of a whale, washed up on a beach nearby, is the most impressive exhibit.

Just south of the city centre, moored by the Tay Bridge, Dundee boasts a perhaps more compelling attraction in the **Royal Research Ship Discovery** (April, May & Sept Mon–Fri 1–5pm, Sat & Sun 11am–5pm; June–Aug 10am–5pm; £1.75). Built in Dundee at the turn of this century for Captain Scott's first expedition to the Antarctic in 1901–4, and one of the last traditional British-built sailing ships, the three-masted steam-assisted vessel has only been berthed here since 1986, when it was returned from London (from where Scott set sail) as one of the first, much-hyped steps in the revitalization of the city. A brand new glass exhibition hall, **Discovery Point**, features high-tech audio-visual displays on the *Discovery* and its history.

Despite its three trips to the Antarctic, the ship itself is in excellent shape, with neat ropes, polished woodwork and gleaming metal. Dundee's shipbuilders, used to building whaling boats that had to cut through drifting ice, were renowned for their ability to construct exceptionally strong hulls out of wood. Inside, informative displays illustrate the skills and trades that brought the *Discovery* contract to the city, as well as clarifying the workings of the vessel – visitors get the chance to explore the whole ship, including the individually name-plated cabins of the scientists and officers who accompanied Scott on his voyage.

Further east along the waterfront, past the Tay Bridge at Victoria Dock lies another ship, the wooden frigate **Unicorn** (April to mid-Oct Mon–Fri & Sun 10am–5pm, Sat 10am–4pm; mid-Oct to March daily 10am–4pm; £1.25), dating from 1824 and the oldest British-built warship still afloat. The fact that its 46 guns – only 18 pounder cannons are still on display – were never fired in aggression probably accounts for its survival. Inside it's a bit sparse, but the cannons are all there along with displays on whaling and other maritime pursuits.

## Out from the centre

A mile or so north of town, **Dundee Law** is the plug of an extinct volcano, and, at 571ft, the city's highest point. Once the site of a seventh-century defensive hill fort, it is now an impressive lookout, with views across the whole city and the Tay. It takes thirty minutes to walk to the foot of the law from the city centre, or you can take bus #4 from Albert Square. The climb to the top is steep and often windy – in summer there's a frequent bus service.

Another mile west of Dundee Law, on Balgay Hill in the wooded **Lochee Park,** is the domed **Mills Observatory** (April–Sept Mon–Fri 10am–5pm, Sat 2–5pm; Oct–March Mon–Fri 3–10pm, Sat 2–5pm; free) with astronomy exhibits and telescopic views of the city. The observatory also has special opening times to coincide with eclipses and other unusual planetary movements.

Four miles east of Dundee's city centre lies the seaside settlement of **BROUGHTY FERRY,** now engulfed by the city as a reluctant suburb. It's a pleasant enough little resort, and on land at least far more unspoilt than Dundee.

The level of pollution on the beach itself, however, is pretty dire – all of Dundee's sewage seems to end up here. If you can't bear the sight of this, **Broughty Castle and Museum**, right by the seashore (Oct–June Mon–Thurs & Sat 10am–1pm & 2–5pm; July–Sept Mon–Thurs & Sat 10am–1pm & 2–5pm, Sun 2–5pm; free), is worth a look. Built in the fifteenth century to protect the estuary, its four floors now house local history exhibits, covering the story of Broughty Ferry as a fishing village and the history of whaling, as well as details of local geology and wildlife.

Just north of Broughty Ferry, at the junction of the A92 and B978, the chunky bricks of **Claypotts Castle** (April–Sept Mon–Sat 9.30am–7pm, Sun 2–7pm; free) constitute one of Scotland's most complete Z-shaped tower houses. Built from 1569 to 1588, its two round towers have stepped projections to support extra rooms – a sixteenth-century architectural practice that makes Claypotts look like it's about to topple.

# Eating and drinking

**Eating out** isn't a particularly rewarding activity in Dundee, and many people resort to eating where they're staying or simply checking out the local pub food. The *Royal Oak*, 167 Brook St, has a particularly sophisticated selection, with Thai, Indian and Spanish tapas on the menu. In the centre of town you'll find the *Pancake Place*, 24 Reform St, one of a reliable Scottish chain, and the *Deep Sea*, in Nethergate, for exceptionally good "fish dinners". The Perth Road, heading west out of town, is also a good bet: *Raffles*, no. 18 (☎26344), the city's best restaurant, serves reasonably priced Scottish food with plenty of vegetarian choices, and the *Gunga-Din Restaurant*, at no. 99b, is good for cheap, authentic Indian dishes.

There's no shortage of good **pubs** in Dundee, due in part to the student population. The youthful hangouts along Nethergate are your best bet: try the *Parliamentary Bar*, at no. 134, or *The Ascot Bar*, nearby at 2 Westport, which also doubles up as a live-music venue. The liveliest bars in the centre of town around City Square are the *Mercantile*, 100–108 Commercial St, the predominantly gay *Gaugar* bar on Seagate, and the *Old Bank Bar*, on Reform Street. The city centre can get quite rough, however, especially at weekends.

# Nightlife

When it comes to **nightlife**, Dundee doesn't offer a great deal. *Fat Sams*, 31 South Ward Rd, is the city's best student nightclub, and also has live music; *De Stilhl's*, 4–6 South Ward Rd, caters for an older, less raucous crowd, and there's a Saturday night disco at the *Tay Hotel* in Whitehall Crescent. Check events at the student union (☎28496) for popular bands.

The *Dundee Repertory Theatre* (☎23530), on Tay Square north of Nethergate, has a good programme of contemporary **theatre**, and hosts many of Dundee's **festivals**, which inject much-needed energy into the city. Best of the bunch are the Jazz and Blues Festival in early June and the Folk Festival in early July. The *Royal Scottish Orchestra* and big-name bands play regularly at *Caird Hall* in City Square (☎23141). The *Cannon Film Centre* on Seagate (☎25247) has the latest **cinema** releases, and for art movies and classics there's the *Dundee Film Theatre* in the *Wellgate Shopping Centre* on Victoria Road (☎23141).

# Around Dundee

There are a handful of sights within easy reach from Dundee in the southern corner of Tayside. North of the city, over the Sidlaw Hills, **Meigle** has one of Scotland's foremost collections of Pictish stones, while the splendid **Glamis Castle** was the setting of Shakespeare's *Macbeth*.

## Meigle

Hourly buses run from Dundee to the tiny village of **MEIGLE**, fifteen miles northwest in the fertile bed of the Tay Valley. Housed in a modest former school-building, the **Meigle Museum** (April–Sept Mon–Thurs & Sat 9.30am–7pm, Sun 2–7pm; Oct–March Mon–Thurs & Sat 9.30am–4pm, Sun 2–4pm; 60p) holds some thirty early Christian and Pictish inscribed stones, dating from the seventh to the tenth centuries, found in and around the nearby churchyard. The majority are either gravestones that would have lain flat or cross-slabs, inscribed with the sign of the cross and usually standing. Most impressive is the seven-foot-tall great cross-slab, said to be Guinevere's gravestone, carved on one side with a portrayal of Daniel surrounded by lions, a beautifully executed equestrian group, and mythological creatures including a dragon and a centaur. On the other side various beasts are surmounted by the "ring of glory" – a wheel containing a cross carved and decorated in high relief. The stone is all the more impressive for its deliberate two-tone effect, the slab of sandstone red at the base and merging into grey at the top. The exact meaning and purpose of the stones and their enigmatic symbols is obscure, and why so many of the stones were found at Meigle is also a mystery. The most likely theory suggests that Meigle was once an important ecclesiastical centre which attracted secular burials of prominent Picts.

## Glamis Castle

Four buses a day (40min; £2.90 return) leave Dundee for the ostentatious pink-sandstone **Glamis Castle** (Easter to mid-Oct daily noon–5.30pm; regular 60min guided tours; £3), about a mile north of the village of **GLAMIS** (pronounced "Glahms"). An over-the-top, L-shaped five-storey pile, set in an extensive landscaped park complete with deer and pheasants, this is one of the most famous castles in Scotland – Shakespeare chose it as the setting for *Macbeth,* both the Queen Mother and Princess Margaret were born here, and it is thought to be one of the country's most haunted buildings.

Although much of what you see today, a mêlée of turrets, towers, heraldic embellishments and conical roofs, dates back to about 1606, the first building on this site was a relatively humble hunting lodge, used in the eleventh century by the kings of Scotland. In 1372, King Robert II gave the property to his son-in-law, Sir John Lyon, who built the core of the present building, and his descendants, the Earls of Kinghorne and Strathmore – the fourteenth of which was the Queen Mother's father – have owned the place ever since.

Inside, Glamis is pretty much a stately home in the same vein as any other. There's an ostentatious Dining Room, chock-full of Victoriana, oil paintings and boasting a rich, plaster ceiling, and a Billiard Room draped with masterly Mortlake tapestries. The Great Hall is one of the highlights, with a wedding-cake ceiling, grand paintings and a jester's outfit on display (Glamis was one of the last castles to employ a court jester until he was sacked for an indiscretion with a lady-in-waiting), but probably the most interesting rooms are those that come with juicy anecdotes. The **Crypt**, for example, heaving with armoury and weapons, is said to be haunted by red-bearded Beardie Crawford, who is hidden in its sealed chambers playing cards with the Devil until Doomsday – a punishment for gambling on the Sabbath.

Seventeenth-century frescoes painted by Jacob de Wet adorn the **Chapel**; legend has it that he was so disgruntled by his low reward, a mere £90 for nearly five years toil, that he took revenge by painting Jesus in an undignified hat and St Simon with a pair of glasses. Apparently Lady Janet Douglas (known as the Grey Lady) has haunted the place since she was burnt as a witch. There are more exquisitely embroidered wall-hangings in the **King Malcolm Room**, where Malcolm II probably died in 1034 after suffering mortal wounds inflicted at the nearby battle of Hunter's Hill, while **Duncan's Hall**, the oldest surviving part of the castle, is the room in which Shakespeare's Macbeth murdered Duncan. The Family Exhibition room gives an insight into the lives of the people who have lived at Glamis, with photographs of the Strathmore family, a bizarre model monkey playing a violin, and a watch that is said to have belonged to the Old Pretender, which was stolen by a maid when he stayed here in 1715.

After wandering around the beautiful grounds, it's worth popping into the more humble **Angus Folk Museum**, in the village itself (Easter–Sept daily 11am–5pm; £1.30). Housed in the quaint nineteenth-century Kirkwynd Cottages, it displays a collection of relics from the area's domestic and agricultural life, including an interesting exhibition on bothies – the minuscule, spartan dwellings of local farmhands.

# The Angus coast

Two roads link Dundee to Aberdeen and the northeast coast of Scotland. By far the most pleasant option is to take the slightly longer A92 coast road which joins the A94 at Stonehaven, just south of Aberdeen, a route that can also be followed by bus or train, taking in Arbroath, Montrose and Brechin. The train line hugging this stretch of coast from Dundee is one of the most picturesque in Scotland, stopping at **Arbroath** and the old seaport of **Montrose**. Trains leave at least hourly, and take around twenty minutes to reach Arbroath and a further fifteen minutes to Montrose.

## Arbroath

Since it was settled in the twelfth century, local fishermen have been landing their catches at **ARBROATH**, where the Angus coast starts to curve in from the North Sea towards the Firth of Tay. The **Arbroath smokie** – a line-caught haddock, smoke-cured over smouldering oak chips and then poached in milk – is probably one of Scotland's best-known dishes, and is best eaten the original way, with a knob of butter, rather than in the more fancy pâtés and mousses that are now becoming popular. Although it has a great location, with long sandy beaches and stunning sandstone cliffs on either side of town, Arbroath, like Dundee, has suffered from short-sighted development, its historical associations all but consumed by pedestrian walkways, a mess of a one-way system and ugly shopping centres.

Chiefly due to its harbour, Arbroath had, by the late eighteenth century, become a trading and manufacturing centre, famed for sail-making (the *Cutty Sark*'s sails were made here) and boot-making. Arbroath's real glory days, however, came much earlier in the thirteenth century with the completion of **Arbroath Abbey** (April–Sept Mon–Sat 9.30am–7pm, Sun 2–7pm; Oct–March Mon–Sat 9.30am–4pm, Sun 2–4pm; 60p), whose pink stone ruins, described by Dr Johnson as "fragments of magnificence", stand on Abbey Street, clearly visible from the High Street. Founded in 1178 by King William the Lion, and dedicated to his old schoolmate Saint Thomas à Becket, who he acknowledged as a "sharer of his tribulations" in England, it was completed in 1233, and became an abbey in 1285.

One of the most significant events in Scotland's history occured here, when on April 6, 1320 a group of Scottish barons drew up the **Declaration of Arbroath**, asking the Pope to reverse his excommunication and recognize Robert the Bruce as king, asserting Scotland's independence from the English: "For, so long as one hundred remain alive, we will never in any degree be subject to the dominion of the English". It was duly despatched to Pope John XXII in Avignon, who in 1324 agreed to Robert's claim.

The abbey was dissolved during the Reformation, and by the eighteenth century it was little more than a source of red sandstone for local houses. However, there is still enough left to get a good idea of how vast the place must have been: the semicircular west doorway is more or less intact, complete with medieval mouldings, and the south transept has a wonderful round window, once lit with a beacon to guide ships. The **Abbot's House** has also survived, used as a private dwelling long after the complex was abandoned, and now housing a small museum with exhibits that include an ancient headless statue thought to represent the abbey's founder.

### Around Arbroath: the cliffs and Lunan Bay

There's not much else to see in Arbroath besides the abbey, but there are some great **walks** in the vicinity. Out from the harbour to the north end of Arbroath Promenade, the red sandstone cliffs begin at **Whiting Ness**, stretching endlessly on to the horizon and eroded into a multitude of inlets, caves and arches. The *Arbroath Cliffs Nature Trail Guide*, available free from the tourist office, picks out twenty good viewing points along the first one and a half miles, and also gives details on the local fauna, flora and birds – you may even see puffins. Once the nature trail begins to dwindle, you can continue to the little port of **AUCHMITHIE** by climbing up to the top of the grassy cliff behind the bay and cutting to the right through farmland. A four-mile drive north on the A92 or a fabulous (if windy) seven-mile walk along the cliffs from Arbroath, **Lunan Bay** is a classic sweep of beach with an eroded ruin of a castle and rocky cliffs at either end.

### Practicalities

Arbroath's t**ourist office,** at Market Place right in the middle of town (Jan–March & Oct–Dec Mon–Fri 9.30am–5pm, Sat 9.30am–12.30pm; April–June & Sept Mon–Sat 9.30am–5.30pm; July & Aug Mon–Sat 9.30am–6pm, Sun 1–5pm;

☎0241/72609), will recommend local walks and can book accommodation. **Buses** terminate at the bus station on Catherine Street (☎0241/70646), about a five-minute walk south of the tourist office, while **trains** arrive at the station just across the road on Keptie Street (for enquiries call Dundee ☎0382/28046).

There's little reason to **stay** in Arbroath, but should you want to, try down by the harbour: both *Harbour House Guest House*, 4 The Shore (☎0241/78047; ②), and the *Sandhutton Guest House*, at 16 Addison Place (☎0241/72007; ②), are good options. The harbour is also the place for **eating and drinking**: a number of sea-salty pubs along the harbour front offer Arbroath smokies – the *Commercial Bar* on the seafront is a favourite with local fishermen, or check out the *Smugglers Tavern* on The Shore, where you can also try over 180 varieties of rum.

# Montrose and around

"Here's the Basin, there's Montrose, shut your een and haud your nose." As the old rhyme indicates, **MONTROSE**, a seaport and market town since the thirteenth century, can sometimes smell a little rich, mostly because of its position on the edge of a landlocked two-mile-square lagoon of mud known as the Basin. But with the wind in the right direction, Montrose, now an important North Sea oil base, is a great little town to visit, with a pleasant old centre and a good museum. The Basin too is of interest: it is flooded and emptied twice daily by the tides and is a rich nature reserve for the host of geese, swans and waders who frequent the ooze to look for food.

Montrose locals are known as Gable Endies, because of the unusual way in which the town's eighteenth- and nineteenth-century merchants, influenced by architectural styles they had seen on the Continent, built their houses gable end to the street. Today the wide High Street is split into two separate one-way streets, but Montrose is also riddled with little lanes that lead into quiet courtyards and gardens, and just wandering around the place is a nice enough pastime.

Behind the High Street, in Panmure Place on the western side of **Mid Links** park, the **Montrose Museum and Art Gallery** (April–June, Sept & Oct Mon–Sat 10.30am–1pm & 2–5pm; July & Aug Mon–Sat 10.30am–1pm & 2–5pm, Sun 2–5pm; Nov–March Mon–Fri 2–5pm, Sat 10.30am–1pm & 2–5pm; donation requested) is one of Scotland's oldest museums, dating from 1842. For a small town museum, it has some particularly unusual exhibits, among them the so-called Samson Stone, which bears a carving of Samson (with a peculiarly over-sized jawbone) slaying the Philistines. Dating from around 900 AD, the piece is one of three Pictish stones found about a century ago on a deserted island nearby on the River Esk. On the upper floor, the maritime history exhibits include a cast of Napoleon's death mask and a model of a British man-of-war, sculpted out of bone by Napoleonic prisoners at Portsmouth. Most intriguing, however, is the enigmatic message on a scrap of paper found in a bottle at nearby Ferryden beach in 1857, written by the chief mate of a brigantine eighty years earlier: "Blowing a hurricane lying to with close-reefed main topsails ship waterlogged. Cargo of wood from Quebec. No water on board, provisions all gone. Ate the dog yesterday, three men left alive. Lord have mercy on our souls. Amen".

If you have time, make for the **William Lamb Memorial Studio** on Market Street (July & Aug Sun 2–5pm; other times by arrangement; ☎0674/73232; free), the studio of local sculptor and etcher William Lamb (1893–1951). It shows a variety of his works, including bronze heads of the Queen, Princess Margaret and the Queen Mother, the earnings from which enabled him to buy the studio in the 1930s. Lamb's striking work is made the more impressive by the fact that he taught himself to sculpt with his left hand, having suffered a war wound in his right.

## Around Montrose: the House of Dun

Across the Basin, four miles west of Montrose, is the Palladian **House of Dun** (late April–late Oct daily 11am–5pm; NTS; £2.40, grounds only £1), reachable by way of the regular Montrose–Brechin bus – ask the driver to let you off outside. Built in 1730 for David Erskine, Laird of Dun, to designs by William Adam, the house was opened to the public in 1989 after extensive restoration, and is crammed full of period furniture and objets d'art. Inside, the ornate relief plasterwork is the most impressive feature, extravagantly emblazoned with Jacobite symbolism. You can also see some gorgeous pieces of intricate needlework, stitched by the illegitimate child of King William IV, Lady Augusta, who married into the Dun family in 1827. The most decorative example is strewn across a huge four-poster given to her as a wedding present by her father.

The buildings in the courtyard – a hen house, gamekeeper's workshop and potting shed – have also been renovated. Modern additions include a tearoom and a weaving shed, and a shop where local weavers give displays of their traditional skills.

## Practicalities

The Montrose **tourist office** is in the library on the High Street (April, May & Sept Mon–Sat 10am–5pm; June–Aug Mon–Sat 10am–6pm; ☎0674/672000). **Buses** arrive at Rossie Island Road on the A92 at the south end of town a few minutes' walk from the High Street (☎0674/672805), while the **train** station is on Western Road. For B&B **accommodation**, try *Oaklands*, 10 Rossie Island Rd (☎0674/72018; ②), a neat, stone-built house with comfortable rooms. The *Salutation Inn*, 69–71 Bridge St, is a good **pub** that also serves inexpensive food.

## Brechin

About nine miles inland from Montrose and served by frequent buses, **BRECHIN** is a dull town, its only attraction the stumpy **Cathedral** on Chanonry Wynd. There's been a religious building of sorts here since the arrival of evangelizing Irish missionaries in 900 AD, and the red sandstone structure has become something of a hotch-potch of architectural styles – what you see today chiefly dates from an extensive rebuilding in 1900. The oldest surviving part of the cathedral, the 106-foot Round Tower on the southwest corner, was built as protection against Viking raids (the door is built a secure six feet above the ground). The pointed roof was a later addition, the gentle tapering of the design an impressive engineering feat. Inside you can see various Pictish stones, illuminated by jewel-coloured stained-glass windows.

The library on St Ninian's Square holds Brechin's local **museum** (Mon–Wed & Fri 9.30am–6pm, Thurs 9.30am–7pm, Sat 9.30am–5pm; free), and gives details on the cathedral, local archeology and the town as both a medieval burgh and industrial centre. The **tourist office** is also in St Ninian's Square (April, May & Sept Mon–Sat 10am–5pm; June–Aug Mon–Sat 10am–6pm; ☎03562/3050).

# The Angus glens

Lying on the southernmost edges of the Grampian Mountains' heather-covered lower slopes, the **Angus glens** – or "Braes o' Angus" – are tranquil valleys penetrated by few roads that offer some of the most rugged and majestic landscape of Northeast Scotland.

It's a rain-swept, wind-blown, sparsely populated area, whose links with tourism are fairly new. The first snows nearly always see the roads closed, sometimes as early as October, and in the summer there are ferocious midges to contend with. Nevertheless, most of the glens, particularly Glen Clova, are now well and truly discovered, and at the height of summer you may find yourself in a traffic jam – something that was unheard of a few years ago. The rolling undulating hills and dales attract hikers, birdwatchers and botanists in the summer, grouse-shooters and deer-hunters in autumn and a growing number of skiers in winter. The most useful road through the glens is the A93, which cuts through Glen Shee to Braemar on Deeside (see pp.329–30). It's pretty dramatic stuff, threading its way over Britain's highest main road pass – the **Cairnwell Pass** at 2199ft.

## Glen Shee and Glen Isla

Sprawled over the flanks of four mountains, the skiing area at **Glen Shee**, the most visited and best known of the Angus glens, is probably the largest in Scotland. The place comes into its own during the winter season – January to March – when an increasing number of skiers, predominantly from the cities of Central Scotland – brave the ridiculously cold temperatures and bitter winds. Ever-expanding ski lifts and tows give access to gentle beginners' slopes; experienced skiers can try the more intimidating Tiger run. In summer it's all a bit sad, with lifeless chairlifts, muddy banks, and expanses of woodland cut back for the pistes. Still, hang-gliders take advantage of the cross winds between the mountains and any adventurous walker should still be able to find peaceful hikes.

The tiny town of **BLAIRGOWRIE**, little more than one main road set among raspberry fields on the glen's southernmost tip, is as good a place as any to base yourself – and is particularly useful in winter if you plan to ski. Right on the river, the town's only claim to fame is that St Ninian once camped at Wellmeadow in the town centre, by an ancient watering hole – a spot now marked by a modern well. The **tourist office** is located nearby at 26 Wellmeadow and is open all year (April–June, Sept & Oct Mon–Sat 9.30am–5.30pm, Sun 11am–4pm; July & Aug Mon–Sat 9am–7pm, Sun 11am–6pm; Nov–March Mon–Fri 9.30am–5.30pm, Sat 9.30am–1.30pm; ☎0250/2960). If you need a place to stay, the *Compass Christian Centre*, Glenshee Lodge, seventeen miles north of Blairgowrie (☎0250/885209; ①), is a good place to meet other hikers, although it is not, unfortunately, served by public transport. In town, more conveniently, *The Old Bank House* on Brown Street (☎0250/8872902; ③), is a great B&B with log fires and has a very good, moderately priced restaurant. Those with more money to spend might want to check out the opulent, ivy-covered *Kinloch House* (☎0250/884237; ⑨), one of the area's most prestigious hotels, set in its own vast grounds three miles west of town on the A923. Another accommodation option in the area is the *Blackwater Inn*, about nine miles north of Blairgowrie (☎0250/885234; ②), which also has a good, cheap restaurant, although again this can't be reached by public transport.

Nearly twenty miles north of Blairgowrie, the **SPITTAL OF GLENSHEE**, though ideally situated for skiing, is little more than a tacky service area, only worth stopping at for refreshment. It is, however, handily close to one of the nicest places to stay in the area, the *Dalmunzie House* (☎0250/885224; ⑥), a gorgeous, turreted, Scottish highland sporting lodge, evoking the peace and tranquility that once pervaded this area – to reach it, take the side road west from town.

Dominated by Mount Blair (2441ft), and with a proliferation of woods, **Glen Isla**, east of Glen Shee, is also known as the Green Glen. Along its southern borders on the B954, the River Isla narrows and then plunges some 60ft into a deep gorge to produce the classically pretty waterfall of **Reekie Linn**. It's known as the "smoking fall", either because of the yellow clouds of wild broom that drift overhead in summer, or more probably because of the water mist produced when the fall hits a ledge and bounces a further 20ft into a deep pool known as the Black Dub.

There's an independent **youth hostel**, the *Highland Adventure* (☎057582/238), with dorms and private rooms, at **KNOCKSHANNOCK**, mid-way between the hamlets of **KIRKTON OF GLENISLA** and **DYKENDS**. The hostel runs a pick-up service from **ALYTH** between Glen Shee and Glen Isla; Alyth is also served by buses from Dundee.

# Kirriemuir, Glen Prosen, Glen Clova and Glen Doll

The sandstone town of **KIRRIEMUIR**, known locally as Kirrie, is set on a hill with glens Clova and Prosen as its backdrop. Despite the influx of hunters up for the "season", it's still a pretty special place, a haphazard confection of narrow closes, twisting wynds and steep braes. The main street, Bank Street, has all the appeal of an old film set, its tiled butcher's shop, tartan outlets and haberdasheries somehow managing to avoid being contrived and quaint.

In the nineteenth century this linen manufacturing centre was made famous by a local handloom-weaver's son, J M Barrie, with his series of novels about "Thrums", in particular *A Window in Thrums* and his third novel, *The Little Minister.* The author himself was to become more famous still as the creator of Peter Pan, the little boy who never grew up, which Barrie penned in 1904 – some say as a response to a strange childhood dominated by the memory of his older brother, who died as a child. Barrie's **birthplace**, a plain little whitewashed cottage at no. 9 Brechin Rd (May–Sept Mon–Sat 11am–5.30pm, Sun 2–5.30pm; NTS; £1), displays his writing desk, photos and newspaper clippings, as well as copies of his works. The washhouse outside – romantically billed as Barrie's first "theatre" – was apparently the model for the house that the Lost Boys built for Wendy in Never-Never Land. Barrie chose to be buried at the nearby St Mary's

Espiscopal Church in Kirrie, despite being offered a more prestigious plot at London's Westminster Abbey.

Kirriemuir's small **tourist office** on Bank Street (April–May & Sept Mon–Sat 10am–5pm; June–Aug Mon–Sat 10am–6pm; ☎0575/74097) gives out information on Kirrie and the glens. **Accommodation** in the area is pricy and often booked up during the summer and hunting seasons. Make reservations at *Crepto*, Kinnordy Place (☎0575 72746; ②) or the central *Thrums Hotel*, Bank St (☎0575 72758; ③).

## Glen Prosen

**Glen Prosen**, a couple of miles north of Kirriemuir, is one of the most untouched of the Angus glens. At its start, just beyond Kirrie, a roadside **memorial column** testifies that here, in 1910 and 1911, Captain Scott and fellow explorer Doctor Wilson holidayed before their ill-fated expedition to the Antarctic – local claims, however, that they prepared for the icy reaches of the Antarctic by exploring the glen in the depths of winter are somewhat exaggerated.

Little has changed since Scott was here, and Glen Prosen remains essentially a quiet wooded backwater, with all the wild and rugged splendour of the other glens but without the crowds. To explore the area thoroughly you need to go on foot, but a good road circuit can be made by heading north from Kirremuir to **PEARSIE** and then on to **GLEN PROSEN** village – little more than a kirk and a coffee shop. The two roads that flank this southern section of the glen meet here, and you can return by the less scenic northern road via the Scott memorial.

If you want to **walk**, head out along the footpath between the kirk and the bridge in Glen Prosen village, then take the right fork where the track splits and continue for four miles or so towards Glen Clova. You'll be rewarded with vistas of Glen Prosen's burnt moorland, which varies in shades depending on when it was lit, and the peaks of Glen Clova.

## Glen Clova and Glen Doll

The beautiful rock cliffs, heather slopes and broad valley meadows of **Glen Clova,** on the east side of the B955 from Kirremuir, are billed as a paradise for botanists, though the ever-growing volume of litter-dropping visitors poses an increasing threat to that status, and you'd be better off heading straight on to the more peaceful **Glen Doll**, at the head of the Glen Clova, where the hills reach 3000ft. It's a good base for walkers, with cheap accommodation at the **youth hostel** four miles north of the village of **CLOVA** (mid-March to Oct; ☎05755/236; Grade 2), a restored hunting lodge with good facilities including a squash court. The postbus from Kirriemuir (19 miles south) runs to the hostel on weekday mornings, and takes about ninety minutes. Alternatively, the *Clova Hotel* (☎05755/222; ②) – practically the only building in Clova – also offers dorm accommodation in a genuine bothy (①) and rents out mountain bikes.

A footpath leads from the hotel east to **Glen Esk**, at first passing through birch woodland, and then climbing steeply towards the cliffs before finally encircling **Loch Brandy**. You have to be fit for this five-mile round-trip hike, but the views of the surrounding peaks and the waters of the loch are worth it.

The land around the youth hostel has been planted with conifers, and there are a number of good **forest walks**, of variable length, signposted from the car park – all have fantastic views. For serious walkers there are three major hill paths which converge in Glen Doll: the Kilbo path to Glen Prosen, Jock's Road up to

Braemar and Capel Mounth, which crosses into Glen Muick – but you must be properly equipped with maps, clothing and provisions to undertake any of these. If the Braes o' Angus have grabbed your imagination it's worth visiting the **Glenesk Folk Museum**, sixteen miles north northwest of Brechin via Edzell (Easter–May Mon & Sat 2–6pm, Sun 1–6pm; June–Sept Mon–Sat 2–6pm, Sun 1–6pm; 50p), an old shooting lodge converted into a museum with displays on the history and traditional life of the glens since 1800. Its *Retreat* coffee room is also a welcome sight for parched and hungry walkers.

# THE GRAMPIAN REGION

Comprising the former counties of Aberdeen, Banff, Kincardine and Moray, and covering some 3500 square miles, the fertile **Grampian region** is a land of open and varied country dotted with historic and archeological sights, from neat NTS properties and eerie prehistoric rings of standing stones to quiet kirkyards, serene abbeys and a rash of dramatic castles.

Geographically, Grampian breaks down into two distinct areas: the **hinterland**, once barren and now a patchwork of farms, with high mountains, sparkling rivers and gentle valleys, and the **coast**, a classic stretch of rocky cliff, remote fishing villages and long, sandy beaches.

For visitors, **Aberdeen** is the city of most obvious interest, with its well-kept buildings (it's often voted Britain's cleanest city), museums and gorgeous parks. From here, it's a short hop west to **Deeside**, annually visited by the royal family and a popular holiday area. Beyond lies the quiet of the **Don Valley**, hectic during the ski season, when skiers take to the slopes at the Lecht, but peaceful the rest of the year, and **Speyside**, the centre of a network of more than half of Scotland's malt whisky distilleries. To the north, the **coast** to Nairn offers the most dramatic scenery Grampian has to offer, punctuated by picturesque villages that haven't changed in centuries.

Aberdeen has an **airport**, and **trains** run from here north along the coast to Inverness and to major points further south. **Buses** can be few and far between, often running on schooldays only, but the main centres are well served. By car, signposted **trails** set up by the tourist board make following the Speyside whisky trail and visiting the northeast coast and castles a painless experience.

# Aberdeen and around

Some 120 miles from Edinburgh, on the banks of the rivers Dee and Don and smack in the middle of the northeast coast, **ABERDEEN** is commonly known as the Granite City. The third largest city in Scotland, it's a place that people either love or hate. Lewis Grassic Gibbon, one of the northeast's most eminent novelists, summed it up, "One detests Aberdeen with the detestation of a thwarted lover. It is the one hauntingly and exasperatingly lovable city of Scotland". The beauty of Aberdeen's famous granite architecture is definitely in the eye of the beholder. Some extol the many hues and colours of the grandiose designs, while others see only uniform grey and find the city grim, cold and unwelcoming. The weather doesn't help: Aberdeen lies on a latitude north of Moscow and the driving rain (even if it does transform the buildings into sparkling silver) can be tiresome.

Since the 1970s, oil has made Aberdeen an almost obscenely wealthy and self-confident place – only four percent of Scotland's population live in the city yet it has eight percent of the country's spending power. Despite (or perhaps because of) this, it can seem a soulless city; there's a feeling of corporate sterility and sometimes, despite its long history, the city seems to exist only as a departure point and service station for the transient population of some ten to fifteen thousand who live on the 130 oil platforms out to sea.

That said, Aberdeen's architecture is undeniably striking: a granite cityscape created in the nineteenth century by three fine architects – Archibald Simpson and John Smith in the early years of the century, and, subsequently, Marshall Mackenzie. Classical inspiration and Gothic-revival styles predominate, giving grace to a material once thought of as only good enough for tombs and paving stones. In addition, in the last few years the city's tourist board has tried to restyle Aberdeen's image from Granite City to Rose City. Every spare inch of ground has been turned into a flower bed, the parks some of the most beautiful in Britain. This positive floral explosion – Aberdeen has been debarred from *Britain in Bloom* competitions because it kept winning – has certainly cheered up the general greyness, but nonetheless the new image, just like the first, is always at the mercy of the weather.

Staying in a city of such prosperity has its advantages. There are plenty of good restaurants and hotels, local transport is efficient and nearly all the sights are free, including Aberdeen's splendid **Art Gallery**. The town boasts a genuinely lively **harbour**, and at night the city stays alive with a thriving pub culture and a fair number of theatres, both mainstream and innovative. Outside the city, down to the southern border of Grampian, **Dunnottar Castle** is the main draw. Beyond lies **Fasque House** and the neat village of **Fettercairn**, a good day trip from the city.

## Some history

In the twelfth century, Alexander I noted "Aberdon" as one of his principal towns and by the thirteenth century, it had become a centre for **trade and fishing**, a jumble of timber and wattle houses perched on three small hills, with the castle to the east and St Nicholas' kirk outside the gates to the west.

It was here that **Robert the Bruce** sought refuge during the Scottish Wars of Independence, leading to the garrison of the castle by Edward I and Balliol's supporters. During the night in 1306, the townspeople attacked the garrison and killed them all, an event commemorated by the city's motto "Bon Accord", the watchword for the night. The victory was not to last, however, and in 1337 Edward III stormed the city, forcing its rebuilding on a grander scale. A century later the Bishop Elphinstone founded the Catholic **University** in the area north of town known today as **Old Aberdeen**, while the rest of the city developed as a mercantile centre and important port.

Industrial and economic expansion led to the Aberdeen New Streets Act in 1800, setting off a hectic half-century of development that almost led to financial disaster. Luckily, the city was rescued by a boom in trade: in the **shipyards** the construction of **Aberdeen Clippers** revolutionized sea transport, and gave Britain supremacy in the China tea trade, and in 1882, a group of local businessmen acquired a **steam** tugboat for trawlfishing – sail gave way to steam and fisher families flooded to the city.

By the mid-twentieth century Aberdeen's traditional industries were in decline, but the discovery of **oil** in the North Sea (see overleaf) transformed the place from a depressed port into a boom-town. Lean times in the 1980s shook the city's confidence, and its future is less secure than once thought, but Aberdeen remains an extremely prosperous city – though what will happen when the oil runs out is anybody's guess.

The telephone code for Aberdeen is ☎0224

# Arrival, information and city transport

Aberdeen's **airport**, seven miles northwest of town, is served by flights from most parts of the UK and a few European cities. Bus #27 runs every forty minutes between the airport and the city centre, taking about thirty minutes. Both the **bus** and **train** stations are in Guild Street, in the centre of the city.

Aberdeen is also linked to Lerwick in Shetland, Stromness in Orkney and the Faroe Isles by *P&O* Scottish **ferries**, with regular crossings from Jamieson's Quay in the harbour.

## Information

From the stations it's a two-minute walk up the hill to Union Street, Aberdeen's main thoroughfare, and the **tourist office** at St Nicholas House on Broad Street, just off the north side of Union Street (Jan–May & Oct–Dec Mon–Fri 9am–5pm, Sat 10am–2pm; June & Sept Mon–Sat 9am–6pm, Sun 10am–4pm; July & Aug Mon–Fri 9am–8pm, Sat 9am–6pm, Sun 10am–6pm; ☎632727). They'll book

### OIL AND ABERDEEN

When **oil** was discovered in BP's Forties Field in 1970, Aberdonians rightly viewed it as a massive financial opportunity, and, despite fierce competition from other east coast British ports and communities in Scandinavia and Germany, the city succeeded in persuading the oil companies to base their headquarters here. Land was made available for housing and industry, millions invested into the harbour and offshore developments, new schools opened and the airport expanded to include a heliport, which has since become the busiest in the world.

The city's **population** swelled by 60,000, and earnings escalated from fifteen percent below the national average to a figure well above it. Wealthy oil companies built prestigious offices, swish new restaurants, upmarket bars and shops, but as Aberdeen rode on the crest of this new economic wave its other industries were neglected.

At the peak of production in the **mid-1980s**, 2.6 million barrels a day were being turned out, and the price had reached $80 a barrel – from which it plummeted to $10 during the slump of 1986. The effect was devastating – jobs vanished at the rate of a thousand a month, house prices dropped and Aberdeen soon discovered just how dependent on oil it was. The moment oil prices began to rise again, more bad luck struck with the loss of 167 lives in the **Piper Alpha disaster** and the government implemented an array of much-needed but very expensive safety measures.

Plans have been put forward to avoid such a crisis happening again, but have been shelved following the recent upturn in oil prices, and while the rest of Britain suffers its worst-ever recession, Aberdeen has lower than four percent unemployment and millions have been reinvested into the oil fields. However, the city faces a fierce fight to keep ahead of new **foreign competition** for investment and secure employment for future generations of Aberdonians.

accommodation for you, charging ten percent of the first night's room rate, redeemable at your hotel. They also run tours of the city, sell theatre, train and bus tickets plus a good selection of pamphlets on the best walks in Aberdeen – well worth the small investment of 25p.

You'll find Aberdeen's free monthly listings magazine, the snappily titled *City of Aberdeen Arts & Recreation Listings*, a useful guide to current events in the city – it's available in most of the pubs and shops. The tourist board also produces a free monthly *What's On* leaflet and runs the 24-hour *What's On Line* (☎636363) with recorded events information.

### City transport

Aberdeen is best explored by foot, but you will need to use **local buses** to reach some of the sights, including Old Aberdeen, in the north of the city. Make sure you carry lots of coins: it's a flat fare of 40p and the driver won't give change. If you're planning on seeing a lot, the **Explorer Ticket** is a sensible option – available from bus stations or the city-centre kiosk outside *Marks & Spencer* on Union Street and valid for one day (£3.30) or two days (£5.40). For information on this and other aspects of the local bus services call ☎643000. Maps are available from the tourist office, the kiosk and the bus station.

**Taxis,** which operate from ranks throughout the city centre, are rarely necessary, except late at night. If you don't manage to hail one, call *Mairs Taxis* (☎724040).

## Accommodation

As befits a high-flying business city, Aberdeen has a large choice of **accommodation.** Unfortunately, though, as most visitors *are* here on business, much of it is characterless and expensive, although some of the swankier places sometimes offer good-value weekend deals. Predictably, the best budget options are the **B&Bs** and **guest houses**, most of which are strung along Bon Accord Street and the Great Western Road, linked by buses #17, #18 and #19 to town. If you're really strapped for cash, head for the city's **youth hostel** or try the **student halls** left vacant for visitors in the summer months. For those under canvas there's a **campsite** in the city's suburbs.

### Hotels

**Albert and Victoria Private Hotel**, 1–2 Albert Terrace (☎641717). Listed building at the west end of Union Street – convenient for town centre and quiet at night. ②.

**Brentwood Hotel**, 101 Crown St (☎595440). Spick and span refurbished old hotel south of Union Street. Often full during the week as it's popular with business people. ②.

**Caledonian Thistle Hotel**, Union Terrace (☎640233). The best of the posh hotels – a wonderful Victorian edifice just off Union Street. ⑦.

**Cedars Private Hotel**, 339 Great Western Rd (☎583225). Cheap hotel with friendly atmosphere. ②.

**Craigynn Hotel**, 36 Fonthill Rd (☎584050). Impressive building on the corner of Bon Accord Street. Victorian ambience with an open fire in the winter. The food is great. ③.

**Ferryhill House Hotel**, Bon Accord St (☎590867). One of the most historic pubs in Aberdeen with colourful rooms and good food. ③.

**Mannofield Hotel**, 444 Great Western Rd (☎315888). Charming old granite building, once a posh private house, one mile west of town. Excellent value three-course dinners. ④.

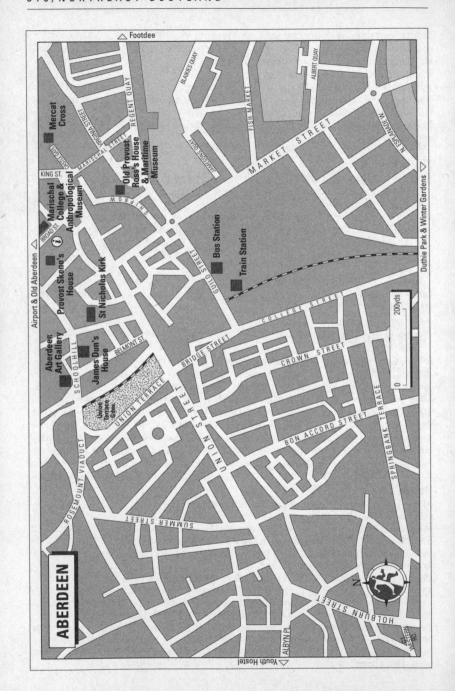

△ Footdee

BLAKIES QUAY

ALBERT QUAY

REGENT QUAY

FISH MARKET

MARISCHAL STREET

Mercat Cross

CASTLE TERRACE

KING ST.

PALMERSTON QUAY

N ESPLANADE W.

Old Provost Ross's House & Maritime Museum

SHIPROW

Marischal College & Anthropological Museum

BROAD ST.

ⓘ

MARKET STREET

Provost Skene's House

Duthie Park & Winter Gardens △

Bus Station

Train Station

GUILD STREET

St Nicholas Kirk

Aberdeen Art Gallery

SCHOOLHILL

BELMONT ST.

James Dun's House

COLLEGE STREET

Union Terrace Gdns

UNION TERRACE

CROWN STREET

BRIDGE STREET

ROSEMOUNT VIADUCT

UNION STREET

BON ACCORD STREET

SPRINGBANK TERRACE

△ Airport & Old Aberdeen

200yds

0

SUMMER STREET

ABERDEEN

N

HOLBURN STREET

ALBYN PL.

GREAT WESTERN RD.

△ Youth Hostel

## B&Bs and guest houses

**Bracklinn Guest House**, 348 Great Western Rd (☎317060). Welcoming Victorian house with elegant furnishings – one of the city's best B&Bs. ①.

**Campbell's Guest House**, 444 King St (☎625444). Highly recommended breakfasts. One mile from the city centre. ①.

**Crynoch Guest House**, 164 Bon Accord St (☎582743). Convenient location in a street lined with guest houses. ①.

**Denmorley House**, Ellon Rd (☎826477). Cheap B&B, right by the Bridge of Don, with great sea views. ①.

**Fourways Guest House**, 435 Great Western Rd (☎310218). A converted manse in the west end of town. ②.

**Klibreck**, 410 Great Western Rd (☎316115). Non-smoking guest house in a stately granite building. ②.

**Salisbury Guest House**, 12 Salisbury Terrace (☎590447). Family-run, comfortable, clean guest house. ①.

## Hostels, campsites and campus accommodation

**Crombie Johnstone Halls**, College Bounds, Old Aberdeen (☎273301). Private rooms in probably the best of the student halls available, in one of the most interesting parts of the city. ①.

**Hazelhead** (☎321268). Five miles west of centre. Grassy campsite with a swimming pool nearby. Follow signs from ring road or take buses #4 or #14. April–Sept. ①.

**King George VI Memorial Hostel**, 8 Queen's Rd (☎646988). Grade 1 SYHA youth hostel with rooms for 4–6, but no café. Closed early Jan to early Feb. Bus #14 and #15 from the train station, or #27, which goes from town to the bus and train station and on to the airport via the youth hostel. Curfew is 2am.

# The City

Aberdeen divides neatly into three main areas. The **city centre**, roughly bounded by Broad Street, Union Street, Schoolhill and Union Terrace, features the unbelievable opulence of **Marischal College**, the colonnaded **Art Gallery** with its fine collection, and homes that predate Aberdeen's nineteenth-century town planning and have been preserved as **museums**. To the south, the **harbour** still heaves with boats serving the fish and oil industries, while north of the centre lies twee **Old Aberdeen**, a village neighbourhood presided over by **King's College** and St **Machar's Cathedral** that is a sanctuary from the rush of the city and harbour.

## The city centre

Any exploration of the city centre should begin at the east end of the mile-long **Union Street**, whose impressive architecture, rather lost among the shoppers and chain stores, finishes up at **Castlegate**, where Aberdeen's long-gone castle once stood, and which these days holds a somewhat scruffy and uninteresting **market** (Thurs–Sat). City life used to revolve around the late seventeenth-century **Mercat Cross**, though it's now dwarfed by mighty granite buildings such as the Salvation Army Citadel and the Town House (fronted by the *Clydesdale Bank*). It's worth a look, however, carved with a unique portrait gallery of the Stuart sovereigns alongside some fierce gargoyles. Nearby, on King Street, the sandstone **St Andrew's Episcopal Cathedral**, where Samuel Seabury, America's first bishop, was consecrated in 1784, offers a welcome relief to the uniform granite.

West down Union Street brings you to Broad Street, and Aberdeen's oldest surviving private house, **Provost Skene's House** at 45 Guestrow (Mon–Sat 10am–5pm; free), dating from 1545. In the sixteenth century all the well-to-do houses in the area looked like this, with mellow stone and rounded turrets – only the intervention of the Queen Mother in 1938 saved Provost Skene's from being demolished like its neighbours. Little has been altered since the Provost of Aberdeen lived here from 1676 to 1685 and the house is now a museum, its fully restored period rooms with oak panelling, fine plaster and well-preserved furniture offering a pertinent glimpse of how a rich Aberdonian merchant lived in the seventeenth century. Don't miss the Long Gallery, where a series of ornate tempera High Church paintings from 1622 show a spirited defiance against the Protestant dogma of the time.

Nearby, on Broad Street, stands Aberdeen's most imposing edifice and the world's second largest granite building after the Escorial in Madrid – the exuberant **Marischal College**, whose tall, steely grey pinnacled neo-Gothic facade is in absolute contrast to the eyesore that houses the tourist office opposite. This spectacular architecture with all its soaring, surging lines has been painted and sketched more than any other in Aberdeen, and though not to everyone's taste – it was once described by a minor art historian as "a wedding cake covered in indigestible grey icing" – there's no escaping the fact that it is a most extraordinary feat of sculpture. The college itself was founded in 1593 by the fourth Earl Marischal, and co-existed as a separate Protestant university from Catholic King's, just up the road, for over two centuries. Charles I endeavoured to reconcile the two as a single entity, but they split again during the Reformation and it wasn't until 1860 that they were united as the University of Aberdeen. The facade fronts an earlier quadrangle designed by Archibald Simpson in 1837–41. After Marischal merged with King's to become the University of Aberdeen in 1860, the central tower was more than doubled in height by Mackenzie in 1893 and the profusion of spirelets added, though the facade was not totally completed until 1906.

Behind the tower, through the college entrance, the Mitchell Hall's east window illustrates the history of the university in stained glass. The fan-vaulted lobby, once the college's old hall, now houses the wonderful **Anthropological Museum** (Mon–Fri 10am–5pm, Sun 2–5pm; free), made up of two large rooms that contain a wealth of weird exhibits, among them a series of Eskimo soapstone carvings, an outrigger canoe carved from a breadfruit tree from Papua New Guinea, a macabre Hawaiian head crafted from basketry and with real dogs' teeth, and a Tibetan prayer wheel. Most bizarre are the high-relief mummy-case of an Egyptian five-year-old girl and a stomach-churning foot, unbound and preserved in brine.

On the corner of Schoolhill and Union Street stands the long **St Nicholas Kirk** (Mon–Fri noon–4pm, Sat 1–3pm; free), actually two churches in one with a solid, central bell tower rising from the middle, from where the 48-bell carillon, the largest in Britain, regularly chimes across the city. There's been a church here since at least 1157, but as the largest kirk in Scotland, it was severely damaged during the Reformation and divided into the West and the East Church, separated today by the transepts and crossing; only the north transept, known as Collinson's aisle, survives from the twelfth century. The Renaissance-style **West Church**, formerly the nave of St Nicholas, was designed in the mid-eighteenth century by James Gibbs, architect of St Martin in the Fields in London's Trafalgar Square. Inside, there's a canopied gallery especially for the city councillors – the most grandiose pew is reserved for the Lord Provost. The **East Church** was rebuilt over the groin-vaulted crypt of the restored fifteenth-century St Mary's Chapel (entered from Correction Wynd), which back in the 1600s was a place to imprison witches – you can still see the iron rings to which they were chained. Take time to explore the large peaceful churchyard, which with its green marble tombs and Baroque monuments seems a million miles from the bustling main street. A little further west up Schoolhill, **James Dun's House** (Mon–Sat 10am–5pm; free) is a smallish, two-storey Georgian house built for the rector of Aberdeen's grammar school in 1769 and now housing contemporary art exhibitions and moderately interesting displays on the city's history.

Opposite, Aberdeen's **Art Gallery** (Mon–Wed, Fri & Sat 10am–5pm, Thurs 10am–8pm, Sun 2–5pm; free) was purpose-built in 1884 to a Neoclassical design by A Marshall Mackenzie. The ground floor features a collection of decorative art that includes Chinese ceramics, Wedgwood pottery and Aberdonian silver, although the first-floor art collection is perhaps more engaging, much of it bequested in 1900 by Alex Macdonald, a local granite merchant who included among his circle the Pre-Raphaelites, Bloomsbury set and a number of Scottish artists. The **Macdonald Room** houses his personal collection of 92 portraits of artists, many of them self-portraits, and most of which he commissioned himself. In the nineteenth-century rooms you can see paintings by Rossetti, Aberdeen-born William Dyce, Blake, Landseer and "Boys" from the Glasgow School, along with Turner's *Ely Cathedral*, while a small group of foreign paintings includes works by the Barbizon School and rich Impressionist landscapes by the likes of Monet and Renoir. As for twentieth-century art, there are pantings by Augustus John, Ben Nicolson, Stanley Spencer, Graham Sutherland, Frank Auerbach and David Hockney among others.

West of the gallery, across the rail bridge, the sunken **Union Terrace Gardens**, bordered by the sparkling white granite houses of Union Terrace, are a welcome relief from the hubbub of heavy traffic on Union Street. In summer you'll catch free brass bands and orchestra performances, making it a great place to have a picnic. From here there are views across to the three domes of the Central Library, St Mark's Church and His Majesty's Theatre, traditionally referred to as "Education, Salvation and Damnation".

### The harbour

The old cobbled road of Shiprow winds from Castlegate, at the east end of Union Street, down to the north side of the harbour. Just off this steep road, well sign-posted, is Aberdeen's oldest surviving building, **Old Provost Ross's House** (Mon–Sat 10am–5pm; free), dotted with numerous tiny windows and boasting the original main doorway set into an arched recess. Actually two houses joined together, it was rescued by the NTS in 1954 and became the **Maritime Museum** thirty years later in deference to the eighteenth-century shipping merchant who once lived here. Through the small rooms, low doorways and labyrinthine corridors it tells in detail the many aspects of Aberdeen's nautical history. A wide range of ship models, some used by shipbuilders during construction, others built in painstaking detail by bored sailors, and still more folded into bottles, litter the place, along with numerous paintings and first-hand oral histories from sea and harbour life. One room focuses on the city's whaling industry between the mid-eighteenth and the mid-nineteenth centuries, while another is devoted to the herring trade. There is also, at the top of the house, an exhibition documenting Aberdeen's move into the oil industry, with a magnificently detailed scale model of a rig.

At the bottom of Shiprow, the cobbles meet Market Street, which runs the length of the **harbour**. Here brightly painted oil-supply ships, sleek cruise ships and peeling fishing boats jostle for position to an ever-constant clatter and the screech of well-fed seagulls. Follow your nose down the road to the **fish market**, best visited early (7–8am) when the place is in full swing. The current market building dates from 1982, but fish has been traded here for centuries – the earliest record dating back to 1281 when an envoy of Edward I's was charged for one thousand barrels of sturgeon and five thousand salt fish.

Back at the north end of Market Street, Trinity Quay runs to the shipbuilding yards and down York Street to the east corner of the harbour. Here you'll come to Aberdeen's "fitee" or **Footdee** (bus #14 or #15 from Union Street), a nineteenth-century fishermen's village of higgledy-piggledy cottages which back onto the sea, their windows and doors facing inwards to protect from storms but also, so they say, to prevent the Devil from sneaking in the back door. Ironically enough, this area, although not dangerous, is now the city's red-light district.

From Market Street it's a twenty-minute bus ride (#6 from Market St or #25 from Union St) to **Duthie Park** on Polmuir Road and Riverside Drive (10am–dusk; free), opened as public gardens in the eighteenth century. The rose garden, known as Rose Mountain due to its profusion of blooms, is great in summer, but the real treat is the Winter Gardens – jokingly held to be a favourite haunt with mean Aberdonians saving on their heating bills. To be fair, the place is most stunning in bad weather, offering a steamy jungle paradise of enormous cacti, exotic plants and even tropical birds.

## Old Aberdeen

An independent burgh until 1891, the tranquil district of **Old Aberdeen**, a twenty-minute bus ride north of the city centre, has always maintained a separate village-like identity. Dominated by King's College and St Machar's Cathedral, its medieval cobbled streets, tiny wynds and little lanes are conserved beautifully, with few cars except along St Machar's Drive, and only one bus (#25 from Union St).

The southern half of the High Street is overlooked by **King's College Chapel** (Mon–Fri 9am–5pm), the first and finest of the college buildings, completed in 1495 with an imposing Renaissance spire. Named in honour of James IV, the chapel's west door is flanked by his coat of arms and those of his queen. The chapel stands on the quadrangle, whose gracious buildings retain a medieval plan but were built much later; those immediately north were designed by Mackenzie early this century, with the exception of Cromwell Tower at the northeast corner, which was completed in 1658. The first thing you notice inside the chapel is that there is no aisle. Within this unusual plan the screen, the stalls (each unique) and the ribbed arched wooden ceiling are rare and beautiful examples of medieval Scottish wood carving. The remains of Bishop Elphinstone's tomb and the carved pulpit from nearby St Machars are also here.

From the college, the cobbled High Street leads a short way north to **St Machars Cathedral** on the leafy Chanonry (daily 9am–5pm; free), overlooking Seaton Park and the River Don. The site was reputedly founded in 580 by

Machar, a follower of Columba, when he was sent by the latter to find a grassy platform near the sea, overlooking a river shaped like a shepherd's crook. This setting fitted the bill perfectly, and the cathedral, a huge fifteenth-century fortified building (only half the length of the original after the collapse of the central tower in 1688), is one of the city's first great granite edifices and a well-known Aberdonian landmark. Inside, the stained-glass windows are a dazzling blaze of colour, and above the nave the heraldic oak ceiling from 1520 is illustrated with nearly fifty different coats of arms from Europe's royal houses and Scotland's bishops and nobles.

Next door to the cathedral, the **Cruickshank Botanic Gardens** (Jan–April & Oct–Dec Mon–Fri 9am–4.30pm; May–Sept Mon–Fri 9am–4.30pm, Sat & Sun 2–5pm; free), laid out in 1898, offer lovely glimpses of the cathedral through the trees. In spring and summer its worth checking out the flowerbeds, but don't bother with the dreary zoological museum.

A wander through Seaton Park will bring you to the thirteenth-century **Brig' o' Balgownie**, which gracefully spans the River Don, nearly a mile north of the cathedral. Still standing, despite Thomas the Rhymer's prediction that it would fall were it ever to be crossed by an only son riding a mare's only foal, the bridge is best visited at sunset – Byron, who spent much of his childhood in Aberdeen, remembered it as one of his favourite places.

Following the river to the mouth of Don over the handsome Bridge of Don will bring you to Aberdeen's **beach**, a lovely curve of perfect clean sand.

# Eating, drinking and entertainment

Aberdeen is certainly not short of good places to **eat**, though you will find it more pricy than elsewhere in Northeast Scotland. Union Street and the surrounding area has a glut of attractive **restaurants** and **cafés**. As for **nightlife**, like most ports-of-call Aberdeen caters for a transient population with a lot of disposable income and a desire to get drunk as quickly as possible. Every time a shop closes down in Union Street it seems to reopen as a loud, flashy bar. That said, there are still a number of more traditional old **pubs** which, though usually packed, are well worth digging out.

## Restaurants and cafés

**Ashvale**, 46 Great Western Rd. One of Scotland's best – and biggest – fish and chip shops, with seating for 300. The fish is best, though they also serve inexpensive stovies, meat pies, etc. Open daily until late.

**Drummonds**, 1 Belmont St (☎624642). Just off Union Street, this is a stylish, moderately priced café and wine bar during the day and a noisy music venue in the evening.

**Elronds Café**, *Caledonian Thistle Hotel*, 10–14 Union Terrace (☎640233). Surprisingly inexpensive lunch and dinner menu, considering its central location in a marble-floored and exclusive hotel.

**The Fortune**, 176 Crown St. Frugal-looking place with good, moderately priced Chinese food.

**Lemon Tree**, 5 W North St (☎642230). Home-made Scottish food. Very reasonably priced, and a buzzing atmosphere with a theatre upstairs.

**Owlies**, Unit C, Littlejohn St (☎649267). Plain French brasserie food, with plenty of vegetarian options. Moderate.

**Poldino's**, 7 Little Belmont St (☎647777). Lively, expensive Italian restaurant.

**Shish Mahal**, 468 Union St (☎643339). Good, moderately priced, Indian food.

**Silver Darling Restaurant**, Pocra Quay, N Pier (☎576229). Excellent, if pricy seafood restaurant in the Footdee. Set lunch around £13.50 or £25 including wine. Closed Sat lunch.

**Wild Boar**, 16 Belmont St (☎625357). Upbeat brasserie with moderately priced vegetarian food, soups and pastas. A popular evening venue. Closed Sat lunch.

## Pubs

**The Blue Lamp**, Gallowgate. Friendly pub with a good jukebox.

**Ferryhill House**, Bon Accord St. Pub with its own garden and very good food.

**Henry J Beans**, Windmill Brae. Yuppie-ish, buzzy bar.

**Ma Cameron's Inn**, Little Belmont St. Aberdeen's oldest pub, though only a section remains of the original. Serves food. Closed Sun.

**The Prince of Wales**, 7 St Nicholas Lane. Aberdeen's most highly regarded pub, with a long bar and flagstone floor. Renowned for its real ales and right in the centre of town, so it often gets crowded.

## Clubs and live music venues

**O'Henrys**, Adelphi Close. Flash club just off Union Street, popular with students in term time.

**The Pelican**, *Metro Hotel*, Market St. Hot and sweaty club with good bands – mainly indie.

## Theatres and concert halls

**Aberdeen Arts Centre**, 33 King St (☎635208). A variety of theatrical productions alongside a programme of lectures and exhibitions.

**Cowdray Hall**, Schoolhill (☎646333). Classical music, often with visiting orchestras.

**His Majesty's**, Rosemount Viaduct (☎641122). Aberdeen's main theatre, in a beautifully restored Edwardian building, with a programme that ranges from highbrow drama and opera to pantomime.

**Lemon Tree**, 5 W North St (☎642230). Avant-garde events with off-the-wall comedians and plays – many are a spin-off from Edinburgh's festival.

**Music Hall**, Union St (☎632080). Big-name comedy and music acts.

# Listings

**Airport** ☎722331.

**Books** *Dillons*, 269–271 Union St (☎210161), has a wide range of arts-oriented books; *Kaos*, 19 Diamond St (☎620212), stocks comics and American crime and sci-fi; and*Waterstones*, 236b Union St (☎571655), boasts a particularly well-stocked Scottish section.

**Bus station** ☎212266.

**Car rental** *Budget* (☎771777) in the airport, and *Caledonian Car and Small Van Hire* (☎584751) on Caledonian Rd just off Bon Accord St in town.

**Chemist** *Boots*, 161 Union St (Mon–Sat 8am–6pm; ☎211592).

**Cinemas** Films on general release are shown at the *Cannon* on Union Street (☎591477) and the *Odeon* on Justice Mill Lane (☎586050).

**Currency Exchange** *Thomas Cook*, 335–337 Union St (Mon–Sat 9.30am–5.30pm; ☎212271).

**Ferries** *P&O* (☎572615).

**Hospital** *The Royal Infirmary*, on Foresterhill, northeast of the town centre, has a 24-hr casualty department (☎681818).

**Maps** *Aberdeen Map Shop*, 74 Skene Street (☎637999).

**Police** The main police station is on Queen Street (☎639111).

**Post Office** Aberdeen's central post office is at 33 Castle St (Mon–Fri 9am–5.30pm, Sat 9am–12.30pm; ☎588260).

**Train station** ☎594222.
**Travel agents** *U Travel*, 110 High St (Mon–Fri 9.30am–4.30pm; ☎273559).

# Southern Grampians

South of Aberdeen, the A92 follows the coast to **Stonehaven**, a dull little town only worthy of mention because of its proximity to **Dunnottar Castle**, a surreal ruin right on the cliffs. Near the Grampian–Tayside border **Fettercairn** is a charming village, with the fascinating **Fasque House**, one time home of prime minister Gladstone, a short drive away.

Stonehaven is easily reached by bus from Aberdeen, but you'll need a car to get to Fettercairn unless you go via Montrose (see pp.309–10) on the Tayside coast.

## Stonehaven and around

A busy pebble-dashed town with little atmosphere, **STONEHAVEN** nevertheless attracts hordes of holidaymakers in the summer because of its sheltered Kincardine coastline. There's little to do here but enjoy the pretty shingle beach, though you could spend an hour or so on the quay at Stonehaven's oldest building, the **Tolbooth** (June–Sept Mon & Thurs–Sat 10am–noon & 2–5pm, Wed & Sun 2–5pm; free), once a store house for Dunnottar Castle (see below) and now a mildly interesting museum of local history and fishing. Generally speaking, however, it is best to give the town a wide berth and head straight for the castle.

Stonehaven's unhelpful **tourist office** is on the main drag, at 66 Allardice St (mid-April to mid-May & Oct daily 10am–1.15pm & 2–5pm; mid-May to June & Sept daily 10am–1.15pm & 2–6.30pm; July & Aug daily 10am–1.15pm & 2–7.30pm; ☎0569/62806). If you want to **stay**, *Arduthie House* is a comfortable B&B on Ann Street (☎0569/62381; ②), or try the *Marine Hotel*, 9–10 Shorehead (☎0569/62155; ②). For **eating**, the *Tolbooth Fish Restaurant*, on the harbour, is pricy but excellent, while *Robert's Bakery*, next to the tourist office, has great sandwiches and cakes. The *Hook and Eye* **pub** on Allardice Street is lively in the evenings.

### Dunnottar Castle

Two miles outside Stonehaven (the tourist office sells a walking guide for the scenic amble) **Dunnottar Castle** (late March–Oct Mon–Fri 9am–6pm, Sun 2–5pm; £1.50) is a huge ninth-century fortress set on a three-sided sheer cliff jutting into the sea – a spot dramatic enough to be chosen as the setting for Zeffirelli's movie version of *Hamlet*. Once the principal fortress of the northeast, much of Dunnottar now stands in ruins, though the scatter of remains are worth a good root around; don't miss the so-called Marischal's Suite, which gives dramatic views out to the crashing sea. Siege and blood-stained drama splatter the castle's past. In 1297 William Wallace burned the whole English Plantaganet garrison alive here, and one of the more gruesome tales from the castle's history tells of the imprisonment and torture of 122 men and 45 women Covenanters in 1685 – an event, as it says on the Covenanters' Stone in the churchyard, "whose dark shadow is for evermore flung athwart the Castled Rock".

Four miles south of Dunnottar Castle, **CATTERLINE** is a clifftop hamlet typical of those along this stretch of coast – worth a visit for the views and the delicious, well-priced lobster at the *Creel* restaurant (☎05695/254).

## Fettercairn and Fasque House

Eight miles southeast on the tiny B9120 (and served by buses from Montrose), the village of **FETTERCAIRN** is renowned for its handsome arch, erected in 1861 after Queen Victoria stayed at the local pub, the *Ramsay Arms* (☎05614/334; ④) – still a good place to stay or to stop for a drink. One mile west, and well sign-posted, the **Fettercairn distillery** (Mon–Fri 10am–4.30pm; free) is Scotland's second oldest, with free tours and the customary free taster at the end.

A short drive north on the Edzel–Banchory road, the once beautiful but now somewhat neglected **Fasque House** (May–Sept Sat–Thurs 1.30–5.30pm; £2) – childhood home of four times prime minister William Ewart Gladstone – is set in grounds filled with deer, pheasants and rabbits. Built in 1809 by Sir Alexander Ramsay, a leading Angus farmer, the estate passed into the Gladstone family in 1829 when Sir John Gladstone, William's father and a rich grain broker, bought the land and added various extensions, developing the gardens and building roads and bridges. Today, in all its intriguing decrepitude, Fasque House offers a great insight into how the affluent landowner lived in the Victorian era. Downstairs, domestic implements litter the place in a refreshingly haphazard manner – you can see old coal scuttles and bedpans and, in the kitchen, an array of enormous copper pans. Upstairs gives the impression of being equally untouched, with a library crammed full of the young Gladstone's books, a splendid Victorian bathroom complete with shower, and bedrooms looking much as the nineteenth-century maids would have left them, with bedcovers turned back.

# Deeside

More commonly known as Royal **Deeside**, the land stretching west of the coast along the River Dee revels in its connections with the royal family, who have regularly holidayed here, at **Balmoral**, since Queen Victoria bought the estate. Eighty thousand Scots turned out to welcome Queen Victoria on her first visit in 1848, but some weren't so charmed – one local journalist remarked that the area was about to be "desolated by cockneys and other horrible reptiles". Today, however, the locals are fiercely protective of their connection with the royal family, forever retelling stories of their encounters with blue-bloods.

Considering she had her pick of the country in which to establish a holiday home, it comes as quite a surprise that this windswept, rainy spot should have attracted her so much. Her visitors thought the same: Count von Moltke, then aide-de-camp to Prince Frederick William of Prussia, observed "It is very astonishing that the Royal Power of England should reside amid this lonesome, desolate, cold mountain scenery", while Tsar Nicholas II whined "The weather is awful, rain and wind every day and on top of it no luck at all – I haven't killed a stag yet". However, Queen Victoria adored the place, and the woods were said to remind Prince Albert of Thuringia, his homeland.

Deeside is undoubtedly beautiful in a fierce, craggy, Scottish way, and the royal presence has certainly put a stop to any unattractive mass development. Villages strung along the A93, the main route through the area, are as picturesque as you'll find anywhere, and the facilities for visitors, who boost the local economy no end, are first class, with a couple of youth hostels, some outstanding hotels and plenty of castles and scenic walks.

*Bluebird Northern* buses from Aberdeen regularly chug along the A93, serving most of the towns on the way to Braemar, past Balmoral to the west; and from June to September the *Heatherhopper* also runs along the A93 on the way to Pitlochry in Perthshire (see *Central Scotland and Fife*).

# From Aberdeen to Banchory

West of Aberdeen is low-lying land of mixed farming, forestry and suburbs. Easily reached from the main road are the castles of **Drum** and **Crathes**, both pleasant stopovers, while the uneventful town of **Banchory** serves as a convenient base if you intend to spend some time in Deeside.

## Drum Castle

Ten miles west of Aberdeen, less than a mile from the A93, **Drum Castle** (mid-April to Sept daily 2–6pm; early–late Oct Sat & Sun 2–6pm; NTS; £3.30) stands in a clearing in the ancient woods of Drum (daily 9.30am–dusk), made up of the splendid pines and oaks that once covered this whole area before mass forest clearance made way for shipbuilding. The castle itself combines a 1619 Jacobean mansion with Victorian expansions and the original, huge thirteenth-century keep. Built initially as a royal fortress, Robert the Bruce gave Drum Castle to his armour bearer, William de Irvine, in 1323 for services rendered at Bannockburn. From that point on, until the NTS stepped in in 1976 (a full 24 generations), the castle was in Irvine hands. To get a sense of the medieval atmosphere of the place, ascend the Turnpike Stair, above the Laigh Hall where a 700-year-old window seat gives views of the ancient forest. The castle also has a peaceful walled rose garden to muse in.

## Crathes Castle and Gardens

Three and a half miles east of Banchory on the A93, **Crathes Castle and Gardens** (mid-April to late Oct daily 11am–6pm; £3; gardens daily 9.30am–dusk; £1.10) encompass a splendid sixteenth-century granite tower house, which appears to have been more for decoration than defence, adorned with flourishes such as overhanging turrets, gargoyles and conical roofs. Its thick walls, narrow windows and tiny rooms loaded with heavy old furniture make Crathes rather claustrophobic, but it is saved by some wonderfully painted ceilings, either still in their original form or sensitively restored; the earliest dates from 1602. Unfortunately, in each room a tartan-kilted Scottish woman recites a well-rehearsed and detailed historical monologue that's difficult to escape, making it necessary to be selective in wandering the rooms – don't miss the Room of the Nine Nobles, where portrayals of great heroes of the past, among them Julius Caesar, King David and King Arthur, are skilfully painted on the beams. More intriguing still is the Green Lady's Room, where a mysterious child's skeleton was found beneath the floor and the ghost of a young girl, sometimes carrying a child, is said to have been spotted – most recently in the 1980s. Here on the ceiling you'll see moral commandments written in Latin, and paintings of grotesque faces and strange designs that make a chilling memento mori. The Muses Room, with portrayals of the nine muses and seven virtues, is also impressive. Beware the "trip stair", originally designed to foil seventeeth-century burglars.

It's easy to spend a day at Crathes. In addition to the castle there's more than one hundred acres of land and an inspired walled garden to explore – the flowers are often bedraggled by the driving rain but the hardy pink Crathes roses and the eccentric hedge-sculptures hold up well.

## Banchory

**BANCHORY**, meaning "fair hollow", is useful as a place to stay. It's easy to laugh at the tourist bumph that claims the "Gateway to Deeside" has an "Alpine feel", but the town does have a certain charm, flanked by hills on one side and the River Dee on the other. It's really just a one-street town, and there's not much to see, though the small local **museum** at the end of High Street (June–Sept Mon–Wed, Fri & Sat 2–5.15pm; free), might warrant thirty minutes or so – especially if you're a fan of local boy James Scott Skinner, fiddler and composer of such tunes as *The Bonnie Lass o' Bon Accord*. Alternatively, you can watch salmon leap all year round from the little footbridge where the Dee joins the Feugh River to the south of town.

The **tourist office** is in the car park on the High Street (mid-April to mid-May & late Sept to late Oct daily 10.30am–1.15pm & 2–5pm; mid-May to mid-Sept daily 10am–1.15pm & 2–6.30pm; ☎03302/2000) and can provide information on walking and fishing in the area. Opposite, *Parkers Lounge Café*, next to the busy nightclub, sells good basic food.

There are several reasonable **hotels** here and in the surrounding countryside. *Banchory Lodge* (☎03302/2625; ④) is a rambling Georgian house just ten minutes' stroll from Banchory at the confluence of the rivers Dee and Feugh. More cheaply, *Burnett Arms Hotel*, 25 High St (☎03302/4944; ②), is a former coaching inn right in town, and the *Old Police House*, 3 Bridge St (☎03302/4000; ③), is a decent **B&B**. Outside Banchory on the Inchmarlo road, the smart *Tor-Na-Collie Hotel* (☎03302/2242; ④) was once a retreat for Charlie Chaplin and his family, and serves splendid Scottish salmon, venison and malt whisky in its upscale restaurant. For **youth hostelling**, the *Wolf's Hearth Hostel* just outside Banchory (☎03398/83460; ①) is open all year. If you're on foot, it's less convenient than Ballater's SYHA (see below), but more than compensates for this with its stunning views.

# Ballater, Balmoral and Braemar

Passing the workaday town of **ABOYNE**, about ten miles west of Banchory, the A9 arrives after another ten miles at the neat village of **BALLATER**, hemmed in by fir-covered mountains. This unassuming place was dragged from obscurity in the nineteenth century when it was discovered that the local waters were useful in curing scrofula, a form of tuberculosis. Scrofula is no longer a problem, but you can still buy Ballater spring water, and the town remains a busy place – these days due to its proximity to Balmoral, which lies eight miles to the west.

It was in Ballater that Queen Victoria first arrived in Deeside by train from Aberdeen back in 1848 – she wouldn't allow a station to be built any closer to Balmoral – Ballater's train station, in the centre of town, is consequently a supremely elegant building, now defunct but still displaying its Victorian timetables. The local **shops**, having provided the royals with household basics, also flaunt their royal connections, sporting oversized royal crests above their doorways.

The **tourist office** is opposite the station in Station Square (mid-April to mid-May & Oct daily 10am–1.15pm & 2–5pm; mid-May to late June and Sept daily

9.30am–1.15pm & 2–6.30pm; late June to Aug daily 9.30am–1.15pm & 2–7pm; ☎03397/55306). Ballater is home to one of the few **youth hostels** in this part of Scotland (mid-March to Sept; ☎03397/55227; Grade 3); you'll find it on the Deebank Road right next to the River Dee and the Fall of Muick, a five-minute walk southeast from the bus station down Dee Street. The best **place to eat** is at the *Mortlach Hotel* (☎03397/55417; ②), where the *Thai Orchid* restaurant has a delicious menu of authentic Thai dishes to eat in and take-away.

### Balmoral Castle and Crathie Church

Originally a sixteenth-century tower house built for the powerful Gordon family, **Balmoral Castle** (May–July Mon–Sat 10am–5pm; £1.50) has been a royal residence since 1852, when it was converted to the Scottish Baronial mansion that stands today. The royal family traditionally spend their summer holidays here, but despite its fame, it can be something of a disappointment even for a dedicated royalist. For the three months when the doors are nudged open the general riff-raff are permitted to view only the ballroom and the grounds; for the rest of the year it is not even visible to the paparazzi who converge en masse when the royals are in residence here in August.

Opposite the castle's gates on the main road, the otherwise dull granite church of **CRATHIE**, built in 1895 with the proceeds of a bazaar held at Balmoral, is the royals' local church. Princess Anne chose the place as the venue for her second marriage to her former equerry, Commander Tim Laurence.

### Braemar

Continuing for another few miles, the road rises to 1100ft above sea level to the upper part of Deeside and the village of **BRAEMAR**, situated where three passes meet and overlooked by a ruined **Castle** (May–Oct daily 10am–6pm; £1.30) of the same name. An invigorating, outdoor kind of place, it's well patronized by committed hikers, although it is probably best known for its Highland Games, the **Braemar Gathering**, held annually on the first Saturday of September. Games were first held here in the eleventh century, when Malcolm Canmore set contests for the local clans in order to pick the bravest and strongest for his army. Attracting "Heavies" – famous Scottish clan members – from around the world, it's an overcrowded, notoriously popular event: Braemar's caber, for the tossing event, is particularly famous, a stripped pine measuring nearly 20ft and weighing 132 pounds. Since Queen Victoria's day it has become customary for successive generations of royals to attend and it is now a huge event, indeed you're unlikely to get in if you just turn up. If you're keen enough to plan that far in advance, tickets are available in about February and March from the Bookings Secretary, BRHS, Coilacrich, Ballater.

If you've come as far as Braemar, it's worth travelling six miles west to the end of the road and the **Linn of Dee**, where the river plummets savagely through a narrow rock gorge. From here there are countless walks, for the casual rambler or full-time hiker, into the surrounding countryside.

Braemar's **tourist office** is in the modern building known as the Mews in the middle of the village on Mar Road (mid-March to mid-May daily 10am–1.15pm; mid-May to June & Sept daily 10am–6.30pm; July–Aug daily 10am–8pm; Oct & Nov 10am–1.15pm & 2–6pm; ☎03397/41600). **Rooms** are scarce in Braemar in the lead up to the gathering, so you'll need to book in advance. *Clunie Lodge*

*Guest House*, on Clunie Bank Road (☎03397/41330; closed April & Dec; ①) on the edge of town, is a good **B&B** with lovely views up Clunie Glen, and there's a **youth hostel** at Corrie Feragie on the Glenshee Road (Jan–Oct; ☎03397/41659; Grade 1). For **drinking**, the *Invercauld Arms* in the middle of town is a youthful hangout with a pool table.

# The Don Valley and the Lecht

The quiet countryside around the **Don Valley**, once renowned for its illegal whisky distilleries and smugglers, used also to be a prosperous agricultural area. As the region industrialized, however, the population drifted towards Dundee and Aberdeen, and nowadays little remains of the old farming communities but the odd deserted crofter's cottage. From Aberdeen, the A944 heads west towards **Alford**, where it meets the River Don; they then continue together past ruined castles into the Upper Don Valley and the heather moorlands of the eastern Highlands. The Lecht Road, from Corgaff to the hilltop town of **Tomintoul**, rises steeply, making the area around it, simply known as the **Lecht**, an ideal skiing centre.

## Alford

**ALFORD**, 25 miles west of Aberdeen, only exists at all because it was chosen, in 1859, as the terminus for the Great North Scotland Railway. Now the only reason to come here is to see the **Grampian Transport Museum** on the Main Street (April–Sept daily 10.30am–5pm; early to mid-Oct Sat & Sun 10.30am–5pm; £1.50), a large and rather soulless display of transport through the ages. Unusual exhibits include the *Craigevar Express*, a strange, three-wheeled steam-driven vehicle developed by the local postman for his rounds before the invention of the engine, and, incongruously, a beautiful Art Deco Belgian dance organ with over four hundred pipes and a full set of drums. You'll also see traction engines, a 1902 dogcart used for transporting gun dogs, a portable steam engine and hundreds of other more familiar vehicles from fire engines to horse-drawn carriages.

Practically next door is the terminus for the **Alford Valley Railway** (April, May & Sept Sat & Sun 11am–5pm; June–Aug daily 11am–5pm; ☎09755/62326), a two-foot narrow-gauge train that runs for about a mile from Alford Station through wooded vales to the wide open space of **Murray Park**; the return journey takes an hour. The station is also home to the **tourist office** (April–June & Sept–Oct daily 10am–5pm; July & Aug daily 10am–6pm; ☎09755/62052).

### Craigievar Castle

About six miles south of Alford, **Craigievar Castle** (May, June & Sept daily 2–6pm; July & Aug daily 11am–6pm; NTS; £2.40) is a wonderful place, a pink mass of fantasy turrets, gables, balustrades and cupolas bubbling over from the top three storeys. It looks as though an architect, drunk on whisky, was allowed to let rip, but was actually built by William Forbes, a Baltic trader known as Willy the Merchant, in 1626, in a period when castles were no longer needed for defence, and architects could go wild with whatever whimsy they desired. Today Craigievar stands with very few additions, and the interior, with a vaulted medieval-style hall, is just as fabulous.

# Kildrummy and Corgarff Castles

Ten miles west of Alford stand the thirteenth-century stone ruins of **Kildrummy Castle** (April–Sept Mon–Sat 9.30am–7pm, Sun 2–7pm; Oct–March Sat 9.30am–4pm, Sun 2–4pm; 60p). Although there's little to see here today, Kildrummy has seen some particularly hideous moments of conflict. During the Wars of Independence Robert the Bruce sent his wife and children here for their own protection, but the castle blacksmith, bribed with as much gold as he could carry, set fire to the place and it fell into English hands. Bruce's immediate family survived, though his brother was executed and the entire garrison hung, drawn and quartered. Meanwhile, the duplicitous blacksmith was rewarded for his help by having molten gold poured down his throat. Other sieges took place during the subsequent centuries: Balliol's forces attacked in 1335, Cromwell took over in 1654 and the sixth Earl of Mar used the castle as the headquarters of the ill-fated Jacobite risings in 1715. Following John Erskine's withdrawal Kildrummy became redundant and it was abandoned as a fortress and residence and fell into ruin. Beside the ruins is a Scottish Baronial-style castle built in 1901, now the *Kildrummy Castle Hotel* (☎09755/71288; ④), with all the trappings associated with a mansion house – wood-panelled rooms, Victorian furniture and a great garden.

Ten miles southwest, **Corgarff Castle** (April–Sept Mon–Sat 9.30am–7pm, Sun 2–7pm; Oct–March, contact key-keeper; HS; £1) is by no means a romantic ruin, little more than a rather ugly white house set within a vaguely interesting star-shaped wall, but it too has an eventful history. Built in 1537 – the wall was added in 1748 – it was first attacked in 1571, during a religious feud between the Forbes, family of the laird of the castle, and the Gordons, who torched the place killing the laird's wife, family and servants. In 1748, in the aftermath of Culloden, the Hanoverian government turned Corgarff into a barracks – note the musket loops in the wall – in order to track down local Jacobite rebels, and finally, in the mid-nineteenth century, the English Redcoats were stationed here with the unpopular task of trying to control whisky smuggling. Today there's little to see inside, but the place has been restored to resemble its days as a barracks, with stark rooms and rows of hard, uncomfortable beds.

# Tomintoul

Just past Corgarff, at Cock Bridge, the road leaps up towards the ski slopes of the Lecht, and, four miles further on, **TOMINTOUL**, at 1150ft the highest village in the Scottish Highlands. A planned village dating from 1779, its long, thin layout and uniform stone buildings don't make it a particularly beautiful place; it's useful, however, as a starting – or resting – point for walkers, or as a base for skiing the Lecht area in January and February.

In the central square the **tourist office** (April, May & Oct Mon–Sat 10am–5.45pm, Sun 2–5.45pm; June & Sept Mon–Sat 9.30am–6.15pm, Sun 2–6.15pm; July & Aug Mon–Sat 9.30am–7.15pm, Sun 10am–1pm & 2–7.15pm; ☎08074/285) also acts as the local **museum** , with mock-ups of an old farm kitchen and a smithie, and some information on local wildlife and geography (same hours; free).

If you need a place **to stay**, you could try the **youth hostel** on Main Street (mid-May to Oct; no phone; Grade 3), or the more luxurious *Glenavon Hotel* on the main square (☎08074/218; ②), whose bar doubles as the local nightspot. Tomintoul's one B&B is *Conglass Hall* on Main Street (☎08074/291; ①). For

---

**SKIING THE LECHT**

The Lecht offers dry ski slope skiing all year; snow skiing, however, is only possible in January and February. Experienced skiers won't find much to tax them, but for learners the gentle slopes are a good introduction. The Lecht is also Scotland's only ski area to offer floodlit **night skiing**. Lift passes cost £9.50 a day for adults, £7.50 for a half day. Ski and boot rental costs £9 a day from the ski school at the base station (☎09756/51440), who also provide tuition for £5 an hour, £12 for four one-hour sessions.

For **information on skiing and road conditions** here call ☎0975/651440 or the *Ski Hotline* (☎0891/654657).

---

**eating,** the *Clockhouse* bistro on Main Street serves great food and also houses a traditional craft shop.

# North of the Don

About thirteen miles northeast of Tomintoul, **Dufftown** lies at the heart of Speyside, and is a far more amenable base for following the malt whisky trail than nearby **Keith,** a relative ghost town, as is the ancient burgh of **Huntly**, east of Dufftown. **Inverurie**, further towards Aberdeen, is the best centre for walking and exploring castles such as Fyvie to the north.

## Dufftown

The cheery community of **DUFFTOWN**, founded in 1817 by James Duff, the fourth Earl of Fife, proudly proclaims itself "Malt Whisky Capital of the World", and indeed it exports more of the stuff than anywhere else in Britain.

What little activity there is in town centres around Main Square, where the four main streets converge. For maps and information on the **whisky trail**, head straight to the **tourist office** inside the rather handsome clock tower on Main Square (April, May & Oct Mon–Sat 10am–5.45pm; June & Sept Mon–Sat 9.30am–6.15pm, Sun 2–6.15pm; July & Aug Mon 9.30am–12.30pm & 1.30–6.45pm, Tues–Sat 9.30am–6.45pm, Sun 10am–12.30pm & 1.30–6.45pm; ☎0340/20501). Also on the square, the *Morven* offers good, cheap B&B **accommodation** (☎0340/20507; ①), while the *Fife Arms Hotel* (☎0340/20220; ②) is a good-value traditional hotel with large rooms. Alternatively, there's the *Davaar* B&B, Church St (0340/204640; ②), which also offers excellent, traditional Scottish meals.

For **eating**, try the *Glenfiddich Café* just beyond the tourist office, or, for more substantial meals, the popular *Task of Speyside*, also on the square. Next door is the *Mason Arms* pub, with a busy pool room, patronized mainly by young people. The *Grouse Inn* round the corner is quieter, and has a good selection of whiskies.

## Huntly

Situated on a low plain surrounded by hills, **HUNTLY**, a small town ten miles east of Dufftown and on the main train route from Aberdeen to Inverness, has little going for it today apart from its proximity to the Malt Whisky Trail. There's been a castle here, however, since the twelfth century. It was the power centre of the Gordons, who ruled from **Huntly Castle** (April–Sept Mon–Sat 9.30am–7pm,

## THE MALT WHISKY TRAIL

Speyside's **Malt Whisky Trail** is a clearly signposted seventy-mile meander around the region via eight distilleries. In this so-called Golden Triangle lies the largest concentration of malt-whisky-making equipment in the world. Unless you're seriously interested in whisky, it's best to just pick out a couple that appeal, although the truly unique claims of each malt make it difficult to choose one over another. Hopefully the list below will help.

All the distilleries offer a guided tour (usually free) with a tasting to round it off – if you're driving you will be offered a miniature to take away with you. Indeed, travelling the route by car is probably the best way to do it, but for those without their own transport, the *Speyside Rambler* offers a connecting service to some of the distilleries during the summer; for more information call ☎0343/544222. Alternatively you could rent a mountain bike for around £10 a day from *Mini-Cheers*, 5 Fife St, Dufftown (☎0340/20559).

**Cardhu**, B9102 at Knockando (May–Sept Mon–Sat 9.30am–4.30pm; Oct–April Mon–Fri only; free). This distillery was established over a century ago, when the founder"s wife, Helen Cumming, was nice enough to raise a red flag to warn local crofters when the authorities were on the lookout for their illegal stills. Tamdhu distillery (see below) is just on the other side of the B9102, so you can easily combine the two.

**Glenfarclas**, off the A95, 17 miles southwest of Keith (June–Sept Mon–Fri 9am–4.30pm, Sat 10am–4pm, Sun 1–4pm; Oct–May Mon–Fri only; £2). Includes an exhibition in four languages and a gallery for watching the cask-filling. The whisky here has been described as going down "singing hymns".

**Glenfiddich**, A941 just north of Dufftown (April to mid-Oct Mon–Sat 9.30am–4.30pm, Sun noon–4.30pm; mid-Oct to March Mon–Fri only; free). Probably the best known of malt whiskies, and the most touristy of the distilleries. Unlike the other distilleries on the trail, Glenfiddich is actually bottled on the premises – prepare yourself for the lethal-smelling bottling plant. The gift shop sells a 50-year-old bottle, a snip at £5000. Right beside the car park you'll see the unspectacular ruins of Balvenie Castle.

**Glen Grant**, Rothes (May–Sept Mon–Fri 10am–4pm; free). Back in 1840, when it was established, this was Speyside's largest producer, but today this is one of the least interesting stops on the trail. Children under 8 not admitted.

**Glenlivet**, B9008, 10 miles north of Tomintoul (April–Oct Mon–Sat 10am–4pm; free). First licensed distillery in the Highlands, following the 1823 Act of Parliament which aimed to reduce illicit distilling and smuggling. Good display of old whisky tools and artefacts. Children under 8 not admitted.

**Strathisla**, Keith (mid-May to mid-Sept Mon–Fri 9am–4.30pm; free). A small old-fashioned distillery claiming to be Scotland's oldest (1786) and situated in a highly evocative highland location on the strath of the Isla river. The malt itself is pretty rare, and used as the heart of the better-known Chivas Regal blend.

**Tamdhu**, off the B9102, 8 miles west of Craigellachie at Knockando (April, May & Sept Mon–Fri 10am–4pm; June–Aug Mon–Sat 10am–4pm; £2). Houses a splendid collection of over 130 different whiskies. The distillery plant is viewed from a special gallery.

**Tamnavoulin-Glenlivet**, Tomnavoulin, under 4 miles northeast of Tomintoul on B9008 (late March to May & Sept to early Nov Mon–Sat 9.30am–4.30pm; June–Aug Mon–Sat 9.30am–4.30pm, Sun 10am–4pm; free). On the banks of the River Livet, the visitor centre is housed in a converted old wool-carding mill.

Sun 2–7pm; Oct–March Mon–Sat 9.30am–4pm, Sun 2–4pm; HS; £1), a ten-minute walk from the town centre, down Castle Street and through an elegant arch. Set in a peaceful clearing on the banks of the Deveron river, this is one of the smallest and prettiest castles in the area, despite being rather skeletal. Built over a period of five centuries, it has sheltered the likes of Robert the Bruce and James IV (who attended a wedding here), and in 1562 became the headquarters of the counter-Reformation in Scotland. After the Battle of Corrichie, brought about by the fourth earl's third son's wish to marry Mary, Queen of Scots, and which effectively brought the Gordons' 250-year rule to an end, the castle was pillaged and its treasures sent to St Machars Cathedral in Aberdeen. The castle suffered again during the Civil War, when its Irish garrison were starved into submission and the men were then hanged and their officers beheaded. Meanwhile the Earl of Huntly, who had supported Charles I and declared "you can take my head off my shoulders, but not my heart from my sovereign", was shot against his castle's walls with his escort, after which the place was left to fall into ruin.

Today you can still make out the twelfth-century motte, a grassy mound on the west side of the complex, separated from the outermost wall by a wide ditch within which the foundations of a stone tower house built in 1400 can be traced. The main castle ruin, with its splendid doorway fronted by an elaborate coat of arms, dates from the mid-fifteenth century, though its impressive bay windows are much later additions. In the basement, a narrow passage leads to the prisons, where medieval graffiti of tents, animals and people adorn the walls.

Seven miles south of Huntly and served by the occasional bus, the modest chateau-style **Leith Hall** (May–Sept daily 2–6pm; early to late Oct Sat & Sun 2–6pm; £2.40) is worth visiting even when closed for a wander around its 286-acre grounds (daily 10am–dusk). Since 1650 home to the Leith and Leith-Hay family, the vast estate of varied farm and woodlands includes ponds, eighteenth-century stables, a bird-observation hide and signposted countryside walks. Inside, you can see personal memorabilia of the successive Leith lairds, along with an array of grand furniture and paintings. Three of the lairds, the sixth, seventh and eighth, were in the armed services overseas, so anyone with military interests or a penchant for British imperial history will have a field day.

### Practicalities

Huntly's **tourist office**, 7a The Square (mid-May to June & early to mid-Sept Mon–Sat 10am–12.30pm & 1.30–5.45pm; July & Aug Mon–Sat 10am–12.30pm & 1.30–6.15pm, Sun 2–6.15pm; ☎05422/2634), is most useful for finding accommodation – they charge you ten percent, redeemable on the first night's stay.

One of the area's best **B&Bs** is *Faitch Hill Farmhouse* (☎046688/240; ②), four miles outside town at **GARTLY**, which has won numerous awards for outstanding cooking and hospitality. In Huntly itself, the *Dunedin Guest House*, 17 Bogie St (☎0466794/164; ②), is a good bet, or for more luxury, you could try *Huntly Castle Hotel* (☎0466/792696; ③), the former home of the Duke of Gordon, which stands just behind the castle ruins.

# Inverurie and around

From Huntly the A96 sweeps southeast to the coast, where some seventeen miles west of Aberdeen, the granite town of **INVERURIE** makes the most convenient base for visiting a number of relics and castles in the area. The tiny **tourist office** is in the town hall on Market Place (early April to May & Oct daily 10am–1.30pm & 2–5pm; June & Sept daily 10am–5pm; July & Aug daily 10am–6pm; ☎0467/20600). Despite its size, it has a large stash of leaflets useful for finding the local relics and monuments which are often badly signposted.

The closest of the ruined castles, within walking distance of the centre, towards the south end of town, is the **Bass**. What appears today to be two unimpressive large tufted mounds in the middle of a field, with stairs leading to the 60ft summit, was in fact the first Norman motte and bailey castle in this part of Scotland, constructed in 1160 by David, the youngest brother of King Malcolm IV.

## Bennachie

The granite hill **Bennachie**, two miles west of town, is possibly the site of the Mon Graupius, Scotland's first ever recorded battle in 84 AD when the Romans defeated the Picts. At 1733ft, this is one of the most prominent tors in the Grampian region, and is traditionally embarked upon by walkers from near the **Chapel of Garioch** (pronounced "Geery") off the A96 about five miles northwest of town. Allow two hours for the hike up Bennachie, and try to avoid the weekends when it can be busy – from the top you can see every ancient monument in the district and wonderful vistas of Aberdeenshire.

## Maiden Stone and Loanhead Stone Circle

Six miles northwest of Inverurie on the B9001, the spooky **Loanhead Stone Circle** has been standing in this beautiful location since 5000 or 4000 BC. Ten upright stones and a recumbant enclose a low ring cairn; the amount of bones buried below – the remains of over thirty people – suggest that the circle was used for rituals around 1500 BC. A couple of miles further northwest, protruding from the edge of a field, the **Maiden Stone** is a 10ft Pictish gravestone, carved from red granite and inscribed with, among other things, dragons, an elephant, a comb and a mirror. No one quite knows who was buried here, but legend has it as the daughter of a laird who died in mysterious circumstances during her elopement.

## Fyvie Castle

Some thirteen miles north of Inverurie and on the bus route, stands the huge, ochre mansion of **Fyvie Castle** (May & Sept daily 2–6pm; June–Aug daily 11am–6pm; early Oct Sat & Sun 2–6pm; NTS; £2.40). Scottish Baronial to the hilt, Fyvie's fascinating roofscape sprouts five curious steeples, one for each of the families who lived here from the thirteenth to the twentieth century. Beginning life as a typical courtyard castle, with a protective wall over six feet thick, over the ensuing centuries the place met with considerable architectural expansion. The Chancellor of Scotland bought Fyvie in 1596 and was probably responsible for the elaborate south front with its gables and turrets; his grandson sympathized with the Jacobites and, following his exile, the estate was confiscated and handed over to the Gordons. In 1889 the castle was sold to the Forbes-Leith, a local family who had made a fortune in America and who were responsible for the grand Edwardian interior. The exquisite dining room is nowadays rented out for corporate entertaining by oil companies who hob-nob among the Flemish tapestries, Delft tiles and the fine collection of paintings that includes feathery Gainsborough portraits and twelve works by Sir Henry Raeburn.

# The coast to Nairn

The coastal region of Northeast Scotland from Aberdeen to Inverness is a rugged, often bleak, landscape which is in parts virtually inaccessible. Still, if the weather is good, it's well worth spending a couple of days meandering through the various little fishing villages and the miles of deserted, unspoilt beaches. Keen walkers have the best run of the area; some of the cliffs are so steep that you have to hike considerable distances to get the best views of the coast.

Most visitors bypass **Peterhead** and **Fraserburgh**, the two largest communities, and head instead to smaller places such as **Cruden Bay** with its good beach, or the idyllic village of **Pennan** and nearby **Cullen**. The other main attractions are the working abbey at **Pluscarden** and the whacky Findhorn Foundation near **Forres**.

This area is fairly well served by buses, and trains from Aberdeen and Inverness stop at Elgin, Forres and Nairn. Even so, it's preferable to have your own transport for reaching some of the best, far-flung places.

## Pitmedden Gardens to Peterhead

Fourteen miles north of Aberdeen, just on the outskirts of Pitmedden village, the **Pitmedden Gardens** (April–Sept daily 10am–6pm; £1.50) are the creation of Alexander Seton – formerly Lord Pitmedden, before James VII removed his title as punishment for opposing his Catholicism. Seton spent his enforced retirement on perfecting an elaborate garden project he had begun in 1675, and today the utterly orderly gardens, 471 feet square, have been restored to their seventeenth-century pattern, comprising an upper and lower enclosure filled with floral designs, neat box hedges, pavilions, fountains and sundials. In the lower garden (best viewed from the terrace), the layout of three of the flowerbeds mimics those of Holyroodhouse in Edinburgh, while the fourth flowerbed, with its crest of arms, and the weather vane, surmounted by soldiers, are tributes to Seton's father who died fighting against the Covenanters in Aberdeen. Entrance to the gardens also takes in the **Museum of Farming Life**, where you'll see old tools and a chilly, dark bothy that was once home to the workers of the 100-acre Pitmedden estate.

### Tolquhon Castle
One of the area's most secluded ruins, **Tolquhon Castle** (April–Sept Mon–Sat 9.30am–7pm, Sun 2–7pm; Oct–March Mon–Sat 9.30am–4pm, Sun 2–4pm; 60p), is tucked away off a dirt track a mile or so northwest of Pitmedden.

Of the medieval remains, the gatehouse facade is the most prepossessing; very much intact, it has a handsome arched portal protected by drum towers and enriched with all manner of sculpted figures and coats of arms. You can still make out what each room was used for: the kitchen has two huge ovens gouged out of the wall, and one of the bedrooms is complete with a dungeon with an ominous trapdoor – even in the sixteenth century, responsibility for law and order still fell on the local laird and at any one time there could have been eight or nine prisoners below.

To the right of the castle, along another mud track, is a converted farmhouse turned **art gallery** (Mon–Wed, Fri & Sat 11am–5pm, Sun 1–5pm) exhibiting a variety of local art and some expensive jewellery and crafts.

## Haddo House and Gardens

Four miles north of Pitmedden, the huge Palladian mansion of **Haddo House** (mid-April to Oct daily 2–6pm; NTS; £2.40), completed to a design by William Adam in 1735, is set in a wonderful 177 acres of woodland, lakes and ponds. Since 1731 Haddo has been the seat of the Gordons and several earls and marquesses of Aberdeen – the grounds, now home to otters, red squirrels, pheasants and deer, were created from a wasteland by the fourth earl in the early years of the last century. The house is now renowned for staging local music, drama and arts: check with the NTS in Aberdeen (☎0224/641122) for details of the high-quality productions.

## Cruden Bay and around

When the A952 juts east towards Peterhead and the coast, it passes **CRUDEN BAY**, an averagely pretty village with a sandy beach that makes a good starting point for two excursions along the coast. The first, three miles or so south, is the huge pink granite ruin of **Slains Castle**, whose stark beauty overlooking the sea is said to have inspired Bram Stoker to write *Dracula*. This eerie castle, built in 1597 but remodelled in Gothic style in the nineteenth century, is surprisingly badly signposted; it can be reached in about thirty minutes by walking along Cruden Bay's main Bridge Street and through the car park at the end, from where you should just head for the sea and along the cliffs.

In the opposite direction, a precarious three-mile walk along the cliff north of Cruden Bay brings you to the **Bullers of Buchan**, a splendid 245ft deep-sea chasm, where the ocean gushes in through a natural archway eroded by the sea. This is some of the finest cliff scenery in the country and attracts a variety of nesting sea birds. A rough (and not particularly safe) footpath leads from the car park past some old cottages to the very edge of the chasm.

# Peterhead and around

Unless you have a particular penchant for baked-bean factories and power stations, **PETERHEAD**, the most easterly mainland town in Scotland, is best avoided. It calls itself a spa town, but don't let that fool you into imagining anything picturesque: as the busiest white-fish port in Europe, with annual catches valued at over $75 million, the harbour is a mass of rusted, dented and dripping boats which gently ooze oil into the murky waters.

Fishing, along with a high-security jail, used to be Peterhead's sole source of income until the arrival of the oil industry in the 1970s. The town's population increased rapidly from 13,000 to 18,000 and though the community is now one of the richest in Britain, many inhabitants say they regret the passing of the less money-orientated days of the past – a yen for the old days that is also evident in the use of the Scottish dialect, Doric.

The oldest building in Peterhead is the four-hundred-year-old **Ugie Salmon Fish House** on Golf Road at the mouth of the River Ugie, at the north end of town (Mon–Fri 9am–noon & 2–5pm, Sat 9am–noon; free), where you can watch the traditional (and extremely malodorous) smoking of salmon and trout in what is actually Scotland's oldest fish-smoking house – the finished product is for sale at reasonable prices. Peterhead's only other attraction is the **Arbuthnot Museum** on St Peter Street (Mon–Sat 10am–noon & 2–5pm; free), whose array of coins and Eskimo artefacts was collected by the local trader Adam Arbuthnot, born in 1773. The history of local whaling, weaving, cooperage and granite quarrying is also highlighted.

Peterhead's **tourist office** is on Broad Street (April, June, Sept & Oct Mon–Sat 10am–5pm; July & Aug Mon–Sat 10am–6pm, Sun 2–5pm; ☎0779/71904), and should you be inclined to **stay** in Peterhead, the most comfortable hotel is the modern *Waterside Inn* (☎0779/71121; ④), set on the banks of the River Ugie at the edge of town on the A952 towards Fraserburgh. For **eating**, fish and chips is your best bet: the *Tasty Plaice*, on Station Road, does great fish suppers.

## Aden Country Park

From Peterhead, a direct bus travels the nine miles to the 230-acre **Aden Country Park** (daily 9am–dusk; free), just beyond Mintlaw. Laid out in the grounds of an old aristocratic estate, the park includes woodlands, a lake, a river and a huge variety of plant and animal life, and also boasts the **North East of Scotland Agricultural Heritage Centre** (May–Sept 11am–5pm; April & Oct Sat & Sun noon–5pm; free). The main feature of this living history museum is Home Farm, a unique semicircular farmstead built around the beginning of the nineteenth century. A pastoral atmosphere is generated with sound effects of crowing, clucking, mooing and neighing, along with the occasional song, and in the horseman's cottage you'll see demonstrations of traditional homebaking. There's also a thoughtful exhibition on farming techniques from the early primitive, backbreaking farm clearings to today's high-tech machines.

# Fraserburgh and the north coast

Ten miles or so north of Aden Park, **FRASERBURGH** is a large unattractive town in the same vein as Peterhead, though its economy still relies only on fishing. An eighteenth-century lighthouse protrudes, oddly enough, from the top of the little sixteenth-century **Fraserburgh Castle** – beware of the weather here: the highest wind speeds in the country, 140mph, were recorded on this spot in 1989.

Though there's little reason to hang around, you can pick up local information from Fraserburgh's **tourist office**, in Saltoun Square (April to mid-Oct Mon–Sat 10am–5pm, Sun 2–5pm; July & Aug Mon–Sat 10am–6pm, Sun 11am–5pm; ☎0346/28315). The *Coffee Shoppe*, 30 Cross St, is a great little place for sandwiches, soup and cakes.

It is best to continue on to the hamlet of **PENNAN**, about twelve miles west of Fraserburgh, along a particularly beautiful stretch of coast road lined with pretty churches and cottages and affording the occasional, startling glimpse of the sea below. A right turn down a steep and hazardous decline leads to Pennan, which came into the limelight when village scenes from the successful British film *Local Hero* were filmed here in 1982. There's little to do here but enjoy the view; if the weather is good you can spot the occasional shoal of porpoise.

Pennan's sole place **to stay** is the *Pennan Inn* (☎03466/201; ④), one of the single row of lovely whitewashed cottages huddled together along the seafront and built right into the cliff face. The inn can arrange fishing and boat trips, and its **restaurant** is excellent, serving fantastic mussels along with a wide range of whiskies – you'll need to book in advance.

## Macduff and Banff

Heading west along the coast from Pennan brings you after ten miles to **MACDUFF**, a famous spa town during the nineteenth century and now with a thriving and pleasant harbour. Just over the River Devoron via a beautiful seven-arched bridge is **BANFF**, where you'll find the extravagant **Duff House** by the golf course (April–Sept Mon–Sat 9.30am–7pm, Sun 2–7pm; 60p), an elegant Georgian Baroque house built to William Adam's design in 1730. Originally intended for one of the northeast's richest men, William Braco, who became Earl of Fife in 1759, the house was clearly built to impress, and could have been even more splendid had Adam been allowed to build curving colonnades either side; Braco's refusal to pay for carved Corinthian columns to be shipped in from Queensferry caused such bitter argument that the laird never actually came to live here and even went so far as to pull down his coach curtains whenever he passed by. Plans are afoot to use the high-ceilinged rooms inside to exhibit a select range of pictures from the National Galleries of Scotland.

**Banff Links beach** to the west of town, is great when it's warm. The other beach, at the mouth of the Deveron, is susceptible to strong currents, and swimming is best avoided. Banff's **tourist office**, which also serves Macduff, is at Collie Lodge, St Mary's car park (April–June & Sept to mid-Oct daily 10am–5pm; July & Aug 10am–6pm; ☎0261/812419).

# Cullen

Twelve miles west of Banff, past the quaint village of **PORTSOY**, renowned for its green marble once shipped to Versailles, is **CULLEN**, served by bus from Aberdeen. The town, strikingly situated beneath a superb series of snaking rail viaducts, is made up of two sections – Seatown, by the harbour, and the new town on the hillside. There's a lovely stretch of sand, pleasantly sheltered from the winds by the hills behind Seatown, where the colourful houses huddle end-on to the sea – confusingly numbered according to the order in which they were built.

Cullen's lovely old **kirk**, about a twenty-minute walk from the centre, dates back to the 1300s, and is still packed out on a Sunday morning. Inside you'll see an ornate lairds' enclosure for the likes of the Duffs and Ogilvies who worshipped here; Alexander Ogilvie, who expanded the church in 1543, is buried in an ornate tomb, and there are a few lairds' graves in the yard, though the holiday apartments beyond the wall rather ruin the atmosphere.

For accommodation, most of the **B&Bs** are set back from the seashore on Seafield Place. They're all much of a muchness, but no. 11 is friendly and comfortable (☎0542/40819; ①). There's little action in the evening; a drink and a fish supper at the local pub is probably your best bet.

# Elgin and around

Inland, about fifteen miles southwest of Cullen, the lively market town of **ELGIN** grew up in the thirteenth century around the River Lossie. It's an appealing place, still largely sticking to its medieval street plan, with a busy main street opening out onto an old cobbled marketplace and a tangle of wynds and pends.

On North College Street, just round the corner from the tourist office and clearly signposted, is the still lovely ruin of **Elgin Cathedral** (April–Sept Mon–

Sat 9.30am–7pm, Sun 2–7pm; Oct–March Mon–Sat 9.30am–4pm, Sun 2–4pm; 60p). Once considered Scotland's most beautiful cathedral, rivalling St Andrews in importance, today it is little more than a shell, though it does retain its original facade. Founded in 1224, the three-towered cathedral was extensively rebuilt after a fire in 1270, and stood as the region's highest religious house until 1390 when the so-called Wolf of Badenoch (Alexander Stewart, Earl of Buchan and illegitimate son of Robert II) burnt the place down, along with the rest of the town, in retaliation for being excommunicated by the Bishop of Moray when he left his wife. The cathedral survived this onslaught, but went on to suffer even more during the post-Reformation, when all its valuables were stripped and the building was reduced to common quarry for the locals. Unusual features include the Pictish cross slab in the middle of the ruins and the cracked gravestones with their *memento mori* of skulls and cross bones.

In the High Street the **Elgin Museum** (April–Sept Tues–Fri 10am–5pm, Sat 11am–4pm; free), along with the usual local exhibits, has a weird anthropological collection including reptilian skulls, a shrunken head from Ecuador, a headhunter's basket decorated with monkey skulls, and Indian sculptures. Strangest of all is the grinning mummy from Peru, thought to have been a princess.

Elgin's other museum is just outside the centre on the A941, where a converted mill makes a wonderfully light and airy venue for the **Moray Motor Museum** (April–Oct daily 11am–5pm; £1), a collection of some 25 ancient, fully polished vehicles including a 1929 Rolls Royce Phantom, a 1920 Jaguar, a 1914 Renault, a wonderful old Bentley and a selection of motorbikes with their side cars.

## Practicalities

Elgin is well served by public transport, with the Aberdeen–Inverness train stopping here several times a day. The **bus station** is at the opposite end of High Street (☎0343/544222), while the **train station** (call Inverness ☎0463/238924 for information) is slightly less convenient on the south side of town on Station Road (turn left out of the station and head along Hay Street to reach the centre).

The **tourist office**, 17 High St (Jan–March, Nov & Dec Mon–Fri 9.30am–5pm; April–May & Oct Mon–Fri 9.30am–5.45pm, Sat 9.30am–1pm & 2–5.45pm; June & Sept Mon–Sat 9.30am–6.15pm, Sun 2–5.15pm; July & Aug Mon–Sat 9.30am–7.15pm, Sun noon–5.45pm; ☎0343/542666), sells a *Town Trail* leaflet that's useful for exploring Elgin, and will also book **accommodation**. The quiet *Carronvale*, 18 South Guildry St (☎0343/546864; ②), is one of the nicest **B&Bs** in town; for more luxury, the castle-like *Mansion House Hotel* (☎0343/548811; ⑥) is one of the most exclusive in the region.

## Pluscarden Abbey

About seven miles southwest of Elgin, **Pluscarden Abbey** (daily 5am–10.30pm; free) looms impressively large in a peaceful clearing off an unmarked road. Founded in 1230 for a French order of monks, the abbey remains a working facility, its serene interior wafting with the scent of incense and flooded with red and gold light from stained-glass windows. In 1390 Pluscarden was another of the properties burnt by the Wolf of Badenoch; recovering from this, it became a priory of the Benedictine Abbey of Dunfermline in 1454 and continued as such until monastic life was suppressed in Scotland in 1560. The abbey's revival began in 1897 when the Catholic antiquarian, John, third Marquis of Bute, started to repair the building. His son donated it, in 1948, to a small group of Benedictine monks from Gloucester, who are still in the process of restoring the place, having introduced modern additions such as the splendid stained glass.

## The Findhorn Foundation

Continuing the spiritual theme, but on a slightly weirder note, is the **Findhorn Foundation** on the B9011, about ten miles east of Elgin (Mon–Sat 9am–5pm, Sun 2–5pm; free). Particularly well known in Germany, Scandinavia and the States, the Findhorn is a magnet for well-heeled hippies from around the world. Set up in 1962 by Eileen and Peter Caddy (see below), the foundation has blossomed from its early core of three adults and three children into a full-blown community, with classes and facilities for hundreds of people. Bizarrely enough, despite its enormous growth, the foundation is still situated on the town's caravan and camping park (April–Oct; ☎0309/690203), creating an incongruous combination of holidaymakers with bucket and spade camping alongside "Findhorners" with their incense and love beads.

# Forres and Nairn

**FORRES,** one of Scotland's oldest agricultural towns, is of little note except for its pretty, flower-filled parks.

The 20ft **Sueno Stone**, on the eastern outskirts of town, is one of the most remarkable Pictish stones in Scotland, now housed in a glass case to prevent

---

### THE FINDHORN FOUNDATION

Following a conversation with God just over thirty years ago, Eileen Caddy upped sticks with her husband Peter and friend, Dorothy Maclean, and settled on a caravan site just outside Forres. Dorothy Maclean believed she had a special relationship with what she called the "devas", in her own words "the archetypal formative forces of light or energy that underlie all forms in nature – plants, trees, rivers etc.", and the three set about creating, from this unpromising sandy soil, a rich garden that produced outsize vegetables and flowers. Dorothy Maclean has since left the foundation, and the gardens, though beautiful, are not quite as outstanding as they once were.

The Original Caravan is now something of a shrine, surrounded by the eyesores of various temporary buildings. Despite its shantytown appearance the foundation is quite wealthy: it has 150 members and over eight thousand visitors attending courses a year, mostly from America, Australia or northern Europe, all of whom must promise to remain vegetarian, drug-free and teetotal while on site. The rules are broken on Fridays, when fish is served (even though the foundation believes that fish has a "depressing effect on the identity") and on Christmas Day, when everyone eats turkey. Every conceivable spiritual therapy available is on offer at Findhorn, from acupuncture through to Holotropic Breathwork, an odd process that involves up to two hours of hyperventilation intended to lift people into "an expanded mystical and spiritual dimension" – although it usually results in violent shaking, coughing, vomiting, and a host of other unpleasant side effects.

The foundation's talk of building a "planetary village" has sent the majority of people in Findhorn into a state of high anxiety, with a local justice of the peace declaring "Behind the benign and apparently religious front of the old Findhorn Foundation lies a hard core of New Agers experimenting with hallucinatory techniques marketed as spirituality". Last year, after considerable opposition from the locals, plans to become a public company (with a £5 million share flotation), and build a holistic health centre, have all gone by the wayside, as have attempts to ban a critical book that claimed the foundation "has settled for secondary values that yield prestige, power, and a comfortable lifestyle" and branded its leaders as "ignorant, deluded and inept".

further erosion. The stone was found buried in 1726 and mistakenly named after Swein Forkbeard, King of Denmark, though it more probably commemorates a battle between the people of Moray and the Norse settlers in Orkney. Carvings on the east face can be read as one of the earliest examples of war reportage, with the story told from the arrival of the leader and his guard at the top to the decapitated corpses of the vanquished at the bottom.

Forres has a small **tourist office** (April, May & Oct Mon–Sat 10am–5.45pm; June & Sept Mon–Sat 9.30am–6.15pm, Sun 2–5.15pm; July & Aug Mon–Sat 9.30am–6.45pm, Sun noon–5.45pm; ☎0309/72938), tucked away in the town's pitifully dull **Falconer Museum** (May, June, Sept & Oct Mon–Sat 10am–5.30pm; July & Aug Mon–Sat 9.30am–6.30pm, Sun 2–5pm; Nov–April 10am–4.30pm; free) on Tolbooth Street, just off High Street. **Buses** stop outside St Leonard's Church on High Street. Call *Northern Scottish* in Elgin (☎0343/544222) for details of buses heading east, and *Highland Scottish* in Inverness for details of services to the west. If you want to **stay** in Forres, try the *Tormhor* **B&B**, 11 High St (☎0309/673837; ③), which has large, comfortable rooms in a Victorian house overlooking splendid flower-filled gardens.

## Nairn

Apparently one of the driest and sunniest places in the whole of Scotland, **NAIRN** began its days as a peaceful community of fishermen and farmers. The former spoke Gaelic, the latter English, allowing James VI to boast that a town in his kingdom was so large that people at one end of the main street could not understand those at the other end. Nairn became popular in Victorian times, when the train line offered a convenient link to its revitalizing sea air and mild climate, and today it still relies on tourism: its windy, coastal golf course, the **Links**, is one of the most popular in Scotland, just as well, as the Moray Firth, on the edge of which Nairn sits, has become a notorious pollution blackspot of late.

Nairn's helpful and well-stocked **tourist office** is at 62 King's St (April & May Mon–Thurs 10am–5pm; late May to late June & early Sept to late Oct Mon–Sat 10am–5pm, Sun 11am–4pm; late June to early Sept Mon–Sat 9am–6pm, Sun 10am–5pm; ☎0667/52753). For **accommodation**, *Greenlawns*, 13 Seafield St (☎0667/52738; ①), is a small **B&B** filled with antiques; although more expensive, the *Golf View Hotel* (☎0667/52301; ④), overlooking the golf course and sea, is also good value.

## travel details

### Trains

**Aberdeen** to: Arbroath (every 30min; 1hr); Dundee (every 30min; 1hr 15min); Edinburgh (1–2 hourly; 2hr 35min); Elgin (hourly; 1hr 40min); Forres (hourly; 1hr 55min); Glasgow (1–2 hourly; 2hr 35min); Huntly (hourly; 45min); Inverurie (hourly; 20min); Keith (hourly; 1hr); Montrose (every 30min; 45min); Nairn (hourly; 2hr 5min); Stonehaven (every 30min; 15min).

**Dundee** to: Aberdeen (every 30min; 1hr 15min); Arbroath (hourly; 20min); Montrose (hourly; 15min).

**Elgin** to: Forres (hourly; 15min); Nairn (hourly; 25min).

### Buses

**Aberdeen** to: Arbroath (hourly; 1hr 20min); Ballater (hourly; 1hr 45min); Banchory (hourly; 55mins); Banff (hourly; 1hr 55min); Braemar (4–6 daily; 2hr 10min); Crathie (for Balmoral) (4–6 daily; 1hr 55min); Cruden Bay (hourly; 50min); Cullen (hourly; 1hr 50min–2hr 30min); Dufftown (2 weekly; 2hr 10min); Dundee (hourly; 2hr); Elgin (hourly; 2hr 35min–3hr 40min); Forfar (2 daily; 1hr

20min); Forres (5 daily; 2hr 35min); Fraserburgh (hourly; 1hr 20min); Fyvie (hourly; 1hr); Huntly (2 daily; 1hr 35min); Inverurie (4 daily; 45min); Macduff (hourly; 1hr 50min); Mintlaw (for Aden Park) (hourly; 50min); Montrose (hourly; 1hr); Nairn (5 daily; 2hr 50min); Peterhead (every 30min; 1hr 15min); Pitmedden (hourly; 50min); Stonehaven (every 30min; 25–45min).

**Ballater** to: Craithie (June–Sept 3 weekly; 15min); Tomintoul (June–Sept daily; 1hr).

**Banchory** to: Ballater (June–Sept 2 weekly; 45min); Braemar (June–Sept 2 weekly; 1hr 20min); Crathie (June–Sept 2 weekly; 1hr); Spittal of Glenshee (June–Sept 2 weekly; 2hr).

**Dufftown** to: Elgin (7 daily; 1hr); Keith (5 weekly; 40min).

**Dundee** to: Aberdeen (hourly; 1hr 50min); Arbroath (every 15min; 40min–1hr); Blairgowrie (every 30min; 50min–1hr); Forfar (every 30min; 30min); Glamis (2 daily; 40min); Kirremuir (hourly; 1hr 10min); Meigle (hourly; 40min); Montrose (hourly; 1hr 15min).

**Elgin** to: Aberdeen (1 daily; 3hr 15min); Forres (every 30min; 20min); Huntly (3 daily; 50min); Inverurie (3 daily; 1hr 45min); Nairn (4–6 daily; 40min); Pluscarden (daily; 20min); Tomintoul (June–Sept daily; 1hr 15min).

**Forres** to: Elgin (5 weekly; 55min); Findhorn (every 30min; 20min).

**Fraserburgh** to: Banff (2 daily; 55min); Macduff (2 daily; 45min).

**Montrose** to: Brechin (hourly; 20min).

**Peterhead** to: Cruden Bay (every 30min; 20min).

### Ferries

**Aberdeen** to: Lerwick, Shetland (daily; 14hr); Stromness, Orkney (weekly; 10hr); Faroe Islands (weekly; 22hr).

### Flights

**Aberdeen** to: Dundee (1 daily; 35min); Edinburgh (4 daily; 40min); Glasgow (3 daily; 45min); London (Heathrow 8 daily, Stansted 3 daily, Gatwick 4 daily; 1hr 30min).

# CHAPTER EIGHT

# THE HIGHLANDS

Scotland's **Highlands** cover the northern two-thirds of the nation and encompass some of its most fabulous scenery: mountains, glens, lochs and rivers contrast with moorland and fertile farms, and the whole sparsely populated area is surrounded by a magnificent and varied coastline. The region falls naturally into two halves: the north is far-flung, wild and remote, and most tourists head for the more accessible – and more varied – south.

The Highland landscape is without doubt the main attraction of the region, and you may be surprised at just how remote much of it is. Cutting across the heart of the **Southern Highlands**, the **Great Glen** provides an obvious focus for your travel, linking the long thin sliver of **Loch Ness**, in the centre of the region, and the key towns of Inverness on the east cost, and Fort William in the west. From here it's possible to branch out to some fine scenery, most conveniently the great mass of **Glen Coe**, but also the remote and tranquil **Ardnamurchan peninsula** and the lochs and glens that lead up to **Kyle of Lochalsh** – the most obvious route to Skye (see p.367). In the opposite direction, south of the Great Glen, the ski resort of **Aviemore** is the most obvious – if not the most appealing – base for visiting the spectacular **Cairngorm Mountains**.

The **Northern Highlands** are at their isolated best on the western side, where the high peaks of Suilven and Canisp lead on to the delights of the north Sutherland coast. All of this is in marvellous contrast to the green and more fertile eastern region, where farm and woodlands run down to the many sandy beaches along the **Dornoch**, **Cromarty** and **Moray Firths**, and the ecologically unique boglands of the **Flow Country** that stretch across the interior of the northeast corner.

Of the major urban centres of the Highlands, **Inverness** makes an obvious base for much of the region, with its good facilities and transport links, while on the western coast **Fort William**, with Ben Nevis rising behind, and the planned eighteenth-century port of **Ullapool** are both well placed for exploring large tracts of splendid countryside – though be warned that none of these towns are particularly endearing places in themselves. In the northeast, **Thurso** is a solid

## SAFETY IN THE SCOTTISH HIGHLANDS

The **mountains** of the Scottish Highlands, while not as high or as steep as the Alps, are so far north that weather conditions – including blizzards and icy winds of up to 100mph – can be fatal. In 1993, some 54 climbers died, many of them inexperienced walkers who did not realise the levels of danger involved. It's essential to take proper precautions. *Always* put safety first: never underestimate just how fast the weather can change (or how extreme the changes can be), and be sure to set out properly equipped, with warm and waterproof clothing, decent footwear, a compass, all the maps you might need, and some food in case you get stuck. Make sure, too, that someone knows roughly where you have gone and when you expect to be back.

stone town with a regular ferry service to the Orkneys, and the old port of **Wick** was once the centre of Europe's herring industry. Further south lie **Dornoch**, with its sandstone fourteenth-century cathedral, and **Cromarty**, whose vernacular architecture ranks among Scotland's finest.

**Getting around** the Highlands generally, particularly the remoter parts, is obviously easiest if you've got your own transport, but with a little judicious forward planning (and enough time to spare) you can see a surprising amount using **buses** and **trains**, especially if you fill in with postbuses. The infamous A9, a fast but notoriously dangerous road, is a key route into the area, sweeping north from Inverness; in the west, the A832, which follows the line of the Great Glen, and the A835, which leads north across the interior, are the main arteries.

---

### ACCOMMODATION PRICE CODES

Throughout this book, accommodation **prices** have been graded with the numbers below, according to the cost of the least expensive double room in high season. The bulk of the recommendations will fall in categories ② to ⑥; recommendations in the highest categories are limited to places that are especially attractive. Bear in mind that many of the swanky hotels often slash their tariffs at the weekend when the business types have gone home, and that many of the cheaper places will also have more expensive rooms. Note that in our accommodation listings price codes are not given for youth hostels – they all come into the lower end of the ① category.

| ① under £20 | ④ £40–50 | ⑦ £70–80 |
|---|---|---|
| ② £20–30 | ⑤ £50–60 | ⑦ £80–100 |
| ③ £30–40 | ⑥ £60–70 | ⑧ over £100 |

---

# THE SOUTHERN HIGHLANDS

The **Southern Highlands** of Scotland encompass the country south of a line drawn roughly from **Kyle of Lochalsh** on the west coast to **Inverness** on the east and down to follow the upper half of the **Spey Valley** west past Loch Laggan to **Fort William** and **Glen Coe**.

On the east coast, **Inverness** is by far the biggest town in the Highlands, a good base for day trips and a jumping-off point for the more remote parts of the region. To some extent, the area around the **Moray Firth** is a commuter belt for the town, but it also boasts a lovely coastline and some of the region's best castles and historic sites. The gentle, undulating green landscape is well tended, good-looking and tranquil: a fertile contrast to the mountains that virtually surround the area.

Slicing through the region – indeed virtually cutting the north of Scotland in two – the **Great Glen**, formed by volcanic action some four hundred million years ago is now filled with three lochs: **Loch Ness**, at nearly thirty miles by far the longest, **Loch Lochy**, and the saltwater **Loch Linnhe**. The latter forms a natural geographical barrier to the relatively undiscovered **Ardnamurchan peninsula**, which offers a huge range of scenery, lots of wildlife and flora and a scatter of crofting towns. Further up this coast, **Kyle of Lochalsh** is the easiest access point for **Skye**. To get there, unless you take the boat up the **Sound of Sleat** via **Mallaig**, you have to backtrack through Fort William, **Glen Moriston** and **Glen Shiel** – magnificent country with superb hiking and climbing.

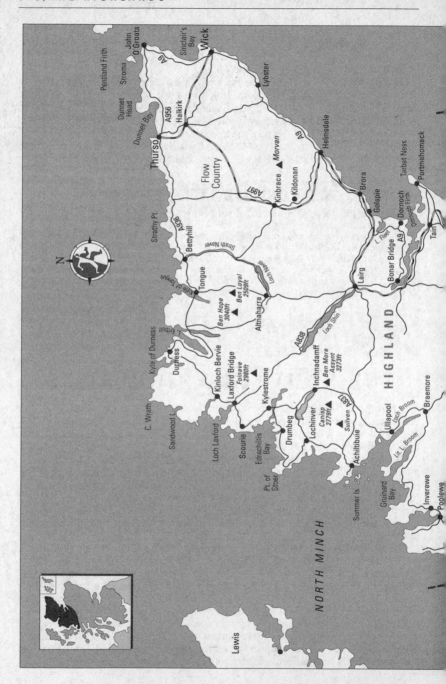

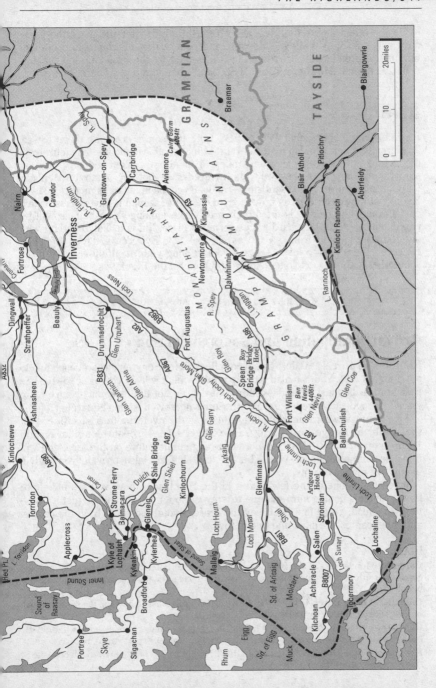

On the other side of the glen, the **Monadhliath Mountains** mark the boundary with the **Spey Valley**. This wide and open valley, offering varied outdoor pursuits in breathtaking surroundings, is backed by the brooding and magnificent **Cairngorm Mountains**, one of Scotland's better-known wilderness areas.

# Inverness

It's likely you'll approach **INVERNESS** from the south, dropping down to sea-level from the heather-clad plateau of the Monadhliath Mountains. The journey to the centre is less scenic, passing miles of unattractive light industry and car showrooms, but once beyond this Inverness is not an unattractive place. Dramatically crowned by a sandstone castle, it retains much of its medieval street layout (although some areas have been developed), while the River Ness, which cuts through the centre, is lined with prosperous-looking stone houses. With a population of 42,500, it's hardly an enormous place, but is usually bustling with out-of-towners come from as far as Thurso and Kyle for a day's shopping. However, there's not a lot to see, and before long your attention is likely to be wandering to the less exploited slopes and glens of the Highlands.

> The telephone code for Inverness is ☎0463

## Arrival, information and accommodation

Inverness **airport** is at Dalcross, seven miles from the city; an airport coach meets most flights (£2). You can also pick up a **taxi**, which will set you back £8–10. The **bus station** lies just behind Academy Street, one of the three city-centre main streets not pedestrianized; the **train station** is nearby on Station Square.

Five minutes' walk from the station towards the river, the **tourist office** is on the corner of Bridge Street and Castle Street (Mon–Fri 9am–5pm, Sat & Sun 10am–4pm; ☎234353). They have a wide range of literature on the area, and will book accommodation for you. The friendly staff can also provide you with a useful free map of the city.

Inverness is one of the few places in the Highlands where you're unlikely to have problems finding **somewhere to stay**, although in July and August it's wise to book ahead. You'll find B&Bs by the score, a youth hostel right in the centre, and three campsites, including one in town.

### Hotels

**Columba Hotel**, Ness Walk (☎231391). Huge, central hotel opposite the castle and just across the bridge from the town centre, with a mixed clientele of tourists and business people. ⑥.

**Cuchullin Lodge Hotel**, 43 Culduthel Rd (☎231945). Established hotel on the southern side of town with a large, pretty garden and good food. ④.

**Glen Mhor Hotel**, 10 Ness Bank (☎234308). Large, welcoming riverside hotel with friendly owners and a popular restaurant. Five min from the centre. ④.

**Riverside House Hotel**, Ness Bank (☎231052). Victorian hotel on the riverbank opposite St Andrews Cathedral. ③.

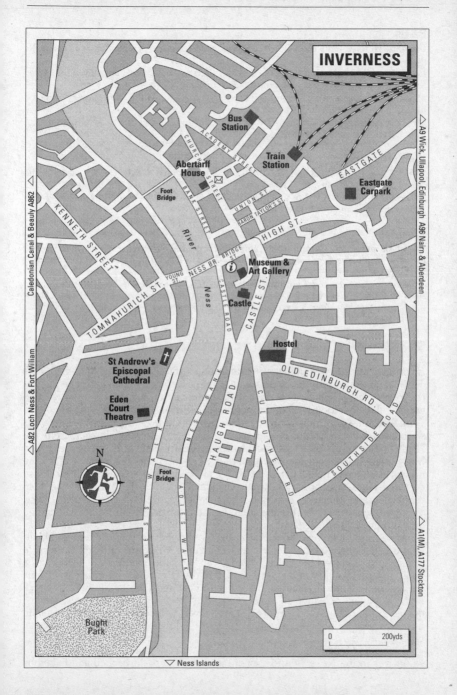

INVERNESS

Bus Station

Train Station

EASTGATE

Eastgate Carpark

Abertarff House

CHURCH STREET

ACADEMY STREET

BANK STREET

Foot Bridge

UNION ST.

BARON TAYLOR'S ST.

HIGH ST.

River

KENNETH STREET

Caledonian Canal & Beauly A862

A9 Wick, Ullapool, Edinburgh A96 Nairn & Aberdeen

TOMNAHURICH ST.

YOUNG ST.

NESS BR.

BRIDGE ST.

Museum & Art Gallery

CASTLE ROAD

Castle

CASTLE ST.

Ness

Hostel

St Andrew's Episcopal Cathedral

OLD EDINBURGH RD.

Eden Court Theatre

NESS BANK

HAUGH ROAD

CULDUTHEL RD.

SOUTHSIDE ROAD

A82 Loch Ness & Fort William

A1(M), A177 Stockton

N

NESS WALK

Foot Bridge

LADIES WALK

Bught Park

0          200yds

▽ Ness Islands

## B&Bs

**Clisham House**, 43 Fairfield Rd (☎239965). Comfortable non-smoking guest house, a 15-min walk from the centre. ③.

**Edenview**, 26 Ness Bank. (☎234397). Spacious B&B as well situated as many of the expensive hotels, a 5-min walk from the centre and overlooking the river. ③.

**Mrs Gillan**, 5 Ladies Walk, Island Bank Rd (☎225406). Right on the river and very comfortable. A 10-min walk from the town centre. ②.

**Mrs MacKenzie**, 5 Crown Circus (☎224222). Solid stone house in a residential area 5min from the city centre. Lots of home comforts. ②.

## Youth Hostels

**SYHA Hostel**, Old Edinburgh Rd (☎231771). Big and busy Grade 1 youth hostel in the centre of town; check in early. Closed Jan.

**Inverness Student Hotel**, 8 Culduthel Rd (☎236556). A 50-bed independent hostel with laundry facilities and free breakfast.

## Camping

**Bught Caravan and Camping Site**, Bught Park (☎236920). Inverness' main campsite, on the west bank of the river near the city centre. Good facilities, but it can get very crowded at the height of the season.

**Bunchrew Caravan and Camping Park**, Bunchrew, three miles west of Inverness on the A862 (☎237802). Well-equipped site on the shores of the Beauly Firth, with hot water, showers, launderette and shop. It's very popular with families so you'll probably have to contend with hordes of screaming kids.

# The City

Inverness' horizon is dominated by its **Castle** (mid-May to Sept Mon–Sat 9am–5pm), a predominantly nineteenth-century red sandstone edifice perched above the river. The original castle was at the core of the ancient town, which had rapidly developed as a port trading with Europe after its conversion to Christianity by St Columba in the sixth century. Two famous Scots monarchs were associated with the castle: Robert the Bruce wrested it back from the English during the Wars of Independence, destroying it in the process, and Mary, Queen of Scots had the governor of the second castle hung from the ramparts after he had refused her entry in 1562. This second castle was also destined for destruction, held by the Jacobites in both the 1715 and the 1745 rebellions, and blown up by them to prevent it falling into government hands. Today's imposing but hardly inspiring pile houses the Sheriff Court; you can go in, but there's little to see.

There's nothing very remarkable to see in the rest of Inverness either, although it's worth taking a look at the **Inverness Museum and Art Gallery**, in the same building as the tourist office (Mon-Sat 9am–5pm; free), which gives a good general overview of the development of the Highlands. Informative sections on geology, geography and history cover the ground floor, while upstairs you'll find a muddled selection of silver, taxidermy, weapons and bagpipes. On the opposite side of the river, the large **St Andrews Episcopal Cathedral** was built in 1866. The interior is pretty ordinary, though it does claim an unusual octagonal chapter house.

The banks of the River Ness make for a good stroll; you can walk half a mile or so upriver to the **Ness Islands**, an attractive public park reached and linked by

Edwardian bridges and laid out with mature trees and shrubs. Further up-stream, the river runs parallel with the **Caledonian Canal**, designed by Thomas Telford in the early nineteenth century as a link between the east and west coasts joining Loch Ness, Loch Lochy and Loch Linnhe. Today its main use is recreational, and there are **cruises** through part of it to Loch Ness. These run from early May to mid-September; you can get full details from *Jacobite Cruises*, Tomnahurich Bridge, Glenurquhart Rd (☎710188).

# Eating, drinking and nightlife

Finding good **food** in Inverness can be a problem. You certainly won't starve, but neither will you go home telling your friends about the city's gastronomic delights. Most of the best food is served in the restaurants in the big hotels, so it's best to book. Otherwise, you'll have to depend on all the usual fast-food outlets.

## Restaurants

**Bishop's Table Restaurant**, Eden Court Theatre. Upmarket self-service restaurant that is part of the theatre complex and has a nice bar and views down to the river. Imaginative food, with good salads, quiches, soups and a speciality dish daily.

**Castle Restaurant**, 41 Castle St. Central restaurant, open all day with a great variety of good, inexpensive Scottish home-cooking.

**Dunain Park Hotel Restaurant**, Dunain Park (☎224532). Award-winning Scots-French restaurant in a country house hotel set in lovely gardens on the river just southwest of town. Not at all cheap, but a good choice for a leisurely dinner.

**Glen Mhor Hotel Restaurant**, 9 Ness Bank (☎234308). Brasserie serving Scottish food for lunch and dinner; particularly generous, moderately priced Sunday lunches.

**Loch Ness House Hotel Cluny Restaurant**, Glenurquhart Rd (☎231248). Hotel restaurant that welcomes non-residents and serves Scottish specialities, including venison and grouse in season, and the ubiquitous haggis.

**Pizza Gallery**, 1 Bridge St. A cheerful, family-run, inexpensive pizza parlour that is actively nice to kids.

**Rose of Bengal**, Ness Bank. This northern outpost of the subcontinent, down on the riverbank, provides standard Indian food and tandoori when haggis palls.

**Whitecross Restaurant**, Muirtown Locks (☎240386). Small, friendly restaurant using local ingredients to produce imaginative Scottish food. Closed Sun dinner & Mon.

## Pubs and clubs

Inverness has a good selection of **pubs**, many of which have occasional live music. Locals head for the lively *Market Bar* off Church Street, and the *Academy* in Academy Street; the *Phoenix*, in the same street, is popular too. The *Eagle* in Baron Taylor Street and the *Gunsmith* in Union Street are central and perfectly good.

If you want to **dance**, *Babourouskie's* in Young Street is a reasonable nightclub, while the *Cummins Hotel* in Church Street organizes ceilidhs during the summer – fun, if a little touristy.

# Listings

**Car rental** *Europcar* (☎462374) has an office at the airport; in town there's a *Hertz* (☎711479) in the train station on Station Square.

**Chemist** *Boots*, Eastgate Shopping Centre (Fri–Wed 9am–5.30pm, Thurs 9am–7pm; ☎225167).

**Currency Exchange** *Thomas Cook*, 9–13 Inglis St (Mon–Fri 9am–5.30pm; Sat 9am–5pm; ☎711921).

**Post Office** 14–16 Queensgate (Mon–Thurs 9am–5.30pm, Fri 9.30am–5.30pm. Sat 9am–12.30pm; ☎234111).

# The Moray Firth

East of Inverness lies the fertile, sheltered coastal strip of the **Moray Firth**, its many historic sites and castles easily accessible as day trips from Inverness. Both the countryside and the amount of attractions around here make a good contrast to the purely scenic splendours you'll encounter once you head further north into the Highlands. The A96 traverses this stretch and it's well served by public transport.

## Culloden

Five miles east of Inverness, the windswept moorland of **Culloden** (site open all year, visitor centre Feb–Nov 10am–4/5.30pm; NTS; free), saw the last great battle on British soil on April 16, 1746, a turning point in the history of the Scottish nation, when the Jacobite cause was finally defeated. The second Jacobite rebellion had begun on August 19, 1745, when the standard was raised at Glenfinnan on the west coast; shortly after, Edinburgh had fallen into Jacobite hands, and Bonnie Prince Charlie had started his march on London. The English, however, had appointed the well-respected Duke of Cumberland to command their forces, and this, together with bad weather and lack of funds, forced the Jacobites to retreat north. They ended up at Culloden, where, ill-fed and exhausted after a pointless night-march, they were also hopelessly outnumbered by the English. The open, flat ground of Culloden Moor was also totally unsuitable for the Highlanders' style of courageous but undisciplined fighting, which needed steep hills and lots of cover to provide the element of surprise, and they were resoundingly defeated. After the battle, in which 1200 Highlanders were killed, Bonnie Prince Charlie fled west to the hills and islands, where loyal Highlanders sheltered and protected him. He eventually escaped to France, leaving his erstwhile supporters to their fate – and, in effect, the end of the clan system. The clans were disarmed, the wearing of tartan forbidden and the clan chiefs became landlords greedy for higher and higher rents. Within a century Highland life had changed out of all recognition.

Today you can walk freely around the battle site; flags mark the positions of the two armies, and **clan graves** are marked by simple headstones. The **Field of the English**, for many years unmarked, is a mass grave for the English troops; and nearby, a stone marks the spot where the Duke of Cumberland is said to have watched the proceedings. Thirty Jacobites were burnt alive outside the old **cottage** next to the visitor centre; inside, it has been restored to its eighteenth-century appearance, with a taped soundtrack of Gaelic music. The **visitor centre** itself provides background information through detailed displays and a slide show about the '45 generally and Culloden in particular.

In April, on the Saturday closest to the date of the battle, there's a small commemorative **service**. The visitor centre has a reference library, and will check for you if you think you have an ancestor who died here. For more on Culloden and the Jacobites, see "History" in *Contexts*.

## Cawdor Castle

Eight miles northeast of Culloden, the pretty, if slightly self-satisfied village of CAWDOR is the site of **Cawdor Castle** (May–Sept daily 10am–5pm; £3), half a mile east of town. Featuring in Shakespeare's *Macbeth* – the fulfilment of the witches' prediction that Macbeth was to become Thane of Cawdor sets off his tragic desire to be king – the castle is a real fairy-tale affair of towers, turrets and crenellations whimsically shooting off from the original fourteenth-century keep. The Cawdors have lived here for six centuries, and there are plenty of signs of life as you tour the interior, along with the usual stately-home tapestries, pictures and good furniture. The lively guidebook gives a blow-by-blow description of everything on view, as well as a comprehensive family history. Look out for the Thorn Tree Room, a vaulted chamber complete with the remains of an ancient tree. According to Cawdor family legend, the fourteenth-century Thane of Cawdor dreamt he should build on the spot where his donkey lay down to sleep after a day's wandering – the animal chose this tree and building commenced right away.

## Fort George

It's about eight miles from Cawdor Castle to **Fort George** (April–Sept Mon–Sat 10am–6pm, Sun 2pm–6pm; Oct–March Mon–Fri 10am–4pm; £2.50) on the tip of the headland nine miles west of **Nairn**, an old holiday resort (see p.342). Considered by military architectural historians to be one of the finest fortifications in Europe, the fort was built between 1747 and 1769 as an impregnable base for George II's army, in case the Highlanders should attempt to rekindle the Jacobite cause. By the time it was finished all was peaceful, and it has been in use as a barracks ever since.

Much of the fort is taken over by the **Regimental Museum of the Queen's Own Highlanders**, whose large collection of weapons, uniforms, medals and coins covers most of the major campaigns fought by the British in the last two centuries. The **chapel** is also worth a look, squat and solid outside and all light and grace within. In summer there's often a **pipe** or **military band** playing.

Walking on the northern, grass-covered casemates look out into the estuary – you may be lucky enough to see the school of dolphins, which regularly comes in with the tide.

## Brodie Castle

Eight miles east of Nairn, just off the A96, **Brodie Castle** (April–Sept Mon–Sat 11am–6pm, Sun 2–6pm; NTS), dating from 1567, is a classic Z-shaped Scottish tower house set in lovely grounds with drifts of daffodils in spring. Although it's now the property of the NTS, the 25th earl of Brodie still lives here, and his presence very much contributes to the albeit slightly stagey country-house atmosphere. The huge, light and airy drawing room with its view of the garden is often used for piano concerts. Inside there are all the rooms you'd expect; a panelled dining room with fabulous plasterwork, several bedrooms complete with four-posters, and a massive Victorian kitchen and servants quarters, all linked by winding passages. The collections of furniture, porcelain and especially paintings are outstanding, with works by Jacob Cuyp and Edwin Landseer, among others. To end your trip there's a **tearoom**, where the staff dish out splendid home-baked cakes.

### West of Inverness: the Beauly Firth

West from Inverness, the Moray Firth becomes the **Beauly Firth**. Since the opening of the **Kessock Bridge** in 1982 this whole area has become something of a backwater, but the A862 which runs beside the sea and gives good views north and west, is an alternative to the fast A9 route north.

**BEAULY** lies at the head of the Firth on the Beauly River, one of Scotland's great salmon rivers. It's a quiet, stone-built town, with one main street widening out into a spacious square, and the ruins of the thirteenth-century **Beauly Priory** off to one side (daily 10am–5pm, £1.50). The town is worth an hour or so; take in *Campbells of Beauly* tweed shop, where you'll find serious Scottish shopping in a wonderfully old-fashioned interior.

If you want to stay, *Ellangowan*, on Croyard Road (☎0463/782273; ②), offers B&B accommodation, while the *Lovat Arms Hotel* (☎0463/782862; ⑥) is an incredibly comfortable traditional hotel.

# Aviemore and the Cairngorms

The ski resort of **Aviemore**, backed by the **Cairngorm Mountains**, lies in the upper part of the **Spey Valley**, about twenty miles southeast of Inverness. This is a beautiful, diverse region, where water, heather and woodland – a superb mix of Caledonian pine, silver birch and juniper – abound, and the landscape ranges from picture-postcard prettiness to truly awe-inspiring grandeur, easily absorbing the thousands of annual visitors. The village of Aviemore itself isn't up to much, but the 4000ft summit plateau of the Cairngorm, the main peak of the range, is often snow-capped, providing stunning mountain scenery on a grand scale – and occasionally good skiing. Most of the area is privately owned by the **Glen More Forest Park** and **Rothiemurchus Estate**, who provide between them a plethora of year-round facilities for outdoor enthusiasts, with masses of **accommodation** of all types. Both bodies actively encourage the recreational use of their land, which gives you the freedom to go virtually anywhere you want.

## Aviemore

**AVIEMORE** was first developed as a resort in the mid-1960s, as the brutal concrete **Aviemore Centre** bears witness: a rundown assortment of cavernous concrete buildings and incongruous high-rise hotels on the edge of the **village** proper. The village itself, a sprawling jumble of traditional stone houses and tacky tourist shops, isn't much better, but if you can brave all this, Aviemore does make a good base from which to explore the valley, and once you're out of town the countryside makes up for a lot.

### Practicalities

Aviemore's **train station** is just north of the **tourist office** on the main drag, Grampian Road (Mon–Sat 9am–5pm; ☎0479/810363). They offer an accommodation-booking service, free maps and endless leaflets on local attractions. **Accommodation** is not a problem around here. In Aviemore there's the *Balavoulin Hotel* (☎0479/810672; ③) and the *Ver Mont Guest House* (☎0479/810470; ②) on Grampian Road. There are also plenty of B&Bs to choose from:

*Valleyfield*, Craig-na-Gower Ave (☎0479/8111485; ②), is particularly good. There's a large official **youth hostel** very close to the tourist office (☎0479/810345; Grade 1), while at **GLENMORE**, in the Glenmore Forest Park a few miles east of Aviemore, the well-signposted *Badaguish Centre* (☎0479/861285), housed in three log cabins, has dorm beds for sixty people. There's another youth hostel at the *Loch Insh Watersports Centre* (☎0540/651272), beautifully sited beside the loch about six miles south of Aviemore near the village of **KINCRAIG**. You could, alternatively, base yourself at **Kingussie**, a quiet village on the other side of Loch Insh (see overleaf).

All the hotels do run-of-the-mill **bar food**. The *Old Bridge Inn*, down by the river below the bridge on the way to Loch Morlich, has more choice than most, as does the *Gallery Bistro* right in the centre of **INVERDRUIE**, a tiny village a mile southeast of Aviemore on the road to Loch Morlich.

## Skiing in Aviemore

Scottish skiing on a commercial scale first really took off in Aviemore. By European and North American standards it's all on a tiny scale, but occasionally snow, sun and lack of crowds coincide and you can have a great day. *Highland Guides*, in Inverdruie (☎0479/861276) sell equipment and maps.

The **Cairngorm Ski Area** is about eight miles from Aviemore, above Loch Morlich in Glenmore Forest Park. It's well served by **buses** from the village, and you can **rent skis** from the *Day Lodge* at the foot of the ski area (☎0479/861261), which also has a shop, a bar and restaurant, and sells tickets for the four chair-lifts and dozen or so drag-lifts.

If there's lots of snow, the area around Loch Morlich and into the Rothiemurchus Estate provides enjoyable **cross-country skiing** through lovely woods, beside rushing burns and even over frozen lochs. If you really want to know about survival in a Scottish winter, you could try a week at **Glenmore Lodge** (☎0479/861276) in the heart of the Glen More Forest Park at the east end of Loch Morlich. This superbly equipped and organized centre, run by the Scottish National Sports Council, offers winter courses in hill-walking, mountaineering, alpine ski mountaineering, avalanche awareness and much besides.

To add to the winter scene, there's a herd of **reindeer** at Loch Morlich, and the **Siberian Husky Club** hold their races in the area.

## Summer activities

In summer, the main activities around Aviemore are **watersports**, and there are two centres that offer sailing, windsurfing and canoeing. The *Loch Morlich Watersports Centre* (☎0479/810310), five miles or so east of Aviemore at the east end of the loch, rents equipment and offers tuition in a lovely setting with a sandy beach, while, up-valley, the *Loch Insh Watersports Centre* (see above) offers the same facilities in more open and less crowded surroundings.

**Riding** and **pony trekking** are on offer up and down the valley; try the *Ballintean Riding Centre* (☎0540/65132) in Kingussie (see overleaf), or the *Carrbridge Trekking Centre* on Station Road in Carrbridge, a few miles north of Aviemore (☎0479/84602).

**Fishing** is very much part of the local scene; you can fish for trout and salmon on the River Spey, and the Rothiemurchus Estate has a stocked trout-fishing loch at Inverdruie, where success is virtually guaranteed.

## Walking

Walking is an obvious attraction in the Cairngorms. If you want to walk the **high tops**, it makes sense to take the chairlift up from the *Day Lodge* (see previous page). Follow the usual rules: take proper equipment, a map, a compass, extra food and warm clothing and remember to leave word of where you're going and what time you expect to be back.

There are some lovely **low-level** walks in the area. It'll take you about an hour or so to walk round pretty **Loch an Eilean**, with well-marked paths, off the B970, the back road to Kingussie. A longer walk starts at the near end of Loch Morlich. Cross the river by the bridge and follow the dirt road, turning off after about twenty minutes to follow the signs to Aviemore. The path goes through beautiful pine woods and past tumbling burns, and you can branch off to Coylumbridge and Loch an Eilean. Unless you're prepared for a 25-mile hike, don't take the track to the Lairig Ghru, which eventually brings you out near Braemar. The routes are all well marked and easy to follow and depending what combination you put together can take anything from two to five hours.

Another good shortish walk leads along well-surfaced forestry track from **Glenmore Lodge** up towards the **Ryvoan Pass**, passing **An Lochan Uaine**, known as the "Green Loch" and living up to its name with its amazing colour. The track narrows once past the loch and leads east towards Deeside, so retrace your steps if you don't want a major expedition.

# Around Aviemore

**KINGUSSIE** (pronounced "Kinusie"), lies fourteen miles south of Aviemore and is far less developed, little more than one main street. Beyond its usefulness as a place to stay, its chief attraction is the excellent **Highland Folk Museum** (April–Oct Mon–Sat 10am–6pm, Sun 2pm–6pm; Nov–March Mon–Fri 10am–3pm; £2). An absorbing collection of buildings, exhibitions and artefacts covering every aspect of Highland life, the complex includes a farming museum, an old smoke-house, a mill, a Hebridean "blackhouse" and a traditional vegetable garden, while every day in summer there's a demonstration of various traditional crafts. Across the river are the ruins of **Ruthven Barracks**, the best preserved of the garrisons built to pacify the Highlands after the 1715 Rebellion and stunningly floodlit at night.

Kingussie's seasonal **tourist office** is on King Street off the High Street (May–Sept Mon–Sat 9am–5pm; ☎0540/661297). If you want to base yourself here, try *Dhumor House*, 67 High St (☎0540/661809; ②), *Arden House* on Newtonmore Road (☎0540/661369; ②), or the *Scot House Hotel* next door (☎0540/661351; ③). The *Cross Restaurant*, in a converted tweed mill nearby on Tweed Mill Brae (March–Nov & Christmas; ☎0540/661166) is one of the best **restaurants** in the region, serving imaginative, innovative cooking using prime local ingredients such as salmon and Angus beef – expensive but well worth it. You'll find **bar food** at the hotels, and good fish and chips at the *Café Volante* on the High Street.

**Buses** run from Aviemore and Inverness to the tiny Georgian town of **GRANTOWN-ON-SPEY**, about fifteen miles northwest of Aviemore, which, if you've got your own transport, makes another good base for exploring the area. All activity is concentrated by the attractive central square, where there's a seasonal **tourist office** in the High Street (May–Sept Mon–Sat 9am–5pm,

☎0479/2473) and plenty of **accommodation** – the *Cumbrae*, South St (☎0479/
3216; ②), *Tyree House Hotel* (☎0479/2615; ③), *Garden Park Guest House*,
Woodside Ave (☎0479/3235; ③) and *The Hawthorns*, Old Spey Bridge (☎0479/
2016; ③), are all comfortable and good value. Just south of town on the Aviemore
Road, the *Craggan Mill Restaurant* serves decent food; for more substantial
meals, the *Ravenscourt House Hotel* restaurant on Seafield Avenue (☎0479/2286)
serves Scottish specialities – definitely worth a try.

# The Great Glen

The **Great Glen** rips through the Southern Highlands from Inverness diagonally
across to Fort William, not particularly spectacular in itself, but providing an
obvious and rewarding route from the east to west coast. Of its three long,
sliver-thin lochs, the most famous is Loch Ness, home to the mythical beast,
linked to the other two, Loch Linhe and Loch Lochy, by the **Caledonian Canal**,
dug in the early 1800s by Thomas Telford to enable ships to pass between the
North Sea and the Atlantic without having to navigate Scotland's treacherous
northern coast.

## Loch Ness

**Loch Ness'** fame has little to do with its appearance. It's long and it's fairly beautiful, but if it weren't for its legendary inhabitant, **Nessie**, the **Loch Ness
Monster**, you'd probably drive past without a second glance – especially as the
busy A82, which runs southwest along the north shore of the loch to Fort
William, is the main route to the west coast, and gives little opportunity to stop.

Nessie's been around a long time. She was first mentioned in St Adamnan's life
of St Colomba, written in the seventh century. Apparently, on his way to
Aberdeen, the saint calmed her down after she attacked one of his monks, and
since then numerous people have claimed a sighting. The present-day interest,
however, is probably greater outside Scotland than in, and is very much a twentieth-century phenomenon, dating from the 1930s when sightings were reported
during the construction of the A82. Numerous appearances have been reported
since, with descriptions ranging from a giant humpbacked beast breaking the
surface of the water to a long snake arching above its surface, but even the most
hi-tech surveys have failed to come up with conclusive evidence.

### Drumnadrochit and Lewiston

Situated on a verdant, sheltered bay fifteen miles from Inverness,
**DRUMNADROCHIT** is practically the first chance to draw breath as you head
down Loch Ness on the busy A82. **Cruises** of the loch begin from here: they
leave two or three times daily from **Temple Pier**, and last about an hour (£3.50).

The **Official Loch Ness Monster Exhibition Centre** (daily 10am–6pm; £4)
gives a history of the sightings over the years, backed up by film, photographs
and statistics, and explains how sonar has been increasingly used to try and cover
the whole of the area of the loch with underwater soundings to pinpoint anything
that might be there. Regular cruises set off from here also, predictably focusing
on "Nessie" lore.

Most photographs allegedly showing the monster have been taken a couple of miles further south, around the fourteenth-century ruined lochside **Castle Urquhart** (daily 10am–5pm; £2). Built as a strategic base to guard the Great Glen, the castle played an important role in the Wars of Independence. It was taken by Edward I of England and later held by Robert the Bruce against Edward III, only to be blown up in 1692 to prevent it from falling to the Jacobites. It's pretty dilapidated today, but looks particularly splendid floodlit at night when all the crowds have gone.

By far the nicest **hotel** around Drumnadrochit is the *Lewiston Arms* in the adjoining village of **LEWISTON** (☎0456/450225; ③), an old inn with a big garden – turn right at the *Esso* petrol station. Otherwise there's the family-run *Benleva Hotel* (☎0456/450288; ③) beside the loch. For **B&B**, *Linne Dhuinn*, in Lewiston (☎0456/450244; ②), has comfortable non-smoking rooms, while *Borlum Farm*, beyond the *Esso* petrol station towards the loch (☎0456/450358; ③), has doubles with great views. Near the latter, signposted from the main road, there's the *Loch Ness Backpackers Lodge* at Coiltie Farmhouse (☎0456/450807), who have double rooms (①) along with standard dorm accommodation. They also organize tours and walking groups, useful if you haven't got your own transport.

All the hotels have **bar food**; in Drumnadrochit the *Glen Restaurant*, and the *Hungry Piper*, 200yd or so further down the road, cater for hundreds with basic food, while *Fiddlers Bistro*, next door to the *Glen*, is more upmarket, with grills and salmon on offer.

### Glen Urquhart and Glen Affric

You can head northwest from Drumnadrochit on the A831 through **Glen Urquhart**, a fairly open glen with farmland giving way to scrubby woodland and heather as you near **CANNICH**. There's a **youth hostel** here (May–Oct; ☎04565/244; Grade 2) that makes a good base for seeing **Glen Affric**, claimed by many to be Scotland's loveliest glen – real calendar stuff, with a rushing river and pine and birch woods opening out onto an island-studded loch, which was considerably enlarged after the building of the dam, one of many hydroelectric schemes around here. The glen is great for picnics and pottering, particularly on a calm and sunny day, when the loch is still, reflecting the myriad islands and surrounding hills. The **hiking** possibilities are tremendous, with another **youth hostel** (June–Oct; no phone; ungraded) only accessible by foot, about nine miles along the track which takes you through Kintail to Shiel Bridge on the west coast (see p.366).

### Invermoriston and Glen Moriston

**INVERMORISTON** is a tiny, attractive village on the shore of Loch Ness, from where you can follow well-marked woodland **trails** past a series of grand waterfalls. Dr Johnson and Boswell spent a couple of nights here planning their journey to the Hebrides; nowadays you could stay at the *Glenmoriston Arms Hotel* (☎0320/51206; ⑤), an old-fashioned inn with more than one hundred malt whiskies on offer at the bar.

If you're driving on from Invermoriston to the west coast, roads are good; this is a main commercial (and tourist) route, as there is no access to this stretch of coast from the south. It's a bleak, somewhat awesome stretch through **Glen Moriston** and beside Loch Cluanie, with serious peaks on either side and little sign of human habitation as the road climbs.

## Fort Augustus and the south side

The south of Loch Ness is far more attractive than its opposite end, the road skirting the water's edge and giving plenty of chances to pull off for a little monster-spotting. **FORT AUGUSTUS**, at the loch's southwestern tip, was named after George II's son, later to become the Duke of Cumberland of Culloden fame, and was built as a barracks after the 1715 Jacobite rebellion. Today, it's a tiny village, dominated by the **Benedictine Abbey** founded on the ruins of the original fort in 1876. The abbey has housed a Catholic boys school for many years: its spacious and peaceful church is always open. You can also view the comings and goings on the **Caledonian Canal** from here, as it leaves Loch Ness.

If you want to **stay**, the *Old Pier* (☎0320/6418; ②) is a great B&B right on the loch; there are log fires in the evenings – often very welcome even in summer – and home-cooked dinners. The small, friendly *Caledonian Hotel* (☎0320/6256; ④) is centrally situated and overlooks the abbey, while the good-value *Brae Hotel* (☎0320/6289; ③) lies in wooded surroundings. The *Whitebridge Hotel* in **STRATHERRICK** behind the hills (☎04563/226; ②) is right off the beaten track, and great value.

Other than bar food at the hotels, there isn't a vast choice of **eating** possibilities in Fort Augustus, but *The Moorings Restaurant*, right by the canal, serves adequate and inexpensive food, as does the *Coffee Shop*, opposite the garage, which churns out homebaking and good soup all day.

## Loch Lochy

The fast A82 runs down the south side of **Loch Lochy** towards Spean Bridge and Fort William, giving fine views across the loch to the steep slopes of **Ben Tee** on its northern side. At Spean Bridge the minor B8004 branches down to **GAIRLOCHY**, lying at its west end, where you once more encounter the **Caledonian Canal** – you can walk easily anywhere along this stretch of the canal, although the easiest access point is where the B8004 crosses it. The countryside along this last section of the Great Glen is gentle, and a little unexciting, with the valley opening out as you approach the sea. The canal debouches into the sea via a series of eleven locks, known as **Neptune's Staircase**, which cover a drop of 80ft and presented Telford with quite an engineering challenge. At this point you are only a couple of miles from Fort William itself.

It's worth a detour round the north side of Loch Lochy to lonely **Loch Arkaig**, a twenty-minute drive that takes you through a pass, ablaze with rhododendrons in early summer, into country that feels a hundred miles from anywhere.

# Fort William and around

The area around **Glen Coe** and **Fort William** gives a taste of the blend of rugged mountain and tranquil sealoch so typical of the Northern Highlands. The gentler, more rounded mountains of the southwest start to give way to altogether more dramatic scenes: with **Ben Nevis**, at 4406ft Britain's highest peak, looming broodily over **Loch Linnhe,** a long sealoch at the southern end of the Great Glen and the Caledonian Canal, with the peaks of the Ardnamurchan peninsula rising from its western shore. This part of the Highlands is steeped in history: Fort William was founded in 1655 and named in honour of William III, and was successfully held by government troops during both the Jacobite risings, while the country to the southwest is inextricably associated with Bonnie Prince Charlie's fleeings after Culloden. Glen Coe is known worldwide for the infamous massacre of 1692 as much as for its magnificent scenery.

Nowadays the whole area is unashamedly given over to tourism, and Fort William itself often swamped by the sheer weight of bus tours, but, as always in the Highlands, within a thirty-minute drive you can be totally alone.

# Fort William

With its stunning position along Loch Linnhe and Ben Nevis rising behind, **FORT WILLIAM** should be a gem. Sadly, ribbon bungalow development and an ill-advised dual carriageway have wrecked the shore, out-of-place modern buildings mar the outskirts, and the High Street is largely given over to tourist-targeted stores selling tacky tartan souvenirs and mass-produced knitwear.

Fort William's downturn started in the nineteenth century, when the original fort, which gave the town its name, was demolished to make way for the train line. Today there's very little to detain you in the town centre, although it's worth taking at least a short look at the **West Highland Museum**, on Cameron Square, just off the High Street (Mon–Sat 9am–5pm; July & Aug also Sun 2pm–5pm). This splendid, old-fashioned and idiosyncratic collection, housed in a crumbling building, covers virtually every aspect of Highland life and makes a refreshing change from the endless audiovisuals of state-of-the-art museums. There's a good section on Highland clans and tartans, and among an interesting selection of Jacobite relics a secret portrait of Bonnie Prince Charlie, seemingly nothing more than a blur of paint, which resolves itself into a portrait when viewed against a brass cylinder.

## Glen Nevis and Ben Nevis: walks and climbs

A ten-minute drive out of town, **Glen Nevis** is a classic Highland glen complete with sparkling river, low-ground grazing with Highland cattle, mixed woodland

---

### THE TARTAN MYTH

Contrary to some expectations, Highlanders are not permanently swathed in **tartan**. Along with such cries as "Och aye the noo" and "Hoots mon and awa" the tartan image is a relic of the nineteenth-century Romanticism, for which Sir Walter Scott has much to answer (see p.115).

Before 1745 Highlanders certainly wore tartan, usually a huge single piece of cloth, which was belted around the waist and draped over the upper body, rather like a knee-length toga. But no clan claimed any specific pattern as its own. Instead, clansmen were recognized by the clan emblem, usually a plant, they wore in their hats. A famous contemporary painting of the Battle of Culloden shows eight warriors sporting over twenty tartans between them, none of which is recognizable today.

After George IV's visit to Edinburgh in 1822 tartan caught on in a big way, helped, later in the century, by Queen Victoria's passion for anything Scottish. Specific "setts" were allocated to specific clans, new patterns were dreamt up and complicated rules laid down for who was entitled to wear what and when.

Today, hardly anyone wears the kilt as everyday dress – very few Highlanders even own a kilt, they're so expensive. Indeed, it's a fact that many of the proudest tartan-wearing Scots haven't set foot in Scotland, let alone the Highlands, for years.

and surrounded by high hills and the bulk of Ben Nevis itself. Quite apart from its natural beauty, it's also the starting point for the **ascent** of Scotland's highest peak and you can **rent** both **mountain equipment** and **mountain bikes** on the spot.

The tourist office in Fort William has excellent maps of the ascent of **Ben Nevis**, which begins at the *Achintee* farmhouse, from where an easy path zigzags up the right of the **Red Burn**. The **summit** is a flat plateau with the ruins of the Observatory which used to stand there. The round trip can take anything from four to six hours, and, despite the numbers tackling it, you should remember to be properly equipped and leave word of when you left.

If you don't fancy a hike up the mountain, a great low-level walk runs from the end of the road at the top of the glen. The good but very rocky path leads through a dramatic gorge with impressive falls and rapids, then opens out into a secret hanging valley, carpeted with wild flowers, with a high waterfall at the far end. It's a pretty place for a picnic and if you're really energetic you can walk on over **Rannoch Moor** to **Corrour Station**, where you can pick up one of the four daily trains to take you back to Fort William. If you're keen to do some serious planned walking, contact Donald Watt (☎0397/704340), the leader of the Lochaber Mountain Rescue Team, who organizes half- and whole-day walks.

# Around Fort William

Seven miles northeast of Fort William on the A82, the Nevis Range boasts Scotland's only **cable car** system, in the **Aonach Mhor** ski area – a popular attraction during the summer off-season. The ride gives an easy approach to some high-level walking, but for most tourists it simply provides an effortless means to rise 2000ft and enjoy the spectacular views from the terrace of the self-service **restaurant** at the top.

From nearby **ROY BRIDGE**, a narrow road leads off the A86 up **Glen Roy**, where a viewpoint a couple of miles up gives a clear sight of the **Parallel Roads**: not roads at all, but the startlingly defined marks left on the hillsides as a glacial lake gradually shrank.

### Glen Coe

Stern and breathtakingly beautiful, **Glen Coe**, sixteen miles south of Fort William on the A82, is one of the best known of the Highland glens and has been the property of the NTS since the 1930s. In 1692 the glen was the site of a famous massacre, after Alastair MacDonald, chief of an unruly and cattle-stealing clan, missed the deadline for taking an obligatory oath of allegiance to William III. This gave the authorities the excuse they needed "to root out that damnable sept (clan)", and government troops were billetted on the MacDonalds. Entertained by the clan with traditional hospitality – a matter of honour in the Highlands – after ten days, on a bitter winter's night, they turned on their hosts, slaying about thirty-eight and causing more than three hundred to flee in a blizzard.

Today, the glen is virtually uninhabited, and provides outstanding **climbing** and **walking**. Many famous mountaineers have gained experience on the demanding **Buachaille Etive Mhor** and its neighbouring peaks. The NTS runs a **visitor centre** (April–Oct 10am–5.30pm) that provides information on outdoor pursuits.

## Fort William area practicalities

**Fort William** is easily reached by **bus** and **train** from Inverness. The **stations** are next door to each other at the east end of the High Street. If you're **driving**, parking can be a nightmare: try the big car park down beside the loch, at the west end of town. The **tourist office**, just off the High Street in Cameron Square (Mon–Fri 9am–5pm, Sat 9am–4pm; ☎0397/703781), will book accommodation for you, and also give out a good, free town map.

There's plenty of **accommodation** in the Fort William area. Of the **B&Bs**, *Finisgaig*, Alma Rd (☎0397/702453; ②), a traditional stone-built house up the hill behind the town centre, offers very good value; *Torgulbin*, on Cameron Road behind the High Street (☎0397/702220; ②), is more modern but has a quiet location. Another good bet is *The Grange*, on Grange Road (☎0397/705516; ③), which has three doubles with private bathrooms in an old house with a nice garden. The *Cruachan Hotel*, on Achintore Road (☎0397/702022; ③), is an attractive hotel overlooking the loch, five minutes' walk from the centre; or you could try the comfortable *Alexandra Hotel*, The Parade (☎0397/702241; ③), one of the oldest hotels in town. If you want to stay right in the centre of Fort William, the *Grand Hotel*, on the High Street (☎0397/702928; ⑤) is perfectly comfortable, if a little dreary.

The *Glen Nevis* **youth hostel** (May–Oct; ☎0397/702336; Grade 1) is an easy walk from town, set in stunning surroundings close to Ben Nevis. There are also two independent youth hostels: the *Achintee Farm Hostel,* near the official hostel (☎0397/702240), is well equipped, with laundry facilities and a TV, and sleeps 24. In **CORPACH**, a Fort William suburb on the road to Mallaig, you'll find *The Old Smiddy*, Station Rd (☎0397/772467), a very comfortable bunkhouse that sleeps twelve people. If you're **camping**, head for the spacious *Glen Nevis Caravan and Camping Park* (☎0397/702191), pleasantly situated two miles up Glen Nevis with hot showers, a shop and restaurant.

Most **eating** places in Fort William are pretty basic. The *Good Food Stop* at the *Alexandra Hotel* does inexpensive grills, fish and pasta and is open all day. *McTavish's Kitchen* in the High Street is cheap and cheerful, full of tourists and with nightly **Scottish entertainment**. The pick of the bunch is the *Crannog Seafood Restaurant* on the pier, where oysters, langoustines, prawns and salmon are cooked with flair in an elegantly converted fish store; the wine list is also excellent, although the prices make it best kept for a treat.

# The west coast: Morven to Kyle of Lochalsh

The remote southwest corner of the Highlands, stretching from the **Ardnamurchan peninsula** up to **Mallaig**, is a dramatic, lonely region, an unfriendly mix of bog, mountain and moor dotted with lochs and fringed by white sand beaches giving splendid views over to Skye and the Hebrides. Its Gaelic name translates as the "Rough Bounds", implying a region geographically and spiritually outside the prevailing currents of thought and behaviour, and, mainly due to its geography, it has always been sparsely populated, with just a few scattered crofting townships clinging to the coast and the shores of the freshwater lochs. Even if you haven't got a car, you should spend a few days here exploring by foot – there are so few roads that some determined hiking is almost inevitable. The stretch of coast **north of Mallaig** is just as attractive, passing the isolated

**Glenelg** peninsula as it heads towards **Kyle of Lochalsh**, the main departure point for Skye. However, there is no road from Mallaig to Glenelg, and most visitors approach from Invermoriston on Loch Ness (see p.358).

The best way into the southwest corner of this region, if you've got your own transport, is to cross **Loch Linnhe** on the ferry to **Corran**, a five-minute crossing with boats running continuously all day (cars £3.80, foot passengers 75p). You can then head west and north to Mallaig. If you're using public transport, there are occasional buses, usually school or post buses, which run at odd times of day. Fairly frequent **buses** and **trains** run from Fort William to Arisaig and along the stretch of coast up to Mallaig, and there's a regular bus service from Inverness to Kyle of Lochalsh via Invermoriston on Loch Ness.

## Morven

From the ferry landing point at **Corran**, the road follows the shore of Loch Linnhe for a few miles on the A861, giving uninterrupted views across its beaches to Glen Coe. The road rises through desolate **Glen Tarbert** and gradually drops down to the sea at **Loch Sunart**, where you can pick up the B884 which crosses this bleak and empty part of the Rough Bounds, known as **Morven**.

The road descends south through the wooded valley of **Glen Geal** to **LOCHALINE**, a remote community on the **Sound of Mull**, with the ruins of **Ardtornish Castle** a thirty-minute walk down the coast to the south. The village has a salty air, with a pier, ship's chandler and diving school, and is much used as an anchorage by yachtsmen cruising the west coast. Its tiny *Lochaline Hotel* (☎0967/421657; ③) serves good bar food, including venison.

## Sunart and Ardgour

The regions of **Sunart** and **Ardgour** make up the country between **Loch Shiel**, **Loch Sunart** and **Loch Linnhe**: the heart of Jacobite support in the mid-eighteenth century. There are no roads in the interior so this is real hiking country; you'll need an OS map and compass to plan your route.

One of two villages in the region, **STRONTIAN** is a pretty place grouped round a green on an inlet of the **Loch Sunart**. There are numerous birds and woodland wildlife to watch for and a huge variety of wild flowers, at their best in late May, June and July. The seasonal **tourist office** (daily 9am–5pm; ☎0967/2131) will book accommodation, but if you want to try for yourself, *Carm Cottage* (☎0967/2112 or 2268; ②) offers B&B in a modern house in the village. The *Strontian Hotel* (☎0967/2029; ④) is pretty and comfortable, while the more upmarket *Loch Sunart Hotel* (☎0967/2471; ⑤) occupies a splendid site right by the water. You can get **meals** in the hotels and good home-baking at the *Spinning Farm Park*, where they sell their own knitwear. **SALEN**, eight miles further down Loch Sunart, is a prosperous, slightly twee yachting port-of-call.

## The Ardnamurchan peninsula

The tortuous road from Salen leads into the **Ardnamurchan peninsula**, one of the most remote places on the British mainland, comprising a varied landscape of woods, water, rocky hills and grassy slopes, bog and heather, hidden coves and open moorland.

Five miles or so from Salen, the tiny settlement of **GLENBORRODALE** houses the enormously expensive *Glenborrodale Castle Hotel* (☎09724/266; ⑨), complete with helicopter pad and solarium. More accessible is the **Glenmore Natural History Centre** (April–Oct 10am–5pm; £2.50), a good introduction to the wildlife of Ardnamurchan, whose chief attraction is its stunning audiovisual display – Michael McGregor, who runs the centre, is a brilliant photographer, whose work features on many postcards. Tasty home-made snacks are served in the **tearoom**.

The district's main village, however, is **KILCHOAN**, nine miles further on, a straggling crofting township with a marvellous sense of isolation. A **ferry** runs six times a day in summer from here to Tobermory on Mull, and there's a summer-only **tourist office** (☎09723/222) which will help with accommodation and information. You can stay at either the *Meall mo Chridhe Hotel* (☎09723/238; ④) or the nearby *Sonachan Hotel* (☎09723/211; ④). For **B&B**, *Mrs MacPhail* (☎09723/322; ③) and *Mrs Scott* (☎09723/250; ③) are both good, and their rates include dinner.

Beyond Kilchoan the road continues to wild and windy **Ardnamurchan Point**, with its unmanned **lighthouse** and spectacular views west to Coll and Tiree and across to the north of Mull. For truly unforgettable vistas, head towards the shell-strewn sandy beach of **Sanna Bay**, about three miles north of the point. From here you can see the Small Isles looming to the north, circled by gulls, terns and guillemots – particularly stunning in early summer, when the machair is carpeted with thrift and clumps of wild iris.

# Moidart

North of the peninsula, Moidart's main town is **ACHARACLE**, an ancient crofting settlement lying at the sea end of **Loch Shiel**. It's an attractive place, surrounded by gentle hills, and the scattered houses form a real community, with several shops, a post office, and plenty of **places to stay**. In the centre of the village you could try the *Ardshealach Lodge* (☎096785/301; ③), which has good-value doubles, or the *Loch Shiel Hotel* (096785/317; ③) where you can get reasonable bar food. *Belmont* (☎096785/266; ②) is a comfortable B&B. Acharacle's village hall is often used for ceilidhs: look out for the notices in the shops.

A mile north of Acharacle, a side road branches off the A861, winding for three miles or so past a secluded loch and through rhododendron thickets to **Loch Moidart**, a calm and sheltered sealoch. At the road end is **Castle Tioram**, reached over a sandy causeway. The thirteenth-century castle was the seat of the MacDonalds of Clanranald, and destroyed by their chief in 1715 to prevent it from falling into Hanoverian hands while he was away fighting for the Jacobites. Today, the surviving walls and tower enclose an inner courtyard and a few chambers.

Back on the A861, the fast new road, funded by the EC, whips you north and along the shores of **Loch Ailort**, a startling turquoise sealoch surrounded by barren and inhospitable hills. The *Glenuig Inn* at the sea end of the loch (☎06877/219; ③) is remote but welcoming, and serves wonderfully fresh fish.

# Morar

Beyond Loch Ailort, in the region of **Morar**, you're back in civilization; getting around is easier, and there are train and bus links to Fort William.

**ARISAIG**, scattered round a rock-strewn sandy bay, is the best base for exploring this bit of the coast. There's nothing in the way of specific "attractions" but if the weather's good you can spend hours wandering about the beaches and ambling along the quiet roads, or make the quick hop over to the Small Isles (see *Skye and the Western Isles*); contact Murdo Grant (☎06875/224).

Accommodation is plentiful. *Kinloid Farm House* (☎06875/669; ②) is one of several B&Bs, while in the more upmarket range, the *Arisaig Hotel* (☎06875/210; ⑤) is an old-established inn with good food. Just outside Arisaig at **BEASDALE**, the *Arisaig House Hotel* (☎06875/626; ⑨) is one of Scotland's best-known country-house hotels with superb food.

The eight miles of coast north of Arisaig is a stunning stretch of white-sand beaches backed by flowery machair, with barren granite hills rising straight up behind. However, the views are somewhat blighted by the string of abandoned old cars, decrepit caravans and piles of rusting metal and general rubbish that characterize this stretch of the coast. The next village of any significance is **MORAR**, where scenes from the film *Local Hero* were shot. **Loch Morar** – rumoured to be the home of Morag, a lesser-known rival to Nessie – runs off to the east, linked to the sea by what must be one of the shortest rivers in Scotland. There's excellent-value **B&B** at *Glenancross* (☎0687/294; ②) and *Cooaindaauch* (☎0687/2406; ②). The *Morar Hotel* (☎0687/2346; ⑤) offers a little more luxury and serves **food**.

# Mallaig

A busy, noisy fishing port whose houses struggle for space with the great lumps of granite which run right down to the sea, **MALLAIG** is not a pretty town. But as a jumping-off point to Skye and the Western Isles (see p.273), it is always crowded with visitors – looked upon with some ambivalence by locals.

It's a compact place, very much concentrated around the harbour, where you'll find the **tourist office** (Mon–Sat 9am–5.30pm; ☎0687/2170) – who will book accommodation for you on the Small Isles – and the **bus** and **train stations**. Unsurprisingly, there are plenty of **places to stay**. For an excellent B&B with real Highland hospitality, try *St Margaret's* on the Glasnacarcoch road (☎0687/2106; ②), or, right on the harbour, *Haco Cottage* on East Bay (☎0687/2434; ②). Also on the harbour you'll find a good **independent youth hostel** called *Sheena's Bunkhouse* (☎0687/2764), and the wonderfully dated *Marine Hotel* (☎0687/2217; ④). Up the hill overlooking the sea, the *West Highland Hotel* (☎0687/2210; ⑤) is another good, delightfully old-fashioned option, with splendid views. The obvious thing to **eat** in Mallaig is fish, available at all the **hotels**, straight off the boats. For a real taste of Highland pub life try the *Marine Bar* or the *Central Bar*, both on the harbour, when the boats are in.

If you're hanging around in the rain waiting for a ferry or train, you could fill in forty minutes or so at **Mallaig Marine World**, north of the train station near the harbour (daily 9am–7pm; £2.50), where tanks of sea creatures share space with informative exhibits about the port.

### Knoydart peninsula

Mallaig is the only feasible departure point for the unrivalled wilderness of the **Knoydart peninsula**, the northernmost of the Rough Bounds, which has no roads, but wonderful climbing and hiking. Ask at the harbour for Bruce Watt, whose boat, the *Western Isles*, makes two runs across daily and gives you a couple of hours ashore. About 45 people live on the peninsula; if you want to stay, rates at the *Marriotts'* guest house (☎0687/2347; ②) include dinner, often a fabulously fresh fish meal. They also have a tearoom for day visitors, and you can **camp** on the flat ground behind their house.

## The Glenelg peninsula

The **Glenelg peninsula**, jutting out into the Sound of Sleat north of Mallaig, is an isolated and little-known crofting area, only really accessible on the fast A87 from the east. A row of little whitewashed houses, surrounded by mature trees comprise **GLENELG** village, about four miles up the coast, where during the summer, there's a **ferry** across to Skye (May–Sept Mon–Sat 9am–5pm, further details on ☎0599/81302). The *Glenelg Inn* (☎0599/82273; ④) is a good place to stay, and you can sample fresh seafood in the bar. The road continues further down the coast to **ARNISDALE** on Loch Hourn, passing the tiny hamlet of **SANDAIG**, where Gavin Maxwell lived with his otters in the Fifties and wrote *Ring of Bright Water*.

The ruins on the right as you enter the village are the remains of **Bernera Barracks**, built as a garrison for government troops to subdue the Highlands in the eighteenth century, and a virtual twin to those at Kingussie (see p.356). Nearby, **Glenelg war memorial** is hard to miss: a huge bronze group with angels, laurel wreaths and weeping women along with a kilted Highland soldier.

## Loch Duich

On the northern end of the peninsula, skirted on its northern shore by the A87, **Loch Duich** is high on the tourist trail, with buses from all over Europe thundering down the sixteen miles from **SHIEL BRIDGE** to Kyle of Lochalsh on their way to Skye. The most dramatic approach to the loch is from the east, through Glen Shiel, where the dramatic mountains known as the **Five Sisters of Kintail** surge up to heights of 3000ft – a familiar sight from endless tourist brochures, but a dramatic one nonetheless. With the hills enfolding both sides of the loch, it's sometimes hard to remember that this is, in fact, the sea. There's a **youth hostel** just outside Shiel Bridge at **RATAGAN** (March–Oct; ☎0599/81243; Grade 2).

Ten miles northwest of Shiel Bridge stands **Eilean Donan Castle** (Easter–Oct daily 9am–5pm), an over-photographed structure that was originally built in the thirteenth century but destroyed in 1719 during one of the minor Jacobite risings. What you see today mainly dates from the 1930s, and houses a variety of Jacobite and clan relics whose charm is rather hard to detect between the attentions of the crowds who descend on the place throughout the summer. Less than a mile away, in the minuscule hamlet of **DORNIE**, there's **food** at the *Clachan Inn* on Francis Street, and, if you want to stay the night, the *Castle Inn*, also on Francis Street (☎059985/205; ④) is a comfortable option. For a little more luxury, head north out of the village to the *Loch Duich Hotel* (☎059985/213; ⑤), which has splendid doubles overlooking the loch. Both places serve **food.**

## Kyle of Lochalsh

Seven miles west of Eilean Donan Castle, **KYLE OF LOCHALSH** is a busy town, both the main departure point for Skye and a rail terminal. Straggling down the hill towards the pier and train station, it's not particularly attractive – concrete buildings, rail junk and myriad signs of the fishing industry abound – and is ideally somewhere to pass through rather than linger. However, until the new **Skye Bridge** opens in 1995, this may be the last thing you're able to do. Ferries run non-stop day and night across to Kyleakin on Skye (see p.277), but the lines of traffic, especially in July and August can be horrific, with vehicles trailing back down the coast and waits of up to four hours. Aim to cross very early or very late, and avoid weekends. The bridge is being built a little north of Kyle; approach roads are being built that will bypass the village.

### Practicalities

**Buses** stop at the pier. Two per day run to Glasgow via Fort William; and two run Monday to Saturday to Inverness via Invermoriston, with one on Sundays. These routes can become very crowded, so it's a good idea to book through *Skye-Ways Express Coach Services*, Ferry Pier (☎0599/4328). **Ferries** run non-stop every ten minutes or so from 7.30am to 9.30pm and every thirty minutes through the night, except from 2–3am.The train station is about five minutes south of the pier and there are three **trains** every day to Inverness. The Inverness–Kyle **train line** is a train enthusiast's dream, curving up north through Achnasheen and Glen Carron.

The **tourist office** (daily 9am–5pm; ☎0599/4276) is about five minutes' walk up the hill from the train station towards the pier, in the monster car park on the headland. They can help with **accommodation** and have plenty of maps, leaflets and information on the area – if you're heading for Skye, it makes sense to get them to book you a room ahead on the island.

If you're catching an early ferry, it might be a good idea to **stay** in Kyle of Lochalsh. The *Kyle Hotel*, on Main Street (☎0599/4204; ⑤), is a traditional middle-ground hotel, but if you're feeling flush splash out at the *Lochalsh Hotel* (☎0599/4202; ⑧), a wonderfully situated place looking out at Skye, with fabulous seafood and an air of dated luxury. The *Wholefood Restaurant* on the Plockton road has good, moderately priced, fresh seafood and vegetarian meals.

# Plockton

Just north of Kyle, at the sea end of **Loch Carron**, lies **PLOCKTON**, a self-consciously pretty village full of yachtsmen, prosperous second-home owners and tasteful craft shops. The uniqueness of the light here has made it something of an artists community, and it's also firmly on the tourist trail; you can **sail**, **windsurf** and take **seal-spotting** cruises from here.

If you want **to stay**, the *Haven Hotel* near the seafront (☎059984/223; ④) is friendly, and renowned for its food, while the *Creag-nan-Daroch Hotel* on Innes Street (☎059984/222; ④) makes a comfortable alternative. The *Plockton Hotel*, Harbour St (☎059984/274; ⑥), is right in the centre and serves good seafood. Down the road back to Kyle the *Tingle Creek Hotel* (☎0599/4430; ⑤) specializes in huge plates of solid home-cooking. Of the fifteen or so B&Bs, *The Shieling* (☎059984/282; ③) and *Mrs Rowe*, 25 Harbour St (☎059984/356; ③), are both good bets.

For **food**, *The Old Schoolhouse* serves reasonably priced steaks and seafood and vegetarian options, and the *Buttery*, part of the grocer's on the corner of the main street by the sea, is open all day for snacks and inexpensive meals. All the hotels are happy to feed non-residents.

# THE NORTHERN HIGHLANDS

The huge, sparsely populated **Northern Highlands** cover the whole of Scotland north of a line running northeast from Kyle of Lochalsh to Inverness. It's a diverse region, with a geographically clear east–west division: the mountains, moor and water of the west offer a chance to pursue outdoor activities away from the crowds, contrasting with the compact villages of the gentler, more fertile land to the east. The rocky, boggy interior, virtually uninhabited and traversed by few roads, has its own desolate beauty.

The arrival of the Vikings in the ninth century was of great importance. They called this area the "South Land" – from which the modern district of Sutherland takes its name – and established a firm clan system, with clansmen holding land owned by their chiefs in return for rent or service. After Culloden, the Clearances emptied most of the inland glens of the far north, however, and left the population clinging to the coastline, where a herring-fishing industry developed.

The **Wester Ross** district, flanking the west coast up as far as the fishing port of Lochinver, is the most visited part of the region. Beyond here, in the more remote region of **Sutherland**, you'll see fewer visitors and get a truer sense of isolation. The flatter, more fertile east – **Easter Ross** – doesn't have to rely to such an extent on tourism; indeed the Black Isle, in particular, just north of Inverness, is one of Scotland's richest farming regions. North of here, in the northeast corner, away from the inevitably busy but rather tawdry focus of John o' Groats, **Caithness** is a deserted and unexplored region, encompassing one of the world's acknowledged great wilderness areas.

### Getting around the Northern Highlands

The eastern half of the Northern Highlands is far better served by **public transport** than the west, with good **train** and **bus** services right up to Wick and Thurso. Buses run along the north coast from Thurso to Durness in Sutherland. To get west, you can go by bus from Inverness to Ullapool, Gairloch and Lochinver, though you may have to backtrack to Lairg to get up and down the coast. The whole area is crisscrossed by **post buses**, which sometimes run at odd times, but do allow you to reach otherwise inaccessible corners. **Driving** around here is unproblematic: the roads aren't busy, though frequently single track, calling for thoughtful driving. Remember to refuel whenever you can, as pumps are few and far between.

# Wester Ross

For many people, **Wester Ross**, which covers the area down the west coast from Loch Inver in the north to Loch Carron in the south, and stretches inland as far as the Fannich mountains, epitomizes the Highlands. It's got mountains, lochs, beaches and islands, with some attractive little towns and townships thrown in. It's easy to reach and has plenty of accommodation to offer; but even in the height of summer you can escape all signs of life very quickly. The weather ranges from stupendous to diabolical: you can't count on a sunny morning meaning a fine day. Beware too, as always in this part of Scotland, of the dreaded midge.

# The Applecross peninsula

The most dramatic approach to the Applecross peninsula (the English-sounding name is actually a corruption of the Gaelic *Apor Crosan*, meaning "estuary") is from the south, along the **Bealach na Ba Pass**. Crossing the forbidding hills behind **KISHORN** and rising to 2000ft, with a gradient and hair-pin bends worthy of the Alps, this route is not for the timid. The other way in is from the north, a beautiful and slow coastal road from **Shieldaig** on **Loch Torridon**, with great views across to Skye.

The sheltered, fertile bay of **APPLECROSS** village comes as a surprise after the bleakness of the moorland approach. It's a beautiful place; you can wander along roadsides banked with wild iris and orchids and explore beaches and rockpools. The *Flowertunnel Restaurant* serves inexpensive food and freshly baked bread. There's camping at the restaurant, or you can stay at the cosy *Applecross Inn* (☎05204/262; ③), right beside the sea. From Applecross, the road continues down the coast to other little crofting settlements, finishing at **TOSCAIG**, with its pier and harbour full of inquisitive seals.

# Loch Torridon to Loch Maree

**Loch Torridon** marks the northern boundary of the Applecross peninsula, its awe-inspiring setting backed by the great, menacing mountain masses of **Liathach** and **Beinn Eighe**. Geologically, the greater part of this area is composed of the reddish Torridonian sandstone, whose beds can be seen on the precipices of Liathach; there are also numerous deeply eroded and ice-smoothed corries. Much of Beinn Eighe is forested with Caledonian pinewood, which once covered the whole of the country, and houses pinemarten, wildcat, fox and badger – you may even see buzzards and golden eagles. There's also a wide range of flora, with the higher rocky slopes producing spectacular natural alpine rock gardens.

If you want to spend a couple of days around here, there's a **youth hostel** in the village of **TORRIDON** (March–Oct; ☎0445/791284; Grade 1), and, four miles west, **SHIELDAIG**, an attractive little lochside village off the main road, has the

---

**WALKING AROUND TORRIDON**

There are difficult and unexpected conditions on virtually all hiking routes in the Torridon area, and the weather can change very rapidly. If you're planning to do the magnificent ridgewalk along the seven peaks of **Liathach**, or want to tackle the strenuous traverse of **Beinn Eighe**, it makes most sense to join a hike organized by the **NTS**: for details contact Seamus MacNally on ☎0445/791221.

If you do want to go it alone, one possible route takes you behind Liathach and down Coire Dubh to the main road in Glen Torridon. This is a great, straightforward walk if you're properly equipped, covering thirteen miles and taking in superb landscapes. Allow yourself the whole day. Start at the stone bridge on the Diabaig road along the north side of Loch Torridon. Follow the Abhainn Coire Mhic Nobuil burn up to the fork at the wooden bridge and from here head east to the pass between Liathach and Beinn Eighe. The path becomes a bit indistinct in the boggy area studded with lochans at the top of the pass, but the direction to go is clear and once over the watershed the route is easy to follow. Down the Coire Dubh burn the track improves; you ford the burn and follow its west bank down to the Torridon road, from where it's about four miles back to Loch Torridon.

---

**THE RED DEER**

The red deer, which lives on the open mountains and moorlands of Scotland, is Britain's largest wild animal, standing 4ft high at the shoulder. Red deer meat, or venison, is becoming increasingly popular, the demand for which is being partly met by farmed deer.

The wild female deer, or hind, bears one calf in early summer, which remains with its mother for at least two winters before joining a group, or herd, of its own sex. The sexes live separately except during the rutting season which runs from mid-September to late October, when the male deer, or stags, will attempt to gather groups of hinds by aggressive roaring and fighting, using their body weight and antlers. These antlers are an annual growth, and their size, and the number of points, vary from year to year. A stag with twelve points is known as a "Royal" and will reach his prime at about six or seven years old.

Red deer are agile and graceful, with phenomenally keen smell and hearing. They were once hunted by bears and wolves, but today have no natural predators. This, coupled with a recent succession of mild winters, has led to a rapid increase in numbers, and deer-stalking (always a popular activity, especially in Victorian times when bridges, roads and lodges were built to facilitate the sport) has become big business in the region. Whatever your views on blood sports, it's certainly arguable that the existence of a healthy and stable deer population is of great ecological importance to the Highland region; and the economic benefits can hardly be overstated.

---

traditional *Tigh-an-Eilean Hotel* (☎05205/251; ⑤) with great views. *Alligin*, on the north of Loch Torridon (☎0445/791256; ②), offers B&B; nearby *Inveralligin* (☎0445/791280) charges the same.

About eight miles north of Loch Torridon, **Loch Maree**, dotted with Caledonian pine-covered islands, is lovely. This is some of Scotland's great deer-stalking country: the remote, privately owned *Letterewe Lodge* on the north shore, accessible only by boat, lies at the heart of a famous deer forest. In the nineteenth century Loch Maree had a regular boat service: there were no roads west, so train passengers alighted at Achnasheen, just to the east, and sailed down the loch to reach Poolewe and Gairloch. Queen Victoria stayed a few days here at the *Loch Maree Hotel* (☎044584/288; ⑤), which still has an indubitably respectable air.

# Gairloch

Three buses weekly run the two-and-a-half-hour trip from Inverness to the west coast crofting town of **GAIRLOCH**, perched on the northeastern shore of the loch of the same name. If you can tear yourself away from the countryside, take time to visit the **Gairloch Heritage Museum** here (Easter–Sept daily 10am–5pm; free), whose eclectic, appealingly ragbag displays cover geology, archeology, fishing and farming, and range from a mock-up of a croft-house to an amazing early knitting machine. Probably the most interesting section, however, is the archive, a unique range of photographs, maps, genealogies, lists of place-names and thousands of hours of taped recollection, mostly in Gaelic, made by elderly locals.

The coast here, lined with tempting sandy beaches, is stunning. *Gairloch Cruises* (☎0445/2175) run bird-watching and sightseeing cruises from the harbour on the south side of town, while nearby, the *Gairloch Watersports Centre* (☎0445/2131) holds classes in windsurfing and water-skiing, and also rents equipment. **BADACHRO**, on the south side of the loch, is the base for *West Highland*

*Marine* (☎044583/291), who offer sailing, canoeing and sea-angling. They can take you diving too, and run a useful sea taxi service back across to Gairloch.

## Practicalities

If you don't have your own transport you'll have to depend upon **post buses** – which run right round both sides of the loch – since everything's scattered over quite an area. There's a good range of **accommodation** in Gairloch, and the centrally situated **tourist office** (☎0445/2130) will help with bookings. The *Millcroft Hotel* (☎0445/2375; ④), right in the village, offers lovely views and very good seafood; decent meals are also served at the friendly *Old Inn* (☎0445/2006; ⑤) near the harbour and set back from the main road. In **Badachro**, the traditional *Badachro Inn* (☎044583/255; ④), by the harbour, has a salty charm, and of the many **B&Bs**, *Duisary*, along the bay on the main road (☎0445/2252; ②), gives excellent value for money.

**Eating** shouldn't be a problem: all the hotels do **bar food**. Pricier options include the *Steading Restaurant*, attached to the Gairloch museum, while the *Mountain Restaurant*, overlooking the sea along the bay beyond the museum, dishes out moderately priced steaks and grills.

# Poolewe

It's a fifteen-minute hop by bus over the headland from Gairloch to the trim little village of **POOLEWE**, on the marvellously sheltered **Loch Ewe** at the mouth of the River Ewe, as it rushes down from Loch Maree. A small side road runs along the south of the loch to **COVE**, where you'll find an atmospheric cave that was used by the "Wee Frees" as a church right into this century. It's quite a perilous scramble up, however, and there's little to actually see when you get there.

The *Pool House Hotel* (☎044586/272; ⑦), right by the sea, is a bit overpriced; better to try the old-fashioned *Poolewe Hotel* (☎044586/241; ⑤), on the road to Cove. For B&B in Poolewe, try *Tigh-na-Moine* (044586/242; ②), or the *Cove* (☎044586/377; ②), in a croft signposted from the main road. There's also an excellent NTS **campsite** between the village and Inverewe Gardens (April–Oct ☎044586/229).

## Inverewe Gardens

Half a mile across the bay from Poolewe, on the A832, **Inverewe Gardens** (daily 9am–sunset; NTS; £3) are the most visited place in Wester Ross, a unique pocket of lush glades and colourful flowers and shrubs in contrast with the barren wildness of the rest of the coast. Work began in 1865 to transform this rocky, boggy moor into the fabulous outland it is today; the **visitors centre** (April–May & Sept–Oct Mon–Sat 10am–5pm, Sun 2pm–5pm; June–Aug Mon–Sat 9.30am–6pm, Sun noon–6pm) has a display outlining the history of the development of the garden, as well as a smallish, reasonable restaurant.

Although as far north as Hudson's Bay in Canada, this part of the coast enjoys a mild climate, and frosts are so rare that exotic blooms from as far away as South America and New Zealand can flourish. Mid-May to mid-June is the best time to see the **rhododendrons** and **azaleas**, while the **herbaceous garden** reaches its peak in July and August, as does the wonderful Victorian vegetable and flower garden beside the sea.

Inverewe is very much a wild garden, with little twisting paths. It's also big; allow at least two hours to do it justice and be prepared to do a lot of walking – there are regular guided **garden walks** every weekday from April to October.

# Gruinard to Ullapool

Occasional buses run the twenty-mile stretch along the A832 from Poolewe past **Aultbea**, a small NATO naval base, to the head of **Little Loch Broom**, surrounded by a salt-marsh covered with carpets of flowers in early summer. The road more or less follows the coast, offering fabulous views and passing a string of tiny, anachronistic villages. During World War II, **Gruinard Island**, in the bay, was used as a testing ground for biological warfare, and for years was ringed by huge signs warning the public not to land. The anthrax spores released during the testing can live in the soil for up to a thousand years, but in 1987, after much protest, the Ministry of Defence had the island decontaminated and it was finally declared "safe" in 1990.

The road heads inland before joining the A835 at **Braemore Junction** above the head of **Loch Broom**: three buses a day stop here on their run between Inverness and Ullapool. The stretch from the head of the loch to Ullapool is one of the so-called **Destitution Roads**, built to give employment to local people during the potato famines of the nineteenth century.

There are a couple of **hotels** along here: the bleak, modern *Ocean View Hotel* at Laide (☎04455731/385; ③) looks pretty tacky, but the position is great, and it's good value. The *Dundonnell Hotel* (☎085483/366; ⑤) at the head of Little Loch Broom, is more upmarket; you can stop at either for a meal in the bar. The *Sailmhor Croft* (☎085483/224) on the loch is an independent youth hostel, with room for sixteen; they also do B&B (①).

# Ullapool

**ULLAPOOL** was founded by the British Fishery Society in 1788 on a sheltered arm of land jutting into Loch Broom. This grid-plan town is still an important fishing port, though its ferry link to Stornoway on Lewis (see pp.286–7) means that in high season the town's own personality is practically swamped by the vast numbers of visitors. This is the best place to stay in the region if you haven't got your own transport – buses run here from Inverness, and there's plenty of accommodation.

### Arrival, information and accommodation

Ullapool is planned on a grid system. The two main streets are **Shore Street**, along the sea, and **Argyle Street**, parallel to Shore Street further inland. **Buses** set you down at the pier, in the centre of town, from where it's easy to get your bearings. The well-run **tourist office** (Easter–Nov Mon–Sat 9am–5pm, Sun 1pm–6pm; ☎0854/612135), directly opposite the bus stop, offers all the usual information, as well as an accommodation-booking service. If you're heading on to the Outer Hebrides, there are three **ferries** daily from Monday to Saturday; the trip takes three and a half hours.

With so many tourists using it as a base, Ullapool has plenty of **accommodation** with numerous hotels, guest houses and B&Bs, plus a nicely situated campsite and a youth hostel.

**Altnaharrie Hotel** (☎085483/230). Famous and select hotel across the loch from town – you're collected by boat from town. Rates, though high, include a splendid gourmet dinner. ⑨.

**Arch Inn**, 11 W Shore St (☎085461/2454). One of Ullapool's oldest inns, built right on the harbour-side, and offering comfortable rooms. ④.

**Ardale**, Market St (☎085461/2220). Good-value central B&B in a modern family home. ②.

**Brae Guest House**, Shore St (☎085461/2421). Great guest house in an immaculately maintained traditional building right on the lochside. ③.

**The Ceilidh Place**, W Argyle St (☎085461/2886). Tastefully decorated, popular hotel at the far end of one of Ullapool's main streets. Laid-back atmosphere. ④.

**Dromnan Guest House**, Garve Rd (☎085461/2333). Small, comfortable guest house with great views of the surrounding mountains and loch. ③.

**Ferry Boat Inn**, Shore St (☎085461/2366). Traditional inn right on the waterfront with a friendly atmosphere and good food. ③.

**Riverside Hotel**, Quay St (☎085461/2239). Good-value family-run place with home-cooked food. ③.

## The Town

There's little to actually do in Ullapool, but the wide eighteenth-century streets, signed in English and Gaelic, make for a pleasant stroll, and if you're into gift shops and knitwear you won't be disappointed. What action there is you'll find by the **harbour**, which is genuine and salty, particularly when the boats are in. In winter the loch is crammed with Russian and Eastern European **factory fish processing boats**, whose crews, known as "Klondykers", stream through town staggering under the weight of hi-tech audio equipment, crates of fruit and boxes of coffee. Local people welcome these visitors, and you'll spot Russian notices announcing local events as well as the Cyrillic "Welcome to Ullapool" sign.

The **Ullapool Museum** (April–Oct Mon–Fri 10am–5pm; free), on W Argyle St, features exhibits on crofting, fishing, and local religion. There's also interesting stuff on emigration: during the Clearances, Ullapool was one of the ports through which evicted crofters left to start new lives in Canada, Australia and New Zealand.

### Eating and drinking

**Altnaharrie Hotel** (☎085483/230). Even if you can't afford to stay in this swanky hotel on the other side of the loch you should splash out on eating here – its international cuisine is outstanding. Very expensive.

**Arch Inn** 11 W Shore St (☎085461/2454). Reasonable bar food in a nice atmosphere.

**The Ceilidh Place**, W Argyle St (☎085461/2886). Imaginative bar food served to a background of classical music. There's also a moderately priced restaurant, serving traditional Scottish food.

**Ferry Boat Inn**, Shore St (☎085461/2366). Fish and seafood restaurant by the water's edge, serving good food at moderate prices.

**The Frigate**, Shore St. Inexpensive wholefood bakery on the seafront, specializing in vegetarian food and good lunches.

**Harbour Lights Hotel**, just south of town on the A835 (☎085461/2222). Family-oriented restaurant specializing in seafood, fish and steaks.

# Lochinver to Kylestrome

About fifteen miles north of Ullapool, the workaday village of **LOCHINVER** marks the start of two routes to **KYLESTROME**. The first, the appalling single-track B869 that veers its way over rock, bog, and past endless lochans, gives access to one of the most beautiful stretches of coast in Scotland, offering deserted beaches and wonderful coastal walks. **ACHMELVICH**, a tiny settlement about five miles north of Lochinver, is reached by a side road off the B869. It's a remote and peaceful place, with a pure white-sand beach on which you're allowed to camp, and a **youth hostel** (March–Oct; ☎05714/480; Grade 3) with room for forty people.

Another five miles or so up the coast you can walk out to **POINT OF STOER**: access is signposted just south of the tiny hamlet of **CLASHNESSIE**, which has fine views across its bay. The straightforward walk takes about thirty minutes; on the way you'll see lots of seabirds and the dramatic rock stack of the **Old Man of Stoer**. The village of **DRUMBEG**, a few miles further on, is surrounded by fish-filled lochs which make it a target for trout-fishing enthusiasts. It's so small you could easily miss it, but it does house the *Drumbeg Hotel* (☎05713/236; ⑥), which is popular with fishermen and tourists alike, and an excellent value B&B, *Culkein* (☎05713/257; ②), right out on the point.

The fast way north from Lochinver to Kylestrome is along the A837, which hugs the banks of **Loch Assynt**, passing the ruins of **Ardvreck Castle**, a MacLeod stronghold from 1597 that fell to the Seaforth MacKenzies after a siege in 1691. The grey stone remains are unsafe, but quite impressive to look at from a distance. To the south lies **Inverpolly Nature Reserve**, a wild protected area of moorland and lochs that rises to two of Scotland's most majestic peaks in **Suilven** (2399ft) and **Canisp** (2779ft), both more often than not swathed in mist. From the castle head north on the A894 to reach the sea end of **Loch Glencoul**, at the head of which is Britain's highest waterfall, the 650-foot **Eas-Coul-Aulin**. The easiest way to see it is to take a boat trip; the walk is a tough two hours even for experienced walkers. *Statesman Cruises* run three or four boats a day from the pier at Kylestrome; the trip takes about two hours and costs £7.50.

# Kylestrome to Durness

From Kylestrome the A838 follows the coast for about eight miles to the village of **SCOURIE**, on a sheltered bay with a sandy beach. You can **stay** at the comfortable *Scourie Lodge* (☎0971/502248; ②); the *Scourie Hotel* (☎0971/502396; ④), although pricier, is also good value. There's a **campsite**, too, with good facilities and overlooking the bay (☎0971/502060).

Scourie is the jump-off point to **Handa Island**, an RSPB seabird sanctuary; *Scourie Boats* (☎097150/2011) run trips out to the island from Monday to Saturday; they'll take you fishing as well. From Scourie the road sweeps inland through the starkest area of the Highlands; rocks piled on rocks, bog and water create an alien landscape, and the stony coastline looks increasingly inhospitable – there's no public transport at all on the twenty-mile stretch from here to Durness.

Eight miles or so north of Scourie, at **RHICONICH**, you can branch off the main road to **KINLOCHBERVIE**, an important fishing port crouching among the rocks in a dauntingly inhospitable landscape. Trucks from all over Europe come here to pick up fish and shellfish. If you want to **stay** here, the *Old Schoolhouse Restaurant and Guest House* (☎097152/1383; ⑤) provides moderately priced home-cooked meals in comfortable surroundings, and the *Kinlochbervie Hotel* (☎097152/1275; ⑧) is well known for its excellent food.

From Rhiconich, the road cuts diagonally across to the **Kyle of Durness**, leaving **Cape Wrath** accessible only to the most adventurous. If you want to visit this wild and impressive headland, named from the Viking *hvarf*, meaning "turning point", it's possible to combine a **ferry** (contact Mr Morrison on ☎0971511/376 or Mrs MacKay on ☎0971511/287) across the Kyle with a **minibus** which runs along the rough track that leads out to the cape. A visitors centre is planned in the near future; go now, while it's still untouched.

## Durness and around

**DURNESS** village is the centre of several crofting communities and is served by daily **post buses** and a daily **bus** from Thurso. There's good **hiking** along this coast; the walk to **Faraid Head**, which juts out northwest from Durness, is easy and pretty. It starts two miles from the village centre at **Balnakeil Church**, an eighth-century ruin (incredibly, the Vatican still holds church records from here that date from 1190), and continues along the beach and through the dunes, finally following the cliffs out to the point, where you'll see many sea birds, including vaguely comical puffins.

A couple of miles east of Durness, the **Smoo Cave** is a large limestone cave with a **waterfall** towards its rear – worth a look, though quite honestly not as spectacular as the tourist board would have you believe.

### Practicalities

Durness has an enthusiastic **tourist office** (March–Oct Mon–Sat 9am–5pm; ☎097181/259) right in the centre of the village who can help with **accommodation**. Of the several **hotels** clustered together in the village, the *Far North Hotel* (☎0971511/221; ④) and the *Parkhill Hotel* (☎0971511/209; ③) are best value, while *Puffin Cottage* (☎0971511/208; ②) is a welcoming **B&B** in a traditional croft house. There's also a **youth hostel** (May–Oct; ☎0971511/244; Grade 3), a mile and a half east of town, and **camping** at *Sango Sands Caravan and Camping Site* on Harbour Road (☎0971522/262), which has the added advantage of a good **bar** and **restaurant**. The *Cape Wrath Hotel* (☎0971511/212; ⑤), right by the ferry point to the cape, is solid and dependable, if a little pricy. **Eating** options are confined to hotel bar food.

# Eastern Sutherland and Caithness

**Eastern Sutherland and Caithness** together cover the northeastern tip of mainland Scotland, jutting out into the North Sea from a rough line drawn between Durness and Dornoch on the east coast. The region is divided quite neatly into two by the boundary between the two areas, marked by the **Ord of Caithness**, a high mass of moorland stretching up from the east coast north of Helmsdale. Until the Clearances, the semi-fertile valleys along the rocky, boggy, loch-studded Sutherland coastal stretch supported a relatively large population; today, however, more people live in Caithness, where the landscape is flatter, gentler and greener, good grazing for cattle and sheep, and the climate is considerably drier.

Caithness is the most heavily visited of the two areas, served by good **train** and **bus** services up the east coast to **Wick** and **Thurso**, and **buses** along the north coast from **Durness**. Inland, it's a different story: the only public transport is provided by erratic **post buses**.

## WALKING AROUND SUTHERLAND

If you're an experienced hiker or even climber, the Sutherland region has some stern tests in store. If you're up to it, the most obvious peaks in Sutherland to go for are **Quinag, Suilven, Canisp, Arkle, Foinaven, Ben More Assynt** and **Ben Loyal.** These are magnificent hills, but they involve tough walking. Be sure to be properly prepared, with a good OS map, a compass, and the right equipment – good boots, warm clothes and waterproofs.

If you're not experienced, **coastal walks** are a better bet. One of the best is the full day's walk from **Cape Wrath** down to **Oldshoremore** via **Sandwood Bay**, the most northerly sandy beach on the coast, with impressive rock stacks. You can get the minibus the eleven miles out to Cape Wrath (see p.374) and walk south; don't try it south-north though – if the weather closes in the bus stops running.

An easier option is to approach Sandwood from the south, off the Oldshoremore road. Go straight on past the "Blairmore" sign over the cattle grid; the track is signposted to the right alongside a house. It's an easy and beautiful walk.

On the flatter east coast, walking is correspondingly easier, with more numerous tracks. If you want to walk in the ecologically unique **Flow Country**, with its desolate watery wastes, *Hidden Hills* organize informative guided walks in the area: contact them on ☎04312/640.

Bear in mind, too that everywhere in the Northern Highlands during the **deer-stalking season** (August 20–October 20) access to some areas may be limited. At other times of the year the major landowners normally welcome walkers.

# The Sutherland coast to Thurso

It's a long 37-mile slog along the north coast from Durness to the pretty town of **TONGUE**, the landscape ranging from harsh around the deep and sheltered **Loch Eriboll**, to the lusher, more friendly scenery of the **Kyle of Tongue**.

There are plenty of pretty coastal walks around the Kyle; if you want to **stay** in Tongue, *Rhian Cottage* (☎084755/257; ②) and *Woodend* (☎084755/332; ②) are good B&Bs; the *Ben Loyal Hotel* (☎084755/216; ⑤) and the *Tongue Hotel* (☎084755/206; ⑤) are more luxurious options. Both do **bar food**. There's also a **youth hostel** a mile north of the village (March–Oct; ☎084755/301; Grade 2).

From Tongue you can head forty miles or so south towards Lairg (see p.382), skirting the edges of the **Flow Country**, which covers much of the interior of Caithness and spreads into Eastern Sutherland. This huge area of bogland came into the news a few years ago when ecology experts, responding to plans to transform the area into forest, swooped down and drew media attention to the threat to this fragile landscape, described by one contemporary commentator as of "unique and global importance, equivalent to the African Serengeti or Brazil's rain forest". Some forest was planted, but the environmentalists eventually won and the forestry syndicates have had to pull out.

**BETTYHILL** is one of North Sutherland's major crofting villages, stretching along the estuary of the River Naver (a famous salmon river), and down the coast to a splendid beach. In the village, the **Strathnaver Museum** (Easter–Sept Mon–Sat 10am–1pm & 2pm–5pm; £1.50), housed in the old church, is mildly interesting, full of locally donated bits and pieces, including a room dealing with the rigours of the Clearances. You can also see some Pictish stones, and an early Bronze Age beaker, found in nearby Strathnaver and proved to be over 3800 years old. Bettyhill's **tourist office** (March–Sept Mon–Sat 9am–5pm; ☎06412/342) can book **accommodation** for you. The *Bettyhill Hotel* (☎06412/352; ③) is right in the centre of the village and pretty basic; half a mile away, right near the windswept beach, the friendly *Farr Bay Inn* (☎06412/230; ③) has more character, and they do excellent **bar food**.

As you cross the border into Caithness, the north coast changes dramatically; the hills disappear to be replaced by fields fringed with traditional stone hedges of Caithness flagstone and some good beaches. At the attractive hamlet of **MELVICH** the A897 cuts south through the open valleys of Strath Halladale and the Strath of Kilodonan, both of which offer excellent salmon fishing, to **Helmsdale** on the east coast (see p.380).

Five miles east of Melvich, **DOUNREAY** Nuclear Power Station is a major employer in Caithness, and there are worries over what will happen when the fast reactor closes in 1994. If you're interested, there's a permanent exhibition detailing the processes (and unsurprisingly the benefits) of nuclear power, and you can take a tour (Easter–Sept daily 10am–5pm; free).

# Thurso

Approached from the isolation of the west, **THURSO** looks like a major metropolis. In fact, it's simply a small service town, grey and tidy, with well-planned streets and the higgledy-piggledy remnants of the fishing port it once was around its long bay. Traill Street is the main drag, turning into High Street at its northern end. There's not much to see, and most people are only here on the way to the Orkney ferry, which leaves from nearby Scrabster.

The town dates from Viking times, when it was the major gateway to the mainland. Later Thurso traded with the Baltic and Scandinavian ports, exporting meal, beef, hides and fish. If you've got time to fill, look at the ruined twelfth- to sixteenth-century **Old St Peter's Kirk**, in the old part of town, near the harbour on the way to the **beach**. You could also visit the average display at the **Thurso Heritage Museum** on the High Street (Mon–Sat 10am–5pm; 50p).

## Practicalities

It's a ten-minute walk from the **train station**, down Princes Street and Sir George Street, to the **tourist office** on Riverside Road (Mon–Fri 9am–5pm, Sat 9am–1pm; ☎0847/62371). The **bus station** is virtually next door: buses run from here to both Inverness and Durness. **Ferries** run daily from adjoining Scrabster to Orkney. You can book ahead through *P&O Scottish Ferries*, Aberdeen (☎0224/572615) or through any tourist office in Caithness or Sutherland. If you just fancy a day trip to Orkney, *Thomas & Bews* at John O' Groats (☎095581/353) run a daily passenger ferry across during the summer.

There's no shortage of good-value **accommodation** in Thurso: the tourist office has a full list. On Traill Street, both the *Central Hotel* (☎0847/63100; ③) and the *Royal Hotel* (☎0847/63191; ③) are good value. Of the B&Bs *Mrs Oag*, 9 Couper Street, east of High Street (☎0847/64529; ②), and *Mrs Bews*, 21 Durness St (☎0847/63906; ②), west of High Street, are welcoming places that serve huge breakfasts. **Food**, though not adventurous, is always fresh and great value. Most of the restaurants are in the hotels; though *Johnston's Café*, on Traill Street, is good for quick snacks, and the *Leisure Centre*, at the sea end of Traill Street, does food all day. The *Marine Inn* by the harbour serves more than adequate bar food, and if you're looking for an enjoyably rowdy local **pub**, the *Central* on Traill Street is a good bet. The *Upper Deck*, right by the harbour at Scrabster, does brilliant steaks and wicked puddings; it's moderately priced and handy for the ferry.

**Nightlife** is as limited as you'd expect, but the *Pentland Hotel* on Princes Street hosts a Highland Night once a week, and there are occasional concerts and ceilidhs at the town hall on the High Street. Ask at the tourist office for a copy of the unmissable monthly, *What's On in Caithness*.

# Dunnet Head to Duncansby Head

Despite the plaudits that John O' Groats customarily receives, Britain's northern-most mainland point is in fact **Dunnet Head** – situated around the far side of **Dunnet Bay**, an impressive sweep of sandy beach backed by dunes about six miles outside Thurso. The bay is becoming well known by **surfers**, and even in the winter you can usually spot intrepid figures far out in the Atlantic surf.

For **Dunnet Head**, turn off at **DUNNET**, at the east end of the bay, onto the B855, which runs four miles over windy heather and bog to the Head. The cliffs are startling, with weirdly shaped isolated rock stacks, known as geos, and a huge variety of sea birds, and on a clear day you can see the whole coastline from Cape Wrath to Duncansby Head and north to the Orkneys. The *Northern Sands Hotel* (☎084785/270; ⑥), in Dunnet village, is worth a stop, if only to eat in the restaurant; its Italian owner produces home-made pasta, very popular with the locals who flock here.

Familiar from endless postcards, **JOHN O' GROATS** comes as something of an anticlimax, little more than a windswept grassy slope leading down to the sea, and dominated by an enormous car park packed with tour buses and giftshops that offer a wide array of pastel candles, satin-covered coathangers and ceramic puffins. John O' Groats gets its name from the Dutchman, Jan de Groot, who

---

## WALKING IN CAITHNESS

If you want to **climb** one of the interior hills it's best to check with the **tourist office**, as Caithness landowners aren't as welcoming as they are in Sutherland. The **Caithness Field Club**, a local walking group based in Wick, welcomes visitors and runs regular walks all season. You could also try asking at the Wick tourist office since the Caithness Director of Tourism is a very keen walker who's delighted to offer suggestions.

The Flow Country, which occupies much of the lower ground in inland Caithness, is half-water, half-bog, with amazing flora and fauna. But walking in bog isn't much fun, besides being ecologically damaging, and if you want to **hike** a bit you should stick to the **coasts**, where the walking is easy, often on grass, with fabulous **birdlife** thrown in.

There's a nice, fairly strenuous half-day's walk down the coast from **Duncansby Head** to **Freswick**, about seven miles away. The cliffs on this stretch are truly impres-sive, and you'll see lots of geos – stacks that have eroded away from the original cliff-line. These impressive formations are also crammed with **birds** – watch out for **terns**, which can be very aggressive during their breeding season in early summer. You'll need to take the **OS 1:50,000 map no. 12** for this one; there isn't a marked path all the way.

South of **Wick** there are more good **coastal walks**, and with a map you can follow the coast for miles, passing the remnants of fishing villages and harbours, reminders of the herring-fishing boom of the last century. If you're pining for a few trees, **Dunbeath Strath**, 22 miles south of Wick, has pleasant and gentle walks up the wooded valley. You'll need two to three hours to do the round trip.

On the **north coast**, anywhere around **Dunnet** offers great opportunities. One of the best half-day walks is from **St John's Head**, east of Dunnet, to **Scotland's Haven**, which you could extend in either direction. This energetic cliff-top walk offers wide coastal views, magnificent cliffs and birds and a major **seal colony** as a bonus.

obtained the ferry contract for the crossing to the Orkneys in 1496. The eight-sided house he built for his eight quarrelling sons is remembered by the octagonal tower of the *John O' Groats Hotel*, good as a stop-off for a quick drink. There's also a **tourist office** (April–Oct Mon–Sat 9am–5pm; ☎095/581 373) just by the car park.

If you're disappointed by John O' Groats, head on a couple of miles to **Duncansby Head**, which, with its lighthouse, magnificent grassy cliffs and terrific walking has a lot more to offer. The **birdlife** here is wonderful and south of the Head there are some very fine cliffs, from where the Orkneys look about a stone's throw away.

# Wick

Originally a Viking settlement called *Vik*, after the creek on which it stands, **WICK** has been a Royal Burgh since 1140. It's actually two towns, Wick proper and **Pultneytown**, immediately south across the river, a messy, rather rundown nineteenth-century community planned by Thomas Telford in 1806 for the British Fisheries Society, formed to encourage evicted crofters to take up fishing.

Wick's heyday as the busiest herring port in Europe, when it exported tons of herring to Russia, Scandinavia and the West Indian slave plantations, is long gone, but it's still a bustling, friendly little town, with a good range of shops and facilities, and a solid Victorian town centre. Pultneytown, lined with rows of fishermens' cottages, is also worth a wander, not least for the **Wick Heritage Centre**, in Bank Row near the harbour (Tues–Sun 10am–5pm; £1). Housed in a row of old fishery buildings, this little museum is crammed with lots of good stuff on the herring industry, and a huge photographic collection covering the town's history from the 1880s.

Three miles north of Wick, rising steeply from a needle-thin promontory, the dramatic fifteenth- to seventeenth-century ruins of **Sinclair** and **Girnigoe castles** functioned as a single stronghold for the Earls of Caithness – in 1570 the fourth earl, suspecting his son of trying to murder him, imprisoned him in the dungeon here until he died of starvation.

### Practicalities

The **train** station and **bus** stops are next to each other behind the hospital. Frequent **local buses** run to Thurso and up the coast to John O' Groats; the **post buses** serve the inland villages. Wick also has an **airport**, a couple of miles north of the town, with direct flights from Edinburgh, Aberdeen and Orkney and connections further south (☎0955/2294).

From the train station head across the river down Bridge Street to the **tourist office**, which is just off the High Street (Mon–Fri 9am–5pm, Sat 9am–1pm; ☎0955/2596). They give out a full accommodation list, along with lots of maps and leaflets. There are plenty of **places to stay**; right next door to the tourist office, the *Wellington Guest House*, 41–43 High St (☎0955/3287; ③), is excellent value, as is the modern *County Guest House*, 101 High St (☎0955/2911; ②). The *Harbour Guest House*, 6 Rose St (☎0955/3276; ②), lies in a tiny road off the Inner Harbour in Pultneytown, and offers comfortable rooms in a lovely old building.

As for **eating**, the *Lamplighter Restaurant* on the High Street serves enormous helpings of imaginative food; in the same building, *Houston's* cheerfully churns out good burgers. The *Lorne Restaurant*, near the Heritage Centre, is moderately priced and produces more than adequate servings of meat and two veg, but is open in the evenings only. There are also a couple of cafés, *Jasmine's* and *Gravelli's*, at either end of the High Street, that are both good. Of Wick's **pubs**, the *Camps* at the east end of the High Street is beery, noisy, and sometimes has **live music**. The *Black Stairs*, by the harbour, is another possibility; down here you'll also find the *Waterfront*, which has food and dancing.

## The east coast: Wick to Golspie

From Wick, the fast A9 follows the coast south along grassy cliffs and over the **Ord of Caithness** all the way to Dornoch. **LYBSTER**, fourteen miles south of Wick, is well worth a look: a nineteenth-century planned village built to house the inland tenants evicted during the Clearances, it prospered during the herring boom and now has a windswept and melancholy charm. A long, wide, usually deserted street leads down to the natural **harbour**, where you can bargain with the fishermen for a lobster.

There are lots of prehistoric brochs, cairns, and standing stones along this stretch of the coast – the best known are at **CAMSTER** and **Loch Stemster**, just inland from **Latheron**, eighteen miles south of Wick.

Some five miles further south, the main road goes through **DUNBEATH**, a scattered crofting community, with a fine harbour and a privately owned fifteenth-century **Castle**. The author Neil M Gunn was born here; you can find out more about him and the area generally at the **Dunbeath Heritage Centre** (Easter–Oct Mon–Sat 10am–5pm; £2).

The A9 leaves the coast near **OUSDALE** to climb the **Ord of Caithness**. Until the last century this was a pretty impregnable obstacle, and even now the bleak and desolate road gets blocked during winter storms. **HELMSDALE**, five miles or so south, is another old herring port, built to house the evicted inhabitants of **Strath Kildonan** behind it. Today, the sleepy-looking grey village attracts thousands of tourists, most of them to see the **Timespan Heritage Centre**, set beside the river (Easter–Oct Mon–Sat 10am–5pm, Sun 2pm–5pm; £2.50). It's a remarkable venture for a place of this size, telling the local story from prehistoric times to the present through hi-tech displays, sound effects and an audiovisual programme.

Helmsdale's **tourist office** (April–Sept Mon–Sat 10am–5pm; ☎04312/640) will help with accommodation. Most of the B&Bs are on the outskirts of town; *Torbuie*, in Navidale (☎04312/424; ②), and *Hazlebank*, in Westhelmsdale (☎04312/427; ②), both offer comfortable rooms. There's also a **youth hostel** (May–Oct; ☎04312/577; Grade 3), about half a mile north of the harbour. For **food**, try the pink, frilly and beflowered *Mirage Restaurant* opposite the Timespan Heritage Centre. The owner is clearly a Barbara Cartland fan; and in fact the prolific author does indeed stay near Helmsdale every year.

From Helmsdale the A897 runs up the Strath to the north coast, following the path of the Helmsdale river, a strictly controlled and extremely exclusive salmon river frequented by the royals. Some eight miles up the Strath at **BAILE AN OR** (Gaelic for "goldfield"), gold was discovered in the bed of the Kildonan Burn in 1869; a gold-rush ensued, hardly on the scale of the Yukon, but quite bizarre in the Scottish Highlands. A tiny amount of gold is still found every year; if you fancy **gold-panning** yourself, pick up a free licence and the relevant equipment from Helmsdale's village shop near the Timespan Heritage Centre.

## THE ATLANTIC SALMON

**Salmon**, whose Latin name, *salmo salar*, means "leaper", have been renowned in Scotland since at least the seventh century, when the Picts carved them on their symbol stones; a thousand years later dried and salted salmon were important exports.

The **lifespan** of the salmon is unique. The fish hatch in rivers in early spring and remain in fresh water until they are two or three years old, when they migrate downstream to the sea. They then move to feeding grounds in the North Atlantic, which they share with young salmon from the rivers of the rest of Europe and the eastern American seaboard. Following this, they return hundreds of miles to the river of their birth, some after only one winter in the sea, when they will weigh 4–9 pounds, others after two or more seasons, by which time their weight reaches 9–18 pounds. Once back in their native fresh water, salmon will not feed until they spawn in November, cutting nests or "redds" in the gravel beds of the river and starting the cycle all over again. After spawning the majority die; the few that survive go back to the sea where they can grow to as much as 44 pounds before returning once more to spawn. The British record weight caught on rod and line is 64 pounds.

Salmon **fishing** in Scotland is an expensive sport, and the value of a rod-caught fish is many times that of those commercially netted or farmed. Fishing rights change hands at considerable prices, and the rents charged to anglers on productive stretches can run into thousands of pounds for a week's fishing.

**Stocks** of Atlantic salmon are in decline, threatened not only by anglers but also by floods, pollution and predators, seals, disease and poachers. Indeed there's a fear that some rivers may soon have insufficient breeding stock to maintain a population – a sad end for a fish that was once so plentiful that servants and apprentices were reputed to insist they were served it no more than three times a week.

The small grey town of **BRORA**, on the coast twelve miles south of Helmsdale, doesn't have much to offer, but it's accessible by **bus** and **train** and it does have *Capaldi's* on the High Street, which sells brilliant home-made Italian ice cream. A mile or so north of the town you'll find the **Clynelish Distillery** (Mon–Fri 9.30am–4.30pm; free), where they'll give you a guided tour and a free dram.

Five miles down the A9, and also on the train route, lies the long, grey town of **GOLSPIE**, the administrative centre for Sutherland, a status that does little to relieve its dullness. It does, however, boast a lovely sandy beach and a golf-course. Overlooking the sea a mile north of town, **Dunrobin Castle** (May Mon–Thurs 10.30am–12.30pm; June–Sept Mon–Sat 10.30am–5.30pm, Sun 1–5.30pm; Oct Mon–Sat 10.30am–4.30pm, Sun 1–4.30pm; £3.50) is approached down a long, wooded drive. The northernmost of Scotland's big houses, it's the seat of the Sutherlands, at one time Europe's biggest landowners, and responsible for many of the Clearances. Though part of the house dates from the fourteenth century, there were considerable additions in the eighteenth century, and most of what you see today dates from Victorian times. The interior is overwhelming and muddled, crammed full of fine furniture, paintings, including two Canalettos, tapestries and *objets d'art*, all displayed in a mausoleum-like gloom.

You can't miss the 100ft high **Monument** to the first Duke of Sutherland on the summit of the 1293ft **Beinn a'Bhragaidh**, just beyond Golspie. Oddly enough, it was erected in the 1820s by subscription from his tenantry, many of whom had been, or were about to be, evicted. It's worth the steep, wet and rocky climb to the top of the hill for the wonderful views south along the coast past Dornoch to the Moray Firth and west towards Lairg and Loch Shin. If you want to tackle it, take the road opposite *Munro's TV Rentals* in Golspie's main street: this leads up the hill and past the fountain to a farm. From here, follow the Beinn a'Bhragaidh footpath (BBFP) signs along the path into the woods. It's steep; and there's no view until you're out of the trees, about ten minutes from the top. Allow about ninety minutes strenuous walking for the round trip.

## Lairg

Four miles south of Golspie, the road cuts fourteen miles west through **Strath Fleet**, with its attractive river, woodlands and farms, to **LAIRG**, a bleak and scattered town at the eastern end of lonely **Loch Shin**, surrounded by vast wastes of moorland. On a fine day this subtle landscape can be beautiful, in the rain it's easy to find it deeply depressing.

Lairg is predominantly a transportation hub, and there's nothing to see in town, although there are many traces of early settlement nearby. A **tourist centre** is planned which will fill you in on the area's history, including the impact of the local Clearances, but until then the main event in Lairg is the annual August lambsale, the biggest one-day sale in Europe, when thousands of sheep from all over the north of Scotland pass through the market.

### Practicalities

Lairg is a major transit point, and, lying as it does at the hub of Sutherland's **road system**, is distinctly hard to avoid. The A838 runs northwest the forty miles or so to Laxford Bridge, traversing Loch Shin and some of the loneliest country in the Highlands: if you're heading for Cape Wrath this is by far the quickest route. Another option is the A836 which heads north, skirting the edge of the Flow Country, to Tongue on the north coast, another forty-mile journey. A few miles south of Lairg the A837 pushes west through lovely Strath Oykel, to Lochinver on the coast, a journey of just over forty miles. For non-drivers, Lairg is on the main **train** line and is the centre of several **post bus** routes. Trains arrive north of the main road along the loch, while buses stop right on the loch.

There's no tourist office in Lairg, and no real reason to stay, but should you need a **B&B**, try *Strathwin* (☎0549/2487; ②), or *Park House* (☎0549/2208; ②), both signposted from the main road, or the croft of *Mrs Gray*, at 97 Lower Toriboll, about five minutes' drive from the town centre (☎0549/2489; ②). Five miles or so south of town, at **CULRAIN**, *Carbisdale Castle* is a very opulent **youth hostel** (Feb–Nov; ☎054982/232; Grade 1).For **food** you're going to have to eat where you sleep, or alternatively try the fish and chip shop on the main road.

# Easter Ross and the Black Isle

The peninsulas of **Easter Ross** and the **Black Isle** are ringed by the waters of the lovely Dornoch, Cromarty and Moray Firths. It's a sheltered and civilized landscape, the rolling land of the interior giving way to a pretty coast lined with prosperous farms. Lacking the scenic grandeur of the west, this is a relatively neglected area, despite being easily accessible by road and the bridges across the Cromarty and Dornoch Firths.

Coming from Inverness, **Dingwall**, **Tain** and **Bonar Bridge** are on the **train line** to Wick; **buses** run to these and also to **Dornoch** and **Lairg**. If you want to get to the **Black Isle**, there are local buses from Inverness.

# Dornoch and around

Well-heeled **DORNOCH** lies some fourteen miles south of Golspie on a flattish headland surrounded by sanddunes. It's very much a holiday town, with solid Edwardian hotels, trees and flowers in profusion, miles of **sandy beaches** giving good views across the Dornoch Firth to the Tain peninsula, and a superb **golf course**, ranked eleventh in the world.

Dating from the twelfth century, Dornoch became a Royal Burgh in 1628. The oldest buildings are all grouped round the spacious **Square**, where you'll find **Dornoch Cathedral**, built of local sandstone and founded in 1224. It's on a tiny scale as cathedrals go, but worth a quick look. The original building was horribly damaged by marauding MacKays in 1570, and much of what you see today was restored by the Countess of Sutherland in 1835, though her worst Victorian excesses were removed this century, when the interior stonework was returned to its original state. Opposite, the fortified sixteenth-century **Bishop's Palace** is a fine example of vernacular architecture, with stepped gables and towers, and has been refurbished as a swanky hotel (see below). Next door, the **Old Town Jail** (Mon–Sat 10am–5pm; free) has a mock-up of a nineteenth-century cell and a book shop. Incidentally, in 1722 Dornoch saw the last burning of a witch in Scotland, an event commemorated by the **Witch's Stone**, which you'll find just south of the Square.

**Strath Carron** runs west from **ARDGAY**, south of Bonar Bridge – about a twenty-minute drive from Dornoch. At the top of this lovely valley lies **Croick Church**, in whose churchyard tenants evicted during the Clearances were forced to shelter as their homes burnt. They scratched their messages on the church windows: you can still make out the words "Glencalvie people was here May 24 1845".

## Practicalities

Buses stop in the Square, where you'll also find Sutherland's main **tourist office** (Mon–Sat 9am–1pm & 2pm–5pm; ☎0862/810400). There's no shortage of **accommodation**. The *Trentham Hotel* near the golf course on the northeast edge of town (☎0862/810391; ③) is friendly and comfortable, if a bit staid; if you fancy a splurge, head for the *Dornoch Castle Hotel* (☎0862/810216; ⑤) in the Bishop's Palace on the central square. Of the B&Bs, *Fiona MacLean*, 11 Gilchrist Square (☎0862/811024; ②), and *Tordarroch*, on Castle Street (☎0862/810855; ②), both offer good value in pretty stone houses near the square. For **food**, the stultifyingly floral restaurant in the *Mallin House Hotel*, north of the main square on Church Street (☎0862/812335), is terrific, and the *Cathedral Café* serves delicious soup and delicious baked goodies.

# The Tain peninsula

Across the Firth from Dornoch, the little sandstone town of **TAIN** is tucked into the hillside overlooking the sea. This was the birthplace of Saint Duthus, a saint who inspired great devotion in the Middle Ages: **Malcolm Canmore** established a sanctuary here in the eleventh century, and in 1360 **St Duthus Collegiate Church** was built, visited annually by James IV, who usually arrived here fresh from the arms of his mistress, Janet Kennedy, whom he had conveniently installed in Moray. There's not a great deal to see in town; the centre is dominated by the sixteenth-century **Tolbooth** with its old bell, and local history is detailed in the unremarkable **Tain and District Museum** on Castle Brae, just off the High Street (Easter–Sept Mon–Sat 10am–4.30pm; free).

If you want to **stay** around Tain, and have money to spend, you could try the Scottish Baronial *Mansfield House Hotel* (☎0862/892052; ⑤), which also serves good **food**. *Strachan's Restaurant*, on the High Street, is open all day, dishing up good, inexpensive Scots food.

Although few people bother to explore as far east of Tain as **Tarbat Ness** on the tip of the peninsula, if you're driving it's well worth putting aside a couple of hours to make the detour. The village of **PORTMAHOMACK** is a green, windswept place, sprawling down the hill and round a sheltered bay full of sailing boats – check out **Tarbat Old Church**, with its odd tower and balustraded entrance at the back. There's a lighthouse at the point, reached along narrow roads running through fertile farmland, with huge views of the surrounding red sandstone cliffs covered in gorse.

If you do make it here, you could have **lunch** at the *Oystercatcher*, which serves up lobster and home-made soups and salads; they also have a few **rooms** available too (☎086287/560; ②). Otherwise, if you want to stay, you could try the *Castle Hotel* (☎086287/263; ③) with good-value doubles overlooking the water.

# The Cromarty Firth to Strathpeffer

South of the Tain peninsula, the **Cromarty Firth** has always been recognized as a perfect natural harbour. During World War I it was a major **naval base**, and today its sheltered waters are used as a centre for rig repair for the North Sea oilfields. The fifteen-mile stretch of the fast A9 from Tain to **ALNESS** passes several villages which have boomed with the expansion of the oil industry, notably **INVERGORDON**, on the coast just west of Nigg Bay.

The extraordinary edifice on the hill behind **EVANTON**, ten minutes west along the A9 from Alness, is the **Fyrish Monument**, built by a certain Sir Hector Munro partly to give employment to the area, and partly to commemorate his own capture of the Indian town of Seringapatam in 1781 – hence the design, resembling an Indian gateway. If you want to get a close-up look, it's a tough two-hour walk through pinewoods to the top.

Most traffic now takes the upgraded A9 north, bypassing the small provincial town of **DINGWALL**. It's a tidy, dull place; a solid market and service town with one long main street that's bustling all day and moribund by dinner time. If you need to **stay** the night, *Victoria Lodge*, Mill St (☎0349/62494; ②), and *Fyrish*, Ferry Rd (☎0349/64233; ②), are fine for a night's B&B.

**STRATHPEFFER**, a Victorian spa-town surrounded by hills and trees nine miles west of Dingwall, is a much better bet. During its heyday, this was a renowned European health resort complete with a **Pump Room**, where visitors could chat while they sipped the water. Today, sadly, several of its fine buildings are in a sorry state, although two or three mammoth faded hotels remain. Activity is concentrated around the main square, where you can sample sulphur-laden water at the **Water Sampling Pavilion**.

There's a **tourist office** (Easter–Nov Mon–Sat 10am–5pm; ☎0997/21415) in the square, with information on points west as well as local areas. Strathpeffer's **hotels** are very popular with bus tours, but often have room: the vast *Ben Wyvis*

(☎0997/421323; ③) is adequate and stands in nice grounds east of the main square on the Dingwall road, while north of the main square, a converted Victorian villa, complete with turrets, houses the *Holly Lodge Hotel* (☎0997/421254; ④). Nearby, the *Inver Lodge* (☎0997/421392; ②) and *Francisville* (☎0997/421345; ②), both west of the main square, offer good **B&B**.

### Routes onward from Strathpeffer

Beyond Strathpeffer, the A834 joins the A835 at **CONTIN**, running fast through high open country and fringing the southern edge of **Loch Glascarnoch** as far as Ullapool. On the way, stretch your legs at **Rogie Falls**, following a series of well-marked paths down to where the water cascades over tree-lined rocks and boulders. Just beyond **GARVE**, about nine miles west of Strathpeffer, the A832 will take you down Strath Bran, with a further choice of route to either Gairloch or Kyle of Lochalsh.

Heading south from Contin the A832 runs through **MUIR OF ORD**, an unexciting town visited in huge numbers for the **Glen Ord Distillery** (Mon–Fri 9.30am–5pm; free). From here you can head through Beauly back to Inverness or strike east to explore the Black Isle.

# The Black Isle

Sandwiched between the Cromarty Firth and Beauly Firth, the **Black Isle** is not an island at all, but a fertile peninsula, packed with prosperous farms, big houses and stands of deciduous woodland. It probably gained its name because of its mild climate: there's rarely frost, which leaves the fields "black" all winter. There are some attractive small towns and great views along the shoreline, but the real treat is the town of **CROMARTY**, sheltered by impressive headlands in the northeast corner, a perfect example of an eighteenth-century Scottish sea-port forced out of business by the arrival of the rail line, featuring a set of large merchant houses and rows of workers' cottages that have led to it being referred to as "the jewel in the crown of Scottish vernacular architecture".

The best way to get a sense of the town is to head straight for the excellent museum in the old **Cromarty Courthouse** on Church Street (Easter–Oct 10am–6pm; Nov–Easter noon–4pm; £2), which tells the history of the town using audiovisuals and animated figures (not as dreadful as they sound, and kids love them). They also issue you with a personal stereo, a tape and a map for a walking tour around the town. Hugh Miller, the nineteenth-century stonemason turned geologist and writer, was born in Cromarty and his **birthplace**, a narrow, cramped thatched cottage nearby on Church Street (April–Sept Mon–Sat 10am–1pm & 2–5pm, Sun 2–5pm; NTS; £2), has been restored to look as it did when he lived there, with a small collection of his personal belongings. Once you've seen that you've really seen Cromarty, although before you move on bear in mind that Bill Fraser will take you out in his boat to see the **porpoises** and bottle-nosed dolphins just off the coast: if you're interested, contact him on ☎03817/323.

If you want to **stay** in this secluded corner, the *Retreat*, on Church Street (☎03817/400; ②), and *Mrs Robertson*, 7 Church St (☎03817/488; ②), are both excellent B&Bs in lovely old houses: they only have a few rooms so it's best to book ahead. For more luxury, the *Royal Hotel* right by the harbour (☎03817/217; ⑤) has comfortable rooms and serves splendid, innovative **food**.

Leaving Cromarty, it's an easy drive along the north shore of the Black Isle, with its scores of **sea birds**, back to join the A9 at Culbokie. An alternative is to take the small **car ferry** north across to Nigg (April–Oct every 30min). Failing that, head down the eastern shore to **FORTROSE**, in a soft and pretty landscape and boasting more fine examples of vernacular architecture, with red sandstone and colour-washed houses dating from the eighteenth century, and a lovely yew-studded green with a ruined **Cathedral**.

**ROSEMARKIE**, a one-street village just north of Fortrose, is thought to have been evangelized by St Boniface in the early eighth century (indeed the whole of the Black Isle is particularly noted for its Pictish Christian sites). If you're inter-ested in such things, check out the **Groam House Museum**, housed in an attrac-tive eighteenth-century building on the main road through the village (May–Oct Mon–Sat 11am–5pm; £1.50), which displays some powerful Pictish Stones, notably the Rosemarkie Cross Slab, a highly decorated eighth-century stone, as well as running regular films on local topics such as the Picts and the so-called Brahan Seer, a seventeenth-century fortune-teller whose enigmatically worded prophecies foretold, among other things, the arrival of steam power, the building of the Caledonian Canal, and the depopulation of the Highlands. He came to a nasty end in 1660, when he "saw" the absent husband of the Countess of Seaforth dallying with a French beauty; the Countess had him burnt at Fortrose in a barrel of tar.

## travel details

**Trains**

**Aviemore** to: Inverness (9 daily Mon–Sat, 4 Sun; 40min); Newtonmore (9 daily Mon–Sat, 4 Sun; 20min).

**Dingwall** to: Helmsdale (3 daily Mon–Sat; 2hr); Inverness (3 daily Mon–Sat; 25min); Kyle of Lochalsh (3 daily Mon–Sat; 1hr 55min); Lairg (3 daily Mon–Sat; 1hr 10min); Thurso (3 daily Mon–Sat; 3hr 20min); Wick (3 daily Mon–Sat; 3hr 20min).

**Fort William** to: Arisaig (4 daily; 1hr 10min); Crianlarich (3 daily; 1hr 40min); Glenfinnan (4 daily; 55min); Mallaig (4 daily; 1hr 25min).

**Inverness** to: Aviemore (9 daily Mon–Sat, 4 Sun; 40min); Dingwall (3 daily Mon–Sat; 25min); Edinburgh (7 daily Mon–Sat, 2 Sun; 3hr 30min); Kyle of Lochalsh (3 daily Mon–Sat; 2hr 40min); Lairg (3 daily Mon–Sat; 1hr 40min); London (5 daily Mon–Sat, 2 Sun; 8hr 35min); Thurso (3 daily Mon–Sat; 3hr 45min); Wick (3 daily Mon–Sat; 3hr 45min).

**Kyle of Lochalsh** to: Dingwall (3 daily Mon–Sat; 1hr 55 min); Inverness (3 daily Mon–Sat; 2hr 30min); Plockton (3 daily Mon–Sat; 20min).

**Lairg** to: Dingwall (3 daily Mon–Sat; 1hr 10min); Inverness (3 daily Mon–Sat; 1hr 40min); Thurso (3 daily Mon–Sat; 2hr 5min); Wick (3 daily Mon–Sat; 2hr 5min).

**Mallaig** to: Arisaig (4 daily; 15min); Fort William (4 daily; 1hr 25 min); Glenfinnan (4 daily; 35 min).

**Newtownmore** to: Aviemore (9 daily Mon–Sat, 4 daily Sun; 20min); Inverness (9 daily Mon–Sat, 4 Sun; 55min).

**Thurso** to: Dingwall (3 daily Mon–Sat; 3hr 20min); Inverness (3 daily Mon–Sat; 3hr 45min); Lairg (3 daily Mon–Sat; 2hr 5min).

**Wick** to: Dingwall (3 daily Mon–Sat; 3hr 20min); Inverness (3 daily Mon–Sat; 3hr 45min); Lairg (3 daily Mon–Sat; 2hr 5min).

**Buses**

**Aviemore** to: Grantown-on-Spey (5 daily; 40min); Inverness (10 daily; 40 min); Newtownmore (10 daily; 20min).

**Dornoch** to: Inverness (3 daily; 1hr 10min); Thurso with connections for Wick (3 daily; 2hr 20min).

**Fort William** to: Drumnadrochit (8 daily; 1hr 30min); Fort Augustus (8 daily; 1hr); Inverness (8 daily; 2hr); Mallaig (1 daily; 2hr).

**Gairloch** to: Dingwall (3 weekly; 2hr); Inverness (3 weekly; 2hr 20min).

**Inverness** to: Aberdeen (4 daily; 2hr 55min); Aviemore (10 daily; 40min); Fort William (8 daily; 2hr); Gairloch (3 weekly; 2hr 20min); Kyle of Lochalsh (2 daily Mon–Sat, 1 Sun; 2hr); Lochinver

(1 weekly; 2hr 30min); Nairn (2 daily Mon–Sat; 50min); Newtownmore (10 daily; 55min); Oban (2 daily Mon–Sat; 4hr 15min); Perth (10 daily; 2hr 35min); Thurso (2 daily Mon–Sat, 1 Sun; 2hr 30 min); Ullapool (3 daily Mon–Sat; 1hr 25min); Wick (3 daily Mon–Sat; 1hr 55min).

**Kyle of Lochalsh** to: Inverness (2 daily Mon–Sat, 1 Sun; 2hr).

**Lochinver** to: Inverness (1 weekly; 2hr 15min).

**Mallaig** to: Fort William (1 daily; 2hr).

**Thurso** to: Bettyhill (1 weekly; 1 hr 20min); Inverness (2 daily Mon–Sat, 1 Sun; 2hr 30min); Wick (2 daily Mon–Sat, 1 Sun; 35min).

**Wick** to: Inverness (2 daily Mon–Sat, 1 Sun; 2hr 55min); Thurso (2 daily Mon–Sat, 1 Sun; 35min).

**Ferries**

**To Kyle of Lochalsh**: Mallaig–Kyle of Lochalsh (3 weekly).

**To Mull**:Kilchoan–Tobermory (7 daily Mon–Sat).

**To Skye**: Mallaig–Armadale (3 daily Mon–Sat).

**To the Small Isles**: Mallaig–Eigg, Rhum, Muck, and Canna (3 weekly).

**To Lewis**: Ullapool–Stornoway (5 Mon; 3 Tues–Sat).

**To Orkney**: Scrabster–Orkney (2 daily Mon–Sat).

# CHAPTER NINE

# ORKNEY AND SHETLAND

Arching out into the North Sea, in the face of furious tides and bitter winds, Scotland's **northern isles** gather neatly into two distinct and very different clusters. To the south, just a short step from the Scottish mainland, the **Orkney Isles** are low-lying rounded mounds, rising gently from the sea. This group of more than seventy islands is heavily cultivated, sparsely populated and supremely fertile. In the warmth of spring and summer, the days are long and skies enormous, the meadows thick with wild flowers and the seashore alive to the sound of millions of sea birds. Another sixty miles to the north the remote **Shetland Isles** present a much fiercer prospect. Exposed to the full force of the elements these islands are chiselled from jagged rock; here steep cliffs rise straight out of the water to form barren heather-coated hills, while narrow voes (a Shetland equivalent of a Norwegian fjord) cut deep into the land. It's a forbidding, powerful landscape, in which the population clings to the margins, huddled along the seashore and depending largely on oil and fish for their livelihood.

Life in both island groupings is, perhaps not surprisingly, intimately linked to the sea, a source of sustenance or, occasionally, disaster, as well as delivering a series of invaders over the years, who have either arrived from the south or across the north sea from Scandinavia. Both Orkney and Shetland have a long and turbulent history of occupation and are littered with interesting archeological remains, evidence of the range of North Atlantic cultures which have used the islands as a refuge.

For the visitor, both groups of islands offer superb walking, birdwatching, fishing, diving and sailing. Despite the inroads of the oil industry the environment remains astonishingly pristine, and the islands have a fantastic elemental beauty, whether it's in the lush meadows of Orkney or the windswept cliffscapes of Shetland. They also harbour a fantastic and heroic history, in a world in which survival itself has always been a major achievement, and the sea always holds the promise of unexpected adventure, filling the past and the present with magical, salty tales.

---

### ISLAND WILDLIFE

Both sets of islands support massive **bird populations**: during the breeding season sea birds easily outnumber people, the high cliffs packed with guillemots, puffins, gulls and razorbills. Smaller migrants drop in on their way to and from their breeding grounds and inland you'll see merlins, peregrine falcons, short-eared owls, curlews and oyster-catchers. The cry of birds is ever present and along the shoreline they flutter and glide in every direction, while the sea itself is home to an abundance of **marine life**, including otters and seals. We've noted the best RSPB reserves in the text, as well as the opportunities for spotting marine life.

# ORKNEY

Just a short step from John O' Groats, the **Orkney Islands** are a unique and fiercely independent grouping. The landscape here is kinder and more accommodating than that of Highland Scotland, supporting a superb abundance of plants, flowers and wildlife. When Orcadians refer to "Mainland" they're talking about their largest island rather than the rest of Scotland, and throughout their history the islands have turned their backs on that barren land to the south and been linked, instead, to a broader international arena – thanks largely to the sea. In the words of Orkney's most famous living poet, George Mackay Brown:

*Orkney lay athwart a great sea-way*
*from Viking times onwards, and its lore*
*is crowded with sailors, merchants, adventurers,*
*pilgrims, smugglers, storms and sea-changes.*
*The shores are strewn with wrack, jetsam,*
*occasional treasure.*

Orkney has a remarkable history of occupation, dating back to prehistoric times and bearing witness to a long succession of North Sea cultures. The islands are excellent farmland, and the shortage of timber and abundance of easily worked sandstone prompted early inhabitants to build solid stone structures, many of which are now amazingly well preserved. There is little that's grand or extensive, but hundreds of small archeological sites do give an interesting feel for the struggle of daily life here.

Small communities began to settle in the islands some four thousand years before Christ, and the village at **Skara Brae** on Mainland, which was inhabited around 3000–2000 BC, is one of the best preserved Stone Age settlements in Europe. Elsewhere the islands are scattered with chambered tombs and stone circles, a tribute to the sophisticated religious and ceremonial practices taking place here some two thousand years before Christ. More sophisticated **Bronze Age** inhabitants built hundreds of compact seaside villages known as **brochs**, protected by walls and ramparts, many of which are still in place. Later, the Picts arrived, and the remains of several of their early Christian settlements can still be seen, the best at the **Brough of Birsay** in the west Mainland, where a group of

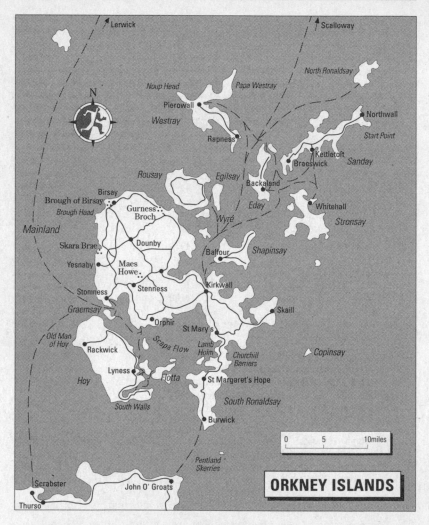

**ORKNEY ISLANDS**

small houses are gathered around the remains of an early church. Later, around the ninth century, **Norse** settlers from Scandinavia arrived, and the islands became Norse earldoms, forming an outpost of this powerful and expansive culture that was gradually forcing its way south. The last of the Norse earls was killed in 1231, but they had a lasting impact on the islands, leaving behind the great St Magnus Cathedral in **Kirkwall**, one of Scotland's most outstanding pieces of medieval architecture.

After the departure of the Norsemen, the islands became the preserve of **Scottish earls**, who exploited and abused the islanders, although a steady increase in sea trade did offer some chance of escape. French and Spanish ships sheltered here in the sixteenth century, and the ships of the **Hudson Bay**

**Company** recruited hundreds of Orcadians to work in the Canadian fur trade. The islands were also an important staging post in the **whaling industry** and the **herring boom**, which brought hundreds of small Dutch, French and Scottish boats to fishing villages throughout the islands.

More recently, the naval importance of **Scapa Flow** brought plenty of money and activity during both world wars, and left the seabed scattered with **wrecks** and the clifftops dotted with gun emplacements. Since the war, things have quietened down somewhat, although in the last two decades the **oil industry**, which now has a large terminal on the island of **Flotta**, and **European Community** funding have brought surprise windfalls to the islands, stemming the flow of young people to the south. Meanwhile, many disenchanted southerners have become "incomers" moving north in search of the purity and simplicity of island life.

## Where to go

Rolling out of the sea "like the backs of sleeping whales", the Orkney Isles offer excellent **walking**, with beautiful arching white-sand beaches. In spring and summer the meadows and clifftops of Mainland are a brilliant green, shining with wild flowers, while huge skies and long days pour light onto the land and sea – a sharp contrast to the bleak enormity of the outlying islands or even the savage moorland of the western Highlands. The largest island, known as the **Mainland**, is joined by a causeway to the southern island of **South Ronaldsay**, and centres on the capital of **Kirkwall**; although you'll most likely arrive at the port of **Stromness**, an old fishing town on the far western shore of Mainland that serves as Orkney's main ferry terminal. Mainland divides into fairly distinct western and eastern sections, both of which are relatively heavily populated and intensely farmed. Further afield, the **smaller islands** (linked to Mainland by regular ferries) are bleaker and wilder: the southern island of **Hoy**, the second largest in the archipelago, presents a superbly dramatic landscape, with some of the highest seacliffs in the country; more exposed still are the ten **northern isles** – low, elemental outcrops, sprawled out into the ocean.

Though obviously the main attraction, there is more to the Orkneys besides the landscape and location, and most of the islands are scattered with interesting **archeological** and **historical** remains, testifying to the astonishing range of influences that have been brought to bear here. Many of the older archeological sites, including the **Stones of Stenness** and **Meas Howe**, are concentrated in the central and eastern parts of Mainland, although more modern points of interest include the magnificent **Cathedral** in Kirkwall, the **Italian Chapel** on Lamb Holm and the **naval museum** on Hoy. Even the surrounding seabed, which is littered with wrecks, presents interesting **diving** opportunities, particularly in Scapa Flow. There is also some excellent **fishing** in both salt and fresh water, with the rivers and lochs offering some of the best trout and sea trout fishing in Britain.

## Getting there

Orkney is connected to the mainland by three **ferry routes**. *P&O Scottish Ferries* (☎0856/850655) run two car ferry services to Stromness: one from Aberdeen (8hr) and a shorter route from Scrabster (1hr 45min), a few miles outside Thurso on the north coast. There's also a passenger-only service, operated by *Thomas & Bews* (☎0955/81353), from John O' Groats to Burwick on South Ronaldsay (45min). To get to the mainland ferry ports, there are **trains** from Inverness as far as Thurso (for Scrabster) and Wick, from where buses run to John O' Groats.

There are also regular **flights** to Orkney: *Logan Air* (☎0856/873457) fly to Kirkwall, Orkney's airport, from Glasgow, Edinburgh and Wick, *British Airways* (☎0345/2221111) from London, Birmingham, Glasgow, Edinburgh and Inverness, with onward connections to Sumburgh in Shetland.

### Getting around
Despite the fact that the islands are small, **getting around** can be something of a problem without your own transport, as many of the most interesting areas are fairly remote and **bus** services, while reasonably efficient, only connect the main towns. **Cycling** is a cheap and effective option as distances are short and hills are low, although wind and rain can be a serious drawback. Bikes can be hired in Kirkwall, Stromness and on some of the smaller islands. If you'd rather drive, **car rental** is also available in Kirkwall and Stromness.

An excellent inter-island **ferry** service is operated by the *Orkney Island Shipping Company*. They have frequent daily sailings to Hoy and once-daily sailing to and from all of the northern isles, each of which can conveniently be visited as day trips (except North Ronaldsay, which only has a weekly service on Friday). *Logan Air* (☎0856/872494) also fly from Kirkwall airport to Westray, Papa Westray and North Ronaldsay.

# Kirkwall

Sheltered at the base of a steep horseshoe bay, the old heart of Orkney's capital, **KIRKWALL**, huddles around the base of the St Magnus Cathedral. The town has two principle focal points: the **harbour**, which bustles with ferries, cargo ships, yachts and fishing boats, and the main shopping street, **Albert Street**, which twists back towards the cathedral through a tight knot of paved streets, old stone houses and narrow, twisting alleys.

By Orkney standards, Kirkwall is a bustling metropolis, and indeed it is a busy market town and home to the island's most important businesses, its more exotic restaurants and better-stocked shops, as well as two distilleries. It's also an interesting place to spend some time, with its unusual, quietly impressive architecture and a gentle, unhurried atmosphere, and makes an ideal base from which to explore Mainland or make day trips to the northern isles.

## Arrival, information and accommodation

Most visitors come to Orkney **by sea** (from either Scrabster or Aberdeen), and arrive at the ferry terminal in Stromness, in the southwest corner of Mainland. Ferries are met by buses to Kirkwall (40min), although if you'd rather stay in Stromness the ferry terminal is within walking distance of all hotels and youth hostels. Arriving **by plane**, the airport is about three miles southeast of Kirkwall on the A960. It's not served by buses, but a taxi into town should only set you back about £5.

**Kirkwall** itself is an easy place in which to orientate yourself as there's really only one main street – **Albert Street** – and the prominent spire of the St Magnus Cathedral clearly marks the town centre. The **tourist office**, on Broad Street beside the cathedral graveyard (daily 8am–8pm; ☎0856/872856), books accommodation and gives out an excellent free leaflet on the town, the *Kirkwall Heritage Guide*, which takes you through all the buildings of interest.

If you're planning to **stay** in Kirkwall, **B&B** is as ever an alternative. The tourist office keeps an extensive list of houses offering accommodation and can book you in (for a ten percent fee which is deducted from the money that the owners receive). If you'd rather not book through the tourist office, or are planning to arrive when they are closed, head out along the Cromwell road, which runs along the waterfront at the eastern side of the bay, where there are several decent B&Bs, including *Craigwood* (☎0856/872006; ①). Other good, central B&Bs are: *Mrs Bain*, 6 Frasers Close (☎0856/872862: ①), *Briar Lea*, 10 Dundas Crescent (☎0856/872747; ①), *Mrs Moore*, 7 Matches Square (☎0856/872440; ①) and *Mrs Forsyth*, 21 Willowburn Rd (☎0856/874020; ①).

## Hotels and youth hostels

**Albert Hotel**, Mounthoolie Lane (☎0856/876000). An old stone building, recently refurbished to modern standards, right in the heart of the town. ②.

**Ayre Hotel**, Ayre Rd (☎0856/873001). A friendly, family-run establishment on the waterfront west of the *Kirkwall Hotel*. ②.

**Kirkwall Hotel**, Harbour St (☎0856/872232). On the harbour front, Orkney's most imposing Victorian hotel struggles hard to achieve the appropriate grandeur. Closed Christmas week. ③.

**Kirkwall Youth Hostel**, 1 Old Scapar Rd (☎0856/872243). On the Orphir Road just over half a mile south of the centre of town.

**St Ola Hotel**, Harbour St (☎0856/873477). Good-value harbour-front hotel, humble neighbour of the *Kirkwall Hotel*. ①.

**West End Hotel**, Main St (☎0856/87 2368). Built in 1824, this is nowadays not too smart but is certainly comfortable and welcoming. ②.

# The Town

Towering above the rest of the town, the **St Magnus Cathedral** (daily 9am–1pm & 2–5pm) is the very heart of Kirkwall, and its most intriguing conventional sight, a totally unique building which employs traditional architectural techniques but gives them a distinctive Orkney twist. The building was begun in 1137 by the Orkney Earl Kol of Agdir, who decided to make full use of a growing cult surrounding the figure of his uncle Magnus Erlendson. Magnus had shared the earldom of Orkney with his cousin Hakon Paulson from 1103, but Hakon grew jealous of his cousin's popularity and had him killed in 1115. When Magnus's body was buried in Birsay a heavenly light was said to have shone overhead, and his grave soon became a place of pilgrimage attributed with miraculous powers and attracting pilgrims from as far afield as Shetland. When Kol of Agdir finally took over the earldom he built the cathedral in his uncle's honour, moving the centre of religious and secular power from Birsay to Kirkwall.

The first version of the cathedral, which was built using yellow stone from Eday and red stone from Mainland, was somewhat smaller than today's structure, which has been added to over the centuries, with a new east window in the thirteenth century, the extension of the nave in the fifteenth century and a new west window to mark the buildings 850th anniversary in 1987. Today the soft sandstone is badly eroded, particularly around the doorways, but it's still an immensely impressive building, its shape and style echoing the great cathedrals of Europe. Inside, the atmosphere is surprisingly intimate, the pink sandstone columns drawing you up to the exposed brickwork arches, while around the walls a series of gravestones and monuments include the bones of Magnus himself, a monument to the dead of HMS *Royal Oak* (which was torpedoed in Scapa Flow in 1939 with the loss of 833 men – see pp.401–2), the tomb of the arctic explorer John Rae, who was born in Stromness, and a collection of gravestones from the sixteenth and seventeenth centuries, inscribed with chilling carvings calling on the reader to "remember death waits us all, the hour none knows".

Alongside the church are the ruined remains of the **Bishop's Palace** (April–Sept Mon–Sat 9.30am–7.30pm, Sun 2–5pm). Built in the twelfth century for Bishop William of Old, the palace consisted of a main hall for ceremonial occasions and a tower which probably served as the bishop's private residence. The palace was rebuilt in the late fifteenth century and restored in the sixteenth, by Bishop Robert Reid, the founder of Edinburgh University. Today the walls and tower still stand, and a narrow spiral staircase takes you to the top for a good view of the cathedral and across Kirkwall's rooftops.

The neighbouring **Earl's Palace**, which dates from 1600, is rather better preserved, its style blending medieval fierceness with the ornate elements of French Renaissance architecture. With its dank dungeons, massive fireplaces and magnificent central hall, it is a much grander building than the Bishop's Palace and has an impressive solidity. Inside, a series of excellent displays analyse the uses of the various rooms, and it's easy enough to imagine the way in which the earl lived here and conducted his ruthless business. The roof is missing, but many domestic details remain, including a set of medieval toilets and the stone shelves used by the clerk to do his filing.

The turreted towers of the Earl's Palace echo those of the Victorian **Town Hall**, opposite the cathedral. Nearby, **Tankerness House** (May–Sept Mon–Sat 10.30am–12.30pm & 1.30–5pm, Sun 2–5pm, Oct–June Sun 2–5pm only; £1), a former home for the clergy that has been renovated countless times over the years, first in 1574 and most recently in the 1960s, houses the **Museum of Orkney History**, a simple but informative museum that takes takes you through Orkney history from the very beginning – well worth a look before you visit the main archeological sites. Amongst its collection, there are some unusual artefacts, including a collection of ba balls (used in a traditional Orkney street game, played every year on Christmas and New Year's days), Pictish board games, an Iron Age bone shovel and early bowls made from whales' vertebra. In addition, there are a couple of rooms which have been restored as they would have been in 1820, when the building was a private home, together with a space for temporary exhibitions. The **gardens** of Tankerness House (which can be entered either from the house itself or from a gate on Tankerness Lane) are open to the public, and on a warm summer afternoon they are thick with the buzz of bees and brilliant blooms.

Further afield (a mile or so south of the town centre on the Holm Road), but well worth the walk, is the **Highland Park** distillery, billed as "the most northerly legal distillery in Scotland". The distillery has been in operation for more than two hundred years, although it was closed during World War II, when it was used as a military food store and the huge vats served as communal baths. You can decide for yourself whether the taste still lingers by partaking of the regular guided tours of its beautiful old buildings and the customary free dram afterwards (Easter–Oct, Mon–Fri 10am–4pm; £2).

# Eating and drinking

Kirkwall offers a surprisingly international selection of **cafés and restaurants**, all within a few minutes of Albert Street, including Orkney's Chinese and Indian restaurants, as well as a US-style burger bar. Most of the food on offer is solid, cheap and uninspiring, with local fish disappointingly rare. Incidentally, if you're looking for the finest Orkney cuisine then you should know that the *Creel Restaurant* in St Margaret's Hope is probably the best in the islands (see p.403).

**Buster's Diner**, 1 Mounthoolie Place. American-style diner that serves rather average pizza, burgers, sandwiches and pancakes. Inexpensive.

**Chez Rejane**, Anchor Building, Bridge St. Kirkwall's only real alternative eating venue, serving delicious home-made wholemeal cakes and vegetarian meals. Closes at 6pm. Inexpensive.

**Empire Chinese Restaurant**, 51 Junction Rd. A poor second best to the Golden Dragon. Standard, inexpensive Chinese menu in a very bland setting, more a takeaway with seats than a restaurant.

**Golden Dragon**, 25a Bridge St. The better of Kirkwall's two Chinese restaurants, with good, standard fare, situated on the second floor behind the *Kirkwall Hotel*. Moderate.

**International Takeaway**, Bridge St. A reasonable alternative if all you want is a basic, stand-up lunch – international fast-food specialities such as fish and chips, burgers, etc.

**Kirkwall Hotel**, Harbour St. Harbour-front restaurant with a French-tinged menu that is as grand as the building. Moderately expensive.

**Mumataz Indian Restaurant**, 7 Bridge St. A welcome addition to Kirkwall's international eating possibilities, serving all that you'd expect from an Indian restaurant, as well as some solid British meals. Pretty reasonably priced too.

**Pomona Cafe**, Albert St. Orkney's most authentic greasy spoon cafe, little changed in the last 20 years, and serving tea, cakes, pies, sandwiches, toasties and simple meals in delightful surroundings.

**St Magnus Cafe**, Broad St. Opposite the cathedral, this is a simple community café serving tea, sandwiches, soups and simple meals. Closes early evening.

**Treanabies**, 16 Albert St. Easy-going restaurant serving a good breakfast, sandwiches, baked potatoes, pasta and pizza, and other inexpensive basic meals.

**West End Hotel**, Main St. Excellent and good-value bar meals – scampi, steak and the like.

# Listings

**Banks** There are branches of all the big Scottish banks on the main street.

**Bike rental** *Paterson's*, Tankerness Lane (☎0856/873097).

**Bookshops** *J M Stevenson*, at the corner of Bridge St and Albert St, or secondhand from 54 Junction Rd.

**Bus companies** *Causeway Coaches* (Kirkwall to St Margaret's Hope, ferry terminal; ☎0856/ 83444); *James D Pearce* (Kirkwall to Stromness; ☎0856/872866); *Rosie Coaches* (Kirkwall to Tingwall and Evie; ☎0856/75227).

**Car rental** *J&W Tail*, Sparrowhawk Rd (☎0856/872490); *Peace's,* Junction Rd (☎0856/ 872866); *W R Tullock*, Castle St (☎0856/874458).

**Currency exchange** In addition to the main banks, the tourist office in Broad Street runs an exchange service that is open daily 8am–8pm in the summer.

**Fishing tackle and diving equipment** *Eric Kemp*, 31–33 Bridge St (☎0856/872137).

**Golf** Kirkwall's golf club, an exposed course to the west of the town with good views of the bay, "welcomes visitors".

**Laundry** *Launderama*, Albert St (Mon–Fri 8.30am–5.30pm, Sat 9am–5.30pm).

Post office Junction Rd (Mon–Fri 9am–5pm, Sat 9.30–12.30am).
Travel agents *Pickfords*, 15 Broad St (☎0856/873734); *Ridgeway Travel*, 67 Albert St (☎0856/873359).

# Western Mainland

The great bulk of **Western Mainland** is Orkney's most fertile, productive ground, fringed by some spectacular coastline, and over the centuries it has played host to a succession of cultures, all of which have clearly left their mark, ranging from the prehistoric village of Skara Brae to the battered concrete huts which mark the remains of Twatt military airfield, a large RAF base in World War II.

Today this part of the island is still heavily farmed, although there are few real villages, with most of the farms and houses scattered across the land. There are still some areas, however, which are too barren to cultivate, and the high ground and wild coastline are protected by several interesting wildlife reserves, while a handful of small lochs offer superb trout fishing.

## Evie and the Broch of Gurness

Overshadowed by the great wind turbines on Burgar Hill, the little village of **EVIE**, on the north coast of Mainland, looks out across the turbulent waters of **Eynhallow Sound** towards the island of Rousay. At the western end of the white sands of Evie, the **Broch of Gurness** (April–Sept Mon–Sat 9.30am–6.30pm, Sun 11.30am–6.30pm; Oct–May Mon–Sat 9.30am–4.30pm, Sun 2–4.30pm; £2) is the best preserved of more than five hundred pre-Christian-era villages dotted across the islands – like the others built to a simple pattern, with a compact group of homes clustered around a central tower. The walls and partitions of the houses are astonishingly well preserved, as is the main tower, which was probably retreated to in times of attack, with its thick, fortified walls and independent water supply.

To the south of Evie, a small road climbs high over the shoulder of **Burgar Hill**, skirting along the side of the huge **RSPB Birsay Moors Reserve**, which embraces most of Burgar Hill and reaches down to the marshland and the shores of Lowrie's Water. The high heather-coated ground provides good hunting for kestrels, merlins and hen harriers, while the loch is used as a nesting site by red-throated divers. The moor is also a source of traditional fuel, and you can make out the areas in which peat is cut, with small stacks often drying on the hillside.

## Birsay: the Earl's Palace, Brough of Birsay and Kirbuster Farm Museum

The parish of **BIRSAY**, which stakes out the extreme western tip of Mainland, was the centre of Norse power in Orkney for several centuries, until the earls moved to Kirkwall following the construction of the cathedral. Today a tiny cluster of homes is gathered around the ruins of the **Earl's Palace** at Birsay, which was built in 1574 at the back of a beautiful little bay. The crumbling walls and turrets retain plenty of their grandeur, although there is little remaining evidence of domestic detail. When it was occupied, the palace was surrounded by flower and herb gardens, a bowling green and archery butts. By comparison, the smaller Earl's Palace in Kirkwall seems fairly humble.

Just over half a mile northwest of the palace is the **Brough of Birsay**, a small Pictish settlement on a tidal island that can be reached during the two hours each side of high tide. Don't get stranded, unless you plan to camp, in which case make sure you're well provided for. The focus of the village was the twelfth-century **St Peter's Church**, the shape of which is mapped out by the remains of its walls.

Two miles east of Birsay, at **KIRBUSTER** (between the Loch of Hundland and the Loch of Bardhouse), the **Kirbuster Farm Museum** (March–Oct daily 10.30am–12.30pm & 1.30–5pm, Sun 2–5pm) is worth a short detour, offering a fairly interesting insight to the hardships of life on an Orkney croft in the last century, when open peat fires filled the rooms with smoke and roofs were protected with heather thatch. Housed in a traditional old structure, with cold stone floors, blackened cooking pots over the fire and fish fillets drying in the smoke, the display is arranged to show the dramatic improvements in croft life which took place last century; one room has bare stone walls and a fire in the centre of the room, while the other has wallpaper and a fireplace.

## Skara Brae

A few miles south of Birsay, the beautiful white curve of the **Bay of Skaill** provides a sheltered break in the cliffs that is home to **Skara Brae** (April–Sept Mon–Sat 9.30am–6.30pm, Sun 11.30am–6.30pm, Oct–May Mon–Sat 9.30am–4.30pm, Sun 2–4.30pm; £2), the remains of a small fishing and farming village that was inhabited between 3000 and 2500 BC and rediscovered in 1850 after a fierce storm by the laird of Skaill (whose massive seventeenth-century home, now converted into self-catering flats, is set a little way behind the bay).

The village is very well preserved, its houses, many of which still stand, huddled together and connected by narrow passages which would have been covered over with turf. For centuries it was buried in the dunes, which protected an astonishing array of domestic detail, including dressers, fireplaces, beds and boxes, all carefully put together from slabs of stone. Archeologists have discovered two distinct types of house: an earlier, smaller structure, built around a central hearth, with beds built into the wall; and larger, later homes that have the beds in the main living area with cupboards behind them. Other evidence shows that the inhabitants were settled farmers eating sheep, cattle and grain, as well as fish and shellfish, and using lamps fuelled by the oil from whales, seals and sea birds.

## Maes Howe, the Stones of Stenness and the Ring of Brodgar

The main road leads back towards Kirkwall via the village of **DOUNBY**, a quiet, former market town, and skirts the shores of Loch Harray (Orkney's most famous trout loch), to reach the great neolithic burial chamber of **Maes Howe** (April–Sept Mon–Sat 9.30am–6.30pm, Sun 11.30am–6.30pm; Oct–May Mon–Sat 9.30am–4.30pm, Sun 2–4.30pm; £2). The chamber occupies a central position on Mainland and is proof-positive of the ingenuity of prehistoric communities in Orkney. It dates from 2750 BC, and is astonishingly well preserved, thanks partly to the massive slabs of sandstone it was constructed from, the largest of which weighs over three tons. The central chamber is reached down a long stone passage and contains three cells built into the walls, each of which was plugged with an enormous stone. When the tomb was opened in 1861, it was found to be virtually empty, thanks to the work of generations of graverobbers, who had only left behind a handful of human bones. It is known for certain that the Vikings broke in here in the twelfth century, probably on their way to the crusades, because they left behind large amounts of graffiti. These runic inscriptions, cut into the walls of the main chamber and still clearly visible today, have a wonderful spontaneity, with phrases such as "Many a beautiful woman has stooped in here, however pompous she might be" and "These runes were carved by the man most skilled in runes in the entire western ocean."

The area surrounding Maes Howe was a religious centre for Orkney's Stone Age inhabitants, and there are a number of remains dating back to that era, the closest of which, the **Stones of Stenness**, lie just over a mile to the west of Maes Howe – the remains of a circle of twelve rock slabs, the tallest of which is over 16ft high. Less than half a mile from these, the **Ring of Brodgar** is a nearly complete ring of 27 stones, beautifully sited on a narrow spit of land between two lochs.

## West Mainland practicalities

The best alternative to Kirkwall as a base for the western Mainland is the village of **Dounby** and the *Smithfield Hotel* right on the main village crossroads (☎0856/77215; ②), a friendly, family establishment with bar and restaurant. Out at Birsay, the *Barony Hotel* (☎0856/72372; ②) is an excellent fishing hotel on the north shore of the Loch of Boardhouse. Alternatively you could try the *Merkister Hotel* (☎0856/77515; ②), at the northern end of Loch Harray off the A968, another good hotel with a bent towards fishing. Among the **B&Bs**, in Birsay you might try *Links House* (☎0856/76221; ①); in Evie *Woodwick House* (☎0856/75330; ①); and in Dounby there's *Dounby House* (☎0856/77535; ①).

If you're just passing through in search of somewhere to rest your weary feet and get a bite to eat, the *Smithfield Hotel* in Dounby, and the *Dale Kitchen* in Evie, are both cosy places, with delicious cakes, soups and sandwiches and warming peat fires. For something more substantial, try the restaurant at Tormiston Mill beside Maes Howe.

# Stromness

*The Orkney I was born into was a place
Where there was no great distinction between
the ordinary and the fabulous; the lives of
living men turned into legend.*
            Edwin Muir

Orkney's great harbour town, **STROMNESS** is perhaps more than anywhere else in the islands the historical heart of the islands. It was here, in the shelter of Hamnavoe, or Haven Bay, on the edge of the great natural harbour of Scapa Flow, that ships from all around the world came and went, sweeping the town into a series of booms, unloading a cargo of sea tales and embarking hundreds of Orcadians on weird and wonderful expeditions.

French and Spanish ships sheltered in Hamnavoe as early as the sixteenth century, and for a long time European conflicts made it safer for ships heading across the Atlantic to travel around the top of Scotland rather than through the English Channel, many of whom called in to Stromness to take on food, water and crew. Crews from Stromness were also hired for herring and whaling expeditions for which the town was an important centre. By 1842 the town was a tough and busy harbour, with some forty or so pubs and reports of "outrageous and turbulent proceedings of seamen and others who frequent the harbour." The herring boom brought hundreds of small boats to the town, along with thousands of young women who gutted and pickled the fish before they were packed in barrels, and by the end of the nineteenth century, this, coupled with the naval significance of the location, had made Stromness into an important harbour town – something it remains, serving as Orkney's main ferry terminal and as the headquarters of the Northern Lighthouse Board.

## Arrival, information and accommodation

However you **arrive**, you'll have no trouble finding your way around as there's really only one street, although it does change its name several times, starting in the north as John Street, and finishing up as South End in the south, with several variations in between. The **tourist office** (Mon–Sat 8am–8pm, 6pm Thurs, Sun 9am–4pm; ☎0856/850716) is in the ferry terminal building on John Street, a couple of minutes' walk away.

Among **places to stay**, the town's first-ever hotel, the *Stromness Hotel*, Victoria St (☎0856/850610; ②), is the most imposing building in town, although it's a touch shabbby inside these days. Other options include the *Royal Hotel* (☎0856/850342; ②) and the *Oakleigh Hotel* (☎0856/850447; ②), two fairly dour hotels situated opposite each other on Victoria St. Perhaps the most attractive location is *Brae's Hotel* (☎0865/850495; ①), on a hill above the southern end of town.

**B&Bs** are plentiful, including the *Ferry Inn* (☎0856/ 850280; ①), *Plainstones*, 130 Victoria St (☎0856/850225; ①), and a handful of others – the tourist office has details. If you'd rather stay outside town, try *Brettobeck Farm* in Kirbister (☎0856/ 850 373; ①), just under four miles north of the town, just off the A967, or *Stenigar*, on the Ness Road at the southern end of Stromness (☎0856/850438; ①).

Stromness also has an official **youth hostel**, on Helly Hole Rd (March–Oct; ☎0856/850589; Grade 2), signposted from the car park outside the *Stromness Hotel*, but it's fairly strictly run, with a curfew and single-sex dorms. Alternatively there's *Brown's Hostel*, 45–47 Victoria St (☎ 0856/850661), an independent youth hostel with bunk beds in shared rooms and kitchen facilities; it's also open all day, and there's no curfew.

## The Town

Clustered along the shoreline, Stromness is a tight network of alleyways and slate roofs, crowded onto the lower slopes of **Brinkie's Brae**, which looms up from the harbour front. The single main street, paved with great flagstones and called various names, among them John Street and Victoria Street, winds along behind the waterfront, from which narrow alleys meander up the hill. Originally all of the waterfront houses had their own piers, from which merchants would trade with passing ships; the **cannon** at the southern end of town (on South End) was fired to announce the arrival of a ship from the Hudson's Bay Company. Today the trade in American rice and Canadian fur has moved on, but the site of the cannon still gives magnificent views of the harbour, and there are a number of reminders of the town's trading heyday. **The Wharehouse**, now home to the *P&O* and tourist offices, was originally built in the 1760s to store American rice, while at the southern end of town, on the Ness Road, **The Doubles** is a large pair of houses on a raised platform that were built as a home by Mrs Christian Robertson with the proceeds of her shipping agency, which sent as many as eight hundred men on whaling expeditions in one year.

For a more systematic account of the town's past, the **Stromness Museum**, off the main street at the southern end of town (Mon–Sat 10.30am–5pm; 80p), houses a collection of salty artefacts gathered from shipwrecks and arctic expeditions, including crockery from the German fleet, beaver fur hats, Cree Indian cloth and part of the torpedo that sunk the HMS *Royal Oak*. Further south, on the main street, is **Login's Well**, a famous watering-point for passing ships – now closed but marked by a plaque commemorating the great expeditions that took their water here. The **Pier Arts Centre**, right on the waterfront, (Sept–May Mon–Sat 10.30am–12.30pm & 1.30–5pm), gives a more contemporary account of Orkney life, home to the agent of the Hudson's Bay Company in the nineteenth century, and now restored to become an important focus of artistic life in the islands. It has regular exhibitions, often featuring painting and sculpture by local artists.

## Eating and drinking

Like any harbour town, Stromness is a good place to **eat and drink**, with plenty of options scattered around the small town centre. The *Ferry Inn* on John Street, beside the tourist office, is a small but popular restaurant, serving good, solid meals of fish, steak and scampi – nothing fancy but the food is good and filling, and inexpensive. *The Coffee Shop*, on the north side of the car park, behind the *Ferry Inn*, is a friendly little café which offers enormous breakfasts, lunches, sandwiches, vegetarian dishes, afternoon tea, cakes and pies – though it closes at 5pm, as does the *Peedie Coffee Shop* on Victoria Street, the town's oldest establishment.

More expensively, the *Hamnavoe Restaurant* at 35 Graham Place (☎0856/850606) is perhaps Stromness' smartest, making full use of local produce including shellfish, fish and beef, and some delicious vegetarian dishes, all served up at very moderate prices. *The Cafe*, on Victoria Street in front of the *Stromness Hotel* on the south side of the car park, with a good harbourside location, is a less pricy option for dinner, serving simple, inexpensive meals of burgers, pizza, pasta and sandwiches. The *Valhala Restaurant*, in the bar of the *Stromness Hotel*, serves a solid but uninspiring menu, including steak, spaghetti and haddock.

## Listings

**Banks** There are branches of the *Bank of Scotland* and *Royal Bank of Scotland* on the main street.

**Bike rental** *Brown's Hostel*, 45 Victoria St (☎0856/850661).

**Car rental** *Brass's Self Drive*, Pierhead Office, John St (☎0856/850750).

**Laundry** Behind the *Ferry Inn*, next to the coffee shop on the north side of the car park (Mon–Sat 9am–5pm).

**Post office** Victoria St (Mon–Fri 9am–1pm & 2–5.15pm, Sat 9am–12.30pm).

**Shopping** For food, the *Argo's Bakery* on Victoria Street, has a wide range of the basics and their own excellent bread and biscuits, while *Foodoodles*, also on Victoria Street, is a delicatessen offering cheeses, salamis and made-to-order sandwiches. For fishing tackle and advice head for *WS Sinclair*, just above the car park on John Street. For books, *JL Broom*, *John Rae*, or *Scapa* secondhand bookshop, are all on the main street.

# Eastern Mainland and South Ronaldsay

Southeast from Kirkwall, a narrow spur of Mainland juts out into the North Sea and is joined, thanks to the ambitious Churchill barriers, to the smaller islands of Burray and South Ronaldsay. The land here is densely populated and heavily farmed, but there are several interesting fishing villages and a scattering of unusual historical relics.

## Eastern Mainland

At its eastern edge, the landscape of Mainland, at least of the northern shore, breaks up into a series of exposed peninsulas, the first of which, **Rerwick Head**, is marked by the remains of World War II gun emplacements; **Mull Head** – the furthest east – is an **RSPB reserve** with a large colony of sea birds, including arctic terns, that swoop on unwanted visitors, screeching threateningly. The reserve is open to visitors at all times (although without your own transport it is hard to reach). There is a car park at the end of the road (a continuation of the B9050), which is about half a mile from the cliffs. A mile and a half south of the reserve, and a short walk from the car park, is **The Gloup**, an impressive collapsed sea cave: the tide still flows in and out through a natural arch making the strange gurgling noises that some say give the cave its name; others claim that it stems from the Old Norse *gluppa*, "a chasm".

On the south coast, just east of the village of **ST MARY'S**, is the **Norwood Museum** (May–Sept only; £2), a collection of antiques that is the life's work of 81-year-old Norrie Wood, a local stonemason who started collecting antiques at the age of thirteen. Only about half of the collection is on display, but it's a fascinating and eccentric selection of bits and pieces from around the world, including pottery, painting, medals, furniture, cutlery, clocks, even a narwhale's tusk, all housed in a grand Orkney home. Sadly Norrie Wood is now blind, but his daughter-in-law, Cilla, gives excellent guided tours of the house.

## The Churchill barriers

The presence of the huge naval base in **Scapa Flow** during both world wars presented a very tempting target to the Germans, and protecting the fleet was always a nagging problem for the Allies. During World War I, blockships were sunk to guard the eastern approaches, but in October 1939, just weeks after the outbreak of World War II, a German U-boat managed to manoeuvre past the blockships and torpedo the battleship HMS *Royal Oak*, which sank with the loss of 833 lives. (The U-boat captain claimed to have acquired local knowledge while fishing in the islands before the war.)

Today the wreck of the *Royal Oak*, marked by an orange buoy off the **Gaitnip Cliffs** (on the west coast of the west Mainland, just off the A961 between Kirkwall and St Mary's), is an official war grave. Its sinking convinced the First Lord of the Admirality, Winston Churchill, that Scapa Flow needed better protection, and in 1940 work began on a series of **barriers** to seal the waters between the mainland and the string of islands to the south – the tiny uninhabited **Lamb Holm** and **Glimpse Holm**, and the larger **Burray** and **South Ronaldsay**. Special camps were built to accommodate the 1700 men involved in the project; their numbers were boosted by the surrender of Italy in 1942, when Italian prisoners of war were sent to work here. Besides the barriers, which are an astonishing feat of engineering when you bear in mind the strength of Orkney tides, the Italians also left behind the beautiful **Italian Chapel** on Lamb Holm. This, the so-called "miracle of Camp 60", must be one of the greatest adaptations ever, made from two Nissen huts, concrete, barbed wire and parts of a rusting blockship. The chapel deteriorated after the departure of the Italians, but its principal architect, Domenico Chiocchetti, returned in 1960 to restore the building, and today it is beautifully preserved and Mass is said regularly.

## South Ronaldsay

At the southern end of the barrier is **South Ronaldsay**, a low-lying island, heavily populated and intensely farmed. The island has a number of old fishing villages, of which the first, **ST MARGARET'S HOPE**, takes its name from Margaret, the maid of Norway, who died here in November 1290 while on her way to marry Edward II – then Prince Edward. Margaret had already been proclaimed the queen of Scotland, and the marriage was intended to unify the two countries. Today St Margaret's Hope is a lovely little gathering of houses at the back of a sheltered bay, and it makes an excellent base from which to explore the area. The village has two small museums. The **Wireless Museum**, on the entrance road (April–Sept daily 10am–7pm), is a small private collection of communications equipment from the war, which has some fairly obscure exhibits including a picture of naval women dancing in costumes made from balloon fabric. The village **Smithy** has also been turned into a museum, with a few exhibits relating to this now defunct business.

Despite the fact that it is heavily cultivated, South Ronaldsay also offers some excellent walking, particularly out on the **Howe of Hoxa**, where there is a small broch and a beach at the **Sands O'Right** – the scene of an annual ploughing match in August, in which local boys compete with miniature hand-held ploughs. Further south, seals and their pups can be seen in the autumn in **Wind Wick Bay**, and there is an ancient chambered burial cairn, known as the **Tomb of the Eagles**, at the southeastern corner of the island, where human remains were found alongside eagles' bones. Finally you reach **BURWICK**, where a passenger ferry connects South Ronaldsay with the Scottish mainland at John O' Groats.

## Practicalities

**Getting to and from South Ronaldsay** isn't easy without your own transport. There are four daily buses (40min) between Kirkwall and St Margaret's Hope, and all ferries arriving at Burwick are met by buses from Kirkwall. However, off the main road you'll have to rely on walking and hitching.

The best **base** for exploring the Eastern Mainland and South Ronaldsay area is without question St Margaret's Hope, and the *Murray Arms Hotel*, a restored village inn (☎0856/83205; ②). There is also somewhat upmarket B&B accommodation at *The Creel*, on Front Street (☎0856/83311; ③), home also to a fine restaurant (see below), and *The Anchorage*, right on the seafront (☎0856/83456; ①). Simpler and cheaper are *Blanster House*, a friendly family home on the main road just south of the village (☎0856/83549; ①), or *Windbreck*, a modern house to the west of the village (☎0856/83370; ①). For really cheap accommodation, head for the *Hiker's Hostel* (no phone) in **HERSTON**, a tiny village at the western edge of the island on the south side of Widewall Bay.

When it comes to **eating**, bar meals are available at the *Commodore Hotel* just east of St Mary's village. In St Margaret's Hope, good meals are on offer at the *Murray Arms Hotel*, while *The Coach House* next door is a good café selling meals, home-made cakes and fine cups of tea. *The Creel Restaurant* in St Margaret's Hope (see p.395) is perhaps the best restaurant in the Orkneys – it has been showered in awards and serves superb local seafood and meat at moderate to expensive prices.

# Hoy

**Hoy**, Orkney's second largest island, rises sharply out of the sea to the southwest of Mainland – perhaps the least typical of the islands but certainly the most dramatic, its north and west sides made up of great glacial valleys and mountainous moorland rising to the 1500-foot-high mass of Ward Hill and the enormous seacliffs of St John's Head. This part of the island, though a huge expanse, is virtually uninhabited, with the remains of one small village, Rackwick, nestling dramatically in a bay between the cliffs; and most of Hoy's six hundred or so residents live on the eastern shore of the island, a narrow strip of fertile land that is home to the scattered villages of Lyness and Longhope.

## Around the island

Much of Hoy's magnificent landscape is embraced by the **RSPB North Hoy Reserve** (which covers most of the northwest end of the island), in which the rough grasses and heather harbour a cluster of arctic plants and a healthy population of mountain hares, as well as merlins, kestrels and peregrine falcons, while the more sheltered valleys are nesting sites for snipe and arctic skua. The best access to the reserve is from the single-track road which follows the **White Glen** across the island to Rackwick. Along the way, the road passes the **Dwarfie Stane**, an unusual solid-stone tomb which dates from 3000 to 2000 BC. A couple of miles further on, the road passes the end of a large open valley which cuts away to the north and along which a footpath runs to the village of **HOY** at the island's northwest tip. On the western side of this valley is the narrow gulley of **Berriedale**, which supports Britain's most northerly native woodland, a huddle of birch, hazel and honeysuckle.

The main road across Hoy reaches the sea at the tiny hamlet of **RACKWICK** on the west coast of the island, a humble scattering of crofts which boldly face the Atlantic weather, flanked by towering sandstone cliffs. Rackwick's crofting community went into a steady decline in the middle of this century: its school closed in 1954 and the last fishing boat put to sea in 1963, after which three of the four-man crew were too old to take on the Atlantic surf. These days many of the houses have been renovated as holiday homes and the savage exposure of the place has provided inspiration to a number of artists and writers, including Orkney's George Mackay Brown, who wrote that "when Rackwick weeps, its grief is long and forlorn and utterly desolate." A small **museum** (open all times), beside the walkers' hostel (see p.405), tells a little of Rackwick's rough history, and the croft of **Burnmouth Cottage**, just behind the beach, which has been traditionally restored to provide accommodation to walkers, gives a good idea of how things used to be.

The cliffs at Hoy's western end are some of the highest in the country, and provide ideal rocky ledges for the nests of thousands of sea birds, including guillemots, kittiwakes, razorbills, puffins and shags. During the nesting season they are alive with noise and activity. Standing just offshore is the **Old Man of Hoy**, reachable by footpath (4 miles) from Rackwick, a great sandstone column some 450ft high, perched on an old lava flow which protects it from the erosive power of the sea. The Old Man is a popular challenge for rock climbers, and a 1966 ascent was the first televised climb in Britain.

On the opposite side of Hoy, along the sheltered **eastern shore**, the high moorland gives way to a gentler environment which is similar to that of the other islands. Hoy marks the western boundary of **Scapa Flow** and during both world wars it played an important role in its defence, with several substantial gun emplacements along its eastern shore. At **LYNESS**, which was the main naval base, the naval cemetery is surrounded by the scattered **remains** of hundreds of concrete structures, which served as hangers and storehouses during the war, and some of which are now used as barns and cowsheds. Among these are the remains of what was – incredibly – the largest cinema in Europe. Perhaps the most unusual of the remaining buildings is the concrete facade of the old *Garrison Theatre*, on the main road to the south of Lyness, formerly the grand front-end of a huge Nissen hut, which housed the theatre but disappeared long ago. The old pump station, which stands beside the new Lyness ferry terminal, has been turned into a **Visitors Centre** (Mon–Fri 9am–4pm, Sat & Sun 10.30am–3.30pm; £1) – basically a local museum displaying an interesting collection of pictures and photographs showing how busy the area was during the wars, as well as an assortment of wartime bits and pieces, including torpedoes, flags, guns, propellers and a paratrooper's folding bicycle.

Further south still, the secure waters of **North Bay** cut a deep inlet, a narrow spit of sand connecting north Hoy with **South Walls**, a fertile peninsula which is more densely populated. The bay itself is ringed with farms and homes and on its south side is the quiet little village of **LONGHOPE**. There is also evidence of early conflict here, with two **Martello towers** that mark the island's southeastern outcrops of Hackness and Crockness, as well as the **Hackness battery**, built between 1813 and 1815 to guard against American privateers during the Napoleonic wars. The eastern tip of the island looks out over treacherous waters and is marked by the **Cantick Head Lighthouse**, while the churchyard at **OSMUNDWALL** contains a monument to the crew of the Longhope lifeboat who died in 1969 when their boat overturned in strong gales on its way to the aid of a Liberian freighter. The entire eight-man crew were killed, leaving seven widows and ten orphans.

## Practicalities

Two **ferry services** run to Hoy: a simple, summer-only, passenger service from Stromness harbour to the village of Hoy at the northwest edge of the island (Mon–Fri 4 daily), and a roll-on roll-off car ferry from Houton on Mainland to Lyness and Longhope on Hoy (6 daily).

If you're planning to **stay over** in Hoy, and with time it does make more sense than visiting on a day trip, good B&Bs include *Stonequoy Far*, Lyness (☎0856/79234; ①), *Burnhouse Farm*, Longhope (☎0856/70263; ①), and *Glebelands*, Longhope (☎0856/70245; ①). More upscale, though not greatly more expensive, there's the *Royal Hotel*, on the main road in Longhope (☎0856/70276; ①), once the favoured hangout of the likes of King George V and the Prince of Wales in 1945, and little changed since then. The island also has three **walkers' hostels**: the *Hoy Outdoor Centre*, just up from the pier in the village of Hoy (☎0856/873535; mid-May to mid-Sept), which offers comfortable dorm accommodation; the *Rackwick Outdoor Centre* in Rackwick (☎0856/873535), which has bunk beds with blankets but no sheets, and a kitchen; and, also in Rackwick, down on the shore, the beautiful *Burnmouth Cottage* (always open; free), an old restored croft that is open to walkers. There's no electricity or bedding, but there is a fireplace and plenty of driftwood.

For **sustenance**, try the new pub in the village of Hoy, down by the post office, and in Lyness you can get food and drink at the *Anchor Bar*. There are shops in Hoy, Lyness and Longhope. Food is also available from the café in the Lyness visitors centre, which is the best place for a warming bowl of soup.

# The Northern Isles

Scattered loosely off the northwestern side of Mainland, Orkney's **Northern Isles** are swept by fierce wind, tide and weather. Their spidery form is a product of this battering, and their stark beauty is based on a simple combination of rock and sand. All of the islands, except North Ronaldsay, can be visited as day trips from Kirkwall, using the excellent ferry service.

## Shapinsay

Just a few miles northwest of Kirkwall, **Shapinsay** is the most accessible – and most systematically developed – of the northern isles. The Balfour family, who had made a small fortune in India, constructed their Baronial castle here in the 1850s, by extending an eighteenth-century farmhouse. They also reformed the island's agricultural system and built **BALFOUR** village to house workers on the estate, a neat and disciplined development with a row of identical cottages. **Balfour Castle** is a mile or so from the centre of the village, hidden among the trees, although you should be able to see it from the ferry as you come in. Though somewhat smaller than many of the Highland castles, it is still an imposing building, a strange mix of architectural styles, bristling with extensions, towers and turrets. If you want to see inside, **tours** are organized on Wednesday and Sunday afternoons by the tourist office in Kirkwall and must be booked in advance.

Elsewhere the island is heavily cultivated, although there are some nice walks along the shoreline to stretches of sand at the **Bay of Furrowend** in the east and the great sweep of **Veantrow Bay** in the north, which opens out towards the islands of Eday and Westray. (Both are a couple of miles from the ferry terminal.) There is also a **goat farm** at East Lairo (daily except Thurs 12.15–3pm; £1.50 per party; ☎0856/71271, call to arrange transport from ferry), where you can meet a herd of prizewinning goats and sample their milk, cheese and yoghurt.

### Practicalities

Just thirty minutes from Kirkwall by ferry, Shapinsay is an easy day trip, but if you'd prefer to stay for a while, **B&B** is available at *Grinigoe* (☎0856/71256; ①), up in the northwest corner of the island. If you're just here for the day, the tea and sandwiches available at the *Smithy Café* in Balfour village are your best bet for lunch.

# Rousay, Egilsay and Wyre

Just over half a mile away from Mainland's northern shore, the island of **Rousay** is dominated by high, heather-covered moorland. It's one of the most interesting of the smaller isles, home to a number of intriguing archeological sites, as well as being one of the more accessible. There are no villages or settlements to speak of, but a single road runs around the edge of the island, connecting a string of small farms and providing an excellent circuit either on a bicycle or by car. In any case it's easy enough to reach the main points of interest on foot from the ferry terminal in the southeast corner of the island.

Only the coastal fringes of the island are cultivated, and the central section is dominated by a cluster of rolling hills, the highest of which is the 750-foot-high **Blotchnie Field**. This high ground offers good hillwalking, with superb panoramic views of the islands, as well as excellent birdwatching: a sizeable section of moorland at the southern end of the island (a short walk from the ferry terminal) is a protected area in the **RSPB Trumland Reserve**. Here you may well catch a glimpse of merlins, hen harriers, peregrine falcons and red-throated divers, although the latter are more widespread just outside the reserve on one of the island's three lochs, which also offer good trout fishing. The north and western sides of Rousay are guarded by two sets of steep cliffs, separated by the sands of **Saviskaill Bay**, and again provide spectacular walks and good birdwatching, with puffins, gulls, kittiwakes and arctic terns all nesting here in the summer.

The southern side of Rousay is home to the bulk of the island's archeological remains, strung out along the shores of the turbulent waters of the **Eynhallow Sound**, which runs between the island and the Mainland. Of these the furthest from the ferry terminal (about 6 miles) is the **Midhowe Cairn**, known as "the great ship of death", a well-preserved communal burial chamber, dating from the third century BC and measuring more than 98ft in length. The central chamber, which is like a stone corridor, is partitioned with slabs of rock, with twelve compartments on each side. Archeologists discovered the remains of 25 people inside the tomb, generally in a crouched position with their backs to the wall. Other smaller tombs are scattered along this coast, including the unusual **Taversoe Tuick** (just off the road a mile or so west of the ferry terminal), a two-storey circular structure with two entrances.

A couple of hundred yards south of the Midhowe Cairn is the **Midhowe Broch**, the well-preserved remains of a fortified Iron Age village which date from the first century AD, and the best preserved of the six brochs that have been found along this shore. It's also thought to be one of the earliest brochs in the Orkneys, with a compact layout that suggests it was a fortified family house rather than a village.

There is evidence of more recent occupation at the **Knowe of Swandro** (on the shore about a mile south of Midhowe), where archeologists have unearthed the remains of a Norse farmstead of the eleventh or twelfth century, although there isn't much to see today. A variety of artefacts have been found here, including bone remains from which scientists were able to roughly determine the diet of the average person at the time – a rather unhealthy, vegetable-free mixture of seal, grouse, sea birds, whales, otters and deer. Nearby lies **The Wirk**, the remains of a grand ceremonial hall from the thirteenth or fourteenth century, and the abandoned **St Mary's Church** (on the coast a mile south of Midhowe), which dates from the sixteenth century but was abandoned in 1820, when the island was suffering rapid depopulation.

Despite its long history of settlement, Rousay is today home to little more than two hundred people, as this was one of the few parts of Orkney to suffer Highland-style clearances. General Traill Burroughs, who owned the island and built **Trumland House** here in 1873 (in the trees above the ferry terminal), decided that he preferred sheep to people and built a wall to keep the two apart, driving the crofters onto the narrow shoreline. The poet Edwin Muir, who was brought up on the neighbouring island of Wyre, described the move in the poem, *The Return*.

> *Their eyes knew every stone*
> *In the huge heartbreaking wall*
> *Year after year grown*
> *Till there was nothing at all*
> *But an alley steep and small,*
> *Tramped earth and towering stone....*

## Egilsay and Wyre

Sheltering close to the eastern shore of Rousay are two low-lying smaller islands, each of which contains some interesting historical remains and both of which are visited by the Rousay ferry as it passses – providing someone has asked the captain to stop. The larger of the pair, **Egilsay**, is dominated by the ruins of the **St Magnus Church**, built on a prominent position in the middle of the island in the twelfth century, probably on the site of a much earlier version. The church, now missing its roof, is the only surviving example of the traditional round-towered churches of Orkney and Shetland and was built as a shrine to the saint who was murdered here in 1115 – a **cenotaph** marks the spot, about a quarter of a mile southwest of the church. Over on **Wyre** are the remains of **Cubbie Roo's Castle**, a twelfth-century Viking stronghold, and the neighbouring **St Mary's Chapel**, a ruined twelfth-century church, of which only a single wall remains.

## Practicalities

Rousay makes a good day trip from Mainland with regular ferry sailings (from Tingwall) and bus connections to and from Kirkwall. Some ferry sailings call in at Egilsay and Wyre, but in most cases they only do so if someone specifically asks to be dropped off there – to arrange this, and to make sure that they come back for you later, call the ferry terminal in Tingwall (☎0856/75360).

On Rousay itself the best place to eat is the *Pier Restaurant*, right beside the ferry terminal at the southeastern tip of the island and serving good food and coffee; if you phone in advance, they will pack you a delicious picnic of crab, cheese, fruit and bannock bread. In the evenings, the restaurant functions as the island's principle pub. The only **hotel** on the island is the *Tavasoe Hotel*, a couple of miles west of the ferry terminal at Frotoft, (☎0856/82325; ②), a modern building added onto an old croft. The hotel has a restaurant, which caters for vegetarians, and a bar. **B&B** is available at *Maybank* (3 miles west of the ferry terminal, ☎0856/82225; ①), while *Trumland Farm* (a mile or so west of the ferry teminal, ☎0856/82252; ①) has a three-bed self-catering cottage to rent. You can rent bikes from *Helga's*, Rousay, behind the *Pier Restaurant* at the ferry terminal (☎0856/82293).

# Eday

Similar in many ways to Rousay and Hoy, the smaller island of **Eday** is dominated by a great block of heather-covered upland, with farmland confined to a narrow strip of coastal ground. Oddly enough, the island is a net exporter of raw materials: peat cut on the high ground is sent to the other northern isles for fuel, and yellow sandstone quarried from the island was used to build the St Magnus Cathedral in Kirkwall.

The island is very sparsely inhabited, and the nearest approximation to a village is the small gathering of houses at **CALFSOUND** in the north, which has the island's only pub. Unless you arrive by plane and touch down at London airport (right in the middle of the island), you'll probably come ashore at the ferry terminal in **BACKALAND**, at the island's southern tip. The southern end of the island offers some great walking, both on the high ground of **Ward Hill** and **Flaughton Hill** and along the jagged western shoreline to the sheltered curve of the **Sands of Mussetter**. However, the most dramatic cliffs are to be found in the far north (6 miles from the ferry terminal) at **Red Head**, which also gives great views of the other islands and of the uninhabited **Calf of Eday** – itself home to some massive bird colonies.

The northern end of the island is also the focus of Eday's archeological heritage. The best way to explore this part of the island is to follow the signposted **Eday Heritage Walk**, which starts at the **Eday Community Centre** on the main road in **HAMMARHILL** (where there is a shop and a display explaining the island's history). The walk, covering around five miles and taking about three hours, follows the road up the north side of **Mill Loch** to the **Stone of Setter**, Orkney's most spectacular standing stone, around 15ft high and occupying a focal point in the landscape. From here, you can climb the Vinquoy Hill to reach the finest of Eday's chambered cairns, the **Vinquoy Chambered Cairn**, which has been partially restored and has a similar structure to that of the Maes Howe tomb on Mainland, with large blocks of stone supporting the inside walls and four tomb chambers set into them. From here you can either head back to the shop or continue north to the dramatic cliffs of **Red Head** and then walk around the coast to **Carrick House** (June–Aug Tues & Thurs; for times call ☎0857/2260), the grandest home on the islands, built by the laird of Eday in 1633 and once the prison of the pirate John Gow, whose ship *The Revenge* ran aground on the island. Gow had sent four heavily armed men to demand assistance at the scene of the wreck, but they were lured into the island's pub and overpowered while drinking. Gow and his crew were subsequently sent to London and hanged in 1729.

## Practicalities

Eday's ferry terminal is at **Backaland pier** in the south, making it fairly inconvenient for visiting the more interesting northern section of the island, although if you haven't got your own transport you should find it fairly easy to get a lift with someone on the ferry.

B&B **accommodation** is available at *Skaill Farm*, a traditional farmhouse just south of the airport (☎0857/2271, closed April & May; ①), *Greentoft* on the eastern side of Ward Hill in the south (☎0857/2269; ①) and self-catering at *Carpaquoy* (☎0857/2262). The **hotel** just north of London airport is run by *Eday Community Enterprises* (☎0857/2248; ①), who also operate a youth hostel and café (Sun lunch noon–2pm). You can rent bikes from *Millbank* (☎0857/2205) near the post office.

# Stronsay

A three-pronged shape to the southeast of Eday, **Stronsay** is a beautiful, low-lying island that for a long time lived off its herring and kelp industries; indeed at one time, at the end of the eighteenth century, the kelp business employed some three thousand people on the island, and during the 1880s Whitehall harbour was one of the main Scottish centres for the curing of herring caught by French, Dutch and Scottish boats, with three hundred boats working out of the port. By the 1930s, however, the herring stocks had been severely depleted and the industry began a long decline.

Today Stronsay supports a sizeable population of farmers, and boasts some interesting bird and plant life and a scattering of vague archeological remains. The only village is **WHITEHALL**, made up of a couple of rows of small fishermen's cottages, and blessed with a hotel and pub. Unless you arrive by plane (at the airstrip at the northern end of the island), it's from here that you'll set out to explore. Stronsay has few real sights, but like all of these northern isles it offers some fantastic walking. The low-lying central land is almost entirely given over to farming and it's on the coast that you'll see the island at its best, where the cliffs are home to several sea bird colonies and seals bask on exposed rocks at low tide. On the island's western arm there are two broad, arching beaches, the **Bay of Holland** and **St Catherine's Bay**, while over in the east there's a small bird reserve on the shores of **Mill Bay**, just south of Whitehall. Birdwatching is at its best here in September and October, when easterly winds bring migrants such as thrushes, warblers, flycatchers and wrynecks.

## Practicalities

Stronsay is served by a twice-daily ferry service to Whitehall. The island has one very welcoming **hotel**, *The Stronsay Hotel* (☎0857/6213; ①), on the quayside in Whitehall; the bar here serves simple meals. For ornithologists, the *Stronsay Bird Reserve* (☎0857/363) offers full board (②), bed and breakfast (①) or camping on the shores of Mill Bay. B&B is also available at *Clifton House* (☎0857/378; ①) and Airy (☎0857/231; ①). You can **rent cars** (from DS Peace, ☎0857/335) or **boats** (from J Stevenson, ☎0857/341).

# Sanday

As its name suggests, **Sanday** is the most insubstantial of the Northern Isles, a great drifting dune strung out between several rocky points. The island's tight bays and clean white sands are the finest in Orkney, and in dry, clear weather it's a superb place to spend a day or two.

The island has a long history as a shipping hazard, with hundreds of wrecks smashed against its shores, although the construction of the **Start Point Lighthouse** in 1807, on the island's exposed eastern tip, has reduced the risk for seafarers. Today the islanders survive largely from farming and fishing, supplemented by a small knitting business, based at Wool Hall in Lady Village and a rabbit farm at Breckan, which specializes in the production of Angora wool.

The shoreline supports a healthy seal and otter population, and behind the beaches are stretches of beautiful open grassland, thick with wild flowers during the spring and summer. The entire coastline presents the opportunity for superb walks, with tight, sand-filled bays protected by jaggy outcrops of rock. Two good landmarks to head for are the **Start Point Lighthouse**, right out at the island's eastern tip a good seven miles from the ferry terminal, and the chambered cairn at **Quoyness** (on the peninsula to the east of the ferry terminal – about a mile), which dates from the third millennium BC. The main chamber is 13ft long and holds six small cells, which contained bones and skulls.

### Practicalities

**Ferries** to Sanday arrive in **KETTLETOFT**, a little gathering of houses which is the nearest thing to a village; the **airfield** is just north of here. **Accommodation** is available at *The Belsair Hotel* (☎0857/5206; ①). Car, caravan and trout-fishing boat **rental** is available from Mrs Main (☎0857/5331).

# Westray and Papa Westray

A pair of exposed islands on the western side of the group, **Westray** and **Papa Westray** bear the full brunt of the Atlantic weather. The southern end of **Westray**, where ferries put in, is relatively gentle, while at the northern end the island rises more sharply, forming dramatic cliffs. Whether or not you're a birdwatching enthusiast, the cliffs of **Houp Head** are very dramatic indeed, particularly when a good westerly swell is up, packed with nesting sea birds during the summer months. The open ground above the cliffs, which is grazed by sheep, is superb maritime heath and grassland, carpeted with yellow, white and purple flowers.

Westray has a fairly stable population of seven hundred or so, producing superb beef, scallops, shellfish and a large catch of whitefish, with its own small fish-processing factory. The main village is **PIEROWALL** in the north, where there's a handful of impressive ruins, including the seventeeth-century **Notland Castle**, which stands just inland of the village, and the medieval parish church of **St Mary's** (on the northern side of the village), both of which can be visited at all times.

Across the short Papa Sound, the neighbouring island and former medieval pilgrimage centre of **Papa Westray** is connected to Westray by the world's shortest scheduled flight – two minutes in duration, less with a following wind. Try and stroll out to the **Knap of Howar**, on the western shore, a Neolithic farm building from around 3500 BC that makes a fair claim to being the oldest standing house in Europe, and the remains of **St Boniface's Church**, dating from the twelfth century. On the northern tip of the island there's yet another **RSPB reserve** which plays host to one of the largest arctic tern colonies in Europe, as well as arctic skuas, razor bills and guillemots.

## Practicalities

If you're **staying in Westray**, the *Pierowall Hotel* (☎0857/7208; ①), on the seafront in Pierowall, is a typical northern isle hotel – simple, informal, but extremely welcoming, and something of a centre of island social life. A touch more upmarket is the *Cleaton House Hotel*, on the main road a few miles south of Pierowall (☎0857/7508; ②), which also has a bar and restaurant. **B&B** accommodation is available at *Sand O'Gill* (☎0856/7374; ①), or at *Bonni Min* (☎0857/7436; ①). On **Papa Westray**, the island's community runs a self-catering youth hostel at *Belthane House* (no phone; ①) and can arrange B&B on some farms (☎0857/4267).

Back on Westray, you can rent **bicycles** from *Sand O'Gill* (☎0856/7374) and if you'd like to play Westray's eccentric **golf course**, just behind Pierowall, clubs can be hired from *Tulloch* general store.

# North Ronaldsay

Isolated by the treacherous waters of the North Ronaldsay Firth, **North Ronaldsay**, Orkney's most northerly island, has a unique outpost atmosphere, brought about by its extreme isolation. Measuring just three miles by one and rising only 66ft above sea level, the island is almost overwhelmed by the enormity of the sky, the strength of wind, and of course the ferocity of the sea – so much so that its very existence seems an act of tenacious defiance.

Despite these adverse conditions, North Ronaldsay has been inhabited for centuries. Today the population is mostly over sixty, but the island is still heavily farmed, the land dotted with old-style crofts, their roofs made from huge flagstones. With no natural harbours and precious little farmland, the islanders have been forced to make the most of what they have and seaweed has played an important role in the local economy. During the eighteenth century kelp was gathered here, burnt in pits and sent south for use in the chemicals industry. The island's sheep, which are a unique breed, tough and goat-like, feed mostly on seaweed, giving their flesh a dark tone and a rich, gamey taste. A drystone **dyke** running around the edge of the island keeps them off the farmland, although some argue that the dyke isn't there to keep the sheep out but to keep the people in. During the clipping and dipping season the islanders herd the sheep into stone "punds" in what is one of the last acts of communal farming practised in Orkney.

The largest buildings on the island are **Holland House**, which was built by the Traill family who bought the island in 1727, and the **lighthouse**, which towers over 125ft in height, and is the only feature which really interrupts the horizon. If you'd like to visit the lighthouse, give the keeper a call (☎0857/3225).

Grey and common **seals** are common on the island and it serves as an important stopping off point for **migratory birds** passing through on their way to and from breeding grounds in Iceland, Greenland and Scandinavia. The peak times of year for migrants are from late March to early June and from mid-August to early November, although there are also many breeding species which spend the spring and summer here, including gulls, terns, waders and cormorants.

## Practicalities

The *North Ronaldsay Bird Observatory*, at Twingness Croft on the southwest tip of the island (☎0857/3267; ①), was established in 1987 by adapting a croft to wind and solar power. It offers full board **accommodation** with a packed lunch, either in dormitories or private rooms. **B&B** accommodation is available at *Garso*, in the northeast (☎0857/3244; ①), or at *Roadside* (☎08573221; ①), both of which have self-catering cottages. *Garso* also operates a car rental and taxi service. **Camping** is possible, but you must ask the permission of landowners. You can rent **bicycles** from *Airfield Goods and Services* (☎0857/3220), by the airfield in the west of the island.

# SHETLAND

Scattered across the ocean, and stuck away in a box on most maps, the **Shetland Isles** are Britain's most remote and northerly corner – closer to Bergen in Norway than to Edinburgh, let alone London. Exposed to all the ferocity of the elements, they are a very different place indeed to Orkney: the land is tough and barren, rising steeply from the sea in a jagged pattern of complex cliffs, sea caves and stacks. The sea cuts into the island at every opportunity, with narrow inlets, similar to Norwegian fjords, while the land itself rises swiftly to high, rocky ground, coated in a thin layer of heather and rough grass, that offers little shelter for potential farmland. The bulk of the population is scattered along the shore, relying on the sea for their livelihood.

The weather is as wild as you'd expect, with severe winds and heavy rainfall, although during summer the sun barely sets and the sky is always illuminated by the "summer dim" a translucent night light. In winter, conversely, there are only a very few hours of daylight. To alleviate the depression that can sink in during these months, the Shetlanders stage the "Up-Helly-Aa", a festival on the last Tuesday in January – a huge and very drunken affair, during which a model of a Viking longship is burnt (see below).

Surprisingly, perhaps, the islands have been inhabited since prehistoric times. There is considerable evidence of Bronze and Iron Age occupation and of Pictish settlers, all of whom left their mark on the place, including some very well preserved brochs and the remains of stone-built villages. In medieval times Shetland was linked at various times with Orkney, Faroe and Norway, and was attacked, invaded and ruled by all three, although for the most part the islands were part of the Norwegian state. With the decline of Norwegian rule came the Scots, who acquired Shetland as part of a dowry paid by King Christian of Norway to finance his daughter's marriage. The Scottish earls gradually imposed themselves on the islands, building some impressive castles, until finally, with the Act of Union in 1707, the Shetlands became part of Britain.

Today the islands are still linked to the wider North Sea community, indeed in the summer there are as many visitors from Scandinavia as Britain. Fishing and oil are the main industries, both conducted on a heavy, industrial scale that has created something of a boom in Lerwick and left much of the harbour scarred by rapid construction work – although the islands have benefitted accordingly. It's this blend of the traditional and the modern which makes Shetland such an intriguing destination: astonishingly up-to-date in some ways, but also a world of its own, utterly dependent on its own resources.

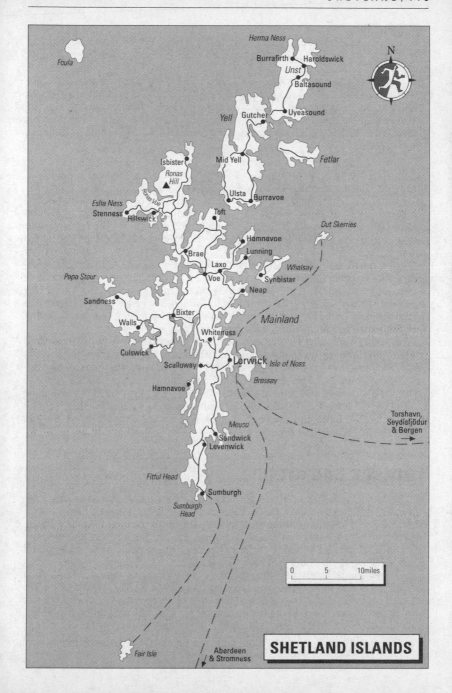

SHETLAND ISLANDS

## Where to go

Whatever else you do in Shetland you're sure to be based, at least for a day or two, in **Lerwick**, the only town of any size and the hub of all transport and communications. The town has a certain industrial energy to it, thanks to the presence of the oil industry, but is also a pleasant fishing port with a fair selection of shops, pubs, hotels and restaurants. From here you can visit large parts of Shetland with ease in less than a day. Across on the west coast is the old capital of **Scalloway**, where the ruins of Scalloway Castle look out on a busy, modern fishing town, while to the east are the islands of **Bressay** and **Noss**, the latter a superb RSPB reserve which is home to thousands of gannets and puffins during the summer months.

To the **south** of Lerwick, a narrow finger of land runs some twenty miles to **Sumburgh Head**; here the land is relatively hospitable and the landscape is scattered with historical remains, including the Iron Age **Mousa Broch** and the ancient community of **Jarlshof**, where there is evidence of continuous habitation for some three thousand years. The south also contains two striking natural features: the RSPB reserve of **Spiggie Loch**, which is home to waders, ducks and swans, and **St Ninian's Isle,** connected to the mainland by a spit of fine, white sand.

To the **north** and **west** the mainland is bleaker and more sparsely inhabited, although the scenery, particularly to the west, opens out in scale and grandeur as it comes face to face with the Atlantic. Among the most dramatic areas are **Esha Ness** and **Ronas Hill**. Further north still, the northern isles of **Yell**, **Unst** and **Fetlar** reach up into the North Sea, populated by small fishing communities that feel dominated by the hostility of the environment.

The empty landscape of Shetland supports an impressive array of birds and wildlife and there is excellent **walking** and **birdwatching** throughout the islands, with RSPB reserves on most of the islands, but particularly on the remote western isles of **Foula** and **Fair Isle**, both of which support a unique culture and way of life. The waters in and around the islands also present excellent opportunities for **fishing**. The voes and lochs of Shetland were once famous for their salmon and sea trout fishing, and although stocks of these are now declining, the hill lochs are still packed with superb brown trout.

# Lerwick and around

For Shetlanders, there's only one place to shop, meet and do business and that's "da toon", **LERWICK**. Very much the focus of life in the islands, Lerwick, like Shetland itself, is a place dominated by the sea, owing its very existence to the superb natural anchorage of **Bressay Sound**. During the summer months, the harbour is always busy with freighters, ferries, factory ships and trawlers, and sprawled along the harbour front are a series of rough, industrial areas, all undergoing rapid transition as they struggle to meet the changing needs of the fishing and oil industries. Away from the seafront, Lerwick is a small provincial centre and market town, with a population of just over seven thousand, almost a third of Shetlanders, and a single shopping street that shuffles with activity on Saturdays. Little has changed here in the last hundred years, and the centre of town still has a compact, stone-built solidity, dominated by strong Victorian architecture, with narrow alleyways climbing the hill behind.

Lerwick began life as a fishing town, catering to the Dutch herring fleet in the sixteenth and seventeenth centuries, which brought as many as twenty thousand men into town, giving it a reputation for "great abomination and wickedness". By the beginning of the nineteenth century, with the addition of Scottish fleets, it was a major centre for fishing, whaling, trading and smuggling, crowded with trading posts, known as lodberries, each with its own pier, and said to be riddled with secret tunnels and illicit storehouses. In 1839 a visitor from Faroe declared "everything made me feel that I had come to the land of opulence." Most of the increasingly squalid lodberries were swept away in the late nineteenth century, and, although you can still see some of the old waterfront buildings to the south of the *Queen's Hotel*, the original Victorian harbour is now only used by private yachts and pleasure boats – the real heavy industry having established several new docks to the north. Nevertheless the large houses and grand public buildings established by the Victorians still dominate, including the two grand hotels, the impressive town hall and the Anderson High School.

# Arrival, information and accommodation

**Arriving** in Lerwick is a fairly straightforward business: the town is small enough to be easily understood and everything is within walking distance. Arriving **by ferry** you'll come ashore at the *P&O* ferry terminal at the northern end of town, about a mile and a half from the town centre. If you arrive **by plane**, you will land at Sumburgh Airport on the southern tip of the island – about twenty miles from Lerwick, to which it's connected by a regular bus. Arriving **by bus** in Lerwick, you'll come into town along Church Road and stop at Market Cross behind the old harbour, the very centre of town, before going on to the **bus station** on Commercial Road, half a mile to the north.

The **tourist office**, centrally situated at Market Cross on Commercial Street, (Mon–Sat 8am–6pm; ☎0595/3434), is a good source of current information, and, for a £1 fee, staff will book your **accommodation**, which is sometimes in short supply during the summer months. They will always know what the situation is, and should be able to track down the very last vacant bed, although you'd be well advised to book somewhere in advance during peak times.

There are lots of good **B&Bs** so there's really no excuse for being caught short. Of a fair number of decent places, try *Woosung*, 43 St Olaf St (☎0595/3687; ①), *Mrs Mona Tulloch*, 50 St Olaf St (☎0595/2468; ①), or *Mrs Goudie*, 78 King Harald St (☎0595/2384; ①).

**Campers** should head for the *Clickimin Caravan and Camp Site*, Lochside, (mid-April to Sept; ☎0595/4555) – a new camp site next to a leisure centre and with plenty of facilities, including good hot showers and a laundry.

## Hotels

**Glen Orchy House**, 20 Knab Rd (☎0595/2031). A guest house that's almost a hotel – licensed, with excellent home cooking. ②.

**Grand Hotel**, middle of Commercial St (☎0595/2826). An old Victorian-style building in the centre of town, recently modernized, and boasting its own nightclub "Posers". Not as grand as the name implies. ⑤.

**Queens Hotel**, south end of Commercial St (☎0595/2826). Lerwick's finest shoreside hotel in a beautiful old building with comfortable accommodation and a good restaurant. ⑤.

**Shetland Hotel**, Holmsgarth Rd (☎0595/5155). An ugly monster behind the ferry terminal, favoured by oil workers and package tourists, but its modern rooms have all the trimmings and it boasts a swimming pool. ⑥.

**Carradale Guest House**, 36 King Harald St (☎0595/5411). Large, comfortable family home, with evening meals available – another upper range B&B. ①.

**Knysna Guest House**, 6 Burgh Rd (☎0595/4865). Comfortable and centrally located, with residents' kitchen, really an upmarket B&B. ①.

# The Town

Lerwick is firmly focused on **Commercial Street**, which still runs through the core of the old town and is the main shopping street. Until the middle of the nineteenth century the street hugged the shoreline, and the alleyways dropped down to the sea, but since then the sea has been pushed back to make way for harbour improvements.

At its south end, Commercial Street passes beneath the solid walls of **Fort Charlotte** (June–Sept daily 9am–10pm; Oct–May daily 9am–4pm; free), built in 1665 to protect the harbour during the war with the Dutch. The fort was reconstructed in the 1780s and again in the late nineteenth century, and today is home to the Territorial Army. The building is also open to the public, and its solid battlements give great views across the harbour.

Up above Commercial Street, right on top of the hill, stands the grand Victorian **Town Hall** (Mon–Fri 10am–noon & 2–3.30pm; free), a magnificent building with stained-glass windows and superb stone carvings that blends the grandeur of a Gothic castle with the stern reverence of a church – a classic Victorian public building. Across the road, the **Shetland Library and Museum** (Mon, Thurs & Fri 10am–7pm, Tues, Wed & Sat 10am–5pm; free) houses an interesting range of Shetland artefacts relating to the islands' archeology and in particular to the heroic struggle of the fishing industry. Some exhibits demonstrate superb local eccentricity, including a stone carving by Adam Christie (1869–1950), a Shetlander who is perhaps best known for his application to patent a submarine made from glass so that it couldn't be seen by the enemy.

Finally, Lerwick still likes to bask in its Viking heritage, and every January the town holds a spectacular and wildly drunken fire festival, the Up-Helly-Aa, complete with fantastic costumes and the torching of a model Viking ship – worth catching if you can brave the weather. The boat is constructed in a workshop on St Sunniva Street and during the summer months hosts the **Up-Helly-Aa Exhibition** (May–Sept Tues & Sat 2–4pm, Fri 7–9pm; £1), which includes a model longship and a collection of photographs of previous festivals.

## Eating and drinking

Despite its distant location, Lerwick has a surprising selection of ethnic restaurants, including two Indian restaurants and a Norwegian café. However, there is little really good food here, and the superb local seafood usually comes wrapped in batter.

**The Candlestick Maker**, 33 Commercial Rd. Lerwick's most international menu, with pizzas, burgers, seafood and steaks. Moderately priced.

**Central Bakery**, 124 Commercial St. Small café inside the bakery, serving soup, sandwiches, pies and cakes. Good for lunch – it closes at 4pm.

**Grand Hotel**, Commercial St, beside Market Cross. Standard bar meals featuring inexpensive scampi, fish and chips and the like, and a somewhat smarter restaurant offering local beef and seafood.

**Havly Centre**, 9 Charlotte St. A Norwegian Christian centre catering to both fishermen and tourists. Friendly and very comfortable, and not at all evangelical, serving coffee, sandwiches, cakes and soups.

**D&G Leslie**, upstairs in the Ellesmere Stores, Market Cross, Esplanade. This central café is always alive with the buzz of video games and the cries of small children, serving cheap sandwiches, pies and baked potatoes. Closes at 8pm, 6pm at weekends.

**Noost Restaurant**, 86 Commercial St. Simple, cheap meals – fish and chips, lasagne and shepherd's pie, though unfortunately it closes at 5pm.

**Puffins**, Mounthooly St. A simple, inexpensive café serving sandwiches and home-baked cakes – strictly no smoking. Closed Sun, and it closes at 4.30pm normally, though is open until 7pm in summer.

**Queens Hotel**, south end of Commercial St. Relatively elaborate and tasty bar meals and a good restaurant serving local seafood, meat and vegetarian dishes.

**Raba Indian Restaurant**, 26 Commercial Rd. Excellent, small Indian restaurant, more popular than its larger rival a couple of blocks to the north. Open late by Lerwick standards. Inexpensive/moderate.

**The Skipidock Inn**, Toll Clock Shopping Centre, North Rd. Fast food-style bar meals in the modern, soulless setting of a small shopping centre.

## Listings

**Banks** The big banks all have branches on Commercial Street.

**Bike rental** Available at *Puffins*, on Mounthooly Street (Mon–Sat 9am–4.45pm; ☎0595/5065), and *Eric Brown*, 68 Commercial St (Mon–Sat 9am–5pm, closed Wed; ☎0595/3733).

**Car rental** *Bolts Car Hire*, 26 North Rd (☎0595/2855); *John Leask & Sons,* Esplanade (☎0595/3162); *Star Rent-A-Car*, 22 Commercial Rd( ☎0595/2075) – all of which have offices at the airport.

**Fishing Tackle** *Rod and Line*, 91 Harbour St (☎0595/5055).

**Laundry** *Lerwick Laundry*, 36 Market St (☎0595/3043).

**Post office** On Commercial St (Mon–Fri 9am–1pm & 2–5.15pm, Sat 9am–2.30pm).

**Travel agent** *John Leask,* Esplanade (☎0595/3162).

## Around Lerwick

Lerwick is an ideal place to base yourself for a few days; the surrounding countryside is very beautiful, and there are a number of good day trips that you can make from here, or if you just want to take an evening stroll then walk out to the headland of **South Ness**, which gives wonderful views of Bressay Sound.

### Clickimin Broch

To the west, about a mile from the town centre, Lerwick is bordered by the **Loch of Clickimin**, which was the site of a substantial settlement for a thousand years or so around the time of Christ. Perched on an outcrop in the middle of the loch is the solid stone tower of the **Clickimin Broch** (always open; free), which began life around 700 BC as a small farmstead and was later enclosed by a defensive stone wall. The main tower served as a defensive castle and probably rose to a height of around 50ft, although today it is reduced to about 10ft, and has two small entrances, one at ground level and the other on the first floor, all carefully protected by outer defences and smaller walls. The broch was originally sited on a small island and reached by an artificial causeway but the water-level has fluctuated over the years and was lowered in the nineteenth century. Today it is possible to walk here on dry land, although the waters of the loch surround it on three sides, adding to its magical atmosphere.

Archeologists working on the site have unearthed an interesting array of domestic goods that suggest the inhabitants were engaged in international trade, including a Roman glass bowl, thought to have been made in Alexandria around 100 AD.

## The Böd of Grimista

In earlier times the seasonal nature of the Shetland fishing industry meant that the summer months were the time to do business, and from the fifteenth century onwards Hanseatic traders from Bremen, Hamburg, Gdansk and other Baltic ports built trading posts in the islands, known as böds, which they opened during the season. The merchants traded directly with the fishermen, exchanging luxuries such as tobacco and alchohol for herring, mackerel, haddock and cod.

Established rather late in the day, the **Böd of Grimista,** about a mile and a half north of the centre of Lerwick, along the Holmsgarth Road (June–Aug Wed–Sun 9am–1pm & 2–5pm; £1), dates from the eighteenth century, and is now surrounded by oil-rig service stations. The building has been completely restored, even down to the wooden storm shutters. The ground floor was originally used as an office and fish-curing station, while the trader and his family lived upstairs. This particular böd was also the birthplace of Arthur Anderson, a merchant seaman who became Shetland's first member of parliament and one of the founders of the *P&O* shipping company.

## Bressay and Noss

Shielding Lerwick from the full force of the North Sea is the low-lying fertile island of **Bressay**, reachable by way of an hourly ferry from Lerwick harbour (from the ferry point just north of the old Victoria pier). In its heyday Bressay had a population of more than a thousand, and was renowned for producing the best milk and butter in Shetland, as well as being a breeding stud for Shetland ponies, which were sent south to work in the mines. Today the island is a big, bare lump, with some high hills and cliffs to the south, which offer good walking, although nothing to rival Noss.

Just off Bressay's western shore, the smaller uninhabited island of **Noss**, home to an enormous colony of sea birds, was declared a national nature reserve in 1955 and is today owned by Scottish Natural Heritage who operate an inflatable dinghy ferry service from Bressay (May 15–Aug 26 daily 10am–5pm; £1 return) – wait at the dock and they'll come and pick you up, although in bad weather you should check with the tourist board that the service is running. Noss is an excellent day trip from Lerwick: you can walk around the island in a couple of hours, climbing high onto the top of the **Noup of Noss**, a massive 500-foot seacliff which faces out into the North Sea. During the spring and early summer the cliffs are packed with gannets, puffins, guillemots, shags, razorbills and fulmars, while the central moorland provides nest sites for skuas, who appear to have absolutely no fear of humans and aggressively dive-bomb any unwanted intruders.

# Scalloway and the West Mainland

The small town of **SCALLOWAY**, just over six miles from Lerwick, is Shetland's Atlantic gateway, facing into the oncoming storms and backed by a ring of steep hills. The town is dominated by the imposing ruins of **Scalloway Castle**, built in 1600 by the Scottish earl, Patrick Stewart, using forced labour, and designed by Andrew Crawford, who was also responsible for the earl's Palace in Kirkwall on Orkney. Scalloway has always been an active fishing post, and, although now somewhat overshadowed by Lerwick, there are still large quantities of cod, haddock and whiting landed here, and the town is now home to the **North Atlantic Fisheries College**, a large modern building which stands on a point overlooking the harbour. Scalloway also has its own small **museum** (May–Sept Tues, Wed, Fri & Sun 10am–1pm & 2–5pm; free), with various displays relating the town's history, including an excellent account of the so-called "Shetland Bus", which ferried people and equipment to and from the Norwegian resistance during World War II.

## The West Mainland

Jutting out into the Atlantic, the **western arm of the Mainland** is almost cut off by several deep, fjord-like voes, forcing you to skirt their shores and climb the steep-sided ridges which separate them. At its heart, the West Mainland is a low-lying outcrop, scattered with hundreds of tiny lochs and rising finally to **Sandness Hill** (750ft) before it plunges into the Atlantic. This dramatic craggy cliffscape is superb for walking, but not so good for living and it's an isolated area, most of the crofts gathered along the southern shore of the Mainland. The only real village is **WALLS**, clustered around a small natural harbour. It has a small, local **museum** (mid-May to mid-Sept Wed, Fri & Sun 1–6pm; free), with an interesting and eclectic gathering of local finds, the fruits of an original schoolboy's collection, along with an exhibition of Shetland knitting.

## Papa Stour

A couple of miles off the Mainland lies the little island of **Papa Stour**, which still supports a population of some 32, having staged a dramatic recovery since 1970 when the island's school closed and all sixteen inhabitants were past childbearing age. Amazingly, the island supported more than three hundred people in the early nineteenth century, and in early times it is thought to have been home to both a Christian community and a leper colony. Following the 1970 population crisis, it became known as the "Hippy Isle" after a number of young British incomers in search of peace and solitude settled here. A hardy handful stayed on and today the island's population is stable and its future seems secure.

The island is made up of a variety of volcanic rocks, with a wild coastline of high cliffs, stacks and superb sea caves. Desperate for farmland the inhabitants have "scalped" the eastern side of the island, dragging the soil onto its more sheltered western side, which is now very fertile. The *Shetland Islands Council* operates a **ferry** to Papa Stour from West Burrafirth five days a week during the summer, and on Friday and Saturday you can visit the island as a day trip, as there is a return ferry in the afternoon.

## Practicalities

There are only two **hotels** in the West Mainland: *Burrastow House* in Walls (☎0595/71307; ④), a fine old eighteenth-century house that offers bed, breakfast and an excellent dinner; and the *Westings Hotel*, a modern family-run hotel at Wormadale on the A971 (☎0595/84242; ②), with superb views across Whiteness Voe. There are, however, plenty of **B&Bs**, including *Effirth*, Bixter (☎0595/81204; ①); *Greenquoy*, Selivoe, Bridge of Walls (☎0595/81347; ①); *Hogan*, Bridge of Walls (☎0595/71375; ①), *Trouligarth*, Walls (☎0595/71373; ①) and *Grundale*, Kergord, Weisdale (☎0595/72298; ①). For really **cheap accommodation**, head for the *Böd of Nebister* in Whiteness, an old trading hut which has been converted to provide simple accommodation (April–Oct; ①) in an eight-bed dormitory – book through the tourist office in Lerwick.

When it comes to **eating**, most B&Bs do an evening meal as well as breakfast as the chances are you'll be a fair distance from the nearest pub. However, simple evening meals are available from the *Norseman's Inn* (☎0859/72304), Voehead, Weisdale and from *Burrastow House* (☎0859/71307) in Walls.

The sparsity of population can also make **getting around** fairly hard going if you do not have your own transport. From Lerwick there are hourly buses to Scalloway (20min), and a less frequent service to Walls (4 daily; 45min), Weisdale and Culswick (daily; 1hr 30min).

# Southern Mainland

**South of Lerwick** the mainland extends in a long, thin peninsula, never more than a few miles wide, which comes to an end at the jagged rocks of Sumburgh Head. It's a wild and beautiful area, rich in archeological interest, and has yielded some of Shetland's most impressive treasures. Heading south, the main road (A970) clings to the eastern side of the peninsula, hugging the contours and passing through several small, scattered settlements.

Off the eastern shore, the small island of **Mousa** is the home of Britain's best preserved broch – the **Broch of Mousa**. Together with a matching structure on Mainland, of which very little remains, this imposing tower, which has an internal staircase, guarded the Mousa Sound and has managed to defy the wind and rain for more than two thousand years. Today the broch is home only to a small colony of storm petrels, although in the eighteenth century there were eleven families living on Mousa, and the remains of a few other simple buildings still stand on the island, including a small water mill. There's also a small quarry, which provided the flagstones for the streets of Lerwick. During the summer, daily trips are run to Mousa from the nearby hamlet of **SANDWICK**, by Tom Jamieson (☎0950/5367).

Heading south from Sandwick, and crossing over onto the western side of the peninsula, lies another small islet, the spectacular **St Ninian's Isle**, which is linked to Mainland by a narrow sweep of white sand – a feature known locally as a "tombolo". The island is currently uninhabited, but there are the ruins of a twelfth-century church here, and in 1958 a hoard of Pictish silver was unearthed on the island by students from Aberdeen University. The silver was hidden in a larch box, and as larch didn't grow in Britain until the eighteenth century it's thought that the box must have originated in Europe.

Continuing south, the **Spiggie Loch RSPB Reserve** is a lovely stretch of reedy water, separated from the sea by a narrow spit of sand. The loch is home to several families of swans and is a popular bathing spot in the event of a warm summer's day.

Further south still, the land rises to the clifftops of **Fitful Head**, a jagged outcrop on which the Lithuanian oil tanker, **The Braer**, ran aground in a fierce storm on January 5, 1993, spilling some 83,000 tons of oil into the surrounding waters. The bow of the *Braer* still pokes out above the waves – best viewed from the small bay between Garth's Ness and Siggar Ness.

Back on the main road, there are signs to the **Croft House Museum** in **BODDAM** (June–Sept daily 10am–1pm & 2–5pm; £1), west of the main road about five miles north of Sumburgh airport. Here an old stone-built Shetland croft has been recreated with traditional furniture and household items, including spinning wheels, high-backed Shetland chairs, baskets woven from heather fibres and a Shetland fiddle.

South of Boddam, the main road arrives at **Sumburgh airport**, Shetland's most important airfield, and marking the southern tip of the island. The airfield is always busy with helicopters and aircraft shuttling to and from oil fields in the North Sea, and also serves as Shetland's main passenger airfield (only flights to Foula and Fair Isle use the Tingwall airfield, just north of Lerwick). To the west of the airfield, **Jarlshof** (May–Sept daily 9.30am–6.30pm; £2; in winter the grounds are open at all times) is one of Shetland's most important archeological sites, occupied for some three thousand years from Neolithic to Viking times and now extensively excavated. The remains are fairly sparse, but from them you can work out the floorplans of these ancient homes, ranging from the oval form of Bronze Age houses to a sixteenth-century hall.

## Practicalities

There are several excellent **hotels** in the South Mainland, including the small family-run *Barclay Arms Hotel* in Sandwick (☎0950/5226; ②), the modern *Swan Hotel* in Levenwick, on the A970, just south of its split with the B9122 (☎0950/2250; ②), and the *Sumburgh Hotel* (☎0950/60201; ③) – Shetland's equivalent of an airport Hilton, with an ugly extension tacked onto the old laird's house to accommodate all those extra oilmen – beside Jarlshof and the airport this is certainly the most convenient.

There are also plenty of **B&Bs** in Sandwick, including *Thistle Cottage* (☎0950/5513; ①), *Marelda* (☎0950/5379; ①) and *Solbrekke* (☎0950/5410; ①). Further south, B&B is available at *Columbine* (☎0950/60582), in the village of North Voe, just south of Boddam to the east of the main road, or at *Colsa* (☎0950/60503; ①) in the village of Scousburgh – over on the east coast on the B9122, a mile or so south of St Ninian's Isle. The **cheapest** accommodation in the area is at the *Cunningsburgh Community Club* (no phone), which operates as a **youth hostel** in the summer months, with dormitory beds, fine showers and a well-equipped kitchen – book through the tourist office in Lerwick.

Public **transport** in the South Mainland is relatively straightforward by Shetland standards. There are ten daily buses from Lerwick to Sumburgh airport (45min), and others that run from Lerwick to Sandwick (30min) and Sumburgh, via Bigton and the east coast, passing St Ninian's Isle and the Spiggie Loch.

# Northern Mainland

**North of Lerwick**, the bulk of the Mainland rises and rolls through a series of large open valleys – virtually uninhabited, with all the grandeur of the Scottish Highlands. There's very little out this way, and the main road pushes north across the open ground, occasionally dropping in on small coastal settlements.

## The Northwest: Sullom Voe, Esha Ness and Ronas Hill

The main road divides at the sheltered tip of the **Olna Firth**, where the village of **VOE**, a tight huddle of homes gathered on the shore, has a somewhat Scandinavian appearance, dominated by a brightly painted wooden building beside the pier – a link perhaps to the fact that the Norwegian Whaling Company was based here from 1904 to 1928.

From Voe the road heads north to **Booth of Toft**, the ferry terminal for the island of Yell (see p.424), while another branch cuts west to **BRAE**, a surprisingly large village which was hugely extended in the 1970s to accommodate the workforce for the expanding oil industry. Today it is still thriving, its fortunes very much linked to the nearby **Sullom Voe Terminal** – the largest of its kind in Europe. The longest voe in Shetland, Sullom Voe has always attracted the interest of outsiders in search of a deep-water harbour. During World War II it was home to the Norwegian airforce and an RAF seaplane base; and the oil industry moved in here in the mid-1970s when two one-hundred-mile pipelines were laid to connect the terminal with the Brent and Ninian oilfields. During the construction phase some seven thousand people worked at Sullom Voe, and the terminal now has the capacity to handle 69 million tons of oil a year, enough to meet nearly three-quarters of Britain's energy needs. Despite this, the terminal keeps very much to itself these days, its huge storage tanks now buried into the hillside, and there is little evidence of any activity apart from the constantly burning flares and the comings and goings of the massive supertankers.

From Brae, a spit of land extends west across the narrow slither of **Mavis Grind**, the point at which the North Sea is said to meet the Atlantic. Beyond this spit the peninsula fans out into an empty, jagged expanse, focused on the old fishing village of **HILLSWICK**, home to Shetland's oldest pub, *The Booth*, and to the *St Magnus Hotel*, a fine Victorian building which has lost a little of its atmosphere thanks to a recent refit (see p.423). Further west, the road comes to an end at **ESHA NESS**, a gnarled rocky point marked by a lighthouse and a small museum at the restored trading booth of **Tangwick Haa** (May–Dec Mon–Fri 1–5pm, Sat & Sun 11am–7pm), which tells the history of this remote corner and its role in the dangerous business of deep sea fishing. In the days when local men put to sea in small, open boats they would sell their catch at the Haa and buy supplies here before setting off again.

The most northerly section of the Mainland here is an exposed peninsula, strewn with granite boulders, on which little soil has managed to settle in the bitter winds. The land rises to the impressive, barren height of **Ronas Hill** – around 1500ft – from the top of which you can look back over the Mainland, north along the coast of Yell, or out into the daunting expanse of the Atlantic. This is certainly one of the most dramatic parts of Shetland, and climbing Ronas Hill is an exhausting but rewarding experience. To the south of Ronas Hill, the land drops away into the narrow, sheltered waters of **Ronas Voe**, while on the western side the power of the sea has created massive seacliffs and the beautiful arching shingle bay of **Lang Ayre**.

## The Northeast: Lunna Ness and Whalsay

The sheltered shores of the **Northeast Mainland** have always been relatively heavily populated, protected from the worst of the weather but with access to some of the finest fishing waters. However, nothing could protect the small boats from the ocean, and in December 1900, 22 fishermen from the area were lost in a single storm, known locally as the **Delting Disaster**.

The large Lunna estate, which occupies the narrow finger of land known as **Lunna Ness**, acted as a base for the "Shetland Bus" during World War II (see p.419). Today the headquarters of the operation, **Lunna House**, in the village of **VIDLIN**, a traditional manor house built in the late seventeenth century, is a guest house (see below). Also in Vidlin is the simple **Lunna Church**, which dates from 1753, but has been rebuilt a couple of times since then. A small hole in the building's outside wall is a "leper's hole", built so that they could listen to the service.

A couple of miles offshore, the island of **Whalsay** is one of Shetland's most successful fishing communities. For centuries the men of Whalsay have been putting to sea in search of whales, fish and shellfish. In the eighteenth and nineteenth centuries the island was a major centre for herring fishing, but when herring stocks declined the people of Whalsay were some of the first to adapt. Today the island remains a thriving and self-reliant fishing community, with some of the most modern fishing vessels in the Scottish fleet, as well as its own net manufacturer, salmon farm and fish-processing plant, making it one of the most wealthy parts of Shetland.

## Practicalities

Of Northern Mainland **hotels**, the _Busta House Hotel_, in Brae (☎0806/22506; ⑤), is a grand old estate house that offers luxurious accommodation, one of the best hotels in Shetland; the S*t Magnus Bay Hotel*, Hillswick (☎0806/23371; ③), is a historic Victorian establishment, if somewhat refurbished inside, and is an ideal base for exploring the wilder shores of the west Mainland. In the Northwest *Lunna House* in the village of Vidlin (☎0806/7237; ①) is an old laird's house converted into a guest house. The _Valleyfield Guest House_, Brae (☎0806/22563; ②), a modern bungalow just outside Brae, is a glorified, relatively luxurious B&B.

As for straight **B&Bs**, in Voe you'll find a welcome at *Hardanger* (☎0806/8357; ①), in Brae at *Vaddel* on Busta Road (☎0806/22407), and further west still in Esha Ness at *Braewick Cottage* (☎0806/623385; ①), just off the B9078 overlooking Brae Wick. On the east side, at the southern end of Lunna Ness in Lunning, there's *Skeo Green* (☎0806/7302; ①).

There are also a couple of good **youth hostels**: the _Voxter Centre_, on the shores of Voxter Voe, a couple of miles north of Brae, open to groups of six or more (☎0806/22417); and the _Sail Loft_ in the village of Voe, which has been converted to provide basic, budget accommodation – you need your own sleeping bag – book through the tourist office in Lerwick.

When it comes to **eating** in this part of the islands you'll find that all B&Bs offer an evening meal as well as breakfast; otherwise you'll have to eat at one of the hotels, although food is also available at the **pubs** in Brae and Hillswick.

# The Northern Isles: Yell, Fetlar and Unst

Stepping out into the wilds of the North Sea, the **Northern Isles** of Shetland are predictably exposed and windswept, with a wild, elemental beauty of their own. Amongst these rolling hills and craggy cliffs you'll find that people are welcoming and the landscape has a solid defiance, weathered by centuries of fierce storms. The islands are connected to each other and to the Mainland by a series of good ferries, while an occasional bus (one or two a day) links the small scattered settlements. Before setting out in this direction, however, you should plan well and book your accommodation, as there are few options.

## Yell

The largest of the three Northern Isles, **Yell** hasn't historically had good write-ups: the writer Eric Linklater described it as "dull and dark", while the Scottish historian Buchanan claimed it was "so uncouth a place that no creature can live therein, except such as are born there." It's certainly true that the rolling moors of Yell are exposed and featureless in comparison to the fertile glens and rocky crags of Unst and Fetlar, but the island does have some interesting corners. It is virtually split in two by a pair of narrow voes, which provide superb natural harbours – during World War II German submarines sheltered here with little danger of being discovered. On the northern side of of one of these voes, the Whale Firth, is the **Lumbister RSPB Reserve**, home to merlins and skuas. In spring and summer the reserve blooms with wild flowers and in a narrow gorge known as the **Daal of Lumbister**, there's a lush growth of honeysuckle, moss campion and wild thyme.

Yell is an important fishing centre with its own fleet operating from the largest village, **MID YELL**, sited on one of Yell's natural harbours. In earlier times much of the industry was based around the southern end of the island, and the island's oldest building, the **Haa of Brough**, built in 1672 (May–Sept Tues, Wed, Thurs & Sat 10am–4pm & Sun 2–5pm; free), was once a major trading post, with the old road passing through a pair of arches which separated the two halves of the building. Today the road has been moved and widened and half of the Haa has disappeared, while the other half is now a local **museum and café**, with an interesting collection of local bits and pieces relating to fishing, whaling and crofting, as well as some information on the island's fauna and flora.

These days much of the deep sea fishing activity has moved to the other end of the island, where ships call in to take on ice and diesel at the pier in **CULLIVOE** – to the north of Mid Yell and close to some of the island's most spectacular scenery. To the west of Cullivoe is the magnificent **Gloup**, a secretive, narrow sandy voe at the northern tip of the island, sheltered by steep cliffs. In the nineteenth century this was one of the largest fishing stations in the islands, and the fishermen here were famous for "their daring spirit and recklessness" – although even they were no match for the great storm of July 1881, which claimed six of their boats, and the lives of fifty-eight men. A **monument** overlooking the voe commemorates the dead with a sculpture of a woman and child looking out to sea.

# Fetlar

The most fertile of the Northern Isles, known in fact as the "Garden of Shetland", **Fetlar** is a lush green hunk of land, coated with wild flowers and playing host to an abundance of birdlife during the summer months, although the bulk is still covered in rough grass and heather. The island name derives from the Norwegian word for "fat land", and local people have suffered as a result of its repuation: in the early nineteenth century almost all the land belonged to two landowners, who cleared off the crofters to make way for sheep; a high wall was built across the island and the crofters given forty days to leave their land. As a result the lairds were able to build two impressive homes, one at **Brough Lodge**, a great Gothic sprawl with towers and battlements, and the other, **Leagarth House**, a more modest villa which had a fantastic walled garden and a large glass conservatory for exotic house plants. Today the island is still endangered by depopulation, with just under one hundred residents, and the community council has taken the brave step of advertising for incomers. The only settlement of any size is **HOUBIE**, where there is a small **Interpretative Centre** (May–Sept Thurs, Sat & Sun 2–5pm) which gives an insight into the island's history, and, if you're in need of refreshment, a **tearoom** at the post office.

The island also offers superb **birdwatching** and some wild, coastal scenery, particularly in the west and south of the island. Access to the north side is restricted as the area is a sensitive **RSPB reserve**; it was here, in 1967, that a pair of snowy owls bred for the first time in Britain. Over the next eight years the birds raised twenty chicks, although since then only females have been seen on the island. If you want to visit the reserve contact the warden on ☎0957/83246.

The island was also, incidentally, once home to white-tailed eagles, and a local tale tells that in the early years of the nineteenth century one of the birds stole a baby from a croft in Unst and carried it to its clifftop nest on Fetlar. A local man, Robert Nicolson, was lowered on a rope and retrieved the child, unharmed. Later in life, when the little girl had grown into a woman, the two met again and married – their descendants still live on Fetlar.

# Unst

The island of **Unst** has a population of around a thousand, although four hundred or so of these are service personnel who work on the RAF base here, staffing the radar and listening out for any uninvited intruders. The island's main village and only pub is at **BALTASOUND**, an important herring-fishing post around the turn of the century, and the remains of the curing stations can be seen on both sides of the voe. The island is scattered with other, older historical remains, including brochs, a standing stone, the solid walls of **Muness Castle** (a mile east of Uyeasound at the southeast corner of the island), which dates from 1598, and the twelfth-century **Kirk of Lund** – which overlooks the sandy bay of Lunda Wick in the southwest. The most dramatic scenery is down the isolated west side of the island and at its northern tip, and there are a number of beautiful sandy beaches, particularly **Skaw** and **Burrafirth** in the north, **Lunda Wick** in the southwest and **Sand Wick** in the southeast. There are also two **nature reserves**, one at **Hermaness**, where the steep cliffs provide nest sites for some 100,000 sea birds, including gannets, puffins and skuas (not to mention some spectacular views), and another at **Keen of Hamar**, which is home to a number of rare arctic plants.

Unst is home to Britain's most northerly pub and post office, but it does not, sadly, offer you the chance to be Britain's most northerly person – a privilege reserved for the three keepers of the **Muckle Flugga lighthouse**, a mile or so off the northern tip of the island. Beyond here is **Out Stack**, Britain's most northerly island.

## Practicalities in the Northern Isles

To get to the Northern Isles from Kirkwall you simply head north on the A968 to **Booth of Toft**, from where the ferry runs (hourly; 10min) to **Belmont** in the south of Yell. Buses from Kirkwall to Toft (1hr) run once or twice a day, crossing on the ferry and continuing north across **Yell**, then crossing another ferry to **Unst** and on to Burrafirth (3hr from Lerwick) in the far north. Between **Gutcher** in north Yell and **Belmont** in Unst another ferry shuttles back and forth (hourly; 10min) and there is a ferry (3–4 times daily; 30min) to Fetlar from Gutcher.

On **Yell**, **hotel accommodation** is available at the *North Isles Motel* at Sellafirth (☎0957/84294; ①), a rather unusual building that appears to be built from a series of portacabins; alternatively there's the *Pinewood Guest House* at South Aywick in east Yell (☎0957/2077; ②), a little ten-bed hotel with fine views of Fetlar and Unst. There are also a number of homes that offer **B&B**, including; *Hillhead*, Burravoe (☎0957/82274; ①), *Lumiere*, Ulsta (☎0957/82281; ①), *Glenlea*, Burravoe (☎0957/82317; ①) and *Crurafield House*, Mid Yell (☎ 0957/21332; ①).

On **Fetlar**, **B&B** is in short supply, only offered at *Gord* (☎0957/83227; ①). In **Unst** there are two **hotels**: the *Baltasound Hotel* (☎0957/81334; ③) and the *Clingera Guest House* (☎ 0957/81579; ①), both in the village of Baltasound. The only other options are **B&B** at *The Barns* in New-Gord (☎0957/85249; ①), or the independent **youth hostel** in Uyeasound (no phone; ①), which is excellent value and has a selection of rooms, hot showers, gas heating and a well-equipped kitchen.

# Fair Isle

Stuck out in the ocean, halfway between Orkney and Shetland, **Fair Isle** is in a world of its own. The north end of the island rises like a wall, with all the fertile ground concentrated in the south and east, where **The Haven** is the island's only safe harbour.

Fair Isle is perhaps most famous for its **birds**: the island provides a refuge for thousands of **migrating birds** and a temporary home to huge numbers of **nesting sea birds**, including skuas, terns, fulmars and puffins. Two important migratory routes converge on the island and over 340 species have been recorded here, taking a welcome break as they head to or from the Arctic. A team of ornithologists working at the **Fair Isle Bird Observatory** record, trap and ring the birds as they pass through.

Ownership of the island has shuttled between Shetland and Orkney over the years. It's said that the Orkneyman Stewart of Brough won the island in a game of cards in the 1770s, but it was returned to Shetland ownership a century later. Due to its bird populations, the island fell under the control of the NTS in 1954, and today has a population of around seventy – a tiny number, but at least up on the all-time low of just forty-four in the 1950s, when outright evacuation was seriously considered. Since then improvements have included the installation of a wind generator and the construction of a harbour to accommodate a regular ferry service.

The ferry from Lerwick arrives on the west side of the island near the bird observatory and although there's no village, as such, on the island, there is a noticeable gathering of houses at **STONYBRECK** in the south. Here a small **museum** in the **George Waterston Memorial Centre** gives an interesting insight into the island's history.

Fair Isle **knitting** is internationally renowned and is very different from traditional Shetland knitting. The designs date back to Viking times and the elaborate use of colour is traditionally linked to the wreck of a Spanish ship in 1588, from which all 465 people on board landed safely. The Spaniards are said to have introduced Moorish designs, although many of those credited to the Spaniards were, in fact, already in use. Today Fair Isle knitting is produced by a cooperative and there are knitting demonstrations in the community hall in Stonybreck.

## Practicalities

The *Shetland Islands Council* operate **ferry services** to Fair Isle from Sumburgh (May–Sept Tues, Sat & alternate Thurs; rest of year Tues only) and Lerwick (on specified dates every couple of weeks). Between April and October *Loganair* operate **flights** from Tingwall airport on Mainland (6 miles northwest of Lerwick) to Fair Isle on Monday, Wednesday, Friday and Saturday – single fare £31.

**Accommodation** on the island is fairly limited. The most popular destination for birdwatchers is the *Fair Isle Lodge and Bird Observatory* (April–Oct; ☎035/ 12258; ② full board), which offers excellent home cooking and a bed in either a dormitory or a private room. The centre carries out scientific research on the island and visitors are always welcome to lend a hand. **B&B** is available in the beautiful eighteenth-century *Auld Haa* (☎ 035/12264; ①) – a former trading booth for fishermen – or at *Schoolton* (☎035/12250; ② full board).

# Foula

Defying wind and tide, the tiny island of **Foula** rises steeply from the sea about 14 miles to the southwest of mainland Shetland. The island leans into the west wind, with massive cliffs facing the onslaught, but drops off in the east, where all the fertile land is concentrated and most of the inhabitants live. Foula is dominated by these dramatic high cliffs: the **Kame** (1241ft) is the second highest vertical cliff in Britain, while the highest peak, the **Sheug** (1379ft), offers superb views of the island, as well as the entire west coast of Shetland and much of Orkney. The wind rips across the top of these exposed heights and often generates whirlwinds, known as "flans" which can tear down the hills with tremendous force.

Foula has been inhabited since prehistoric times, and the island's isolation has ensured a resilient conservatism. Local people still haven't made the transition between the Julian and Gregorian calendars, celebrating Old Yule on January 6 and New Year's Day on January 13. Foula's population peaked at around two hundred at the end of the nineteenth century, but has fluctuated wildly over the years, dropping to three in 1720, following an epidemic of "muckle fever"; today the island has a resident population of around forty people, as well as 1500 sheep, a handful of Shetland ponies and a unique species of field mouse, all of whom are vastly outnumbered by the visiting bird population, which is estimated at some half a million. During the spring and summer, the cliffs are packed with puffins, guillemots, gannets, fulmars and razorbills, while the island is also visited by skuas, eider ducks, red-throated divers and the rare leach's petrel.

# Practicalities

**Ferry** services to Foula run from Scalloway (May–Sept on alternate Thurs; 3hrs) and Walls (May–Sept on Tues, Sat and alternate Thurs; Oct–April on Tues only; 2hrs 30min), with single fares for a bargain price of £1.25. *Loganair* also have **flights** four times a week from Tingwall airport between March and October, for a single fare of £17.

B&B **accommodation** is available at *Leraback* (☎039/333226; ①), or you can rent an entire cottage, sleeping six, from Mrs Holbourn (☎039/333232; £70 per week). For budget travellers, the cheapest accommodation on the island is at the small *Ristie Hostel* (☎039/333233; ①), which has its own kitchen. If you are either camping or staying in a youth hostel, you must bring supplies with you from the mainland as there is little provision on the island itself.

## travel details

### ORKNEY

**Buses**

**Kirkwall** to: Houton (5–6 daily; 30min); St Margaret's Hope (4 daily; 40min); Stromness (hourly; 40min); Tingwall (3 daily; 25min).

**Ferries**

**Burwick** to: John O' Groats (passengers only, 2–4 daily; 40min).

**Kirkwall** to: Shapinsay (4–6 daily; 45min); Eday, Stronsay, Sanday, Westray and Papa Westray (1–3 daily; 1-2hr); North Ronaldsay (1 weekly).

**Lyness** to: Hoy, Flotta and Graemsay (11 daily; 35–65min).

**Stromness** to: Aberdeen (daily in summer, 3 weekly in winter; 8hr); Hoy (passengers only, 2–3 daily; 30min); Scrabster/Thurso (daily, except Sun in winter; 1hr 45min).

**Tingwall** to: Egilsay, Rousay and Wyre (16 daily; 30min).

**Flights**

**Kirkwall** to: Aberdeen (daily; 45min); Eday (Mon, Wed, Fri 2 daily; 12min); Edinburgh (daily; 1hr 55min); Glasgow (daily; 2hr 15min); Inverness (daily; 40min); North Ronaldsay (Mon–Sat 2 daily; 40min); Papa Westray (Mon–Sat 2 daily; 25min); Sanday (Mon–Sat 2 daily; 11min); Stronsay (Mon–Sat 2 daily; 18min); Westray (Mon–Sat 3 daily; 12min).

### SHETLAND

**Buses**

**Cullivoe** to Ulsta (2 daily; 1hr 15min).

**Lerwick** to: Brae (7 daily; 35min); Hamnavoe (2 daily except Sun; 30min); Hillswick (daily; 1hr 15min); Laxo (1 or 2 daily; 1hr); Sandwick (5 daily except Sun; 45min); Scalloway (11 daily except Sun; 15min); Sullom Voe (7 daily; 35min); Sumburgh (5 daily; 1hr); Unst (daily; 2hr 40min); Vidlin (2–3 daily except Sun; 30min); Walls and Sandness (2–5 daily; 45min); Weisdale and Culswick (daily; 1hr 20min); Yell (daily; 2hr 20min).

**Sullom Voe** to: Toft (daily Mon–Fri; 15min).

**Unst, Yell and Fetlar**: Nicebus community transport route varies daily (☎Baltasound 224).

**Yell** to: Lerwick (daily; 2hr 20min).

## Ferries

**Bressay** to: Noss (May–Aug, inflatable dinghy shuttles 10am–5pm daily except Mon and Thurs).

**Fetlar** to: Mainland, either Yell or Unst (5 daily; 30min).

**Lerwick** to: Aberdeen (via Orkney, 2 weekly; 10hr); Bergen (weekly in summer); Bressay (21 daily; 5min); Fair Isle (11 yearly; 4hr 30min); Out Skerries (2 weekly; 2hr 20min).

**Sandwick** to: Mousa (April–Sept, daily tour).

**Scalloway** to: Foula (May–Sept fortnightly; 3hr).

**Sumburgh** to: Fair Isle (weekly; 2hr 40min).

**Toft (Mainland)** to: Yell (27 daily; 20min).

**Vidlin** to: Out Skerries (3 weekly; 1hr 30min); Whalsay (11–17 daily; 30min).

**Walls** to: Foula (May–Sept 3 weekly, otherwise once; 2hr 30min).

**West Burrafirth** to: Papa Stour (May–Sept daily; 35min).

**Yell** to: Unst (16–22 daily;10min).

## Flights

**Sumburgh** to: Aberdeen (4 daily; 1hr); Unst (March–Oct, Mon–Fri, 1 flight; 25min).

**Tingwall** to: Fair Isle (March–Oct, Mon, Wed, Fri, Sat, 2 flights; 25min); Foula (March–Oct, Mon, Wed, Fri, Sat, 1 flight; 15min); Out Skerries (March–Oct, Mon, Wed, Thurs, Sat, 1 flight; 15min); Papa Stour (April–Oct, Tues, 1 flight; 10min); Unst (March–Oct, Mon–Fri, 1 flight; 25min).

# PART THREE

# THE
# CONTEXTS

Scottish Primrose
(Primula Scotica)

# THE
# HISTORICAL
# FRAMEWORK

## PREHISTORIC SCOTLAND

Scotland, like the rest of prehistoric Britain, was settled by successive waves of peoples arriving from the east. These first inhabitants were **hunter-gatherers**, whose heaps of animal bones and shells have been excavated, amongst other places, in the caves along the coast near East Wemyss, in Fife. Around 4500 BC, **Neolithic farming peoples** from the European mainland began moving into Scotland. To provide themselves with land for their cereal crops and grazing for their live-stock, they cleared large areas of upland forest, usually by fire, and, in the process, created the characteristic moorland landscapes of much of modern Scotland. These early farmers estab-lished permanent settlements, some of which – like the well-preserved village of **Skara Brae** on Orkney – were near the sea, enabling them to supplement their diet by fishing and to develop their skills as boat builders. The Neolithic settlements were not as isolated as was once imagined: geological evidence has, for instance, revealed that the stone used to make axe-heads found in the Hebrides was quarried in Northern Ireland.

Settlement spurred the development of more complex forms of religious belief. The Neolithic peoples built large chambered burial mounds or **cairns**, such as those at **Maes**

**Howe** on Orkney. This reverence for human remains suggests a belief in some form of afterlife, a concept that the next wave of settlers, the **Beaker people**, certainly believed in. They placed pottery beakers filled with drink in the tombs of their dead to assist the passage of the deceased on their journey to, or their stay in, the next world. The Beaker people also built the mysterious **stone circles**, thirty of which have been discovered in Scotland. Such monuments were a massive commitment in terms of time and energy, with many of the stones carried from many miles away – just as they were at Stonehenge in England, the most famous stone circle of all. One of the best known Scottish circles is that of **Callanish** on the Isle of Lewis, where a dramatic series of monoliths (single standing stones) form avenues leading towards a circle made up of thirteen standing stones. The exact function of the circles is still unknown, but many of the stones are aligned with the posi-tion of the sun at certain points in its annual cycle, suggesting that the monuments are related to the changing of the seasons.

The Beaker people also brought the **Bronze Age** to Scotland. Bronze, an alloy of copper and tin, was stronger and more flexible than its predecessor flint, which had long been used for axe-heads and knives. New materials led directly to the development of more effective weapons, and the sword and the shield made their first appearance around 1000 BC. Agricultural needs plus new weaponry added up to a state of endemic warfare as villagers raided their neighbours to steal livestock and grain. The Bronze Age peoples responded to the danger by developing a range of defences, among them the spectacular **hill forts**, great earthwork defences, many of which are thought to have been occupied from around 1000 BC and remained in use throughout the Iron Age, sometimes far longer. Less spectacu-lar but equally practical were the **crannogs**, smaller settlements built on artificial islands constructed of logs, earth, stones and brush, such as Cherry Island in Loch Ness.

Conflict in Scotland intensified in the first millennium BC as successive waves of **Celtic** settlers, arriving from the south, increased competition for land. Around 400 BC the Celts brought the technology of **iron** with them and, as Winston Churchill put it, "Men armed with iron entered Britain and killed the men of bronze". These fractious times witnessed the construction of hundreds of **brochs** or fortified towers. Concentrated along the Atlantic coast, particularly in Sutherland and Caithness, the brochs were drystone fortifications (built without mortar or cement) often over forty feet in height. Some historians claim they provided protection for small coastal settlements from the attentions of Roman slave traders. The double stone walls of **Doune Carloway**, a broch on Lewis, still stand, even in their ruined state, at over thirty feet high. The Celts continued to migrate north almost up until Julius Caesar's first incursion into Britain in 55 BC.

At the end of the prehistoric period, immediately prior to the arrival of the Romans, Scotland was divided among a number of warring Iron Age tribes, who, apart from the raiding, were preoccupied with wresting a living from the land, growing barley and oats, rearing sheep, hunting deer and fishing for salmon. The Romans were to write these people into history under the collective name Picti, or **Picts**, meaning painted people – after their body tattoos.

## THE ROMANS

The Roman conquest of Britain began in 43 AD, almost a century after Caesar's first invasion. By 80 AD the Roman governor, Agricola, felt secure enough in the south of Britain to begin an invasion of the north, building a string of forts across the Clyde–Forth line and defeating a large force of Scottish tribes at Mons Graupius. The long-term effect of his campaign, however, was slight. Work on a major fort – to be the base for five thousand men – at Inchtuthill, on the Tay, was abandoned before it was finished, and the legions withdrew south. In 123 AD the **Emperor Hadrian** decided to seal the frontier against the northern tribes and built **Hadrian's Wall**, which stretched from the Solway Firth to the Tyne and was the first formal division of the island of Britain. Twenty years later, the Romans again ventured north and built the **Antonine Wall** between the Clyde and the Forth. This was occupied for about forty years, but thereafter the Romans, frustrated by the inhospitable terrain of the Highlands, largely gave up their attempt to subjugate the north, and instead adopted a policy of containment.

It was the Romans produced the first written accounts of the peoples of Scotland. In the second century AD, the Greco-Egyptian geographer Ptolemy drew up the first known map of Scotland, which identified seventeen tribal territories. Other descriptions were less scientific, compounding the mixture of fear and contempt with which the Romans regarded their Pictish neighbours. Dio Cassius, a Roman commentator writing in 197 AD, informed his readers that:

*They live in huts, go naked and unshod. They mostly have a democratic government, and are much addicted to robbery. They can bear hunger and cold and all manner of hardship; they will retire into their marshes and hold out for days with only their heads above water, and in the forest they will subsist on barks and roots.*

## THE DARK AGES

In the years following the departure of the Romans, traditionally put at 450 AD, the population of Scotland changed considerably. By 500 AD the **Picts** were confined to eastern Scotland, between Fife and the Moray Firth. Today their settlements can be generally determined by place names with a "Pit" prefix, such as "Pitlochry", and by the existence of carved symbol stones, like those found at Aberlemno in Angus. To the west, between Dumbarton and Carlisle, was a population of **Britons**. Many of the Briton leaders had Roman names, which suggests that they were a Romanized Celtic people, possibly a combination of tribes maintained by the Romans as a buffer between the Wall and the northern tribes, and peoples pushed west by the Anglo-Saxon invaders landing on the east coast. Both the Britons and the Picts spoke variations of P-Celtic, from which Welsh, Cornish and Breton developed.

On the west coast, to the north and west of the Britons, lived the **Scotti**, Irish-Celtic invaders who would eventually give their name to the whole country. The first Scotti arrived in the Western Isles from Ireland in the fourth century AD, and about a century later their great king, Fergus Mor, moved his base from Antrim to Dunadd, near Lochgilphead, where he founded the kingdom of Dalriada. The Scotti spoke Q-Celtic, the precursor of modern Gaelic. On the east coast, the Germanic **Angles** had sailed north along the coast to carve out an enclave in

East Lothian around Dunbar. The final addition to the ethnic mix was also non-Celtic. In the eighth century, **Norse** invaders began to arrive, eventually settling the Orkneys, the Shetlands, the Western Isles and the extreme northeast corner of the mainland.

The next few centuries saw almost constant warfare among the different groups. The main issue was land, but this was frequently complicated by the need of the warrior castes, who dominated all of these cultures, to exhibit martial prowess. Military conquests did play their part in bringing the peoples of Scotland together, but the most persuasive force was **Christianity**. Many of the Britons had been Christians since Roman times and it had been a Briton, Saint Ninian, who conducted the first missionary work among the Picts at the end of the fourth century. Attempts to convert the Picts were resumed in the sixth century by Saint Columba, who, as a Gaelic-speaking Scotti, demonstrated that Christianity could provide a bridge between the different tribes.

Christianity proved attractive to pagan kings because it seemed to offer them extra supernatural powers. As Saint Columba declared, when he inaugurated his cousin Aidan as king of Dalriada in 574, "Believe firmly, O Aidan, that none of your enemies will be able to resist you unless you first deal falsely against me and my successors". This combination of spiritual and political power, when taken with Columba's establishment of the island of **Iona** as a centre of Christian culture, opened the way for many peaceable contacts between the Picts and Scotti. Intermarriage became commonplace and the Scotti king, Kenneth MacAlpine, who united Dalriada and Pictland in 843, was the son of a Pictish princess — the Picts traced succession through the female line. Similarly, MacAlpine's creation of the united kingdom of **Alba**, later known as **Scotia**, was part of a process of integration rather than outright conquest. Kenneth and his successors gradually extended the frontiers of their kingdom by marriage and force of arms until, by 1034, almost all of what we now call Scotland was under their rule.

## THE MIDDLE AGES

By the time of his death in 1034, **Malcolm II** was recognized as the king of Scotia. He was not, though, a national king in the sense that we understand the term, as under the Gaelic system, kings were elected from the *derbfine*, a group made up of those whose great-grandfathers had been kings. The chosen successor, supposedly the fittest to rule, was known as the *tanist*. By the eleventh century, however, Scottish kings had become familiar with the principle of heredity, and were often tempted to bend the rules of *tanistry*. Thus, the childless Malcolm secured the succession of his grandson **Duncan** by murdering a potential rival *tanist*. Duncan, in turn, was killed by **Macbeth** in 1040. Macbeth was not, therefore, the villain of Shakespeare's imagination, but simply an ambitious Scot of royal blood acting in a relatively conventional way.

The victory of **Malcolm III**, known as Canmore ("bighead"), over Macbeth in 1057 marked the beginning of a period of fundamental change in Scottish society. Having avenged his father Duncan, Malcolm III, who had spent the previous seventeen years at the English court, sought to apply to Scotland a range of ideas he had brought back with him. He and his heirs established a secure dynasty based on succession through the male line and introduced **feudalism** into Scotland, a system that was diametrically opposed to the Gaelic system, which rested on blood ties: the followers of a Gaelic king were his kindred, whereas the followers of a feudal king were vassals bought with land. The Canmores successfully feudalized much of southern and eastern Scotland by making grants to their Norman, Breton and Flemish followers, but beyond that, traditional clan-based forms of social relations persisted.

The Canmores, independent of the local nobility, who remained a military threat, also began to reform the **church**. This development started with the efforts of Margaret, Malcolm III's English wife, who brought Scottish religious practices into line with those of the rest of Europe and was eventually canonized. **David I** (1124–53) continued the process by importing monks to found a series of monasteries, principally along the border at Kelso, Melrose, Jedburgh and Dryburgh. By 1200 the entire country was covered by a network of eleven bishoprics, although church organization remained weak within the Highlands. Similarly, the dynasty founded a series of **royal burghs**, towns such as Edinburgh, Stirling and Berwick, and bestowed upon them charters recognizing them as centres of trade. The charters usually granted a measure of self-government, vested in the town corporation or guild, and the monarchy hoped this liberality would both encourage loyalty and increase the prosperity of the kingdom. Scotland's Gaelic-speaking clans had little influence within the burghs, and Scots – a northern version of Anglo-Saxon – had become the main language throughout the Lowlands by 1550.

The policies of the Canmores laid the basis for a cultural rift in Scotland between the Highland and Lowland communities. Before that became an issue, however, the Scots had to face a major threat from the south. In 1286 **Alexander III** died, and a hotly disputed succession gave Edward I, the king of England, an opportunity to subjugate Scotland. In 1291 Edward presided over a conference where the rival claimants to the Scottish throne presented their cases. Edward chose John Balliol, in preference to Robert the Bruce, his main rival, and obliged John to pay him homage, thus turning Scotland into a vassal kingdom. Bruce refused to accept the decision, thereby continuing the conflict, and in 1295 Balliol renounced his allegiance to Edward and formed an alliance with France – the beginning of what is known as the "Auld Alliance". In the conflict that followed, the Bruce family sided with the English, Balliol was defeated and imprisoned, and Edward seized control of almost all of Scotland.

Edward had shown little mercy during his conquest of Scotland – he had, for example, had most of the population of Berwick massacred – and his cruelty seems to have stirred a truly national resistance. This focused on **William Wallace**, a man of relatively lowly origins who forged an army of peasants, lesser knights and townsmen that was fundamentally different from the armies raised by the nobility. Figures like Balliol, holding lands in England, France and Scotland, were part of an international aristocracy for whom warfare was merely the means by which they struggled for power. Wallace, by contrast, led proto-nationalist forces determined to expel the English from their country. Probably for that very reason Wallace never received the support of the nobility, and, after a bitter ten-year campaign, he was betrayed and executed in London in 1305.

With Wallace out of the way, feudal intrigue resumed. In 1306 **Robert the Bruce**, the erstwhile ally of the English, defied Edward and had himself crowned king of Scotland. Edward died the following year, but the unrest dragged on until 1314, when Bruce decisively defeated a huge English army under Edward II at the battle of **Bannockburn**. At last Bruce was firmly in control of his kingdom, and in 1320 the Scots asserted their right to independence in a successful petition to the pope, now known as the **Arbroath Declaration**.

In the years following Bruce's death in 1329, the Scottish monarchy gradually declined in influence. The last of the Bruce dynasty died in 1371, to be succeeded by the "Stewards", hence **Stewarts**, but thereafter a succession of Scottish rulers, culminating with James VI in 1567, came to the throne when still children. The power vacuum was filled by the nobility, whose key members exercised control as Scotland's regents while carving out territories where they ruled with the power, if not the title, of kings. At the close of the fifteenth century, the Douglas family alone controlled Galloway, Lothian, Stirlingshire, Clydesdale and Annandale. The more vigorous monarchs of the period, notably **James I** (1406–37), did their best to curb the power of such dynasties, but their efforts were usually nullified at the next regency. **James IV** (1488–1513), the most talented of the early Stewarts, might have restored the authority of the crown, but his invasion of England ended in a terrible defeat for the Scots – and his own death – at the battle of Flodden Field.

The reign of **Mary, Queen of Scots** (1542–67) typified the problems of the Scottish monarchy. Mary came to the throne when just one week old, and immediately caught the attention of the English king, Henry VIII, who sought, first by persuasion and then by military might, to secure her hand in marriage for his five-year-old son, Edward. Beginning in 1544, the English launched a series of devastating attacks on Scotland, an episode Sir Walter Scott later called the "Rough Wooing", until, in the face of another English invasion in 1548, the Scots – or at least those not supporting Henry – turned to the "Auld Alliance". The French king proposed marriage between Mary and the Dauphin Francis, promising in return military assistance against the English. The six-year-old queen sailed for France in 1548, leaving her loyal nobles and their French allies in control, and her husband succeeded to the French throne in 1559. When she returned thirteen years later, following the death of Francis, she had to pick her way through the rival ambitions of her nobility and deal with something entirely new – the religious Reformation.

## THE REFORMATION

The **Reformation** in Scotland was a complex social process, whose threads are often hard to unravel. Nevertheless, it is quite clear that, by the end of the sixteenth century, the established church was held in general contempt. Many members of the higher clergy regarded their relationship with the Church purely in economic terms, and forty percent of known illegitimate births (ie those subsequently legitimized) were the product of the "celibate" clergy's liaisons.

Another spur to the Scottish Reformation was the identification of Protestantism with anti-French feeling. In 1554 Mary of Guise, the French mother of the absent Queen Mary, had become regent, and her habit of appointing Frenchmen to high office was seen as part of an attempt to subordinate Scotland's interests to those of France. There was considerable resentment, and in 1557 a group of nobles banded together to form the **Lords of the Congregation**, whose dual purpose was to oppose French influence and promote the reformed religion. With English military backing, the Protestant lords succeeded in deposing the French regent in 1560, and, when the Scottish Parliament assembled shortly afterwards, it asserted the primacy of Protestantism by forbidding the Mass and abolishing the authority of the pope. The nobility proceeded to confiscate two-thirds of Church lands, a huge prize that did much to bolster their new beliefs.

Even without the economic incentives, Protestantism was a highly charged political doctrine. Luther had argued that each individual's conscience was capable of discerning God's will. This meant that an hierarchical priesthood, existing to interpret God's will, was unnecessary and that the people themselves might conclude their rulers were breaking God's laws, in which case the monarch should

be opposed or even deposed. This point was made very clearly to Queen Mary by the Protestant reformer **John Knox** at their first meeting in 1561. Subjects, he told her, were not bound to obey an ungodly monarch.

Knox, a Protestant exile who returned to Scotland in 1559, was a follower of the Genevan reformer Calvin, who combined Luther's views on individual conscience with a belief in predestination. He argued that an omnipotent God must know everything, including the destinies of every human being. Consequently, it was determined before birth who was to be part of the Elect, bound for heavenly glory, and who was not, a doctrine that placed enormous pressure on its adherents to demonstrate by their godly behaviour that they were of the Elect. This was the doctrine that Knox brought back to Scotland and laid out in his Articles of Confession of Faith, better known as the **Scot's Confession**, which was to form the basis of the reformed faith for over seventy years.

Mary ducked and weaved, trying to avoid an open breach with her Protestant subjects. The fires of popular displeasure were kept well-stoked by Knox, however, who declared "one Mass was more fearful than if ten thousand enemies were landed in any part of the realm, of purpose to suppress the whole religion". At the same time, Mary was engaged in a balancing act between the factions of the Scottish nobility. Her difficulties were exacerbated by her disastrous second marriage to **Lord Darnley**, a politically inept and cruel character, whose jealousy led to his involvement in the murder of Mary's favourite, David Rizzio, who was dragged from the queen's supper room at Holyrood and stabbed 56 times. The incident caused the Scottish Protestants more than a little unease, but they were entirely scandalized in 1567, when Darnley himself was murdered and Mary promptly married the **Earl of Bothwell**, widely believed to be the murderer. This was too much to bear, and the Scots rose in rebellion, driving Mary into exile in England at the age of just 25. The queen's illegitimate half-brother, the Earl of Moray, became regent and her son, the infant James, was left behind to be raised a Protestant prince. Mary, meanwhile, became perceived as such a threat to the English throne that Queen Elizabeth I had her executed in 1587.

Knox could now concentrate on the organization of the reformed Church, or **Kirk**, which he envisaged as a body empowered to intervene in the daily lives of the people. **Andrew Melville**, another leading reformer, wished to push this theocratic vision further. He proposed the abolition of all traces of Episcopacy – the rule of the bishops in the Church – and that the Kirk should adopt a **Presbyterian** structure, administered by a hierarchy of assemblies, part-elected and part-appointed. At the bottom of the chain, beneath the General Assembly, Synod and Presbytery, would be the Kirk session, responsible for church affairs, the performance of the minister and the morals of the parish. In 1592, the Melvillian party achieved a measure of success when Presbyteries and Synods were accepted as legal church courts and the office of bishop was suspended.

**James VI** (1567–1625) disliked Presbyterianism because its quasi-democratic structure – particularly the lack of royally appointed bishops – appeared to threaten his authority. He was, however, unable to resist the reformers until 1610, when, strengthened by his installation as James I of England after Elizabeth's death in 1603, he restored the Scottish bishops. The argument about the nature of Kirk organization would lead to bloody conflict in the years after James' death.

## THE RELIGIOUS WARS

Raised in Episcopalian England, **Charles I** (1625–49) had little understanding of Scottish reformism. He believed in the Divine Right of Kings, an authoritarian creed which claimed the monarch was God's representative on earth and, therefore, his authority had divine sanction, a concept entirely counter to Protestant thought. In 1637, Charles attempted to impose a new prayer book on the Kirk, laying down forms of worship in line with those favoured by the High Anglican Church. The reformers denounced these changes as "Popery" and organized the **National Covenant**, a religious pledge that committed the signatories to "Labour by all means lawful to recover the purity and liberty of the Gospel as it was established and professed".

Charles declared all the "Covenanters" to be rebels, a proclamation endorsed by his Scottish

bishops. Consequently, when the king backed down from military action and called a General Assembly of the Kirk, the assembly promptly abolished the Episcopacy. Charles pronounced the proceedings illegal, but lack of finance stopped him from mounting an effective military campaign – whereas the Covenanters, well-financed by the Kirk, assembled a proficient army under Alexander Leslie. In desperation, Charles summoned the English Parliament, the first for eleven years, hoping it would pay for an army. But, like the calling of the General Assembly, the decision was a disaster and Parliament was much keener to criticize his policies than to raise taxes. In response Charles declared war on Parliament in 1642.

Until 1650 Scotland was ruled by the Covenanters and the power of the Presbyterian Kirk grew considerably. Laws were passed establishing schools in every parish and, less usefully, banning trade with Catholic countries. The only effective opposition to the theocratic state came from the **Marquis of Montrose**, who had initially supported the Covenant but lined up with the king when war broke out. His army was drawn from the Highlands and islands, where the Kirk's influence was weakest. Montrose was a gifted campaigner who won several notable victories against the Covenanters, but the reluctance of his troops to stay south of the Highland Line made it impossible for him to capitalize on his successes, and he was eventually captured and executed in 1650.

Largely confined to the peripheries of Scotland, Montrose's campaigns were a side-show to the **Civil War** being waged further south. Here, the Covenanters and the English Parliamentarians faced the same royal enemy and in 1643 formed an alliance. Indeed, it was the Scots army who captured Charles at Newark in Nottinghamshire, in 1646. There was, however, friction between the allies. Many of the Parliamentarians, including Cromwell, were **Independents**, who favoured a looser form of doctrinal control within the state Church than did the Presbyterians, and were inclined towards religious toleration for the law-abiding sects outside the state Church. In addition, the Scots believed the English were tainted with **Erastianism** – a belief in placing the secular authority of Parliament over the spiritual authority of the Church.

The Parliamentarians in turn suspected the Scots of hankering for the return of the monarchy, a suspicion confirmed when, at the invitation of the Earl of Argyll, the future Charles II came back to Scotland in 1650. To regain his Scottish kingdom, Charles was obliged to renounce his father and sign the Covenant, two bitter pills taken to impress the population. In the event, the "Presbyterian restoration" was short-lived. Cromwell invaded, defeated the Scots at Dunbar and forced Charles into exile. Until the restoration of 1660, Scotland was united with England and governed by seven commissioners.

Although the restoration of **Charles II** (1660–85) brought bishops back to the kirk, they were integrated into an essentially Presbyterian structure of Kirk sessions and Presbyteries, and the General Assembly, which had been abolished by Cromwell, was not re-established. Over three hundred clergymen, a third of the Scottish ministry, refused to accept the reinstatement of the bishops and were edged out of the Church, forced to hold open-air services, called **Conventicles**, which Charles did his best to suppress. Religious opposition inspired military resistance and the Lowlands witnessed scenes of brutal repression as the king's forces struggled to keep control in what was known as "The Killing Time". In the southwest, a particular stronghold of the Covenanters, the government imported Highlanders, the so-called "Highland Host", to root out the opposition, which they did with great barbarity.

Charles II was succeeded by his brother **James VII** (James II of England), whose ardent Catholicism caused a Protestant backlash in England. In 1689, he was forced into exile in France and the throne passed to **Mary**, his Protestant daughter, and her Dutch husband, **William of Orange**. In Scotland, William and Mary restored the full Presbyterian structure and abolished bishops, though they chose not to restore the political and legal functions of the Kirk, which remained subject to parliamentary control. This settlement ended Scotland's religious wars and completed its reformation.

## THE UNION

Although the question of Kirk organization was settled in 1690, the political issue of the relationship between the Crown and the Scottish Parliament was not. From 1689 to 1697, William was at war with France, partly financed by Scottish taxes and partly fought by Scottish soldiers. Yet many Scots, mindful of the Auld Alliance, disapproved of the war and others suffered financially from the disruption to trade with France. There were other economic irritants too, principally the legally sanctioned monopoly that English merchants had over trade with the English colonies. This monopoly inspired the **Darien Scheme**, a plan to establish a Scottish colony in Panama. The colonists set off in 1698, but, thwarted by the opposition of both William and the English merchants, the scheme proved a miserable failure. The colony collapsed with the loss of £200,000 – an amount equal to half the value of the entire coinage in Scotland – and an angry Scottish Parliament threatened to refuse the king taxes as rioting broke out in the cities.

Meanwhile, in the north, the Highlanders blamed William for the massacre of the **MacDonalds of Glencoe**. In 1691, William had offered pardons to those Highland chiefs who had opposed his accession, on condition that they took an oath of allegiance by New Year's Day, 1692. Alasdair MacDonald of Glencoe had turned up at the last minute, but his efforts to take the oath were frustrated by the king's officials, who were determined to see his clan, well known for their support of the Stewarts, destroyed. In February 1692, Captain Robert Campbell quartered his men in Glencoe and, two weeks later, in the middle of the night, his troops acted on their secret orders and slaughtered as many MacDonalds as they could. Thirty-eight died, and the massacre caused a national scandal, especially among the clans where "Murder under Trust" – killing those offering you shelter – was considered a particularly heinous crime.

The situation in Scotland was further complicated by the question of the succession. Mary died without leaving an heir and, on William's death in 1702, the crown passed to her sister **Anne**, who was also childless. In response, the English Parliament secured the Protestant succession by passing the Act of Settlement, which named the Electress Sophia of Hanover as the next in line to the throne. The Act did not, however, apply in Scotland, and the English feared that the Scots would invite James Edward Stewart back from France to be their king. Consequently, Parliament appointed commissioners charged with the consideration of "proper methods towards attaining a union with Scotland". The project seemed doomed to failure when the Scottish Parliament passed the **Act of Security**, in 1703, stating that Scotland would not accept a Hanoverian monarch unless they had first received guarantees protecting their religion and their trade.

Nevertheless, despite the strength of anti-English feeling, the Scottish Parliament passed the **Act of Union** by 110 votes to 69 in January

1707. Some historians have explained the vote in terms of bribery and corruption. This certainly played a part (the Duke of Hamilton, for example, switched sides at a key moment and was subsequently rewarded with an English Dukedom), but there were other factors. Scottish politicians were divided between the Cavaliers – Jacobites (supporters of the Stewarts) and Episcopalians – and the Country party, whose Presbyterian members dreaded the return of the Stewarts more than they disliked the Hanoverians. There were commercial considerations too. In 1705, the

## THE HIGHLANDS

The country that was united with England in 1707 was itself divided by the Highland Line. The people of north and west Scotland spoke Gaelic, rather than Scots, and were mostly pastoralists, moving their sheep and cattle to highland pastures in the summer, and returning to the glens in the winter. They lived in single-room dwellings heated by a central peat fire and sometimes shared with livestock, and in hard times they would subsist on cakes made from the blood of their live cattle mixed with oatmeal. Highlanders supplemented their meagre income by raiding their clan neighbours and the prosperous Lowlands, whose inhabitants regarded their northern compatriots with a mixture of fear and contempt. In the early seventeenth century, Montgomerie, a Lowland poet, suggested that God had created the first Highlander out of horseshit. When God asked his creation what he would do, the reply was "I will doun to the Lowland, Lord, and thair steill a kow".

It would be a mistake, however, to infer from the primitive nature of Highland life that the institutions of this society had existed from time immemorial. This is especially true of the **"clan"**, a term that only appears in its modern usage in the sixteenth century. In theory, the clan bound together blood relatives who shared a common ancestor, a concept clearly derived from the ancient Gaelic notion of kinship. But in practise many of the clans were of non-Gaelic origin – such as the Frasers, Sinclairs and Stewarts, all of Anglo-Norman descent – and it was the mythology of a common ancestor, rather than the actuality, that cemented the clans together. Furthermore, clans were often made up of people with a variety of surnames, and there are documented cases of individuals

changing their names when they swapped allegiances.

At the upper end of Highland society was the **clan chief** (who might have been a minor figure, like MacDonald of Glencoe, or a great lord, like the Duke of Argyll, head of the Campbells), who provided protection for his followers: they would, in turn, fight for him when called upon to do so. Below the clan chief were the **chieftains of the septs**, or sub-units of the clan, and then came the **tacksmen**, major tenants of the chief to whom they were frequently related. The tacksmen sublet their land to **tenants**, who were at the bottom of the social scale. The Highlanders wore a simple belted plaid wrapped around the body – rather than the kilt – and not until the late seventeenth century were certain tartans roughly associated with particular clans. The detailed codification of the **tartan** was produced by the Victorians, whose romantic vision of Highland life originated with George IV's visit to Scotland in 1822, when he appeared in an elaborate version of Highland dress, complete with flesh-coloured tights.

Victoria and Albert continued the mythology, designing a tartan for royal usage and increasing national interest in the supposed – in fact, invented – traditions of Scotland. John and Charles Sobieski published their pseudo-scholarly *Vestiarium Scoticum* (Scottish Dress), which contained drawings of over fifty clan tartans, all of them fake. At the same time the kilt acquired an enormous sporran, and was to be worn with black shoes and a newly designed jacket. It was, however, only possible to romanticize the clans because they were no longer a threat. Victoria's fantasies were bought and paid for by the bloody work of "Butcher" Cumberland on Culloden field (see p.352).

English Parliament had passed the Alien Act, which threatened to impose severe penalties on cross-border trade, whereas the Union gave merchants of both countries free access to each other's markets. The Act of Union also guaranteed the Scottish legal system and the Presbyterian Kirk, and offered compensation to those who had lost money in the Darien Scheme.

Under the terms of the Act, both parliaments were to be replaced by a new British Parliament based in London, with the Scots apportioned 45 MPs and 16 peers. There were riots when the terms became known, but no sustained opposition.

## THE JACOBITE RISINGS

When James VII/II was deposed he had fled to France, where he planned the reconquest of his kingdom with the support of the French king. In 1702, James' successor, William, died and the hopes of the Stewarts passed to his cousin James, the "Old Pretender" (Pretender in the sense of having pretensions to the throne, Old to distinguish him from his son Charles, the "Young Pretender"). The Crown passed to Anne, however, and after her death and the accession of the Hanoverian George I, the first major **Jacobite uprising** occurred in 1715. Its timing appeared perfect. Scottish opinion was moving against the Union, which had failed to bring Scotland any tangible economic benefits. The English had also been accused of bad faith when, contrary to their pledges, they attempted to impose their legal practices on the Scots. Neither were Jacobite sentiments confined to Scotland. There were many in England who toasted the "King across the water" and showed no enthusiasm for the their new German ruler. In September 1715, the fiercely Jacobite John Erskine, Earl of Mar, raised the Stewart standard at Braemar Castle. Just eight days later, he captured Perth, where he gathered an army of over 10,000 men, drawn mostly from the Episcopalians of northeast Scotland and from the Highlands. Mar's rebellion took the government by surprise. They had only 4000 soldiers in Scotland, under the command of the Duke of Argyll, but Mar dithered until he lost the military advantage. There was an indecisive battle at Sheriffmuir in November, but by the time the Old Pretender arrived the following month, 6000 veteran Dutch troops had rein-

forced Argyll. The rebellion disintegrated rapidly and James slinked back to exile in France in February 1716.

The **Jacobite uprising of 1745**, led by James' dashing son, Charles Edward Stewart (Bonnie Prince Charlie), had little chance of success. The Hanoverians had consolidated their hold on the English throne, Lowland society was uniformly loyalist and even among the Highlanders Charles only attracted just over a half of the 20,000 clansmen who could have marched with him. Nevertheless, after a decisive victory over government forces at Prestonpans, Charles made a spectacular advance into England, getting as far as Derby. London was in a state of panic: its shops were closed and the Bank of England, fearing a run on sterling, slowed withdrawals by paying out in sixpences. But Derby was as far south as Charles got. On December 6, threatened by superior forces, the Jacobites decided to retreat to Scotland. The Duke of Cumberland was sent in pursuit and the two armies met on **Culloden Moor**, near Inverness, in April 1746. Outnumbered and out-gunned, the Jacobites were swept from the field, losing over 1200 men compared to Cumberland's 300 plus. After the battle, many of the wounded Jacobites were slaughtered, an atrocity that earnt Cumberland the nickname "Butcher". Jacobite hopes died at Culloden and the prince lived out the rest of his life in drunken exile.

In the aftermath of the uprising, the wearing of tartan, the bearing of arms and the playing of bagpipes were all banned. Rebel chiefs lost their land and the Highlands were placed under military occupation. Most significantly, the government prohibited the private armies of the chiefs, thereby effectively destroying the clan system.

## THE HIGHLAND CLEARANCES

Once the clan chief was forbidden his own army, he had no need of the large tenantry that had previously been a vital military asset. Conversely, the second half of the eighteenth century saw the Highland population increase dramatically after the introduction of the easy-to-grow and nutritious potato. Between 1745 and 1811, the population of the Outer Hebrides, for example, rose from 13,000 to 24,500. The clan chiefs adopted different policies to deal with the new situation. Some encouraged emigration, and as many as 6000 Highlanders left for the Americas between 1800 and 1803 alone. Other landowners developed alternative forms of employment for their tenantry, mainly fishing and kelping. **Kelp** (brown seaweed), was gathered and burnt to produce soda ash, which was used in the manufacture of soap, glass and explosives. There was a rising market for soda ash until the 1810s, with the price increasing from £2 a ton in 1760 to £20 in 1808, making a fortune for some landowners and providing thousands of Highlanders with temporary employment. Other landowners developed **sheep runs** on the Highland pastures, introducing hardy breeds like the black-faced Linton and the Cheviot. But extensive sheep farming proved incompatible with a high peasant population, and many landowners decided to clear their estates of tenants, some of whom were forcibly moved to tiny plots of marginal land, where they were to farm as **crofters**.

The pace of the **Highland Clearances** accelerated after the end of the Napoleonic Wars in 1815, when the market price for kelp, fish and cattle declined, leaving sheep as the only profitable Highland product. The most notorious Clearances took place on the estates of the Countess of Sutherland, who owned a million acres in northern Scotland. Between 1807 and 1821, around 15,000 people were thrown off her land, evictions carried out by Patrick Sellar, the estate factor, with considerable brutality. Those who failed to leave by the appointed time had their homes burnt in front of them and one elderly woman, who failed to get out of her home after it was torched, subsequently died from burns. The local sheriff charged Sellar with her death, but a jury of landowners acquitted him – and the sheriff was sacked. As the dispossessed Highlanders scratched a living on the acid soils of some tiny croft, they learnt through bitter experience the limitations of the clan. Famine followed, forcing large-scale emigration to America and Canada and leaving the huge uninhabited areas found in the region today.

The crofters eked out a precarious existence, but they hung on throughout the nineteenth century, often by taking seasonal employment away from home. In the 1880s, however, a sharp downturn in agricultural prices made it difficult for many crofters to pay their rent. This time, inspired by the example of the Irish Land League, they resisted eviction, forming the **Highland Land Reform Association** and the **Crofters' Party**. In 1886, in response to the social unrest, Gladstone's Liberal government passed the **Crofters' Holdings Act**, which conceded three of the crofters' demands: security of tenure, fair rents to be decided independently, and the right to pass on crofts by inheritance. But Gladstone did not attempt to increase the amount of land available for crofting and shortage of land remained a major problem until the **Land Settlement Act** of 1919 made provision for the creation of new crofts. Nevertheless, the population of the Highlands has continued to decline during the twentieth century, with many of the region's young people finding city life more appealing.

## INDUSTRIALIZATON

**Glasgow** was the powerhouse of Scotland's **Industrial Revolution**. The passage from Glasgow to the Americas was much shorter than that from rival English ports and a lucrative trans-Atlantic trade in tobacco had developed as early as the seventeenth century. This in turn stimulated Scottish manufacturing since, under the terms of the Navigation Acts, the Americans were not allowed to trade manufactured goods. Scottish-produced linen, paper and wrought iron were exchanged for Virginia tobacco and, when the American Revolution disrupted the trade in the 1770s and 1780s, the Scots successfully turned to trade with the West Indies and, most important of all, to the production of cotton textiles.

Glasgow's west coast location also gave it ready access to the sources of raw cotton in the Americas, while the rapid growth of the British Empire provided an expanding market for its finished cloth. Initially, the city's **cotton industry**, like the earlier linen industry, was organized domestically, with spinners and weavers working in their homes, but increased demand required mass production and a need for factories. In 1787, Scotland had only nineteen cotton mills; by 1840 there were nearly two hundred.

The growth of the textile industry spurred the development of other industries. In the mid-eighteenth century, the **Carron Ironworks** was founded near Falkirk, specializing in the production of military munitions. Here, the capital and expertise were English, but the location was determined by Scottish coal reserves, and by 1800 it was the largest ironworks in Europe. The basis of Scotland's **shipbuilding** industry was laid as early as 1802, when the steam vessel *Charlotte Dundas* was launched on the Forth–Clyde canal. Within thirty years, 95 steam vessels had been built in Scotland, most of them on Clydeside. The growth of the iron and shipbuilding industries, plus the extensive use of steam power, created a massive demand for **coal** and pit shafts were sunk across the coal fields of southern Scotland.

Industrialization led to a concentration of Scotland's **population** in the central Lowlands. In 1840, one third of the country's industrial workers lived in Lanarkshire alone, and Glasgow's population grew from 17,000 in the 1740s to over 200,000 a century later. Such sudden growth created urban overcrowding on a massive scale, and as late as 1861, 64 percent of the entire Scottish population lived in one- or two-room houses. For most Clydesiders, "house" meant a couple of small rooms in a grim tenement building, where many of the poorest families were displaced Highlanders and Irish immigrants, with the Irish arriving in Glasgow at the rate of one thousand a week during the potato famine of the 1840s.

Nevertheless, by the late nineteenth century a measure of prosperity had emerged from industrialization, and the well-paid Clydeside engineers went to their forges wearing bowler hats and starched collars. They were confident of the future, but their optimism was misplaced. Scotland's industries were very much geared to the export market and, after **World War I**, they found conditions much changed. During the war years, when exports had been curtailed by a combination of U-Boat activity and war production, new industries had developed in India and Japan, and the eastern market for Scottish goods never recovered. The postwar world also witnessed a contraction of world trade, which hit the shipbuilding industry very hard and, in turn, damaged the steel and coal industries. By 1931, for instance, pig iron production was at less than 25 percent of its 1920 output.

These difficulties were compounded by the financial collapse of the early 1930s and, by 1932, 28 percent of the Scottish workforce was unemployed. Four hundred thousand Scots emigrated between 1921 and 1931, and those who stayed endured some of the worst social conditions in the British Isles. By the late 1930s, Scotland had the highest infant mortality rate in Europe, while some thirty percent of homes had no WC or bath. There was a partial economic recovery in the mid-1930s, but high unemployment remained until the start of **World War II**.

## THE LABOUR MOVEMENT

In the late eighteenth century, conditions for the labouring population varied enormously. At one extreme, the handloom weavers, working from home, were well-paid and much in demand, whereas the coal miners remained serfs, bought and sold with the pits they worked in, until 1799. During this period, the working class gave some support to the **radical movement**, those loosely connected groups of reformers, led by the lower middle class, who took their inspiration from the French Revolution. One of these groups, "The Friends of the People", campaigned for the extension of the right to vote, and such apparently innocuous activities earnt one member, Thomas Muir, a sentence of fourteen years transportation to Australia.

In 1820, the radicals called for a national strike and an insurrection to "show the world that we are . . . determined to be free". At least 60,000 workers downed tools for a week, and one group set off for the Carron Ironworks to seize arms. The government were, however, well prepared. They slammed radical leaders into prison and a heavy military presence kept control of the streets. The strike fizzled out and three leading radicals, all weavers, were later executed.

The 1832 Scottish Reform Act extended the franchise to include a large proportion of the middle class and thereafter political radicalism assumed a more distinctive working-class character, though its ideals still harked back to the American and French revolutions. In the 1840s, the **Chartists** led the campaign for working-class political rights by sending massive petitions to Parliament and organizing huge demonstrations. When Parliament rejected the petitions, the more determined Chartists – the "physical-force men" – urged insurrection. This call to arms was not taken up by the Scottish working class, however, and support for the Chartists fell away. The insurrectionary phase of Scottish labour was over.

During the next thirty years, as Scotland's economy prospered, skilled workers organized themselves into craft **unions**, such as the Amalgamated Society of Engineers, dedicated to negotiating improvements for their members within the status quo. Politically, the trade unions gave their allegiance to the Liberal Party, but the first major crack in the Liberal–Union alliance came in 1888, when **Keir Hardie** left the Liberals to form the Scottish Socialist Party, which was later merged with the Independent Labour Party, founded in Bradford in 1893. Scottish socialism as represented by the ILP was ethical rather than Marxist in orientation, owing a great deal to the Kirk background of many of its members. But electoral progress was slow, partly because the Roman Catholic priesthood consistently preached against socialism.

In the early years of the twentieth century, two small Marxist groups established themselves on Clydeside: the **Socialist Labour Party**, which concentrated on workplace militancy, and the party-political **British Socialist Party**, whose most famous member was the Marxist lecturer John MacLean. During World War I, the local organizers of the SLP gained considerable influence by playing on the fears of the skilled workers, who felt their status was being undermined by the employment of unskilled workers. After the war, the influence of the shop stewards culminated in a massive campaign for the forty-hour working week. The strikes and demonstrations of the campaign, including one of 100,000 people in St George's Square in Glasgow, panicked the government into sending in the troops. But this was no Bolshevik Revolution – as Emmanuel Shinwell, the seamen's leader and future Labour Party politician, observed, "[the troops] had nothing much to do but chat to the local people and drink their cups of tea". The rank-and-file may have had little interest in revolution, but many of the activists did go on to become leaders within the newly formed Communist Party of Great Britain.

The ILP, now an affiliated part of the socialist **Labour Party**, made its electoral breakthrough in 1922, when it sent 29 Scottish MPs to Westminster. They set out with high hopes of social progress and reform, aspirations that were dashed, like trade union militancy, by the 1930s Depression. At the 1945 general elec-

tion, Labour won forty seats in Scotland and, in more recent times, the Party has dominated Scottish politics with the gradual eclipse of the Scottish Conservatives: in 1955 the Conservatives held thirty-six Scottish seats, while in 1993 they had just eleven.

Labour's position in Scotland is not, however, completely secure. The ILP MPs of the 1920s combined their socialism with a brand of Scottish nationalism. In 1924, for instance, the MP James Maxton had declared his intentions to "make English-ridden, capitalist-ridden Scotland into the Scottish socialist Commonwealth". The Labour Party maintained an official policy of self-government for Scotland, endorsing home rule in 1945 and 1947, but these endorsements were made with less and less enthusiasm. In 1958, Labour abandoned the commitment altogether and adopted a unionist vision of Scotland, much to the chagrin of many Scottish activists.

In 1971, **Upper Clyde Shipbuilders** stood on the brink of closure, its demise symbolizing the failure of traditional Labour politicians to revive Scotland's industrial base, which had resumed its decline after the end of World War II. In the event, UCS was partly saved by the work-in organized by two Communist shop stewards, Jimmy Reid and Jimmy Airlie. After fourteen months, the work-in finally succeeded in winning government support to keep part of the shipyard open, and Scots saw the broadly based campaign waged on its behalf as a national issue – Scottish industries set against an indifferent London government. Many socialist Scots, like James Jack, General Secretary of the Scottish TUC, moved towards some form of nationalism.

## THE NATIONALISTS

The **National Party of Scotland** was formed in 1928, its membership averaging about 7000 people, mostly drawn from the non-industrial parts of the country. Very much a mixture of practical politicians and left-leaning eccentrics, such as the poet Hugh MacDiarmid, in 1934 it merged with the right-wing Scottish Party in 1934 to create the **Scottish National Party**. The SNP, after years in the political wilderness, achieved its electoral breakthrough in 1967 when Winnie Ewing won Hamilton from Labour in a by-election. The following year the SNP won 34 percent of the vote in local government elections and gained control of Cumbernauld, successes which had repercussions within both the Labour and Conservative parties. Both began to work up schemes to give Scotland a measure of self-government, and the term "Devolution" was coined. The objective in both cases was to head off the nationalists.

When the Conservatives came to power in 1970, Edward Heath, the prime minister, shelved plans for devolution because the SNP had only secured a twelve percent share of the Scottish vote. The situation changed dramatically in 1974, when Labour were returned to power with a wafer-thin majority. The SNP held seven seats, which gave them considerable political leverage. Devolution was back on the agenda. The SNP had also run an excellent election campaign, concentrating on North Sea oil, which was now being piped ashore in significant quantities. Their two most popular slogans, "England expects . . . Scotland's oil" and "Rich Scots or Poor Britons?" seemed to have caught the mood of Scotland.

The Labour government put its devolution proposals before the Scottish people in a **referendum** on March 1, 1979. Thirty-three percent voted "Yes" and thirty-one percent "No", a majority in favour but not by the required forty percent. It seems likely that Labour's proposals fell short because, cobbled together at Westminster for reasons of expediency, they failed to define exactly what a "Yes" vote would mean — and all sorts of interpretations were offered during the referendum campaign. But the exercise did bring about a change within the Labour Party, which is now committed to a Scottish Parliament, and throughout the 1980s and into the early 1990s, the overwhelming majority of Scots have consistently voted for parties committed to self-rule. Only the Conservatives have held the unionist line, and they're less popular in Scotland than ever.

Whether self-rule will be granted, and, if so, in what form, remains to be seen. Even the SNP is not completely clear, but they have their own divisions, with left-wingers such as Jim Sillars struggling with more conservative elements within the Party.

## THE FUTURE

Whatever political system emerges in Scotland, and whatever party stands at its head, Labour or Nationalist, the Scottish nation faces an uncertain future. New industries established in the 1960s to replace the old traditional heavy industries are now themselves in decline, and more recent high-tech enterprises have also failed to generate much employment. Even the valuable oil industry, producing £5 million a day in exports, hasn't been able to soak up the unemployed, and the fishing industry, very profitable up until the mid-1980s, now finds itself in difficulties as the European Community places further limits on the Total Allowable Catches (TACs), and skipper-owners struggle to repay mortgages taken out to buy new vessels.

The consequences of this long-term industrial decline are visible in every indicator of national well-being, and, in the short term at least, it's difficult to see how the trend can be reversed. Tourism, of course, remains crucial to Scotland's economic well-being, and it can only be hoped that the devolution of power from Westminster — if and when it comes — will be enough to kickstart the nation's economy into the 21st century.

# THE WILDLIFE OF SCOTLAND

A comprehensive account of Scotland's wildlife would take a whole book to cover; what follows is a general overview of the effects of climate and human activity on the country's flora and fauna.

## CLIMATE

Scotland's mountains are high enough to impose harsh conditions, especially in the Highlands, and the **Cairngorm plateau** (the largest area of high ground in the whole of Britain) is almost arctic even in summer. Despite this, however, since the easing of the Ice Age about 10,000 years ago, Scotland has developed a rather complex climate, and some areas of the country are quite mild.

The Atlantic tempers conditions on the west coast, and in winter the warmish water of the Gulf Stream swings north, so that at **Inverewe**, for example, you'll find incongruously lush gardens blooming with subtropical plants. Inland, the weather becomes more extreme, but what restricts plant life on many Scottish hills is not the cold so much as the stress of wind and gloomy cloud cover. **Ben Nevis**, for example, is clouded and whipped by 50mph gales for more than two-thirds of the year, and as a result, the tree line – the height to which trees grow up the slopes – may be only 150 feet above sea level near the west coast, but up to over 2000 feet on some of the sheltered hillsides inland.

## A BRIEF HISTORY

After the Ice Age, "arctic" and "alpine" plants abounded, eventually giving way to woody shrubs and trees, notably the Scots pine. Oak and other hardwood trees followed in some places, but the **Scots pine** remained the distinctive tree, spreading expansively to form the great **Caledonian Forest**. Parts of this ancient forest still remain, miraculously surviving centuries of attack, but it is only comparatively recently that attempts at positive conservation have been made.

Early **settlement**, from the Picts to the Norsemen, led to clearance of large areas of forest, and huge areas were burnt during the clan wars. When centuries of unrest ended with the Jacobite defeat at Culloden in 1745, the glens were ransacked for timber, which was floated downriver to fuel iron smelting and other industries. The clansmen had had a free-booting cattle economy, but during the infamous **Clearances**, both the cattle and the defeated Highlanders were replaced by the more profitable sheep of the new landlords. As also happened on the English downland and moorland, intensive sheep grazing kept the land open, eventually destroying much woodland by preventing natural regeneration.

In Victorian times **red deer** herds, which also graze heavily, provided stalking, and when rapid firing breech-loading guns came into general use around the 1850s, **grouse** shooting became a passion. It's strange to think of birds changing the scenery, but grouse graze heather and thus large areas are burnt to encourage fresh green growth. No tree saplings survive and the open moorland is maintained.

The flatter **lowlands** are now dominated by mechanized farming; barley, beef, turnips and potatoes conspire against wildlife, and pollution and development are as damaging here as elsewhere. Even the so-called **"wilderness"** is under threat. Its own popularity obviously holds dangers, and the unique flora of the Cairngorm peaks, for example, is in danger of being stamped out under the feet of the summer visitors using the ski lifts. But even more damaging than tourism is **conifer planting**. In recent decades, boosted (if not caused) by generous grant aid and tax dodges, large areas of open moorland have been planted with tightly packed monocultural ranks of foreign conifers, forbidding to much wildlife. Coniferization is particularly threatening to large areas of bogland in the "Flow Country" of Caithness and elsewhere, areas that are as unique a natural environment as the tropical rainforests. For these and other similar habitats, registration as an **SSSI** – a Site of Special Scientific Interest – has proved barely adequate, and the only real safeguard is for such areas to be owned or managed by organizations such as **Scottish Nature** (the national agency) or the **Scottish Wildlife Trust**, the **Royal Society for the Protection of Birds** and similar voluntary groups.

## WILD FLOWERS

Relic patches of the Scots pine Caledonian Forest, such as the Black Wood of Rannoch and Rothiemurchus Forest below the Cairngorms, are often more open than an oak wood, the pines, interspersed with birch and juniper, spaced out in hilly heather. These woods feature some wonderful wild flowers, such as the **wintergreens** which justify their name, unobtrusive **orchids** in the shape of creeping lady's tresses and lesser twayblade, and, in parts of the northeast especially, the rare beauty of the **twinflower**, holding its paired heads over the summer **needle litter**.

You'll also find old oak woods in some places, especially in the lower coastward lengths of the southern glens. Here the Atlantic influence encourages masses of English bluebell, **wood anemone** and other spring flowers. (In Scotland the English bluebell is known as the **wild hyacinth**, the Scots keeping the name "bluebell" for the summer-flowering English harebell that grows in more open ground.) Scotland, or at least lowland Scotland, has many flowers found further south in Britain – **maiden pink**, orchids, **cowslip** and others in grassy areas. Roadside flowers, such as **meadowsweet** and **meadow buttercup**, **dog rose**, **primrose** and **red campion**, extend widely up through Scotland, but others, such as the **white field rose** and **mistletoe**, **red valerian**, **small scabious**, **cuckoo pint** and **travellers joy** (and the elm tree), reach the end of their range in the Scottish central lowlands.

Scotland's mountains, especially where the rock is limey or basic in character, as on Ben Lawers, for example, are dotted with arctic–alpine plants, such as mountain **avens**, with their white flowers and glossy oak-like leaves, and handsome **purple saxifrage**, both of which favour a soil rich in calcium. Here as elsewhere, the flowers are to be found on ledges and rock faces out of reach of the sheep and deer. Other classic mountain plants are **alpine lady's mantle** and **moss campion**, which grows in a tight cushion, set with single pink flowers.

Higher up on the bleak wind-battered mountain tops, there may be nothing much more than a low "heath" of mosses and maybe some tough low grasses or rushes between the scatterings of rubble. Because this environment encourages few insects, such plants are generally self-fertilizing and some even produce small plants or "bulbils" in their flower heads instead of seed.

A variety of ferns shelter in the slopes amid the tumbled rock screes or in cracks in the rock alongside streams. In Scotland's damp climate, you'll also see many ferns on lower ground, but some, the **holly fern** for one, are true mountain species. **Lichens**, too, are common on exposed rocks, and in the woods bushy and bearded lichens can coat the branches and trunks.

**Bogs** are a natural feature of much of the flatter ground in the Highlands, often extending for miles. Scottish bogland comprises an intricate mosaic of domes of living bog moss (sometimes bright green or a striking orange or yellow), domes of drier, heathery peat, and pools dotted in between. The wettest areas give rise to specialized plants such as **cranberry**, **bearberry** and also the **sundews**, which gain nutrients in these poor surroundings by trapping and absorbing midges on the sticky hairs on their flat leaves.

At sea level, the rivers spawn estuaries; these and some sea lochs are edged with **salt-marshes**, which in time dry out to "meadows" colourful with **sea aster** and other flowers. The west coast, especially the cliffs of Galloway, shimmer blue with **spring squill** as soon as the winter eases, while the Galloway shore marks the southernmost limit of **Scots lovage**, a celery-scented member of the cow parsley family. A relic of arctic times, the **oysterplant**, with blue-grey leaves and pink bell flowers, also grows here, as it does on the shores of Iceland and Scandinavia.

Scotland has some wonderful **sand dune** systems, which on the back shores harden into grassy patches often grazed by rabbits to create a fine turf.

## BIRDLIFE

It might seem unexpected to find birds nesting at over three thousand feet, but in Scotland the wind is strong enough to blow patches of icy ground clear of snow, enabling birds to make their homes on the mountains. The **dotterel**, a small wader with a chestnut stomach, is a rare summer visitor to the Cairngorms and other heights – in the Arctic it nests down to sea level. Even rarer is the **snow bunting**, the male black and white, the female brownish – perhaps only ten pairs nest on Scotland's mountains, although they are seen much more widely around the coasts in winter, when the male also becomes brown.

More common on the heights is the **ptarmigan**, shy and almost invisible in its summer coat, as it plays hide and seek amongst the lichen-patched boulders – you're most likely to see it on the Cairngorms, as it ventures out for the sandwich crusts left by the summer visitors using the ski lifts. It is resident up here, and moults from mottled in summer to pure white in winter.

The ptarmigan's camouflage helps protect it from the **golden eagle**. This magnificent bird ranges across many Highland areas – there are perhaps three hundred nesting pairs on Skye, the Outer Hebrides, above Aviemore and Deeside, and in the northwest Highlands, each needing a territory of thousands of acres over which to hunt hares, grouse and ptarmigan. The **raven** also has strong links with the mountains, tumbling in crazy acrobatics past the rock faces.

Where the slopes lessen to moorland, the domain of the **red grouse** begins. This game bird not only affects the landscape but also, via the persecution of gamekeepers, threatens eagles and other birds of prey, although they are all theoretically protected. The **cuckoo** might be heard as far as northern Scotland – one of its favourite dupes, the **meadow pipit**, is fairly widespread on any rough ground up to three thousand feet. **Dunlin** and other waders nest on the wet moorlands and boglands, where the soft land allows them to use their delicate bills to probe for insects and other food.

You'll come across many notable birds where pine woods encroach onto open moor. One such is the **black grouse**, with its bizarre courtship rituals, when both sexes come together for aggressive, ritualistic display in a small gathering area known as a "lek". The **capercaillie**, found deeper in the forest and perhaps floundering amongst the branches, is an unexpectedly large, turkey-like bird, about three feet from bill to end of tail, which also has a flamboyant courting display. A game bird, it was shot to extinction but reintroduced into Scotland from Europe in 1837. Other birds that favour the pine woods are the **long-eared owl**, many of the **tit** family (including the crested tit in the Spey valley), the **siskin** and the **goldcrest**. The Speyside woods, especially, are a stronghold of the **crossbill**, which uses its overlapping bill to prise open the pine cones.

Scottish **lochs** are as rich in birdlife as the moorlands that embrace them. After fifty years of absence, the **osprey** returned and is now breeding and fishing the waters of Loch Garten and elsewhere. In addition to common species such as **mallard** and **tufted duck**, you might also see **goosander**, **red-breasted merganser** and other wildfowl. The superbly streamlined fish-eating **red-** and **black-throated divers** nest in the northwest, while the **great northern diver**, with its shivery wailing call, is largely a winter visitor on the coasts, though one or two pairs may occasionally nest.

Scotland is also strong on **coastal birds**. **Eider duck** gather in their thousands at the mouth of the Tay, and the estuaries are also a magnet for **waders** and **wild geese** in winter: the total population of barnacle geese from the Arctic island of Spitsbergen winter in the Solway estuary and on the farmland alongside. Other areas to head for if you're interested in seabirds are remote cliffs such as St Abb's Head in the Borders, and the many offshore **"bird islands"**, which although often little more than bare rock, attract vast colonies that fish the sea around them. Some have their own speciality – **Manx shearwaters** have vast colonies on Rhum for example, while the Shetland isle of Foula has about a third (three thousand pairs) of all the **great skuas** breeding in the northern hemisphere. Remote St Kilda is also stunning, with snowstorms of **gannets**, **puffins**, **guillemots**, **petrels** and **shearwaters**.

In addition to Scotland's resident bird population, and the winter and spring migrants, the western coasts and islands often see transatlantic "accidentals" blown far off course, which give rise to inbred **subspecies**. St Kilda is of particular interest to specialists, not only for its sheer numbers of resident birds but also for the **St Kilda wren**, a distinct subspecies. In northern and parts of eastern Scotland the English all-black carrion crow is replaced by the **"hoodie"** or hooded crow, also found around the Mediterranean, with its distinctive grey back and underparts. Where the ranges of carrion crow and hoodie overlap, they interbreed, producing offspring with some grey patches of plumage.

## MAMMALS

By the mid-eighteenth century, much of Scotland's wild animal life — including the Scottish **wolf**, **beaver**, **wild boar** and **elk** — had already disappeared. Although the indigenous **reindeer** was wiped out in the twelfth century, more recently a semi-wild herd of Swedish stock was reintroduced to the slopes of the Cairngorms above Aviemore. Of two other semi-wild species — **Highland cattle** and **Shetland ponies** — the first is a classic case of breeding fitting conditions (they can survive in snowy conditions for fifty days a year) while the second, the smallest British native pony, probably arrived in the later stages of the Ice Age when the ice was retreating but still gave a bridge across the salt water. There are feral **goats** in some places, but probably the most interesting of such animals is the **Soay sheep** of St Kilda. This, Britain's only truly wild sheep, notable for its soft brown fleece, can be seen as a farm pet and in wildlife parks — and is even used to graze some nature reserves in the south of Britain.

Although there are **sika** and **fallow deer** in places, and **roe deer** are widespread, Scotland is the stronghold of **wild red deer** herds, which, despite culling, stalking for sport and harsh winters, still number more than quarter of a million head. By origin a woodland animal, they might graze open ground — of necessity when the forest has been cleared — but they also move up to high ground in summer to avoid the biting flies and the tourists, and to graze on heather and lichens.

The **fox** is widespread, as are the **mole** and **hedgehog**, but the **badger** is rather more rare. The **wild cat** and **pine marten** live in remote areas, hiding away in the moors and forests.

The former, despite its initial resemblance to the family pet, is actually quite different — larger, with longer, striped fur, and a blunt-ended bushy tail that is also striped. The agile cat-sized pine marten, although hunted by gamekeepers, is maintaining reduced numbers, preying on squirrels and other small animals.

Native red **squirrels** are predominantly found in the Highlands, where they are still largely free from competition from the grey, which began to establish themselves about a century ago and now have a strong presence in many lowland areas. **Rabbit** and **brown hare** are widespread, as are the **blue** or **mountain hare** in the Highlands, usually adopting a white or patchy white coat in winter. The north Scottish **stoat** also dons a white winter coat, its tail tipped with black, when it is known as ermine. Although Scotland is too far north for the dormouse and the harvest mouse, **shrews**, **voles** and **field mice** abound, and though there are few bats, the related **pipistrelle** is quite widely seen.

You may also be lucky enough to encounter the **otter**, endangered in the rest of Britain. In Scotland, the otter is found not only in the rushing becks but more often along the western coast and islands where it hunts the seashore for crabs and inshore fish. The otter is not to be confused with the feral **mink**, escaped from fur farms to take up life in the wild; these mink are a scourge in some areas, destroying birds.

**Whales** and their kin are frequent visitors to coastal waters and **seals**, including the shy grey seal, are quite common. However, in the hitherto virgin sea lochs of the west coast, both the seals and the coastal otters are under threat from the spread of **fish farms** (for salmon and sea trout). Not only are they poisoned by the chemicals used to keep the trapped fish vermin-free, but they also face the threat of being shot by the fish farm owners when they raid what is to them simply a natural larder.

## FISH, REPTILES, INSECTS

Quite apart from the Loch Ness monster, Scotland has a rich water life. The Dee and other rivers are famous **salmon rivers**, fished when the salmon swim upstream to breed in their ancestral gravel headwaters. The fish leap waterfalls on the way, and many rivers which have been dammed or barricaded have "salmon ladders" to help them – these make great tourist attractions. The **sea trout** is also strongly migratory, the **brown or mountain trout** less so, although river or stream dwellers do move upstream and lake dwellers up the incoming rivers to spawn. Related to these game fish is the **powan or freshwater herring**, found only in the poorer northern basins of Loch Lomond, and possibly a relic from Ice Age arctic conditions. The richer southern waters of Loch Lomond and others similar contain **roach**, **perch** and other "coarse" fish.

Although the **adder** is common, the **grass snake** is not found in Scotland. Both **lizards** and the snake-like **slowworm** (in fact a legless lizard) are widespread, as are the **frog** and **toad**; the natterjack toad, however, is seen rarely this far north.

Scottish boglands are notable for their **dragonflies**, which prefer acid water, and **hawkers**, **darters** and **damselflies** feature in the south. One Scottish particular is the **blue hawker**, common in parts of the western Highlands. As for **butterflies**, some of the familiar types from further south – common blue, hairstreaks and others – are scattered in areas where conditions are not too harsh. One species with a liking for the heights is the **mountain ringlet**, only seen elsewhere in the Lake District and in the Alps, which flies above 1500 feet on the Grampians. Adapted to quite harsh conditions, it is clearly a relic of early post-glacial times. Another mountain butterfly, the **Scotch argus**, no longer found in England or Wales, is widespread in Scotland, and the **elephant hawk moth** can be seen in the Insh marshes below the Cairngorms.

# *BOOKS*

Wherever a book is in print, the UK publisher is given first in each listing, separated, where applicable, from the US publisher by an oblique slash. Where books are published in only one of these countries we have specified which one; when the same company publishes the book in both, its name appears just once. Out of print titles are indicated as o/p – these should be easy to track down in second-hand bookshops.

## ART AND ARCHITECTURE

**David King** *Complete Works of Robert and James Adam* (Butterworth-Heinemann). Comprehensive and scholarly look at the work of the Adam brothers.

**Charles McKean, David Walker and Frank Walker** *Central Glasgow* (Mainstream/State Mutual Book Company). An architectural romp through the city centre and West End, with plenty of photographs and informed comment.

**Duncan MacMillan** *Scottish Art 1460-1990* (Mainstream). Lavish overview of Scottish painting with good sections on landscape, portraiture and the Glasgow Boys.

**Alistair Moffat and Colin Baxter** *Remembering Charles Rennie MacKintosh* (Colin Baxter Photography Ltd). Illustrated biography of Scotland's most celebrated early twentieth-century architect, artist and designer.

**Alastair Smart** *Allan Ramsay 1713–1784* (National Gallery of Scotland). Good study of one of Scotland's most representative eighteenth-century artists, written by a leading Ramsay scholar.

## HISTORY, POLITICS AND CULTURE

**Ian Adams and Meredith Somerville** *Cargoes of Despair and Hope* (John Donald Publishing). Riveting mixture of contemporary documents and letters telling the story of Scottish emigration to North America from 1603 to 1803.

**Ian Bell** *Dreams of Exile* (Mainstream/Holt). Admirable biography of Robert Louis Stevenson that seeks to explain his work in terms of Scottish emigration, exile and escape. Does a good job of balancing the real man against his over-romanticized image.

**Hugh Cheape** *Tartan: The Highland Habit* (National Museums of Scotland/University of Washington Press). The history of tartan from medieval times to the invention of the exclusive clan identity in the nineteenth century.

**David Daiches, ed**. *A Companion to Scottish Culture* (Polygon/Holmes & Meier). More than three hundred articles interpreting Scottish culture in its widest sense, from eating to marriage customs, the Scottish Enlightenment to children's street games.

**Margaret George** *Mary, Queen of Scotland and the Isles* (Macmillan/St Martin's Press). Thoroughly researched novel, telling the perennially romantic story of Mary, Queen of Scots, with a wealth of detail.

**Rosemary Goring** *Chambers Scottish Biographical Dictionary* (UK Chambers). More than two thousand mini biographies of important Scots, both well-known and utterly obscure, in fields such as law, medicine, education, the Church, music and the stage.

**Magnus Linklater and Robin Denniston** *Anatomy of Scotland* (UK Chambers). Social history essays on the workings of Scotland over the past 45 years, covering everything from the law to pop music.

**Michael Lynch** *Scotland: A New History* (UK Pimlico). Probably the best available overview of Scottish history, going right up to 1991 and the bid for a national parliament.

**James MacKay** *Burns: A Biography of Robert Burns* (Mainstream). Recent attempt to clear the myths surrounding Scotland's most famous poet, including those created by the man himself.

**Charles McKean** *Edinburgh* (UK Canongate). Lively, lyrical account of the development of Scotland's capital right up to the present.

**John McLeod** *No Great Mischief If You Fall* (Mainstream). Gloom and doom on the rape of the Highlands; an enraging, bleak but stimulating book debunking some of the myths held by the Highland industry.

**Frank McLynn** *Bonnie Prince Charlie* (UK OUP). Huge, very readable and more or less definitive biography.

**Ann McSween and Mick Sharp** *Prehistoric Scotland* (Batsford/New Amsterdam Books). Thematic introductory guide to many of Scotland's prehistoric sites, with atmospheric black-and-white photographs and imaginative illustrations.

**Andrew Marr** *The Battle for Scotland* (UK Penguin). Decent history of Scottish politics, from nineteenth-century Radicalism to demands for home rule in the 1990s.

**John Prebble** *Glen Coe; Culloden; The Highland Clearances* (Penguin/Secker & Warburg, Penguin/Athenum o/p, Penguin/Secker & Warburg o/p). Emotive and subjective accounts of key events in Highland history. Essential reading for Jacobite sympathizers.

**John Purser** *Scotland's Music* (Mainstream). Comprehensive overview of traditional and classical music in Scotland – thorough and scholarly but readable.

**T C Smout** *A History of the Scottish People 1560–1830* and *A Century of the Scottish People 1830–1950* (Fontana/Scribner o/p; Fontana/Yale University Press). Widely acclaimed volumes for those keen to delve deep into the complexities of Scottish history.

**Tom Steel** *Scotland's Story* (UK Fontana). Good people-based introduction written to accompany a popular British television series.

## GUIDES AND PICTURE BOOKS

**Kathleen Cory** *Tracing Your Scottish Ancestry* (Polygon/Genealogical Publishing Co). A practical guide to how to research your roots.

**Joe Fisher** *The Glasgow Encyclopedia* (UK Mainstream). The essential Glasgow reference book, covering nearly every facet of this complex urban society.

**Magnus Magnusson and Graham White, eds**. *The Nature of Scotland – Landscape, Wildlife and People* (Canongate). Glossy picture-based book on Scotland's natural heritage, from geology to farming and conservation. Good section on crofting.

**Oscar Marzaroli** *Glasgow's People: 1956–1988* (UK Mainstream). Wonderful collection by Glasgow's most sympathetic photographer.

**Richard Muir** *The Coastlines of Britain* (UK Macmillan). An exploration of all aspects of Scotland's varied coast with chapters on cliffs, beach, dunes, flora and fauna.

**Anne Shade** *Scotland for Kids* (Mainstream). Indispensable advice on where to go and what to do with children in Scotland, written by a mother of two.

## FOLKTALES AND LEGENDS

**Margaret Bennett** *Scottish Customs from the Cradle to the Grave* (UK Polygon). Fascinating and sympathetic extensive oral history.

**Michael Brander** *Tales of the Borders* (UK Mainstream). Part social history and part guide book, a collection of romantic nineteenth-century Border tales retold and put into historical context.

**Alan J Bruford and Donald Archie McDonald, eds**. *Scottish Traditional Tales* (UK Polygon). A huge collection of folk stories from all over Scotland, taken from tape archives.

**Anne Ross** *Folklore of the Southern Highlands* (Batsford). A comprehensive collection, with sections on clan lore, witchcraft, spells and taboos, festivals and scores of obscure customs.

**Jennifer Westwood** *Albion: A Guide to Legendary Britain* (UK Grafton). Highly readable volume on the development of myth in literature, with a section on Scottish legends.

## MEMOIRS AND TRAVELOGUES

**James Boswell** *The Journal of a Tour to the Hebrides* (Penguin/OUP o/p). Lively diary account of a journey around the islands taken with Samuel Johnson, written by his biographer and friend.

**Jack Caplan** *Memories of the Gorbals* (Pentland Press). Stories of growing up Jewish in 1930s Glasgow. Occasionally verges on the sentimental, but all in all an absorbing, personal view.

**Derek Cooper** *Hebridean Connection* (UK Fontana). Written in the 1970s, at a time of economic crisis, Cooper's refusal to romanticize Highland culture and his obvious love for the region make this a compulsive, moving read.

**James Hunter** *Scottish Highlanders* (Mainstream). Attempts to explain the strong sense of blood-ties held by people of Scottish descent all over the world; lots of history and good photographs.

**R F MacKenzie** *A Search for Scotland* (UK Fontana). Mixture of autobiography, reflection and polemic; rambling, emotional and unstructured, it reflects the author's lifelong love of Scotland.

**Tom Morton** *Spirit of Adventure: A Journey Beyond the Whisky Trails* (Mainstream). Offbeat and funny view of Scotland's whisky industry as seen from the back of a motorcycle in appalling weather.

**T C Smout and Sydney Wood** *Scottish Voices 1745–1960* (UK Fontana). A fascinating collection of contemporary personal accounts on aspects of Scottish life, including school, work, fishing, farming, religion and sex.

**Douglas Sutherland** *Born Yesterday: Memories of a Scottish Childhood* (Canongate). Childhood memories of growing up in the 1920s and 30s in the Orkneys, Aberdeenshire and the Moray Firth.

## FOOD AND DRINK

**Michael Brander** *Essential Guide to Scots Whisky* (Canongate). A history of whisky from the days of the illicit distillers to the present day, along with a directory of malt.

**Catherine Brown** *Scottish Cookery* (UK Chambers). Practical, easy-to-follow recipes with interesting background notes on the history of Scottish food and ingredients.

**Annette Hope** *A Caledonian Feast* (UK Mainstream). Authorative and entertaining history of Scottish food and social life from the ninth to the twentieth century. Lots of recipes.

**Charles McLean** *The Pocket Whisky Book* (UK Mitchell Beazley). A tiny, thorough, fact-filled book covering malt, grain and blended whiskies, plus whisky-based liqueurs.

**F Marian McNeill** *The Scots Kitchen* (UK Mercat Press) and *The Scots Cellar* (UK Lochar). The first is a definitive, learned and entertaining guide to the history of Scots cooking, the second a history on the consumption and appreciation of whisky, ale and wine, with some good, alcoholic recipes.

## FICTION

**Iain Banks** *The Crow Road* (UK Abacus). Funny, pacy and imaginative book about growing up in Scotland in the twentieth century, by the author of the acclaimed, visceral *The Wasp Factory*. Full of Scottish landscapes, along with the sick coincidence and grim humour that typify Banks' work.

**D K Broster** *The Jacobite Trilogy* (UK Penguin). Tear-jerking trilogy centred round the tribulations of the Jacobite supporters.

**John Buchan** *The Complete Richard Hannay* (UK Penguin). This one volume includes *The 39 Steps*, *Greenmantle*, *Mr Standfast*, *The Three Hostages* and *The Island of Sheep*. Good gung-ho stories with a great feel for Scottish landscape. In the US, both OUP and Godine publish various editions of the Hannay stories.

**Moira Burgess and Hamish Whyte, eds**. *Streets of Stone* (Mainstream/Salamander). Anthology of contemporary Glaswegian short stories.

**Lewis Grassic Gibbon** *A Scots Quair* (Penguin/Schocken). A landmark trilogy, set in northeast Scotland during and after World War I, and seen through the eyes of Chris Guthrie, "torn between her love for the land and her desire to escape a peasant culture". Strong, seminal work.

**Alasdair Gray** *Lanark* (Canongate/Braziller o/p). Somewhat self-indulgent post-modern fantasy, telling the adventures of a male art student in the grim, apocalyptic town of "Unthank", a thinly veiled analogy for present-day Glasgow.

**Neil M Gunn** *The Silver Darlings* (UK Faber & Faber). Probably Gunn's most representative and best-known book, evocatively set on the northeast coast and telling the story of the herring fishermen during the great years of the industry. Other examples of his romantic, symbolic works include *The Lost Glen, The Silver Bough* and *Wild Geese Overhead.*

**James Hogg** *The Private Memoirs and Confessions of a Justified Sinner* (Penguin). Complex, powerful mid-nineteenth-century novel dealing with possession, myth and folklore, as it looks at the confession of an Edinburgh murderer from three different points of view.

**A L Kennedy** *Looking for the Possible Dance* (UK Secker & Warburg). Young Scottish writer dissects the difficulties of human relationships on a personal and wider social level.

**Alexander MacArthur and Kingsley Long** *No Mean City* (UK Chambers). Classic story of razor gangs in 1935 Glasgow.

**William McIlvanney** *A Gift from Nessus* (UK Mainstream). Moral tale set in 1960s Glasgow that counterposes the outward trappings of materialism with the emptiness of our inner life.

**Compton Mackenzie** *Whisky Galore* (Penguin). Comic novel based on a true story of the wartime wreck of a cargo of whisky on a Hebridean island. Full of predictable stereotypes but still funny.

**Neil Munro** *The Complete Edition of the Para Handy Tales* (UK Birlinn). All the epic adventures of the famous Clyde tugboat and her crew in one volume.

**Colin Nicolson, ed.** *Iain Crichton Smith: Critical Essays* (Edinburgh University Press). A good introduction to the life and works of one of Scotland's leading contemporary writers, who writes poetry and novels in Gaelic and English.

**Sir Walter Scott** *The Waverley Novels* (Penguin & OUP). The books that did much to create the romanticized version of Scottish life and history. Titles include *Old Mortality, The Heart of Midlothian, The Fair Maid of Perth* and *The Antiquary.* For more on Scott, see p.114.

**Muriel Spark** *The Prime of Miss Jean Brodie* (Penguin/Harper Collins). Wonderful evocation of middle-class Edinburgh life and aspirations, still apparent in that city today.

**R L Stevenson** *Dr Jekyll and Mr Hyde; Kidnapped; The Master of Ballantrae; Weir of Hermiston* (Penguin/Vintage; Penguin/Signet; Penguin/OUP; Penguin). More nineteenth-century tales of Highland adventure. For more on Stevenson, see p.79.

**Nigel Tranter** *The Bruce Trilogy* (Coronet/ Hodder & Stoughton). Massive tome by prolific and hugely popular author on Scottish themes.

**Jeff Torrington** *Swing Hammer Swing* (UK Minerva). Gripping contemporary account of working-class Glasgow, centred around the tale of a week in the life of Tam Clay. Winner of the 1993 Whitbread prize for fiction.

## POETRY

**Robert Burns** *The Complete Illustrated Poems, Songs and Ballads* (UK Lomond Books). Facsimile edition of the works of Scotland's most famous bard. OUP publish much of Burns' work in the US.

**Douglas Dunn, ed**. *The Faber Book of Twentieth-Century Scottish Poetry* (Faber & Faber). All the big names and some lesser known works.

**Douglas Dunn** *Scotland: An Anthology* (UK Fontana). Wide-ranging anthology featuring both Scottish writers and outsiders that attempts to provide a background to past and present notions of Scottish nationality.

**Liz Lochhead** *Bagpipe Muzak* (UK Penguin). A great collection of monologues and poems examining contemporary everyday life from a deceptively simple angle.

**Hugh MacDiarmid** *Complete Poems* (edited by Michael Grieve and W R Aitken; Carcanet/ Penguin o/p). Complete works of Scotland's finest modern poet.

**William MacGonagall** *Poetic Gems* (UK Duckworth). Compulsive selection of works by Scotland's much-loved worst poet.

**McCaig, Morgan, Lochhead** *Three Scottish Poets* (UK Canongate). One volume of Scotland's three best-known modern poets.

**John McQueen and Tom Scott, eds**. *The Oxford Book of Scottish Verse* (OUP). Claims to be the most comprehensive anthology of Scottish poetry ever published.

**Tom Scott, ed**. *The Penguin Book of Scottish Verse* (UK Penguin). Good general selection.

## OUTDOOR PURSUITS

**Bartholomew Walks Series** (UK Bartholomew). The series covers different areas of Scotland including Perthshire, the Borders and Fife, Loch Lomond and the Trossachs, Oban, Mull and Lochaber, and Skye and Wester Ross. Each booklet has a range of walks of varying lengths with clear maps and explanations.

**Exploring Scotland's Heritage Series** (UK HMSO). Detailed, beautifully illustrated series with the emphasis on historic buildings and archeological sites. Books include Orkney and Shetland, the Highlands, Grampian, Fife and Tayside, and Lothian and the Borders.

**Andrew Barbour** *Atlantic Salmon* (Canongate). Complete and easy-to-read rundown on all aspects of the life-cycle of this fascinating fish and its place in the Scottish economy.

**Hamish Brown, Rennie McOwan and Richard Mearns** *Great Walks* (Ward Lock/ o/p). More a reference book than a field guide, with lots of photos and hand-drawn maps. Sections on walking in the Borders, the Highlands and the islands.

**Andrew Dempster** *Classic Mountain Scrambles in Scotland* (UK Mainstream). Guide to hill walks in Scotland that combines straightforward walking with some rock-climbing.

**Michael Madders and Julia Welstead** *Where to Watch Birds in Scotland* (Christopher Helm). Comprehensive region-by-region guide with maps, details on access and habitat and notes on what to see when.

**Hamish McInnes** *West Highland Walks vols 1–4* (UK Hodder & Stoughton). Good walks and accompanying maps, with a text that incorporates history and legend.

**Cameron McNeish** *The Munro Almanac* (Neil Wilson Publishing/Lochar). A complete pocket guide to all Scotland's Munros giving details on access, maps, routes and accommodation information.

**Oleg Polunin** *Collins Photoguide to the Wild Flowers of Britain and Northern Europe* (UK Collins). An excellent, easy to use field guide.

**Robert Price** *Scotland's Golf Courses* (Mercat Press/Macmillan). A thorough lowdown on Scottish courses for serious golfers, with good photographs.

**Bill Robertson** *The Scottish Mountain Guide* (UK Mainstream). Packed with information on all the hills over 2000ft, a good field guide for planning a trip to the Scottish mountains.

**Wainwright in Scotland** (Michael Joseph/ Viking Penguin). Scottish walks in the same inimitable style and presentation as the famous Lake District series.

**Brendan Walsh** *Scottish Cycling Guide* (UK Mainstream). Selection of cycling tours covering the northwest and the islands.

# *LANGUAGE*

**Although Gaelic remains a living language, even in the *Gàidhealtachd* or Gaelic-speaking areas of the Western Isles, parts of Skye and a few scattered islands of Argyll, every encounter you are likely to have with locals will be conducted in Scots, a form of "English" whose peculiar accent, vocabulary and grammar have led many to declare it, too, to be a separate language.**

Scottish **Gaelic** (*Gàidhlig*, pronounced "Gallic") is one of only four Celtic languages to survive into the modern age (Welsh, Breton and Irish Gaelic are the other three). Manx, the old language of the Isle of Man, died out earlier this century, while Cornish was finished as a community language way back in the eighteenth century. Scottish Gaelic is most closely related to Irish Gaelic and Manx – hardly surprising given that it was introduced to Scotland from Ireland around the third century BC. From the fifth to the twelfth centuries, Gaelic enjoyed an expansionist phase, gradually becoming the national language, thanks partly to the backing of the Celtic church in Iona. At the end of this period, Gaelic was spoken throughout what is now Scotland, but from that point onwards it began a steady decline.

Over the next few centuries, even before union with England, power, religious ideology and wealth gradually passed into non-Gaelic hands. The royal court was transferred to Edinburgh and an Anglo-Norman legal system was put in place. The Celtic church was Romanized by the introduction of foreign clergy, and, most importantly of all, English and Flemish merchants colonized the new trading towns of the east coast. In addition, the pro-English attitudes held by the Covenanters led to strong anti-Gaelic feeling within the Church of Scotland from its inception.

The two abortive Jacobite rebellions of 1715 and 1745 furthered the language's decline, as did the Clearances that took place in the Gaelic-speaking Highlands from the 1770s to the 1820s, which forced thousands to migrate to central Scotland's new industrial belt or emigrate to North America. Although efforts were made to halt the decline in the first half of the nineteenth century, the 1872 Education Act gave no official recognition to Gaelic, and children were severely punished if they were caught speaking the language in school.

Current estimates put the number of Gaelic speakers at 80,000 (just below two percent of the population), the majority of whom live in the *Gàidhealtachd*, with an extended Gaelic community of perhaps 250,000 who have some understanding of the language. In the last decade or so the language has stabilized, thanks to the introduction of bilingual primary and nursery schools, and a huge increase in the amount of broadcasting time given to Gaelic-language programmes. The success of rock bands such as *Runrig* has shown that it is possible to combine traditional Gaelic culture with popular entertainment and reach a mass audience.

While Gaelic has undergone something of a renaissance, **Scots**, or "Lallans", as spoken by the "English-speaking" majority of Scottish people, is still struggling for recognition. Scots is, of course, closely related to the English spoken south of the border, since it began life as a northern branch of Anglo-Saxon. In the early fifteenth century, it replaced Latin as the country's main literary and documentary language, but has since been drawn closer to southern varieties of English. Many people reject the view that it is a separate language at all, considering it to be, at best, an artificial amalgamation of local dialects. Robbie Burns is the most obvious literary exponent of the Scots language, but there has been a revival this century led by poets such as Hugh MacDiarmid. (For examples of the works of both writers, see "Books".)

## GAELIC GRAMMAR AND PRONUNCIATION

Gaelic is a highly complex tongue, with a fiendish, antiquated grammar and, with only eighteen letters, an intimidating system of spelling. Pronunciation is actually easier than it appears at first glance – one general rule to remember is that the **stress** always falls on the first syllable in a word. The general rule of syntax is that the verb starts the sentence whether it's a question or not, followed by the subject and then the object; adjectives generally follow the word they are describing.

### SHORT AND LONG VOWELS

Gaelic has both short and long vowels, the latter being denoted by an acute or grave accent.

**a** as in c**a**t; before nn and ll, like the *ow* in b**ow** (of a boat)
**à** as in b**a**r
**e** as in p**e**t
**é** like the *ai* in r**ai**n
**i** like the *ee* in str**ee**t, but shorter
**í** like the *ee* in fr**ee**
**o** as in p**o**t
**ò** like the *a* in the enthr**a**l
**ó** like the *ow* in b**ow** (of a boat)
**u** like the *oo* in sc**oo**t
**ù** like the *oo* in l**oo**

### VOWEL COMBINATIONS

Gaelic is littered with diphthongs, which, rather like in English, can be pronounced in several different ways depending on the individual word.

**ai** like the *a* in c**a**t, or the *e* in p**e**t; before dh or gh, like the *ee* in str**ee**t
**ao** like the *ur* in s**ur**ly
**ei** like the *a* in m**a**te
**ea** like the *e* in p**e**t, or the *a* in c**a**t, and sometimes like the *a* in m**a**te; before ll or nn like the *ow* in b**ow** (of a boat)
**èa** as in h**ea**r
**eu** like the *ai* in tr**ai**n, or the *ea* in f**ea**r
**ia** like the *ea* in f**ea**r

**io** like the *ea* in f**ea**r, or the *ee* in str**ee**t, but shorter
**ua** like the *ooe* in w**ooe**r

### CONSONANTS

The consonants listed below are those which differ substantially from the English.

**b** at the beginning of a word as in **b**ig; in the middle or at the end of a word like the *p* in **p**air
**bh** at the beginning of a word like the *v* in **v**an; elsewhere it is silent
**c** as in **c**at; after a vowel it has aspiration *before* it
**ch** always as in lo**ch**, never as in **ch**urch
**cn** like the *cr* in **cr**owd
**d** like the *d* in **d**og, but with the tongue pressed against the back of the upper teeth; at the beginning of a word before e or i, like the *j* in **j**am; in the middle or at the end of words like the *t* in cat; after i like the *ch* in **ch**urch
**dh** before and after a, o or u an aspirated *g*, rather like someone gargling; before e or i like the *y* in **y**es; elsewhere silent
**fh** usually silent; somtimes like the *h* in **h**ouse
**g** at the beginning of a word as in **g**et; before e like the *y* in **y**es; in the middle or end of a word like the *ck* in so**ck**; after i like the *ch* in lo**ch**
**gh** at the beginning of a word as in **g**et; before or after a, o or u rather like someone gargling; sometimes after i like the *y* in ga**y**, but often silent
**l** after i and sometimes before e like the *l* in lot; elsewhere a peculiarly Gaelic sound produced by flattening the front of the tongue against the palate
**mh** like the *v* in **v**an
**p** at the beginning of a word as in **p**et; elsewhere it has aspiration *before* it
**rt** pronounced as **sht**
**s** before e or i like the *sh* in **sh**ip; otherwise as in English
**sh** before a, o or u like the *h* in **h**ouse; before e like the *ch* in lo**ch**
**t** before e or i like the *ch* in **ch**urch; in the middle or at the end of a word it has aspiration *before* it; otherwise as in English
**th** at the beginning of a word, like the *h* in **h**ouse; elsewhere, and in the word *thu*, silent

## GAELIC PHRASES AND VOCABULARY

The choice is limited when it comes **teach-yourself Gaelic** courses, but the BBC *Can Seo* cassette and book is perfect for starting you off. Drier and more academic is *Teach Yourself Gaelic* (Hodder & Stoughton), which is aimed at bringing beginners to Scottish "O" grade standard. *Everyday Gaelic* by Morag MacNeill (Gairm) is the best phrasebook around.

### BASIC WORDS AND GREETINGS

| | | | | | |
|---|---|---|---|---|---|
| yes | *tha* | night | *oidhche* | music | *ceòl* |
| no | *chan eil* | here | *an seo* | book | *leabhar* |
| hello | *hallo* | there | *an sin* | tired | *sgìth* |
| how are you? | *ciamar a tha thu?* | this way | *mar seo* | food | *lòn* |
| OK | *tha gu math* | that way | *mar sin* | bread | *aran* |
| thank you | *tapadh leat* | pound/s | *not/aichean* | water | *uisge* |
| welcome | *fàilte* | tomorrow | *a-màireach* | milk | *bainne* |
| come in | *thig a-staigh* | tonight | *a-nochd* | beer | *leann* |
| goodbye | *mar sin leat* | cheers | *slàinte* | wine | *fion* |
| goodnight | *oidhche mhath* | yesterday | *an-dé* | whisky | *uisge beatha* |
| who? | *cò?* | today | *an-diugh* | post office | *post oifis* |
| where is...? | *càit a bheil...?* | tomorrow | *maireach* | Edinburgh | *Dun Eideann* |
| when? | *cuine?* | now | *a-nise* | Glasgow | *Glaschu* |
| what is it? | *Dé tha ann?* | hotel | *taigh-òsda* | America | *Ameireaga* |
| morning | *madainn* | house | *taigh* | Ireland | *Eire* |
| evening | *feasgar* | story | *sgeul* | England | *Sasainn* |
| day | *là* | song | *òran* | London | *Lunnain* |

### SOME USEFUL PHRASES

| | | | |
|---|---|---|---|
| It's a nice day | *tha latha math ann* | Do you speak Gaelic? | *a bheil Gàidhlig agad?* |
| How much is that? | *dè tha e 'cosg?* | What is the Gaelic for? | *Dé a' Ghàidhlig a tha air?* |
| What's your name? | *dè 'n t-ainm a th'ort?* | I don't understand | *chan eil mi 'tuigsinn* |
| Excuse me | *gabh mo leisgeul* | I don't know | *chan eil fhios agam* |
| What time is it? | *dé am uair a tha e?* | That's good | *'s math sin* |
| I'm thirsty | *tha am pathadh orm* | It doesn't matter | *'s coma* |
| I'd like a double room | *'se rùm dùbailte tha mi 'g iarraigh* | I'm sorry | *Tha mi duilich* |

### NUMBERS AND DAYS

| | | | | | |
|---|---|---|---|---|---|
| 1 | *aon* | 11 | *aon deug* | Monday | *Diluain* |
| 2 | *dà/dhà* | 20 | *fichead* | Tuesday | *Dimàirt* |
| 3 | *trì* | 21 | *aon ar fhichead* | Wednesday | *Diciadain* |
| 4 | *ceithir* | 30 | *deug ar fhichead* | Thursday | *Diardaoin* |
| 5 | *còig* | 40 | *dà fhichead* | Friday | *Dihaoine* |
| 6 | *sia* | 50 | *lethcheud* | Saturday | *Disathurna* |
| 7 | *seachd* | 60 | *trì fichead* | Sunday | *Didòmhnaich/* |
| 8 | *ochd* | 100 | *ceud* | | *La na Sàbaid* |
| 9 | *naoi* | 1000 | *mìle* | | |
| 10 | *deich* | | | | |

### SURNAMES

The prefix **Mac** or **Mc** in Scottish surnames derives from the Gaelic, meaning "son of". In Scots Mac is used for both sexes, but in Gaelic, women are referred to as Nic, for example:

*Donnchadh Mac Aodh*   Duncan MacKay          *Iseabail Nic Aodh*   Isabel MacKay

## GEOGRAPHICAL AND PLACE-NAME TERMS

The purpose of the list below is to help with place-name derivations and with more detailed map reading.

|  |  |
|------|---------|
| **ach** or **auch**, from **achadh** | field |
| **ail**, **aileach** | rock |
| **Alba** | Scotland |
| **ault**, from **allt** | stream |
| **ardan** or **arden**, from **àird** | a point of land or height |
| **bal** or **bally**, from **baile** | town, village |
| **balloch**, from **bealach** | mountain pass |
| **bad** | clump of trees |
| **bagh** | bay |
| **bàrr** | summit |
| **beg**, from **beag** | small |
| **ben**, from **beinn** | mountain |
| **blair**, from **blàr** | field or battlefield |
| **cairn**, from **càrn** | pile of stones |
| **craig**, from **creag** | rock |
| **cnoc** | hill |
| **coll** or **colly**, from **coille** | wood |
| **corrie**, from **coire** | round hollow in mountainside, whirlpool |
| **cruach** | bold hill |
| **dubh** | black |
| **dun** or **dum**, from **dùn** | fort |
| **drum**, from **druim** | ridge |
| **ess**, from **eas** | waterfall |
| **eilean** | island |
| **fin**, from **fionn** | white |
| **gair** or **gare**, from **geàrr** | short |
| **garv**, from **garbh** | rough |
| **glen**, from **gleann** | valley |
| **gower** or **gour**, from **gabhar** | goat |
| **inch**, from **innis** | meadow or island |
| **inver**, from **inbhir** | rivermouth |
| **ken** or **kin**, from **ceann** | head |
| **knock**, from **cnoc** | hill |
| **kyle**, from **caolas** | narrow strait |
| **lag** | hollow |
| **loch** | lake |
| **meall** | round hill |
| **mon**, from **monadh** | hill |
| **more**, from **mór** | large, great |
| **rannoch**, from **raineach** | bracken |
| **ross**, from **ros** | promontory |
| **rubha** | promontory |
| **sgeir** | sea rock |
| **strath**, from **srath** | broad valley |
| **tarbet**, from **tairbeart** | isthmus |
| **tir** or **tyre**, from **tìr** | land |
| **torr** | hill, castle |
| **traigh** | shore |

# A SCOTTISH GLOSSARY

**AULD** Old.

**AYE** Yes.

**BAIRN** Baby.

**BEN** Mountain peak.

**BONNIE** Pretty.

**BOTHY** Primitive cottage or hut; farmworker's or shepherd's mountain shelter.

**BRAE** Slope; hill.

**BRIG** Bridge.

**BROCH** Circular prehistoric stone fort.

**BURN** Small stream or brook.

**BYRE** Shelter for cattle; cottage.

**CAIRN** Mound of stones.

**CARSE** Riverside area of flat alluvium.

**CEILIDH** Social gathering involving dancing, drinking, singing and story-telling.

**CLAN** Extended family.

**COVENANTERS** Supporter of the Presbyterian Church in the seventeenth century.

**CORBETT** Mountain between 2500 and 3000ft high.

**CORBIE-STEPPED** Architectural term; any set of steps on a gable.

**CORRIE** Circular hollow on a hillside.

**CRAIG** Steep peak or crag.

**CRANNOG** Celtic lake or bog dwelling.

**CROFT** Small plot of farmland with house, common in the Highlands.

**CROW-STEPPED** Same as *corbie-stepped*.

**DOLMEN** Grave chamber.

**DRAM** Literally, one-sixteenth of an ounce. Usually refers to a small measurement of whisky.

**DRUM** Narrow ridge.

**DUN** Fortified mound.

**FIRST-FOOT** The first person to enter a household on *Hogmanay* (see below).

**FIRTH** Narrow inlet.

**GILLIE** Personal guide used on hunting or fishing trips.

**GLEN** Deep, narrow mountain valley.

**HARLING** Limestone and gravel mix used to cover buildings.

**HOGMANAY** New Year's Eve.

**HOWE** Valley.

**HOWFF** Meeting place; pub.

**INCH** Small island.

**KEN** Knowledge; understanding.

**KILT** Knee-length tartan skirt worn by Highland men.

**KIRK** Church.

**KYLE** Narrow strait or channel.

**LAIRD** Landowner; aristocrat.

**LAW** Rounded hill.

**LINKS** Grassy coastal land; coastal golf course.

**LOCHAN** Little loch or lake.

**MACHAIR** Sandy, grassy, lime-rich coastal land, generally used for grazing.

**MANSE** Official home of a Presbyterian minister.

**MUNRO** Mountain over 3000ft high.

**MUNRO-BAGGING** Sport of trying to climb as many Munros as possible.

**PEEL** Fortified tower, built to withstand Border raids.

**PEND** Archway or vaulted passage.

**PRESBYTERIAN** The official (Protestant) Church of Scotland, established by John Knox during the Reformation.

**SASSENACH** English.

**SHINTY** Simple form of hockey.

**SNP** Scottish National Party.

**SPORRAN** Leather purse worn in front of a kilt.

**STRATH** Broad flat river valley.

**TARTAN** Check-patterned woollen cloth, particular patterns being associated with particular clans.

**THANE** A landowner of high rank; the chief of a clan.

**TREWS** Tartan trousers.

**WEE** Small.

**WYND** Narrow lane.

**YETT** Gate or door.

# INDEX

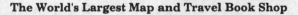

# SLEEP EASY
## BOOK AHEAD

**IBN** INTERNATIONAL BOOKING NETWORK

**Belfast**
0232 324733

**Glasgow**
041 332 3004

**Dublin**
01 301766

**London**
071 836 1036

**Washington**
0202 783 6161

**Canada**
FREEPHONE 0800 663 5777

**Australia**
02 261 1111

**New Zealand**
09 379 4224

Call any of these
numbers and your
credit card secures a
good nights sleep ...

in more than 26 countries

up to six months ahead

with immediate confirmation

HOSTELLING
INTERNATIONAL

*Budget accommodation you can **Trust***

# You are A STUDENT

## You travel THE WORLD

## You want TO SAVE MONEY

# Here's how

The International Student Identity Card

Available at Student Travel Offices Worldwide.

Entitles you to discounts and special services worldwide.